WASHINGTON'S NEW POOR LAW

Welfare Reform and the Roads Not Taken— 1935 to the Present

WASHINGTON'S NEW POOR LAW

Welfare Reform and the Roads Not Taken— 1935 to the Present

Gertrude Schaffner Goldberg
Sheila D. Collins

The Apex Press
New York

Published by The Apex Press, an imprint of the
Council on International and Public Affairs,
Suite 3C, 777 United Nations Plaza, New York,
NY 10017 (800-316-2739), www.cipa-apex.org.

Library of Congress Cataloging-in-Publication Data

Goldberg, Gertrude S.
    Washington's new poor law : welfare reform and the roads
not taken—1935 to the present / Gertrude Schaffner
Goldberg, Sheila D. Collins.
      p. cm.
    Includes bibliographical references and index.
    ISBN 0-945257-84-8 (alk. paper) — ISBN 0-945257-83-X
(pbk. : alk. paper)
      1. Public welfare—Government policy—United States—
    History—20th century. 2. Federal aid to public welfare
    —United States—History—20th century. 3. Welfare
    recipients—Employment—United States. 4. United
    States. Personal Responsiblity and Work Opportunity
    Reconciliation Act of 1996. 5. United States—Politics
    and government—20th century. 6. United States—Social
    conditions—20th century. 7. United States—Economic
    conditions—20th century. I. Collins, Sheila D. II. Title.

HV95.G57 2000
362.5'8'0973—21   00-030634

Typeset by Peggy Hurley
Printed by Thomson-Shore, Inc., an employee-owned company.
Printed in the United States of America

In memory of Bertram M. Gross

1912-1997

Brilliant and passionate
lifelong champion of
full employment

Table of Contents

Acknowledgments

For more than a decade, we have had the opportunity of working closely with a group of scholars, mostly economists, who share not only our commitment to economic justice but also our view that the most promising route to that goal is jobs at livable wages for all who want to work. They have taught us a great deal about economics, politics, and past efforts to achieve full employment. They have shared their knowledge and encouraged our scholarship. We are particularly grateful to Helen Lachs Ginsburg and to Philip Harvey, who in addition to their support, carefully read and critiqued the manuscript.

Bertram Gross, to whom we dedicate this book, had a hand in drafting the Full Employment Bill of 1945 and the original Humphrey-Hawkins Bill of 1974, the legislation that would have guaranteed a job for all, but which were enacted without an enforceable right to work. He encouraged us to write our first book, *Jobs for All: A Plan for the Revitalization of America* (by Sheila D. Collins, Helen Lachs Ginsburg, and Gertrude Schaffner Goldberg, The Apex Press, 1994). We are inspired by his relentless, lifetime advocacy of full employment.

Our publisher, Ward Morehouse, a tireless advocate for justice, suggested that we write this book. Although we sometimes have rued the day when we agreed to take on such a task, we thank Ward for setting us on a course that ultimately taught us so much more about work, welfare, and the recent history of our country.

We thank Mark Greenberg, staff attorney, Center for Law and Social Policy in Washington, D.C., for reviewing the chapters of the book dealing with the events leading up to the repeal of Aid to Families with Dependent Children, the passage of the new welfare law, the Personal Responsibility and Work Opportunity Reconciliation Act of 1996, and the consequences of what goes by the name of welfare "reform." Professor June Axinn brought to a reading of the manuscript in its early stages her extensive knowledge of the history of American social welfare that is revealed in the successive editions of *Social Welfare: A History of the American Response to Need,* which she co-authored with Mark Stern (5th ed., Allyn & Bacon, 2001).

We have built on the scholarship of Winifred Bell whose *Aid to Dependent Children* (Columbia University Press, 1965) did so much to illuminate the early history of ADC, particularly the mechanisms by which black women and children were denied assistance on the basis of thinly veiled racial criteria. And no one who writes about the subject is without debt to Frances Fox Piven and Richard A. Cloward whose *Regulating the Poor* (New York: Pantheon, 1971) transcended the largely descriptive studies that preceded it and identified not only the functions of relief but the economic and political forces that give rise to it. We thank Judith Russell for lending us her dissertation, "The Making of American Antipoverty Policy: The Other War on Poverty" (Columbia University, 1992), which helped us to understand why the antipoverty program of the 1960s eschewed a job-creation strategy.

We appreciate the opportunity to have presented a draft of our final chapter to the Columbia University Seminar on Full Employment and to the Seminar's chairs, Helen Lachs Ginsburg, Sumner R. Rosen, and June Zaccone, for giving us this chance to benefit from the critiques of the members of the Seminar. Our thanks also to the Columbia University Seminars Program and its tireless director, the late Dean Aaron Warner, for a grant that enabled us to undertake this research.

We appreciate and, in making final revisions, have taken into account comments by Joel Blau, Heather Boushey, and Richard Cloward who critiqued the book at a panel discussion before its publication.

We thank Professor Robert Cherry of Brooklyn College for sharing his knowledge of the effects of tight labor markets on minorities.

Finally, we wish to thank our editor, Gabrielle Sindorf, and typesetter, Peggy Hurley, who were assigned this project after a series of unfortunate events and who did yeoman work in pulling together a complicated manuscript.

CHAPTER 1

Washington's New Poor Law and Welfare Repeal: Introduction and Overview

In August 1935, President Franklin Roosevelt signed the Social Security Act (SSA), the cornerstone of the American welfare state. After wielding the presidential pen, Roosevelt declared that had no other bill been passed by Congress, "this session would be regarded as historic for all time."[1]

Another Democratic president, Bill Clinton, signed a new welfare law 61 years later that repealed part of the SSA: Title IV, Aid to Families with Dependent Children (AFDC). Clinton, too, claimed historical significance: "Today we are taking a historical chance to make welfare what it was meant to be: a second chance, not a way of life." The *New York Times* took a different view: "Clinton Signs Bill Cutting Welfare."[2] The new law, the Personal Responsibility and Work Opportunity Reconciliation Act (PRWORA), was expected to reduce funding for low-income programs by nearly $55 billion from its passage until the year 2000.[3]

Replacing AFDC, the nation's entitlement to single women and their children, was a new program whose name tells the tale: Temporary Assistance for Needy Families (TANF). Lest there be any misunderstanding of congressional intent, the PRWORA explicitly states that TANF "shall not be interpreted to entitle any individual or family to assistance. . . ."[4] Strict work requirements for those on assistance and lifetime limits on the receipt of TANF benefits are the hallmarks of the measure that was said to make work, not welfare, "a way of life." So are new restrictions on government aid to many legal immigrants.

1

Welfare as We Knew It: Myths and Reality

Candidate Bill Clinton's 1992 campaign promise to "end welfare as we know it" both reflected and exacerbated national concern over a program that had never been popular. Indeed, welfare "crisis" is a term that had been applied to AFDC more than once since 1935. The program had been amended many times, both expanding and restricting its provisions, but never before had repeal been seriously considered.

What accounts for the timing and the extent of change? Was AFDC too costly? Does the timing of repeal imply that the United States was less able to pay the welfare bill in the 1990s than in the six preceding decades? Why were work requirements imposed? Were they imposed because most recipients were unwilling to work? Were welfare benefits so generous that work did not pay? Were limits on receipt of benefits a response to the rolls being flooded with long-term dependents? Was multigenerational recipience the norm? Did the "brood-mare" epithet, bestowed on welfare mothers by Louisiana Senator Russell Long a quarter-century ago, reflect welfare recipients' procreation patterns? And what about the racial composition of AFDC? Was the typical welfare mother African–American? Were immigrants disproportionately milking the system?

Assume you are as ignorant of the national debate that preceded welfare repeal as ideal jurors selected for a notorious criminal case. Do the following allegations against welfare fit the facts about AFDC and its beneficiaries? Was the welfare "crisis" myth or reality?

MYTHS

Myth 1: Welfare Was Expensive

Spending for the AFDC program was 1% of the federal budget and .25% of the Gross Domestic Product (GDP). Total spending for all programs for the poor (means-tested benefits), including those for the elderly as well as the disabled, was 11.9% of the federal budget, compared to 18.0% for post-Cold War defense expenditures.[5]

Myth 2: The U.S. Could Not Afford the Welfare Bill

Contrary to the perception that the nation was suffering from deficient and declining national resources, the real Gross Domestic Product (GDP) per capita of the United States more than doubled between 1960 and 1996, and was 29% higher than in 1980. The gains in recent years had gone to the top, but total national wealth had nonetheless increased. The federal deficit had been declining in real terms and as a percentage of GDP, and the national debt, or accumulated deficits, was just under 50% of GDP in 1996, compared to over 100% at the end of World War II.[6]

Myth 3: Welfare Benefits Were Too Generous

In January 1996, combined benefits of AFDC and food stamps fell below the official U.S. poverty level ($12,516 for a family of three) in all 50 states; the median state provided benefits equal to 65% of the poverty level.[7] The real, or inflation-adjusted, value of AFDC benefits had been falling for 20 years. Average benefits were 37% lower in 1995 than in 1975.[8]

Work, when it was available, offered more money than meager welfare benefits. Although the value of the minimum wage fell, particularly in the 1980s, it would have provided a year-round, full-time worker with $8,840 in 1996 (before it was raised in October of that year), plus an Earned Income Tax Credit of $3,556 (for two children), bringing the family income to $12,396 or nearly equal to the three-person poverty line. Compare this with the national median of 65% of the poverty level for AFDC and food stamps combined—which means families in one-half the states received less.

Myth 4: Welfare Spawned Large Families

In 1994, over 70% of families receiving AFDC had one or two children (43% had only one child, and 30% had two). Only 10% of the families had more than three children.[9]

Myth 5: Welfare Created Chronic and Intergenerational Dependency

Of AFDC caretakers (mostly mothers), 75% did not get AFDC as children, and another 16% received it infrequently. Only 9% of the caretakers grew up in families who used welfare frequently.[10]

Most families received AFDC for 2 years at a time or less, and total usage for the majority was 36 months or less. However, owing to the insecurity of the low-wage labor market, most returned for a subsequent spell on welfare.[11] At any one time, the majority of recipients were long-term clients, albeit a minority of the total number who went on the rolls over the period in question.[12]

Myth 6: Too Generous Welfare Caused Single Parenthood and Teen Pregnancy

Poverty and unemployment, not the level of public assistance, have been associated with single parenthood and teenage pregnancy. Benefit levels have declined sharply over the past 20 years, but rates of single parenthood have continued to increase. European nations with much lower rates of teenage pregnancy than the United States provide much more income support.[13]

Myth 7: Welfare Mothers Did Not Work

Nearly 75% of AFDC recipients were in the labor market, either combining welfare with low earnings, working some of the time and receiving welfare between jobs, working limited hours and looking for work, or looking for work the entire time.[14]

Myth 8: There Were Enough Jobs for All

Early in 1997, more than 16 million Americans who wanted to work full-time were either unemployed or forced to work part-time. Even in areas where unemployment levels were below national averages, job vacancy surveys found three to five persons needing work for every available job. In neighborhoods where welfare recipients lived and could be expected to work, the numbers were considerably larger.[15]

Myth 9: Immigrants Come to the U.S. to Take Advantage of Welfare and Overuse It

"Most research has found that immigrants are overwhelmingly drawn by the hope of better jobs, not by U.S. benefit programs. When job prospects dim, many (especially Mexicans) return home."[16] Although immigrants are likely to suffer more economic dislocation than established groups, nonrefugee legal immigrants of working age are about equally likely to receive public benefits as their citizen counterparts—5.1% for immigrants, compared to 5.3% for citizens.[17]

Myth 10: AFDC Was for Blacks

In 1994, when welfare reform was being hotly debated, only a little over one-third of AFDC recipients were black (36%). However, over one-half (56%) were either black or Hispanic.[18] Should it be surprising that African–American and Hispanic single-mother families were disproportionately dependent on welfare? Their rates of poverty in 1996 were 51.0% and 59.7%, respectively, compared to 36.9% for their white counterparts.[19]

Education did not pay off for women of color to the extent that it did for white men and women. In 1992, black women with high school diplomas had poverty rates three times that of white females with the same level of education (30.6% vs. 9.8%), and with some college they had poverty rates slightly higher than those of white males who did not complete high school (18.0% vs. 17.3%). Hispanic women with a bachelor's degree had higher poverty rates than white males with only a high-school education (7.3% vs. 6.9%) and were more than twice as likely to be poor as white women in the same educational category (7.3% vs. 2.7%).[20]

REALITY

The disparity between these "facts" and the arguments put forward by critics of AFDC suggest that the welfare crisis "is not a verifiable entity but a construction that sustains ideological interests."[21] James Galbraith maintains that financial and commercial interests have misapplied the word "crisis" to a number of conditions with the same underlying purpose: "in order to legitimize the reduction of social welfare and social security programs, to withdraw resources from the social to the private realm."[22] Policy analysts, welfare law experts, and welfare advocates constructed their own arsenals filled with facts to destroy the ideological construction on which welfare "reform" was based, but the myths failed to surrender to this counterattack.[23]

Political scientists refer to "policy learning" as a kind of "feedback" in which "past policies serve as models for future policies or ones to avoid."[24] Such "learning" is, of course, often constructed, not on knowledge, but on falsification and myth. Welfare had often been the subject of such "policy learning" during its 61-year history. Why, in the mid-1990s, was AFDC not simply castigated or amended, as in the past, but repealed? This book addresses that question.

The Welfare Reform Tradition

"Reform" seems like an unlikely word for PRWORA. Changes in public policy that promote justice, economic well-being, and democratic rights and values are often designated reforms. To historian Richard Hofstadter, the Progressive and New Deal periods in American history were periods of reform—when government used its power to initiate social insurance and collective bargaining rights for workers, to protect women and children against industrial abuses, to restrain and regulate monopolies, and to extend the suffrage to women.[25] This is not the kind of reform usually associated with welfare, either yesterday or today.

A second meaning of reform is punishment of individuals or restriction of their rights in order to improve their characters or behaviors, as in "reform school." This type of welfare reform has a long tradition, dating back at least to nineteenth-century measures that restricted the receipt of relief in both England and the United States.

Before the advent of modern social insurance, it was rare for policymakers to admit that able-bodied applicants for relief were victims of involuntary unemployment or other circumstances beyond their control. Traditionally, those responsible for welfare policy assumed that personal deviance or character flaws were responsible for the economic dependence of able-bodied persons—"sturdy beggars" in the parlance of the early relief statutes or poor laws.

Historian Paul Slack points to surveys of the poor in the closing years of the sixteenth century that found lots of poor, laboring persons who were not able to live off their labor, but "there was no recognition here that people wandering or loitering might be trying to find work, not to avoid it." Slack also points out that even if unemployment were acknowledged, relief in the form of work was unusual.[26] Writing of later, but not dissimilar, policies in the United States, Philip Harvey concludes that "prior to the New Deal, the view of joblessness that dominated American law was behavioralist in that it assumed both the cause and cure for joblessness lay in the behavior of jobless individuals themselves."[27] The very availability of welfare was—and still is—thought to create the need for it, and personal deficiencies are deemed not only causes of the need for relief, but its results.

More often than not, welfare reform spells reductions of benefits and punitive treatment of recipients in the name of improving their characters. In 1834, poor-law reform in England attempted to end the system of supplementing the wages of workers who otherwise might have gone hungry or migrated to industrial cities, leaving farmers without sufficient hands.[28] The claim by the English Poor Law Commissioners was that it was "a bounty on indolence and vice."[29] The same reform denied assistance in their own homes (outdoor relief) to able-bodied men and required them to surrender their freedom and enter the workhouse, a quasi prison for the unemployed and underemployed (indoor relief), in order to get public aid.[30] This was the alternative, regardless of whether work were available or wages sufficient. The 1834 poor-law reform established the principle that relief for able-bodied males was to be less desirable—"less eligible" was the term—than the wages of the lowest-paid independent laborer. The workhouse, like modern workfare, clearly met that test.

English poor-law reform was aided initially by good harvests and a boom in railroad construction, just as PRWORA got underway in a period of uncharacteristically low levels of unemployment. Nineteenth-century welfare reform in England reduced relief substantially for able-bodied men, and hard times a decade later did not return the rolls to prereform levels.[31] Interestingly, the public-welfare historian, Blanche Coll, used quotation marks around the word, "reform," when referring to the 1834 repeal of the old poor law.[32] It could be argued that the 1996 repeal of AFDC did to women what the 1834 reform did to men.

In the United States, nineteenth-century leaders of private charity were also welfare "reformers." They attempted to limit both public and private relief. What the dependent poor needed was "not alms but a friend." This was the motto of the Charity Organization Societies (COS), which arose in U.S. industrial cities in the last decades of the nineteenth century. Volunteer "friendly visitors"—later social caseworkers—went to the homes of the indigent and attempted to correct the moral lapses believed to be the causes of pauperism or economic dependence: lack of sobriety, prudence, industry, and providence.[33] The dependent poor, or paupers, were *in*dolent, *im*pecunious, *in*ebriate, *im*moral, *un*worthy.

Under the banner of "charity," late nineteenth-century welfare "reformers" conducted successful campaigns to abolish public relief to the poor in their own homes (outdoor relief) in most of the large cities of nation. [34] The founder of the New York COS and one of the nation's leaders in welfare "reform" stated the case against outdoor relief in this way:

> There should be a sure refuge from starvation. So far as this refuge is furnished from the funds raised by taxation, however . . . the only safe way to provide it is under such stringent conditions that no one shall be tempted to accept it except in an extremity, and under such conditions, also, as will as soon as possible make the recipient of help able to support himself again. . . . I mean that relief should be indoor relief, inside the doors of an institution. . . .[35]

These "reformers" organized private charity to prevent duplication and overlap in the provision of relief, along with providing the counsel of a friendly visitor. Like their contemporary counterparts, these reformers were concerned with "welfare dependency," but not with poverty, and they, too, were willing to increase economic hardship in order to reduce relief rolls. One result of organized charity's campaigns to abolish public outdoor relief was to break up families and institutionalize their children.[36] With good reason, historian Michael Katz holds that welfare "reform" in the United States has consistently meant restriction and repression. "Indeed, it is only a slight exaggeration to say that the core of most welfare reform in America since the early nineteenth century has been a war on the able-bodied poor; an attempt to define, locate, and purge them from the rolls of relief."[37]

Washington's New Poor Law

With its repeal of the right to government assistance, the nation's new welfare legislation evokes memories of the "poor laws" that persisted with varying degrees of harshness until the passage of the SSA of 1935. In 1934, a social-welfare historian, Edith Abbott, had written that most state poor laws were "survivals of the old statutes adopted more than a century ago in one state after another, following old colonial laws, which in the beginning, had followed the general principles of the English Poor Law."[38] PRWORA is, in some important respects, a reversion to the pre–New Deal poor laws. Although there were exceptions, of course, in times of depression or extremely high unemployment, United States poor laws characteristically—

- Denied outdoor relief to able-bodied dependents whether or not jobs were available

- Provided work, if at all, under coercive conditions—often in a workhouse or poorhouse

- Assumed that able-bodied paupers were unworthy and responsible for their dependency

- Assumed that the very availability of relief caused the need for it

- Required relatives (other than parents), often poor and ill themselves, to assume responsibility for their kin

- Lacked a concept of relief as a right or entitlement, even for those deemed unemployable or "worthy" of assistance

- Were financed and administered by local authorities and consequently differed not only among states, but within them as well

- Denied assistance to strangers and recent arrivals to the community, partly as a means of limiting local financial responsibility

- Denied recipients political and civil rights in return for a meager dole.[39]

Prior to the Great Depression, poorhouses were either the primary or only form of relief in more than one-half the states. On the eve of the SSA, over one-fourth of the states still denied relief recipients the right to vote or hold public office.[40]

Like previous proponents of "welfare reform," the writers of the nation's new poor law are concerned with the morality of the indigent. The "Findings" or legislative rationale preceding the provisions of PRWORA decry what the framers of the act call "the crisis in our Nation"—the public dependency, school failure, violent crime, and juvenile delinquency that arise from the moral transgressions of unmarried AFDC recipients, their sexual partners, and their offspring:

Marriage is the foundation of a successful society. The increase
in the number of children receiving public assistance is closely
related to the increase in births to unmarried women. . . . Surveys of teen mothers have revealed that a majority of such mothers
have histories of sexual and physical abuse, primarily with older
adult men. . . . Areas with higher percentages of single-parent
households have higher rates of violent crime. Therefore, in light
of this demonstration of the crisis in our Nation, it is the sense
of the Congress that prevention of out-of-wedlock pregnancy and
reduction in out-of-wedlock birth are very important government
interests and the policy contained in . . . [the section on TANF]
is intended to address the crisis.[41]

Soon after these "Findings" were approved by the president
and the Congress, another national "crisis" ensued, one stemming
from the moral lapses of those who enacted this legislation—extra marital sex between the chief executive and a much younger
woman (an intern in the White House) and subsequent revelations
about the transgressions of several members of Congress.

Welfare Repeal: Right, Left, and Center

Whether on the political Right or Left, almost everyone disliked AFDC, but there were deep divisions over the nature and
source of its problems. The conservative architects of the new welfare
law rationalized "reform" by arguing that excessive benefits cause
rising fertility rates among single mothers and that a "permissive"
welfare state had created a serious decline in the incentive to work.
Such arguments are based on the assumption that there are adequate labor-market alternatives to economic dependency and that
welfare recipients have simply failed to make use of these abundant opportunities for economic self-sufficiency. Therefore, strict
work requirements and behavioral sanctions are needed to goad
the indolent into joining the rest of hardworking America.[42] Legal
immigrants are denied aid based on the assumption that they are
disproportionately dependent on government and are consuming
resources that could be used by our own citizens. Cutbacks, in
any case, are necessary because welfare is unaffordable.

Liberal scholars join conservatives in condemning "welfare
dependency." However, where conservatives trace its origins to
the allegedly dysfunctional behavior and culture of the welfare
population, liberals (including many "welfare advocates") attribute
it to the immediate structural environment that has stripped the

poor of their ability to compete. [43] They point to such recent environmental changes as job losses from deindustrialization, the new high-tech requirements of the emerging labor market, and the loss of middle-class role models, institutions, and cultural norms from central city ghettos. In effect, liberals argue that the welfare poor, like the "Third World" of neoclassical development theory, have failed to keep up with modernity. [44] For the most part, liberals' prescriptions for change involve narrowly targeted human-resource development programs to prepare welfare recipients for the labor market, such as, education, training, family planning, job-readiness skills, transportation, child care, relocation assistance, and other services.

Neither liberals nor conservatives have considered or proposed measures to deal with fundamental defects in the economic system, notably the chronic insufficiency of jobs at decent pay that is documented on many pages of this book. A case in point is Senator Daniel Patrick Moynihan, once a liberal and later a neoconservative. While pinpointing black male unemployment as a problem underlying the economic dependency of black women, Moynihan has never put forth a program for job creation or full employment. In the words of a student of neoconservatism: "Fundamental irrationalities in the economic system he does not consider at all." [45]

Critics on the Left view welfare as a symptom of a capitalist system that must keep the lives of some in a state of controlled poverty so that others may grow rich. Yet, even if they are severely critical of some welfare policies, many on the Left find relief preferable to the alternatives of hunger and extreme deprivation. Frances Fox Piven and Richard Cloward, who contend that historically the function of relief has been to regulate and control the poor, nonetheless maintain that "a relief explosion is a reform just because a large number of unemployed or underemployed people obtain aid . . . many of . . . [whom] would otherwise be forced to subsist without either jobs or income." [46] In contrast to earlier Leftist writers, who emphasized the cooptative functions of the welfare state, Piven and Cloward saw welfare as a means of reducing the reserve army of labor and of providing alternatives to any job at any wage. [47] In the mid-1980s, Piven and Cloward joined Fred Block and Barbara Ehrenreich in calling for an expanded welfare state rather than an emphasis on job creation. Although they did not underestimate the consequences of unemployment or underemployment, Piven, Cloward, Block and Ehrenreich rejected a policy of full employment, associating it, in the context of the Reagan era, with "tough, low-paying, and otherwise undesirable jobs."[48]

Despite her Left-feminist critique of relief policy as "regulating the lives of women," Mimi Abramovitz also supported liberalized welfare rather than welfare "reform."[49] In a defense of welfare written for the Bertha Capen Reynolds Society, "a national organization of progressive social workers," Abramovitz and Fred Newdom conceded that "advocates would like to end those aspects of 'welfare as we know it,' which are harmful to clients"—such as perpetuating poverty through low benefits. Whereas welfare "reform" would limit the length of time on welfare and "[make] the period as difficult as possible," Abramovitz and Newdom wanted to liberalize AFDC, to improve labor-market conditions, and to empower recipients rather than restrict their benefits and rights still further.

The Argument of the Book

This analysis of work and welfare differs significantly from conservative and liberal perspectives. It repudiates the stream of individualistic analyses characteristic of conservatives that heaps scorn and blame on poor women, especially women of color. It also challenges the liberal view that it has been only recent changes in the circumstances of the poor that have led to their alleged "dependency." Contrary to these views, we argue that major responsibility for the economic dependence and chronic poverty of millions of women and children falls on the shoulders of the labor market, on inadequate employment opportunities, for both men and women, that persisted for all but the war years in the 1940s, 1950s, and 1960s. This chronic shortage of good jobs could have been eliminated by visionary social policies that were proposed but never enacted—the roads not taken. Because the root causes of poverty and economic dependency are too few jobs, and even fewer ones that pay living wages, real welfare "reform" requires jobs for all at family-supporting incomes. By contrast, PRWORA, despite its name, is not about "work opportunities." It is only about work requirements.

This argument also parts company with prominent spokespersons on the Left who recognize that jobs are either in short supply or short on rewards, but who do not believe that full employment is either feasible or desirable.[50] Some others on the Left give lip service to the full-employment ideal but fail to make employment the centerpiece of their policies or strategies or, in any case, have not seriously sought to build a movement for full employment.

Neither, for that matter, have civil-rights organizations. Although they have consistently espoused a "dual agenda" of "jobs and freedom," they have not mobilized equally for both.[51] Civil, rather than economic, rights have been the centerpiece of their movement strategies. At best, a half-hearted partner on behalf of policies benefiting the working class as a whole was a labor movement bereft of its more idealistic and militant ranks by the anti-Communist purges of the 1940s and 1950s.[52]

UNDEREMPLOYED WORKING CLASS OR *UNDERCLASS*?

In recent years, the term *underclass* has been coined to differentiate welfare mothers and some other "disreputable" people from the mainstream.[53] Theories that place primary emphasis on the personal deficiencies, deviancies, and pathologies of the poor are inadequate explanations of their plight. Perhaps the rich, in the phrase attributed to F. Scott Fitzgerald by Ernest Hemingway, are "different from you and me," but the poor differ from the rest of the population in circumstance more than in character.

A convincing case can be made for thinking of people on welfare as an underemployed working class rather than an "underclass." As Jacqueline Jones has shown, at least from the Civil War to the present, those now termed America's *underclasses* are people who have been systemically dispossessed of their livelihoods through racial and gender discrimination in the workplace, economic dislocations, and deliberate government policies.[54] Either they cannot find jobs, or, when they do work, they labor at jobs that pay low wages and are subject to frequent layoffs.

The valuable research of Kathryn Edin and Laura Lein[55] reveals that the majority of welfare mothers had work experience. Yet, Edin and Lein nonetheless categorize poor mothers as "work-reliant" and "welfare-reliant." Such dichotomies are perhaps understandable analytically. When carried into the popular media, however, they add to the long-standing splintering of the working class.

Sociologist Mark Rank, who did both qualitative and quantitative studies of welfare families in Wisconsin, began his research with the view that they were different from other people, but the data led him to emphasize the similarities between the families in his study and the rest of the population:

> Perhaps the most salient theme to emerge from this study is that
> the welfare recipient is fundamentally not much different from
> you or me. There is a tendency to view welfare recipients as
> significantly different from the rest of us. . . . After spending
> 10 years on this project, I have come to a much different con-
> clusion. These are people who work just as hard as the rest of
> us, care just as much about their future and their children's future,
> and hope to get ahead just as much as the next fellow. The dif-
> ference lies not within them, but primarily within their position
> in relation to the larger forces found in our society.[56]

In contrast to liberals and conservatives, who contend that the
labor market, if not already capacious enough to employ everyone who needs a job, will do so with continued economic growth,
we demonstrate the opposite: Throughout most of the history of
AFDC, there were never sufficient jobs at decent wages for men
and women of working age. Job vacancy surveys, even in areas of
the country with low rates of unemployment, repeatedly demonstrate that there are not enough jobs of any kind for those who
seek them, much less living-wage jobs.[57] For much of the time in
recent decades, the Federal Reserve Board has raised interest rates
and thus increased unemployment in order to stave off inflation.
Cynically, the nation then treats the long-term victims of this policy
as if they were responsible for their unemployment. And without
enough jobs to go around, Washington, in the name of welfare
"reform," has imposed a work requirement and a denial of relief
to those who do not comply.

If environments condition behavior, we might assume that people
who are without work for long periods of time are likely to become socialized to their condition, and they will either lose the
capacity to work or fail to acquire the necessary discipline. However much the expected may occur, there is considerable evidence
of the opposite response. Typically, many jobless applicants queue
up when jobs become available, among them women and men who
express the desire to come off welfare and to be able to pay their
bills.[58] Economist Richard Freeman has shown that when employment opportunities expand in local labor markets, the percentage
of economically disadvantaged young men who are employed rises
substantially. Indeed, "employment of black youth is particularly
sensitive to the state of the local labor market."[59] Similarly, Paul
Osterman, who studied the impact of full employment in Boston
in the 1980s, concluded that "it is very clear that the poor did

respond to economic opportunity when it was offered."[60] Ironically, the essays of Freeman and Osterman appear in a volume entitled *The Urban Underclass.* Their findings, instead, support our assumption that there is an underemployed working class rather than an ingrained, dependent, and culturally different "underclass."

ARE WORK REQUIREMENTS EVER FAIR?

The United States has had entitlements to welfare for various population groups, but it has never had an entitlement to work, an opportunity for everyone to practice the work ethic so revered in American culture. Would a work requirement be fair if we had such an entitlement? The question, we believe, needs to be reframed: Is a work requirement necessary to prevent malingering? And are the services of every able-bodied person needed?

Although many disadvantaged workers queue up in long lines for jobs when they become available, there is probably a residual group of people who have been deeply damaged by poverty, by "jobless ghettos" with few stably employed role models, and by schools that do not educate.[61] Yet, William J. Wilson, who acknowledges and details the personal deficiencies of black youths subjected to the harsh environments of "jobless ghettos," concludes that "in a tight labor market the status of all workers—including disadvantaged minorities—improves because of lower unemployment, higher wages, and better jobs."[62] With unemployment at a three-decade low in 1999, opportunity, indeed, was dipping down into the former "jobless ghettos," and employers and unions were lifting barriers and courting and training women as well as ghetto residents.[63]

Before we can determine the size and nature of the residual group who will not take advantage of such opportunities, we must first sustain fiscal, monetary, and labor-market policies that are conducive to employing everyone who wants to work. Along with stimulative fiscal and monetary policies that generate sufficient jobs, there must be labor-market measures that offer education and training in relation to available opportunities for employment, as well as job and career information, vocational guidance, and relocation allowances.[64] Such labor-market policies not only assist individual workers but contribute to important requisites for continuing full-employment policies—economic efficiency and the control of inflation. However, education, training, and job placement services do not create jobs and are no substitutes for the economic policies that make for full employment.[65]

What about work requirements for individuals who choose to provide care to the very young and the very frail in their families? Such care is vital work—a service not only to families but to the community, and it should be compensated through some form of public income support, such as paid parental or dependent-care leave. Public policy, as exemplified by welfare reform, moved in the opposite direction and in tandem with rising unemployment and increasing rhetoric about family values.

On the other hand, many who have family-care responsibilities may wish to work, either full- or part-time, providing that they have access to affordable and quality substitute care. Such provisions must be part of any full-employment policy—and for all employed parents, not only those on welfare. To require parents to be employed in the absence of such a guarantee—both of day care for preschoolers and after-school care for grade-school children—is an inhumane and reckless public policy.

Do we need the services of every "able-bodied" man and woman? Without a doubt, there is much need that is not being met by either the public or private sector. Filling gaping holes in low-cost housing, child care, and public transportation would only scratch the surface of unmet needs in a civilized community. There is currently no national inventory of the need for vital goods and services in all of the communities across the land or of the number of jobs that would be required to meet those needs. Individual communities have undertaken surveys and found that to meet needs in such areas as child care, home maintenance and rehabilitation, mass transportation, and water and environmental improvements, many new jobs would have to be created.[66]

We assume that a commitment to full employment would require a permanent, standby public employment program for those who do not find work in the market or government sectors and that such a program would begin by assessing the job and community needs gaps. A policy of providing a "work benefit" through a permanent, standby public employment program for those who exhaust unemployment benefits and are still without work was, in fact, envisioned by Franklin Roosevelt and other New Dealers, but not enacted.[67]

The public employment programs of the Great Depression and the Comprehensive Employment and Training Administration (CETA) of the 1970s—which will be reviewed in Chapters 3 and 6 of this book—were different from the workfare programs that are being required of some welfare recipients. Nancy Rose, who recognizes some of the shortcomings of public-works projects like the Works Progress Administration (WPA) of the New Deal and CETA, nonetheless labels them "fair work." In contrast to workfare, the "fair work" programs are voluntary.[68] Workfare participants work off their benefits, earning no more than public assistance allowances, and they are without some of the workplace rights of "regular" workers. By contrast, CETA was entirely separate from relief even though it was targeted to the disadvantaged in its later phases. WPA workers had to be eligible for relief, but they were paid a "security wage" that was higher than assistance levels but less than the rate in nonsubsidized employment. CETA workers were sometimes paid "prevailing wages" for similar work.[69] Even with wage constraints in its later years, CETA compensation was well above relief levels.

A workfare requirement is certainly unjust. But what of a fair-work requirement? If and when an entitlement to work is created, then it will be possible to test the assumption that we make: that work requirements are unnecessary when there are sufficient jobs for all who are able-bodied, who do not choose to be occupied for all or part of the work day in family care and for whose children good, affordable care is available. If there remain unfilled jobs and a sizeable residual group who is unwilling to work, not occupied in family care, and unreceptive to humane programs to encourage the work ethic, then policymakers will be in a better position to address the question of work requirements.

GENDER AND COLOR

As the "Findings" for the PRWORA reveal, it is the behavior of women living and breeding without a husband, along with their abusive sexual partners, that constitutes the "crisis" for which current welfare "reform" is the solution. Perhaps the reference to "abusive partners" in the "Findings" reflects a newfound consciousness among welfare reformers that it takes two to make a child. Yet, such statements obscure the economic reasons why so many welfare fathers are neither breadwinners nor husbands. Moreover, it is poor women and their children who suffer the main scorn and the main economic losses of welfare "reform." Indeed, tougher child-support procedures, the law's punishment for the abusive men, often puts battered women at greater risk.[70]

As feminist scholars have documented, impugning the sexual morality of poor, single mothers and punishing them for their behavior and failure to conform to a married-couple standard or "family ethic" is frequent in the annals of relief.[71] Drawing on the pioneering research of Winifred Bell, our account of the early years of ADC shows how illegitimacy became a pretext for denying assistance to the offspring of single mothers. This was also a racist policy, given higher rates of out-of-wedlock parenthood among blacks.[72] However, the result of this harassment, as Piven and Cloward have observed, was to force more poor women into the low-wage labor market, typically the cotton fields. The rhetoric was dominated by family concerns, but program changes or attributes were shaped by the requisites of the labor market.[73]

At the same time that relief policy has inadequately protected poor women, the labor market has either excluded them or offered them a secondary or marginal status, particularly if they were women of color. The fathers of their children have, in many cases, suffered severe labor-market disadvantages, and AFDC policy, throughout its history, as previously mentioned, deprived most poor, two-parent families of assistance. The framers of the PRWORA bemoaned the fact that 89% of the children receiving benefits lived in homes in which no father was present[74]—quite disingenuous in view of the fact that federal law had largely confined benefits to single-parent families throughout the 60-year history of AFDC. Denying eligibility to two-parent families meant that if fathers were either marginally employed or jobless, mothers and children were better off financially without them.

Racism, as already suggested, must be considered in any attempt to understand the kind of language that has shaped welfare discourse and the social policies that flow from it. Michael Katz argues that a number of forms of exclusion—including employer preference, the racism of white unions in keeping out blacks and Latinos, as well as Jim Crow laws and de facto patterns of segregation—have combined to prevent disproportionate numbers of blacks and Latinos from obtaining the ethnic employment niches that enabled other disadvantaged or immigrant groups to become upwardly mobile.[75] Thus, they have suffered a disproportionate share of the unemployment, underemployment, low wages, and economic insecurity that have been endemic to our economy in both good times and bad. This historic exclusion helps to explain, in turn, the dispro-

portionate dependence on welfare of African–Americans and Hispanics.

In sum, the rhetoric of welfare "reform" is based on three assumptions that we refute in this book:

1. Welfare recipients are an "underclass"—basically so lazy or
   demoralized by a culture of poverty that they must be treated
   with "tough love" in order to get them to work.

2. The low-wage labor market into which welfare recipients are
   expected to "graduate" is sufficient not only to support them
   and their families but to provide even traditionally disadvantaged minorities and women with paths out of poverty.

3. Working at any job at any wage is preferable to "dependency,"
   even for the mothers of very young children.

Outline of the Book

The poor laws, observed the English historians J. L. Hammond
and Barbara Hammond, were a system of employment as well as
a system of relief.[76] This book examines the relationships between
labor-market and public-assistance policies from the Great Depression until the present. The book proceeds chronologically,
from the enactment of Aid to Dependent Children (ADC) as Title
IV of the Social Security Act of 1935, through its repeal in 1996
and the first 4 years of its replacement, TANF.

Chapter 2, "Aid to Dependent Children Is Born," covers the
formative years of ADC, 1935–1960. It reveals that in the 1930s,
a decade of many social movements, there was none in behalf of
poor women and children. Little noticed at the time of its enactment, ADC rode into the SSA on the coattails of programs for the
elderly and the unemployed that enjoyed widespread public support. Within the federal government, the U.S. Children's Bureau
was the agency that studied and monitored the state mothers'-aid
programs (enacted in the decades prior to the Great Depression)
on which ADC was modeled. Leaders of the Children's Bureau made
the case for a public-assistance program for dependent children,
drafted the ADC legislation, and testified on its behalf. Like mothers'-
aid programs, but in contrast to emergency relief in the first years
of the Roosevelt administration, ADC was largely restricted to children
of single mothers.

Planners of the SSA took a maternalist approach—women were nurturers and men were breadwinners.[77] They argued that federal funds would enable ADC to succeed where state mothers'-aid programs had failed. Intended to free single mothers from the breadwinner role so that they could perform the nurturing role, mothers'-aid programs had been funded so meagerly that most poor, single mothers were either not aided at all or forced to supplement very low benefits with employment. Although SSA planners proposed that federal grants to the state be contingent on their providing adequate assistance benefits, that stipulation was stricken by southern legislators intent on maintaining a low-wage labor pool. States were also given leeway to make mothers' moral suitability a condition of eligibility, and this amounted to carte blanche for states to deny benefits to families with children born out of wedlock, hence to black families in which such family composition was more prevalent. Suitable homes criteria resulted in denial of ADC to disproportionate numbers of black women and children throughout the formative years of the program. ADC served more blacks than mothers'-aid, but, until the 1960s, far fewer than the number who needed it.

Chapter 3, "Welfare Law and Labor Law: The Formative Years," identifies the fluctuating employment conditions for men and women between 1935 and 1960. New Dealers claimed that employment assurance was more important than income support. They established work programs of unprecedented size, albeit not large enough to cure the massive unemployment of the Great Depression, and for reasons that we ponder, did not make employment assurance part of the nation's permanent legislation for economic security. The work programs were discontinued when World War II temporarily absorbed the unemployed. During the war years, the nation experienced a brief period of full employment and with it a decline in the welfare caseloads. Full employment, however, was not a governmental policy but a by-product of waging a world war.

Although favored in opinion polls by the majority of Americans, a policy of full employment in peacetime that was also endorsed by both presidential candidates in 1944 and passed by the Senate was rejected by the House of Representatives. We explore the reasons why a "road" that would have obviated much unemployment, economic dependency, poverty—and welfare—was not taken, despite the wondrous economic consequences of wartime full employment for civilians and for national income.

Although a number of factors boosted consumption in the immediate postwar years, unemployment rose, although nowhere near prewar levels. It went up more in the 1950s, particularly among African–Americans. With it emerged a racial gap in unemployment rates that persists to this day. During these years, although the need for relief grew, assistance, particularly for blacks, was woefully inadequate. When unemployment returned, there were no work programs, only unemployment insurance to cushion its effects. Unemployment insurance, however, mainly relieves the short-term unemployment of stable workers. Thus, for the chronically and marginally unemployed and many in industries not covered by unemployment insurance, there was either public assistance or nothing at all.

Chapter 4, "Expanding Economy and Exploding Relief Rolls," shows how AFDC policies were liberalized in the 1960s, and how groups long excluded from assistance—both before and after 1935— became eligible. The Kennedy administration began with an effort to reduce dependency through professional casework services that was followed, not by a reduction of the relief rolls, but by a concurrent expansion of both the economy and public relief. The Department of Labor documented the severe subemployment in the nation's ghettos, even during the low unemployment years of the 1960s. Yet, the most obvious strategy for economic opportunity—the assurance of jobs at decent wages, the "road" that had been eschewed by postwar policymakers—was again bypassed. Chapter 4 explains why, for a second time, this particular "road" was not taken.

Two social movements that might have forced the issue were the National Welfare Rights Organization (NWRO) and the Civil Rights Movement. Yet neither did. The principal historian of the NWRO claims that most welfare mothers wanted to work, but the NWRO was hamstrung by its male leadership who supported the traditional sexual division of labor. As a result, NWRO fought for higher benefits and guaranteed incomes for its membership but not for sufficient jobs at living wages for all. Although "Jobs and Freedom" were the twin rallying calls of the 1963 March on Washington, most of the efforts of civil-rights activists were focused on civil and voting rights. Toward the end of his life, Martin Luther King, Jr., moved toward an emphasis on jobs and economic justice. Had his assassination not occurred, the first U.S. movement for full employment might have been born.

The pressure of NWRO and of the community-action programs of the antipoverty war resulted in a big increase of the welfare rolls. Many African–Americans who had been denied eligibility by racist-inspired moral criteria of eligibility and other stratagems began to collect benefits. The increased number of African–Americans on the rolls and the fact that the movement for welfare rights consisted largely of black women made AFDC particularly vulnerable to the media-hyped and politically exploited fears of working-class whites that arose in response to the gains of the Civil Rights Movement, black riots in the nation's cities, and new economic worries.

The 1970s was a transitional decade for social policy. Chapter 5, "Setting the Stage for Welfare[1] Reform, 1967–1980," sketches the structural and ideological climate that helps to explain the mix of progressive and reactionary tendencies exhibited by policymakers during the decade. It begins with the collapse of the Bretton Woods system, the international trade and currency regime that had provided the postwar world with high growth and had made possible a tenuous accord with labor, which in turn had provided some political support for limited expansion of the welfare state.

The chapter then examines the political responses of both the business community and the political elite to the slower growth and stagflation associated with this collapse: the increased politicization of business interests; the replacement of Keynesian economics with conservative monetarist and supply-side policies; a virulent ideological and institutional attack on both organized labor and the welfare program and its recipients; and the development of a harsher conception of the welfare poor that would soon eclipse the milder ones that had dominated the thinking of New Deal policymakers and their progeny. The chapter marks the growth of the "New Right"—a political/religious movement that shifted the center of gravity of the Republican party farther to the Right and created disarray among ideological liberals, setting the stage for a more punitive round of welfare "reform" in the ensuing decade.

Chapter 6, "Enter Welfare 'Reform,' 1967–1980," traces the attempts to "reform" the welfare system that began in the late 1960s and continued throughout the next three decades. It reviews presidential proposals for modest, guaranteed incomes, analyzes the political responses to them, and describes the more punitive welfare "reforms" that were part of the backlash. Chapter 6 also traces the emergence of the initially modest income supplement for working-poor families—the Earned Income Tax Credit—that was already eclipsing federal expenditures for AFDC by the time of its repeal. Presidents Nixon and Carter were seen by some observers as unwilling to spend the money or political resources to achieve the modest income guarantees they had proposed. These measures were, in any case, rejected by congressional conservatives, particularly southerners, who felt they would threaten the traditional low-wage economy of their region.

In analyzing the public policies of the 1970s, Chapter 6 also explores the feeble, ultimately unsuccessful or short-lived attempts of Congress to take the "road" toward job creation and full employment. These were stymied by growing concern over inflation and new definitions of full employment that trivialized joblessness among women, youth, and blacks. Social scientists played a role in rationalizing these conservative social policies, among other things, inventing the notion of a "natural rate of unemployment." For a third time, the "road" appeared on the map, but economic policy took a different turn.

With conservative ideas gaining ground, the stage was set for the election of Ronald Reagan and the political triumph of a more punitive approach to the welfare poor. Chapter 7, "The Final Act: Welfare's Repeal," shows that the Reagan administration's disingenuous creation of a huge federal deficit—the product of tax reductions and hiked defense spending—also became an excuse for reductions in further domestic spending. While moving toward the repeal of welfare, Reagan was unable to accomplish it. Instead, there followed the repressive workfare "reforms."[78] Starting with the work-oriented but ultimately futile Family Support Act (FSA) of 1988, the Reagan, Bush, and Clinton administrations encouraged a series of state "waivers" of federal welfare rules for the purpose of welfare "reform." Increasingly punitive, they were harbingers of the welfare "reform" (PRWORA) that was to come. By the time PRWORA was passed, 43 such waivers had been granted.[79] The PRWORA represented the culmination of over 30 years of welfare "reform" and the near triumph of the New Right's attempts to strip away the New Deal's social legacy. But it was also the failure of the social imagination of both liberals and progressives in bypassing roads that could have led to a different destination. This failure left advocates for the poor trying desperately to hold on to a past program that even they could not wholeheartedly support.

Chapter 8, "Washington's New Poor Law: Part I," explores the

effects of the repeal of AFDC and of its replacement, the PRWORA
of 1996. After 4 years of welfare "repeal," it is possible to project
its impact by considering evidence from studies of the waiver
experiments that preceded it, from the provisions of the bill itself, and from the evidence of this initial period of implementation. Although there have been some improvements over the old
program, by and large the picture is not a hopeful one for the poor.
While public officials tout dramatic drops in the welfare rolls as
signs of the program's success, the more appropriate measure of
success is the ability of welfare recipients to support themselves
and their families with dignity and the opportunity for economic
and social advancement. By this measure, the program appears to
be failing, even in years of unusually low unemployment.

After explaining what the bill does and does not do, Chapter
8 examines the effects of the devolution of responsibility for the
poor to 50 state governments and many more county and city
governments. Most state and local governments have not been friends
of poor and oppressed people, and since the 1930s, disadvantaged
minorities have usually looked to Washington for whatever relief
they could get.[80] Four years into welfare reform, we find a mixed
picture. States have drastically reduced their welfare rolls, are moving
more welfare clients into work than ever before, and are providing them with more resources. However, they have not been successful in providing them with family-supporting jobs, even in a
time of relatively low unemployment. A number of states have adopted
harsher penalties and are discouraging people from applying for
welfare in the first place. Many of the poor have even lost access
to benefits like food stamps and Medicaid. Chapter 8 also explores
the dangers inherent in the drive toward privatization of services,
the punitive and often ineffectual restrictions placed on welfare
recipients, and the false assumptions about the capacity of the labor
market to provide an exit from poverty that underlie the work requirement of the new law.

To base welfare reform on a program to achieve economic self-
sufficiency through work involves ensuring not only that there
are enough good jobs but that the new workers are equipped to get
and hold them. Chapter 9, "Washington's New Poor Law: Part II,"
explores the law's weak commitment to education and training and
the problems policymakers will encounter as they attempt to move
most of their caseloads into the labor market. The architects of
the PRWORA ignored both the law of unintended consequences

and the combined effects of welfare repeal with cuts in other safety-net programs. Chapter 9 examines these consequences and explores one final effect of the new law: the discriminatory impact of welfare reform on immigrants, people of color, and poor women. All of these changes add up to the latest round in an old war against the poor. While the full effects of this war were masked by the strong economy and low unemployment of the late 1990s, as well as by the fact that most welfare recipients had not yet reached their limit on receipt of benefits, there is no telling what will happen when the next recession occurs and there remains only an enfeebled safety net.

Chapter 10, "Real Welfare Reform: The Roads Not Taken," summarizes the conditions that led to welfare repeal: the basic attributes of AFDC that made it politically vulnerable, the burden of the labor-market contexts in which it operated, the lost opportunities for reform of both welfare and work and their political consequences, and finally some immediate conditions that hastened its extinction. Theorists of social welfare have debated whether its social-control functions primarily enforce the work ethic or the family ethic,[81] and, based on our study of work and welfare since 1935, this final chapter takes a critical look at the class, gender, and racial lenses that have previously been applied to the relief system. The chapter then turns to two types of policy goals and political action. The first of these we refer to as "The Politics of Welfare Repair," which deals with the promising renewal of advocacy by low-income groups sparked by the repeal of AFDC. The second is real welfare reform—work reform—whose constituency is potentially much broader than that of welfare.

Since the repeal of AFDC, interest in job creation has begun to take hold among welfare advocates, although full employment as a national policy—not just for welfare recipients—still seems beyond their ken. Nor have policymakers pledged themselves to hold down the unemployment rate, much less lower it further. Real full employment would improve wages, perhaps obviating the rising need for a wage subsidy like the Earned Income Tax Credit. A tighter labor market should make it easier to revive the institutional bulwarks of living wages and job security that were partially torn down in the last three decades. In any case, real full employment is not simply jobs for all but a qualitative as well as quantitative goal, including living wages, such benefits of civilized society as universal health insurance and child care, and a humane workplace.

In arguing for full employment as the focus of reform, we are aware that no society has come close to eradicating poverty, particularly for women and their families, without substantial income transfers. In Sweden, where full employment reigned for more than 60 years, it was the combination of jobs for all, decent wages, and a generous welfare state that provided an escape from poverty for single mothers and their children and that made the workplace friendly to families.[82] In some countries, the welfare state has achieved low levels of poverty without full employment.[83]

Heavy reliance on income transfers, however, is less desirable than full employment and may be politically inadvisable. Countries with rising national incomes, although financially capable of offsetting the effects of increasing unemployment, may well choose not to do so.[84] In any case, with full-employment policies, social policy is freed, to a great extent, from compensating for unemployment and its attendant ills and can more readily finance such policies as universal health insurance, paid parental leaves, family allowances, and quality child care for all. The social attributes of employment for all who want to work, however, are important and transcend its fiscal advantages for the welfare state.

The final chapter explores the case for a government commitment to full employment at decent wages as both a moral and human-rights imperative and a sound economic investment that will have broad benefits for more than just the poor. It addresses many of the issues of fiscal and monetary policy as well as the questions associated with globalization that would have to be considered in carrying out such a policy. Finally, it addresses the question of why there has never been a full-scale, successful movement for full employment in the United States and explores political strategies that would move the country toward a policy of livable-wage jobs for all.

In the final analysis, the obstacles to full employment and jobs at livable wages are not primarily economic or technical. Economic and technical rationales are the excuses political and economic elites use to avoid facing what is at heart a moral and spiritual issue—their inability to share more equitably the common wealth of the nation. As the United States enters the twenty-first century, richer than ever before in its history, it has the opportunity to provide to all its people that source of dignity and security so essential to democracy and international peace—and so long avoided by American policymakers—a socially useful job at a living wage. It could fulfill the dream of an "Economic Bill of Rights" that Franklin Roosevelt proposed more than a half century ago, when this country was very much less wealthy, and which began with two essential guarantees: "the right to a useful and remunerative job" and "the right to earn enough to provide adequate food and clothing and recreation." The Economic Bill of Rights recognized that "true individual freedom cannot exist without economic security and independence." The realization of these *economic rights* would make it easier to solve most of the serious social problems that continue to plague us. The paramount question is, then, do we have the political will?

CHAPTER 2

————⟨∥∥⟩————

Aid to Dependent Children Is Born

The architects of the Social Security Act (SSA)—President Franklin Roosevelt and members of his cabinet who served on the Committee on Economic Security (CES)—preferred that relief be in the form of work. Roosevelt maintained that continued dependence on relief "induces moral disintegration" and that "work must be found for the able-bodied but destitute workers." In a 1935 message to Congress laying out principles for a massive public-employment program, Roosevelt expressed the administration's determination to "preserve not only the bodies of the unemployed from destitution but also their self-respect, their self-reliance and courage and determination."[1] Thus, only a few weeks before proposing the SSA, the landmark legislation that established the American welfare state, Roosevelt declared: "The federal government must and shall quit this business of relief."[2]

Predicting that the economy would not absorb all the unemployed, the CES recommended that public-employment programs "be recognized as a permanent policy of the government and not merely as an emergency measure."[3] Ironically, the actual policies of the federal government turned out to be just the opposite of those articulated by Roosevelt and his close associates. In less than a decade, the work programs of the New Deal were history. By contrast, the direct-relief programs established by the SSA either exist to this day or have been replaced by other federal or federal-state public assistance programs. Instead of quitting the "business of relief," the federal government quit the business of work relief.

Hardly noticed at the time was the relief measure that later became synonymous with welfare—Aid to Dependent Children (ADC), Title IV of the Social Security Act.[4] Along with Old Age

Assistance (Title I) and Aid to the Blind (Title X), ADC was for persons considered unemployable and therefore not eligible for work relief.[5] Most mothers of dependent children were, in fact, able-bodied, but ADC was based on the assumption that fathers should be breadwinners and mothers nurturers. According to congressional testimony by Edwin E. Witte, executive director of the CES, "unemployment compensation, work programs—nothing of that kind—will help these families. They are families without a breadwinner in them, except for the mother, who is needed to care for the children."[6]

This chapter identifies the economic and political forces that gave rise to the SSA and explains how ADC, with no organized clientele or mobilized constituency outside the federal government, came to be included in the nation's permanent social-welfare programs. It traces the history of ADC's formative period, its first quarter century: how it was established during the New Deal, liberalized incrementally in the late 1930s and under the Fair Deal of President Harry S. Truman, and maintained with some modest, statutory improvements, although with less national oversight, under the Republican administration of Dwight D. Eisenhower.[7] The chapter shows how ADC both reflected and transcended its direct predecessors, the mothers' or widows' pensions that had been established in most states in the decades preceding the Great Depression, how it buried some poor-law traces, and bore the mark of some others. The chapter also recounts how low benefits and restricted eligibility failed to substitute for the male breadwinner, or pater familias, and thus did not enable most poor women to assume the "traditional" female role. And it shows that, despite the existence of ADC, millions of poor families, including nearly all with two parents in the home, continued to be deprived of aid and dignity.

Chapter 3 also deals with the period from 1935 to 1960, but from the perspective of labor-market conditions for both men and women. It shows how many poor men, although expected to work, were often unemployed or underemployed and without government work relief. Single mothers, although not expected to work, were frequently forced to do so because of low ADC benefits and restrictive eligibility conditions.

The Great Depression and the Birth of ADC

The 1930s was an era of social movements, but there was no movement for poor mothers and their children.[8] How then can we explain the inclusion of ADC in the Social Security Act of 1935? Advocacy for extension of existing, state mothers'-aid programs by leaders of the U.S. Children's Bureau, the opportunity for change afforded by economic collapse, and the political response to that crisis account for the passage of ADC—despite its lack of an organized constituency outside the federal bureaucracy. Programs for the elderly and, to a lesser extent, the unemployed enjoyed widespread, organized support. ADC rode into the Social Security Act on the coattails of popular movements of the elderly and the unemployed.

THE MOTHERS'-AID MODEL

In 1909, at the urging of Progressive-era reformers, President Theodore Roosevelt convened the White House Conference on Dependent Children.[9] One of the recommendations of the conference was passage of a pending bill to establish a Children's Bureau in the federal government that would collect and exchange ideas and information on child welfare or, as Roosevelt later put it, that would serve as a "recognized and authoritative source of information upon . . . subjects related to child life."[10] Three years later, the bureau was created and placed, a year after its establishment, in the newly created Department of Labor. Had there been no agency within the federal government representing the interests of children, it is unlikely that ADC would have been included in the SSA.[11]

Between 1870 and 1900, an earlier wave of welfare "reform" virtually abolished relief to the poor in their own homes in most of the nation's largest cities.[12] As a result, thousands of families were broken and their children institutionalized.[13] The White House conference resolved that "except in unusual circumstances, the home should not be broken up for reasons of poverty, but only for considerations of inefficiency or *immorality*" (italics added).[14] Mothers' aid, initially called widows' pensions, was thus established in the decades after the White House conference of 1909. By 1935, these programs for single mothers and their children existed in 41 states.[15]

State widows'-pension programs were an attempt to carry out the principles of the White House conference. However, as the CES pointed out in making the case for federal funds, limited amounts of money had kept the state-assistance programs from realizing the goal of "releas[ing] from the wage-earning role the person whose natural function is to give her children the physical and affectionate guardianship necessary. . . ." Federal grants-in-aid, they concluded, were "imperative . . . if the mothers' care method of rearing fatherless families is to become nationally operative."[16]

The Children's Bureau had no formal responsibility for the state mothers'-aid programs, but in carrying out its function of conducting research on the condition of children, the leaders of the Children's Bureau were in a position to know just how limited these programs were.[17] It was a report by Katharine Lenroot and Martha Eliot, bureau chief and assistant bureau chief, respectively, on which the CES based its recommendations for ADC. Lenroot and Eliot argued that attempts to provide security for the unemployed would not benefit families whose breadwinners were absent. For these groups of families, they concluded, "special provision must be made."[18]

ECONOMIC AND POLITICAL CRISIS

As its name implies, the Great Depression was an unprecedented economic crisis threatening the political stability of the country. Historian Eric Goldman contrasts it with a severe nineteenth-century depression:

> It started like 1873. On October 29, 1929, scrambling, yelling traders dumped 16,410,000 shares of stock on the New York Stock Exchange, and the United States refused to believe what it was watching. A nation returned to the cult of captains of industry, did not expect its gods to fail it. . . . The Thirties, like the Seventies, had finally admitted that the captains of industry did not have the situation in hand.

> But having started so much like '73, the new depression soon took on far grimmer lines. All the things that had shocked the country in the Seventies reappeared in doubly disturbing form. Small businesses were going down at a rate never before approached, and the number of farmers losing their lands was nearing the three-quarters-of-a-million mark. . . . The pillaging and bloodshed of the strike of 1877 had been disquieting, but in the early

Thirties, food riots were becoming common, 15,000 angry veterans milled around the national Capitol, and in the Midwest,
where the Seventies had produced nothing more violent than Green-
back speeches, farmers dragged from his bench a judge who tried
to foreclose mortgages, beat him, then strung him up until he
fainted.[19]

Between 1929 and 1932, the nation whose business was business lost faith in its economic and political leaders. When it came
to relieving the suffering of millions of unemployed and destitute
people, President Herbert Hoover was unyielding and even denied their misery in order to rationalize his inaction.[20] Hoover held
that second only to preventing hunger and suffering (for which
he would have called upon "every resource of the federal government") was to maintain at full strength "our great benevolent agencies
for character building, for hospitalization, for care of children and
all their vast number of agencies of voluntary solicitude for the
less fortunate." His third task was "to maintain the bedrock principle of our liberties by the full mobilization of individual and
local resources and responsibilities."[21] In Hoover's view, it would
not be necessary to violate the American creed by providing direct federal relief because his administration was "effectively
preventing hunger and cold."[22]

The facts tell a different story. New York City relief payments
averaged $2.39 a week and could accommodate only about one-
half of the unemployed. The Philadelphia Community Council described the situation in July 1932 as one of "slow starvation and
progressive disintegration of family life."[23] A social worker from
a voluntary agency in the same city told a Senate subcommittee
of shocking, but nonetheless daily, occurrences of homelessness
because relief funds did not cover rent.[24]   Clarence Pickett, executive
secretary of the American Friends Service Committee, testified before
a House subcommittee that people in West Virginia were breaking
into the storehouses and stealing supplies.[25] The collapse of the
nation's banking system on the eve of Roosevelt's inauguration
was still another sign of breakdown. Not to mention that 13 million persons, or about one-fourth of the work force, were unemployed. Labor Secretary Perkins depicted a crisis that clearly met
Hoover's criterion for summoning the resources of the federal
government:

> It is hard today to reconstruct the atmosphere of 1933 and to evoke
> the terror caused by unrelieved poverty and prolonged unemployment.

> The funds of many states and localities were exhausted. The le-
> gal debt limit of many states had been reached, and they could
> borrow no more, even for so urgent a matter as relief. The situ-
> ation was grim in city, country, and state. Public welfare officers
> had reached the end of their rope. . . . The federal government
> and its taxing power were all one could think of.[26]

To New Deal historian Arthur M. Schlesinger, Jr., it was "not just a matter of staving off hunger. It was a matter of seeing whether a representative democracy could conquer economic collapse. It was a matter of staving off violence, even (at least some so thought) revolution."[27]

Although he sounded some of the same notes as his rival for the presidency, especially the goals of a balanced federal budget and sound currency, Franklin Roosevelt differed from Herbert Hoover in acknowledging the severity of conditions and in the emergency relief policies that he immediately initiated. As governor of New York, Roosevelt had experimented at the state level with some of the measures that later became hallmarks of the early New Deal. Providing cash assistance and public employment, the Temporary Emergency Relief Administration (TERA) in New York was followed by the Federal Emergency Relief Administration (FERA) in Washington, and the top welfare aides, Relief Administrator Harry Hopkins and Labor Secretary Frances Perkins, had served him earlier as governor. Moreover, according to Schlesinger, Roosevelt was "the single national political leader to identify himself with the social-insurance cause."[28]

In providing emergency relief, the New Deal made a major break with tradition.[29] The first big change was federal funding. Whereas the poor laws were the province of local and state governments, FERA either shared the costs of direct relief with the states or, if the states were without the resources, paid the whole bill. Under FERA, the federal government bore approximately 70% of total relief costs.[30] Federal resources enabled FERA to serve unprecedented numbers of destitute persons—for example, over three and one-half times the number of families assisted by state mothers'-aid programs.[31]

Second, FERA rules called for "sufficient relief to prevent physical suffering and to maintain minimum living standards"; average relief grants for the country as a whole about doubled from May 1933, when FERA was initiated, to January 1935.[32] According to a representative of the American Association of Social Workers,

"perhaps the greatest thing that has been done to the worker by
the Federal Emergency Relief Administration is that it has for the
first time given assistance . . . that was way over and above anything that we have known in our state poor laws."[33]

Third, in addition to assisting persons considered unemployable, FERA provided both work relief and direct assistance to
employable persons.[34] From the last quarter of the nineteenth century
until the 1930s, public aid for employable persons had been largely
indoor relief, that is, inside the poorhouse or a comparable institution.[35] For a time, then, the federal government offered direct
relief to both the employable and the unemployable poor—a policy
that would end with the Social Security Act.

Less than 2 years after inaugurating the New Deal, Roosevelt
announced that he was planning a permanent security program.
One factor in favor of significant reform at that moment was the
unprecedented victory in midterm elections for the party occupy-
ing the White House. That win in both houses of Congress prompted
FERA Administrator Harry Hopkins to exult: "Now or never, boys—
social security, minimum wage, work programs. Now or never."[36]

Widespread strikes and demonstrations by industrial workers
and the unemployed in 1934 and continuing, albeit at a diminished level, into 1935 are another part of the political context of
the SSA. In Schlesinger's view, the conflict between business and
labor (in 1934) over the right to organize and bargain collectively
"approached civil war" in some communities. Referring to employers' resistance, he wrote: "Never had American businessmen
hired so many private police, strikebreakers, thugs, spies, and agents
provocateurs. Never before had they laid up such stores of tear
gas, machine guns, and firearms."[37]

What were the forces opposing reform? The business community was no longer prostrate, grateful to its rescuers, or willing to
concede being saved by government intervention.[38] Opposed to
government fiscal policies and to increased government regulation, such as the Securities Exchange Act, was the American Liberty
League. Dominated by northern industrialists like Du Pont and
General Motors executives, the league served as "a vehicle for
anti-New Dealers of both parties."[39] In the spring of 1935, the
organized business community, through the U.S. Chamber of Commerce, vigorously opposed the Social Security Bill.[40] Republican
members of the House Ways and Means Committee, who were present
for the vote, said "nay" to it.[41] Jill Quadagno emphasizes that

representatives of the monopoly sector of capital, if not in favor
of government responsibility for old-age security, were much less
opposed than the smaller, competitive business sector, and, seeing its passage likely, did their best to influence the shape of the
legislation.[42] In any case, business was much less unified in its
opinion of the SSA than of the National Labor Relations (Wagner)
Act, also passed in 1935.[43]

The American state structure with its divided powers at the
national level was a restraint on New Deal reform. Perhaps the
most formidable potential foe of legislation expanding the power
of the federal government was the Supreme Court. Likely allies
of the administration, reformers such as Justice Louis Brandeis,
were wary of big government as well as big business. These liberals united with conservatives on the bench to invalidate some
major New Deal programs.[44] And certainly the prospect of such a
fate for Social Security may have limited federal control over
permanent income-support programs.

Congress, the other part of the government triad, had some
outspoken conservative voices, New Deal adherents, and some others
who were to the left of the Democrat in the White House. Legislators like Senators Robert Wagner of New York and Robert M.
LaFollette, Jr., of Wisconsin had striven vainly for social-minded
policies in the 1920s and early 1930s. Others were pushing the
administration further: the populist senator from Louisiana, Huey
Long, whose "share-the-wealth" proposal Roosevelt coopted in the
Wealth Tax Act of 1935; Congressman Ernest Lundeen, whose
"Workers' Unemployment, Old-age and Social Insurance Act" featured
benefits at the average-wage level for all jobless persons, regardless of the reasons for unemployment, under a democratic plan
allowing for local representation by recipients; Senator Hugo Black,
who wanted insurance programs to be financed by more progressive taxes instead of the regressive payroll taxes favored by administration and business proponents; and Representative John
McGroarty, whose proposed legislation embodied the Townsend
Plan that called for a universal benefit of $200 a month for all
unemployed persons over 60, providing they spent it in the next
30 days.

Although it could not be called a movement with a mass following like the Townsendites, the American Association for Labor Legislation (AALL) had developed social-insurance concepts
in the decades preceding the Great Depression and influenced those

who framed and ultimately implemented the SSA.[45] Advocates of
social insurance, like I. M. Rubinow and Abraham Epstein, favored higher benefits and more significant income distribution.

Edith Abbott, dean of the School of Social Service Administration at the University of Chicago, decried the policy of returning to states with insufficient resources those destitute persons not
eligible for federally aided assistance (not aged, blind, or dependent children) and for whom work relief was either unavailable or
unsuitable.[46] Also exerting pressure and in time forming an un-
easy coalition with Townsend and Long was the radical, fascistic
"radio priest," Father Coughlin, who first considered the New Deal
"Christ's Deal" but later turned against it for failing to make more
radical changes.[47]

These pressures for more radical reform provided the administration with a strategy for gaining passage of the SSA. "Congress," observed the *New York Herald Tribune*, "was being told it
would get Townsend or Long if it failed to pass the Economic Security
Bill. . . ."[48] Frances Perkins later recalled that "one hardly real-
izes nowadays how strong was the sentiment in favor of the Townsend
Plan and other exotic schemes for giving the aged a weekly income."[49] In the *New York Times*, there were references, like that
of Speaker of the House Joseph W. Byrns, to the "mountainous
piles of letters with which Congress is deluged by supporters of
the Townsend and Lundeen plans."[50]

Added to this mixture of conflicting forces was the powerful
president himself. If not a fiscal conservative, Roosevelt often
acted like one, notably in cutting back the WPA in 1937, a policy
that contributed to the slump, the "depression within the depression," the next year that significantly reduced confidence in the
New Deal.[51] Or did the president go slowly because he believed
that the American people were unprepared for a permanent reform, despite the experience of a depression that did not abate
until the federal government intervened? Yet the receptivity to
social insurance and labor legislation had changed. According to
New York Senator Robert Wagner, he seemed to be living in a
different world.[52]

In June 1933, only a few months after taking office, the New
Deal president told a *New York Times* reporter: "We'll be social-minded
enough in another year to make a beginning in a great social reform which must be carefully adapted to our special conditions
and needs." Whatever changes in the public mind that 3 years of

depression had wrought, Roosevelt nonetheless held that "a nation has to be educated to the point where reforms can be assimilated without dangerous spasms of indigestion."[53] The American ethos of individualism was one in which welfare and security, particularly if these entailed expansion of federal authority, were alien. Perhaps Roosevelt was not being overly cautious in judging that the Great Depression had not shattered the American creed of self-sufficiency. A year later, Oswald Garrison Villard, the editor of the Left-leaning *Nation* wrote, "it will be wise leadership as well as sound strategy if the President makes use of the next six months to prepare the public mind for his programs of advanced social legislation. . . ."[54]

While the times were favorable to social security, Roosevelt's effort to build consensus for reform is a prime example of presidential leadership of public opinion.[55] In the year preceding passage of the SSA, President Roosevelt and his lieutenants built support for a value inimical to the American creed and showed its compatibility with traditional beliefs of the frontier nation. In one of his famous fireside chats, in November 1934, Roosevelt told his radio audience, "I prefer and am sure you prefer that broader definition of liberty to which we are moving forward to greater freedom, to greater security for the average man [*sic*] than he has ever known before."[56] Urged to "discuss the matter in as many groups as possible," Labor Secretary Perkins made more than 100 speeches during the year prior to passage of the Social Security Act, "always stressing social insurance as one of the methods for assisting the unemployed in times of depression and in preventing depressions."[57]

The administration emphasized security obtained through social insurance, not public assistance. The most innovative programs of the SSA were Old Age Insurance and Unemployment Insurance (Titles II and III), both financed through payroll taxes. The planners of the SSA were initially resistant to continuing federal aid to unemployable persons but yielded because poverty was widespread and local and state resources for poor relief depleted[58]— not to mention intense political pressure from the elderly. For the poor elderly, blind, and dependent children, the federal government would provide partial funding of relief through its general revenues. However, other needy people would once again be dependent on state and local governments with inadequate resources to care for them.

Beyond Mothers' Aid—but How Far?

ADC borrowed from existing mothers'-aid programs but transcended them. What follows is a comparison of the two programs with regard to such attributes as coverage and types of benefits provided. Perhaps the greatest change was partial financing by the federal government. Liberalization also came during the Truman administration when ADC became an entitlement. However, despite greatly increased black recipience, ADC often abetted racism, particularly through the use of moral qualifications for eligibility that disproportionately excluded African–Americans.

COVERAGE

ADC provided broader coverage of poor families than mothers'aid, but it still left out the majority of poor families with dependent children. One reason for ADC's broader coverage was its availability in vastly more jurisdictions than mothers' aid. Since state mothers'-aid laws were often permissive rather than mandatory, many localities failed to offer benefits. Relatively little state money was available for these programs, and depending so largely on local funds, they assisted only a fraction of those in need.[59] At no time before passage of the Social Security Act did more than one-half the counties in the country provide mothers' pensions.[60] In contrast, the SSA stipulated that if a state were to get ADC funds, the program must be mandatory and in effect in all political subdivisions of the state.[61]

As the name Aid to Dependent Children implies, the planners of the SSA switched the focus in family assistance from mothers' to children's aid. The *Report of the Committee on Economic Security* pointed out that what it proposed were "not primarily aids to mothers, but defense mechanisms for children."[62] This had the effect of drawing attention away from mothers' behavior and may have facilitated coverage of unmarried mothers.

Mothers' pensions were initially confined to widows and orphans.[63] In fact, during the early years, they were often known as "widows' pensions." Even in the early thirties, when one-half of the 41 states with mothers'-aid laws covered deserted families, more than four-fifths of the families served were, in fact, widows and their children.[64] Nonetheless, in her testimony to Congress, Katharine Lenroot conveyed the impression that mothers' aid was more inclusive than it was in reality. For example, she provided a table entitled *Conditions under which mothers' aid may be granted* showing that 39 of 49 jurisdictions permitted aid to "any mother" or to "deserted" mothers.[65] Formally this was the case, but actually, as noted, very few families other than those of widows were served. At the same time, Lenroot emphasized continuity with past American experience and held that the provisions for children's security in the bill "build upon experience that has been well established in this country."[66] She pointed out that the eligibility standards called for in the bill "would be broad enough to include all families where there is only one adult person, and that person needed for the care of children under 16. . . ."[67] Yet, if these standards were implemented, the new legislation would deviate significantly from the nation's experience with mothers' aid.

The Social Security Act did have broader eligibility standards than mothers' aid. The SSA contained no reference to the marital status of the adult with whom the dependent child would live. A dependent child was defined as one who is deprived of parental support, not only by death but by "continued absence from the home, or physical or mental incapacity of a parent."[68] Secretary of Labor Frances Perkins, who thought in terms of widows or married women with disabled or deserting husbands but not unwed mothers, reportedly felt misled by the Children's Bureau.[69]

Broader though it was, ADC's definition of a "dependent child" still did not include children in two-parent families who were deprived of support by the unemployment or insufficient wages of one or both of those parents. A definition of dependent children, advanced by the FERA, that would have extended coverage to children in two-parent families in which the father was unemployed, hence to virtually to all families requiring relief, was turned down by the CES.[70] As a result, ADC was confined to "fatherless families," and it remained overwhelmingly a program for single-mother families until its repeal. The SSA planners maintained that families other than those without breadwinners would be helped by provisions for the unemployed through private industrial recovery or a works program or, in the future, unemployment compensation.[71] While a portion of adults in two-parent families were covered by work-relief programs during the Depression and more were employed during the brief periods of full- or near-full employment during wartime, this was never the case in peacetime. Nor did unemployment compensation reach the most disadvantaged workers.

CASH BENEFITS

The SSA stipulated that "'aid to dependent children' means money payments with respect to a dependent child or dependent children."[72] For at least a century, as the poignant title of Michael Katz' history of American social welfare suggests, the poor had lived "in the shadow of the poorhouse."[73]

That shadow was erased for poor people covered by the Social Security Act—by its stipulation that public assistance programs were to provide cash or money payments. Mothers' aid, too, provided cash benefits but, as shown, it was much more limited in coverage than ADC. Even the ground-breaking FERA had permitted both cash and benefits in kind.[74]

LOW BENEFITS

Most of the women who had managed to qualify for mothers' aid were nonetheless forced to work for wages.[75] The reason for this—and one that would become important in ADC as well—is that benefits were often too low to support a family. In families receiving mothers' aid, the children often worked too, despite the fact that its benefits were supposed to cushion the impact on family income of state laws outlawing child labor. Meager mothers'-aid benefits, concludes historian Stephanie Coontz, contributed to a "system [that] did not so much subsidize domesticity as endorse low-paid, part-time, irregular work for women in marginal labor markets."[76] This description of mothers' aid also fits ADC and, to an even greater extent, its replacement, TANF.

Despite some liberalization, ADC benefits remained low. Benefits were paltry, even with Washington sharing the costs of the program with the states. Low benefits persisted despite the fact that the federal government increased its share of program costs in 1939 and five additional times between 1946 and 1956. The lower the benefit, the smaller the number of eligible families. Low benefits thus meant that large numbers of needy families were excluded from coverage because their incomes were above the benefit levels. They were thus obliged to depend on the labor market or other sources of income.

As first drafted, the SSA (then the Economic Security Bill) required the monthly benefit "to provide, when added to the income of the family, a reasonable subsistence compatible with decency and health."[77] Under the leadership of Senator Harry Byrd of Virginia, the Senate deleted from the bill these attempts to set minimum standards. None of the public-assistance titles in the SSA—ADC, OAA, and Aid to the Blind—required the states to meet standards of minimum adequacy in order to receive federal funds. According to Wilbur Cohen, Byrd was responsible for the bill's "most significant long-range loss . . . the fatal blow that still prevents any effective nationwide quantitative standards in federal-state welfare. . . ."[78] Byrd argued against requiring adequate benefits because of the financial burden it would impose on states like his own Virginia and on what he referred to as the "dictatorial power" of the federal administrator over what the state would be permitted to do.[79] In arguing against a minimum standard for OAA, Representative Howard W. Smith, also of Virginia, called attention to the potential threat to cheap labor:

> You take the average laborer on the farm, . . . and his earning capacity on an average over the past times has been from $20 to $30 a month. To put him on a pension at sixty-five of $30 a month is not only going to take care of him, but a great many of his dependents . . . who could much better be employed working on a farm.[80]

Economic historians Lee J. Alston and Joseph Ferrie maintain that deleting "reasonable subsistence" standards is an indication that class factors—to keep both white and black agricultural labor cheap and dependent on southern landlords—were more important than the racial motives.[81] However, CES executive director Witte wrote that "at least some southern Senators feared that this measure might serve as an entering wedge for federal intereference with the handling of the Negro question in the South."[82] In any case, although the SSA required states to set a standard of need in assistance programs, it did not require them to meet that standard in providing assistance, and in 1950, less than one-half the states fully met their own standards of need in any of the federally aided public-assistance programs.[83]

Washington did even less to encourage states to meet standards of minimum adequacy for dependent children than for the elderly. Whereas the federal government would reimburse states half the benefit paid to a recipient of Old Age Assistance, up to a limit of $30 a month, it would only reimburse one-third of an ADC benefit, up to $18 for the first child and up to $12 for each of the other dependent children in a family.[84] This meant Washington would contribute up to $15 a month for the elderly poor, compared to $6 a month for the first child and $4 a month for the other poor, dependent children in a family. The 1939 SSA amendments raised the federal share to one-half of $18 a month for the first child and one-half of $12 for each additional child; the proportions of the grant as well as the maximum amounts in which Washington would share were raised in 1946 and 1948.[85] The House Ways and Means Committee turned down President Truman's 1948 proposal that the federal government "match more fully the higher payments which many states find necessary to meet the needs of recipients" and that the federal grants be related to the financial resources and needs of the state.[86] Despite that defeat, federal shares were increased in 1952 and 1956, and grants were varied in relation to states' ability to pay in 1958.[87]

In ADC's first 15 years, grants were not given to the mother or other relative with whom the child was living. Thus, the children's grants had to be shared with the adult. Although interested in relieving the mother from the breadwinner role, framers of the SSA evidently gave little thought to her bread. Was this an unanticipated consequence of the efforts by child advocates to draw attention away from mothers and toward children?

Edwin Witte, the executive director of CES, had a different interpretation. He pointed out to congressional leaders that it was "utterly illogical to expect a mother and a child under 16 to live on $18 per month when old age assistance grants of $30 per month for an individual were contemplated in the same Act"; that this was a justified criticism was acknowledged, though no change was made. The reason? Witte believed it was because "there was little interest in Congress in the aid to dependent children."[88] Fifty years afterward, Wilbur Cohen, secretary of Health, Education and Welfare (HEW, now Health and Human Services [HHS]) under President Lyndon Johnson, wrote: "No one foresaw the dimensions or significance ADC was to have as 'the welfare program' in later years."[89]

The difference in organized support for children and the elderly and in consequent congressional and executive interest is reflected in the size of average benefits in 1940: $9.43 per recipient of ADC, compared to $20.10 per OAA recipient.[90] The Truman administration recommended—and Congress enacted in the 1950 Amendments—federal matching grants for one needy relative living with the dependent child.[91] Yet, in 1959, the gap between average OAA and ADC benefits was about as wide as it was in 1940.[92]

Clearly, this is not merely a reflection of the differing needs of the two age groups but of the disparity in their political clout. OAA, moreover, was largely "white," and ADC, although largely white, too, was disproportionately African–American.

As administered in the South, the ADC program, observed historian Jacqueline Jones, probably could not sustain a family whose mother did not work. However, she points out, ADC allowed at least some black women in the urban north to withdraw from the paid labor force and to improve the quality of family life as a result. "New-Deal welfare programs afforded an opportunity to place family considerations over the demands of white employers."[93] Reports of county ADC supervisors in the early days of the program reveal, on the one hand, an "intense desire not to interfere with local labor conditions" and to have employable Negro mothers continue their "usually sketchy seasonal labor or indefinite domestic service rather than receive a public-assistance grant." On the other hand, aid was given to Negro families in another county because "the scale of wages and employment opportunities for Negroes are [*sic*] so extremely low that without these grants the children would undoubtedly starve."[94]

Researchers Gordon Blackwell and Raymond Gould called attention to the fact that "the income of ADC families in 1950 was still far from adequate to assure a level of living compatible with minimum health and decency." At the time, the average payment per ADC recipient was $17.64 a month, about 60% of the lower of two urban standards proposed by Blackwell and Gould.[95] Studying ADC in the late 1950s, the Advisory Council on Public Assistance reported continuing failure to meet standards of adequacy in the program for dependent children.[96] Only one-fifth of the states met full need by their own standards. Just one state met 100% of need under a standard based on food costs.

With benefits so low, recipients were probably forced to supplement their incomes with earnings or other income sources, and many others who were poor by all but the most meager standards had incomes too high to qualify for ADC. Recent research by Kathryn Edin and Laura Lein found that many families' supplemented benefits too small for subsistence with employment that very few of them reported fully, if at all, to welfare departments.[97] Thus, we infer that families may well have worked and not reported it in earlier decades, particularly since earnings were deducted from welfare checks, dollar for dollar, until 1962, when work expenses

could first be taken into account, and 1967, when the first $30
and one-third of the remainder of total monthly income could be
disregarded.[98] The structure of the program was such that recipients had no incentive to work unless off the books, especially in
the early decades. Although the tax was less than 100% after 1967
(67%), the incentive was modest. Some additional support for our
inference that recipients were indeed working comes from a study
in Philadelphia that found that nearly 90% of welfare mothers had
been or were working in 1962.[99]

RESIDENCE REQUIREMENTS

Residence requirements, or settlement laws as they were called
in earlier times, were hallmarks of the poor laws in England and
were transported to North America by British colonists. By denying relief to newcomers or persons who had not established residence in a particular jurisdiction, settlement laws limited local
financial responsibility in a system entirely financed by local
governments. Settlement laws were also believed to keep paupers
from migrating to places where benefit levels were higher. The
most punitive of these statutes made it possible to eject from a
parish persons who, in the opinion of the authorities, might in the
future become dependent. In the eighteenth century, Adam Smith
wrote: "There is scarce a poor man in England of 40 years of age
. . . who has not in some part of his life felt himself most cruelly
oppressed by this ill-contrived law of settlements."[100]

The Social Security Act permitted the states to impose residence requirements on the very young. Under Title IV, states could
deny assistance to a child who had resided in the state less than
a year or, if born in the state within a year preceding application,
whose mother had lived there less than a year.[101] During the late
1950s, particularly, state residence requirements were strictly
enforced, thus keeping new, African–American migrants to northern cities off the rolls.[102]

Elimination of state residence and citizenship requirements
as a condition for federal matching funds was another recommendation of the Truman administration that was rejected by a Democratic Congress.[103] According to the Public Assistance Advisory
Council (1960), "the great majority of states have residence requirements that, with much resultant hardship, exclude many fi-

nancially needy persons from public assistance."[104] In 1968, the National Advisory Commission on Civil Disorders, appointed by President Lyndon Johnson, commented that residence requirements probably did little to discourage migration but "frequently served to prevent those in greatest need—desperately poor families arriving in a strange city—from receiving the boost that might give them a fresh start."[105] Migrant workers were among those particularly oppressed by residence requirements. Without access to the safety net, they were obliged to work for any job at any wage. In 1969, when the Supreme Court declared residence laws unconstitutional, HEW estimated that between 125,000 and 175,000 additional recipients would be added to the rolls.[106]

ENTITLEMENT

During the formative period of ADC, many of the states were short of funds and consequently closed intake until a vacancy was created by a case closing. Thus, like mothers' aid and the poor laws, ADC did not begin as an entitlement in the sense of serving every family who met eligibility standards. The 1950 amendments to the SSA changed that. Passed during the administration of President Harry Truman, the 1950 amendments required state plans to provide that "all individuals wishing to make application for aid to dependent children shall have the opportunity to do so, and that aid to dependent children shall be furnished with reasonable promptness to all eligible individuals."[107]

With the repeal of AFDC in 1996, Congress, as we noted in Chapter 1 (see p. 1), rescinded the entitlement to welfare for needy families with children that had been part of the statutes for 36 years. In advocating for ADC, Grace Abbott, a former chief of the Children's Bureau and professor of public welfare at the University of Chicago, emphasized what continuous availability of assistance could do for families: "Usually the children are really nice children and the families are nice families, if they could just be put on a permanent basis of knowing that the money was coming, and plan for it. It would make great difference in the security of these families."[108] Repealing the AFDC entitlement in 1996—in the name of "welfare reform"—was a throwback to the poor laws and the very antithesis of social security for children.

STATE WORK REQUIREMENTS

ADC's state work requirements also enforced low-wage work. Despite planners' goal of releasing mothers from the wage-earning role, the SSA was silent about the employment of adults who cared for eligible, dependent children. States, therefore, were free to deny assistance to recipients when local employers needed their services, and southern states, particularly, availed themselves of the opportunity. For example, in 1943 Louisiana adopted a policy of refusing assistance to all applicants or recipients of ADC so long as they were needed in the cotton fields. In one parish, children as young as 7 were covered by this policy, and, expectedly, most of the families to whom it applied were black.[109] In the early 1950s, Arkansas adopted a similar policy requiring able-bodied mothers and older children to accept employment whenever it was available.[110] Whether or not states adopted work requirements formally, public-welfare agencies "in the interest of economy and in an effort to make a showing in reduction of the number of cases, were shortsightedly forcing mothers to accept paid employment outside of the home, with little real consideration of the individual needs of their children. . . ."[111]

Work requirements were not confined to southern states. A hearing convened by the Illinois State Advisory Committee of the U.S. Commission on Civil Rights in 1966 revealed that African–Americans in southern Illinois were routinely denied aid during certain seasons of the year and forced to work for $.50 an hour.[112] Thus, even during the years when the stated intent of federal policy was to free poor, single mothers from the role of breadwinner, many mothers, often African–American women, were forced into the low-wage labor market. In this respect, ADC functioned similarly to mothers' aid.

Racism

Exclusion based on race was another characteristic of mothers' aid that found its way into ADC. In 1931, black, single-mother families received only 3% of total mothers' pensions, and some counties, even entire southern states, denied these mothers aid altogether.[113] By contrast, black children made up 14% of children accepted for ADC in 1937–1938 and, although still not served in proportion to their need, were a significant proportion of the children accepted for aid in southern states.[114] Nonetheless, a number of states were adept at denying ADC to eligible African–Americans. And as Chapter 4 shows, soon after blacks came onto the ADC caseload in numbers commensurate with their need and deprivation during the 1960s, the program found itself in jeopardy. Indeed the federal government attempted to impose some restrictions that resembled those common in southern states during the early years of ADC.

MORAL ELIGIBILITY

An important carryover from mothers' aid was the use of moral criteria to determine eligibility for assistance. "Mothers' aid," writes historian Linda Gordon, "honor[ed] the quintessential female labor, mothering."[115] Yet, it was not mothering per se that was "honored." Eligibility depended on a mother's worthiness or ability to provide a "suitable home." To be eligible for a pension, a mother had to be "a proper person, physically, mentally and morally fit to bring up her children."[116]

From the inception of ADC, states restricted eligibility on moral grounds that were not stipulated in the federal statute. As Winifred Bell points out, "The Social Security Act did not require that children live in 'suitable homes' or have 'fit parents' in order to qualify for assistance."[117] These "suitable-homes" policies, however, were consistent with the congressional intent that "a state may . . . impose such other eligibility requirements—as to means, moral character, etc.—as it sees fit."[118] Interestingly, although the Children's Bureau and the social-work profession supported suitable-homes policies over the years, Lenroot and Eliot's report to the CES makes no recommendation regarding a suitable-homes policy.[119] Federal authorities and the Child Welfare League of America, which included directors of most state public-welfare agencies, favored suitable home criteria but associated them with "standards of care and health fixed by state laws."[120] However, by not forbidding the use of moral criteria and allowing state discretion, the federal statute opened the door for the use of suitable-homes policies for exclusion ostensibly based on morality but actually based on race. "Suitable homes," according to Patterson, was "a euphemism for those with illegitimate children."[121] Since out-of-wedlock births were more prevalent among blacks than whites, states found ways—without directly discriminating by race—to deny ADC to black women and their children.

Winifred Bell, who carefully detailed these and other devices to limit ADC caseloads, concluded that the primary functions of moral eligibility criteria were: "(1) to restrict the growth of the caseload; and (2) to inhibit ADC coverage of Negro and illegitimate children who because of their family composition were more apt to qualify than were white children with two able-bodied parents in the home."[122] An important indication that these laws were punitive is that children in homes declared "unsuitable" by local welfare departments were seldom removed and placed in more "suitable" homes.

In 1959, Florida passed a law that included seven conditions of unsuitability, six of which were traditional types of neglect.[123] The seventh included promiscuous conduct in or outside the home and having an illegitimate child after receiving an assistance payment. All but 73 of the 5,000 families alleged not to be providing a "stable moral environment" were black, even though whites were nearly 40% of the total caseload.

In 1960, Louisiana went overboard to reduce its caseload through "suitable-homes" policies.[124] No assistance was to be provided to any child whose mother had given birth to an illegitimate child after receiving assistance without satisfactory evidence that illicit relationships had ceased and the home was suitable. Louisiana Governor Jimmie H. Davis explained that the state's Suitable Home Law was "designed to take off the welfare rolls those who made it their business to produce illegitimate children."[125] The entire Louisiana ADC caseload was reviewed. Within a few months more than 6,000 families were notified—without mentioning their statutory right to appeal—that their checks would be discontinued. The result: loss of benefits to more than 30,000 adults and children. Of the children cut off, 95% were black, although black children were just 66% of Louisiana's ADC caseload.[126]

In the last days of the Eisenhower administration, HEW Secretary Arthur F. Flemming ruled that states could not deny assistance to a needy child on the basis of unsuitable home conditions without making provisions to put the child in a foster home or provide for food and shelter in another way.[127] As a *New York Times* editorial put it, "if a state finds a home is 'unsuitable' because of the presence of an illegitimate child or children, the responsibility remains for the state to provide a 'suitable home' if it wants to continue to get federal ADC funds."[128] In making his ruling, Secretary Flemming pointed out that seven other states—Georgia,

Arkansas, Mississippi, Texas, Florida, Virginia, and Michigan—had suitable-homes laws that might conflict with his resolution.[129] Congress upheld the Flemming Ruling, but Bell reveals that it accomplished almost nothing because states turned to other vague and discriminatory tests.[130]

State "man-in-the-house" rules also limited eligibility for ADC. According to Piven and Cloward, man-in-the-house rules in the South were directed almost exclusively against blacks. This policy, they point out, denied a man the support of his family and forced him to take subminimum work.[131] If a man were in the house, public-assistance departments assumed the man was a substitute father and that the children were therefore not "deprived of parental support." This also became a suitability issue since it presumably involved promiscuity and illegitimacy. The infamous midnight raids in which public-assistance workers would visit and search for men in the houses of clients were devices for detecting the presence of substitute fathers. The substitute-parent ploy was used by states throughout the 1950s to reduce caseloads.

The Advisory Council on Public Assistance, appointed in 1959 by Secretary Flemming, concluded that, rather than being a cause of increasing rates of single motherhood, ADC was "a reflection of their existence. . . ."[132] The Advisory Council favored continuing aid to children who were born out of wedlock or victims of a deserting parent and expanding the program to all needy children outside institutions.

Congressional concern for moral eligibility did not end with the Flemming ruling. As Chapter 1 noted, Congress trotted out moral criteria to justify welfare repeal. Children growing up in single-parent homes—like the vast majority of children on AFDC—were prone to a host of social problems and antisocial behavior.[133] In other words, Congress was continuing to accuse welfare mothers of not providing suitable homes for their children and, thus, to restrict aid to them.

CHANGING CASELOAD, GROWING UNPOPULARITY, AND THE ATTACK ON PUBLIC WELFARE

Contrary to common misperception, the majority of the early ADC caseload were not the children of "respectable" widows. In the late 1930s, 43% of the ADC caseload consisted of families with a deceased father, but in the majority (57%) fathers were incapacitated or absent from the home for other reasons. The proportion of families with an unmarried mother was very low in the early years, perhaps owing to the slow process of change from more restrictive mothers'-aid laws.[134]

One consequence of the 1939 Amendments to the SSA, which extended Old Age Insurance to dependents and survivors (widows and orphans) of insured workers, was to increase the proportion of the ADC caseload whose mothers were divorced, separated, or never-married. As a result of these amendments, more than two out of five of the ADC families headed by a widow were transferred to the Old Age and Survivors' Insurance.[135] Why were more than half not transferred? The reason is that many lower income men, particularly African–Americans, worked in jobs not then covered by Old Age and Survivors' Insurance.

Increases in desertion, divorce, and out-of-wedlock births in the years following World War II were another development that contributed to changes in the composition of the ADC caseload. The nation's divorce rate more than doubled between 1939 and 1946; it had fallen by 1948, although not to prewar levels. The rate of out-of-wedlock births rose over 70% between 1939 and 1947 and showed no signs of abating in the late 1940s.[136]

Trends that were depriving children of parental support were associated with social and economic dislocations. War, with its disruption of family life, was certainly a factor; so was the exodus from the rural south of increasing numbers of landless, agricultural workers, among them African–Americans who were vulnerable not only to the vicissitudes of poverty and migration, but to racial discrimination as well. Writing in the 1950s, Phyllis Osborn pointed to problems that are always inherent in mass migration of persons whose impoverishment undermines their ability to support their children: lack of education and trade skills and racial discrimination in employment.[137]

By 1948, African–Americans were three times as likely to live apart from their spouses as whites.[138] In their 16-state study of ADC caseloads, Alling and Leisy found that the proportion of African–American families on the rolls had increased by 46% between 1942 and 1948, no doubt a reflection of the growing rate of black single motherhood.[139] Among 6,500 ADC families in 38 states in 1950–1951, African–American mothers were 48% less likely than white recipients to be widows, 57% more likely to be deserted by their husbands, and four times as likely to be unmarried or to have out-of-wedlock children.[140]

Thus, changes in family composition and the coverage of some widows—particularly white women—and their children through social insurance had much to do with the change in the clientele of the ADC caseload. By 1951, fathers in one-half (52%) of ADC families were absent for reasons other than incapacity, and only about one-fifth (21%) were deceased.[141]

As ADC became more African–American and more concentrated among those whose need was associated with socially disapproved behavior, it increasingly became a target of criticism.[142] Phyllis Osborn referred to "what has often seemed to be an organized effort to discredit the ADC program,"[143] speculating that "the recent devastating attacks were to a considerable extent associated with desperate efforts to unseat an administration that had been in power in the national government for 20 years." She observed that the virulence of the attacks had subsided since the 1952 elections. In his 1953 social security message, President Eisenhower had stated that "the human problems of individual citizens are a proper concern of our government" and that "to reduce both the fear and the incidence of destitution to the minimum . . . are proper aims of all levels of government, including the federal government."[144]

Axinn and Levin attribute "the attack on public welfare" to rising costs and changing composition of the assistance rolls—fewer elderly and more families with dependent children. There was also the changing image of the adult recipient of assistance from the worthy elderly and widows to women who had children out of wedlock.

What accounts for states' increased leeway to invoke punitive measures? According to Axinn and Levin, it resulted from the Eisenhower administration's shift toward state discretion and away from centralized federal authority.[145] Earlier in the decade, prior to the Eisenhower presidency, the federal Bureau of Assistance upheld a provision of the SSA, but Congress overruled it. The Bureau had withdrawn funds from Indiana when it violated the statutory protection of recipients' privacy by reverting to the poor-law practice of making public their names and the amounts of their payments. However, in 1951 Congress permitted this violation of the SSA with no loss of federal funds.[146]

The attack on public welfare rose to a high pitch in the so-called "Newburgh Crisis." In 1961, the city manager of this Hudson River town in New York State announced a code of welfare regulations

that "included in one package many of the devices being used across
the country to control the size of welfare rolls and to reduce welfare
expenditures."[147] Intended as a crackdown on "welfare chiseling"
by "undesirable newcomers"—recent African–American migrants
from the South—the code included loss of benefits for able-bodied
adult males who refused municipal work, denial of relief to voluntary job leavers, substitution of vouchers for cash payments, and
termination of relief to unwed mothers who had another child out
of wedlock.[148] Judging that the code would be in violation of the
SSA as well as state laws, the New York State Social Welfare Board
ordered Newburgh not to implement these regulations, and Governor Nelson Rockefeller expressed disapproval of the stringent
code.[149] However, the code was not without its supporters. For
example, a *Wall Street Journal* editorial lamented: "It's a fine
commentary on public morality in this country when a local
community's effort to correct flagrant welfare abuses is declared
illegal under both state and federal law"; Senator Barry Goldwater
(R-Ariz.), who would be the Republican standardbearer in the next
presidential election, heartily approved of the Newburgh initiative.[150] (Chapter 3 discusses the Kennedy administration's response
to the issues raised by Newburgh.)

Rising costs contributed to the attack on welfare. These were
the result of population growth, liberalization of benefits, changing family composition, migration, higher unemployment, and the
expansion of the program to more jurisdictions.[151] A bigger contributor to higher ADC costs than the increase in caseloads was
the rise in benefit levels. Piven and Cloward point out that although the national average benefit level rose almost by one-half,
the rolls rose only 17%.[152] Much of the rise in benefits was attributable to keeping up with inflation. ADC benefits, although higher,
nonetheless remained meager.[153] Focusing on the entire public-assistance caseload, Axinn and Levin make a similar point to that of
Piven and Cloward, namely that costs rose more steeply than the
number of beneficiaries.[154]

Rising costs were a concern to liberals as well as conservatives. Former Connecticut Governor Abraham Ribicoff, later secretary
of HEW under the Kennedy administration, told a congressional
committee: "I can tell you that from my own experience in six years
as Governor that there were few problems that were as frustrating
and as bothersome as the whole problem of welfare costs. . . .
Welfare costs keep going up every year."[155] Although there was

concern over rising caseloads, the increase was modest compared to that of the following decade when, as we shall show, many families who would have been denied assistance in the 1950s were added to the rolls. Deterrent practices reminiscent of both the poor laws and mothers' aid—such as residence requirements and moral criteria of eligibility—help to explain the relatively modest rise in caseloads in a time of increasing unemployment, social dislocation, and single parenthood.

GENERAL ASSISTANCE: THE LAST RESORT

General assistance is the last resort of needy individuals and families not eligible for federally aided programs—most two-parent families, childless couples, and single adults who are neither disabled nor elderly. Like state and local relief under the poor laws, general assistance has always been meager in coverage and benefit levels.[156] As a federal government monograph states: "From a national point of view, the decentralization of general relief led to a substantial reduction in relief standards," particularly in the South.[157] Since the emergency relief programs of the Great Depression, the federal government has provided no money for general relief or to those individuals and families not covered by the categorical programs of the SSA. Nor does Washington require the states to assist them. Even where general assistance is available, observed the Advisory Council on Public Assistance in 1960, "more often than not by any standard it is insufficient."[158] In 1959, the director of the federal Bureau of Public Assistance wrote, "there are still many persons throughout the country with serious financial needs for which no resources are yet available."[159] For them, the labor market, however lean, was the primary source of income.

Along with his 1948 recommendations regarding public assistance, President Truman proposed that Washington extend matching funds to all needy individuals, regardless of category or reason for their economic dependency. This had been proposed by the National Resources Planning Board and the Wagner-Murray-Dingell bills of 1943 and 1945 that Congress did not pass.[160] Arthur J. Altmeyer, then chairman of the Social Security Board, considered congressional rejection of President Truman's proposal one of the major shortcomings of the 1950 amendments to the SSA.[161]

As unemployment increased later in the 1950s, this failure to provide assistance to two-parent families as well as to single adults who were neither disabled nor elderly caused severe hardship to growing numbers of poor people. Federal policy that provided funds for assistance to single-parent families but not to two-parent families with an unemployed parent clearly created an incentive for unemployed men to desert their families or not to marry the mothers of their children. Federal policy carried on the mothers'-aid tradition of passing judgment on the sexual morality of women. It also confined its support to single-mother families and denied assistance to able-bodied poor men and their dependents altogether.

Summary: The Formative Years

ADC maintained some features of the poor laws but was nonetheless an advance over the mildly progressive mothers'-aid programs. The states would administer public assistance and set benefit levels. The means test would continue to be imposed. But there were important changes: a permanent contribution by the federal government, the stipulation that benefits must be in cash, and additional limits on poor-law practices that had made the loss of civil and political rights the price of a meager dole. After 15 years, moreover, ADC became an entitlement. Nonetheless, low benefits and restricted eligibility meant that the intention of supporting a division of labor in the family that had never held among the poor was thwarted. For many of these women, neither family patriarchy nor state patriarchy availed.[162]

Initially, the SSA excluded most blacks and women from the insurance programs and covered them, if at all, with these modified poor laws. Social insurance was extended to many women in 1939, not in their own right, but as dependents and survivors of insured workers. However, the putative breadwinners of many poorer women were not covered by Old Age and Survivors' Insurance, and that meant, among other things, that these women did not benefit as dependents or survivors either. Southern legislators succeeded in retaining state control of important public-assistance policies and led the fight to beat back New Dealers attempts to require adequate benefits. State control of public assistance meant, as we have shown, states' rights to continue to practice racism, sexism, and economic oppression. Suitable-homes policies punished black women for failure to conform to the family ethic, but the result was also economic—a looser labor market and lower wages. As the Newburgh "crisis" demonstrated, making African–Americans the targets of welfare crackdowns was not confined to the South.

Sometimes violating both the letter and spirit of the SSA and other times moving into the vacuum of unstated policies, states mounted an attack on ADC and its clients hardly more than a decade after it began. Indeed, assaulting ADC was chronic, from the 1940s to its repeal. Even during the 1950s, when growth in the rolls was modest—we will show that it was much too small in relation to mounting need—welfare bashing was "in." What distinguishes the 1940s and 1950s from recent decades is that successive administrations, though they permitted violations of the SSA and policies that discriminated against women of color, continued to express support for the program and to make modest improvements despite these attacks. Of particular interest in view of later developments was endorsement of federal responsibility for reducing both the fear and incidence of destitution by the first Republican president since the passage of the SSA.

Modest increments in federal financing were enacted in the formative years of ADC. These were federal matching of higher proportions of the benefits to children and inclusion of mothers' or caretakers' grants, thereby acknowledging their right to assistance. One liberalization of the federal matching formula was enacted in 1956 under the Republican administration of Dwight Eisenhower, and the variable federal matching percentage was introduced 2 years later during the same presidency. Eisenhower, though more conservative than his New Deal and Fair Deal predecessors, did not attempt to dismantle their programs. He has been characterized as "a conservative caretaker for the Democratic order."[163] When it came to relieving unemployment, however, he did, as the next chapter will show, diverge significantly from the New Deal.

The establishment of a federal bureaucracy to monitor its implementation was an important consequence of the passage of the SSA. With expertise and access to legislators, these bureaucrats were able to achieve incremental improvements, even in a relatively conservative age.[164] In addition to the changes in funding, 1950 witnessed the extension of coverage to a new group of unemployable adults, the disabled, and the first payments to suppliers of medical or remedial care to AFDC recipients were an early step toward Medicaid.

Extending coverage to employable adults other than single mothers would have gone beyond these incremental changes. The most important advance in public assistance in the early New Deal, one that was introduced by FERA but rolled back with the SSA, was federal support for all those in need, regardless of the cause. President Truman's proposal to decategorize public assistance or to provide benefits to all who needed them was turned down at the committee level in a Democrat-controlled House of Representatives. In 1935, the federal government did not "quit" the "business of relief." Instead, it terminated its funding of aid based on need alone and gave its backing to the traditional distinctions between the "worthy" and "unworthy" poor. It was the latter who would be neglected by economic and social policies alike.

CHAPTER 3

Welfare Law and Labor Law: The Formative Years

T he relationship between public assistance and the labor market
is both complex and critical to understanding ADC. The
previous chapter pointed out that many mothers whose children
received aid were not, in fact, freed from the breadwinners' role.
Low benefits, eligibility restrictions, and state work requirements
forced many poor women to support themselves independently and
others to supplement their meager grants with wages. Although
the SSA did not exclude children on the basis of their parents'
marital status or their race, states found ways to deny assistance
to black children born to unmarried women. Adults in the families
so excluded also became dependent on the labor market and other
nongovernmental sources of income.

Single parenthood is often born of unemployment. Economic
prospects influence whether parents marry at all as well as whether
they stay married.[1] This is particularly the case when public assistance is confined to single-parent families or to those in which
one or both parents are incapacitated. Thus, the present or past
labor-market position of "welfare fathers"—not married to their
children's mothers, divorced, separated, or deserting and paying
insufficient or no child support—is pertinent to any discussion of
public assistance. In addition, the former labor-market status of
deceased parents, as already discussed, determines whether and
how well their dependents are covered by social insurance or whether
they are consigned to the more demeaning and stingier
public-assistance programs. Finally, employment and earnings of
both parents in a married-couple household are particularly critical, given the lack (until the recent growth of the EITC) of government support for poor families with two, able-bodied parents
in the home.

During the first 25 years of ADC, from 1935 to 1960, employment conditions for men and women fluctuated. From the beginning of the program until the end of World War II, the federal government either provided work opportunities for a portion of the unemployed or, in order to wage a world war, fully employed the population. Although the Roosevelt administration mounted the largest public employment programs in history during the Great Depression, work programs served only a portion of the unemployed at any one time, and job-creation programs did not become a permanent government function. In the immediate postwar period, Congress rejected full employment. Unemployment reappeared and became increasingly serious for young workers and for black men and women after the Korean War. From the mid-1950s on, the consequences of federal failure to provide work for the unemployed on a permanent basis, which had been masked during the two wars, became apparent but was largely neglected not only by social policies but by economic policies as well.

Why Were Work Programs Limited and Temporary?

Federal relief administrator Harry Hopkins wanted a permanent work program because he believed that for years to come "there will remain . . . as the responsibility of government, a standing army of able-bodied workers who have no jobs."[2] Secretary of Labor Frances Perkins, who chaired the CES, wrote that both Roosevelt and Hopkins "had the idea of a permanent work-relief program, perhaps instead of Unemployment Insurance." But it had not been written into the law, and, commenting in the mid-1940s, Perkins pointed out that "unemployment insurance stands alone as the protection for people out of work."[3] Although Hopkins did not succeed in persuading the CES, Roosevelt, or Congress to write work assurance into the Economic Security Bill, he continued to argue that the problem of unemployment would not be solved by temporary measures.[4]

New Deal historian Irving Bernstein wrote that "throughout its history, both the President and the Congress considered WPA (Works Progress Administration) a 'temporary' if not 'emergency' agency, slated for oblivion as soon as severe unemployment disappeared." This, Bernstein pointed out, was reflected in 1-year appropriations that made long-term planning by WPA impossible. However, since unemployment did not disappear and even grew worse during the recession of 1937–1938, WPA survived until World War II, when joblessness did disappear for a time.[5]

Arthur J. Altmeyer, chairman of the technical board of the CES, recalls that FDR wanted a worker who exhausted unemployment benefits and was still unemployed to be entitled automatically to a work-relief job.[6] Yet, in alluding to a 1937 Senate Special Committee to Investigate Unemployment and Relief, Altmeyer recalls that "it was recognized that the emergency work-relief program known as the Works Progress Administration was not a permanent solution of the unemployment problem, and it was hoped that, with the continuing recovery from the Great Depression permanent solutions could be found." However, with unemployment again rising in 1937, "the committee decided the time had not yet arrived when it would be feasible to replace existing emergency programs with permanent ones."[7]

Tracing the emergence of the idea of the right to work in the United States, Peter Bachrach held that Roosevelt "was never willing to ask for more than temporary appropriations designed to employ only a minority of those who were unemployed."[8] Early in 1936, the Works Progress Administration employed more than 3 million people when the average number unemployed that year was 9 million.[9] New Deal historian William Leuchtenburg writes that "by any standard, [WPA] . . . was an impressive achievement, [but] it never came close to meeting Roosevelt's goal of giving jobs to all who could work."[10] Referring to all the work programs of the federal government, a monograph prepared by the Division of Research for the WPA said as much:

> Since 1935 the total number given employment on various public work programs has ranged from a low of 2.3 million to a high of 4.6 million. Large as these figures are, at the peak they represented less than half of the number estimated as unemployed. Indeed, throughout this period these programs have averaged only between one-quarter and one-third of the estimated unemployed . . . . [11]

In December 1940, for example, there were 2 million persons employed on WPA projects and three times that many—6 million unemployed men and women—searching for work.[12] Roosevelt's reluctance to employ more of the jobless, despite his stated preferences for work programs over relief, is believed to have stemmed from the costliness of work relief, his desire to balance the budget, and opposition from business and conservative politicians who considered that it was competitive with private industry and drove up wage rates by paying relief workers too much.[13] There was also opposition in farm areas, particularly in the South, where planters complained that work relief made it impossible to get cheap farm labor.[14]

Conservative fears were first voiced against the truly innovative Civil Works Administration (CWA), which began late in 1933, employed 4 million people by January 1934, and was disbanded later that year.[15] Conservatives in the administration and Congress persuaded Roosevelt that it was too costly and that it "was highly suggestive of the right to work."[16] By this, they meant it might lead to pressure for a permanent and expanded work program— not only from the 4 million CWA workers but also from millions of unemployed workers without government-created jobs. Roosevelt also felt CWA could create a permanent dependent class and that its continuance might imply that the country would be in a permanent depression.[17] Even though unemployment was 25% and CWA employed only about one-third of the jobless at wages well below the national average, business interests, particularly in the South and in construction, the type of work done by most CWA workers, accused CWA of providing too much job security, too high wages, and too lax a work environment.[18]

There is disagreement over why the longer-lasting WPA was terminated in 1943. While Edwin Amenta holds that Roosevelt ended WPA in order to appease conservatives who had made big gains in the 1942 congressional elections, Edward Berkowitz and Kim McQuaid write that "programs such as WPA . . . made little sense in an economy engaged in the mammoth public-works project called World War II."[19] Similarly, Nancy Rose holds that "a shortage of labor for the time being ended the need for government programs in which people were put to work."[20]

Although she does not discount the role of the "political class struggle" in opposition to work programs and the defeat of full employment, Theda Skocpol gives weight to some other factors. She holds that "efforts at bureaucratic state building and administrative reform since the Progressive Era have not facilitated national economic planning for full employment."[21] The state and local opposition to directives from Washington that Skocpol cites was, no doubt, a factor in congressional opposition to work programs. However, a class factor, what Nancy Rose refers to as "unremitting attack (on New Deal work programs) from the business sector,"[22] seems a far more formidable foe of employment assurance than the consequences of deficient state structures. Significantly, with intense, organized pressure from the elderly, the Roosevelt administration bypassed the state and local governments and established a permanent, wholly federal program of Old Age Insurance. Moreover, in contrast to ADC and Old Age Assistance, both of which built on state pension programs for single mothers and the elderly, there was no U.S. model or existing bureaucratic structure for Old Age Insurance. Skocpol also points to internal contradictions within the Democratic party, the opposition between entrenched southern conservatives and urban liberals in the North. Yet, these contradictions are at most intervening factors, derivative of opposing class interests in which liberal forces were either too weak or not fully committed to employment assurance. Of course, we do not know what the alignments would have been had World War II not cured what were still very high levels of unemployment.

Sexism, Racism, and New Deal Employment Policies

Those who planned permanent and temporary social welfare programs in the 1930s were chiefly concerned about male breadwinners who had usually been stably employed but who were now unemployed in large and unprecedented numbers. Indeed, "for many Americans of both sexes, kicking women out of the labor force was the solution to unemployment."[23] In fact, New Deal historian Irving Bernstein writes that "perversely the most important public-policy issue of the decade was the movement to deny jobs to married women."[24] Not surprisingly, New Deal work programs were designed primarily for white males. Treating single mothers as unemployables who needed government income support is perfectly consonant with this emphasis on employment for males.

Women, generally, and particularly both men and women of color, were overrepresented among the underserved. When women did get a slot in a work program, they were paid lower average wages than white men, $3 a day for women compared to $5 for men.[25] Under WPA, wages varied by the zones into which the country was divided and, within these, by occupation and urban or rural residence. The original payment schedule ranged from $19 a month for unskilled labor in the rural South to $94 a month for technical and professional workers in the urban areas of the north and west.[26] The majority of unskilled African–American workers were located in the zone with the lowest minimum wage for such workers.[27] In the deep south, young African–American men had difficulty getting into the Civilian Conservation Corps (CCC) and were largely in segregated camps when they did gain admittance; even a committed civil-rights advocate like Harold Ickes, who headed the Public Works Administration (PWA), was forced to discriminate on its projects in the South.[28]

Since the New Deal, work-relief programs concentrated on construction projects, in which positions were overwhelmingly male.[29] Moreover, positions were limited to one member per family, the male if he were present and employable. Women were about one-fourth of the workforce but had only one-sixth of WPA slots and an even smaller proportion of the earlier work programs of FERA.[30] Unemployment and Old Age Insurance, the two nonstigmatized and most innovative programs of the SSA, were directed toward the occupations in which white men were employed; as noted, workers in agricultural and domestic service, many of them women and blacks, were not insured. Seventy percent of those employed in these two occupations were African–Amercian.[31] Thus, blocked access to employment opportunities meant exclusion from the more desirable income-support programs or the social insurances.[32] Women and African–Americans were relegated to stigmatized and underfunded public-assistance programs.

World War II and Full Employment

Unemployment was 25% in 1933 and fell under the Roosevelt administration but never below 14% until 1941, when it was still almost 10%. The following year, the rate fell sharply to 4.7%, and for 3 years thereafter the country experienced "full" employment (1.9% in 1943 and 1945, 1.2% in 1944). Between 1940 and 1945, when the war ended, unemployment fell by 7 million. Moreover, the number of persons in the armed forces surged by 11 million in those years, and civilian employment grew by over 5 million.[33]

Women increased their labor-market participation from nearly 11 million in 1940 to 19.5 million at the peak of war production. Yet, historian Alice Kessler-Harris cautions against exaggerating the increase in women's labor-force participation over and above expected increments.[34] For a brief span of time during the war emergency, the positive contributions of women to the labor force became the focus of public attention. This was in marked contrast to the 1930s, when women had to apologize for paid work and present it as a last resort to preserve family life.

Older, married women contributed most of the increase in women's employment during the war, but mothers, including many with young children, also joined the labor force. The big rise in mothers' employment led to recognition of the need for certain types of support services. Under funds provided by the Community Facilities Act of 1941 (Lanham Act), more than 1.5 million children of mothers employed in defense industries were cared for in vacant stores, private homes, churches, an assortment of other dwellings, and, after considerable controversy, in centers constructed with federal funds. The number of children served by these Lanham Act funds was more than the number in all other kinds of day care as late as the middle 1970s.[35]

The brief period of wartime full employment brought new jobs and new responsibilities in the workplace to women, but not equal wages. In 1944, women's wages in manufacturing were 60% of men's wages.[36] Consequently, women who attempted to support themselves and their families were at great disadvantage. In 1948, a year of high wages, almost 25% of families supported by single women had total annual incomes of less than $1,000, compared to 10% of families with male breadwinners.[37]

Despite the need for labor in war production, African–Americans had to threaten militant action—a march on Washington—in order to break into these industries, even at the lowest levels. Their threat led President Roosevelt to sign an executive order creating a Fair Employment Practices Commission (FEPC) in 1941. But it was widely violated. Racial clashes and mounting minority militancy led to a second FEPC, and ultimately African–Americans and other people of color benefited from the greatly increased demand for both civilian and military employment.[38]

The number of African–Americans in civilian jobs increased by almost 1 million between 1940 and 1944, and 700,000 more entered military service. The principal movement was from agriculture and domestic service and from the lines of the unemployed into industrial work. African–Americans began the war with wages about one-half those of whites and had moved up to three-fourths by 1944.[39] The unemployment rates of African–American women dropped significantly during the war, as did the numbers employed in low-paid, low-status work. Often fighting discrimination, they were able to take advantage of tight labor markets and substantially increase their employment as factory operatives and clerical, sales, and professional workers.[40]

Economic gains from full employment were significant, particularly when one considers that it lasted only 3 years and had been preceded by the decade of the Great Depression. Prosperity lifted all income groups, but poorer persons gained most.[41] As for poverty, the proportion of the population with annual after-tax incomes under $2,000 was halved.[42] "Of major consequence for income redistribution," according to social-welfare historians June Axinn and Herman Levin, "was the influx of women into the labor force and the shift of blacks from farm to higher-paying factory jobs."[43]

In the years of declining unemployment and poverty, the ADC rolls also fell. This was true even though the number of jurisdictions in which the program operated grew, the age limit of children for whom the federal government would provide ADC funds was increased, and benefits rose modestly.[44] The rate of children under 18 receiving ADC fell by nearly one-third (31%) between 1942 and 1945—from 23 to 15 per 1,000.[45]

The Defeat of Full Employment

A formidable combination of factors favored continuation of the policy of full employment after the war. The brief and happy holiday from unemployment contrasted sharply with the decade preceding the war. The fear of another depression was the specter constantly raised by Senator James Murray, one of the Senate's chief proponents of full-employment legislation.[46] During the Senate hearings on the Murray-Wagner Full Employment Bill, moderate Democrat Joseph C. O'Mahoney provided an example of this thinking: "Are we going to have to depend upon another war to take the economy above the depression line, if another depression comes?"[47] A large proportion of the public favored government creation of jobs for everyone who wanted but could not get one in the private sector.[48] Government assurance of employment had been an important recommendation of the National Resources Planning Board (NRPB), one of the centers of Keynesian thinking in the late 1930s.[49] Spending the money required for full employment had been helped along by the war, which, as Leuchtenburg points out, had "freed the government from the taboos of a balanced budget and revealed the potentialities of spending."[50]

Following the recommendations of the NRPB for an Economic Bill of Rights, Roosevelt, in his 1994 State-of-the-Union address, called for "the right to a useful and remunerative job" as the first of these guarantees.[51] The platforms of both parties in 1944 endorsed the principle of federal responsibility for providing "jobs for all."[52] Roosevelt's Republican opponent in the 1944 presidential election, Governor Thomas E. Dewey of New York, declared himself in favor of full employment and held that the government was obligated to provide sufficient jobs when necessary, although his support for the latter was evidently qualified.[53]

Perhaps the war experience convinced FDR that a much bolder government approach to job creation was necessary and feasible. He eloquently articulated the Economic Bill of Rights in his state-of-the-union message and reiterated it and the need for 60 million jobs during the 1944 presidential campaign. Nevertheless, he neither endorsed the full-employment legislation introduced by Senator James Murray in 1945 nor sponsored an alternative bill. Indeed, in his definitive legislative history of the Employment Act of 1946, Stephen Kemp Bailey reveals that Roosevelt's overriding goal of gaining bipartisan congressional support for the United Nations made him wary of creating disunity by promoting full employment. So he "followed this hands-off policy until his death."[54] We will never know whether Roosevelt would have thrown his prestige and support behind full employment after the war ended and the threat of unemployment returned.

In the wake of Japan's surrender in August 1945, and consequent concern for conversion to a peacetime economy, President Truman declared the full-employment bill (introduced earlier that year) a "must."[55] A number of businessmen, industrialists, and bankers joined organized labor, major religious organizations, welfare groups, the Conference of Mayors, some veterans' organizations, and many other individuals and organizations in support of the bill during Senate hearings later that month. At that time, the opposition of the Chamber of Commerce and the National Association of Manufacturers was perfunctory.[56] The internationalist segment of the capitalist class, represented by the Council on Foreign Relations and the Committee for Economic Development, supported the bill because it seemed an assurance against a decline in the American economy that could lead to a worldwide depression.[57]

International developments also contributed to the push for full employment. The British Labour Party had won a landslide election only weeks before, and testimony of each of the bill's sponsors called attention to these results in Britain and considered full employment capitalism's alternative to socialism.[58] Competition from socialism and the real possibility that more war-shattered European states would fall to communism were already apparent. Winston Churchill delivered his famous "iron curtain" speech in Truman's home state of Missouri early in 1946.

Advocates for the rights of African–Americans recognized the importance of full employment. Representatives of leading civil-rights organizations testified in favor of the original bill and urged their members to support it. At a meeting of 35 national labor, civic, religious, and professional organizations convened by the bill's sponsors to discuss a nationwide campaign for its passage, Judge William H. Hastie, a board member of the National Association for the Advancement of Colored People (NAACP), made these prescient remarks: "The Negro [the term then used for blacks or African–Americans] has the most to lose if the objectives [of the Murray-Wagner Bill] are not achieved. The fact must be brought home to minority groups that they will never be able to make progress unless there are adequate jobs for people."[59]

The powerful, numerous, and diverse voices and forces in favor of full employment and government job assurance were not enough to secure a permanent commitment to jobs for all. Subsequent American history might have been different had Congress voted for full employment, but the 1945 bill that called for jobs for all "had to go through a Congress run by moderate to conservative Democrats reflexively skeptical of neo-New Dealish nostrums."[60]

The strategy of the bill's framers was interesting. The legislation would not guarantee full employment or any specified number of jobs, nor was it an appropriation or job-creation measure. It declared that "all Americans able to work and seeking work have the right to useful, remunerative, regular, and full-time employment."[61] How was this to be accomplished? It was to be the responsibility of the federal government to provide such volume of federal investment and expenditures as would be needed to assure full employment if private, state, and municipal enterprises were not sufficient to provide work for all who wanted it.[62] It was this key "compensatory" action by the federal government—to be accomplished procedurally through a National Production and Employment Budget prepared by the executive—that was removed from the bill in order to win support, including that of leading conservative Senator Robert A. Taft.[63] Nonetheless, sponsors felt that one of the amendments to the bill, which passed the Senate by a wide margin of 71 to 10, had retained the key obligation for government spending to achieve the objective of full employment.[64]

On the other hand, the future vice president, Alben Barkley, then a senator, was skeptical. Barkley complained that the full-employment bill "now promised anyone needing a job the right to go out and look for one."[65] Whatever the interpretation of the Senate's action, a conservative House of Representatives, dominated by business interests and particularly concerned about a possible threat to cheap farm labor, watered the bill down beyond recognition.[66]

A forecast of the salutary consequences of full employment suggests why employers and their proxies in government would resist it:

> Our experience with periods of labor shortage indicates that its first effect is greatly to increase the bargaining power of labor, both individually and collectively. This results in steady improvement of wages and working conditions, up to the limit set by productive capacity. It means that employers must seek to make employment attractive, since the workers are no longer motivated by the fear of losing their jobs. A shift of workers from the less pleasant and remunerative occupations occurs, so that standards are raised at the lower levels. . . .
>
> The status of labor will improve, since employers can no longer rely upon the discipline of discharge to enforce authority. The tendency will be for labor to have more participation in industrial and economic policy.[67]

Instead of full employment, the Employment Act of 1946 promised "maximum employment," and the government commitment was limited to "all practical means consistent with the needs and obligations of national policy."[68] One senator observed that the final bill implied that "we will see that you have a job if something doesn't interfere."[69] The Conference Report of the Congress, which specifically rejected the term "full employment," cited the substitute Bill of the House that declared: "the function of Government is to promote, and not to assure or guarantee employment."[70] Although it eschewed full employment, the Employment Act of 1946 established administrative structures for national economic planning: the Council of Economic Advisers and the Joint Economic Committee of Congress. The structures that could facilitate employment assurance are in place, but the policy of full employment is not.

Scholars disagree regarding the commitment of the new president and his potential for gaining passage of a genuine full-employment bill.[71] Given the political persuasion of Congress and the original bill's potential for modifying industrial power relationships and democratizing capitalism, it is unlikely that full employment could have been won in the absence of a mass movement in its favor and the related circumstance of a return to mass unemployment. For all the organizational support behind the Murray-Wagner insurance bill and favorable popular opinion regarding job guarantees, there was nothing like the popular mobilizations that have created the necessary pressure for women's suffrage, old-age insurance, and expansion of labor and civil rights. An impressive array of human-rights, liberal, labor, women's, and social-welfare organizations had supported the forerunner of the Full Employment Bill in 1944, but Bailey points out that of these, only two, the Union for Democratic Action (organized in 1941 for the major purpose of uniting labor and liberal groups behind an aggressive anti-Fascist foreign policy) and the National Farmers' Union, backed it enthusiastically.[72] Significantly, both labor federations, the AFL and the CIO, although on record as supporters, were concerned lest legislation that seemed idealistic detract from issues of greater immediate concern, such as unemployment-compensation, minimum-wage, and antidiscrimination legislation.[73]

Public approval of a concept such as full employment is not necessarily tantamount to support for specific legislation embodying that principle. As noted, in 1944, two-thirds of the respondents in a *Fortune* poll were in favor of the proposition that the federal government should, if necessary, assure jobs for all. However, in July 1945, about the same proportion (69%) of those polled in the second congressional district in Illinois, in the heart of Chicago, had not heard of any bill before Congress that would plan for enough jobs for everyone after the war. Like respondents to the *Fortune* poll, the vast majority of these Chicagoans (83%) were in favor of a bill that would assure jobs through the use of federal funds, but about the same proportion had not heard of the Murray-Wagner Full Employment Bill.[74]

The postwar recession that might have made it impossible for politicians to turn down full employment was avoided for several reasons: pent-up consumer demand, created by years of depression and wartime shortages; money saved during the prosperous war years when consumer goods were scarce; and the G. I. Bill, which cushioned the effects of demobilization by providing education and training for veterans, loans for their purchase of homes, businesses, or farms, unemployment insurance, and employment services.[75] What also served to avert mass unemployment was the firing of many women workers, the closing of federal child-care centers, and a propaganda campaign against women who wanted to work outside the home that succeeded in returning many to their jobs in the home.[76]

While the more conservative make-up of the House undoubtedly contributed to its rejection of the full-employment guarantee enacted by the Senate, the different circumstances in which the two versions of the bill were passed is another factor in the outcome. The Senate voted in September 1945, just 1 month after the surrender of Japan, when the return of mass unemployment threatened the country. By 1946, as Helen Ginsburg observes, "the expected postwar depression had not happened. . . . The first wave of postwar strikes had started, fueling anti-labor feeling."[77] With the specter of mass unemployment fading considerably, political pressure for a fuller employment guarantee also abated.[78] Just as the fear of unemployment had created support for jobs for all, the drive for full employment faced a roadblock when an unemployment crisis failed to appear.[79] As Richard Neustadt observed: "if experience . . . had not dispelled the specter of postwar unemployment, much more might have been done with Truman's program of September 1945 [full employment and a number of other unrealized goals of the New Deal]."[80]

Joblessness, although not at prewar levels, in fact, did return. It began with a near doubling of the unemployment rate between 1945 and 1946. Yet, the unemployment rates were still under 4% until 1949, when the rate was almost 6%. Following a respite during the Korean War, unemployment rates thereafter never went below 4% and actually averaged 5.2% during the 7 peacetime years of President Eisenhower's administration.[81] Defense spending dropped after tripling in real terms between 1950 and 1954, but Cold War expenditures remained more than twice the pre-Korean War figure throughout the 1950s.[82] Although military spending is less labor-intensive than domestic spending and has been seen by some experts to have depleted the economy and crowded out vital government investment in the civilian sector, there is no doubt that United States unemployment would have been higher in these years had it not been for the size of the military budget.[83]

African–Americans, Young Workers, and
Women in the Postwar Economy

Decline in the labor-market status of African–Americans and young workers in the years following the Korean War prosperity of 1950 to 1953 is of particular relevance to the history of ADC. Writing in the mid-1960s, Arthur M. Ross concluded that "the period since the end of the Korean War has been one of retrogression rather than progress for the Negro."[84] The Korean War prosperity of 1950–1953, Ross pointed out, gave African–Americans a chance to maintain and extend their wartime economic gains. African–American unemployment was 8.5% in 1950 but below 5% for the 3 war years, dipping to 4.1% in 1953. For the rest of the Eisenhower years, however, it averaged 9.4%, more than twice the 4.5% rate for whites. Despite 4 years of uninterrupted economic growth, black unemployment in 1964 was 9.8%, more than double the white rate.[85]

What accounts for rising unemployment among blacks? In both the 1940s and 1950s, about 1.5 million blacks migrated to northern cities.[86] Conditions, however, were less favorable in the latter decade. In the 1940s, despite discrimination, labor markets were often tight, and opportunities expanded in production work, even for those with few skills and relatively little education. By the 1950s, blacks had begun to catch up with whites in manufacturing, but manufacturing jobs increased more slowly between 1950 and 1960 than in the previous decade. Speaking in 1963, former Secretary of Commerce Luther H. Hodges gave an important reason for the black decline: the persistence of long-standing racist hiring practices. Consequently, African–Americans were largely excluded from white-collar occupations that had accounted for 97% of the employment increase since 1947.[87] Three recessions between 1954 and 1961 left African–Americans further behind. Moreover, government housing and transportation policies had concentrated African–Americans in cities, the very places that were losing jobs or experiencing slow job growth. As employment opportunities moved to the suburbs, African–Americans were barred from them by discrimination, low income, or lack of transportation.[88]

After 1953, teenage unemployment worsened, especially among African–Americans. Youth unemployment (16–19 years) was under 10% in 1948, and again from 1951 to 1953, but from 1954 to 1960 it averaged 13.1%. The racial gap in teenage unemployment widened, reaching nearly 2:1 in 1958 and 1959.[89] The labor-force participation rates of teenagers (14–19) of both races fell off from 1950 to 1960, but the decline was sharper among blacks.[90]

Psychologist Kenneth Clark wrote poignantly of the effect of underemployment on the black man who "is required to face the fact that he cannot protect his children or be the agent through which they will be adequately fed or clothed or educated."[91] Clark observed that what may appear to be irresponsibility or neglect can be interpreted as "the anguished escape of the Negro male from an impossible predicament."[92] Since he cannot function well as a husband and father, he may simply withdraw. The next chapter shows how black unemployment and its grim consequences were largely overlooked, even by the War on Poverty.

How did women, generally, and African–American women, particularly, fare in the postwar economy? During the 1950s, women continued their historic ascent in labor-force participation.[93] Writing late in the decade, economist Eveline M. Burns, formerly research director of the National Resources Planning Board, pointed out a consequence of the increased tendency of mothers of young children to take paid employment. It had led to a questioning of the original conception of the ADC program regarding the desirability of having mothers at home while children are still young.[94] Yet, a few years later, in 1960, only 20.2% of ever-married women with children under 6 years were in the labor force, and even fewer, 14%, were employed full time, which would certainly have been necessary if lower-paid women were to become self-supporting.[95] The question raised by Burns would nonetheless continue to be asked as the labor-force participation of mothers soared in the following decades.

Without denying the serious problem of unemployment and declining labor-force participation of young black men, it is important to call attention to the picture for young black women. Many of these women had to support themselves, and others were needed to contribute substantially to family income in married-couple households. In the 1950s, the unemployment rates of black women climbed by more than 20%, somewhat more than the increase for black men. Young black women between 14 and 19 years of age lost almost as much ground as their male counterparts (62% compared to 67% increase in unemployment). Among young black adults, 20–24 years of age, women's unemployment rates grew at a higher rate than men's.[96]

Although blacks of both sexes were disproportionately disadvantaged

in the labor market, most of the unemployed have always been white
because blacks are a minority of the population. In 1950, there were,
on average, 2.6 million unemployed whites, compared to fewer than
600,000 blacks. Ten years later, following the deterioration of the
position of blacks in the labor market, whites still made up nearly
80% of the unemployed.[97]

Unemployment and Economic Dependency

With the return of higher unemployment, the ADC rolls began
to rise. The rate per 1,000 children under the age of 18 more than
doubled between 1945 and 1961.[98] What contributed to rising and
falling ADC rates? Driving them up were increases in the economically vulnerable, single-mother population and their declining median incomes relative to those with a husband present.
"In most states," wrote Allison and Leisy, "the increase in the
ADC load seems to be the result of declining employment opportunities for marginal workers, especially women and children."[99]

The increasing number of single-mother families was also related to the return of unemployment and to lack of public assistance for two-parent families with unemployed fathers. As James
Sundquist observed:

> In each recession . . . a major new category of needy families
> appeared—families of men still jobless after their unemployment
> insurance benefits had expired. The anomaly was that if the family
> remained together it was ineligible for federally-aided assistance,
> but if the father disappeared his wife and children could apply
> for Aid to Dependent Children (ADC).[100]

As pointed out in the preceding chapter, Congress turned down
President Truman's proposal to extend aid to all needy families
with children.

Despite the increasing need for public assistance, state measures such as "suitable-homes" and residence policies prevented
many families who did meet eligibility criteria, particularly African–American women and children, from getting relief. Thus,
notwithstanding increases in the size of the caseload and in relief
expenditures, only one-fifth to one-sixth of the nation's poor got
public assistance under programs of the SSA and state general-
assistance programs in the 1950s.[101]

Liberal legislators, led by Senator Paul Douglas, attempted

to attack the employment problem by providing economic stimuli to depressed areas. In both 1958 and 1960, public-opinion surveys asked respondents whether they agreed or disagreed that "the government in Washington ought to see to it that everybody who wants to work can find a job." In both surveys, nearly three-fifths either agreed strongly or agreed but not very strongly.[102] Business representatives in the administration were against the proposal. And President Eisenhower, discounting public opinion, twice vetoed bills providing loans and grants for retraining unemployed workers and for public facilities needed by depressed areas or communities to attract industries. Interestingly, congressional opponents of this legislation sometimes charged that unemployment was so widespread that a national rather than an area approach was needed, even as they fought against national measures.[103]

Summary: The Roads Not Taken

The most notable failure of postwar reform was the defeat of full employment. What the New Deal did under the pressure of prolonged depression was not to be continued. Nor would the country again see the near full employment that occurred, not as a government policy, but as a byproduct of waging a world war. Full employment had been good for those on the home front, but it was defeated by business interests that had profited by it but were unwilling to continue to share prosperity and power. The ability of certain segments of the business community to influence the House of Representatives was decisive. The task of business opponents was simpler because potential advocates of full employment were not sufficiently committed or mobilized. That, in turn, is related to the fact that recurrence of depression-level unemployment, the domestic emergency that might have stimulated mass support, failed to materialize.

The New Deal and its successor, Fair Deal, failed to assure full employment or the continuance of public-employment programs. Unemployment insurance, a New Deal legacy, is a bulwark against destitution but confined to the short-term unemployment of stable workers. Thus, for the chronically and marginally unemployed, and for many in industries not covered by unemployment insurance, there was either public assistance or nothing at all. As shown, ADC rolls increased, but the majority of poor families remained unaided and were forced to compete in a labor market that was chronically unable to absorb them in peacetime. By keeping the low-wage labor market loose, relief policy served capital. The rise in ADC rolls in the 1950s should be compared to the far greater surge in the next decade when unemployment was falling rather than rising. It is this rapid and steep rise in the relief rolls that most Americans considered a "crisis" and only welfare-rights advocates regarded as "reform."

The next chapter relates and explains this startling rise of relief in a time, not of depression, but of unprecedented general prosperity. This provides further insight into the history just recounted—when ADC grew, but hardly in proportion to need. It shows how the nation, given another opening for reform, bypassed the road to full employment once again. Further, it shows how policymakers eschewed the choices that might have reduced the bitter racial inequality and much of the need for perennially unpopular relief. The road not taken would have prevented many of the social pathologies that continue to plague us today.

CHAPTER 4

Expanding Economy and
Exploding Relief Rolls

T o some observers of the American welfare state, the combination of exploding relief rolls and declining unemployment rates in the 1960s seemed to imply that "the welfare
rolls have a separate life outside of the national job market."[1] This
was a change from earlier decades, when caseloads fell in response
to declining unemployment, particularly during World War II and
the Korean War.[2]

Should it have been so surprising that the relationship between
declining unemployment and falling caseloads disappeared in the
prosperous 1960s? Labor-market conditions are not the sole determinants of increases and decreases in the receipt of public assistance. Welfare rolls also respond to changes in public opinion,
family composition, attitudes and assertiveness of prospective relief
recipients, and judicial, legislative, and administrative policies.
All these, with the probable exception of public attitudes toward
welfare, changed during the 1960s. At the same time, despite the
decline in the official unemployment rate, labor-market conditions
continued to play a leading role in the need for AFDC.

This chapter discusses policies specifically directed toward
public welfare, beginning with the initiative of the Kennedy administration to prevent dependence on relief. Additionally, it analyzes
the strategies or types of economic opportunities characteristic of
the war on poverty in the 1960s, including the roads not taken.
The forces that gave rise to this antipoverty program and the relief explosion to which it contributed are also identified. Finally,
this chapter attempts to explain a paradox: a public policy that
claimed to be offering a "hand up" rather than a "handout" but
provided much more of the latter than the former.

The Welfare Initiatives of the Kennedy Administration

The welfare initiatives of the Kennedy administration were both individualistic and liberal. On the one hand, the administration attempted to prevent economic dependency by expanding professional casework services in public-welfare departments. In contrast to the brand of welfare "reform" exemplified by the Newburgh crisis of 1961 and amendments to the Social Security Act later in the decade, the means were nonpunitive but nonetheless individualistic.

Indicative of the Kennedy administration's liberal stance was an expansion of coverage to some two-parent families and the first step toward the in-kind programs for the poor that were to grow to large proportions under his successors.[3] Although more demeaning than cash relief, these benefits in kind added substantially to the resources of the poor.

THE SOCIAL-SERVICE APPROACH

In its social-service initiatives, the Kennedy administration assumed that dependence on relief is more the result of individual deficiency than shortcomings in the economic system. Consonant with abiding American individualism, this policy was also based on beliefs nurtured by generations of social workers: that preventive and rehabilitative services delivered by professional caseworkers could reduce economic dependency. Actually, the 1956 amendments to the SSA, passed under President Eisenhower, had included 50-50 matching provisions to cover the cost of state services to help public-assistance recipients achieve stable family life and self-support, but the states had drawn down very little of this money.[4]

As pointed out in Chapter 2, Connecticut Governor Abraham Ribicoff, appointed secretary of HEW by President Kennedy, had developed a concern over rising costs of public welfare, multi-problem families, and chronic dependency.[5] To advise the administration, Ribicoff appointed an Ad Hoc Committee on Public Welfare, consisting of public and voluntary social-welfare leaders. Their counsel was hardly surprising: "Expenditures for assistance not accompanied by rehabilitation services may actually increase dependency and eventual costs to the community."[6]

In the first presidential address ever devoted entirely to public assistance, John F. Kennedy declared that the reasons for poverty "are often more social than economic."[7] In the year preceding Kennedy's message, unemployment stood at 6.7%, more than double the figure 10 years earlier, and African–American unemployment was double-digit, 12.5%.[8] In 1961, the average, monthly ADC payment for a family (3.8 persons) was $111, or about $1,300 annually, less than one-half the 4-person poverty threshold.[9] Despite this, the million-aire president called, not for more jobs or for benefits that would have made family life supportable, but for family services.

The administration's recommendations, enacted as part of the Public Welfare or Social Services Amendments of 1962, were that a service plan be developed and applied for each child recipient and that services be provided by trained personnel to the extent possible. The federal government would up its contribution for services to 75%. In the Social Services Amendments, the Kennedy administration accepted the view that social-work services could lead to self-care and self-support, thus implying that the personal deficiencies of relief recipients caused their dependency. Described as "social work's response to Newburgh," the amendments none-theless "shared a basic premise with the proponents of the Newburgh plan . . . that the preferred address to the problem of economic dependency was to intervene in the life of the individual family."[10]

Unlike welfare "reform" 5 years later, the federal government imposed no work requirements. Nonetheless, prevention of de-pendency meant that welfare mothers should get jobs. In the address introducing his public-welfare proposals, the president observed that "many women now on assistance rolls could obtain jobs and become self-supporting if local daycare programs for their young children were available."[11]

Along with rehabilitation services to encourage economic independence, the Kennedy administration proposed to deal with other obstacles to mothers' employment. It recommended $5 million in grants to the states for the establishment of daycare in 1962, and $10 million annually thereafter. An additional work incentive allowed recipients to deduct their work expenses from their earn-ings. This was a small step away from the severe work disincen-tive of ADC: the reduction of grants by the amount of recipients' earnings, in effect, a 100% tax. As employed welfare clients used to put it, "we're working for the welfare department."[12]

In the 5 years following enactment of the amendments that were intended to reduce dependency, the number of AFDC recipients rose by more than one-third (36%).[13] The reasons, discussed in the following section, are unrelated to the Social Services Amendments.

Some observers have claimed that the amendments were poorly implemented because there was insufficient social-work personnel to do the job. There may have been some truth in this criticism and in the observation that the demonstration programs were poorly planned and implemented.[14] However, when the assumptions of the Social Services Amendments were tested under ideal conditions, the problem proved to be in conception, not execution. Conducted at one of the country's most outstanding and highly professionalized family-service agencies, this research compared the length of time on AFDC of two randomly selected groups of newly dependent families, one in which recipients got both AFDC and the services of professional caseworkers and another in which they got only cash relief. There were no significant differences in dependency outcomes for the two groups.[15]

EXPANDED COVERAGE

The Kennedy administration also proposed to extend ADC eligibility to some two-parent families. A response to the recession of the late 1950s and the long-term hardships of families in Appalachia,[16] the Unemployed Parent Program (ADC-UP) began as a temporary measure in 1961 and became permanent with the 1967 amendments. However, by that time, the definition of "unemployed parent" had been narrowed so much that only fathers with relatively steady and recent attachment to the labor force were eligible.[17] The more common problems of welfare fathers were sporadic, marginal employment, long-term unemployment with consequent withdrawal from the labor force, and low wages—in other words, the very type of labor-market disadvantages for which the SSA had provided neither social insurance nor job assurance. The families of the men who suffered these conditions were not eligible for AFDC unless fathers were out of the home. Not surprisingly, the number of unemployed parents covered by the AFDC-UP program was about 4% of the family caseload in 1970, owing both to the eligibility restrictions and the fact that fewer than one-half of the states had inaugurated UP programs.[18]

Interested in rehabilitation, Kennedy also called for a Community Work and Training Program (CWT) to allow recipients the opportunity to work for their welfare payments in publicly created jobs.[19] States were required to match federal funds to finance the training programs, but only 12 had developed a CWT by 1967.[20]

In-Kind Support for the Poor

Enactment or expansion of means-tested, in-kind programs, particularly food stamps, Medicaid, and public housing, not only added to the benefits of recipients of cash relief, but extended coverage to new categories of the poor: married-couple families and individuals with low earnings whose needs had largely been ignored by federal public-assistance policies. A clue to how important in-kind benefits would become is the finding of a New York City study that the average family on AFDC in 1974 got over three-fifths of its income from in-kind benefits.[21]

Are in-kind programs equal to their cash value? Should they be counted in calculating poverty rates? Regardless of the answers, they add substantially to the living standards of the poor. Food stamps mitigate extreme interstate disparities in cash benefits. Another asset is that the public feels money is being well spent (e.g., on food for the family rather than beer or worse). Moreover, the interests of recipients can be united with those of powerful providers, such as agribusiness and the health and hospitals industries. On the other hand, in-kind programs restrict choice and, if they are means-tested, stigmatize recipients. The stipulation that benefits were to be in cash, it will be remembered, was one of the progressive features of the Social Security Act.

FOOD STAMPS

A food-stamp program operated during the 1930s but was discontinued in favor of distribution of surplus commodities during the next two decades. In 1961, President Kennedy revived food stamps on a pilot basis. Compared to commodity distribution, food stamps offered recipients more choice, but using the coupons identified them as public dependents at the checkout counter and was therefore stigmatizing. Particularly when families were required to purchase their coupons with the amount of money they were assumed to be able to spend on food, participation in the program was low, despite the fact that the subsidy considerably augmented cash income. Although it was a hedge against hunger, nearly four-fifths of the poor people living in counties participating in the food-stamp program did not claim benefits in 1969.[22]

Severe malnutrition hit the headlines in the late 1960s. Hunger became a national issue, and the Nixon administration responded by federalizing the food-stamp program and liberalizing benefits in 1970.[23] The program grew nearly fourfold, from 3.2 million participants in 1969, when benefits were still meager, to 12.2 million in 1973.[24] Purchase requirements for food stamps were lifted in 1977 under the Carter administration.[25]

Compared with unpredictable medical expenses, food expenses can be anticipated and added to cash relief budgets, thereby increasing recipients' dignity and opportunities for choice. However, if states provide meager cash relief and are reluctant to raise benefits, food stamps can stave off hunger and malnutrition. When food stamps got underway in the sixties, all but six states set their AFDC standards below the federal definition of poverty, and more than two-thirds failed to appropriate the money necessary to meet their own low standards.[26] Clearly, food stamps were a way of putting food into the mouths of persons whom the states were unwilling to feed. Writing before its liberalization, Gilbert Steiner of the Brookings Institution emphasized that food stamps were demeaning and considered it unwise to have resurrected the program in 1961.[27] After Congress facilitated access to the program, the restrictions of choice and stigma nonetheless remained. Yet, in 1980, social-policy expert Robert Nathan characterized the expansion of food stamps as "the most important change in public welfare policy since the passage of the Social Security Act."[28]

MEDICAID

"Probably the foremost legislative achievement of the Johnson Administration" is how Sar Levitan and Robert Taggart describe the passage, in 1965, of Medicare and Medicaid.[29] Medicaid pays for the health care of the poor, elderly, disabled, and families with dependent children, that is, categories of the poor covered by the public-assistance titles of the SSA. Medicare, which covers health care for persons 65 and older and eligible for Old Age and Survivors' Insurance, was championed both by labor and the organized elderly. The main pressure groups for Medicaid were governors and lobbyists for the wealthier northern states who complained of escalating health costs.[30] Medicaid meant that about one-half a state's costs for health care for the poor would be paid by Washington. Some persons not on welfare were covered by Medicaid, although, in 1967, Congress limited coverage to persons whose income did not exceed 133% of a state's AFDC standard.[31] In many states, that was below the poverty level.

Low-Income Housing

Unlike Medicaid and food stamps, housing aid, while substantially expanded in the 1960s, has never been an entitlement. Throughout the history of the program, only a minority of those eligible for housing assistance has been served. In a famous pronouncement in 1937, Roosevelt declared that one-third of the nation was "ill-housed, ill-clad, ill-nourished." Yet, between 1937—when the public-housing program was initiated—and 1960, fewer than one-half million units had been completed.[32] Although the Kennedy administration was sympathetic to more housing production, its appointees reportedly became preoccupied with the development of social services in the projects.[33] While 34,000 subsidized units were produced in 1963, mostly under the low-rent housing program, nearly five times as many units were built in the last full year of the Johnson administration than in the last Kennedy year.[34]

Employment Conditions

Although the overall economic picture was rosy in the second half of the 1960s, it remained dark for some groups. Unemployment rates rose and fell between 1960 and 1963 and then dropped in 5 of the next 6 years. Unemployment for the last 3 years of the decade—ranging from 3.8% in the first 2 years to 3.5% in the last—was comparable to or lower than in the first years after World War II but not quite so low as during the height of the Korean War.[35] These, too, were years of military build up, this time for the war in Southeast Asia. Consistent with population and labor-force growth, the annual average number of unemployed persons was higher than the 1960 count in every year of the decade but one.[36]

While African–American unemployment rates were double-digit from 1958 to 1963, they did drop steadily in the 1960s—again, not to Korean War levels. In the 5% range during the Korean War, African–American unemployment dropped from 9.6% in 1964 to 6.4% in 1969.[37] Youth unemployment, although it, too, responded to economic expansion, did not fall below 12.2% at any time during the 1960s. The lowest rate for young African–Americans was about

double that or nearly one in four.[38] In the mid-1960s, a former
executive assistant to Labor Secretary Willard Wirtz wrote that
"unemployment in nonwhite America was cataclysmic, chronic, and
malignant. . . ."[39]

MEASURING SUBEMPLOYMENT

Wirtz, labor secretary in both the Kennedy and Johnson administrations, recognized how seriously the official unemployment
rate underestimated labor-market disadvantages in the nation's ghettos.
The official rate, which includes only those who are actively looking
for work and employed less than 1 hour a week, greatly under-
states joblessness. Consequently, Wirtz proposed that the department develop an overall measure of economic hardship that would
include "all workers with severe labor market problems whether
or not they were unemployed."[40] The result was a Subemployment
Index that, in addition to persons officially counted as unemployed
by the Department of Labor, encompassed the following:

- Involuntary part-time workers

- The estimated number of discouraged, adult, male workers,
  that is, those who want a job but have stopped looking for
  one

- An estimate of the number of males not counted by the census,
  assuming one-half the missing males to be subemployed

- Full-time workers with annual incomes under the government's
  poverty threshold

Although the Subemployment Index encompasses more economic hardship than the official unemployment rate, the Social
Security Administration's (SSA) poverty threshold, which was one
of its components, underestimates economic deprivation because
it is based on an economy food budget that is admittedly "for
temporary or emergency use when funds are low."[41] Economists
engaged in research on subemployment made a strong case for
the use of a more realistic, lower-level budget developed by the
Bureau of Labor Statistics, which was $6,960 in 1970, compared
to the SSA standard of $4,000.[42]

In November 1966, when national unemployment was 3.4%,
the lowest for that month in 13 years, the Department of Labor

intensively surveyed 10 urban slum areas to determine their subemployment rates. Whereas official unemployment in these areas averaged nearly 10%, subemployment was, on average, more than three times as prevalent, reaching a high of 47% in slum areas of San Antonio. "The subemployment survey," observed economist Helen Ginsburg, "had gone directly to the core of the urban crisis: unemployment and the inability of many workers from slums to earn a decent living."[43] Interestingly, New York and California, with four of the 10 areas included in the subemployment survey, accounted for 40% of the total rise in AFDC rolls during the 1960s.[44]

A Census Employment Survey, using a similar subemployment index, was administered in 51 urban areas as part of the 1970 census. Analyzing the voluminous data from the CES, the Senate Sub-committee on Employment, Manpower, and Poverty found an average subemployment rate of 30.5% for the 51 areas, even when the meager poverty standard of the Social Security Administration was used. This was very close to the results of the smaller Department of Labor survey in 1966, and economists William Spring, Bennett Harrison, and Thomas Vietorisz drew inferences similar to Ginsburg's response to the Labor Department findings: "This is the urban crisis. And it is the subemployment rate which helps us to see the connection between the structure of the labor market and continued poverty and despair—a connection that is masked by the conventional unemployment rate."[45]

There are no subemployment data prior to 1966. When the official unemployment rate was higher, subemployment probably was too, but in any case, what remained in the years of low unemployment was extensive. Since surveys of subemployment did not measure economic deprivation in smaller cities, towns, suburbs, and rural areas, the extent of hardship was still unfathomed by these efforts to document labor-market disadvantages in big-city ghettos.

WOMEN'S UNEMPLOYMENT

The Subemployment Index was not only limited in locale and linked to a meager poverty standard, but it was also gendered. It included only male, discouraged workers, but not women who drop out of the labor market when they cannot find a job. Moreover, to count only involuntary part-time work is to underestimate the number of women who would like full-time work. Although classified as voluntary part-timers, some women have to work fewer hours because they cannot find or afford substitute care for their children.

Some subsequent research on economic disadvantage also has this tendency to overlook the consequences of women's employment. William Julius Wilson and his colleagues, who provide important data on the connection between structural economic changes in the inner city and dependency on welfare, focus on males who are marriageable, that is, those who are employed and between the ages of 15 and 44 years. These researchers relate rising rates of single motherhood among African–Americans between 1960 and 1980 to the declining pool of African–American men who are "marriageable."[46] Yet nonmarriage, divorce, separation, and desertion, although clearly not explained by economic factors alone, seem less likely if women as well as men are stably employed. Young women with poor employment outlooks may lack desirable career alternatives to premature motherhood.[47] It is significant that wives' employment has been found to reduce both female "headship" and poverty among blacks.[48]

The employment picture for young women, particularly African–Americans, was not a pretty one in the 1960s. In 1967, when unemployment stood at 3.8%, the rate for young (18–24 years), out-of-school women with some work experience averaged 23.7% for whites and 37.9%, nearly two-fifths, for blacks.[49] This exceeds the highest overall unemployment rate during the Great Depression. Even with 13 or more years of schooling, young black women had an unemployment rate of 31.9%, only a few points less than high school graduates (34.9%) or those lacking a diploma (35.9%).[50] After careful study of youth employment problems in the late 1960s and early 1970s, a task force assembled by the Twentieth Century Fund called attention to the labor-market disadvantages of young women, particularly blacks.

> The employment problems of black girls, perhaps even more than those of males, are a function of inadequate demand. There are too few jobs for those who want to work, and the openings that are left for black women are the least attractive. Increasing skills and rising levels of labor force participation are not much use when jobs are in short supply.[51]

The task force had a simple policy proposal: "The *sine qua non* for the employment problems of black girls is to increase the number of available jobs and to achieve sustained tight labor markets that could absorb the labor force dropouts as well as the unemployed."[52] In the absence of an expanded supply of jobs, the task force concluded that birth control would be even less useful than improvements on the supply side (e.g., skill enhancement). Indeed, "If all else remained the same, unemployment rates for black women would probably grow worse rather than better if more women became labor-force participants through the prevention of unwanted children."[53] Yet, increasing the labor force participation of women on welfare rather than increasing the demand and rewards for their labor is precisely the policy goal that Congress has followed, with increasing degrees of compulsion—from the 1962 amendments to the SSA through the repeal of AFDC in 1996. Indeed, this is what is meant by welfare "reform."

In concluding this discussion of employment indices relevant to public assistance, we think it important to point out that although African–American unemployment rates were double those of whites every year during the 1960s, white unemployment was numerically much greater. For example, in 1968, there were almost four times (3.8) as many unemployed whites as persons of other races (2,226,000, compared to 591,000).[54] This is not to overlook the fact that black disadvantage was disproportionate and increasingly a source of discontent.

Black protest, as shown in the following section, was an important ingredient in the liberalization of relief policy. This protest resulted in adding to the rolls needy African–American families who had been kept off by exclusionary and deterrent policies of past decades. It also resulted in the addition of needy white families, who were encouraged to claim the benefits for which they, too, were eligible. Blacks had more catching up to do, but somewhat more white than African–American families joined the rolls. Between 1961 and 1967, the AFDC rolls increased by 246,000 white families, compared to 211,000 African–American families.[55]

Explaining the Welfare Explosion

As a result of exclusionary, deterrent, and stingy relief policies, the 1960s began with a backlog of unrelieved family need. As discussed, despite improved economic conditions, subemployment in the ghettos remained at levels that would have been considered a crisis had they been experienced by the rest of the population. What changed in the 1960s was not the existence of need, but the recognition and response to that need. There is a striking contrast between the 1950s, when the phrase, "affluent society," was used to describe the United States, and the 1960s, when, amidst greater affluence and less privation, an American president declared "war on poverty." This is a classic example of the discrepancy between actual social conditions and the societal perception and response to those conditions.[56]

In the 1950s, poverty was what Robert Merton calls a "latent" social problem—a harmful social condition with negative consequences for individuals and society, but not generally recognized as such.[57] The task of explaining how the problem became "manifest" and a matter of national concern is not an easy one. The related puzzles—why long-neglected need was met and why relief rolls "exploded"—are the conundrums that remain debatable, despite much scholarship on the domestic policies of that era.

IMMEDIATE CAUSES OF THE EXPLOSION

Two important works that have analyzed the great expansion of AFDC in the 1960s differ on a number of points, but they agree that changes in the behavior of the poor and in the administration of relief were the immediate detonators of the relief explosion. James Patterson describes these two developments:

> One was a big jump in the percentage of eligible families that applied for aid, reflecting potential clients' much heightened awareness of their rights under the law. The second development was a sharp rise in the percentage of eligible applicants who were in fact assisted. Together, these forces resulted in a fantastic jump in the participation of eligible families in AFDC, from perhaps 33% in the early 1960s to more than 90% in 1971.[58]

Frances Fox Piven and Richard Cloward draw the following, similar conclusions:

> It is no exaggeration to speak of the poor applying for assistance "in numbers heretofore unequalled." Nationally, applications rose from 588,000 in 1960 to 1,088,000 in 1968, an increase of 85 percent.

> As the volume of applications rose, the proportion accepted also rose . . . from 54% in 1960 to 70% in 1968. . . .

> The impact of changing application and approval rates on the welfare rolls was substantial, to say the least.[59]

As assistant for urban affairs in the Nixon administration, Daniel Patrick Moynihan investigated the New York City welfare explosion in which the caseload grew as much in two years, 1965–1967, as it had in the 18 preceding (a quarter-million increase). He found "some indications that caseworkers had become more lenient. The rate of rejection of AFDC applicants had dropped from 40% in 1965 to 23% in 1968." Perhaps recognizing that caseworkers' independent leniency is unlikely to be tolerated to the tune of a quarter-million increase in welfare recipients, Moynihan acknowledged this steep rise might reflect such factors as the policy of a mayor by no means hostile to welfare, "administrative breakdown," more eligible applicants due to more single-mother families, their greater assertiveness, or, the most likely source, in his view, wages too low for the low-skilled male family head to maintain a family. He conceded, though, that "there were no hard answers."[60]

THE SINGLE-MOTHERHOOD FACTOR

Rising rates of single motherhood, partly a reflection of deteriorated employment conditions for younger workers and African–Americans, made more families economically vulnerable and could thus have been a factor in expansion of the welfare rolls. Daniel Patrick Moynihan considered single motherhood an important component of the "tangle of pathology." Then a special assistant to the secretary of labor, Moynihan associated the development of a debilitating, matriarchal family structure with slavery, Reconstruction, urbanization, and male unemployment. He pleaded for treatment of the "tangle of pathology" but offered few policy prescriptions. However, in his highly influential and widely promulgated report, Moynihan strongly advocated changing the behavior of families and downplayed the effects of social reform, declaring that "unless this damage [to the Negro family] is repaired, all the effort to end discrimination and poverty and injustice will come to little."[61]

Single motherhood had been increasing prior to the 1960s, and could not, as Patterson points out, account for a rise in welfare rolls as sudden and as sizable as the one that occurred after 1965.[62] The rate of single motherhood increased 32% from 1960 to 1970, but at the same time, the poverty rate of single mothers decreased 22%. In the next decade, the number of single-mother families escalated more steeply, by 50%, and their poverty rate stayed about the same.[63] If single motherhood were the major factor driving the AFDC caseload, then we would expect the increase in the rolls to have been much greater in the 1970s than in the 1960s. On the contrary, the number of families receiving AFDC increased by a factor of 1.8 in the 1960s and by less than one-half that proportion (68%) in the 1970s.[64] Increased single motherhood, although it enlarged the pool of eligible families, was at most an ingredient in the welfare explosion but not the principal one.

RISE IN BENEFIT LEVELS

Rising benefit levels also increased the number of eligible families. The average benefit per recipient rose by 72% between 1960 and 1970, but the cost of living increased only 9.2%.[65] Patterson estimates that the tendency of wealthier states, particularly, to raise the income levels at which families became eligible for AFDC increased the recipient pool by about 35% between 1967 and 1971, the years of most rapid growth.[66] Liberalization, however, should be put into perspective. In 1970, the average family benefit was only 54% of the meager, 4-person poverty standard.[67]

CIVIL RIGHTS AND THE RISE OF RELIEF

The "rights consciousness of the era" certainly played a role in the relief explosion and was a legacy of the civil-rights revolution.[68] The movement began with demonstrations against denial of essential civil rights in the South, but by the mid-1960s had evolved into a demand for economic rights. Jobs, however, not welfare, were the economic rights emphasized by the movement. The 1963 March on Washington was "for Jobs and Freedom." The "Official Call" for the march, signed by leaders of the major civil-rights organizations, set forth demands for civil rights and for jobs, the latter including a federal public-works program to provide jobs for all the unemployed.[69] Nor was this an isolated incident. Based on their extensive study of principal civil-rights organizations, Hamilton and Hamilton conclude that civil-rights leaders consistently made job creation a high priority in their recommendations to policymakers.[70] The ten demands listed in the Lincoln Memorial Program for the march included "a massive federal program to train and place all unemployed workers—Negro and white—on meaningful and dignified jobs at decent wages."[71] Interestingly, none of the demands pertained to income support or welfare. Platforms or demands are not necessarily where movements place their resources, and although full employment was a stated goal of civil-rights organizations, it was not the issue over which the major battles were fought.

Martin Luther King, Jr., who rose to prominence in the 1955 Montgomery struggle for equal use of public transportation, was slain in Memphis where he had gone in solidarity with striking garbage men. At the end of his life, King was organizing a massive Poor People's March on Washington, and in his latest book, he declared that the "Negro problem" would not be solved until we created either full employment or guaranteed incomes.[72] Sargent Shriver, director of the the federal antipoverty program, regarded the struggle against poverty and for civil rights as "all part of the same battle."[73]

The rights consciousness that had its origins in the civil and then economic struggle of African–Americans inspired a number of other rights movements: the "second wave" of women's liberation, the movements for the rights of the disabled and of gay men and women, and the Welfare Rights movement, which has been called "the social protest of poor women."[74]

THE WAR ON POVERTY AND ECONOMIC OPPORTUNITY

Again, the road was not taken. The War on Poverty gave additional impetus to the "rights consciousness" of the era and increased the propensity of poor people to claim the benefits for which they were eligible. This expansion of relief is an ironic outcome of a War on Poverty whose generals billed it as a means of lessening economic dependency. In signing the Economic Opportunity Act in 1964, President Johnson declared: "We are not content to accept the endless growth of relief rolls or welfare rolls. We want to offer the forgotten fifth of our people opportunity, not doles."[75] Another antipoverty president, Franklin D. Roosevelt, had also claimed to be reducing dependence on "the dole."[76] According to one of the planners of the War on Poverty, "the rejection of an income strategy was assumed to be politically unavoidable and only mentioned in speeches explaining that the Poverty Program was not a handout but a hand up."[77]

But economic opportunity was not defined as employment opportunity any more than it was conceived as increased income support. As one of the poverty warriors wrote: "It was not an in-come-distribution program. It was not a large-scale employment program."[78] In 1964, Labor Secretary Wirtz, who later documented the underemployment crisis in the ghetto, argued that the "single immediate change which the Poverty Program could bring about in the lives of the poor would be to provide the family head with a regular, decently paid job."[79] According to Adam Yarmolinsky, Shriver's chief deputy in planning the antipoverty program, those who developed the program "thought the basic problem of pov-erty was making it possible for people to find and hold decent jobs."[80] Yet, they postponed a job-creation strategy. One reason was they expected the impending federal tax cut to expand em-ployment, including jobs for which the poor could qualify. But they were also concerned about the cost of job creation.[81] More-over, as Margaret Weir illustrates, this preference for tax cuts as fiscal stimuli rather than increased government spending was typical of the brand of Keynesianism that had prevailed in the economic and policy-making circles of the United States and that had been advocated by liberal business leaders.[82]

Nonetheless, as "a last-minute element of the program," plan-ners for the War on Poverty did look for money to fund a job-cre-ation program, evidently adopting Senator Gaylord Nelson's (D-Wis.) proposal to fund a public employment program with cigarette or tobacco taxes.[83] However, Johnson opposed a new tax at a time when taxes were being cut. Ignoring a plea for jobs by Secretary Wirtz, he gave the proposal a cold reception.[84] Perhaps, in addition to the money issue, Johnson remembered the fierce business opposition to direct job-creation programs during the Great Depression and feared such a strategy would undermine the broad base of support, including business, that he sought for his War on Poverty.[85]

Political scientist Judith Russell, who studied archival materi-als extensively, considers this to be the decisive reason for the failure of the War on Poverty to pursue a jobs strategy: "the lack of a clear consensus among experts, early on, about the nature of unemploy-ment and how it related to economic performance and the relationship of these two factors to poverty."[86] Russell's account certainly shows disagreement between Labor Secretary Wirtz and Chairman of the Council of Economic Advisors Walter Heller. The latter favored a tax cut to stimulate the economy rather than targeted job-creation measures. The former believed that a macroeconomic stimulus was essential, but that it would not solve the "hard-core" unemployment central to poverty and characteristic of the ghetto.[87] Adam Yarmolinsky's view, cited previously, suggests that antipoverty planners may have shared Heller's faith in a tax cut and that they considered job creation important but too costly.

Russell also suggests two other reasons why policymakers eschewed substantial job creation: belief that the Labor Department was incapable of administering such a program effectively, and the government's "halting and partial" commitment to the African–American struggle for full economic rights.[88] However, both Kennedy and Johnson administrations established new structures, such as the President's Committee on Juvenile Delinquency and the Office of Economic Opportunity when they favored a policy and judged existing agencies unequal to the task of implementing it.

The employment focus of the antipoverty program was on increasing the employability of poor youth and adults through education and training so that they could take advantage of expanding opportunities. Although it had faith in macroeconomic measures to expand the economy, the administration had supported the Manpower Development and Training Act (MDTA) of 1962 that was originally developed to serve workers displaced by technological change, primarily white males.[89] Later, as the War on Poverty got underway, MDTA was revised to help persons who were unskilled and deficiently educated. The Job Corps, offering intensive remedial education and training to severely disadvantaged teens in a residential setting, and the Neighborhood Youth Corps, providing work and some training to in-school and out-of-school youth, were part of Title I of the Economic Opportunity Act of 1964, the legislation that inaugurated the War on Poverty. With the exception of the Neighborhood Youth Corps, which spent less than $200 million in 1967, these programs were not conceived as efforts to expand jobs but to improve the alleged mismatch between workers' skills and job demands.[90]

"During 1966 and 1967," writes historian David Zarefsky, "it became apparent that the War on Poverty included neither the direct provision of jobs nor the guarantee of eventual employment."[91] Robert Kennedy, then senator from New York, was among those who publicly acknowledged this omission. In the fall of 1966, Kennedy asserted that "no government program now operating gives any substantial promise of meeting the employment crisis affecting the Negro of the cities."[92]

Community Action Programs (CAPs) were the antipoverty

programs that contributed most to the welfare expansion. The most innovative, visible, and controversial interventions of the War on Poverty, CAPs were deliberately designed to challenge the local governments and service-delivery systems that federal planners considered unresponsive to the needs of the poor. Title II of the Economic Opportunity Act of 1964 defines a community-action program as one that contributes to the elimination of poverty through providing a broad range of resources and opportunities to the poor and that is "developed, conducted, and administered with the maximum feasible participation of residents of the areas and members of the groups served. . . ."[93]

The intellectual origins of community action were in the programs of the President's Committee on Juvenile Delinquency (PCJD), particularly its flagship Mobilization for Youth (MFY).[94] PCJD planners had close ties to the office of Attorney General Robert Kennedy. And it was Robert Kennedy who persuaded Sargent Shriver to emphasize community action. Kennedy later testified on behalf of Title II: "Community action programs must basically change the institutions that affect the poor by involving the poor in planning and implementing programs: giving them a real voice in their institutions." [95] Community action meshed with the ethos of African–Americans in the civil-rights movement.[96] Michael Katz considers "community action the method for 'shaking the system' and forcing change on reluctant school administrators, welfare and employment service officials, and even settlement houses and Community Chest leaders. . . ."[97]

Nor was it only the programs funded through CAPs that put pressure on service-delivery systems; other federal programs to combat juvenile delinquency, mental illness, and blighted neighborhoods engaged in similar activities.[98] There were a thousand community-action programs in operation at the peak of the Office of Economic Opportunity (OEO), and although most may have worked relatively harmoniously with local institutions, many did not.[99] Patterson, for example, concludes that the War on Poverty helped to "arouse the poor," adding to what was already being accomplished by the civil-rights movement and "the general rise in expectations in the affluent 1960s."[100]

Legal-services programs, which were part of the CAPs, did much to expand welfare rights and welfare rolls. Patterson considers that legal services, which employed 1,800 lawyers in 850 law offices by 1969, did more than any other OEO program to arouse the poor.[101] Legal services, it should be noted, had its roots in the work of MFY social workers, who identified their low-income clients' need for legal advice on welfare and other civil issues. MFY hired attorney Edward Sparer, who went on to found the Center on Social Welfare Policy and Law (now Welfare Law Center).[102]

Legal-service lawyers not only settled individual grievances of welfare clients but successfully challenged welfare laws and administrative procedures. The Center on Social Welfare Policy and Law, which later got funds from CAPs' Office of Legal Services, either represented the plaintiffs or officially assisted lawyers for the plaintiffs in two of the three Supreme Court cases involving welfare rights.[103] In *King* v. *Smith* (1968), the Court ruled that "substitute fathers" could not be considered actual fathers for purposes of denying eligibility for AFDC. The decision in *Shapiro* v. *Thompson* (1969) was that residency limits violate constitutional rights to travel between states. *Goldberg* v. *Kelly* (1970) held that a fair hearing must precede rather than follow termination of benefits and stipulated basic requirements for the hearings, such as the opportunity to cross-examine adverse witnesses, to be represented by counsel, and to have impartial decision makers. The number of AFDC recipients had more than doubled between 1960 and 1969, that is, prior to these rulings, but the Supreme Court decisions probably contributed to the continued surge in relief—over 75% growth—between 1969 and 1974.[104]

War on Poverty programs not only spurred applications for relief but increased the likelihood of their acceptance. It was no longer lone, uninformed, unassertive welfare clients who inquired about benefits. These clients were now backed by trained advocates, lawyers who could sue, and direct action in the form of marches and sit-ins at welfare centers. According to Piven and Cloward, "A vast array of groups—social workers, churchmen [sic], lawyers, civic organizations, public welfare employees, private foundations, activist students, antipoverty employees, civil rights organizations, settlement house and family agencies, not to speak of organizations of the poor themselves—began to batter the welfare system."[105] According to one report of 11 cities that was conducted by the Department of Health, Education, and Welfare, "A statistically significant relation did exist between CAP expenditures and the *AFDC poor rate*—the higher the [per capita] expenditure the higher the rate [at which poor families were on the rolls]."[106]

THE WELFARE-RIGHTS MOVEMENT

One highly visible expression of aroused consciousness, militancy, and organization of the poor themselves was the rise of a welfare-rights movement in the mid-1960s. The most vocal national organization in the movement and the channel for most welfare protest activities after 1966 was the largely black National Welfare Rights Organization (NWRO) founded by George Wiley, a former associate national director of the Congress on Racial Equality (CORE).[107] The fact that the highly visible and vocal client advocates for welfare rights were black may well have added to the impression that AFDC was an African–American program, notwithstanding the fact that African–Americans, although disproportionately represented, were not the majority of recipients.[108]

The origins of NWRO, according to its historian Guida West, were in both the civil-rights and antipoverty movements. "From the civil-rights movement came its organizers, leaders, liberal supporters, their networks, and their monies. From the poverty movement emerged its theoreticians, other organizers, and federal funds."[109] Federally funded CAPs, Volunteers in Service to America (VISTA), also an OEO program, social-welfare agencies, church organizations, and social-action groups provided organizers, volunteers, and other resources to NWRO.[110] According to one estimate, three-fourths of welfare-rights organizers were antipoverty workers, many of them VISTA volunteers.[111]

NWRO employed the strategies for mobilizing AFDC recipients that had been pioneered at MFY: "solving individual grievances of existing recipients and taking actions on collective grievances."[112] For the first 3 years of its activities, 1966–1969, protests and sit-ins at local welfare departments were the principal strategies that NWRO used against the welfare authorities for solving collective grievances.[113] Guida West believes that the street strategy of NWRO paid off, not only for NWRO members but also for the poor generally; millions of dollars were paid out for many more welfare clients.[114] Until then, welfare systems had deterred many eligible persons from applying. The strategy of NWRO was to keep pressure on local welfare agencies "to do no less than follow existing law."[115]

It is estimated that there were upward of 500 NWRO groups throughout the country in the late 1960s.[116] NWRO members were between 1 and 2% of the families on AFDC.[117] Undoubtedly, there were many more sympathizers and participants in various welfare-rights activities. In any case, the number is extraordinary considering the poverty, stigma, race, and traditional passivity of the clientele.

The extent to which this mobilization of poor women depended on "establishment" support should not be underestimated. It is important to remember that potential beneficiaries were not organized in the 1930s when ADC was enacted, nor did ADC recipients become an organized interest group for 30 years after the inception of the program. It was only with support from the federal government and from powerful nongovernmental agencies that welfare clients became, for a short time, an organized constituency. War on Poverty funds, it should be noted, were not the only source of federal support for NWRO.[118] In a move considered cooptative by some of its adherents, NWRO accepted about half a million dollars from the Department of Labor for involving welfare clients in leadership roles in the Work Incentive Program of AFDC, which it had originally opposed as "slave labor."[119]

Rights consciousness and community action changed the perceptions of some welfare mothers in a way that is best expressed by NWRO members:

When I first came on welfare, I was ashamed, because society has taught us to be ashamed of something like that. . . .

Milwaukee was having civil rights marches . . . and my kids . . . were beginning to see that we were as bad off as most of the people out there, so they told me that they were going on the marches for civil rights . . . when the kids decided that they were going . . . I had to go with them.

That's when I learned of the welfare laws and the Supreme Court decisions and that welfare is a right and not a privilege . . . and I started wanting to learn more about it.

I feel the only way changes will be made, especially in the welfare system, is through poor people, welfare people, organizing and raising a lot of hell . . . which is all we can do.[120]

I went on welfare so I could stay home with the kids because they were getting completely out of control. The baby was three at the time, and he had never really been with me. I had been working since he was born. He couldn't even associate with me, and I just couldn't take that anymore. I decided that until my kids are old enough to realize what work is all about, the government

owes me to bring up my children. The government owes me because
I am raising two boys that I am sure they'll be taking into their
armed services one of these days to fight their damn wars.[121]

We have been forced, due to our sick society, to live as we are
now. Fathers have been driven from their homes because of our
welfare system which won't aid a family if the father is in the
home. And then the government says the poor family is breaking up, and it's the one who's causing it.[122]

THE POLITICS OF ANTIPOVERTY POLICIES

We have shown how federally financed community action helped
not only to mobilize the poor to claim welfare benefits to which
they were entitled but also to exert pressure on local authorities
to accept more applications. What is harder but necessary to account for is why the federal government began the 1960s by trying to reduce relief rolls and dissociated its antipoverty program
from "handouts" but nonetheless financed the community action
program that contributed to a tremendous expansion of what it claimed
to be avoiding.

The war on poverty, writes Richard Polenberg, "did not arise
out of a loud public demand but from a quiet professional one."[123]
It is true that professionals, academics, and their allies in the
foundations formulated and tested community action as well as
some other approaches like the Job Corps and Neighborhood
Youth Corps. Yet, ideas and programs like community action
do not see the light of day, much less become models for public
policies, unless they serve some political purposes. It is widely
recognized that serious and widespread disorder—riots in Watts,
Newark, Detroit, Atlanta—followed rather than preceded the
declaration of the War on Poverty.[124] Yet, fear of disorder and
the need to reward and maintain a constituency that was absolutely vital to Democratic presidential victories rank high among
the many factors that account for a war on poverty and the funding
of community action.

Moved by his encounter with poverty during his presidential
campaign in West Virginia, President Kennedy referred repeatedly
to poverty in his inaugural address and initiated a number of policies
and projects for youth employment, remedial education, aid to
depressed areas, and manpower development and training, not to
mention an extension of ADC.[125] The president conveyed his interest

in the poverty problem to Walter Heller, director of the Council of Economic Advisors (CEA), and asked him for "the facts" in December 1962. Heller, in turn, put his economist colleague, Robert Lampman, to work on a study of poverty that moved the administration further toward a direct attack on poverty by its finding: that there had been "a drastic slowdown in the rate at which the economy was taking people out of poverty."[126] In the spring of 1963, Kennedy was said to be looking for a "comprehensive structural counterpart, taking the form, not of piecemeal programs, but of a broad war against poverty itself . . . which would pull a host of social programs together and rally the nation behind a generous cause." By the fall of 1963, the president had made a firm decision to mount an assault on poverty that would be "the centerpiece of his 1964 legislative recommendations."[127]

Reportedly, Kennedy thought initially in terms of Appalachia and rural poverty and was influenced by the *New York Times* articles on distress in eastern Kentucky as well as by Michael Harrington's book, *The Other America* (or reviews of it), neither of which focused on urban poverty.[128] His own encounter with poverty, moreover, had been in Appalachia. Why, then, did the War on Poverty, which was conceived by the Kennedy administration and carried out by its successor, emphasize urban poverty?

In its "profiles of disorder," the National Advisory Commission on Civil Disorders mentions outbreaks involving both whites and blacks in five cities in 1963. Birmingham was the scene of the most violent encounters that year. The police used dogs, firehoses, and cattle prods against civil-rights marchers; white racists shot at blacks and bombed black residences; blacks retaliated by burning white-owned businesses in black areas; and most alarming and tragic of all, a black church was bombed, killing four young girls in a Sunday school class.[129] In the summer of 1963, 14,000 demonstrators were arrested in the states of the Old Confederacy. Arthur M. Schlesinger, Jr., compared the months of May and June 1963 to an earlier season of revolt: "One had seen no such surge of spontaneous mass democracy in the United States since the organization of labor in the heavy industries in the spring and summer of 1937. Characteristically each revolution began with direct local action—one with sit-downs, the others with sit-ins."[130]

At a 1973 conference on the origins of the War on Poverty, Adam Yarmolinsky, Sargent Shriver's deputy in planning the Poverty Program, attempted to downplay the influence of race or political concerns on Kennedy's interest in an antipoverty program.[131] Speaking at the same conference, Daniel Capron, a former official of the Council of Economic Advisors (CEA) and the Bureau of the Budget, admitted that "we saw, literally, the March on Washington and that sure didn't do anything to cool us off on pushing this embryonic program."[132] In fact, the administration was concerned enough about the March on Washington in August to try to get it called off, and having failed in that effort, to attempt to moderate and control it.[133] Richard Cloward, one of the professors whose theories and program concepts had served as models for the antipoverty program, reminded the conference what had been going on during the months when Kennedy was committing himself to the War on Poverty.[134] Prompted by Cloward and Frances Fox Piven, Yarmolinsky later conceded that the poverty program "was in part a response to profound . . . social movements in the United States."[135] James Button argues that once the antipoverty program was instituted, the increased urgency represented by the black riots led to greater emphasis, especially in the CAP, on urban blacks.[136]

The importance of retaining a black vote that had been absolutely critical to the Kennedy election in 1960 should not be overlooked. Schlesinger, for example, observes that "had only whites gone to the polls in 1960, Nixon would have taken 52% of the vote." In the electoral college, Kennedy could not have carried Illinois, Michigan, Texas, South Carolina, and possibly Louisiana without the African–American vote.[137] Capron pointed out that it would have been "death to bill any kind of program as a help-the-blacks program. But that doesn't mean that we didn't realize that this program was very important in terms of the black vote. . . ."[138] Piven and Cloward suggest that directing services to the ghettos was a way of placating blacks and at the same time not alienating whites so much as with programs that involved integration.[139] Referring to the importance of solidifying the loyalty of urban blacks and the slim margin of Democratic victory in the 1960 election, Zarefsky concludes: "One obvious way to do this was by making them the beneficiaries of federal largesse." But, in order not to alienate whites, "programs in aid of the poor must mute the questions of race, translating it into terms which could command biracial support."[140]

All this does not mean that planners of the federal antipoverty program anticipated that community action would lead to the relief expansion or that they were initially trying to placate disorder with welfare. It is true that African–American women were not the rioters.

If their teenage children were, programs targeted to African–American youth, like the Job Corps, were a direct means of quieting them. But money to their families in the form of relief would also aid disruptive youth. In any case, mounting unrest was viewed particularly by federal elites as "demands for help from a disadvantaged minority group that had little or no access to conventional political channels." The antipoverty program began to respond to two of the more intense upheavals, in Rochester and Los Angeles, by pumping more funds into these cities.[141] To James Button, who studied the political impact of black violence, the model-cities program was in part a "direct response" to the riots, especially the 1965 outbreak in the Watts section of Los Angeles.[142]

Expanding AFDC was probably a relatively easy way to respond to these pressures. It had been clear from the outset that Congress would not fund a new income-support program, even had Johnson espoused the guaranteed-income or negative-income tax proposals that were discussed and favored by some policymakers, intellectuals, and business leaders in the middle 1960s.[143] The welfare explosion put millions of extra dollars into the hands of the ghetto poor without any Congressional action except the establishment of the antipoverty program itself. Johnson, responding to widespread chagrin over the "welfare mess," announced in 1967 that he would establish a Commission on Income Maintenance to study the problem and make recommendations, but he put off establishing the commission until the next year.[144] Probably he stalled long enough to ensure the commission would not make its recommendations until after the 1968 election. Another advantage of AFDC expansion over other kinds of reform, particularly as the Vietnam War became more costly, is that about one-half of the increase in benefits would be picked up by the states.

PUBLIC ATTITUDES

In addition to awakening their fears, protest and riot may have pricked the conscience of American elites. The executives of major national corporations who formed an Urban Coalition with labor, religious, academic, and civil-rights leaders to respond to the urban crisis were not necessarily insincere in their motto, "Give a Damn."[145] Yet, the conversion of economic elites, if the policies of the near future are any indications, was all too brief.

The general public, in any case, did not change its mind. Had the expansion of the welfare rolls been put to a referendum, it is unlikely that it would have passed. As the increasing number of applicants for ADC implies, some poor, single mothers themselves altered their values, particularly the belief that they had a right to relief and to be treated with dignity, despite their dependence on public assistance. Indeed, transvaluation of participants is characteristic of social movements. But that does not mean the public altered its attitudes.

Opinion polls are often hard to interpret, and their results frequently depend on how questions are phrased. With that caveat we point to some evidence that reveals little softening of public attitudes toward economic dependency. A Gallup poll early in 1965 found that 50% of respondents favored denying relief to unwed mothers who had further illegitimate children, and 73% favored giving welfare clients food and clothing instead of cash.[146] In spring 1969, 84% of a nationwide sample of 1,017 adults agreed that too many people were receiving welfare who should be working, and 61% agreed that many women getting welfare money are having illegitimate babies to increase the money they get.[147] When 11 reasons for poverty were grouped according to whether they were individualistic (lack of effort), fatalistic (sickness and physical handicaps), or structural reasons for poverty (failure of industry to provide enough jobs), one-half of the sample placed great emphasis on the individualistic factors, and only a minority viewed societal factors to be of equal importance. The researcher concluded that "although the structural interpretation seems to have emerged in the last several decades as an increasingly important view of poverty . . . it is clear that the individualistic view is still firmly entrenched among average Americans."[148]

Summary: Work, Welfare, and Economic Opportunity

At the beginning of the 1960s, philosopher Charles Frankel coined an aphorism to characterize the state of American welfare: "Our deeds, though behind our needs, are ahead of our thoughts."[149] Deeds and needs drew closer together in the 1960s, although they did not meet, even during a time that combined great economic expansion and intense, if short-lived, commitment to social reform. By the end of the decade, the poverty rate had nearly halved— from 22.2% in 1960 to 12.6% in 1970, but more than 25 million people remained poor in the most prosperous society the world had ever known.[150] Perhaps social attitudes softened slightly for a brief interlude. Yet it was not primarily kinder and gentler thoughts that led to temporary liberalization of relief policies; indeed, the rapidity with which restrictive policies were invoked, beginning as early as 1967, suggests that minds changed modestly, if at all. To some Americans, namely, welfare advocates and clients, community action had led to welfare reform, but they were in the minority. To more Americans, the explosion of the relief rolls was a welfare crisis.

Labor-market deficiencies were well documented by both executive and legislative branches of the federal government during the prosperous 1960s, but this evidence of severely limited economic opportunities failed to influence federal antipoverty policy. Despite recognition of severe subemployment in the ghettos on the part of some high officials, job creation targeted to the inner-city poor was not a strategy of the War on Poverty. The creation of sufficient, adequate-paying jobs would have been a genuine economic opportunity, but government job creation has been a response to recession and depression, not to endemic underemployment in good times. Once again, an employment road that would have offered genuine economic opportunity for the poor had not been taken. Instead, unemployment was treated as a deficiency of human capital or of motivation, education, and training. The "benefit" that would have been a real "hand up" and a genuine "economic opportunity" and that was championed by some members of the administration, including, in time, the director of the antipoverty program, was eschewed—especially by Congress and the president, who had declared unconditional war on poverty. In time, the director of the antipoverty program and top members of his staff made job creation a major component of their plans for abolishing poverty.

Labor-market disadvantage, better documented in the 1960s than ever before, was largely seen in male terms. Subemployment included *male* discouraged workers and the *male* census undercount. An exception was the Twentieth Century Fund report on youth employment that carefully analyzed the employment problems of young, African–American women and viewed job expansion the critical economic strategy for African–Americans of both sexes.

According to NWRO historian Guida West, "adequate benefits and adequate jobs were both high on the poor women's agenda," and many felt NWRO should fight for jobs, better educational opportunities, and child care for mothers, as well as for welfare rights.[151]

Such a program would have offered choices to poor women. West observes, however, that in contrast to the volunteer female activists who were welfare clients, many of the paid men in the movement, including the executive director and founder, George Wiley, supported the traditional division of labor between the sexes. In this regard, although not in their stance toward the moral standards of recipients, the professional welfare advocates of the 1960s resembled the women reformers who, earlier in the century, had championed government support for women's nurturing roles rather than for their breadwinning roles.

Although the War on Poverty was in considerable measure a response to African–American protest, it did not pursue the economic rights preferred by civil-rights advocates. One reason may be that African–American protest, while giving frequent and often eloquent support to employment, and not to welfare, concentrated its resources on civil and voting rights. At the time of his death, Martin Luther King appeared to be moving toward a major emphasis on economic rights, including full employment. However, job creation, with the exception of the March on Washington in the summer of 1963, was not the focus of the great majority of rights protests and movement activity. Thus, one movement advocating economic rights made welfare, not work, its priority, while the other, although supporting job creation and full employment, concentrated its forces elsewhere.

If it seemed politically impossible to provide the most obvious form of economic opportunity, then the next best and most fair-minded policy would have been to acknowledge the need for relief, rather than to expand and denigrate it simultaneously. This policy of giving and grousing, which characterizes the response of the 1960s and, to some extent, FDR's attitude toward the "dole" in the 1930s, ensures disdain and eventual benefit losses for those who depend on grudgingly extended assistance. Had political leaders helped the public to understand why relief was rising in a time of general prosperity, reform might have lasted longer and perhaps even addressed itself to the basic causes of economic insecurity.

CHAPTER 5

Setting the Stage for Welfare
"Reform," 1967–1980

T he period that began in 1967 and ran through the end of the next decade is the Janus face of social policy. On the one hand, the liberal, mildly redistributive legacies of the New Deal and Great Society eras, entrenched in the policy networks that link the federal bureaucracy to congressional committees and interest groups, continued to exert pressure on policy making, especially as economic conditions worsened and the poverty rate began to rise. The temporary political recovery of the Democratic party after the Watergate debacle also assured some continuation of a liberalizing pressure on social policy. But during this period, changes were occurring in the international economy that would profoundly alter the terms of the social-policy debate. The responses of both the business community and politicians to changing economic and geopolitical realities would realign the party system, bringing a new set of political actors to power with a very different economic and social agenda on both sides of the aisle—one that, by 1996, would result in the repeal of welfare.

This chapter begins with a brief analysis of the macroeconomic events that gradually altered the policy climate in Washington. These gave impetus to a new, ultraconservative political movement that, by the end of the decade, would be poised to take power on behalf of a much more repressive view of welfare recipients and of the welfare state in general. It examines: the response of business to the slower growth of the 1970s; the rise in inequality; the discrediting of Keynesianism as an economic policy tool; the resurrection of laissez-faire economic theory; the political mobilization of the business community; accelerating attacks on labor and welfare; poor-law ideology dressed up as a new genre of social theory; the ʋsion of the New Deal Coalition within the Democratic party; ₁nd the rise of a new right-wing political movement composed of business leaders, neoconservative policy wonks, media pundits, religious fundamentalists, and politicians. Finally, the chapter points to another road not taken—the brief opening of an opportunity that the urban rebellions of the late 1960s presented for a massive jobs and urban revitalization program. This neglected opportunity will be discussed in greater detail in the following chapter.

The Macroeconomic Context of Policy Making, 1967–1980

The period that witnessed the opening up of the welfare rolls to greater numbers of claimants was an era of general prosperity that was marked by the almost doubling of average family income as well as a precipitous decline in poverty. In retrospect, this period appears as an aberration in American history, if not also in world history.[1] The period was a product of both the unique conjunction of forces that led the United States to emerge from World War II as the world's most powerful economy as well as the system of international trade and currency arrangements that were drawn up among the allied nations at the Bretton Woods conference in 1944.

The Bretton Woods system, designed not only to advance world trade but also to promote the goal of full employment, had facilitated rising expectations for people across the globe. The United States was at the helm of this new prosperity. American businesses reaped the initial rewards of both fortunate circumstance and government policies of enlightened self-interest. In this optimistic postwar climate, business leaders, aided by the Dixiecrat-GOP alliance in Washington, succeeded in crushing the most militant sectors of the labor movement (those who were most committed to a broad social-welfare agenda and to organizing the unorganized). The large industrial unions were forced to settle—albeit not without constant warfare—for a tacit "social contract" that provided family-supporting wages pegged to cost-of-living increases for a (largely white male) fraction of the American working class. New opportunities for workers in the mainstream economy were aided by government policies like the progressive income tax, the interstate highway system, the G.I. bill, and, to some extent, increased social-welfare benefits for the poor, the elderly, and the disabled.

Military spending was also a fiscal stimulus, notwithstanding its relative inefficiency—in comparison to civilian spending—as a job-creating mechanism.[2]

By the end of the 1960s, however, the postwar regime began to unravel, and the world economy entered a period of relative stagnation and instability.[3] By 1973, the Bretton Woods regime was in ashes, and the United States economy was characterized by two U-turns, one in the poverty rate, which, after declining by 50% between 1959 and 1973, began to rise, and the other a reversal of the trend toward rising real wages and economic growth. By the mid-1970s, economists had coined a new word, "stagflation," to describe the perplexing and persistent combination of high unemployment and inflation that had developed. Stagflation was most prevalent in the United States. According to then dominant economic theory, this was not supposed to happen.[4] When unemployment went up, inflation was supposed to come down. The Nixon, Ford, and Carter administrations all tried a mix of mildly stimulative and contractionary policies, but none of them was able to curb the inflation.

The crisis reflected in these economic events was both economic and ideological. It led to a gradual shift in emphasis among economists from assuring some measure of employment[5] to stemming inflation,[6] and among social policy elites from alleviating poverty to curbing the demands of the poor for a bigger slice of the pie.

The major problem faced by big business during the 1970s was how to increase its profitability and investment capital in the face of stagflation.[7] American firms chose to recoup losses in their rate of profit growth by cutting labor costs.[8] Aided by new technological developments in the electronics, communications, and transportation industries, they accelerated the shipping of their most labor-intensive operations, not just to union-free areas within the United States, but to low-wage countries where they could evade the labor and environmental laws so dearly achieved in this country. For every 100 jobs created between 1969 and 1976, 88 were destroyed through this process, and most of these were in high-wage, unionized sectors.[9] As we show, businesses also sought to hold the growth rate of wages below productivity increases in order to curb inflation, a change from most of the postwar era in which productivity gains were generally shared with workers in the form of higher wage settlements.

The Demise of Keynesianism and the
Return of Laissez-Faire

Economic theory is both a response of academic, business, and policy elites to economic events and a determinant of them. Once translated into public policy, economic theory becomes embedded in a series of ongoing institutions and expectations. Relationships among congressional committees, executive branch agencies, and interest groups (known as "iron triangles") develop to keep programs funded and political support high. Any fundamental change in the economic theory that guides economic and social policy, therefore, requires the destruction of the expectations that it nurtured and the institutional base which had supported it.

Keynesianism—the theory that helped to explain the policy decisions of most western governments in the post-World War II era—posited an active role for government in stabilizing the business cycles and redistributing resources. U.S. policymakers, however, employed a limited form of Keynesianism in comparison to most of their European counterparts. Rather than choosing active labor-market policies as some European nations had, they preferred tax relief and military spending as economic stimuli and narrowly targeted relief programs to mitigate the worst consequences of economic downturns.[10] Nevertheless, this limited form of Keynesianism fit the policy decisions taken throughout the 30-year, postwar period. The core of interest-group support for Keynesian-style social programs was a coalition of labor unions, civil-rights groups, and social-service providers, anchored by the resources and organizational capacity of the trade-union movement. But the end of stability in the international system and the growth of stagflation during the 1970s proved fateful for both the theory and the coalition that had mobilized for government-led solutions to poverty.

The failure of mildly Keynesian efforts to bring the economy back into equilibrium in the 1970s eroded policymakers' confidence in Keynesianism as both a diagnostic and prescriptive policy tool. In the absence of any other economic theory, policymakers adopted two complementary theories that had been developed by conservative economists: "monetarism" and "supply-side," the latter essentially laissez-faire dressed up in new clothing. Both theories, when enacted, had the effect of transferring money to the wealthy.

According to University of Chicago monetarist Milton Friedman, the stagflation of the 1970s was not caused by the untenable imperial reach of the United States and the bloated military budget; nor was it caused by the collapse of the international monetary system or the two oil crises in 1973 and 1979 that were brought on by the decision of the OPEC oil cartel to restrict supply. Rather, the culprit was the Federal Reserve's failure to rein in the money supply.[11]

Jimmy Carter's Federal Reserve chairman, Paul Volker, used monetarist theory as a justification for policy change. Volker argued that the Fed should focus on controlling inflation (of most concern to the Fed's major constituencies, Wall Street and holders of government debt), and to do so it should control the growth rate of the money supply. For 3 years (with no congressional or presidential attempt to overrule his policies), Volker reduced the rate of growth of the money supply; instead of the swift reduction in inflation that monetarists had predicted, interest rates soared, starting the worst recession since the Great Depression.[12] Volker's actions also created a ripple of credit tightening across the entire global economy.[13]

Helen Ginsburg has pointed out that policymakers justified their emphasis on curbing inflation over reducing unemployment through a series of sometimes racist and sexist rationalizations that amounted to claiming that the unemployment rate was really overstated or that it was not all that important. Unemployment, they claimed, fell heaviest on women and youth (or on African–Americans) who now made up a greater proportion of the labor force. Since (white) male "breadwinners" had much lower unemployment rates, unemployment was not so consequential. Another argument was that generous government benefits cushioned the impact of unemployment or acted—as in the case of unemployment insurance and welfare benefits—as an incentive to keep recipients jobless. And finally, they pointed to the underground economy that was probably keeping many of the unemployed afloat.[14] As William Greider observed, however, few Americans understood that monetary policy worked to effectively ration credit according to "the financial girth of the prospective borrowers," and neither elected officials nor the Federal Reserve had any incentive to inform them.[15]

For supply-side theorists like economist Arthur Laffer,[16] the causes of the economic malaise were: the high cost of labor; the expansion of income-maintenance programs that had kept wages artificially high in the face of rising unemployment by making it

easy for people to opt out of the labor market; the excessive regulatory framework that was putting too high a price on the cost of
doing business; and burdensome taxes that were dampening investment.[17] If labor's power could be weakened, if government
spending on social entitlements could be reduced, if regulations
could be loosened, and personal and corporate taxes lowered—so
the theory went—individuals' work efforts would be stimulated,
businesses would have more money to invest in new technologies, factories, and equipment, the economy would grow, and tax
revenues would increase.

The Ideological Offensive

Implementing monetary austerity, curtailing the welfare state,
and setting market forces loose to allocate goods, services, and
credit represented a reversal of the entire postwar policy of using
government to regulate the business cycle so as to place limits on
the tendency of greed to overtake concern for the social good. In
effect, it was erosion of the rather short-lived progressive interpretation of the Constitution, that one of the purposes of government is to "promote the general welfare."

If such a reversal of theory were to be translated into policy,
it would require, first, curtailing the public's growing expectations of government as well as curbing labor's demand for rising
wages. This meant clamping down on what conservative intellectuals described as an "excess of democracy" or a "rising tide of
entitlement."[18] In the business and policy forums of the 1970s could
be found expressions of a fear that the popular aspirations of the
1960s and early 1970s—for greater participation in political life,
for a reduction in economic inequality, and for an end to the U.S.
role as world cop—had gone too far. In his book, *A Time for Truth*,
former Secretary of the Treasury in the Ford administration William Simon, an ardent free-marketeer, expressed his fear that the
country was in "immense danger," that "its very cornerstone, economic and political liberty, had been seriously eroded."[19] In an
address to the Trilateral Commission, one of several elite international forums that were convened during the 1970s to deal with
the crisis in the world economy, Harvard political scientist Samuel
Huntington pined for the day when "Truman had been able to govern
the country with the cooperation of a relatively small number of
Wall Street lawyers and bankers."[20]

The subsequent political and cultural history of the period may be read as the attempt by believers in the doctrine of laissez-faire to relegitimize the "free market" as the most efficient distributor of goods and services. During the years of Keynesian-style government intervention, the "free market" had fallen into disrepute, and big business had lost the public's confidence.[21] In practice, however, laissez-faire did not mean a severance of the economy from the state. In a global economy in which there was no longer a steering mechanism, it was more important than ever that the state assure the capital accumulation process. To do this, it had to loosen the Keynesian controls that had kept the economy somewhat subservient to human needs; instead, it had to use other controls—the Federal Reserve—to assure a continuous flow of capital to large creditors. Thus, a return to the "free market" meant wresting the small measure of influence that representatives of workers, consumers, and advocates for the poor had with the state, and placing the state apparatus more firmly under the influence of corporate and financial leaders.

Doing this, however, might threaten political stability. The system would therefore require relegitimation through a campaign of re-education and mass propaganda. Those groups that had championed the Keynesian agenda would have to be discredited, and the New Deal political coalition, along with the institutions and networks it had erected, would have to be broken apart and some of its constituents pulled into the Republican camp.

The Political and Ideological Mobilization of the Business Community

The need to relegitimize the free market would entail an unprecedented political mobilization of the business community. According to Thomas Edsall,[22] the mobilization was initiated in 1973 and 1974 by a small group of Washington's most influential corporate lobbyists. During the course of the 1970s, key business lobbying organizations were revitalized under the leadership of the Fortune 500, and new ones were formed. In 1970, only a handful of the Fortune 500 companies had Washington lobbyists, but by the end of the decade more than 80% did.[23] A series of ad hoc coalitions was also established to fight for common interests, such as defeat of both the Consumer Protection Agency and labor-law reform. Political Action Committees (PACs) were established to

pool campaign contributions in order to get around limitations that
reforms of the campaign finance system had placed on individual
donations. By the end of the decade, business PACs had greatly
eclipsed labor as major contributors to political campaigns.[24]

By the early 1970s, the decline of party loyalty and congressional
reform had weakened the role of committee chairs, diffusing power
more widely in the Congress. This induced business to develop
a new approach to influencing public policy, based on mobilizing
grassroots opinion rather than lobbying a few key congressional
committee chairs.[25] Thanks to computerized direct-mail technologies,
they could now mobilize their far-flung empire of employees,
subcontractors, customers, and stockholders and direct their voices
to the appropriate legislator. Corporations also turned to advertising,
aimed at promoting not a product, but a set of ideas. In addition,
they began to pour millions of dollars into a host of new and
refurbished foundations, legal organizations, opinion journals,
newspapers, radio and television programs, and "think tanks,"
whose spokespersons were increasingly featured on the
corporate-owned media. Among these groups were the Heritage
Foundation, the John M. Olin Foundation, the American Enterprise
Institute, the Manhattan Institute, the Bradley Foundation, the
Free Congress Foundation, the Washington Legal Foundation, and
the *Washington Times*. Business interests also paid for a series
of weekend seminars at plush retreats on the benefits of a free-
market economy, to which leaders from the political, academic,
and religious communities were invited, without cost to them.
Corporations funded university chairs, television series like
conservative economist Milton Friedman's "Free to Choose," and
curricula for the public schools.

THE ATTACK ON LABOR

To cut its own labor costs as well as to weaken labor's bargaining power and political influence in the Democratic party, business
initiated an aggressive offensive that effectively ended the limited social contract that had been the bedrock of the postwar recovery. It hired union-busting law firms, lobbied to have antiunion
representatives placed on the National Labor Relations Board, de-
certified union elections, threatened workers with plant closures
if they refused to accept wage and benefit reductions, and enforced
stricter work rules. In public pronouncements, politicians and

businessmen blamed labor for taking too big a bite out of profits, thereby destroying business' ability to invest in new plants and equipment. They also blamed double-digit inflation on union demands for wage and benefit hikes. Ronald Reagan's attack on the Air Traffic Controller's Union was a signal that union bashing would be supported at the highest levels of government.

This broad-based attack on labor, along with the transfer of unionized jobs to cheaper labor zones in the U.S. and abroad— abetted by government tax and subsidy policies that promoted such relocation—was effective.[26] By 1981, union membership had dwindled to 22.6% from a high of 32.5% in 1953. It would go down even further in the decade to come, making union density at the beginning of the twenty-first century the lowest in the industrialized world. Of course, not all of the blame for labor's erosion can be laid at the feet of business and government. The purging of the most progressive elements from the AFL-CIO during the Communist witch hunts of the 1940s and 1950s resulted in "business unionism." A tacit agreement not to organize the unorganized was part of the postwar "social contract" to which labor had agreed. Thus, as labor lost jobs to plant closings and business decertification of union elections, it failed to replace them with jobs in newly organized industries in the expanding service sector.

THE ATTACK ON WELFARE

It was harder for business to attack the welfare state openly, for a large part of the middle class benefited from programs like Social Security, unemployment compensation, Medicare, and disability insurance. By the 1970s, these government benefits had become acceptable for millions of people, most of whom contributed to them when they or their breadwinners were employed. It was far easier to attack programs that were politically vulnerable, like AFDC. In time, AFDC, though taking up only about 1% of the federal budget, would become a stand-in for the entire welfare state and the evils of "big government."[27]

The major thrust for the return of laissez-faire came from business leaders and policymakers associated with an ultraconservative wing of the Republican party that had been organizing for a comeback ever since the defeat of their presidential candidate, Barry Goldwater, in 1964. One of the animating forces behind the attack on the welfare state, however, came from a small group of ex-liberal intellectuals—

dubbed neoconservatives—who began to switch sides during the social turbulence of the 1960s.[28] Fearful that the state was coming apart at the seams and that civil society was being corrupted by an antiauthoritarian countercultural revolution, they began to focus their vitriol on the 1960s generation that had led the fight for civil rights, welfare rights, women's rights, and antiimperialism during the 1960s and early 1970s.

Manipulating public confusion over the nature of socioeconomic inequality in the United States, neoconservative apologists maintained that the real divisions in the country were not between the haves and the have-nots, but between "producers" (businessmen, manufacturers, hard-hats, blue-collar workers, and farmers) and a "New Class" of "nonproducers." In the latter category were lumped the major media, liberal foundations, the educational establishment, federal and state bureaucracies, and a permanent welfare class.[29]

With its politically weak constituency and generally negative public image, AFDC became an easy target.[30] While welfare was never a popular program, its targeting for special attack was aided by the increased "coloring" of the welfare rolls in the late 1960s and early 1970s.[31] Although African–Americans are no less committed to the work ethic than whites, black laziness has been an enduring stereotype in the mythology of white racism. As more African–Americans began to claim their overdue entitlement to welfare through a movement that heightened their public visibility, this stereotype reemerged as a salient ingredient in the political culture. Martin Gilens had shown that the symbolic power of welfare "stems in large measure from its racial undertones." It has always been easy to manipulate the never very cohesive American working class along racial lines, especially during economic downturns. Unscrupulous politicians find race-coded issues like welfare useful because they can exploit the power of racial animosity without being charged with race baiting.[32] The success of George Wallace's racially oriented populist campaign in the 1968 presidential election had already convinced the Republican party that the New Deal Coalition could be split along racial lines by linking African–American crime to welfare "dependency" and civil disorder. The campaign strategy worked to get Nixon elected and has been used with some success in Republican campaigns ever since.[33]

As agenda setter, issue framer, and most influential source of Americans' information about the world, the mass media played a major role in making these connections. During the late 1960s and early 1970s, black inner-city poverty received lurid headlines as riots, black power and welfare-rights protests broke out in cities across the country. Exposed night after night to scenes of ghetto turmoil, stories of "welfare chiselers" (which usually featured African–American subjects), and "black-power" militants, many members of the white working class, who were feeling the loss of their own economic security, interpreted government spending on the poor as favoritism to a class of lazy, if not dangerous, and certainly undeserving poor people. According to Martin Gilens, who studied media images of African–Americans over a 43-year period, "black faces are unlikely to be found in media stories on the most sympathetic subgroups of the poor, just as they are comparatively absent from media coverage of poverty during times of heightened sympathy for the poor."[34] Programs like affirmative action only added to the conviction of blue-collar whites that they were being shortchanged. Unable to understand the larger macroeconomic forces that were shaking up their world, they equated their own insecurity with the rise of black aspirations.

As we saw in Chapter 4, neoconservative social theorists like Daniel Patrick Moynihan also used the race card to suggest that there was something inherently dysfunctional about the female-headed African–American family. In elevating this idea to the level of national policy, President Johnson had handed conservatives a perfect tool for splitting the New Deal coalition.

The Rise of the New Right

The rise of poverty in the early 1970s and increases in the welfare rolls came at a time when the country was undergoing profound cultural change. The women's and gay movements were demanding radical alterations in sexual mores, women were moving into the workforce in unprecedented numbers (partly because of declining male wages), and the "black power" movement was challenging whites' unacknowledged, centuries-long position of relative privilege. These cultural challenges were threatening, not only to neoconservative intellectuals associated with prestigious eastern institutions, but to blue-collar and lower middle-class whites whose social status and financial security were already buffeted by economic change. Their anxieties eventually found expression in the rise of the Religious Right, the latest expression of a recurring pattern in

American politics during times of economic and cultural stress.[35] Opportunistic televangelists, seeking to build political/religious empires by using new electronic communications technology, began linking the single motherhood of AFDC clients with a general breakdown in morals and with threats to the traditional (i.e., patriarchal) family.

Again, the mass media abetted the propagandists of the Right. By the late 1970s, the media had coined a term, *the underclass,* to define a subset of the poor who were distinguished, not by their lack of access to resources, but by their behavior. *Time* magazine began the trend in 1977 with its description of an emergent inner-city underclass "more intractable, more socially alien, and more hostile than almost anyone had imagined."[36] Soon, the term was being used by media pundits, conservative social theorists, and establishment research institutes to link a set of behaviors considered pathological with the welfare poor: teenage pregnancy, dropping out of school, drug addiction, family disruption, crime, and juvenile delinquency.[37]

There have always been differences between the household and family structures of whites and African–Americans. Although the rate of single motherhood in the 1970s and early 1980s was increasing slightly faster among whites than among blacks, the fact that a greater proportion of African–American families was headed by women on welfare who lived in neighborhoods where crime and decay were prevalent meant that a term that was based on moralistic and judgmental definitions of the family, as discussed in Chapter 2, would indict the African–American family more than the white.[38] Black welfare mothers were thus held responsible for rearing a generation of school drop-outs, drug dealers, and criminals, as well as daughters who would grow up to be "welfare dependent." As Andrew T. Miller has observed, the concept of the "underclass" was just the latest version of an historic tendency to elide class and race.[39] Perceiving that their pro-big-business economic agenda had a limited market, conservative political strategists learned that they could use the emotionally charged issues of the Religious Right—single parenthood coded as concern for "family values," along with school prayer, abortion, "godless communism," crime, and fear of homosexuality—to drive a wedge into the white, blue-collar, and lower middle-class base of the Democratic party, thereby expanding their electoral base.[40] In this New Right configuration, the conservative social agenda of the Religious Right was linked to the economic and foreign policy agenda of the political Right. The Religious Right's national network of churches and television and radio programs provided the organized troops for the New Right's political campaigns. For its part, the Religious Right's penetration of the Republican party at its highest levels gave it direct access to the legislative halls where it hoped to pass laws that would divert public funds to private religious schools, censor the public airwaves, establish prayer in the public schools, outlaw homosexual activity, and rescind abortion rights for women.[41]

For the Right, the welfare state was not only the cause of moral decay, crime, and "dependency," but the taxes needed to support it were a drain on the country's ability to generate economic growth. In 1978, California passed Proposition 13, an aggressively marketed referendum that sought to reduce middle-class taxes by linking what was in reality a growth in the regressivity of the tax system to the growth in government entitlement programs. Declining wages, inflation, stagnating family incomes, and rising relief rolls—products, as we have seen, of larger macroeconomic forces and misguided government policies—were now collapsed into the single culprit: excessive taxes. Although U.S. citizens enjoyed a considerably lower overall tax burden than their European counterparts,[42] the tax-cutting fever caught on, sweeping legislative halls across the country and becoming one of the key planks in the Republicans' attack on the entire panoply of New Deal and Great Society programs. As the next chapter will show, it would deal the death blow to President Carter's welfare-reform proposals.

Social Theory Reconstructs the Poor

The ideas about the welfare poor that pervaded the nightly news and the pages of neoconservative journals like *Commentary* and *The Public Interest* and that were preached from the pulpits of televangelists found expression, toward the end of the decade, in a new wave of social theory that was the work of a handful of neoconservative intellectuals. Three in particular, who wrote during the 1980s, were instrumental in creating the intellectual legitimacy for the move to repeal the federal entitlement to welfare. Funded by the think tanks and research institutes created with corporate money—like the Heritage Foundation, the American Enterprise Institute, the Manhattan Institute, and the Cato Institute—

obscure social commentators like George Gilder and social scientists Charles Murray and Lawrence Mead rose to instant fame by
combining messages that cleverly appealed to the economically
conservative business constituency of the Republican party and to
the lifestyle-oriented conservatism of the Religious Right. Their
theories deserve some consideration, as many of their assumptions
would become embedded in the welfare reform efforts of the 1980s
and 1990s.

GEORGE GILDER

George Gilder's book, *Wealth and Poverty*, which made the
bestseller list in 1981, was a paean to the capitalist system as the
best of all possible worlds, offering endless opportunities for upward
mobility for those willing to work hard to achieve them. Gilder
attributed poverty to the deficiencies of the poor themselves in
three areas: the failure to work hard; the lack of appropriate family modeling; and the lack of faith, by which he meant, "Faith in
man, faith in the future, faith in the rising returns of giving [Gilder's
definition of working hard], faith in the mutual benefits of trade,
faith in the providence of God [which] are all essential to successful capitalism."[43]

For Gilder, the lack of appropriate family modeling was the
source of the other two failures. The poor, he maintained, are different
because they grow up in single-mother families. Gilder's thesis
rested on a dubious biological theory about the source and nature
of gender difference. Males and females, he argued, differ in their
ability to make use of the opportunity for hard work that capitalism provides. Men's innate, aggressive, sexual drives motivate
them to work hard, but only if they are channeled through monogamous patriarchal marriage. If not, they are dissipated in
impulsive, present-oriented behavior. Because they are child-bearers,
women are oriented toward the future. However, they are distracted
by family care and other concerns and tend not to make earning
money a top priority in their lives. Thus, those most likely to succeed
in a capitalist society are married, monogamous men who can de-
vote long hours to hard work.[44] According to Gilder, poverty persists because of the disproportionate number of unattached males
and female-headed families in low-income communities. The lack
of monogamous, patriarchal family models fails to inspire young
men with a sufficient motivation to work, save, and believe in the

future. Unlike Daniel Patrick Moynihan, who, as we noted in Chapter 4, had attributed the matrifocal African–American family to the legacy of slavery,[45] Gilder argued that the major cause of this "deviant" family structure was the welfare state. By replacing the role of male provider with the state, the welfare system had robbed men of the discipline needed to succeed in a capitalist system.[46] "Only the men can usually fight poverty by working, and all the antipoverty programs—to the extent they make the mother's situation better—tend to make the father's situation worse; they tend to reduce his redemptive need to pursue the longer horizons of his career."[47]

Dismissing racial and gender discrimination as possible sources of poverty, Gilder not only attacked the most visible welfare program, AFDC, but the entire apparatus of the welfare state with the traditional poor-law complaint that the very availability of assistance causes the need for it.

> Unemployment compensation promotes unemployment. . . . Disability insurance in all its multiple forms encourages the promotion of small ills into temporary disabilities, and partial disabilities into total and permanent ones. Social-security payments may discourage concern for the aged and dissolve the links between generations. . . . Comprehensive Employment and Training (CETA) subsidies for government make-work may enhance a feeling of dependence on the state without giving the sometimes bracing experience of genuine work.[48]

Conservatives like Gilder, of course, did not push for nonwelfare measures that would support family life, such as an increase in the minimum wage or jobs for all at decent wages. Gilder's analysis led him to conclude that the welfare state should be reduced, made unattractive, and "even a bit demeaning"[49]—as if the stigma attached to means-tested programs like AFDC and food stamps were not already that. "A sensible program would be relatively easy on applicants in emergencies but hard on clients who overstay their welcome."[50] A minimal, temporary welfare program should be supplemented with a universal system of taxable child allowances. While many liberals and progressives have also suggested universal child allowances—that have existed in a number of European countries—Gilder's proposal rested on his belief that it would reduce the incentive for large families to become female-headed in order to collect welfare. Welfare for two-parent families was an excluded alternative.

Ignoring the alternative of redistributing wealth downward (e.g., through a more progressive tax system), Gilder suggested that the most effective way to deal with poverty is to increase the rate of investment by reducing taxes on the rich. As the economy grows, economic benefits will inevitably "trickle down" to the poor through an increase in the number of jobs. Although he admitted that this would increase inequality, anything less, he argued, would cut American productivity, limit job opportunities, and perpetuate poverty by reducing the work incentive of the poor.[51] Assuming that a bigger pie would inevitably provide enough family-supporting jobs, Gilder ignored the history of workplace discrimination and low-wage work that this book documents and that coexisted even with an expanding national output.

CHARLES MURRAY

Gilder's book was followed by Charles Murray's *Losing Ground: American Social Policy 1950–1980* (1984),[52] written with funding from the conservative Manhattan Institute. While Gilder had blamed American social policy for contributing to indolence and poverty, his attack was largely philosophical. *Losing Ground* purported to present "scientific" documentation of the relationship between liberal social policy and the growth of poverty. Murray sought to demonstrate that increasing poverty rates after 1973 were correlated with three types of events that logically should have reduced the poverty rate: (1) the most dramatic rise in government spending for programs targeted at the poor since the Great Depression; (2) a host of liberal legislation, court decisions, and changes in administrative policy that made it easier for the poor to get government benefits; and (3) a growth in the gross national product that Murray claimed was greater than during the latter part of the 1950s when, he claimed without evidence, the poverty rate was declining.

Ignoring the alternative that poverty would be worse without welfare, Murray concluded that if poverty grew despite increased government help, the programs designed to alleviate poverty must be the source of the problem. His conclusion rested on a belief, totally without a basis in empirical evidence, that people are essentially lazy and amoral and will not work to improve their condition unless coerced into doing so. Liberal social policy, by making it too easy to collect government benefits, had made it profitable and rational for the poor to be both lazy and immoral.[53]

The policy prescription flowing from such an analysis was Draconian. Murray advocated scrapping the entire panoply of social-welfare legislation, with the exception of unemployment insurance. But he went even further in arguing for the reversal of every court decision favoring affirmative action. What would people do without such minimal kinds of support as welfare, food stamps, worker's compensation, Medicaid, subsidized housing, and the like? Murray's answer, like that of his philosophical ancestor, Herbert Spencer, was private charity and local, tax-supported services, but only for the "deserving poor." The rest simply had to sink or swim.

> Billions for equal opportunity, not one cent for equal outcome— such is the slogan to inscribe on the banner of whatever cause my proposals constitute. . . . Some people are better than others. They deserve more of society's rewards, of which money is only one small part. . . . Government cannot identify the worthy, but it can protect a society in which the worthy can identify themselves. . . . I am proposing a triage of a sort, triage by self-selection.[54]

Like Moynihan's report nearly 20 years earlier, *Losing Ground* elicited a flurry of critiques from liberal and progressive researchers who showed his reasoning and analysis of quantitative data to be deeply flawed,[55] and his prescriptions, not only heartless and cruel, but already tried and found to be ineffective.[56] Nevertheless, his approach would find a warm reception in the Reagan White House. In fact, *Losing Ground* was often cited as the Reagan administration's bible.[57] In 1994, Murray and a fellow neoconservative, Richard Herrnstein, were to write *The Bell Curve* (1994),[58] which went beyond *Losing Ground* by resurrecting the old Social Darwinist argument that the poor (now a code word for African–American) were genetically inferior, in which case no amount of social engineering could possibly do any good. Indeed, *The Bell Curve* tore off the thin racist mask of *Losing Ground*. It was clearly blacks who were less worthy or deserving of societal rewards. *The Bell Curve* was funded by the Lynn and Harry Bradley Foundation, a philanthropy that was heavily involved later on in funding the national campaign against affirmative action, attacking President Clinton's attempt to nominate law professor Lani Guinier to the Justice Department, orchestrating the nomination of Clarence Thomas to the Supreme Court, supporting the campaign for school vouchers, and funding the design of Wisconsin's W-2 program of welfare "reform," which became the model for the Personal Responsibility and Work Opportunity Reconciliation Act of 1996.[59]

LAWRENCE MEAD

Although they agreed with Murray's criticisms of the welfare system, few neoconservative policymakers during the mid-1980s were ready to go as far as dismantling the entire safety net. They still faced a Democratic Congress and a public that, while it disliked "welfare," would not have been willing to throw poor people out into the cold.[60] According to Michael Katz, "sophisticated conservatives know the inevitability of big government in modern America. Their problem is to make it work for their ends and to set it on a plausible theoretical and moral base. This was the task begun by Lawrence Mead. . . ."[61]

For Mead, a New York University political scientist and the author of *Beyond Entitlement: The Social Obligations of Citizenship* (1986),[62] the most important function of government is not the protection of civil rights and liberties, the raising of living standards, or the enhancement of democratic participation, but the creation and maintenance of social order, which, along with individual "liberty," has been one of the paramount goals of the New Right and a traditional goal of conservatives. Alarmed by what he saw as a deterioration of social responsibility, especially in the higher crime rates, out-of-wedlock births, and school and work-force incompetencies of the poor, Mead argued that the liberal welfare state is not necessarily too big, it is simply just too permissive:

> They [federal programs for the poor] have given benefits to their recipients but have set few requirements for how they ought to function in return. In particular, the programs have as yet no serious requirements that employable recipients work in return for support. There is good reason to think that recipients subject to such requirements would function better.[63]

To arrive at this conclusion, Mead had to dismiss the impact of larger social forces on poverty: discrimination, chronic job shortages, and low wages. Today's social problems, he asserted, are not, on the whole, due to oppression, and chronic unemployment is not due to a lack of jobs. Without citing any evidence, he pronounced that:

> For both rich and poor alike, work has become increasingly elective, and unemployment voluntary, because workers commonly have other sources of income, among them government programs. Job seekers are seldom kept out of work for long by a literal lack of jobs. More often, they decline the available jobs as unsatisfactory, because of unrewarding pay and conditions.[64]

However, for Mead, such so-called "voluntary" unemployment is a social problem only when it afflicts the poor, not the wealthy. Flouting that other cherished conservative political value, liberty, Mead would require the poor to work off their welfare checks. "Low-wage work apparently must be mandated, just as a draft has sometimes been necessary to staff the military. Authority achieves compliance more efficiently than benefits, at least from society's viewpoint."[65]

Such programs would apply to mothers with children over the age of 3 who would have to find their own day care. Their work would not necessarily have to be well-paid or even rewarding. Noncompliance would result in denial of assistance to the entire family and could possibly be as grave an act against the state as refusal to be drafted. Mead's call for expanding state power to coerce the poor into behaving did not, however, call for expanding state power to ensure that jobs were available.

The political effectiveness of such social theories, reiterated in the pages of conservative journals, in the halls of Congress, and on the talk-show circuits, cannot be overestimated. It reinforced popular stereotypes about the poor and purported to give them scientific credibility. As *New York Times* writer Jason DeParle has pointed out, however, few of the nation's poverty experts—liberal or conservative—have ever bothered to talk to the poor themselves, to learn firsthand what their existence is like and what motivates them, and those few who have done so, have seen their scholarship ignored by policymakers and media pundits.[66]

The White Backlash Reconsidered

Much has been written about the so-called "white backlash" of the late 1960s and 1970s—the alleged U-turn in white public opinion toward the aspirations of African–Americans, centered most sharply on the aspirations of poor African–Americans. Most commentators who have supported the backlash theory—whether conservative, liberal, or progressive—have tended to see it as

inevitable, a natural reaction to the legal remedies chosen to enforce increasingly intimate associations across racial lines, the
"excessive" demands on the welfare state, or as a response to
African–American violence and urban decay. Yet, the period we
have been describing is far more complex than this theory
suggests.

The precipitous decline in support for liberal politicians, the
Democratic party, and President Johnson's policies—beginning with
the loss of 49 seats in the House of Representatives and 4 in the
Senate in the 1966 midterm elections—is hard to attribute to any
one cause.[67] The war in Vietnam, student protests, and the assas-
sinations of progressive leaders certainly played a role. Yet, white
backlash stemming from urban riots, rising crime rates, and federal expenditures for the alleged perpetrators of these problems
may also have played a part. It is worth noting that there was a
drop in the proportion of northern whites who felt Johnson was
either moving "not fast enough" or "about right" on racial integration from 71% in April 1965, before the Los Angeles (Watts
ghetto) riot in August of that year, to 64% the month of Watts, and
40% in September 1966, following uprisings in Chicago, Cleveland, and 41 other cities.[68] An additional piece of data supporting
the backlash theory is the loss of white, working-class support for
the Democratic party in 1968.[69]

Those who downplay the racial backlash theory point to opinion
polls well into the 1970s that found increasing support for racial integration, except for school busing, a subject on which
African–Americans were themselves divided.[70] Moreover, several public opinion surveys conducted in the late 1960s found
majority white approval for massive federal spending to overcome racial inequality despite the occurrence of major violence
in predominantly black and Latino ghettos. The survey of 15
cities conducted for the Presidential (Kerner) Commission investigating the riots concluded:

> There is a willingness among the white population of these northern
> cities to see government play a strong hand in helping bring about
> improvement in the conditions of the cities. . . and this approval
> is not reduced when the purpose of assistance is specifically related
> to the needs of the Negro population and the prevention of ri-
> ots. This superficially simple solution to the problem of urban
> riots—more rigid police control of the Negro areas—is not gen-
> erally seen by white residents as an adequate answer.[71]

James Button, who traced both the liberal response to violence that facilitated the relief explosion that we discussed in Chapter 4 and the riot backlash apparent in congressional elections by 1968, maintains that these findings "suggest why administration officials could increase some ghetto-oriented programs without suffering the consequences of severe political retribution from a large number of whites."[72]

If there had been a moment when instituting a program for jobs and urban revitalization like that recommended by the Kerner Commission was auspicious, it may have been in 1968. As noted, public opinion throughout the 1960s had become increasingly supportive of racial integration, at least in the abstract, and clear majorities of whites supported federal programs to tear down the ghettos and give jobs to all the unemployed, *even when a 10% rise in personal taxes would have been required.* Researchers for the Kerner Commission found it peculiar that neither Congress nor the press recognized this opportunity. In fact, they suggested that the press had oversold the idea of a "white backlash" and that policymakers, not the public, seemed unwilling to initiate and support "a war on poverty that goes far beyond any of the measures seriously considered by recent congresses."[73]

It may be interesting to speculate on what the history of the 1970s would have been like had the policymakers chosen to act on the opportunity with which they were presented in 1968. Of course, the Democrats were embroiled in a divisive and inflationary war in Vietnam. Further, although Robert Kennedy, Willard Wirtz, and Sargent Shriver realized the need for a jobs strategy (see Chapter 4, pp. 89-91), most Democrats and their economic advisors were neither ideologically nor politically prepared to admit that the lack of sufficient jobs at family-supporting wages was a major source of continuing poverty and racial disturbance.[74] It was easier to blame poverty on a "dysfunctional" black family. To have admitted this chronic unemployment and underemployment would have been to admit that the capitalist market—even in relatively good economic times—was dysfunctional, incapable on its own of providing decent jobs for all who needed them.

As it was, the first Nixon administration, as we show in Chapter 6, looked both ways, wooing the constituency of populist segregationist George Wallace but expanding some welfare state programs, including AFDC and food stamps and introducing the first (but very small) public-service, job-creation program since the 1930s.[75]

According to Polenberg, the combined results for Hubert Humphrey, a liberal on economic issues as well as race, and Wallace, who favored federal job-training programs, safeguards for collective bargaining, a higher minimum wage, and adequate medical care for all, could be read as persisting support for New Deal liberalism without racial equality, and Nixon appeared to play this card, too.[76] However, after his second victory in 1972, Nixon, propounding the goals of self-support and self-sufficiency that were to become so prominent in the ensuing decades, turned against the Great Society. Acting like what some would consider the "true Nixon," he proposed a series of radical changes in public-welfare services, including reducing the scope of or dismantling a number of urban development programs, such as Medicaid, education, and training grants, and most of the antipoverty program.[77] Had Nixon's threatened impeachment and resignation not ensued, we might have seen much more curtailment of social welfare than we did.

Rising Inequality

This period of economic restructuring and increasing attacks on the institutions and programs that had sustained a limited welfare state resulted in increasing disparities—between population groups as well as businesses. "Deindustrialization"—the loss of millions of well-paid, unionized manufacturing jobs—resulted in growing unemployment, underemployment, and declining wages throughout the 1970s and 1980s.[78] While deindustrialization affected all workers in labor-intensive industries, African–Americans were disproportionately affected. African–American men who had migrated from the South had been located at the lower levels of heavy industry. During the postwar period of high economic growth, jobs in union plants had enabled some to find a source of stable, family-supporting work. But as they were usually the last hired, they were now the first to be laid off in an extensive process of firings euphemistically called "downsizing." Lacking education and higher levels of skill training, many African–American men were unable to make the transition from blue collar to white collar. They were also excluded by both income and residential segregation from following corporate headquarters when they moved to the suburbs. The result, as William Julius Wilson and others have shown, were central cities left with increasingly concentrated populations of poor people of color.[79]

Immigration, too, may have played a part in rising unemployment and poverty rates, especially for African–Americans. The U-turn in wages and the high average levels of unemployment in the 1970s, 1980s, and early 1990s were concurrent with the arrival of large numbers of newcomers to this "nation of immigrants." As a result of the liberalization of immigration policy that began in 1965, 18 million immigrants, many from impoverished areas of Latin and Central America and Asia, came to the United States between 1971 and 1996.[80] By the mid-1980s, the resident undocumented alien population was estimated at 3–3.5 million.[81] Although the literature on the effects of immigration on native-born workers is mixed, several researchers have concluded that the arrival of so many low-skilled immigrants has probably affected job loss and wage decline for the most disadvantaged native workers, particularly African–Americans. It is hard to avoid the assumption that at the very time the nation was beginning to seriously address the civil and economic rights of African–American citizens, changes in immigration policies exposed them to competition comparable to what earlier generations had experienced with the influx of European newcomers in the late nineteenth and early twentieth centuries.[82]

Rising interest rates and economic uncertainty always fall heaviest on those who can least afford them: small businesses and low-income families. In combination with a tax code that allowed the wealthy to deduct much more of their interest costs than individuals or businesses with lower incomes, the Federal Reserve's credit-tightening policies had the effect of transferring income from the average consumer to the wealthiest, and from small, struggling businesses to the largest, thus furthering inequality and oligopoly in the U.S. economy.[83] While big business complained vociferously about its falling profit rates, it was the "little guys" who took the big hits. For example, from 1972 to 1980, real (inflation-adjusted) median family income did not rise at all, and average hourly earnings rose only 1%. But real personal interest income rose by a whopping 138%, corporate executive pay by 97%, and after-tax corporate profits by 95%.[84]

Summary: From Ideological War to Electoral Victory

By the end of the 1970s, the growing conservative movement had made considerable inroads on the attitudes of American policymakers. The great U-turns in the trajectory of the American

economy were being blamed on greedy unions, lazy welfare recipients, and a welfare state that had grown fat and overly permissive.
In response to economic challenges, such as increased international
economic competition and natural resource cartels in the developing nations, conservatives proposed a strategy that came to be known
euphemistically as "restructuring"—wage freezes; the development
of alternative work arrangements that increased the flexibility with
which workers could be hired, fired, and scheduled; the shift of
capital and labor-intensive production to lower wage areas abroad;
and cutbacks of the welfare state. Instead of stimulating the economy
by increasing the purchasing power of the majority, empowering
labor, and enlarging support for the poor, as Roosevelt had done
in the Great Depression, they proposed just the opposite: clamping down on labor and tightening the tap on the poor.

What economic conservatives understood far better than their
liberal counterparts was that it is not the quality of ideas that matter
so much as the ability to sell them to the public.[85] Sarah Covington,
who examined the influence of about a dozen conservative foundations
during the 1990s for the National Committee for Responsive
Philanthropy, concluded that it would be difficult to overstate their
impact not only on public attitudes and public policy in paving
the way for welfare reform, but also on a dozen other ideas that
have now become or are moving to become public policy.[86]

Liberal foundations, on the other hand, have consistently refused
to support progressive media, think tanks, or public interest groups
that could get another kind of policy message across; nor have
they been willing to fund general support for broad-based progressive organizations or movement-building among working and
lower income groups. Instead, they have funded largely isolated
grassroots efforts or discrete issues and programs. The result, said
Michael Schuman, former staff member of a progressive organization, is a proliferation of short-term projects attached to flimsy
institutions and a fractured Left.[87]

By the end of the 1970s, the New Right had been able to translate
its ideological power into significant electoral victories. Although
Democrats made a comeback after the Watergate scandal, many
of the newly elected Democrats were Democrats in name only, having
been elected from white, affluent suburban districts that had gone
for Nixon in 1972.[88] And Jimmy Carter's advocacy of deregulation, budget balancing, his Federal Reserve chairman's concern
for inflation over unemployment, and his injection of religion into

national affairs paved the way for the even more conservative policies that were to come.[89]

According to Edsall, the elections of 1976 and 1978 "increased the number of ideologically conservative Republicans by a total of 28 members," converting the right wing of the Republican party "from a small and insignificant minority into a substantial block of votes. . . ."[90] These victories were aided not only by the war on labor and the intense ideological campaign that had been waged throughout the decade but by the demise of the internal political control the parties had formerly exercised over candidates and party platforms. The New Right was also aided by new advances in telecommunications technology, which were reshaping the electoral process, making it harder to run for office or to win without big money and media appeal.[91] The 1980s and 1990s would see these and subsequent electoral victories dramatically reshape the policy climate for poor relief.

CHAPTER 6

⌒⌒⌒

Enter Welfare "Reform,"
1967–1980

In view of the mixture of lingering liberalism and emerging conservatism in the late 1960s and early 1970s, it is not surprising that federal leaders responded to the relief explosion with a mixture of repression and reform. Beginning in 1967, Congress enacted work requirements for welfare mothers and a "freeze" directed against illegitimacy. Two presidential commissions and two presidents, Richard Nixon and Jimmy Carter, proposed varying versions of a guaranteed income that seemed reformist to some and regressive to others. Each of these, despite the low benefits that they proposed, had the potential for uniting those falsely dichotomized groups, the welfare and nonwelfare poor. Both plans would also have changed the color of welfare by adding more whites than blacks to the rolls and thereby making it less vulnerable to the developing backlash. Neither presidential proposal was enacted.

With recession and higher levels of unemployment, partly the results of new antiinflation strategies, government job creation and full employment rejoined the legislative agenda, but with no more permanence than in earlier decades. Again, a policy of government-guaranteed full employment that might have erased capitalism's dark shadow was defeated or diluted beyond recognition. Stagflation, the new combination of economic stagnation and inflation that emerged in the 1970s, complicated the already formidable obstacles to progressive welfare reform and full employment.

Perhaps because both were directed to the "deserving" poor, the two least-debated measures for poverty prevention in the 1970s were reformist and lasting. Congress twice rejected presidential proposals to federalize assistance to the working-age poor and their children, but, in 1972, it did approve a federal income guarantee to needy persons who are aged, blind, or disabled (Supplemental Security Income or SSI). Enacted in 1975 and aimed at the worthy, but long-neglected poor who work for low wages, the Earned Income Tax Credit (EITC) initially provided a modest income supplement to poor workers with dependent children. By the late 1990s, however, the EITC was spending more federal dollars than public assistance for needy families (TANF, the successor to AFDC). Largely left out of these reforms were two other disadvantaged groups: stay-at-home mothers and their children and childless men and women with little or no attachment to the labor market. It was these two groups, disproportionately African–American and Hispanic, that came increasingly to be seen as an unworthy "underclass." They would become the victims of the harsher "reforms" that were to follow.

Congressional Initiatives

Although federal funds helped fuel the welfare explosion, Congress tried to stem the expansion to which the War on Poverty had contributed. Having agreed to the strategy of preventing dependency through the provision of social services in 1962, Congress essayed new, increasingly harsh measures with Social Security amendments in 1967 and 1971. Perhaps because civil disorder and explosive conditions in the nation's ghettos made it too risky to do so, Washington did not turn off the spigot, but the rolls stabilized after mid-decade, particularly in view of the rise in unemployment.[1] In 1971, many states began reducing welfare benefits.[2] As the cost of living soared, the states refused to raise their benefits so that over time there were substantial reductions in what had never been a generous program.[3]

THE 1967 AMENDMENTS

With the 1967 amendments, a new Congress took aim at escalating relief rolls and illegitimacy. Chairman of the House Ways and Means Committee Wilbur Mills, a conservative southern Democrat, stated the rationale clearly:

> In 1962 we gave them [the states] options. For five years this load has gone up and up and up, with no end in sight. . . . Are

you satisfied with the fact that illegitimacy in this country is
rising and rising and rising? I am not. We have tried to encourage the states to develop programs to do something about it.
Now we are requiring them to do something about it. . . . If
there are any jobs available for them [recipients], we want them
to have them.[4]

On the restrictive side, Congress enacted a "freeze" on federal matching funds for increased state AFDC costs attributable
to desertion or illegitimacy. Exempted from the "freeze" were the
families of the more "respectable" recipients: widows and unemployed parents in married-couple families. In another effort to clamp
down, the new policy disqualified adults and out-of-school children from AFDC if they refused to accept employment or to participate in training programs without good cause. Indicative of
the extent to which these policies were unduly punitive is the fact
that "voluntary requests for training under the Work Incentives
(WIN) program exceeded the available supply, and compulsion
became unnecessary."[5]

Added to the work requirements were some work incentives.
The 1967 amendments went beyond the 1962 rule allowing for
deductions for welfare expenses: the first $30 of earnings, plus
one-third of the remainder were to be discounted. The new WIN
program would also fund some day care as well as placement, training,
and job creation.

In signing the 1967 amendments, President Johnson tried to
accentuate the positive, calling attention to the work incentives,
day care, and other services that he had recommended to Congress.
At the same time, LBJ alluded to "certain severe restrictions" that
Congress had substituted for some of his recommendations.[6] The
president, who had championed the civil rights cause, was signing
an antiblack measure, for, as Daniel P. Moynihan points out, the
AFDC "freeze" was directed to the problem of illegitimacy, and
the majority of illegitimate births were nonwhite.[7]

In enacting the "freeze," Congress attempted to legislate a form
of moral eligibility reminiscent of the "suitable-homes" policies
pursued by a number of states prior to the brief welfare-rights
era. These state antecedents, as pointed out in Chapter 2, were
also antiblack. In 1961, the outgoing Eisenhower administration
had ruled against state suitable-homes requirements in the absence
of alternative placements for children, but now Congress was writing
moral eligibility into the federal law. When the complexion of the
AFDC caseloads changed for the country as a whole, the federal

government began to treat welfare recipients more like southern states had—with federal complicity—traditionally treated their predominantly African–American caseloads. That the civil-rights president signed legislation directed against African–Americans with only a small demur suggests how short-lived was the national commitment to reducing racism. Joel Handler writes that "welfare became a 'crisis' when AFDC recipients became increasingly black and never married."[8]

Pressured not only by welfare-rights advocates but by officials of states with large welfare caseloads that would have to pick up the costs formerly shared with Washington, both Johnson and Nixon delayed implementation of the "freeze," and in 1969, Congress repealed it at Nixon's request. Yet, even if the thaw came quickly, the message of the "freeze" was clear. Congress would attempt to stem the relief rise with repression as well as incentives, and, in addition to employing the familiar weapon of racism, sexism would also be used to discredit welfare and its recipients. The "freeze" was a warning to unmarried mothers that Congress could get tough with them.[9]

The 1967 work requirements are usually viewed as a reversal of the long-standing policy to support maternal care of dependent children:

> This emphasis on workfare betrayed an ironic shift from the goals of ADC as framed in 1935. The original legislation aimed to help deserving mothers to care for their children at home— to keep them out of the labor force. By contrast, WIN sought to get these mothers to work.[10]

This assessment seems to overlook the fact that for the first 25 years of AFDC, Congress condoned eligibility restrictions, and low benefits had forced many mothers into the low-wage labor market. It also fails to recognize that Washington's intent to have welfare mothers work was already explicit in 1962. Indeed, the change at the federal level was from expectation to requirement of work. One indication that the 1962 amendments encouraged employment is that they allowed welfare recipients to deduct their work expenses from earned incomes before these earnings were deducted from benefits. In fact, the deducted costs of transportation, child care, and the like might well exceed the "thirty and one-third" discounts that were added to these work-expense deductions 5 years later. Moreover, it is clear that prevention and rehabilitation, the watchwords of 1962, meant getting recipients out to work and off the rolls, albeit through counseling and other services rather than coercion. Recall President Kennedy's words in his 1962 speech on public welfare: "Many women now on assistance rolls could obtain jobs and become self-supporting if local day-care programs for their young children were available. . . ."[11] Kennedy had reinforced this expectation by recommending grants to the states to aid in establishing local programs for day care of the children of working mothers.

Thus, work requirements, long imposed by some of the states, became, like the "freeze," a matter of federal policy. In some respects, moreover, the 1967 amendments were improvements over state work requirements. Initially, at least, the government offered both employability and employment opportunities to WIN registrants, along with the right to keep more of their earnings. As Axinn and Levin point out, there were both carrots and sticks in the 1967 amendments.[12]

Day-care provisions accompanied the 1967 legislation, but there were not enough facilities to carry out the ambitious plans of those who sought to move parents from welfare to work, and WIN did not authorize funds for major renovation or construction of new facilities.[13] Writing in 1971, Steiner concluded: "There are not enough facilities—good, bad, or indifferent—to accomplish the day care job envisioned by those congressional and those admin-istration planners who still talk of moving parents from welfare rolls to payrolls. . . ."[14]

To deal with the shortage of child care for children of the increasing number of women employed outside the home, Con-gress passed the Comprehensive Child Care Act of 1971 that provided billions to fund preschool, day-care, nutritional, and other pro-grams for children, not only of welfare mothers but of parents with considerably higher incomes. President Nixon included work re-quirements for welfare mothers in his Family Assistance Plan and had earlier declared himself in favor of a national commitment to child care. Nonetheless, he vetoed the measure. His stated ratio-nale: that it would "diminish parental authority and parental in-volvement with children."[15]

WIN: A LOSER

WIN was not a successful program, either in its initial, rather mild phase (WIN I), or in later stages (WIN II and III), when it placed less emphasis on training or job preparation and more on job placement. As interpreted by officials of HEW, only AFDC-UP fathers, dropouts over 16, and a few mothers of school-age children who had access to free day care ever had to register for work under WIN I.[16] The results of the first years of WIN were meager indeed. Early in 1970, after about 19 months of implementation, WIN data took the shape of a funnel, narrowing with each step of the process from the number screened for possible referral to those who were actually employed after participating in WIN. At the wide end were 1,478,000 screened and at the narrow, 22,000 employed, or less than 1.5%.[17]

Considering that one-sixth of welfare recipients found employment without WIN, these results were not promising.[18] Welfare expert Gilbert Steiner pointed his finger at the limited number of child-care slots in determining major responsibility for these results, whereas manpower specialists Sar Levitan and Robert Taggart put the blame on the critical shortage of jobs for welfare mothers.[19] The findings of a study of WIN during 1973–1975 underscore the importance of job creation. Subsidized public employment was a particularly effective tool for increasing the employment and earnings of welfare recipients. But WIN had only modest success in increasing employment and earnings in the private sector.[20]

Disappointed with the initial results of WIN, Congress passed the "Talmadge" amendments in 1971, requiring all recipients of working age, except women caring for children under age 6, to register for WIN. Further, states that did not place 15% of those registered in jobs were to lose federal funds. Calling attention to the "severe job shortage" and other factors that rendered most welfare mothers either unable to find work or unsuitable for it, social-welfare historian William Trattner, writes: "Rather than pass legislation designed to deal with the causes of the problem or meet the needs of the poor, Congress strengthened the more coercive features of the Work Incentive Program. . . ."[21]

According to the 1974 *Manpower Report of the President*, welfare recipients were usually offered unskilled labor or low-level clerical jobs, typically characterized by high turnover and low wages.[22] Unfortunately, the conclusions of the report were ignored by subsequent welfare "reformers": "Research findings point to a paucity of jobs available to welfare recipients at a sufficiently high wage level to result in the removal of most family heads from the rolls."[23] Denial of labor-market realities for relief recipients is an

old story. Thus, nearly all employers in a survey of rural communities held that jobs were available for welfare recipients—despite the fact that only 2% of these employers actually had job
openings for WIN participants.[24]

Having reviewed the early history of WIN, Gilbert Steiner
predicted that work training and day care would do little to reduce the number of welfare recipients or relief costs. It would be
more realistic, Steiner concluded, "to accept the need for more
welfare and to reject continued fantasizing about day care and
'workfare' as miracle cures."[25] Without serious efforts to create
decent jobs for welfare mothers and fathers, Steiner's recommendation was both sensible and humane.

High-Level—but Unheeded—Advice

Unlike pronouncements by elected and appointed federal officials, several reports commissioned by the federal government
about this time provided a realistic perspective. Two of these
addressed public-welfare issues. Investigating the shocking riots
that tore apart so many major cities in the 1960s, the third of these
reports proposed reform in both work and welfare.

ADVISORY COUNCIL ON PUBLIC WELFARE

The June 1966 report of the Advisory Council on Public Welfare
proposed an adequate level of assistance in every state and, in
place of the categorical approach that excluded many of the poor,
the use of financial need as the sole criterion for eligibility.[26] Appointed
by President Johnson, the council pointed out that although 8 million
persons depended on public assistance, an additional 26 million
lived below the official poverty standard. Further, public-assistance
payments were so low that the U.S. government was "a major source
of the poverty on which it has declared unconditional war."[27] Steiner
called the council's recommendation that social services be expanded
and extended as a matter of right "the last hurrah of the social-
welfare professionals who had long dominated public-assistance
policy development."[28] Nonetheless, the council's recommendations
clearly recognized that relief recipients need a great deal more
than social services.

The council observed that the United States "is . . . distinguished from other countries in the degree to which unprecedented resources combine with . . . unprecedented interdependence to make . . . [protection for those in need] both possible and essential."[29] Thus, the title of their report: *Having the Power, We Have the Duty.*

In addition to having unprecedented resources, the United States was also distinguished in the degree to which it considered the price of relief onerous. As Martin Rein and Hugh Heclo reported, other countries were experiencing comparable welfare expansions in the 1960s without regarding them as negatively as did the United States.[30] According to the Advisory Council, expenditures for public welfare had decreased as a percentage of national personal income and gross national product, even though its dollar costs had risen in recent years.[31] In contrast to the coming era of welfare "reform," the council recommended measures for establishing eligibility "in such manner as to protect their [recipients'] dignity, privacy, and constitutional rights."[32]

NATIONAL ADVISORY COMMISSION ON CIVIL DISORDERS

Appointed in July 1967 by President Johnson, who charged its members to "find the truth and express it in your report," the National Advisory Commission on Civil Disorders was known as the Kerner Commission, after its chairman, Otto Kerner, a Democrat and governor of Illinois.[33] Its vice chairman, New York Mayor John Lindsay, was then a Republican. "Civil disorders" was the euphemism for the severe riots that had broken out in one city after another, among them Los Angeles, New York, Chicago, Newark, Birmingham.

The Kerner Commission's "Recommendations for National Action" began with employment: "Unemployment and underemployment are among the most persistent and serious grievances of our disadvantaged minorities. The pervasive effect of these conditions on the racial ghetto is inextricably linked to the problem of civil disorder."[34] In the "riot cities" the commission found that "Negroes were three times as likely as whites to hold unskilled jobs, which are often part time or seasonal, and 'dead end'—a fact that's as significant for Negroes as unemployment."[35] Consequently, the commission recommended continued emphasis on national economic growth and job creation "so that there will be jobs available for those who are newly trained, without displacing those already employed"; consolidation of existing education, training, job development, and recruiting programs to avoid duplication; and creating 2 million jobs (1 million in the public sector and 1 million in the private sector) in 3 years.[36]

When the commission issued its report in March 1968, the unemployment rate was 3.8%, the lowest for that month since 1953.[37] Clearly, the ghettos needed much more than a reduction or even a relatively low rate of overall, official unemployment. It would take recessions and rising joblessness in the 1970s to get Congress to address the chronic problems of unemployment and underemployment through targeted job creation, but even then, a limited number of jobs for a limited amount of time.

The Kerner Commission also recommended welfare reform. "Our present system of public assistance," it stated, "contributes materially to the tensions and social disorganization that have led to civil disorders." According to the commissioners, the system excluded large numbers of persons in great need who, "if provided a decent level of support, might be able to become more productive and self-sufficient." Interestingly, the commission viewed adequate benefits as a spur to economic independence rather than an invitation to continuing dependence on welfare. Not only did the system exclude many of the poor, but "for those who are included, it provides assistance well below the minimum necessary for a humane level of existence. . . ."[38] The Kerner Commission suggested seven areas of major change, including a federal, minimum-income standard for AFDC at least as high as the official poverty standard, payment of higher proportions of the grants by the federal government, and expansion of the AFDC-UP program which "reaches the family while it is still intact."[39]

In their concluding welfare recommendations, the commissioners pointed "toward a national system of income supplementation."[40] Efforts should be made to develop incentives for fuller employment, they said, by providing necessary supplements for those who work as well as to cover those who cannot work or remain with their children. The EITC would, in time, contribute to the former goal but, as will be shown, it has functioned more to keep the incomes of the working poor from falling even lower, as the minimum wage and wages generally lost ground, than to improve their condition. Like the Advisory Council on Public Welfare, the commission proposed that the only eligibility condition be financial need—in other words, the recommendation of President Truman rejected by Congress in 1950. This policy would have meant that two large and important groups not covered by federal programs would be eligible for public assistance: employed persons working for substandard wages or forced to work part-time, and unemployed persons who are neither disabled, elderly, nor single parents of young children. These recommendations not only reflected growing interest in some form of income guarantee but also anticipated the work of a new Commission on Income Maintenance Programs recently appointed by President Johnson.[41]

COMMISSION ON INCOME MAINTENANCE

Chaired by Ben W. Heineman, top executive of the Chicago and Northwestern Railroads, the Commission on Income Maintenance was still another high-level advisory body that proposed liberalization and a wider federal role in public welfare. Consisting of 21 members, none associated with the existing welfare system, the commission was appointed by President Johnson in January 1968 and directed to "examine any and every plan, however unconventional. . . ." [42] The Heineman Commission delivered its report, *Poverty Amid Plenty*, in November 1969; it recommended an approach very similar to the Family Assistance Plan that had recently been proposed by President Richard Nixon—"*the creation of a universal income supplement program financed and administered by the Federal Government, making cash payments to all members of the population with income needs*" (their italics).[43] The commission was very critical of the deterrent, poor-law features of public assistance, which "often seem designed to restrict benefits through the imposition of residence requirements, tests of 'moral worthiness,' mandatory acceptance of social services, overly stringent asset tests, income limits set below the poverty line, and the like."[44] "A poor substitute for providing adequate cash incomes to the poor," in-kind programs, the commission held, should be phased out and the equivalent assistance given in cash.[45]

Both the commission's plan and President Nixon's recently unveiled scheme (see pp. 140–147) were versions of the Negative Income Tax (NIT). They were descendants of much earlier approaches dating as far back as supplementation of very low wages early in the Industrial Revolution in England. Similar ideas had been proposed in the mid-1940s by the U.S. Treasury Department, by conservative economist Milton Friedman a decade later, and by liberal academics in the 1960s.[46] Friedman was among

those who proposed that the government should provide benefits
to persons whose incomes are too low to pay taxes and to reap
the advantage of personal exemptions and deductions.[47] In his
widely read book, *Capitalism and Freedom*, Friedman recommended
substitution of the negative income tax "for the host of special
measures now in effect," including social security.[48] Christopher
Green's study, issued by the Brookings Institution in 1966, contained detailed proposals for a negative income tax.[49]

All NIT plans include a minimum income guarantee or benefit and taxation of earnings at some specified rate until the benefit is eliminated (break-even point). At that point, the income
tax kicks in. Is adequacy achieved? That depends on the level of
the income guarantee and, for those who work, on the guarantee
and the rate at which earnings below the break-even point are taxed.
Higher guarantees and lower taxes on earnings amount to more
adequate benefits but more expensive programs.

The NIT appealed to leaders of the War on Poverty and to a
number of prominent economists. Within a year of its existence,
the Office of Economic Opportunity (OEO) developed a plan to
end poverty that included income in the form of an NIT as well
as jobs and services.[50] Interestingly, they favored both income support
and employment reforms, obvious strategies that the War on Poverty plans had omitted. Without going through Congress, which
was never shown the plan to end poverty, the OEO financed the
New Jersey Graduated Work Experiment that tested the effects of
various NIT plans on several hundred low-income families.[51]

While the Heineman Commission was at work, 1,200 economists urged Congress "to adopt this year a national system of income
guarantees and supplements" that were "feasible and compatible
with our economic system."[52] A related idea, the guaranteed income, originally without an income test or work requirement, gained
support on the Left in the 1960s. In some cases, proponents of a
guaranteed income held that modern technology would increasingly obviate the need for employment of the unskilled, but it would
not affect the need for income. That would have to be in the form
of a transfer payment. With this rationale, a work requirement made
no sense.[53]

The Heineman Commission proposed a federal income guarantee of $2,400, conceding that the amount was not necessarily
adequate but that it could be implemented.[54] According to a report
issued by the Institute for Research on Poverty of the University

of Wisconsin, an agreement between Nixon administration officials, including Assistant for Urban Affairs Daniel P. Moynihan and members of the commission, was reached in June 1969. In return for continued staff support, the commission would not recommend more than a $2,400 basic benefit for a family of four.[55] The benefit would be reduced by $.50 for every dollar of income from other sources.

Unlike subsequent welfare "reformers" and the Nixon planners, the commission considered work requirements coercive. "Since we do not have employment for all those who want to work, employment tests lose much of their meaning in the aggregate."[56] The commission was convinced that "the poor are not unlike the nonpoor. Most of the poor want to work."[57] A systematic study of how poor people, especially African–American recipients of public welfare, felt about work was conducted at about that time and corroborated the Heineman Commission's views. This research for the Brookings Institution by Leonard Goodwin concluded that there are "no differences between poor and nonpoor when it comes to life goals and wanting to work."[58] Goodwin, however, found that failure in the workplace crushed the hopes of the poor. Thus, women terminated from the WIN program without jobs became more accepting of being on welfare and less inclined to try again.[59]

Heineman and his colleagues maintained that the employment-security triad of the 1930s—employment for the employables, social insurance for those forced out of their jobs, and residual aid for the unemployable and uninsured—was not working.[60] (One reason, of course, was that there were insufficient employment opportunities.) They were also skeptical of the strategies of the War on Poverty that focused primarily on "long-run creation of opportunity" but "did little to affect incomes directly."[61] The commission, which did its work at a time of very low official unemployment, directly challenged the assumption that "everyone who is employable could work at adequate wages," pointing out that one-third of all persons in poor families in 1966 lived in families headed by full-time, employed male workers.[62] The Heineman Commission's proposed guarantee, then, would cover the poorly paid as well as those without income. Thoroughly opposite to stated public policy, which was to prevent economic dependence, the commission concluded that "there must be a larger role for cash grants in fighting poverty than we have acknowledged in the past."[63]

Presidential Initiatives

THE FAMILY ASSISTANCE PLAN

In August 1969, delegates to the Republican National Convention roared approval of their newly nominated standard bearer for his remarks about the welfare explosion: "For those who are able to help themselves, what we need are not more millions on welfare rolls, but more millions on payrolls."[64] That was *candidate* Nixon; the following year *President* Nixon proposed the Family Assistance Plan (FAP), a negative income tax for families with children that would have made more than 12 million additional parents and children eligible for welfare rolls. Political analysis of the FAP debate and defeat is complicated by its mixture of reform and restriction and by the difficulty of avoiding *ad hominem* interpretations of proposals by its presidential sponsor.

The FAP would have established a minimum, federal benefit for families with children. In order to distinguish the FAP from the guaranteed income, which was not considered popular, the administration presented it as "primarily . . . an income supplement to reinforce work efforts and family stability of those who can work but are not able to provide adequately for their families."[65] Nixon himself tried to make a distinction between the administration's plan and a guaranteed income: "A guaranteed income establishes a right without any responsibilities; family assistance recognizes a need and establishes a responsibility. It provides help to those in need and, in turn, requires that those who receive help work to the extent of their capabilities."[66]

This was in contrast to the proposal of the Heineman Commission, which considered it unfair to require work when jobs were not available. Indeed, Nixon is said to have mentioned the words, "work," "jobs," or words rooted in "work" 60 times in his 35-minute speech introducing FAP, and Richard P. Nathan, who served as deputy under secretary for welfare reform in HEW, holds that Nixon was very serious about the work requirement and distinguished FAP from a guaranteed income on that basis.[67] In this speech, Nixon reiterated what he had said often during the campaign: "What America needs is not more welfare but more workfare," but he used the term, not in its current meaning of working for one's welfare benefit, but rather as combining regular employment and a reduced welfare check.[68]

Essentially, FAP adopted the WIN work requirements.[69] Yet, a number of experts have pointed out that FAP was, in fact, an income guarantee, for only one member of a family would lose benefits for refusal to comply with its work requirements.[70] The administration's stated intention was to increase the self-sufficiency of employable recipients by providing more training opportunities and child-care services, but both were very inadequate in relation to the number of eligible mothers and children.[71]

In addition to a cash benefit of $1,600, a four-person family would also have been eligible for $860 of food stamps or a total of $2,460 a year.[72] For the employed parent, there would be an earnings disregard (the first $720 a year), with the remainder taxed at the rate of 50%, up to a break-even point of $3,920 ($3,920-$720 x .50=$1,600). Actually, as Senator John Williams demonstrated in devastating questioning of HEW Secretary Robert Finch when he appeared before the Senate Finance Committee, the effective tax was much higher because of recipients' loss of in-kind benefits as their incomes rose.[73]

Because Washington would assume responsibility for the $1,600 guarantee, FAP would provide fiscal relief to states. Versions of the FAP varied with respect to state fiscal relief and requirements regarding maintenance of existing levels of benefits in the 42 states that already paid benefits higher than the FAP guarantee. The 1969 version required that states spend at least 50% of the current amount for 5 years. Some later versions called for state supplementation with federal sharing of those costs. The final version, HR 1, neither required state supplementation nor provided for Washington's participation in these costs.[74]

FAP would have increased the public-assistance rolls by 4 million employed poor workers. More whites than blacks would be added. The FAP caseload was expected to become 62% white and 38% black.[75] By contrast, the 1969 AFDC caseload was 45.2% black.[76] Many blacks and whites in low-benefit southern states stood to gain. On the other hand, large numbers of welfare recipients in higher benefit states would not.[77]

Why did Richard Nixon propose and for a time support a proposal that "called for the most extensive structural changes in public assistance since the original social security legislation of 1935"?[78] The reasons are complex and still the subject of debate. One reason seems to be the need, particularly for an activist chief executive, to do something about what was perceived as a "welfare mess," if not a "welfare crisis." Even observers who attempted to put the problem in perspective acknowledged that "for more than a decade Americans have lamented their welfare crisis" because costs had tripled since 1960, the welfare population had climbed, and AFDC was seen as a cause of family problems.[79] Rising and seemingly out-of-control welfare rolls are seldom seen as desirable, even if such an expansion provides a modicum of security to long-deprived and hungry people. Daniel Patrick Moynihan, who served under both the Kennedy and Johnson administrations and was an advisor to President Nixon on domestic policies, viewed the welfare situation as a "nationwide problem . . . which, if not out of control, was evidently worsening."[80] Moynihan's overblown rhetoric and efforts to prove the existence of a wholly unprecedented crisis have been challenged, but his very bombast and appeals to Nixon's historic role as a conservative reformer in the tradition of Benjamin Disraeli caught the president's interest and support.[81] Moreover, even one critical of Moynihan's analyses concedes that "by 1969 . . . both popular and professional dissatisfaction with AFDC was so overwhelming that a welfare-crisis mentality would have dominated policy making even if Nixon had resisted . . . [Moynihan's] arguments."[82]

Jill Quadagno argues that FAP was not only a means of reforming the despised welfare system but also a bone to Nixon's "silent majority." It proposed to provide income supplementation to the working Americans whom he had described as forgotten in the concern over the unemployed and the impoverished.[83] Quadagno also emphasizes two other rationales for FAP. First, it would reduce further riots (the Kerner Commission had, as pointed out previously, concluded that AFDC increased tensions) by encouraging young men to marry and form stable, male-headed households.[84] Observing that under FAP training would be geared to males, Quadagno infers that the intent was for "federal policy . . . [to] reinstate black men as household heads by reducing the labor-force participation of black women."[85] However, FAP's adoption of the WIN work requirements for mothers, except those with children under 6 years of age, seems to us to be a move in the opposite direction. It should be pointed out that by not restricting benefits to single parents, relief policy can be neutral with respect to family composition, not necessarily patriarchal. Gearing training to men or failing to provide sufficient child care is, however, not neutral.

While FAP was appealing to working-class Democrats and to

patriarchal family values, it generated opposition among the Southerners whom Nixon also wanted to woo. Quadagno argues that Nixon failed to take into account the effect of FAP on the political and economic structure of the South.[86] Yet, it seems unlikely that so seasoned a politician as Nixon, a former senator and vice president, could have so overlooked the traditional hostility of southern legislators to even the most modest income guarantees or minimally adequate benefit levels.

In one important way, FAP's nationalization of assistance to families and children seems at odds with the Nixon thrust toward more state and less federal responsibility—the "New Federalism." Yet, it has been argued that by assuming more federal financial responsibility, FAP would provide fiscal relief to the states.[87]

How did the public react to FAP? Initially, editorial comment, with the exception of some of the black press, was favorable.[88] Ben Heineman gave FAP good marks, and since Heineman was a Democrat and his Commission on Income Maintenance Programs had been appointed by a Democratic president, this was valuable political support.[89] The NWRO first tried to "Up FAP," but failing that, sought to "Zap FAP."[90] The Nixon proposal would not benefit NWRO's constituents, who were largely welfare mothers in the North.[91] NWRO's Johnnie Tillmon called FAP "disguised repression," pointing out that 42 states plus the District of Columbia were already paying AFDC benefits higher than what FAP proposed. She criticized FAP for discriminating against AFDC women and children in favor of the aged, blind, and disabled; and she pointed out that poor mothers would not be given the choice of staying home with their school-age children or going to work. Rather, they would be required to register for work, regardless of the availability of adequate child care and without designated labor standards for wages and working conditions.[92]

Citing the conclusions of "many researchers and activists" and the view of Guida West already noted in Chapter 4, Linda Gordon holds that "many, perhaps most, 'welfare mothers' would like employment outside their homes."[93] Yet, as we have also pointed out, the goals to which the movement dedicated its resources did not reflect this preference. Indeed, Hamilton and Hamilton emphasize that NWRO's position during the FAP debate was weakened by its failure to emphasize the critical issue of jobs: "A demand for jobs would have dispelled many of the myths and assumptions about welfare dependency . . . [and] would have exposed the hypocrisy

involved in developing a mandated work policy for welfare recipients when it was clear that jobs were not available for all of
them."[94] What Hamilton and Hamilton say about NWRO could be
applied as well to most welfare advocates, at least since the 1960s—
until, handed a *fait accompli* with TANF, they have begun to concern
themselves with job creation.

While it has been argued that low benefits were partly a function of southern states' limited fiscal capacities or low per capita
incomes,[95] Southerners were no more friendly to higher benefits
when Washington offered to pay the bill. "There's not going to be
anybody left to roll those wheelbarrows and press those shirts"
complained Georgia Congressman Phil Landrum.[96] Governor Lester
G. Maddox put it this way: "You're not going to be able to find
anyone willing to work as maids or janitors or housekeepers if
this bill goes through. . . ."[97] "Many white Southerners," wrote
Burke and Burke, "feared that FAP's guaranteed income would shrink
the supply of cheap labor, bankrupt marginal industry, boost the
cost of locally produced goods and services, increase taxes, and
put more blacks into public office."[98] Senate Finance Committee
Chairman Russell Long—of "black-brood-mares-of-AFDC" infamy—
was particularly concerned that the guarantee would pay people
not to work, leaving them time to produce illegitimate children.[99]
A political scientist at Vanderbilt University held that because the
FAP would be administered by the federal government, it would
free many poor African–Americans in the rural South from the intimidation stemming from dependence on local officials and enable
them to exercise their political rights without fear of economic
consequences.[100]

Conservatives in and outside the administration had reservations that were not directly related to the political economy of the
South. Nixon's economic counsel, Arthur F. Burns, was concerned
about any "reform" that added millions more to already swelling
welfare rolls, and Burns was opposed to a guarantee of welfare as
a matter of right rather than based on "disability-related deprivation."[101] Business was divided, with elite organizations like the
Committee for Economic Development in favor. The Chamber of
Commerce and the National Association of Manufacturers split,
with the former against relief to able-bodied adults and convinced
that work requirements would not hold, and the NAM, representing the more capital-intensive firms, endorsing FAP.[102]

Liberals were torn. Although they favored aiding the working
poor and raising standards in low-benefit states, they were inclined

to support NWRO in its Zap-FAP campaign and were, moreover, suspicious of anything Nixon did.[103] Some liberals were concerned about the questions that remain debatable to this day: whether to support a measure that took steps in the right direction and that could perhaps be improved incrementally. More radical critics like Piven and Cloward believed that if FAP had been enacted, it would have been implemented repressively, although they recognized that "the main features appeared liberal, and in some ways were."[104] Perhaps Congress would have indexed FAP to the cost of living, as it did SSI and food stamps, thereby protecting it from the benefit erosion that occurred for 20 years with the nonindexed AFDC. Since FAP would have provided benefits to the working poor, it would have linked the income security of the employed and non-employed poor and made family assistance less vulnerable to political attack. Some liberals in Congress, led by Senator Abraham Ribicoff, HEW secretary in the Kennedy administration, tried hard to reach a compromise with the White House that might have improved and saved FAP.[105]

Civil rights groups first favored FAP, but harsher amendments added in later versions of the plan caused them eventually to testify against it.[106] Civil rights groups, moreover, consistently pointed out that work requirements were unnecessary because welfare recipients wanted to work.[107] The final version of the FAP, HR 1, proposed a minimum wage for recipients that was considerably less than the statutory minimum and that would have been "tantamount to a differential wage for a large portion of the African-American population."[108]

"The only strong and unqualified pressure for . . . [FAP]," wrote Burke and Burke, "came from those who wanted welfare changed, not for reasons of philosophy, but rather for the promise of fiscal relief. These were many of the nation's governors and county officials."[109] Not surprisingly, when alternative sources of fiscal relief were available, they lost interest in FAP.

There is another important reason why FAP got zapped. According to some observers, President Nixon seems to have lost interest and certainly did not exert strong-enough efforts to influence senators.[110]

Nixon's chief of staff, H. R. Haldeman, attributes a more Machiavellian motive to the president in the first round of the FAP debate. According to Haldeman's diary entry for July 13, 1970, Nixon "wants to be sure it's killed by Democrats and that we make big play for it, but don't let it pass, can't afford it."[111] Two years

later, when a new version of the plan was again being considered
by the Senate Finance Committee, Nixon, rather than agree to a
compromise with liberal forces led by Senator Ribicoff that would
have raised the guarantee a few hundred dollars and softened the
work provisions, decided to go into the 1972 election with an issue
to exploit rather than an enacted measure that could be open to
criticism.[112] Burke and Burke, who credited the president with a
"good deed" in introducing FAP, refer to this as "Nixon's desertion."[113] This is Senator Ribicoff's view: "Amid all the rhetoric
about fathers deserting their children, the president deserted FAP,
though he had supported it in 1969 and early 1970. It perished in
1972 from lack of nourishment by the White House."[114] By then,
presidential politics had been added to other reasons Nixon might
have had for killing the FAP. His rival for the presidency in the
1972 election, Senator George McGovern, had proposed an income guarantee that was unpopular with many people, and Nixon
wanted to do nothing to lessen the Democratic candidate's vulnerability by supporting a program that could also be viewed as
an income guarantee.[115]

NWRO claimed a hand in zapping FAP. The welfare-rights group
had brought important liberal and minority allies, like the National
Council of Churches and the Black Congressional Caucus, into the
anti-FAP campaign and, according to NWRO historian Guida West,
"succeeded in building a liberal coalition sufficiently strong to
help kill FAP."[116] Piven and Cloward, who counseled NWRO against
using its resources to lobby against FAP and thereby neglecting
its grassroots base, do not think NWRO influenced the outcome
of FAP.[117] It has even been suggested that NWRO's opposition could
have helped FAP.[118]

Moynihan credits the defeat of FAP (in 1970) to "the triumph
of conservative strategy" on the Senate Finance Committee.[119] In
particular, Moynihan had in mind Senator John Williams' (R-R.I.)
grilling of HEW Secretary Robert Finch on the subject of work
incentives. NWRO's George Wiley said that: "Senator Long had
succeeded in making the bill so repressive that he united all the
liberal forces for the first time to back the Welfare Rights Position."[120] Moynihan's account, however, did not cover the last 2
years of the FAP effort, or in Senator Ribicoff's words, "he left at
half time."[121] Burke and Burke point out that impending passage
of a revenue-sharing bill in 1972 "robbed FAP of its solitary major
political attraction."[122]

The debate over FAP had been a national one. When it began, the forces of disorder were strong, and welfare inequities had been linked to them.[123] FAP held out little to the most disruptive quarters, the African–American ghettos in the North. In mobilizing to oppose FAP, some of the militants left the streets and the grassroots and entered the lobbies of Congress. The debate diverted, divided, and exhausted the NWRO.[124]

By the time the FAP debate was over, the streets had quieted. Perhaps FAP filled the function as a holding operation for the administration—a proposal for wiping up the "welfare mess" and a gesture toward the working poor and the welfare poor in low-benefit states—that served to mollify critics and gave a sense that Washington was not sitting still. The welfare-rights advocates lacked the energy and resources to return to the grass roots or the asphalt to organize for measures that would benefit not only the poorly paid and the welfare poorest, but recipients whose benefits were less meager but by no means sufficient.

While the FAP was bogged down in the Senate Finance Committee in 1971, the Senate unanimously passed the "Talmadge" amendment, effective in 1972, that required AFDC mothers with no children under age 6 to register for work or lose benefits. In practice, this was more a threat than an enforceable requirement. "The principal reason," according to an Urban Institute study, "is that there were always more AFDC recipients who wanted to avail themselves of the services offered by the work-registration program than there were funds available to finance these services."[125] Such threats are considered "good" politics, and they serve to perpetuate the popular view that welfare recipients will not work without coercion.

THE PROGRAM FOR BETTER JOBS AND INCOME

Jimmy Carter also made a campaign issue of welfare. As his secretary of HEW, Joseph Califano, observes: "Cleaning up the welfare mess was the best ear-of-the-listener issue in Carter's campaign lexicon." Candidate Carter, relates Califano, used welfare "reform" to please different folks—sometimes meaning "getting the bums off welfare," other times more money to the poor and fewer degrading procedures, and still others, fiscal relief to the states. As president, Carter wanted comprehensive welfare "reform," but what he did not tell even his HEW secretary at first was that he wanted it for nothing, at no extra cost to the federal budget.[126]

Introduced by Jimmy Carter nearly 5 years after the defeat of Nixon's welfare "reform," the Program for Better Jobs and Income (PBJI) was similar to FAP and directed toward the still unsolved problems in AFDC; it was fairer to the poor but did not inspire nearly so much interest. Like FAP, PBJI bore some resemblance to the Speenhamland system that supplemented very low incomes of rural laborers during the early stages of the Industrial Revolution in England.[127]

President Carter's plan was distinctive in two important respects: It combined income support and job assurance in one program and recognized that it is unfair to expect people to work if there are insufficient jobs or workplace supports, especially child care. While PBJI combined aid for the employed and nonemployed poor in a single program, it divided them into two groups, those expected to work and those not expected to work, with different treatment and income guarantees. Those expected to work would receive wage supplements, including an increase in the recently enacted EITC (see pp. 151–155), federal help in finding employment, or one of 1.4 million special public-service jobs offered through the CETA program (see pp. 157–159) and paying the higher of the federal or state minimum wage. These jobs were reserved for the "principal" earner in families with at least one child; the principal earner would be the person with the highest earnings or the one who worked the most hours during the 6 months prior to application for job-search assistance.[128] Those "not expected to work" included the aged, disabled, blind, and single parents whose youngest child was under 7 years old. The adult in a single-parent family whose youngest child was 7–14 years old was expected to work part time. Thus, certain mothers would still be treated as nurturers rather than breadwinners, although there was a limit to support for full-time nurturing. By combining SSI, AFDC, state-local general assistance, and food stamps in one cash program with a single eligibility standard, PBJI would streamline the income-support system.

For persons expected to work, PBJI would grant $2,300 a year, and for those not expected to work, $4,600. For the former, the first $3,800 of earnings would not be counted toward reduction of benefits, but thereafter, the rate of reduction would be 50% until total income reached $8,400. Those with the higher guarantee would have all earnings taxed at the 50% rate until total income was $8,400. After an unsuccessful, 8-week search for a private or public job, persons expected to work would be eligible for the higher guarantee. As long as they earned over $1,900 a year, persons expected to work would be better off than those not expected to work and not earning income.

"To no one's surprise," writes Patterson, "Carter's proposals ran into the same kind of opposition that had defeated the similar Family Assistance Plan in 1972."[129] PBJI, too, would increase costs, expand the rolls, and raise questions of work incentive.[130] Perhaps the cost is one reason for Carter's failure to support the plan vigorously, for he had been adamant about wanting a zero-cost reform.[131] According to Elizabeth Wickenden, consultant to the Child Welfare League of America, the inner logic of the bill was distorted by "the president's insistence that welfare reform be achieved within the strait-jacket of a balanced budget."[132]

Like FAP, PBJI ran up against the "veto coalition"—the South, business, and the Republican party.[133] Of these, however, only the southern legislators had been monolithic in their opposition to FAP. Whereas FAP pleased the state and local officials who would get fiscal relief, PBJI disappointed even this potential constituency. Actually, Wickenden wrote that PBJI disappointed all major power bases, including the AFL-CIO Executive Council, which found its labor standards wanting. Wickenden's analysis also implied that the number of new job slots created by PBJI was insufficient to accommodate both the unemployed and welfare recipients expected to work.[134] The obvious question is whether it would have been possible to craft a welfare-reform proposal attractive enough for beneficiaries and their advocates to give it their strong support while also being acceptable to some business interests and moderates of both parties.

Advocates of welfare rights responded similarly to the relatively low level of benefits in both FAP and PBJI. The Center on Social Welfare Policy and Law charged Carter's plan with the failure to guarantee an adequate income for all and a decent job for all who wish to work.[135]

Daniel P. Moynihan, then a New York senator, was also critical of PBJI's low benefits and insufficient fiscal relief to cities like New York.[136] Yet, PBJI guaranteed a family whose parents were not expected to work a somewhat higher proportion of the poverty standard than the FAP proposal Moynihan had championed.[137]

PBJI was regarded as patriarchal by some critics. NOW charged Carter with trying "to solve the problems of women in poverty by providing men with jobs."[138] Since special public-service jobs would go to "principal earners" in two-parent families and only to those

single parents expected to work, mothers of preschool children
and women in two-parent households, it was anticipated, would
be denied or have unequal access to these jobs. "The designation
of 'principal wage earner' inevitably results in exclusion of the
woman from priority consideration for job training and placement."[139]
"In defining these categories," write Handler and Hasenfeld, "the
Carter administration acknowledged the changing role of women
but nonetheless maintained the patriarchal domestic code and
confirmed women's inferior position in the labor market."[140] Women
had criticized the Nixon plan for not giving them the choice to
stay home with their children. Arguing that work requirements were
unnecessary because people would work if decent jobs were available,
NOW called for full employment or a job guarantee but also held
that "true welfare reform must include minimum federal benefit
levels that respect the value of work done in the home by providing assistance at an adequate level."[141] In this statement, NOW
supported employment for women and compensation for work in
the home, a policy that would permit mothers choice between the
two types of work.

    While not consistent with women's equality, Carter's plan, in
contrast to FAP, the several WINs, and welfare "reform" in the
1990s, would not have forced mothers to work if there were insufficient jobs, training opportunities, and adequate child care.
PBJI offered higher income guarantees to single mothers not expected
to work than to families in which the adult was expected to work,
but lower incentives to work. Moreover, if those single mothers
worked, their incomes would be subjected to higher cumulative,
marginal tax rates than families with a member expected to work.[142]

    Less interest in PBJI than in FAP is attributable to a number
of differences. One is that the ghettos were quieter and the urgency to "do something" less. Another is that George McGovern's
rout in the 1972 election was associated with his espousal of the
guaranteed income, and legislators may have been reluctant to involve
themselves in a plan, however much less liberal than McGovern's,
that risked unpopularity. Axinn and Levin think the public lost
interest when the deserving poor were taken care of by the passage of SSI, but that seems to overlook the fact that there had
been almost no public interest or congressional debate over that
part of the Nixon plan.[143] According to HEW Secretary Califano,
prospects for passage were promising until the enactment, in June
1978, of California's Proposition Thirteen to slash state property
taxes.[144] As a result, congressional leaders withdrew the legisla-

tion in order to avoid a humiliating defeat for the administration.

There were attempts to revive a modest proposal the following year, but "the President had lost his appetite for welfare reform."[145] Although Senator Moynihan initially pushed for welfare
reform, and referred to the PBJI as "magnificent and superbly crafted"
when it was reintroduced in 1978,[146] he lost interest in a guaranteed income by the following year. Having been concerned with
the poor in low-benefit southern states, New York's Senator Moynihan
was now more interested in the needs of the Northeast and "tired"
of "trying to force on the South a system that its politicians do not
want."[147] Moynihan believed, moreover, that the need for raising
low benefits was less urgent, food stamps having been substantially liberalized in the early 1970s. Since it was no longer thought
that poor people migrated north to get bigger welfare checks, higher
benefits were not needed in the South to deter them from coming.
Finally, recent social research had raised doubts of whether a
guaranteed income would prevent family breakup or provide work
incentives. The Seattle-Denver income-maintenance experiment
appeared to show that extending cash relief to two-parent families broke up more families than relief to single-parent families.[148]
Evidently the interest in preventing single parenthood was greater
than in reducing poverty.

THE EARNED INCOME TAX CREDIT

Accounts of the EITC are omitted from most histories and social-
policy analyses until the 1990s, when scholars began to recognize
that it had become a major income-support program.[149] Because it
began modestly in 1975, the EITC probably did not, at the time,
seem either to substitute for some of the innovative features of
the FAP, particularly in its coverage of workers not receiving public
assistance, or to make that part of the Carter plan less necessary.
In 1994, it was estimated that by the end of the century, federal
expenditures for the EITC would exceed what Washington would
spend for AFDC, and the same holds true for the TANF program
that replaced AFDC in 1996.[150]

The working poor were major casualties of the FAP defeat.
Conservative Senator Russell Long—perhaps the most formidable
congressional obstacle to the FAP—championed the EITC, maintaining that he wanted to keep people from being taxed onto the
welfare rolls.[151] Long's concern over a larger benefit for nonworkers

which could affect willingness to take menial jobs at low pay did not apply to supplementation of earned income, for it would encourage just the opposite. With the EITC, Senator Long and his fellow Southerners did not need to worry about whether maids would iron shirts and "boys" push wheelbarrows. Providing a work bonus was Long's aim. And it was the public, rather than the low-wage employers, who would foot the bill. EITC was supposed to increase the work incentive by "making work pay" or "to enlarge the supply of labor by increasing the relative attractiveness of work (versus welfare)."[152] The share of full-time, year-round workers who earned less than poverty-level wages (equivalent to less than $12,195 per year in 1990) jumped 50% between 1974 and 1990.[153] The EITC cushioned the impact of this decline for many workers and their families and by intent also eased the burden of Social Security and Medicare payroll taxes.[154]

The EITC is a refundable tax credit, paid even if it exceeds the taxpayer's liability. Initially, the EITC was only for families with children, but since 1993, it has provided a small benefit to individuals and childless couples. It is separate from public assistance, and eligibility requires some earned income during a calendar year. Excluded are the long-term unemployed and those caring full-time for young or infirm family members.

The EITC began in 1975 with a maximum credit of $400 for families with annual adjusted gross incomes (AGI) up to $4,000. It became permanent in 1978, was indexed in 1986 during the Reagan administration, substantially increased in 1989 under George Bush, and in 1993, under Bill Clinton. By 1999, the EITC provided a maximum credit of $3,816 for families with two or more children and benefited families with AGI up to $30,580. Adjusted for inflation, the bonus is somewhat more than three times its 1975 value. By providing a substantially higher benefit for two or more children than for one, the 1989 legislation began to address family size. Six states had enacted earned income tax credits by 1992.[155] By 1998, nine states had done so.[156] For example, New York adopted one in 1994 that adds 20% to the federal EITC, bringing the maximum credit for Empire State claimants with two children up to an estimated $4,387 in 1999.[157]

Despite its name, the EITC is largely a form of public assistance rather than a tax credit. In 1998, 86% of total EITC expenditures of $29.4 billion consisted of direct outlays from the federal treasury.[158] The remaining 14% were tax refunds or tax expenditures that show up only as reduced revenues.

Why, with four-fifths of its costs budgeted like traditional public assistance, did the EITC expand during some of the years when welfare was under attack? Not because it shares the political advantages of tax expenditures. EITC benefits were indexed (1986) and substantially increased in real terms (1990 and 1993) because the EITC is directed toward the "deserving" poor whose benefits are seen as "earned."[159] Could a program that included both the deserving poor and those collecting "unearned" benefits, as FAP and PBJI were to do, have enjoyed the political advantage of the EITC, which serves only the former? That difficult question remains unanswered.

Most EITC benefits, about two-thirds, go to the "nonpoor," and over one-third augment incomes of families earning over $20,000 a year.[160] Thus, substantial sums were spent on families with incomes above the poverty standard—albeit a meager one—at the same time that budgets fell sharply in real terms for the most severely disadvantaged families—the traditional welfare clients. Indeed, the fact that the incomes of some poor children with employed parents were being supplemented may have made it easier to reduce commitment to other, even poorer children, whose parents were not employed outside the home. Moreover, families with earnings well below the income for which the maximum credit is paid get very small benefits. A basic issue is whether the allowance is for children. If so, should the source of their parents' incomes be the issue? Children's allowances in other countries are not based on parents' labor-market status and often are not means-tested.

The EITC, although means-tested, escapes the meanness and the stigma usually associated with public assistance. Instead of applying to a public-assistance agency or department, applicants claim credits from the Internal Revenue Service, an agency that interacts with the public generally, not only with the poor. Thus, the EITC has the appearance of universalism, despite its selectivity. This is one of the reasons why the proportion of eligible persons who actually claimed their benefits early in the 1990s was between 81 and 86%, compared to 62–72% for AFDC, and 54–66% for food stamps.[161]

The availability of the EITC may reduce incentives to raise the wages of low-paid workers, thereby contributing downward pressure on the entire wage structure. However, since nearly all claimants get their benefits in a lump sum,[162] they may remain aware of their paltry wages and of the need for a raise. There is little research to date on how recipients perceive and use the EITC, but one study based on a small sample of women in the welfare-to-work transition found that most of the women could not make an explicit link between the EITC and work incentives.[163] Nonetheless, some recent academic research credits the EITC with the dramatic rise in labor-force participation of single women with children since the mid-1980s.[164]

If the EITC does take pressure off the minimum wage, some analysts find this a desirable feature. They point to the possible job-destroying effects of increases in the minimum wage. These, however, have been seriously challenged by recent research.[165] It is also claimed that minimum-wage rises are not well targeted to the poor, again a debatable point.[166] The EITC, as we have already noted, also has targeting limitations in that two-thirds of its benefits go to the nonpoor. While the very poor should remain a priority of public policy, it is important to keep in mind that the poverty standard itself underestimates poverty and that aiding individuals and families with incomes above the poverty line is an antipoverty measure in all but the limited, official definition of the term. The Center on Budget and Policy Priorities, perhaps the prime advocate for the EITC, does not take an either-or approach. The Center regards the EITC and the minimum wage as "two policy pillars."[167]

The minimum wage was already declining in value when the EITC was enacted, and it has sunk much lower since then. Persons who worked full-time, year-round for the minimum wage earned 120% of the three-person poverty level in 1968; just over 100% in 1975; 70% in 1989, when the value of the minimum wage was the lowest since 1950; and 82% in 1998.[168] Interestingly, in 1998, the minimum wage, *plus* the EITC benefit for two children, was 111% of the three-person poverty standard.[169] Thus, rather than bettering the condition of low-income workers, the EITC has served to offset the decline in the minimum wage. Moreover, for families with a minimum-wage worker and more than two children or four or more persons in the family, the EITC does not even provide an escape from official poverty.

The EITC lifts millions of families out of poverty, indeed more than any other antipoverty program. In 1996, 4.6 million people in low-income working families who would have been poor without the EITC were raised out of poverty.[170] Poverty rates for families with children were 16.5% in 1996, when the 1993 increase in benefits was fully phased in, compared to 13.3% in 1975 when the EITC was enacted.[171]

While we are uncomfortable with criticizing any approach that puts money in the hands of the needy, it seems more desirable for workers to earn an adequate wage than to depend on a government transfer. Instead of employers paying the full price of the wage bill, the EITC passes part of the cost onto taxpayers and government at a time when there is reluctance to spend on other programs, notably cash assistance for families with no earnings or housing subsidies for the poor. Not surprisingly, "leading business groups" called upon New York Governor George Pataki to expand the state's income-tax credit. "Businesses," observed a *New York Times* reporter, "like the credit because it effectively raises the incomes of lower-paid workers without any cost to their employers, easing the pressure to raise wages."[172]

Some experts who favor the EITC over the minimum wage are nonetheless critical of its high tax on income or its phase-out rate of 21% for families with two or more children. For families with incomes low enough to receive the maximum credit, the EITC provides a work incentive, an addition to earned income of as much as 40%. For married-couple families with combined incomes of $20,000 or more, there are penalties for extra earnings that could create work disincentives. However, the evidence although limited, suggests that the phase-out of the EITC has little or no effect on hours of work.[173]

Brief Encounters with Job Creation and Full Employment

It took a Great Depression for the United States to acknowledge some of the economic insecurity and unemployment of normal times and to establish a permanent, income-support system. Among the permanent measures enacted in 1935 was insurance for short-term unemployment. The social-security planners believed that when unemployment insurance benefits were exhausted, there should be a "work benefit" or "work provided by the government" instead of extended cash payments.[174] As was pointed out in Chapter 2, the SSA provided neither cash relief nor job programs for long-term unemployment. It approached economic security in terms of income support, thereby splitting social and economic or employment policy. Moreover, many of the lowest-paid workers and disproportionate numbers of African–Americans had been omitted altogether from unemployment insurance because, like Old Age Insurance, it excluded both agriculture and domestic service.[175]

Mitigated for a time by the job-generating effects of hot and cold wars, serious unemployment problems reemerged in the mid-1950s and were disproportionately visited on African–Americans. Congress passed legislation to address employment problems in distressed urban and rural areas, but, as discussed in Chapter 3, the bills were vetoed in 1958 and 1960 by President Dwight Eisenhower. Nor did the 1960s' combination of macroeconomic stimuli and supply-side measures such as MDTA effectively dent the employment problems of the ghettos.

It took a recession and the return of high rates of unemployment for Washington to become directly involved in job creation once again. Increased in response to a subsequent, deeper recession, job-creation programs were eventually targeted to the hardcore unemployed and the disadvantaged instead of to the victims of countercyclical unemployment. Higher unemployment served as an impetus, not only to employment and training programs, but to already pending full-employment proposals, including permanent government responsibility to create jobs for all those who want to work and are not absorbed by the private sector. But once again, government job creation was short-lived. This time it was fear of inflation rather than a substantial reduction of unemployment that accounted for the decline and repeal of employment programs. As for full employment, there was no strong, popular movement backing it, and it is doubtful whether top political leaders ever intended full employment to be more than a symbolic, election-year gesture.[176]

JOB-CREATION PROGRAMS

Public-service employment, the major job-creation measure of the 1970s, had small beginnings in the 1960s. Urban areas lacked the fiscal capacity to meet increasing demands for public service.[177] One approach to the shortage of jobs and public services was public-service employment (PSE). Antipoverty programs had begun to employ neighborhood workers in order to make services more responsive to the needs of low-income communities and clients.[178] Impressed with these services and concerned about job shortages for disadvantaged groups, Frank Riessman and Arthur Pearl recognized that the two needs—for public services and jobs—could be combined to create "new careers for the poor."[179] Initially, Congress responded to this combination of unmet community and worker needs through modest additions to the Economic Opportunity Act, including a New Careers program that trained some of the urban poor for existing public-service jobs. As noted, the Kerner Commission, which investigated the urban riots of the 1960s, called for the creation of 1 million jobs in the public sector as a solution to the endemic poverty of the urban ghettos.[180] Proponents of job-creation programs used the Kerner Commission recommendation to gain support for their programs.[181]

The Nixon administration was willing to deal with underemployment through income support but was quite opposed to government job creation until recession and politics forced its hand. Although President Nixon vetoed a 1970 bill that included authorization of a small public-service-employment component, he signed the Emergency Employment Act (EEA) a year later, when recession, partly brought on by the administration's conservative economic policies, drove unemployment up to 5.9% and cost Republicans losses in the 1970 elections.[182] Serving only 3% of the unemployed (150,000 jobs)—far fewer than the number who lost their jobs due to Nixon administration policies—the EEA was nonetheless important because it was the first general, public-employment program since the Great Depression and the first antirecessionary job program to emphasize public-service employment rather than public works.[183]

Although Nixon stopped supporting public employment after his reelection, he did, under the pressure of Watergate and in return for consolidation and decentralization of existing manpower and training programs, agree to a small jobs component in the Comprehensive Employment and Training Act (CETA) of 1973.[184] During the severe recession of the mid-1970s, when for 3 years unemployment rates were the highest since 1941, employment policy became more focused on work relief. This serious downturn, like the milder recession of 1971, "provided liberals . . . with the leverage they needed over a conservative Republican president [Gerald Ford] to accept a measure he would otherwise have blocked."[185]

CETA grew considerably under the Carter administration. Faced with the new stagflation, Carter's economic advisers considered it more efficient to deal with unemployment through targeted job creation than macroeconomic stimuli that could heat up the economy and exacerbate inflation.[186] Under Carter, CETA reached its zenith of 742,000 public service slots, up from 310,000 under Ford. Still, this represented only about 12% of the more than 6 million unemployed persons in 1978—a much smaller proportion of the unemployed than the WPA served. In the first Carter fiscal year, the CETA budget increased by 70%, and the PSE proportion of CETA funds grew to 60%, compared to 37% in 1975.[187] Nonetheless, CETA was a small program serving a small proportion of the unemployed in a time of growing, mass unemployment. Indeed, with one hand, the government gave a little through CETA job creation, and with the other, it took more away through its restrictive fiscal and monetary policies.

In response to some real or alleged problems of CETA, Congress made changes that crippled it. In its early phases, there was a tendency toward "creaming" or giving jobs to the most employable applicants and toward substituting CETA workers for regular government employees, thus providing fiscal relief to localities. The amount of substitution is itself debatable, but in an atmosphere of severe recession and state initiatives to limit taxes, CETA probably preserved services that would have been cut rather than substituted for them.[188] In late 1978, Congress addressed these problems by restricting eligibility in PSE to the hard-core jobless, keeping wages very low, limiting employment to the least skilled, and requiring prime sponsors (usually local governments) to spend more money on training.

These changes were the political kiss of death for CETA. First, a program for the poor tends to be as unpopular and politically powerless as its clientele. Second, CETA's strongest lobby, local governments, got less fiscal relief and consequently provided less political support.[189] Local government officials were also less than enthusiastic about changes that centralized the program and limited their autonomy, such as strict monitoring by the federal authorities to reduce mismanagement and fraud.[190] Greatly exaggerated, mismanagement and fraud, according to one expert, represented at most 1% of CETA jobs.[191]

The enthusiasm for jobs programs was short-lived. In addition to the consequences of serving a constituency with less political voice in its later years, CETA suffered from a very bad press that distorted its accomplishments. Like the WPA, which was also a favorite whipping boy, CETA was responsible for many useful services.[192] Reviewing CETA reauthorization hearings in 1978, Bullock revealed that hostile critics did not want to hear evidence contradicting their prejudices. Despite reams of studies and other evidence, one of the main influences on Congress was a negative

Readers' Digest article on a boondoggle.[193] Finally, as unemployment rates dropped from 8.5% in 1975 to 6.1% in 1978 and 5.8% in 1979, public concern shifted to rising inflation.

Willing for a few years to create jobs as a countercyclical measure during a period of high unemployment and eventually to target them to the hard-core unemployed, political leaders became less supportive of employment and training programs toward the end of the Carter administration, even when unemployment was climbing.[194] Certainly, political leaders had not accepted the reality of chronic unemployment and underemployment or public responsibility for permanent expansion of jobs. Indeed, a leader with deep ideological resistance to government job creation like Ronald Reagan terminated CETA when unemployment rates were the highest since the Great Depression—and with virtually no public protest.

TOYING WITH FULL EMPLOYMENT

Representative Augustus Hawkins, an influential member of the Black Congressional Caucus from the Watts district of Los Angeles and chair of the House Education and Labor Committee's Subcommittee on Equal Opportunities, was the guiding spirit behind the 1970s effort to guarantee jobs for all. Hawkins' 1-minute address to the House of Representatives, a week after he and Congressman Henry Reuss (D-WI) introduced the Equal Opportunity and Full Employment Bill, conveys not only his human-rights conception of full employment but the depth of his commitment to the goal:

> Assuring full employment is the single most important step in the national interest at this time. . . . An authentic full employment policy rejects the narrow, statistical idea of full employment measured in terms of some tolerable level of unemployment—the percentage game—and adopts the more human and socially meaningful concept of personal rights to an opportunity for useful employment at fair rates of compensation.[195]

The economy was not in recession when Hawkins and Reuss designed and introduced their full-employment bill. As a representative of a black, ghetto district, Hawkins well knew that employment problems are endemic in neighborhoods like Watts, in good times as well as in bad. At the same time, Hawkins saw his bill as more than a benefit to Watts. Full employment was to be the key to reducing many social problems—poverty, inequality, discrimination, crime, welfare—and to improving the living standards of Americans.[196] Soon thereafter, Hubert Humphrey introduced an identical bill in the Senate. In 1975, Humphrey cosponsored a bill with Jacob Javits (R-NY) that called for an Economic Planning Board in the Office of the president that would develop a balanced economic-growth plan based on comprehensive data pertaining to the economy and that would suggest policies for carrying out the plan.[197] With unemployment soaring to the highest postwar level and the Hawkins' bill attracting more support, Humphrey and Hawkins introduced a bill early in 1975 that combined the goal of full employment with a national economic-planning mechanism.

The early Humphrey-Hawkins bills had two outstanding features, both of which were conspicuously missing from the final version enacted in 1978. The original legislation called for a right to a job that would be enforceable in court and required the federal government to create reservoirs of jobs sufficient to employ all those who could not find work in the private sector. Most jobs were to be created by an expansionary economic policy, but the shortfall would be made up through federally financed employment designed by local planning councils.[198] The enforceable right to a job and the reservoirs of jobs for the unemployed were the two provisions of the bill that made the job guarantee real. The former was sacrificed very soon in the legislative process to win the support of AFL-CIO President George Meany, for one.[199] Labor evidently feared this would create a flood of job seekers. In an inflationary time, the expansionary fiscal policies drew fire and were gradually weakened.[200] Since the Act, in its final version, required congressional authorization for job creation, there was virtually no change from the existing situation.

Hawkins had not wanted to play the "percentage game." He did not want to define full employment in terms of an acceptable unemployment rate. Initially, full employment meant a job for everyone willing and able to work, including those not in the labor force; full implementation was to take 5 years.[201] As unemployment rose, the employment goals shrank.[202] Since neither these targets nor the promise of a job for all was any longer enforceable, the change, when it occurred, was largely nominal. As inflation loomed increasingly larger as a public issue, and despite attempts to beat it back by the bill's proponents, the Senate added a specific infla-

tion-reduction goal, although the bill specifically stated that policies and programs for reducing inflation should be designed so as
not to impede achievement of the goals for reducing unemployment.[203]

The Full Employment and Balanced Growth Act of 1978 set
specific goals for unemployment, but these were not mandatory
and were sacrificed to anti-inflation goals and reductions in social spending in both the Carter and Reagan administrations. Soon
after the passage of Humphrey-Hawkins, the White House announced
cuts of 100,000 in CETA PSE slots that were, in turn, denounced
by Congressman Hawkins as a violation of the Act's interim target
of 4% unemployment.[204] In any case, employment and training
programs began to be cut back soon after passage of the Humphrey-
Hawkins Full Employment and Balanced Growth Act of 1978.
Humphrey-Hawkins had set an interim target of 4% unemployment
by 1983; instead, the unemployment rate rose in 1982 to more than
double that target rate—indeed, to the highest level in the postwar period, and joblessness was only slightly lower in 1983, the
target year.[205] It was not until January 2000, 17 years later, that
the *interim* target was reached.

The political battle over Humphrey-Hawkins in the 1970s, Philip
Harvey observes, was "in all essential respects a reprise of its
predecessor," the Murray-Wagner Full Employment Bill.[206] Yet, as
Helen Ginsburg points out, big business and the Republicans had
killed genuine full employment in the 1940s, but in this second
round, "the conservatives didn't have to do much to win their points."[207]
Not that business organizations failed to denounce Humphrey-
Hawkins. The Chamber of Commerce, National Association of Manufacturers, and the Business Roundtable testified against it in the
1976 hearings.[208] However, "liberal" economist Charles Schultze
of the Brookings Institution, Carter's chairman of the CEA, led
the charge against Humphrey-Hawkins, arguing that the control of
inflation took precedence over job creation and that both specific
targets for unemployment and creation of public-service jobs threatened price stability and should be removed from the bill.[209] Early
in 1977, Helen Ginsburg wrote that Schultze's Senate testimony
in the preceding year, reprinted as an op-ed essay in *The Washington Post,* "is widely credited with having killed H. R. 50's [Humphrey-
Hawkins'] chances in the last Congress."[210]

Schultze appears to have taken the position that his view was
scientific and rational whereas the advocacy of full employment,

job creation, and more expansive fiscal policies was political
and constituency-based, that is, a response to the pressure of
organized labor and the civil-rights community. Mainstream
economics was, indeed, moving away from both planning and
expansive fiscal policies. Within the administration, Labor
Secretary Ray Marshall, also an economist, took a position different
from the emerging consensus in the profession. Marshall argued
that public funding of jobs was less costly and less inflationary
than subsidizing unemployment through insurance or welfare.[211]
It is Margaret Weir's view, however, that the bill gave only cursory
attention to how full employment could be achieved without
aggravating inflation.[212] The taint of inflation was certainly a
political liability. Freshmen Democratic Congresspersons, fearing
retaliation for support of an inflationary measure, persuaded the
House leadership not to hold the vote on Humphrey-Hawkins
before the 1976 election.

    In the democratic primaries, Carter and segregationist Gover-
nor George Wallace of Arkansas were the only candidates who
did not support Humphrey-Hawkins. Full employment was scarcely
talked about during the presidential campaign, although Carter
endorsed a version of Humphrey-Hawkins a month before the
election.[213] In return for the support of the frontrunner, the bill
was rewritten with greater emphasis on inflation control, more
reliance on private employment than on public-service jobs, and
the proviso that public-sector jobs would be low-pay in order to
hold down inflation and discourage migration from the private to
the public sector.[214]

    An impressive number of organizations supported Humphrey-
Hawkins. Chaired by Coretta Scott King and Murray Finley, head
of the Amalgamated Clothing and Textile Workers, the National
Committee for Full Employment was founded in June 1974. It
brought together labor, religious, civil rights, black, ethnic, women's,
senior citizens and other groups with a stake in full employment.[215]
Despite the range of this support, full employment came to be
seen as a black issue, promoted primarily by the Congressional
Black Caucus,[216] and that, too, was a political liability, particularly in a time of white backlash. In any case, "the strength of
the movement for full employment was never equal to the task
that had to be done. . . ."[217]

    Indeed, it could hardly be called a movement. Had public support
been widespread and organized, it would have been more diffi-

cult for power brokers like Meany, Carter, and even some liberal
Democrats to render the bill virtually unenforceable in return for
their support.

Summary: Ready for "Righty"

The 1970s began with a Republican president who tried to replace AFDC with a small, guaranteed income, who federalized
and liberalized benefits to the elderly and disabled poor, and under
whose administration the proportion of GDP spent on welfare rose
85%.[218] The decade ended with a Democratic president whose ap-
pointee to the Federal Reserve Board pursued policies that sacrificed employment creation to inflation control; who barely increased
social-welfare expenditures; who favored no-cost welfare "reform"
and failed to fight hard for it in any case; who first expanded but
subsequently cut back public-service employment, even as unemployment rose; and who consistently watered down and then violated full-employment legislation.[219] Gone was the buoyant economy
that had supported a brief period of reform and the imperatives—
both moral and social-control—for reducing poverty. Whereas the
proportion of GDP spent on the military fell by about 35% from
the time Nixon took office until he resigned, the military budget
declined in the first Carter years but rose nearly 11% in the last
2 years for which he was responsible.[220]

Reform of both welfare and employment policies was on the
agenda for the first time in 30 years. Two presidents proposed
welfare reform that would have increased federal responsibility
for assistance and changed its single-parent focus, racial composition, and the proportion of employed recipients. Compared to
AFDC, such reform, although wanting particularly in benefit adequacy, would have broadened the constituency of welfare and
reduced its unpopularity, but neither Presidents Nixon nor Carter
was willing to pay the bill for modest reform. Whether they could
have overcome the political opposition of the "veto coalition" had
they mobilized the substantial political resources of the presidency
is debatable. Instead of the benefit increases proposed by several
high-level government commissions, AFDC budgets began their
steep fall in real terms.

Some prominent members of Congress turned down the road
to employment reform but met substantial roadblocks to their full-
employment initiatives. Although they secured passage of a

full-employment bill, the original destination was hardly recognizable when they got there. Indeed, only a few years later, such "full-employment" policies would offer no obstacle to the first double-digit unemployment rates since the Great Depression.

What followed in domestic and defense policy under the Reagan administration was less a sharp turn to the Right than great acceleration in the direction that had already been taken. Whereas the economic and political climate helped to make a Republican moderately liberal in the late 1960s and early 1970s, it exerted conservative pressure on a Democrat a decade later. The moderate Carter prepared the ground for the reactionary Reagan and the second act in the national drama of welfare "reform."

CHAPTER 7

The Final Act: Welfare's Repeal

T he next act in the drama of welfare reform begins with President Ronald Reagan. The result of the final act, however, was not welfare reform in the positive sense of that word, but rather repeal of the nation's 60 year-old ADC-AFDC program. The *coup de grace* was not delivered by one of the most ideologically conservative presidents this country has ever experienced, but by a Democratic president with the support of one-half of the Democratic congressional delegation. This chapter begins by examining the strategy used by the Reagan administration to dismantle much of the bureaucratic infrastructure that had sustained a safety net for the poor. It next looks at the failed attempt at welfare reform—the Family Support Act of 1988—which represented a compromise between Republicans who wanted a more punitive welfare-to-work program like that suggested by Lawrence Mead and Democrats intent on assuring that if welfare recipients were forced to work there would be adequate support services and transitional aid for them.

Squeezed by recession and lackluster federal support, the Family Support Act never had a chance to prove itself. What followed was welfare reform by default—a series of ever more punitive state initiatives that paved the way for the final assault on the welfare entitlement. This chapter traces the course of welfare repeal as it made its way through both Republican and Democratic administrations to its denouement in the passage of the Personal Responsibility and Work Opportunity Act of 1996. We seek to explain its triumph not only as a political and ideological victory for the conservatives in both parties but as the failure of left-liberal Democrats to organize around a more visionary approach to work, welfare, and economic justice.

The Economic and Social Policy Strategy of the Reagan "Revolution"

The election of 1980 significantly shifted the balance of power in Washington. The Republicans not only won the presidency but also the Senate. Although the House remained in Democratic hands, the Republicans picked up 31 seats, making a coalition between Republicans and southern Democrats much more likely. Flush with what they considered a new "mandate," the Reagan administration set out to accomplish a revolution in social and economic policy—to reduce the welfare state to its bare bones. True believers in the Reagan doctrine, like David Stockman, Reagan's director of the Office of Management and Budget, saw themselves as engaged in a holy crusade. "A true economic policy revolution," he wrote, "meant risky and mortal combat with all the mass constituencies of Washington's largesse—Social Security recipients, veterans, farmers, educators, state and local officials, the housing industry, and many more."[1] The Reagan administration attempted to accomplish this revolution through a variety of procedural and administrative gimmicks, such as changing the eligibility rules for certain programs, shifting authority for selected programs to the states, and offering the budget as a unified package that would have to be voted on by a single "up" or "down" vote. Changes were accomplished in four policy areas: tax reform, deregulation, monetary policy, and reallocation of federal budget dollars.[2]

TAX REFORM

At the center of the 1981 Economic Recovery Tax Act was a reduction in income tax brackets that was sold to the American public as a tax reduction that would benefit the "middle class." (The reduction or elimination of income taxes had long been a goal of conservative free marketeers.)[3] Stockman later admitted that this was a "Trojan horse"—a political deceit used to reduce the top tax rate from 70% (in the 1970s) to 28%.[4]

The result of the Reagan tax reform of 1981 was a massive redistribution of income and wealth, from the lower and middle-income groups to the very wealthy. The top 10% of the population ended up with lower tax rates, while the bottom 90% ended up with higher rates.[5] Between 1980 and 1984, changes in tax policy had left families with incomes of less than $10,000 with a $95 loss, while families making over $200,000 had gained $17,403.[6] During the 1980s, state taxes also added to growing inequality, as rising state sales taxes fell disproportionately on poor families, and as one-half the states with income taxes made them less fair for low- and middle-income earners.[7] In addition to huge tax reductions for the wealthy, the 1981 tax act lowered corporate taxes so much that a survey of 250 giant companies for the 1981–1983 period found that more than one-half of them escaped taxation entirely in at least one of those years, despite large profits.[8] Compared to the 1960s, when average corporate income taxes were 23.4% of all federal revenues, they fell to an average of 8.1% between 1983 and 1986.[9] Lost taxes were estimated to have cost the federal treasury half a trillion dollars.[10] The result of decreased tax revenues, a bloated military budget, and rising health expenditures was a burgeoning federal deficit.

Successive tax reforms (between 1982 and 1993) recovered a portion of the lost tax revenues, but the momentum of the supply-siders had taken its toll. Although debt is not necessarily bad if borrowing is used to stimulate a slow economy, the net effect of the Reagan administration's "fiscal revolution" had been to accumulate a federal debt (much of it owed to foreign creditors) that surpassed those of all other past administrations combined. The size of the debt then became, in the hands of subsequent Republican and some Democratic legislators, a convenient excuse to call for a curb on further social spending.

DEREGULATION

By the time Reagan was elected, the push for deregulation was well underway. Carter had made deregulation a major theme of his administration. He had deregulated the airlines and had begun to deregulate trucking, railroad, and interest rates. Deregulation is not necessarily detrimental.[11] It depends on what is deregulated, how it is done, and how it affects different population groups. However, supply-side enthusiasts in the Reagan administration, with the complicity of members of Congress from both parties who had been influenced by campaign contributions, took deregulation beyond the bounds of either prudence or consumer fairness. The most egregious example was the deregulation of the savings and loan industry. This action is estimated to have cost the public between

$500 billion and $1.4 trillion,[12] and it successfully diverted money from moderate-cost housing to unneeded office complexes and fancy resorts. The results of many other deregulated activities resulted in reckless speculation, corporate sacrifice of long-term goals to short-term profits, and new threats to health, safety, and the environment.

Deregulation affected various sectors of the population differently. Educated, affluent consumers got cheaper products, greater variety, and were able to gain from the high real interest rates (adjusted for inflation) that deregulation made possible. The poor, on the other hand, were hurt by these interest rates, had trouble negotiating the bewildering array of choices now being offered, faced higher minimum deposit requirements at banks, and steeper local phone rates. As in other areas, the net effect of Reagan's deregulation was to shift power and money from the low-income to the wealthy and from workers to corporate management.[13]

MONETARY POLICY

As Kevin Phillips has observed, Republicans have historically supported the penchant of the creditor class for high interest rates and tight money, but Reagan was "committed not simply to traditional conservative politics but to right-wing economic theories and ideologies—and *to radical combinations of these ideas* (author's emphasis)."[14] The combination of tax cuts and tight money policy was one of these radical combinations, for the effects pulled in opposite directions, although both favored the wealthy. The immediate result of the high interest rates and program cuts of 1981 was to throw the country into one of the worst recessions since the Great Depression. The unemployment rate rose at one point to over 10% in 1982, coming back down to the 5% range only at the end of the decade. The Fed's tight money policy resulted not only in a boom in interest-rate returns to the wealthy, but in shrinking industrial production, a steep drop in the housing market, a depression in agriculture, timber, oil, and gas mining, and an overvalued dollar. That overvalued dollar made foreign goods cheaper in the United States and U.S. goods more expensive abroad. American markets were flooded with foreign goods, and the market for U.S. goods abroad shrank, accelerating the so-called "deindustrialization" of the United States that had been in process for some time.

In 1982, an international banking crisis loomed, as Third World debtors threatened to default on their loans. The Federal Reserve Board was forced to abandon its tight money policy. Interest rates came down, and Third World debts were quickly restructured, but the price for poor and working people in both the Third World and the United States was high: IMF-dictated austerity programs for the poorer nations, sending them into deeper poverty and making it more difficult to purchase American goods; increased unemployment for Americans employed in export-related sectors of the economy; and an enormous taxpayer bailout of the banks.

When growth began to pick up, it was the large, established businesses that benefited over small- and medium-sized ones. Much of the new liquidity found its way, not into productive investments to produce more jobs, but into takeovers and mergers that reduced employment and into a variety of new speculative instruments in the stock market.[15]

REALLOCATION OF FEDERAL DOLLARS

David Stockman was a convert to the supply-side economic theories of economists like Arthur Laffer and Milton Friedman. As Stockman wrote in his memoir: "Its vision of the good society rested on the strength and productive potential of free men in free markets. It sought to encourage the unfettered production of capitalist wealth and the expansion of private welfare that automatically attends it."[16] Despite admitting that "the whole thing [supply-side theory] is premised on faith . . . on a belief about how the world works,"[17] Stockman took up the task of designing and implementing an economic program for Reagan that proposed sweeping cuts in domestic programs and taxes, deregulation of industry and finance, and stepped-up military spending, the latter not a little at odds with reducing big government.

Stockman's targets ranged much wider than welfare. His attempt to cut the "waste" and "pork" out of government focused most heavily on the Social Security system on which millions of older Americans relied. "No single issue was as critical to the success of the Reagan Revolution as Social Security reform," he wrote. "A frontal assault on the very inner fortress of the American welfare state . . . was now in order."[18] However, when Congress took its scissors to the budget, the cuts fell heaviest on groups with the least political and economic power—namely the poor and disabled. Social Security's powerful senior lobby preserved the program, albeit with some adjustments that made it less generous. Means-tested benefit programs were singled out for particularly harsh reductions, with AFDC sustaining the largest cut. An estimated 500,000 families may have lost their benefits.[19] The Comprehensive Employment and Training Act (CETA), Washington's first substantial job-creation program since the Great Depression, was killed just as it was beginning to meet its target of providing jobs for the poor.[20] Federal subsidies for low-income housing were cut by 75%, contributing to a new phenomenon in postwar history—widespread homelessness. Despite its being universal, or not confined to the poor, unemployment insurance suffered significant retrenchment, owing largely to the near gutting of the Extended Benefit program. Hundreds of unemployment offices around the country were also closed, making it more difficult for the unemployed to collect the benefits to which they were entitled. The result was that real benefits for the long-term unemployed in the early 1980s were less than one-half of those in the previous recession, despite higher unemployment.[21] According to the Congressional Budget Office, cuts of $30 billion were made in entitlement programs in 1981 and 1982. Cuts in discretionary spending, which includes benefits for the poor such as the Home Energy Assistance Program, housing, and social services, were cut by about $26 billion per year.[22]

More than 60 categorical aid programs were consolidated into block grants and turned over to the states. The New Right consciously chose block grants as a strategy for dismantling the infrastructure of the welfare state. By switching from categorical grants-in-aid targeted at specific constituencies for strictly federally defined purposes, they gave states more flexibility, which often meant the flexibility to reduce programs for the poor. An added bonus was that it weakened the political support for vulnerable programs by breaking up the "iron triangles" of mutual interest among executive branch agencies, congressional committees, and interest groups that had sustained welfare-state programs over the years. As an attendee at a Conservative Caucus briefing put it: The block grant system "is the major strategy conceived in order to pull the rug out from under the liberals and leave them completely powerless or [having] no longer any reason to exist."[23]

Some dismantling of welfare-state programs was accomplished, not through limiting their appropriations, but through administrative changes that declared large numbers of people ineligible.

One of the most tragic examples was the administration's attack on Social Security Disability Insurance and Supplemental Security Income (SSI), which had the effect of ruling as many as 400,000 people—many of them severely disabled—ineligible for their only source of income. The courts eventually overturned this ruling, but the Reagan administration continued to defy the court order. Objections from the states, which were forced to pick up some of the bills, persuaded Congress to reinstate most of the claimants, but not before many had died or become sicker. The mentally ill were especially hard hit and were least equipped to appeal their cases. Some of them may have become part of the homeless problem that emerged in the 1980s.[24]

The poor suffered more severely from the Reagan administration's "reforms." By reducing income and earnings limits, Reagan's policies made 450,000 families ineligible for AFDC.[25] Altogether, some 3 million persons lost food stamps, 300,000 were dropped from Medicaid, and more than 100,000 from SSI. By 1984, some 4 million people had been forced off the rolls of these programs, and many others suffered benefit losses.[26]

A series of hearings around the country, spearheaded by the National Urban League in 1982, revealed widespread suffering as a result of the first round of cuts. A universal thread running throughout the hearings was a sense of people beating their heads against a brick wall. "They were trying to get ahead, but it appeared, at least in their eyesight, that the 'system' was determined to keep them scratching for crumbs. Understandably, they were frustrated, confused, and in many instances, bitter." One hearing participant's statement seemed to sum it up: "We're already poor. We're already starving. Don't just stand there and kill us."[27]

While Reagan succeeded in getting Congress to approve virtually all of his cuts in low-income benefit programs in the first year and about one-fifth in the second, thereafter, the political tide began to shift, and federal reductions virtually ceased. According to Pierson, the steep recession that began in late 1981 reduced confidence in Reagan's economic program and heightened public sympathy for the poor. The result was an acceleration in the usual loss of momentum that presidents experience after their "honeymoon" periods.[28] Stockman saw it in ideological terms: "the cornered and intimidated politicians struck back and stopped the Reagan Revolution dead in its tracks." "Democracy," he admitted, "had defeated the doctrine."[29]

By 1987, a slightly larger proportion of the GDP was being spent for social welfare than in 1980. Some of the programs, particularly Medicaid and food stamps, were expanded.[30] What was different about the social-welfare state at the end of the Reagan years was not so much its size as its composition. Public aid for the poor—food stamps, Medicaid, and the cash benefit programs— had fallen from 15% of total expenditures in 1980 to 13% in 1987. While this may not seem like much, any drop in spending at a time when needs for more social welfare are growing means an actual larger loss.[31] *If Medicaid had been excluded, there would have been a 30% drop.* On the other hand, social-insurance programs—those that are universal and benefit many who are better off as well as the poor—had risen from 47% to 50% of total spending.[32]

One "welfare" package that was not attacked either verbally or with reductions, but in fact was greatly enlarged, was the millions of dollars in military contracts. Even as domestic spending was being curtailed, a record $1.6 trillion was spent on defense over the next 5 years, an expansion of "big-government" that belied the administration's antigovernment rhetoric. It was the largest military buildup in peacetime history.[33]

The cost of shifting federal monies from safety-net programs to the military was not only a loss for welfare recipients but for the working poor, who also depended on many of these programs. The cuts fell disproportionately on African–Americans, Latinos, and women, not only because they used government programs in greater proportion to whites and men, but because, having been shut out of many high-wage sectors of the private economy, they were disproportionately employed in institutions of the welfare state.[34] Shifting money from social spending to the military also involved shifting it from northeastern and midwestern cities and poor rural areas with high concentrations of welfare recipients to more affluent sections in the Sunbelt states, as well as from less-skilled blue-collar workers to better paid, high-tech workers.

Welfare Reform by Default

While Reagan succeeded in his first term in reducing aid to the poor through the use of block grants that disguised budget cuts and administrative changes that reduced eligibility, he had not yet moved toward a full-fledged overhaul of the welfare system. His aim was to implement a plan, similar to one he had initiated as governor of California, that would require all welfare recipients to work in exchange for their welfare benefits, notwithstanding the fact that the California program had been a colossal failure.[35] But legislators, uncertain about both the feasibility and effectiveness of universal workfare, made it an option in the 1981 Omnibus Budget Reconciliation Act. Workfare, many realized, would require more expenditures on education and training, job counseling, health, and day care, as well as efforts to make jobs available and attractive. Yet they were caught in a budget squeeze with a large federal deficit and an administration ideologically committed to reducing government.[36] Thus, states were allowed to experiment with workfare but in a context in which reduced funding had the effect of limiting money available for employment-preparation activities.[37] This pattern of increased emphasis on work, state innovation under federal waivers of welfare regulations, and strict cost containment set the pattern for the rest of the decade and beyond. By 1987, as many as 40 states were exercising their option to operate welfare-to-work programs. Reminiscent of nineteenth-century poor-law "reform," the issue around which welfare debates now often revolved was not how to end poverty but how to end "welfare dependency."

By the end of Reagan's first term, the ability of corporate power and right-wing ideology to set the domestic policy agenda had advanced considerably. This was the case even though programs for the poor recovered some lost ground in the late 1980s. The victory of conservative ideology could be seen in the fact that while the AFDC program (which took up a mere 1% of the federal budget) was held responsible for all manner of evil, the mounting costs of corporate welfare and irresponsibility were virtually ignored.

With the opening of his second term in 1985, Reagan announced his intention to "reform welfare." In response, a number of liberal and conservative public-policy groups launched studies of ways to reform the system. The following year, the National Governors' Association voted to make welfare reform its top priority. The effort was spearheaded by Democratic Governor Bill Clinton of Arkansas and Republican Michael Castle of Delaware—both from low-benefit states. (The maximum benefit for a three-person family in Arkansas in 1985 was only 50% of the national average—$239 a month in 1996 dollars or $2,868 a year—a little over $18 per person per week to purchase housing, transportation, clothing, and other necessities, not to mention a birthday present for the children.)[38]

The result of this renewed interest in reforming welfare was a gathering consensus among policy elites around three points: (1) that the breakdown of the family and inadequate inner-city educational systems were generating a permanently dependent "underclass"; (2) that a reformed system should be based on the concept of reciprocal responsibilities between government and the welfare recipient; and (3) that states should be given greater discretion over certain aspects of welfare policy.[39] While there was agreement on goals, there was little consensus on how to achieve them. Despite the Right's relentless attacks on welfare recipients, public-opinion polls taken in the latter half of the 1980s indicated some softening in attitudes toward the poor and toward welfare.[40]

THE FAMILY SUPPORT ACT OF 1988: TOO LITTLE, TOO LATE

With Democrats now a majority in both houses, it was unlikely Congress would pass the more punitive workfare measures favored by many conservatives. Thus, after intense congressional debate, a compromise, the Family Support Act of 1988, PL 100-485, was worked out. Engineered primarily by New York Senator Daniel Patrick Moynihan, the Family Support Act simultaneously expanded federal mandates requiring states to move their welfare caseloads into work-related programs and increased state discretion in designing those programs.[41] The centerpiece was the Job Opportunities and Basic Skills Training Program (dubbed the JOBS program), requiring states to provide assessment, training, education, work experience, or job-search assistance for welfare recipients. To those charged with administering the program, the Family Support Act represented a dramatic shift in welfare policy from income support to a focus on moving welfare clients toward self-sufficiency.

Unlike the old law, which often made working more expensive than staying on welfare, the Family Support Act sought to make "work pay" by requiring states to provide child care and Medicaid for up to 1 year for families leaving the rolls for work, as well as raising certain earnings disregard limits for those on the rolls. It mandated educational activities, as appropriate, including high school or GED programs and remedial and ESL education to achieve a basic literacy level. While requiring poor family heads to engage in work or work-related activity under threat of sanction, it exempted from work-participation requirements mothers with children under the age of 3 years or, if state child care was not guaranteed, under the age of 6 years.[42] It did not penalize the entire family if the eligible parent defaulted on his/her responsibilities.[43] This was in contrast to the stricter requirements of the PRWORA that would replace it (see Chapter 8). Democrats had gone along with these new work requirements (which, it should be noted, did not create new jobs) in exchange for Republican concessions on federal funding for job training, placement activities, and transitional child care and health coverage.

While hailed by Democrat Thomas Downey, chair of the House Subcommittee on Public Assistance, as "the most significant change in the welfare system since its inception," the Family Support Act was hardly revolutionary.[44] In fact, it represented a compromise between "competing discourses and policy solutions" that had long plagued discussions of welfare policy.[45] As a result, both Right and Left observers found much to criticize.

To conservatives like Murray, the law did not go far enough. It was too generous with its child-care and Medicaid benefits and would encourage women not on welfare to quit their jobs so they could get these benefits. (If this were likely, then benefits should have been universal. The U.S. is almost alone among wealthy industrial nations in not treating benefits like health care as universal "rights.")

Urban League lobbyists complained that "Congress and the White House [had] failed to seize the moment to enact a constructive and humane plan that at least would have opened the door toward self-sufficiency for AFDC families."[46] Some progressive critics were even less delicate. They saw the new law as downright reactionary—"the most punitive and inadequate addition to American welfare since the workhouse."[47]

To one feminist observer, the Family Support Act represented a "tension between two masters that have long ruled in unison: capitalism and patriarchy," brought about by changes that were occurring in the roles of women and the structure of family life. The increased participation of women in the labor market had created a boon for capitalism in the form of cheaper labor: Women are generally paid less, and if women work, men do not have to be paid a "family wage." But patriarchy dictated that women stay at home.[48] In feeding women into the low-wage labor market, the Family Support Act was bowing to the dictates of capitalism, but in freeing women from the necessity of relying on men by providing transitional child care, Medicaid, and increased earnings disregards, it threatened conservative "family values." Perhaps bowing to conservative claims that AFDC was creating disincentives to marriage, the Family Support Act required all states to provide time-limited welfare payments to poor, two-parent families whose "principal earner" was unemployed (AFDC-UP) but required that at least one of the parents participate in a specified program activity for up to 40 hours per week.[49] Still, very few two-parent families were served, even in the last years of the program.[50] The Family Support Act also tried to resolve the tension between capitalism and patriarchy by forcing fathers to contribute to family income through stiffer child-support enforcement and by requiring states to establish paternity and to garnish fathers' wages.

Democratic liberals and organizations like the American Public Welfare Association had gone along with the bill, believing that "it was the best that could be gotten at the time."[51] They congratulated themselves that they had not only averted the worst of the "reform" proposals but had exempted several low-income programs from the automatic budget limits set by the Gramm-Rudman-Hollings Act and had even succesfully increased appropriations for some of them.

According to Felicia Kornbluh, the increased emphasis on making work pay could have been an opening for welfare activists to fight for a more humane solution to the welfare mess. She argued that welfare recipients should demand the training, child care, and health services to which the law entitled them or refuse to work without them. Employers would then be forced to pressure state governments into providing decent services or to stop sanctioning women for nonparticipation. State governments might in turn petition the federal government to take some action.[52]

But the subversive potential never materialized, and the 1988 compromise was destined to be short-lived. First, Reagan's debt burden guaranteed that the amount of federal funds necessary for states to move their welfare clients into education, training, or work-experience programs would not be sufficient. Then governors Bill Clinton and Michael Castle admitted as much when they wrote that "states must rethink approaches to services to get the most from limited resources. . . . In essence, states must continue to do more with less, taking risks and experimenting with new ways of doing business."[53]

Second, the states were erroneously hailed as the new incubators of creative solutions to welfare dependency.[54] In reality, they were engaged in luring companies from other states or in retaining companies with large tax giveaways and other subsidies, but with little permanent employment gains to show for substantial losses of public revenues.[55]

Third, while welfare recipients were now required to engage in education and training, if not work experience, there were little hard data on what kinds of training best equipped welfare recipients for a rapidly changing labor market. The growing percentage of jobs that were based on low-wage services and "flexibility" (a euphemism for temporary and involuntary part-time work) meant that it would be difficult for many welfare recipients to get and hold a job that provided financial stability, let alone upward mobility.

Even as lawmakers were pushing the welfare-to-work proposals, there were several assessments of such programs that showed modest, if any, benefits. For example, a rigorously controlled study of five, small, welfare-to-work experiments in different states by the Manpower Demonstration Research Corporation showed that in four of the states where the demand for labor was relatively high, these programs increased women's employment between 3 and 9% but did not increase the employment of men. Women who participated in the programs increased their total earnings by an average of 19.5%, but men actually lost income. Tempering even these modest findings, however, was the fact that in the fifth state, West Virginia, with one of the highest unemployment rates in the country, there were no increases in regular, unsubsidized employment among the participants and no gains in earnings.[56]

Analyses of two other experiments both hailed by the media as success stories, the GAIN program in Riverside, California, and the Massachusetts Employment and Training Choices Program (ET), revealed more positive, yet still modest, outcomes. In California, after 3 years, participants in GAIN had increased "graduation" from welfare to work by 5 percentage points, while in Massachusetts, 50% of the AFDC caseload got jobs, but most jobs still left the participants in poverty.[57] A later, but broader, study of these early experiments by the Manpower Demonstration Research Corporation found little evidence that they led to consistent employment, higher earnings for welfare recipients, reductions in welfare caseloads, or reductions in welfare benefits paid by states.[58] A report by the General Accounting Office pointed out that JOBS programs were unlikely to end the need for welfare due to factors outside the control of JOBS programs, such as service and funding shortages and poor economic conditions.[59]

One of those outside conditions—recession—hit in October 1990, just as the Family Support Act was about to be implemented. Official unemployment rates in the early 1990s rose as high as 7.7% (mid-1992), and adding underemployment (involuntary part-time workers and discouraged workers who had dropped out of the labor market) doubled the jobless toll.[60]

The onset of recession brought rising welfare rolls and reduced state budgets, pushing states to reduce programs that assisted low-income households. Thirty-nine states and the District of Columbia froze or cut welfare benefits in 1991. States also made cuts in general cash-assistance programs that affected nearly half a million people, about one-third of the general-assistance recipients nationwide. Eleven states cut special-needs payments and/or emergency cash-assistance programs designed to avert homelessness, while 38% of the states that appropriated funds for low-income housing reduced those programs. States cut or froze benefits in the AFDC program again in 1992, 8 states reduced or eliminated general assistance, and SSI benefits for the poor elderly and disabled were either frozen or cut in 26 states that offered them as a supplement to the federal benefit. [61] States were required to match federal funds for the JOBS program but were late in implementing this requirement. As a result, the great majority of states failed to draw down their full federal allocations, even as late as 1994, thus limiting participation in the JOBS program.[62]

Recessions notoriously undermine the best of intentions when it comes to the poor. With one of the more laudable programs in the nation, even Massachusetts was forced to cut back. By 1995, Massachusetts had become one of the "leading states in tough welfare reform."[63] Moreover, the recession of the 1990s differed from other postwar recessions in that even when output began to rise, employment growth continued to lag, giving rise to the phrase, "jobless recovery."[64] The result was that only a very small fraction of the welfare caseload was able to graduate into real jobs.[65]

Despite declining welfare budgets, many Republican governors saw in this shift of welfare responsibility to the states a political goldmine. Committed to lowering taxes in a time of soaring crime rates and other problems related to a weak economy, they needed something to make themselves look good.[66] Welfare had always been a convenient whipping boy. Capitalizing on the public stigma of welfare recipients as "immoral" and "irresponsible," one that had been fed by the conservative pundits of the previous decade, many Republican governors requested waivers from federal regulators to develop programs that turned out to be much more punitive than the Family Support Act.

Wisconsin's Republican governor, Tommy Thompson, in a startling reversal of that state's leadership in progressive social legislation, had been among the first to hitch his reputation to the rising star of welfare reform. In 1987, Thompson pushed through a Democratic-controlled legislature Wisconsin's "Learnfare" program, which reduced benefits to AFDC families whose teenagers failed to attend school a specified number of times. Although preliminary studies showed no improvement in school attendance among students of welfare families who had participated in Learnfare, it proved to be popular with the public,[67] bringing Thompson national fame as an innovator and encouraging him to go further.

THE STATE WAIVER PROCESS: PRESAGING THE "END OF WELFARE AS WE KNOW IT"

In 1992, the number of states requesting federal waivers increased dramatically, following President Bush's State of the Union message.[68] In it, he had expressed a concern about the "narcotic" effects of welfare and vowed to make the state waiver process easier. Bush's sudden concern about welfare may have been an attempt to one-up his opponent in the 1992 presidential race, "New Democrat" Bill Clinton, who had declared his intention to "end welfare as we know it."[69] Pressured by powerful forces bent on balancing the budget, both men may have been influenced by a Congressional Budget Office staff memorandum suggesting that welfare caseloads had taken a sharp upward turn despite the economic recovery.[70] But both candidates also knew from extensive polling that attacking "welfare" made good campaign copy, although when pressed, most people would probably not have gone along with the harsh cutbacks some were proposing.[71]

States requesting waivers used both carrots and sticks to change the behavior of welfare recipients. Moving away from an earlier focus on education and training—partly because research findings had raised questions about the effectiveness of adult basic education as a means of increasing employment among welfare recipients—many began to emphasize rapid job placement. It is always possible to make work more attractive or to increase work incentives by raising wages, but this was not the case in this recessionary period or in the previous decade, when the real value of the minimum wage was allowed to fall to its postwar nadir.[72] In a restricted funding climate, states wanting to move clients rapidly into jobs were more likely to reduce the benefit package so as to make work—any work—more attractive.

While several states sought to loosen federal restrictions, which had made it difficult to move welfare recipients into the labor force (such as limits on earnings disregards, assets, child-care assistance, and medical aid), over one-half imposed stricter penalties for failure to comply with program rules, stricter time limits and work requirements, and penalties for additional childbearing. For example, the Democrat-controlled legislature in New Jersey passed a measure that provided financial incentives for marriage and employment and denied additional welfare payments to women who had children while on welfare. Similar rules were eventually adopted by 23 other states. (Interestingly, there is some evidence that the effect of the New Jersey program was not heightened abstinence, as had been the intention of policy framers, but an increase in abortions.[73]) The Republican-controlled Connecticut legislature passed a bill to roll back benefit levels to the late 1980s, to limit welfare receipt to 21 months, and to fingerprint all welfare recipients. Maryland and Colorado began reducing payments to mothers who failed to have their children immunized, and most bizarre of all, New Hampshire proposed straightening the teeth of welfare recipients on the theory that better looks would lead to better jobs.[74]

On the surface, such punitive measures might seem to be necessary to bring discipline and order to the allegedly "lazy" and "undisciplined" lives of welfare recipients, but they denied the realities of the unreliable, low-wage labor market with which most welfare mothers had to contend. In some cases, they verged on unconstitutional infringements of welfare clients' privacy rights. Lawsuits were filed in several states charging that the experiments violated federal law barring human experiments without informed consent. Critics also pointed out the fallacy of presumably supporting the child while punishing the parent's behavior.[75]

A few sympathetic poverty researchers and journalists began to document the horror stories. For example, one Iowa mother who got a job in a box-making factory was fired when she had to stay home with her sick 5-year-old. When her benefits were then reduced, she was evicted and fled to Ohio to avoid losing her children to foster care.[76] Another died from a stroke after apparently trying to stretch out her blood pressure medicine. Detroit's homeless population increased between 30 and 50%.[77] Thousands of families in Michigan, whose Republican governor, John Engler, had bragged about his state's ability to reduce the welfare rolls, were working their way off welfare, but at wages that still left them 20% below the poverty line for a family of four.[78]

The Clinton Administration: Lurching toward Welfare Repeal

While campaigning for the presidency as a "New Democrat," Bill Clinton not only declared his intention to "end welfare as we know it" but hinted at a 2-year time limit on continued welfare support, thus exceeding earlier campaign promises to clean up the welfare "mess" and profoundly altering the terms of the debate. Until now, one of the few remaining firewalls protecting recipients of AFDC had been the threat of being called a racist if one were antiwelfare. The threat, of course, would come from the Left. According to Clifford Johnson, senior fellow at the Center on Budget and Policy Priorities, Clinton's 1992 campaign razed that firewall. "Here's a Democrat saying we have to 'end welfare as we know it.'"[79]

No one, including welfare recipients themselves, liked the current welfare system, so there were few to speak up for it when the attacks started. According to Patricia Reuss, senior policy analyst with the NOW Legal Defense and Education Fund, "the large liberal advocacy organizations were a day late and a dollar short, and only came on board after 'Newt happened,' but it took them months to recover from the elections and begin realizing that the Personal Responsibility Act was getting passed as they maundered."[80]

So long as the details were not spelled out, nearly everyone was in favor of "reform." Thus, each side could read into a proposal to "end welfare as we know it" its own scenario. Advocates of the poor hoped for a program of stepped-up support for child care, education, training, and possibly even job creation. Hillary Rodham Clinton's advocacy of children as a board member of the Children's Defense Fund gave them some reason to hope. Conservatives, on the other hand, pictured something on the order of Charles Murray's and Lawrence Mead's prescriptions: a temporary-support program designed to expel people as quickly as possible into the private labor market while at the same time regulating their personal behavior. To still others, welfare "reform" was a code phrase for getting tough on blacks. The devil, as it turned out, would once again be in the details.

Peter Edelman, an assistant secretary in the U.S. Department of Health and Human Services, who resigned his post in 1996 over Clinton's signing of the new welfare law, argues that Clinton's first mistake was in calling for an end to the system before the Family Support Act even had a chance to be fully implemented. According to Edelman, it was a case of a campaign sound bite undermining the more nuanced policy planning Clinton had actually intended.[81] However, Clinton was no stranger to the problems associated with welfare "reform." His own attempts as governor of Arkansas to move welfare recipients into the labor market had been a failure.[82]

Clinton's idea for time-limited welfare reform had come from Harvard professor David Ellwood, whom Clinton had brought into the White House to design his program. Ellwood's plan, however, had called for a government commitment to provide the supports necessary to graduate women from welfare to work—child care, child support if fathers did not come through, transportation, training, health care, and, if necessary, jobs.[83] In 1994, wrote Edelman, Clinton clarified his stance on the 2-year time limit in proposed legislation (ignored by Congress) that would have continued welfare payments to recipients who played by the rules but who could not find jobs within that time.[84] But Clinton had already given conservatives an opening he could not close.

Despite Edelman's attempt to give Clinton the benefit of the doubt, Clinton's welfare plan was far tougher on welfare recipients than even President Reagan had proposed.[85] His first-term neoliberal economic program for reducing and "streamlining" government, reforming health care by keeping the private insurance industry satisfied, and providing a weak stimulus program and a tax break for the "middle class" was a continuation of the attack on government of the Reagan era. It was light years away from Roosevelt's visionary 1944 program for an Economic Bill of Rights. The notion that welfare reform ought to be just one part of a comprehensive antipoverty strategy had long since been abandoned, not only by conservatives, but also by many liberal Democrats. So, too, had the idea that cash benefits should be available on the basis of need, whether or not the recipient was deemed "capable" of working.[86] Both Nixon's Family Assistance Plan, coming near the end of a long period of New Deal policy ascendancy, and Carter's Better Jobs and Incomes Programs, their low annual income guarantees notwithstanding, now looked more progressive than the ideas being circulated by this "New Democrat" in the White House.

Thwarted by an increasingly powerful and cohesive Republican party and stymied by a deeply divided Democratic party, the president was unable to persuade Congress either to adopt his anemic economic stimulus program, which inspired a Republican filibuster but little else, or his proposal to put more money into job training and education. For most of his first term, however, Clinton was preoccupied with his clumsy and predictably unsuccessful attempt to pass a national health insurance plan.

Unable to give his own welfare reform proposal the attention it needed, Clinton took the expedient way out, implementing reform through the use of the executive waiver but in line with his preference for greater state discretion over welfare policy. This administrative procedure did not require him to win congressional approval. By granting waivers to the states for program innovations that diverged from federal guidelines, the administration sought to assure its Democratic constituency that some safety nets and national standards were being maintained and at the same time to accede to the devolutionary fever that had seized the Republican party. President Clinton could denounce various congressional Republican proposals for federal welfare reform as too Draconian, while at the same time giving the states permission to do almost everything he had criticized.[87]

But Clinton's desire to please both sides in the welfare debate only fed the growing Republican demand for outright welfare repeal. As Mark Greenberg, senior staff attorney at the Center for Law and Social Policy, observed, the waiver process "has been used to undercut basic safeguards of federal law, and this has contributed to the current environment in which states want no federal standards whatsoever."[88] Douglas Besharov, a policy analyst at the conservative American Enterprise Institute, confirmed this assessment. Besharov crowed that Clinton had accomplished through waivers what no Republican president could have achieved. "It's Nixon in China," he said. "If Clinton had been a Republican, the Democrats in Congress would have stopped these waivers in their tracks."[89]

While some of the inaction of Clinton's first administration

can be traced to his own character flaws (e.g., his need to please
all sides and to win at any cost), even more of it was institutional.
By 1993, responding to pressure from financial markets over rising national deficits, Congress had locked in permanent caps on
future entitlement and discretionary spending, leaving the president little room to maneuver and making it harder to deal with
social problems.[90] This became painfully evident in early 1994 as
the 32-member team Clinton had assembled to draft his welfare
overhaul scheme sought to fashion a plan that provided adequate
support for moving welfare recipients into jobs while adhering to
the budget limits—the illusion of cost-free welfare reform once
again. After a year of often intense internal debate, a consensus
emerged that it could not be done. Providing meaningful support
for single mothers—let alone creating sufficient jobs—would cost
far more (at least in the short-term) than either the administration
or the Republican Congress was willing to spend. Thus, the proposal finally submitted by the Clinton planners in June 1994 was
a greatly scaled-down version of their original plan. Even at that,
the Congressional Budget Office estimated it would cost nearly
$5 billion more than Clinton had allotted.[91]

From the New Deal to the Newt Deal

By November 1994, both the Democratic president and Congress had failed to offer, much less deliver, a visionary program
of economic growth and national revitalization. In their anxiety
over chronic economic stagnation, worsening conditions of work,
and a deterioration in the quality of life, where were Americans
to turn?[92]

Taking advantage of unprecedented media power to manipulate voters' economic anxieties and engage in scapegoat politics,
the Republicans swept the midterm elections in 1994, gaining not
only both houses of Congress (for the first time in 40 years) but
a net of 11 governorships and 15 state houses.[93] Compared with
the 1992 freshman congressional class, this one was even more
heavily skewed to the wealthy and privileged[94] and to a far Right
ideology that railed against "big government's" intrusion in economic affairs but not against its intrusion into the private morals
of women and the poor. Elected to Congress were 73 freshman
Republicans—most of them young, white, and male—who had been
in the vanguard of movements in their states to cut the federal

government and deregulate industry. Moreover, several had ties to the Christian Coalition and some to a more dangerous far Right paramilitary constituency whose antigovernment sentiments had been fostered by years of near-treasonous attacks on government by many who were in the government or had benefited from its largesse.

With control over appropriations and tax policy, the Republicans were now poised to complete the dismantling of the welfare state that they had begun under Reagan. The only possible fly in the ointment would be a veto from an unpopular president who had been running hard to catch up with the Republicans from the moment he came into office.

Pollsters found that only one-sixth of those who went to the polls in November 1994—themselves a minority of all eligible voters—regarded the outcome as "an affirmation of the Republican agenda." Nevertheless, the Republican leadership took the election as a mandate for its slash-and-burn policies.[95] With fanfare reminiscent of a presidential inauguration, Newt Gingrich, the triumphant Speaker of the House and the man who claimed to have created a Republican "revolution," opened the 104th Congress announcing the "Contract with America." The contract was a set of ten ideologically driven platform planks with implementing legislation that, if passed in their entirety, would have represented the most radical restructuring of government since the New Deal. Indeed, Gingrich frequently likened himself to Franklin Roosevelt, if only in the sweeping nature of the government reforms he proposed to pass within the first 100 days.

In contrast to the New Deal, however, the Contract offered no new efforts to prevent deepening poverty, inequality, economic stagnation, or global instability. Instead, it sought to undo the entire legacy of the two previous eras of progressive social reform and to propel the nation forward to a futuristic high-tech economy and backward to a nineteenth-century conception of government—one that served mainly to protect the interests of the rich and powerful. It did this, however, by cloaking itself in populist rhetoric that resonated with ordinary (mostly white) Americans who had been conditioned by almost two decades of anti-"big-government" rhetoric.

The Republicans chose several legislative strategies to accomplish their purpose. First, government spending (with the exception of the military budget) was to be cut. Second, much of the standard-

setting and regulatory authority that was left—especially for social programs—was to be turned over to the states.[96] Third, tax
reforms would redistribute wealth from the poor and middle classes
to the wealthy. Fourth, the regulatory process would be turned
inside out by requiring consumers and environmentalists to prove
that regulations would pass a rigorous cost-benefit analysis before any could be applied.[97] Finally, what states refused to do or
could not do would be left to the private sector.

The pretext for slashing government spending was, of course,
the ballooning national deficit and debt, which, as pointed out,
stemmed largely from Reagan's supply-side policies as well as from
unemployment. Characterizing the debt as a damocles sword hanging
over the heads of future generations, the Republicans—with help
from a number of their conservative Democratic colleagues—sought
to pass a Balanced Budget Amendment to the Constitution. The
amendment would have required the federal government to reduce
the debt to zero by 2002 and to maintain balanced budgets for
every year thereafter. Hardly a voice served to remind the budget
balancers that the debt was 51% of the GDP, compared to well
over 100% at the end of World War II, when it had ushered in an
era of prosperity and growth.[98]

Without the unanticipated, Wall Street-driven growth in the
economy that was to occur later in the 1990s, balancing the budget would have required over $1 trillion in spending cuts over the
next 7 years, a sum budget cutters had never before contemplated.
While poverty programs would suffer disproportionate cuts, without
even greater reductions in the military budget, every social program would eventually have to fall to the budget-cutters' axe:
education, health care, biomedical research, social services, housing,
transportation, the environment, the arts, and even the big prize
that had eluded David Stockman—Social Security. This, of course,
was one of the real intentions of those who proposed the balanced-
budget amendment in the first place, just as it was the intention
of those who created the deficit. As *New York Times* journalist
Jason DeParle observed, Gingrich's interest in a balanced budget
was more than fiscal. "It changes the whole game," Gingrich had
said. "You cannot sustain the old welfare state inside a balanced
budget."[99]

Indicative of the deficit obsession that had overtaken policymakers of both parties, the Balanced Budget Amendment, after passing
the House, was one vote short of Senate passage.[100] The narrow-

ness of the loss, however, virtually guaranteed its reintroduction and gave momentum to the Republican drive for budget reduction by other means.

Among the first, and disproportionately largest, targets for reduction were the safety-net programs for the poor and unemployed: AFDC, food stamps, school lunches, mother-and-child nutrition programs, home-energy assistance, and unemployment insurance. With the exception of Medicaid, SSI, food stamps, and school lunches (the last two of which were saved as federal entitlements largely because of lobbying by powerful agricultural and education lobbies), most of the categorical safety-net programs would be turned into block grants and sent to the states at reduced amounts. Republicans cast their strategy for "devolving power back to state and local governments" as a move toward democracy. Because they are closer to home, they argued, these governments were presumably more accountable to the people.

If balancing the budget were not enough to reduce the size of the federal government, the Republicans' tax-cutting proposals were designed to finish it off. Despite public-opinion polls showing Americans were more concerned with deficit reduction than tax cuts, Gingrich had committed Republicans to balance the budget and provide $189 billion in tax relief over 5 years.[101] Once again, the House Republican plan called for a Trojan horse in the form of a $500-a-year-per-child tax credit for the "middle class" as a way of making palatable a far heftier tax-relief package for the very rich. The Treasury Department, for example, found that about one-half the Contract's tax cuts would go to the richest 10% of U.S. families, and nearly 30% to the top 2%.[102] Some Republicans, however, were pushing to go even further. Majority leader Dick Armey proposed to junk the mildly progressive income-tax code for a regressive flat-tax scheme, while others suggested scrapping the income tax altogether and instituting an extremely regressive sales tax. "Our challenge," said Representative Bill Archer, chair of the House Ways and Means Committee, "is to do no less than pull the current income tax code out by its roots and throw it away so it can never grow back."[103]

The Senate, a more deliberative body led by "old guard" Republicans who had come to power during the waning days of New Deal policy hegemony, eventually modified some of the program cuts. The Senate was also reluctant to enact a tax cut before the budget was balanced. Nevertheless, the die had been cast. Whether or not the "big government" of the New Deal and Great Society eras was ever big enough in proportion to the needs of the nation, the very concept of big, compassionate government was now out; a leaner and meaner state was in.

In the spring and summer of 1995, as the public began to learn what the cutbacks would mean, protests by the poor, feminists, students, state workers, trade unionists, and liberal advocacy groups took place in cities across the country. Antipoverty advocates, who had been struggling for years to win incremental benefits, were left with no recourse but protest once they learned of the wholesale assault their political leaders were making on the disliked but essential AFDC and other poverty programs. But the protests were largely sporadic and uncoordinated, and the media barely paid attention.[104]

Other members of the liberal social-policy network—unions (with the exception of AFSCME, which represents public-service employees, including welfare caseworkers), civil-rights groups, some mainstream women's organizations, immigrant-rights groups— had not actively involved their constituencies in the early stages of the struggle.[105] A range of social-policy research and advocacy groups, like the Center on Budget and Policy Priorities, the Center for Law and Social Policy, the Welfare Law Center, the Urban Institute, and the Children's Defense Fund had sought to persuade Congress and state legislatures of the devastating social and economic costs of the Republicans' plans to balance budgets at the expense of the poor, the sick, and the elderly. But their carefully researched analyses fell on deaf ears and failed to reach the broader public where they might have generated some popular mobilization against the Republicans' agenda. Liberal policy analysts and lobbyists, used to working in an atmosphere where rational persuasion had a place in politics, were taken aback by the Republicans' adherence to emotionally laden mindsets about the poor. Said one such lobbyist, "it was the most difficult lobbying I have ever done. The vast majority of Republican officials simply were unwilling to accept what you said."[106]

Amid the din of Republican celebration, the Democrats' protests could barely be heard beyond the halls of Congress, and the protests, however strident, were enfeebled by media silence. Learning the lessons from their coverage of the Vietnam War protests, the corporate media had discovered they could "manufacture consent"[107] by ignoring dissident voices and distracting the public with daily soap operas of sex, scandal, and violence. Perhaps nothing is so indicative of the weakness of the opposition to the Republican's social agenda as the large Washington, D.C., rally organized by the Children's Defense Fund (CDF) in May 1996. Strongly opposed to "the Contract" and more quietly against time limits on receipt of welfare, CDF has been a consistent advocate for a wide range of antipoverty measures. Yet, while it was able to mobilize thousands of child advocates to descend on Washington, the CDF failed to send a strong political message that the end of an entitlement to government support would mobilize the advocacy community in an extended campaign of active resistance.[108]

From Welfare Reform to Welfare Repeal

Clinton's failure to pass his own welfare overhaul bill while he still had a Democratic Congress virtually guaranteed that the conservative Republicans would exploit his campaign slogan to "end welfare as we know it" to accomplish what they had always wanted: the end of the "culture of entitlement" for poor families with children. With the opening of the 104th Congress in January 1995, displaying all the fervor of the newly proselytized, House Republicans immediately began hearings on their own welfare bill, one of the planks in the Contract with America. As the debate got underway, four major areas of contention emerged. The first and most basic was the issue of entitlement itself. Many liberal Democrats and progressives were aghast at the implication: the end of any entitlement of the poor to government help. Twenty years earlier, former New Dealer and dean of social welfare lobbyists Elizabeth Wickenden had written: "The open-ended authorization [making possible an entitlement] is perhaps the most precious safeguard of individual rights in the present programs, especially for members of minorities and others subject to discriminatory attitudes."[109] Millions of children, the administration pointed out, would be denied benefits if the Republican time limit on benefits were to be enacted, evidently unmindful of the fact that their own president had originally suggested a 2-year time limit. Republicans countered that their welfare plan could increase suffering for some children and families in the short run but would help them in the long run by attacking the "culture of dependency."[110]

The debate was joined by Republican governors who argued that if given a block grant to replace several national entitlement

programs, they could design more effective programs while saving the federal government money. They even proposed freezing
federal welfare spending for several years. To many governors,
eager to increase their own power in the short-term while ignoring the long-term consequences, block grants seemed like the gift
of a lifetime. Yet, critics pointed out that block grants, which are
fixed amounts of money transferred from federal revenues to the
states, do not allow states to adjust to changes in either their fiscal
health (occasioned, for example, by large plant closings, natural
disasters, or demographic shifts) or to macroeconomic changes
such as inflation or recessions.[111] Thus, states could be forced to
choose between meeting the additional needs entirely with state
funds, cutting benefits for all poor families, or denying aid to newly
poor families.

Democratic Governor Howard Dean of Vermont argued that
block grants could further exaggerate the already unfair differences in benefits among the states, giving further discretion to those
states like Mississippi that are notoriously reluctant to help the
poor. Moreover, faced with an estimated annual loss of nearly $100
billion from cuts in federal aid to state and local governments over
the next 7 years, if the Republican "Contract" were to go through
as projected, state and local governments would almost certainly
either have to enact politically unpopular tax increases or slash
services that the middle class had come to expect, such as education, road maintenance, libraries, recreational and environmental
programs, and park maintenance.[112]

Critics further argued that state and local governments had rarely
protected the rights or interests of racial or other minorities—indeed they had often violated them. As Arthur Schlesinger, Jr., has
pointed out, "the growth of national authority [by which he means
the growth of federal welfare programs and federal restrictions on
state attempts to limit civil and political rights]. . . has given a
majority of Americans more personal dignity and liberty than they
ever had before."[113] Nor did history demonstrate that states were
any more accountable to their publics than the federal government.
In fact, most people knew less about their state legislatures than
they did about Congress; fewer people voted in state and local
elections; state tax systems were more regressive than the mildly
progressive federal income tax; and without strict campaign finance reform, lobbying by powerful special interests was just as
likely at the state as at the federal level. Not surprisingly, accord-

ing to Dona Hamilton and Charles Hamilton, civil-rights organizations "adamantly opposed any abdication of responsibility and authority over welfare programs by the federal government."[114]

Furthermore, faced with reduced federal funding, fewer federal regulations, and the pledge by many governors to reduce taxes, states were likely to engage in a race to the bottom when it came to funding services of any kind, let alone politically unpopular safety-net programs. However, all such criticisms fell on deaf ears as conservative Republicans now dominated not only the Congress, but also the National Governors' Association.

A second area of contention was over which pieces of the federal budget would be turned into block grants. Federal programs for the poor encompassed a wide spectrum. Some, like AFDC, were targeted at those thought to be typical of the welfare population—the "unworthy" poor. Others, like the food-stamp program, the school-lunch program, and various housing subsidies benefited many employed persons whose incomes were above the poverty line—a tacit admission by previous legislators that the labor market was, by itself, incapable of providing everyone who worked with a living wage. The question for Congress was which of these programs should remain grants-in-aid and entitlements, and which should be consolidated into block grants and turned over to the states.

In negotiations over the welfare bill, one of the subcommittees of the Republican-dominated House Economic and Educational Opportunities Committee went beyond even the Contract with America. It proposed consolidating nine categorical programs into three broad block grants, giving states responsibility for child care, school meals and various nutrition programs, and repealing all federal health and safety regulations for child care. "The Federal government simply cannot dictate every detail for every state and every local community . . ." said committee chairman, Bill Goodling (R-Pa.).[115] Some Democrats countered that Republicans were destroying successful and popular programs and that without federal oversight, states would abandon their responsibility for the health and safety of poor women and their children in favor of tax reduction. Some of them sought to modify the wholesale repeal of federal responsibility for such programs by offering amendments designed to retain some federal standards, but they were overwhelmingly outvoted. GOP moderates, who a few years before would have rejected such wholesale abandonment of federal protection, were in many cases now voting with their more conservative colleagues.

The third area of contention was over which population groups should be deemed eligible for continued aid. Anti-immigrant sentiment surfaced in Republican proposals to deny any kind of aid to illegal immigrants, all but emergency medical aid to legal non-immigrant foreign residents, and all aid to legal immigrants (with the exception of veterans, refugees, and those over the age of 75 who had lived in the United States for 5 years). Certain persons formerly eligible for SSI and Medicaid were also now deemed ineligible, such as those with a primary diagnosis of alcohol and drug addiction—and particularly heartless, a large category of disabled children, who would no longer qualify for SSI under new, more stringent definitions of "disability."

Still a fourth area of contention was over the Republicans' intention to use sanctions in the welfare bill to impose a two-parent family structure and moral standards on young people by denying, among other things, aid to unwed mothers under the age of 18 and giving cash bonuses to states that reduced their out-of-wedlock births. "The overall goal of federal policy must be to promote responsible parenthood," Robert Rector, a senior policy analyst with the conservative Heritage Foundation, told the legislators. "That means three things: Do not have a child until you are married. Do not have a child until you . . . have a reasonable expectation of supporting a family. . . . And do not have a child until you are . . . emotionally mature"—an admonition reminiscent of another poor-law reformer, Thomas Malthus.[116]

Some Democrats argued that denying aid to unwed mothers would hurt children who could not be held responsible for their parents' behavior. Some Republican antiabortion lawmakers, on the other hand, raised fears that denying cash assistance to unwed teenage mothers and rewarding states for reducing out-of-wedlock births could prompt more abortions. Still other critics, especially those who had done research on out-of-wedlock births, argued that there was no hard evidence that young women had babies so that they could collect meager welfare benefits. The decision of young women to have children, they pointed out, was a far more complex phenomenon that could not be solved simply by cutting off funds.[117]

One of the more controversial planks in the Republican proposal (eventually dropped because of public outcry) sought to deny welfare payments to unwed mothers and let states use the money to operate orphanages and group homes and to promote adoption.

Democratic opponents attacked the plan as Dickensian, demonstrating that orphanages would cost far more than current welfare benefits, and that the orphanage plan exposed the Republicans' hypocrisy regarding so-called "family values."[118] As discussed in Chapter 2, one of the major motivations for the enactment of mothers'-aid programs, the precursors of AFDC, was the determination, as expressed in the principles established in the White House Conference of 1909, that families should not be broken up and the children institutionalized for reasons of poverty alone.

Despite wide-ranging objections, not only from reputable poverty researchers and economic-policy analysts but from most of the country's major religious bodies,[119] on 24 March 1995, the House passed a bill by a 40-vote margin repealing the federal entitlement to welfare. Even the normally moderate *New York Times* had earlier described the proposed plan as "carnage."[120] The bill consolidated dozens of federal social-services programs into five block grants in predetermined lump sums. Cash benefits were to be denied to unwed mothers under 18, mothers already on welfare, noncitizens, drug and alcohol addicts, and many disabled children. As Democrats and some moderate Republicans assessed the damage, they sought to console themselves with the assumption that the more moderate Senate would modify some of the bill's harshest proposals.

But this assumption was ill-founded. In September 1995, 87 of the 100 senators voted to abandon federal welfare guarantees, passing their own bill that was only a little less onerous than the House measure. Republicans were joined by 3 out of every 4 Democrats, who were quoted as holding their noses while voting "yes" because this was "the best bill they could possibly get out of Congress."[121] President Clinton, characteristically talking out of both sides of his mouth, praised the Senate bill, saying that if the effort remained bipartisan, "we will have welfare reform this year, and it will be a very great thing. But if the Congress gives in to extremist pressure . . . they will kill reform."[122] Of the bill's passage, *New York Times* journalist Michael Wines observed: "So begins the final journey of the Great Society, with Lyndon Johnson's political progeny clambering aboard a bandwagon they could have steered but chose not to."[123]

The Senate bill, however, was not yet destined to be the final journey, for welfare reform was to become part of a much larger battle of political wills between the president and the Republican

Congress over balancing the budget. Republicans decided to include many of their welfare provisions in the budget reconciliation bill that came up for a vote later that fall. Reducing the federal deficit in 7 years as Republicans were pledged to do—while adding money to defense, cutting corporate taxes and capital gains for the rich—meant that they would have to cut or slow the growth in spending of everything else. Through an arcane rule associated with the budget reconciliation process, the Democratic minority succeeded at the last minute in eliminating many of the welfare bill's harshest measures—including the 5-year time limit. But Clinton had already vowed to veto the budget bill because it made too many extreme cuts—especially in Medicare, a politically popular program. By including the welfare measure in the budget bill, the Republicans sought to blame Clinton for vetoing a welfare bill he had said he could live with. Twisting the veto to his own purposes, however, Clinton claimed he vetoed the bill because it would impoverish more than a million children.

The Republicans sought to force Clinton into accepting their balanced budget plan by shutting down the government—first for 6 days in November 1995 and for nearly a month from mid-December to early January 1996. While Republicans had hoped to have it both ways—blaming Clinton for the shutdown but also using it to show that we do not need a federal bureaucracy—they quickly learned that the public did care about government. As people saw their relatives and neighbors—government employees—miss paychecks and as Social Security claims offices began to close down, they registered their protests in letters and visits to their representatives, on radio talk shows, and to the media. Moreover, as the budget stalemate dragged on, even a financial community that ordinarily lobbied against government intrusion began to get restive as markets tumbled and veiled hints circulated of international financial collapse if the United States failed to meet its debt payments.

It was one thing to attack government verbally, but it was another to shut it down. Forced to capitulate, the Republicans agreed to resume government functioning. A frontal assault, they had learned, would not work. From now on, they would have to resort to guerilla tactics, targeting for extinction those programs that had only limited or narrow support, while keeping programs that were more visible and popular with the middle class. As one journalist described it: "Call it the 'let 'em eat Vermeer' revolution. The middle class gets its passports and tourist sites; the poor fend for themselves; and corporate campaign contributors, free at last of federal regulation, grab everything that's not nailed down."[124]

It was, however, a pyrrhic victory for Clinton. During the course of the conflict, he had moved inexorably toward the Republican's demand for a balanced budget in 7 years, instead of the longer period he had originally proposed. Unwilling to raise taxes or to touch the defense budget, middle-class entitlements, or corporate perks (many of which were going to his high-flying campaign funders), Clinton, in time, would cave in totally to the Republicans' welfare repeal plan, which, in some important respects, was his own.

In January 1996, the Congress made another try at welfare reform, passing it as a separate piece of legislation. Clinton vetoed this one, saying "it does too little to move people from welfare to work," but also stating that "I strongly support time limits, work requirements, the toughest possible child support enforcement, and requiring minor mothers to live at home as a condition of assistance."[125] Yet, in his State-of-the-Union message, he proposed no new welfare-reform plan, simply urging Congress to send him a bipartisan bill he could sign.

In the third week of July 1996, both the House and Senate passed a third version of welfare repeal. The Senate vote was 74 to 24, with Democrats evenly split for and against. If liberal Democrats had hoped the Senate would produce a less punitive bill than that of the House, they were sorely mistaken. In all major respects the bills were identical: the repeal of a federal entitlement to welfare; the 5-year time limit; the work requirement for those on welfare; and the denial of aid to most legal immigrants.[126] Clinton pronounced the measures "much improved" and, as a sop to the more liberal wing of his party, suggested some amendments that he hoped would be taken up in the conference committee, knowing, however, that key legislators in both houses would oppose them. Jason DeParle, perhaps the most sensitive major-media journalist writing on welfare reform, put in perspective the significance of this last, desperate attempt to save face:

> As the movement to repeal welfare boiled across the Senate last week, a noteworthy chart appeared on the chamber floor. Decorated with a sketch of a creeping infant, it advertised a Democratic amendment to provide vouchers to those children—as many as four million—who could be dropped from government rolls if the bill becomes law.

Through an eerie enumeration, the poster specified what the vouchers could buy:

Clothing

Diapers

Cribs

Medicine

School Supplies

That the Democrats' hopes for the welfare poor has been reduced to a plan to salvage some diapers speaks volumes about the national debate. That the amendment failed says even more.[127]

The ambivalence and confusion within the administration over welfare repeal were reflected in the sharply differing opinions offered by members of the Clinton team. Said one of Clinton's welfare-policy officials, "I hope Armey [Representative Dick Armey, majority leader of the House] can push this bill to the Right in conference" so it will become unacceptable to the president. Some of Clinton's political advisers, on the other hand, said they hoped he would get a bill he could sign.[128]

The Final Act: Welfare's Repeal

By August 1996, the House-Senate conference committee had finished its work. The product, the Personal Responsibility and Work Opportunity Reconciliation Act (PRWORA), was called by Senator Moynihan "the most brutal act of social policy since Reconstruction" and "a social risk that no sane person would take."[129] Moynihan evidently overlooked his own role in creating the ideological momentum for welfare "reform." Indeed, the historical parallel between the "redemption" of southern Bourbon rule after the first Reconstruction and the triumph of racially coded class warfare overthrowing the gains of the "Second Reconstruction" (i.e., the 1960s civil rights/Great Society era) has not been lost on those who know their history.[130]

The PRWORA was approved by more than three-to-one majorities in each house. One-half of the House Democrats and slightly more than one-half of the Democratic senators voted for it. They sought to assuage their consciences over voting for a bill that repealed over 60 years of Democratic legislation in the twisted logic of Orwellian doublespeak. New York Democrat Gary Ackerman's excuse was indicative:

> This is a bad bill but a good strategy. In order to continue eco-
> nomic and social progress, we must keep President Clinton in
> office. . . . We had to show Americans that Democrats are will-
> ing to break with the past, to move from welfare to workfare.
> Sometimes in order to make progress and move ahead, you have
> to stand up and do the wrong thing. If we take back the House,
> we can fix this bill and take out some of the Draconian parts.[131]

Senator Barbara Mikulski (D-Md.), a former social worker for
Catholic Charities and the City of Baltimore, who had gotten her
start in politics as a representative of the working class, justified
her vote for the bill with the notion that the dysfunctional welfare system needed a "wake-up" call. "Without this bill would poor
children be better off? I'm not so sure," she opined.[132] Representative Lynn Rivers of Michigan, who, herself, had become a single
mother at the age of 18, voted for the bill because she did not
want to be seen as an "obstructionist."[133]

Some Democrats were still hopeful that President Clinton
would veto the bill. After all, the bill was little different from
the two he had vetoed previously. Such thinking, however, was
both wishful and naive. Throughout the drawn-out process of debate
over welfare reform, Clinton, who had come into office as a leader
of the conservative, Democratic Leadership Council, had moved
inexorably to the Right. Then, too, this was an election year.[134]
Speaking on condition of anonymity, one of Clinton's administration officials had earlier told the *New York Times*: "AFDC is
the bone that the Clinton White House can throw to the hounds
at the door, the people who want to make radical changes in the
welfare state."[135]

Thus, on 22 August 1996, President Clinton, always the political animal, threw that bone. As three handpicked former welfare recipients and a mostly Republican audience looked on, Clinton
signed the welfare bill in a Rose Garden ceremony, hailing the
decision as an historic chance to "recreate the nation's social bargain
with the poor." Several members of Clinton's welfare reform team
promptly resigned in protest,[136] although they had earlier participated in the waiver process. Welfare advocates, however, hardly
saw the bill as a positive chance to recreate the nation's social
bargain with the poor. Indeed, at the very moment of the Rose Garden
ceremony, they were protesting along the block north of the White
House."[137]

THE FAILURE OF LIBERAL-LEFT WELFARE REFORM

Although advocacy groups had lobbied to mitigate some of the most Draconian measures proposed by the Republican Congress and contributed to the successful efforts to preserve food stamps, SSI, and child welfare as entitlements, they were ultimately out-witted and outgunned by the opposition on AFDC. While the far Right was building a mass-based constituency, liberal advocacy groups for the poor were depending on their lobbyists in Washington to work the incremental changes in legislation and rule making that are the lobbyists' stock-in-trade. Their focus on the fine-tuning of welfare legislation rather than on the broader need for living-wage jobs had left them vulnerable and confused when welfare reformers became more serious about pushing welfare recipients into the labor market and later on simply getting them off the rolls. With the Republican victory in 1994, advocacy groups were left trying to bail out a sinking ship. Said one liberal lobbyist wistfully: "We lost a lot of friends on the Hill. Some Democrats rolled over and played dead. The mood of the country seemed to change in four years."[138]

Advocacy groups were also hampered by the comprehensiveness of the Republican assault. A number of them were organized around defined issues or constituency groups (for example, children, immigrants, people of color, people with disabilities, nutrition, welfare). Although the Washington-based Coalition on Human Needs served as a kind of coordinator, there was too little time to mount the kind of broad-based opposition that was needed. Sharon Daly, vice president for Social Policy of Catholic Charities USA, admitted that it was hard to develop strategies to counter the Republican offensives when "you were opposed to almost everything."[139] Another said she was not surprised about what happened to AFDC but was not expecting the severity of the attack on other programs that served less-stigmatized groups.[140] The director of the Children's Defense Fund's Family Income Division expressed the dilemma her organization faced in May 1996 when they organized their Stand for Children rally. This was "a point of agonizing around here" she said:

> We had a very broad range of participants, were reaching out to new groups like the Girl Scouts, and really were constrained by the coalition-type structure to pitch it very politically. We hoped

this would broaden our constituency over the long run. We're
not sure what was right, whether it will pay off.[141]

The work issue posed difficulties for some of these advocates
and their organizations. Perhaps reflecting the split between economic and social policies that characterized U.S. domestic policy,
most organizations advocating for the poor were narrowly focused
on income support. They tended to call attention to the paucity of
jobs in the U.S. economy in order to discredit work requirements
in welfare-reform proposals rather than to advocate the expansion of employment opportunities that would have benefited both
poor men and women—whether or not they were on welfare. Advocating for jobs, some feared, might make it seem as if they had
joined the camp of favoring the punitive work requirements envisioned by the Republicans. There was concern about the quality of those jobs or work slots, concern that if the work slots were
created, cash assistance would be contracted, and fear about how
mandatory programs were often implemented.[142] Jennifer Vasiloff,
former executive director of the Coalition on Human Needs, reflected on the lessons of welfare reform: "We learned we need to
place bigger emphasis on employment issues and strategies, to
increase opportunities for jobs for lower-skilled folks, and to improve
the lower-wage labor market in general."[143] Catholic Charities USA,
however, was one organization that took the position that "all people
should have the opportunity to participate in our economic system" and that it was necessary to "make work pay."[144]

It might be assumed that welfare reform would have posed a
different dilemma for women's organizations from that confronted
by some of the welfare-rights and antipoverty groups. After all,
employment has been viewed as a sign of women's liberation, and
equality for women in the labor market has been a major focus of
feminism. Why would the movement want to support what amounted
to the right of some women not to work? On the other hand, some
feminists have objected that women's care work should be counted
and compensated. At least in the final years of the assault, if not
earlier, a number of women's organizations opposed welfare "reform."
One visible sign of this was a full-page ad in the *New York Times*
with the title, "A War against Poor Women Is a War against All
Women." The argument was that welfare is the "ultimate security
policy of every woman in America," a means of escaping a brutal
relationship or protection in a job market hostile to women.[145] Although
NOW President Patricia Ireland attracted media attention for a White

House vigil when PRWORA was signed (for which traditional antipoverty advocates were grateful), preserving the entitlement to welfare never gained support among women comparable to that of the annual pro-choice marches in Washington organized by the National Abortion Rights Action League. One reason is that most nonpoor women probably do not feel that welfare is their ultimate security. It is a program for the poor, not for them. Means-tested programs for the poor alone are politically vulnerable for this reason.

Given the disproportionate numbers of blacks on welfare, it is not surprising that civil-rights groups were more consistent in their opposition to the kind of welfare reform that had been proposed for the last 30 years. Yet, despite their testifying repeatedly to that effect,[146] even they shrank from proposing—much less mobilizing grassroots support for—a broad program of guaranteed jobs at decent wages at the time welfare reform was on the agenda. Perhaps, in the conservative climate of the 1980s and 1990s, they felt they would be a voice crying in the wilderness, abandoned even by their traditional allies in the Democratic party. At least that is how the following statement, made in an Urban League document, might be interpreted. "The political climate did not lend itself to an NUL policy that called for a national guaranteed income and full-employment plan to eradicate poverty. To have offered such a proposal . . . would have rendered NUL irrelevant."[147] Thus, to maintain what small leverage they had left, they lobbied in the period before passage of the Family Support Act of 1988 for cost-neutral administrative regulatory changes in the support programs needed to move the most disadvantaged welfare recipients into the labor market—preemployment education and training, child care, transportation, and Medicaid coverage.[148] On the eve of passage of the PRWORA, realizing that the modest changes it had lobbied for had been mostly rejected and that the welfare entitlement would be repealed, the Urban League turned its attention to the question of public job creation.[149] But by then the die had been cast.

Recipient groups, subjected to a relentless Right-wing and media campaign to stigmatize them still more, and without the commitment of resources from more powerful groups that they had enjoyed for a brief period in the rights-conscious 1960s, were, for the most part, not active in their own defense. Those who would pay the heaviest price for welfare reform had no impact on the national debate.

Summary: The Failure of the Liberal Imagination

That the 30-year effort to "reform" welfare ended in its repeal is a product of the political genius of the emerging Republican majority in dressing up in new clothes both shop-worn ideas and failed policies (aided, it is important to note, by millions of dollars in corporate campaign contributions and conservative foundation grants). By the same token, it is the failure of liberal Democrats and foundations to seize on, market, and update the idea of government-guaranteed full employment. This was proposed at various moments in our history, but never enacted. The failure of liberal policymakers and interest groups to mount a strong counteroffensive and of liberal interest groups to unite and mobilize around a program of jobs for all at living wages not only contributed to punitive welfare "reform" but to Democratic defeats in Congress that delivered the votes for repealing the entitlement to government help. During Reagan's presidency, historian Arthur Schlesinger, Jr., wrote that the Democratic party "should dispel the current notion that it is the party of welfare and . . . recover its old identity as the party of jobs."[150] Instead, it became the party of neither.

CHAPTER 8

Washington's New
Poor Law: Part I

The ostensible purpose of the Personal Responsibility and Work Opportunity Reconciliation Act (PRWORA) was to end "welfare dependency" by enabling welfare recipients to graduate into the world of productive and family-supporting work. Presumably, this would eventually result in higher income, new self-esteem, and more "responsible" behavior for these former recipients. Almost 1 year after implementation of the program, Health and Human Services Secretary Donna Shalala pronounced it a roaring success. "Millions of people are moving off welfare," she boasted. "We have the lowest rates we've had since 1969. And the message from the private sector today is that people are not only taking jobs, but they're staying in the jobs at higher rates than other employees coming in."[1]

Secretary Shalala's comments were at best a bit of wishful thinking and at worst an example of the elaborate set of euphemisms and selective use of statistics that have distorted the welfare reform debate from the beginning. To properly evaluate the PRWORA's "success" requires a much more complex analysis than looking only at roll reductions or concluding on the basis of a fraction of the entire caseload that the welfare-to-work programs are indeed working.[2]

Chapters 8 and 9 examine the numerous economic, political, and ethical problems associated with the bill. This is not meant to be a definitive evaluation. Final regulations determining the implementation of the law were not issued until April 12, 1999, and did not go into effect until October 1, 1999. Dozens of discrete studies of the bill's effects are underway across the country, and the full effects will not be known for at least 5 years after implementation. Nevertheless, there is sufficient evidence from the state waiver experiments that preceded it, the results of preliminary studies conducted during the first 3 years of implementation, and the provisions of the bill itself to know that there are problems on the horizon.

In this chapter, after an analysis of the law itself, we take up problems associated with the end of a federal entitlement to poor relief and the dubious assumptions built into the law about the capacity of the labor market to provide self-sufficiency for all of the welfare recipients who will be expected to work in it. In Chapter 8, we look at the law's provision for the kinds of supportive services needed to make a work program successful and at the combined effects of welfare repeal with cuts in other safety-net programs, as well as at the discriminatory impact of welfare reform on particular populations.

The Personal Responsibility and Work Opportunity Reconciliation Act: What Does It Do?

The TANF block grant repealed the entitlement to federal government assistance for poor women and their children.[3] Welfare benefits for families have always been meager, but lifetime limits on the receipt of TANF deprive poor women and their children of the modicum of security they once had. Families lose TANF benefits after 5 years (states are allowed a 20% exemption for hardship cases), whereas the only time limit on the receipt of AFDC was the age of the youngest child in the family. Moreover, the TANF time limits are to be imposed, regardless of whether jobs are available for the parents whose benefits expire. The new law also has strict work requirements for recipients while they are on relief, frequently forcing them to enroll in "workfare" programs that require them to work off their benefits. Because the PRWORA was silent about whether such programs were subject to the Fair Labor Standards Act, until the Labor Department ruled that they were, many welfare recipients began to work under conditions that often violated labor laws and paid them no more than their welfare checks.[4]

In contrast to categorical grants-in-aid like AFDC, block grants are intended to give substantial discretion to the states. In certain areas, this has resulted in positive state innovations. For example, under the old law, welfare applicants were restricted to assets worth $1,000, thus forcing them to pauperize themselves in order to claim welfare. Under the PRWORA, states were allowed to

increase the asset limits; by 1999, 39 states had done so. The
PRWORA also eliminated the federal requirement that states impose
extra eligibility restrictions on two-parent families, a requirement
that effectively confined relief to single-parent families. In 1999,
35 states treated eligibility for two-parent families the same as
for single-parent families, although the PRWORA places stricter
work requirements on two-parent families. A number of states
also increased the earnings disregard level (the amount that can
be earned before benefits are reduced) above that allowed by the
previous law.[5]

However, certain features of TANF—the definition of work activity, the proportions of the caseload to which work requirements
apply, and the amount of time recipients must spend on these "jobs"—
regulate the states more strictly than did AFDC.[6] The Social Security Act limited the harshness of the states in some important
respects, but PRWORA binds them in the opposite direction.[7]

In addition to TANF, the new welfare law repealed Emergency
Assistance for Families and the Jobs Opportunity and Basic Skills
(JOBS) program that had been enacted less than a decade ago as
a means of encouraging the states to provide employment and training
to welfare recipients. In addition, it imposed work requirements
on adult food-stamp recipients who are neither elderly, disabled,
nor rearing dependent children. Also singled out for punishment
were most legal aliens whose rights to primary public benefit programs
had, since passage of the Social Security Act, been basically the
same as citizens. Immigrants who come legitimately to our shores
were barred for 5 years from receiving food stamps or Supplemental Security Income (SSI), the assistance program for needy
persons who are elderly, blind, and disabled. States were given
the choice of deciding current immigrants' eligibility for TANF,
nonemergency medical services under Medicaid, and public social services.[8] A year after passage of the bill, in response to a
wide range of pressure, Congress restored SSI benefits to some
categories of legal immigrants, but the basic restriction on legal
immigrants' rights persists.[9]

The Work Requirement: What Does the Law Say?

While turning over most authority for reforming welfare to the
states, the new poor law revealed its true intentions in the strict
work requirements for which it holds states accountable. Under

TANF, within the first year of implementation, states were required to move 25% of the adults or minor parents in their single-parent caseloads into approved "work activity" and 50% by the year 2002. Two-parent families are held to an even stricter requirement: 75% in fiscal year 1997–1998 and 90% thereafter. Thus, the penalty for two-parent families persists in this form. States have the option of exempting from work requirements single parents with a child under the age of 1 year, but parents can only receive this exemption for a total of 12 months, regardless of whether they are consecutive. Many states, however, decided not to exercise this option, presumably using the threat of work as a deterrent to further childbearing. Five states provide no exemption for the age of a child.[10]

Welfare recipients were required to work a minimum of 20 hours a week for the first 2 years of the law's operation, rising to 30 hours by the year 2000. States have the option of limiting the required hours of work per week for every fiscal year to 20 hours for single parents of a child under the age of 6. In two-parent families, both parents must work—one for 35 hours and the other for at least 20 hours per week.

The law defined "work activity" as any of the following: unsubsidized employment; subsidized private-sector employment; subsidized public-sector employment; work experience if sufficient private-sector employment is unavailable; on-the-job training; job readiness and job-search assistance; community-service programs; vocational educational training; job skills directly related to employment; education directly related to employment or satisfactory attendance at a secondary school for recipients under 20 who lack a high school education; and providing child care to another recipient who is engaged in community-service programs.

The law required states to reduce or deny aid to recipients who refuse to participate in work activity, subject to good cause and other exceptions determined by the state. Thus, states are allowed considerable discretion. However, if a family's aid is reduced or denied, the entire family is affected. This is a big change. Under the old law, if a parent failed to comply with the rules without good cause, grants could be reduced only by the amount attributable to the noncomplying recipient, and conciliation processes were required to try to secure cooperation before the sanction could be imposed.[11] Under the new law, dependent children can be penalized. States may also terminate Medicaid coverage for adults (but

not for their children) whose benefits are terminated due to refusal to work. They may not, however, penalize a single parent
caring for a child under 6 years old if the parent proves he or she
failed to work because child care was unavailable. This, of course,
will be difficult to prove and could lead to some dangerous abuses
as a public television documentary aired in 1998 demonstrated.[12]
Will a mother have to accept any child-care arrangement the state
proposes, even if she feels it is inadequate and may be harmful to
her child?

States that fail to meet the work-requirement quotas will have
their federal grants reduced; but they may reduce their required
participation rates in any year if they reduce their average monthly
caseloads below fiscal year 1995 levels. This is an enormous incentive for states to reduce their caseloads regardless of whether
welfare recipients find jobs or not. It is a reverse of the previous
legislation, which encouraged states to do more—at least up to
federal matching limits. These are the broad outlines of the welfare-to-work program. In the details of implementation lurk a host
of problems.

The End of Entitlement: Will the States
Do a Better Job?

The first set of problems with the new Poor Law involves the
decision to end the federal entitlement to welfare by consolidating several categorical aid programs into a few block grants. Unlike
categorical grants, which are carefully targeted and designated
for specific purposes by the federal government, block grants give
states broad discretion in the use of the money. Under the old
categorical aid programs, no state had provided welfare benefits
large enough to raise families above the federal poverty level.[13]
Nevertheless, the AFDC grant-in-aid, for all its shortcomings, held
the states to important standards that protected clients. For example, in 1950, when Congress required that all individuals wishing
to apply for ADC should have the opportunity to do so and should
be aided if they met eligibility conditions, the program became
an entitlement. This meant that it was more likely that there was
some kind of cash safety net available if recipients played by the
rules. As we pointed out in Chapter 2, the requisite that benefits
be in cash was one of the important, progressive provisions of the
Social Security Act. Under PRWORA, states are free not only to

determine the eligibility rules and definitions of need, but also to transfer money from cash assistance to various noncash media, such as vouchers and subsidies to employment or service providers.

In 1970, the Supreme Court ruled in *Goldberg v. Kelly* that the Constitution's due process clause entitled welfare recipients to notice and a fair hearing before an administrative judge prior to being terminated from AFDC.[14] Although Congress had not amended the Social Security Act to reflect the Court's decision, the Department of Health and Human Services (DHHS) did adopt the *Goldberg* decision in its federal regulations.[15] Now, with no clearly articulated uniform standards by which to judge what is fair, legal challenges to state authorities or abusive local officials have to be fought out city-by-city and state-by-state. According to Mark Greenberg of the Center for Law and Social Policy, in some instances there may even be no legal basis for a challenge to abusive state or local action.[16] Legal challenges were made even more difficult when the same Congress that passed welfare "reform" forbade legal services corporations from handling class-action suits as well as from challenging welfare "reform."[17]

Although the new law gave states freer rein with the money, the strict time and work-related requirements that bind states violate the spirit of a block grant. Moreover, under the old law, federal requirements tried to assure some measure of economic fairness for welfare recipients, although many states balked at meeting them. The new requirements, however, have a different purpose: to get welfare recipients into the labor market as quickly as possible, regardless of the consequences for families or individuals.

OUT OF SIGHT, OUT OF MIND

Within the first 2 years of implementation of the PRWORA, it appeared that the states were only too willing to adhere to these new requirements. Across the country, states bragged about how they had reduced their welfare rolls, as if declining rolls were the main measure of the program's "success." A press release issued by the nation's governors 2 years into welfare reform hailed the pace and initial success of welfare reform, declaring that it had "far exceeded expectations of proponents and skeptics alike."[18] Indeed, family caseloads nationwide fell 47% from August 1996 through December 1999.[19] Dramatic reductions in caseloads, however, do not in themselves offer proof that welfare "reform" has worked.

As the DHHS pointed out, fluctuations in the rolls have usually mirrored changes in national economic conditions, with increases during times of recession and decreases during times of growth and high employment. Other factors unrelated to welfare rules also influence welfare recipiency, such as changing family structures, immigration, and demographic shifts.[20]

During the first 2–3 years of welfare "reform," there was little information on those who disappeared from the rolls. The TANF statute allowed for a phase-in of state data reporting requirements to the DHHS based on when a state implemented its TANF program. States were slow in reporting what was happening to welfare recipients who left the rolls, and, in addition, the reporting system designed by the DHHS posed significant initial challenges to states and to the department itself.[21] Consequently, during the first 2 years of welfare reform, few states were properly tracking recipients who left the rolls.[22] Moreover, public officials in some states even refused to provide independent researchers with the records that would allow them to conduct their own surveys.[23] For many of these families, the strong economy was no doubt responsible, as it has always been, for providing a way off welfare, but it is likely that many others fell into an abyss of deeper poverty.[24] As Christopher Cook has pointed out "in the cold calculus of welfare reform, a closed case means success, regardless of what happens to the recipient."[25]

Although DHHS urged that caution be taken in drawing conclusions from what preliminary data were collected, records from at least 18 early state studies analyzed by the General Accounting Office (as well as from court cases, newspaper articles, and reports from social-service agencies), welfare recipients and others in the field paint a different picture from the upbeat one given by Secretary Shalala and the nation's governors. Most states, it appeared, were using sanctions for rule infractions much more aggressively than they had in the past,[26] and many, in the deterrence mode of the poor laws, were discouraging families from even applying for welfare in the first place. According to some researchers, it is likely that those who were most in need of welfare may have fallen into these two camps.[27]

In Missouri, for example, thousands of welfare recipients were cut from the rolls for refusing to take jobs in one of two of the state's major industries: poultry plants and hog slaughterhouses, where assembly-line jobs require workers to process animal parts at breakneck speed under dangerous and dirty conditions.[28] States were also moving their caseloads into work or work-related programs as quickly as possible, and many were less willing than under the previous legislation to exempt from the work requirement adults with physical and mental impairments and, as we noted, those with very young children.[29]

The preliminary record on job placement looked somewhat hopeful. According to the first comprehensive federal government study of the law's effectiveness, the states had exceeded their mandatory participation rates. An average of 28% of adults on the welfare rolls were engaged in some form of work activity 1 year after the law's passage. "The welfare reform law was designed to promote work, and that's exactly what's happening," boasted Clinton's domestic policy advisor, Bruce N. Reed.[30] Statistics from 18 state follow-up studies revealed even higher numbers—between 61% and 87% finding jobs in a survey published in 1998, and between 50% and 70% in a survey published in 1999.[31] But these figures must be put into perspective. The jobs were not necessarily permanent, and 11 of the 18 studies published in 1998 used samples that were not representative of the entire state's welfare population. The 1999, 18-state survey reported that the 50–70% work rate was around 5–10% higher in a time of record-low overall unemployment than the proportion of recipients who left welfare for jobs under the old AFDC program. The GAO reported that these employment rates "generally exclude families who returned to welfare, which can be a substantial portion of the families who leave welfare."[32]

WORKING IN POVERTY AND INTO DEEPER POVERTY

While some data were collected on former recipients' earnings, the studies did not provide a complete story of hourly wages, number of hours worked, or total family and child well-being.[33] No doubt, the better educated were able to find family-supporting jobs, as they always were in a time of economic growth. And a study of New Jersey welfare leavers showed that tight labor markets enabled 40% of even the lowest-paid to increase their earnings by at least 50%.[34]

But despite increased state efforts to "make work pay," other studies were not as hopeful.[35] Although former recipients tended to work a substantial number of hours—typically more than 30 a week—most were earning less than the poverty level for a family of three, and few received paid vacations, sick leave, or employer-sponsored health insurance or pension plans.

Moreover, most families continued to rely on other forms of public help like food stamps, Medicaid, and child care as well as on family and friends. Between 19% and 30% of these families returned to welfare within a few months.[36] A New York State survey showed that nearly three-fourths of the 480,000 people who had left the rolls of AFDC and Home Relief (general assistance) between July 1996 and March 1997 had not found jobs at all. When New York City's caseload was considered by itself, the percentage without jobs was even higher; and because of the way in which "employment" was defined in the survey (anyone who made $100 or more in 3 months after leaving the rolls), the number of individuals and families suffering severe economic deprivation was probably even greater.[37]

A public television documentary that aired on June 5, 1998,[38] put a human face on the figures behind these statistics. The program followed six women in three states who were facing their states' time limits, all of which were shorter than the federal 5-year limit. The report documented how the approach and then the reality of the welfare cutoffs affected them, providing some insight into what may be the fate of millions of others as the 5-year time limit approaches. Each of these women, faced with a daunting set of multiple handicaps, had made valiant efforts to find jobs, child care, transportation, and help to resolve their problems, which ranged from the lack of a high school education to depression and drug addiction. Yet, by the time they were supposed to become "self-sufficient," not one had a job that promised to lift her out of poverty, and some, although working, were worse off than they had been on welfare, having to depend on food pantries to get their families through the week. Moreover, none of them expected ever to be able to climb out of poverty because of the nightmare of "Catch-22" situations they experienced as they sought to conform to the harsh rules of the new system.

A trend toward deepening poverty among some who leave the rolls is being tracked by a number of organizations. According to the Children's Defense Fund and the National Coalition for the Homeless, among those working and earning money, many were earning *less* than they were before welfare reform went into effect and were increasingly unable to pay for food or rent. Increases in extreme poverty—that is, incomes below one-half the poverty line—were most common among families who were most likely to be moving from welfare to work—single-mothers with some work experience during the year. The Center on Budget and Policy Priorities, blaming the erosion of safety nets, reported that average incomes of the poorest 20% of single-mother families fell from 1995 to 1997, despite a robust economy.[39] Surveys of selected cities conducted each year by the U.S. Conference of Mayors have found increasing uses of food pantries and homeless shelters since welfare repeal was implemented. The majority of the mayors queried in 1997 said that they thought welfare reform played either a major role or was one of several factors causing the increase in hardship. In 1999 and 2000, for example, emergency food assistance increased by an average of 18% and 17%, respectively, over the previous year, and requests for food assistance by families with children increased by an average of 15% and 16%, respectively. Thirty-two percent of those seeking food in 2000 were employed, and 62% of them were families with children. The average demand for shelter in 2000 increased by 15% and for homeless families by 17%—the highest 1-year increase in a decade.[40] New York, with one of the highest welfare caseloads in the nation, was not among the cities responding to the mayors' surveys. But an examination of 13 different studies of New York's welfare leavers revealed even higher levels of reliance on emergency feeding and shelter programs than the national averages. The conclusion of the researchers was that "the [human] consequences go beyond any legitimate vision of welfare reform."[41]

This increased evidence of poverty may be explained by the first national study to test whether each state's new policy choices represent a greater or lesser investment in economic security for recipients than the previous system had provided. Conducted by Tufts University's Center on Hunger, Poverty, and Nutrition Policy, the study showed that more than two-thirds of the states have implemented welfare policies that will make the economic situations of families worse than under the old welfare system. Although conducted quite early in the game, the fact that the Tufts study measured each state's commitment to policies that past research has shown can enhance or inhibit economic security gives the report credibility. Hence, its results are early-warning signals to the policy community. A subsequent report released by the Tufts Center in January 2000 found that despite a continuing economic boom, hunger was becoming such an acute problem that a significant proportion of working families were relying on soup kitchens and food banks to feed themselves. Of families leaving welfare,

the Tufts Center's report that 38% struggle to provide food for
their children.[42]

Another particularly disturbing outcome of welfare "reform"
has been the drop in the number of families receiving Medicaid
and food stamps. While all families with incomes below 33% of
the federal poverty level are eligible for Medicaid, prior to passage of the PRWORA, if a family became eligible for AFDC, it
was automatically put on Medicaid. The PRWORA, however, separated
eligibility for Medicaid from cash assistance. The welfare bill requires
states to continue Medicaid eligibility for every family that meets
the AFDC eligibility criteria used by the state on July 16, 1996
(with the exception of a TANF client who refuses to work). However, researchers have found that many families who leave the rolls
for work were not told by state authorities that they could still collect
Medicaid and food stamps, and many who were diverted from the
rolls did not learn that they might qualify for these benefits.[43] Since
few of the jobs welfare recipients get pay benefits, let alone wages
high enough to afford health care, the health and nutritional needs
of the nation's poor may be declining seriously.

Benefit levels have always varied from state to state, but now
states can differ on a number of other dimensions such as providing benefits in cash. As many states seek to transfer responsibility
for welfare to lower levels of government, wide disparities are
showing up not only between states but within them as well.[44] For
example, differences in the use of eligibility criteria were found
among counties in Alabama with the result that some deterred people
from applying for welfare, while others, using the same rules, declared them eligible.[45]

Idaho's story provides a dramatic example of how one state's
rosy economic statistics can hide the darker reality of life for the
poor. Idaho brags that it has one of the fastest growing economies,
the lowest unemployment rate, the lowest crime rate, and the steep-
est drop in welfare rolls in the nation—77% since 1994; but its
incarceration rate is the third highest in the country and has increased
dramatically. Idaho spends about 5 times as much on keeping people
in prison as it does for overall child welfare (in which it is second
to last in the country). In 1998, the state was spending over 13 times
as much to build a new privately operated prison as it was on overall payments to the poor. It should be no surprise that its rate of
child abuse and neglect was 3 times the national average, and that
60% of its fourth grade pupils read below their grade level.[46]

As critics have pointed out, wider state leeway in the expenditure of funds for the poor could result in a race to the bottom. Currently, several states have been providing more generous benefits than others, thanks to a strong economy and surplus funds that have accrued as a result of declining rolls. But if the economy should turn sour, few states, counties, or cities will want to become a mecca for welfare recipients by offering more generous benefits or conditions than others.[47] Before the PRWORA went into effect, several states had already imposed shorter time limits and more restrictive policies than the federal law requires, and several had reduced the amount of the welfare grant.[48]

THE END OF RED TAPE?

There is no doubt that the old welfare program was oppressive and frustratingly bureaucratic. However, shifting responsibility to the states does not necessarily get rid of the red tape associated with welfare bureaucracies. In fact, it may only increase it, as eligibility rules, time limits, requirements for compliance, and other procedures have become a tangle of thousands of different signals. Devolution of responsibility has not only moved from federal to state, but from state to county and municipal governments and even to private companies.[49]

The new law required a massive shift in the culture, the infrastructure, and expectations of the social service establishment. This required a new set of skills, expertise, training, and services that most systems were ill-equipped to provide. Indeed, as welfare "reform" went into effect, anecdotal evidence of heightened tension and hostility between welfare recipients and equally confused and frustrated local welfare officials appeared to increase.[50] Supporters of Wisconsin's vaunted welfare reform program, W-2, were forced to admit that its "celebrated effort bears only an intermittent likeness to the program of customized employment services outlined in planning documents and praised from the Oval Office on down."[51] Two years into welfare "reform," advocates for the poor in Missouri found that 50% of the paperwork needed to process clients was overdue.[52] A *New York Times* reporter observed that in New York City, where welfare centers have been converted into "job centers," the name change involved little more than political posturing. A draft memo included in a training manual for workers described employment as a "secondary goal," the first being to discourage the poor from applying for welfare in the first place.[53]

Since more decision making is now vested in varying levels of state and local government, the changes introduced are necessarily more complex and involve increased discretion. While a vast research industry is now underway, researchers will have more difficulty evaluating the effectiveness of welfare repeal and making cross-state comparisons than under the old plan.[54]

BLOCK GRANTS: A TICKING ECONOMIC TIME BOMB

Another major problem with block grants is that, unlike the federal entitlement, they do not rise and fall with need. What was once an open-ended grant has been turned into a fixed sum provided annually to the states for 6 years. The formula for what each state receives is based on its federal funding for AFDC benefits and administration, emergency assistance, and the JOBS program in either fiscal years 1995 or 1994, or the average of fiscal years 1992–1994, whichever is higher.

Under the old program, states that spent more for the poor were rewarded with a proportionate increase in federal funding, although matching formulas limited how much the federal government would pay per recipient. However, under the new law, there is no incentive for states to spend more. In order to receive their full share of funds, states are required to spend only 75% of their own fiscal year 1994 expenditures (this is termed "maintenance of effort"), while moving a rising percentage of their caseloads into work or work-related programs; otherwise they face financial penalties.

As they reduce their welfare rolls, states are free to shift a substantial percentage of the money they formerly contributed to welfare into other programs or not to spend it at all. States can transfer up to 30% of the TANF grant into the Child Care Block Grant or the Social Services Block Grant. These block grants represent other pieces of the patchwork of laws and programs that, together, make up welfare "reform." However, states are not required to reserve these funds for TANF recipients only. Thus, Congress provided an incentive for states to move people off the TANF rolls so they can free up that money for other purposes. Some states have been only too willing to use this incentive. A study by the National Campaign for Jobs and Income found that despite the fact that poverty remains high and, for some families, poverty has deepened, 45 states as of September 1999 had at least some unspent TANF money, and a few were using it to pay for tax cuts and other programs that do not benefit poor families. New York, for example, was one of six states to use TANF funds to reduce its own spending on welfare and the state Earned Income Tax Credit.[55]

The assumption behind this policy is that as states move more of their TANF caseloads into the labor market, there will be a reduced need for federal funds. Indeed, many states complained that they were prevented from achieving greater savings because they had to comply with "maintenance of effort" requirements, even though their caseloads decreased dramatically.[56] In 1998, more than one-half the states were unwilling to spend all of the federal money available to them, and six states refused to apply for any of the $3 billion available for welfare-to-work grants for the hardest to employ—this, despite evidence that some families that had left the rolls were falling into deeper poverty.[57] Some states claimed that they simply could not develop programs fast enough to use the money, others said that the "problem" for which the funds were earmarked had disappeared, while others said they were saving the funds for a rainy day. It appeared, 2–3 years into welfare "reform" that states were counting on that unused balance to meet the needs of their poor should a recession occur but were unwilling to re-serve their own funds for such a purpose.[58]

While saving for a rainy day is a laudable purpose, the best way to prevent that rainy day from being worse than it could be is to provide real opportunities for upward mobility for those in poverty now. Moreover, if the money sits unused in Washington, Congress is likely to conclude that it has other uses for it or to give it back as tax relief. Indeed, in March 1999, the Senate Appropriations Committee approved a supplemental appropriations bill that included a $350 million cut in TANF funds as an offset for new spending.[59]

The assumption that states will no longer need federal help for welfare recipients bears examining. Both Congress and state officials seemed to think when they passed the law that the economic growth with low inflation that the nation was experiencing in the latter half of the 1990s would continue indefinitely. The optimism of state officials was buoyed by reduced caseloads resulting from both economic expansion and more restrictive state welfare policies. As a result, for the early years of reform, states were getting more money per recipient than they had been getting in the past.

Yet, neither history nor recent experience warrants such economic optimism. Prior to the stabilizing effects of the New Deal programs, the "free market" produced depressions about every 20 years. Without the purchasing power provided by the Social Security Act, the United States might have faced far more severe recessions in the intervening years than it has to date. In passing the PRWORA, Congress seems to have forgotten not only the lesson of the 1930s, but also our own recent experience with severe recessions, as documented in Chapters 5 and 6.

The federal government set aside $2 billion (over 5 years) in a contingency fund, and the unused TANF fund balance is about $3 billion. Yet even if Congress decides not to use that balance for something else, it is doubtful that the combined amount—$5 billion—would be enough in another recession. During the last one, welfare costs rose by $6 billion in 3 years.

Come the next recession—perhaps more severe because of reduced economic stabilizers—states will either have to divide the money up among more people, deny benefits to many needy people, or find more money from state resources, which could mean raising taxes—a politically unpalatable prospect even in good economic times. Yet even without a recession, the Congressional Budget Office estimated that the amount of money available to the states through TANF would fall $1.2 billion short of what will be necessary to meet the work requirements, not including child-care costs.[60]

Not only will states have less for welfare, but the other budget cuts Congress and the president have enacted come almost entirely from grants to state and local governments. Since states have been getting over 20% of their total revenues from federal grants, those reductions will hurt state budgets. As budget support declines for programs that enjoy broad, middle-class support, states will reduce their funding for the less popular means-tested programs, as they have done in the past.[61] As Robert Matsui (D-Calif.) pointed out: "It's fantasy to believe the states will be able to protect children in poverty. By abdicating responsibility for America's poor to the states, we force children to compete with services like fire and police protection."[62] Hugh Price, president of the National Urban League, also observed: "Years ago we ended mental health treatment as we knew it, and the states never established community-based mental health care."[63] Without a countercyclical infusion of federal funds, the end of the welfare entitlement could well deepen any future recession. Block-granted welfare is a ticking time bomb.

And what happens when the current law comes up for reauthorization in 2002? Will Congress consider reduced welfare loads as having solved the problem of the need for any further federal help for the poor?

Poverty Pirates: The Dangers of Privatization

The PRWORA gives states enormous discretion by stating that TANF funds may be used "in any manner that is reasonably calculated to accomplish the purpose of this part"—the purpose being to provide assistance to needy families; promote job preparation, work, and marriage; prevent and reduce out-of-wedlock pregnancies; and encourage the formation and maintenance of two-parent families.[64] In effect, it opens the door for states to transfer welfare from poor mothers and children to private corporations. Privatization is not necessarily bad. It depends on what the service is, who is delivering it, and the kind of government oversight provided. Moreover, the purchase of services from nonprofit or proprietary providers and the debate over which sector is better positioned to help the poor is not new. Poor relief in the nineteenth and early twentieth centuries was a complex mix of public relief and private charity, and in the last quarter century, privatization had already become a major alternative for delivery of services funded by government.[65] Even before PRWORA went into effect, many states were contracting with private companies for tasks such as child-support enforcement and job training.[66]

Now, however, they can contract out the administration of the TANF block grant, TANF-related services, and the administration of child-care funds. Private, for-profit firms are also lobbying to take over what has been a governmental function at least since 1935: the determination of eligibility for assistance and the amounts of benefits paid. This represents a fundamental shift in how states deliver income support to the poor.[67] The law allows states to contract not only with voluntary and proprietary organizations to provide the services that accomplish its purposes but with religious bodies as well.[68]

While there may be some unexpected benefits to this increasing privatization, there are also new dangers. Even before the law went into effect, corporations like Lockheed Martin (a defense contractor), IBM, Unisys, Andersen Consulting, and Ross Perot's Electronic Data Systems, were providing services in 49 states; and

in Texas, then Governor George W. Bush had asked the federal
government for a waiver so that private firms could take over the
eligibility determination not only for TANF, but for food stamps
and Medicaid as well.[69] "This is one of the biggest corporate grabs
in history," charged Sandy Felder, public sector coordinator for
the Service Employees International Union (SEIU).[70]

For corporations, the rewards are clear. At stake is a new stream
of money that governments now spend to administer welfare programs. Turning welfare administration over to the private sector
relieves states of the headache of having to run welfare systems
which, as we shall show, could fail in the mission of moving welfare
recipients into family-supporting work. Presumably, it will also
keep down costs and thus help reduce taxes.

But the standard free-market arguments for privatization—that
it is more effective and cost-efficient than government—do not
always work for social service delivery.[71] For example, a California child-support enforcement contract won by Lockheed Martin
for $99 million had grown to a $277 million debacle and had to
be canceled in 1997 after only 23 of 58 counties were being served,
with all but $4 million of the loss covered by taxpayers.[72] Non-
governmental organizations, especially those seeking to make profits,
often choose the less difficult or sick clients, known as "creaming" or "cherry picking," a term used to designate the efforts of
HMOs to serve the well elderly. Under such circumstances, comparing effectiveness and efficiency of private and public provision is meaningless. After studying several privatization efforts,
Elliott D. Sclar concluded that the costs of administering the
contracting process and monitoring the work of contractors frequently outweigh the savings from lower internal costs of direct-
service provision. Moreover, the competitive climate that is said
to make companies more efficient often fails to appear, or when
it does in the first round, to disappear in subsequent ones. Sclar
found that, given the unique nature of most services, the contract
evolves into a de facto monopoly favoring those who win the first
round.[73] Cecilia Perry fears that although nonprofit agencies are
in on the first round of contracts, eventually they will not be able
to compete with the large for-profit corporations. "There is something fundamentally wrong," she argues, "with the concept that
companies can amass huge profits from federal and state funds
intended to provide basic human services to poor families."[74]

Moreover, privatization of social services poses dangers for
public workers. Savings from privatization usually involve lower

staff costs, the result of both reduction in numbers and lower salaries. Privatization substitutes nonunionized staff for better paid, often unionized government workers. A 1996 study by the Chicago Institute on Urban Poverty found that in 7 out of 10 public-service categories in that city, privatization drove the wages of entry-level workers below the poverty level.[75] Privatizing public functions is also a disproportionate strike against working- and middle-class women and minority workers, especially African–Americans, so many of whom found a route to upward mobility through government employment.

In fact, government employees in recent years have constituted a large segment of the labor movement. In 1998, only 9.5% of private sector workers were unionized, compared to 37.5% of government workers.[76] As a strike against workers and against the labor movement, privatization complements other policies to weaken the power of workers such as the social welfare cuts and fiscal and monetary policies that loosen the labor market.

"Ironically," Neil Gilbert and Paul Terrell observe, "efforts to revitalize civil society through support of geographically based mediating institutions [such as community-based organizations] are being promoted at the costs of functionally based communities of organized labor, which also constitute powerful mediating institutions of civil society."[77]

For welfare recipients, there are considerable dangers in privatization. Since the law penalizes states that fail to move their welfare populations into approved "work activities" and rewards them for reducing their caseloads, states may be tempted—and corporations will be only too happy—to reduce the caseloads for them, whether or not the welfare recipients get family-supporting jobs.[78] Comparing public and private employees, SEIU's Sandy Felder pointed out,

> A public employee is more likely to be concerned about moving a welfare participant into a long-term employment situation, because that will save the most tax dollars in the long run. A worker for a private company is going to focus on how to get individuals off welfare in the shortest time, no matter what happens to them later, since that is what increases their company's profits and keeps the worker employed.[79]

Observing that "contracting out of governmental responsibility for determining who is eligible for public benefits . . . raises profound concerns about public oversight," the Center on Social

Welfare Policy and Law recommended that "no contract should be constructed so that a contractor profits if eligible persons are deterred from applying or pursuing their applications."[80]

A study of Wisconsin's W-2 program (its equivalent of the TANF program) indicated that fears of privatization may be well-founded. Five private agencies (two for-profit and three nonprofit) were awarded about $142.5 million in contracts the first year to run the program in Milwaukee County, which had 85% of the state's welfare caseload. After 11 months, the agencies amassed a surplus of $31 million by spending less than was allocated to them for expenses, and, under a formula in which they get to keep a proportion of the surplus, they were able to pocket a collective $12.4 million as "profits." According to the American Federation of State, County and Municipal Employees (AFSCME) in Wisconsin, the companies made money by discouraging people from applying for welfare or placing people in a "job-ready" category (not provided for under the law), which meant they were denied benefits, even though they had no income. The "profits" made from saving tax dollars can conceivably go to private shareholders, depriving Milwaukee County of several million dollars it could have used to improve services to clients. In fact, in late 2000, a major scandal erupted in which one of the private-service providers, Maximus, admitted to spending hundreds of thousands of TANF dollars for staff parties, promotional gimmicks, meals and concerts for employees, and travel by employees to secure welfare administration contracts in other states. Goodwill Industries, another provider, was also accused of having used $143,000 on expenses incurred in trying to secure a welfare contract in Arizona.[81]

Privatizing services for the poor poses other dangers. Turning services like caring for children and the elderly into profit-making enterprises threatens to diminish the quality of care in pursuit of the bottom line. While governments have often abused their power, there is at least some public oversight of their practices. Private companies, however, can more easily be shielded from public scrutiny through laws that protect their propriety interests. Indeed, the company responsible for lobbying for the wording in the law that made privatization possible—a for-profit orphanage called the Au Clair School—was accused of mistreating children and evading government oversight.[82] The private nursing-home industry is another case in point. According to Eric Bates, the privatization of nursing homes has been responsible for such egregious violations of patients' rights that legislators who ordinarily come down on the side of 'free enterprise' and against government regulation, have come to advocate government staffing standards."[83] Recent experience in the privatization of state prisons also raises serious doubts about public oversight.[84] Civil libertarians fear that privatization could further erode client privacy rights, since the welfare system asks many more personal questions of its clients than most other American institutions. The government already has a difficult time ensuring that the personal data held by banks, credit companies, and the like remain confidential. With lessened government oversight, it will be difficult to ensure protection for welfare clients should private companies get hold of this kind of information. Again, the spirit of the Social Security Act could be violated, since it had ruled out pauper lists and other poor law practices that infringed on the right to privacy.

Another danger posed by privatization is the increased possibility of political corruption. Private companies are not subject to the requirements of the Freedom of Information or Public Records Acts.[85] Companies bidding for lucrative social service contracts like Lockheed Martin have already been heavily engaged in lobbying state legislators, contributing to political campaigns, and buying the services of former government employees. AFSCME has claimed that corruption scandals contributed to the professionalization of public workers in the first place.[86] By giving much more rein to privatization, PRWORA is likely to increase the revolving-door syndrome so observable in the defense industry—from jobs in government bureaucracies to positions in companies seeking favors from the same public agencies.[87]

While the government has often been cited for waste and corruption, at least there is an accountability system that is permeable to the public. If it wishes, the public can force public officials to change the managers of the bureaucratic systems that are responsible for the waste. In states where private firms have taken over parts of the system, there have been cases of fraud and mismanagement, but the public cannot change these managers.[88] Moreover, as Henry Freedman, director of the Welfare Law Center, observed, once they get in

> a lot of these private companies will have a stranglehold. . . . When a public agency doesn't perform, you improve the training or replace the people who aren't performing. At least you already own the hardware and infrastructure. It will be much

more difficult for the government to start from scratch if the private company walks away with everything when their contract is terminated.[89]

While some of the problems associated with for-profit management of welfare services would be absent if the programs were run by nonprofits, even they are not necessarily corruption-free. In the last few years, the top manager of United Way was found to have been involved in a massive embezzlement scheme, and both United Way and the Hellenic American Neighborhood Action Committee were involved in patronage and graft schemes in the awarding of public-service contracts in New York City.[90]

Where Are the Jobs? The Dubious Premises of the PRWORA

The PRWORA is based on the assumption that the private labor market is capacious enough to absorb all of the welfare recipients who need jobs. Examining the absorption of thousands of new job entrants during the first 2 years of welfare repeal, several researchers are now conducting studies to project the continued capacity of the labor market to employ welfare caseloads. While some are cautiously optimistic, others point out that the type of work is likely to be part-time or temporary and to pay lousy wages.[91]

The assumption that an expanding economy necessarily produces enough jobs or jobs that everyone can live on is not based on empirical data. In order to have an effective jobs-oriented approach to poverty, we need to know the answers to questions such as: How many people want and need full-time jobs but do not have them? How many unfilled jobs are there in the economy at any time? Where are they located? Are the openings for full-time or part-time workers? What are the wages and benefits? What qualifications must workers have to fill them?[92] The truth is, no one can answer these questions with any certainty. We do know, however, as we showed in Chapter 4, that in the "booming" 1960s, subemployment was extensive in low-income areas.

HOW MANY NEED JOBS?

In the first place, we lack adequate information about the number of people needing full-time jobs. This is because of the peculiar way the unemployment rate is measured. Persons working 1 or more hours weekly for pay or profit (or 15 hours of nonpaid employment for a family enterprise) are counted as employed, even if they are working part-time but want full-time work. Persons who have not looked for work in the past 4 weeks are not considered unemployed, regardless of their desire for work. The unemployment statistics count as neither employed nor unemployed all those in the military, or homeless, or working in the underground economy. Many of these people would be in the mainstream civilian labor market were enough jobs at decent wages available. The unemployment statistics do not count those in prison—currently an estimated 1.8 million people—many of whom turn to crime or are incarcerated for drug-related offenses because of the dearth of legitimate opportunities available.[93]

For some groups, like the disabled, the official labor-force survey may considerably understate the job need. For example, according to a 1987 Harris poll, almost 8.5 million working-age disabled persons wanted jobs, but due to a lack of support for the needs of the disabled, most did not engage in a job search. That number far exceeded the Bureau of Labor Statistics' estimate of 1 million disabled persons who wanted jobs but were not actively seeking them, none of whom were even considered "discouraged workers."[94]

Thus, it is more than just welfare recipients who need good jobs. In fact, a more realistic assessment of the truly jobless would more than double the official unemployment rate.[95] According to economist Lester Thurow, properly counted, our true unemployment rate in 1995 was no better than Europe's, and if we added to the unemployed all the underemployed workers, about one-third of the nation's workforce was potentially looking for more work.[96]

HOW MANY JOBS ARE AVAILABLE?

Beyond needing to know how many people need full-time jobs, we also need to know what the demand for workers is at any given time and location. Unlike certain other developed countries, the United States does not regularly collect such job vacancy information. The Bureau of Labor Statistics collects data on the number and characteristics of unemployed persons and on the number and characteristics of occupied jobs. It does not collect data on the number and characteristics of vacant jobs employers are trying to fill. Milwaukee is the only large city in the nation regularly studying job openings to address issues of skill and spatial mismatch.[97]

Job vacancy surveys have occasionally been done for selected periods and regions of the United States. What they show is that *even in good economic times*, there have always been more people looking for jobs than there are jobs available. The author of one such study, Katherine Abraham, commissioner of the U.S. Bureau of Labor Statistics in the Clinton administration, estimated that there were roughly 2.4 unemployed persons for every vacant job during the middle 1960s, when the official unemployment rate averaged 4.5%; an average of close to 4 unemployed persons per vacant job during the early 1970s, when unemployment averaged 5%; an average of 5 or more unemployed persons for every vacant job during the latter part of the 1970s, when unemployment averaged 6–7%; and an average of 8.4 persons for every vacant job in 1982, when unemployment was 9.5%.[98] Recent studies conducted in several regions of the country show similar findings.[99]

Under prodding from the Progressive Caucus, particularly the late Congressman George Brown, Jr. (D-Calif.), and the National Jobs for All Coalition, the Congress appropriated funds in the 1998 budget for the Labor Department to conduct a sample of such job surveys. While these sample surveys were being implemented, the Bureau of Labor Statistics requested and received an appropriation to begin planning for a national job vacancy and turnover survey that would begin in 2002. Although the sample will be too small to permit the level of detail that would identify job availability in specific locations, national level data will give some indication of the relation between job seekers and job openings.

Since most welfare recipients have little education and few skills, job availability, by itself, will not necessarily result in work. There must be an adequate number of entry-level jobs available. In 1997, 92% of 34 cities surveyed by the U.S. Conference of Mayors said there were not enough low-skilled jobs to meet federal work requirements.[100] In the entire Midwest region, there were between two and four workers needing low-skilled jobs for every such opening available.[101]

When work qualifications and experience were considered in the Milwaukee study cited previously, the opportunities for employment dwindled even more. Only 24% of job seekers who lacked a high school diploma or relevant work experience qualified for full-time openings and only 62% qualified for part-time jobs.[102] A study conducted by researchers at Columbia University of job vacancies in the fast food industry in Central Harlem, New York City, in 1993,[103] showed how unlikely it was during recessions for welfare recipients to move into even low-wage jobs. The study demonstrated that there were 14 job seekers for every job available, and because of the oversupply of labor—many workers came from outside central Harlem—the credentials for obtaining these jobs were pushed up.

Jobs for which welfare recipients have the appropriate credentials must be available, and they must be located where the recipient lives and can be expected to work. Only 6% of welfare recipients have cars, and public transportation routes often do not extend to the suburbs where most of the jobs are.[104] The U.S. Conference of Mayors reported that the availability of transportation to work for TANF and food-stamp recipients was a problem in 84% of the 34 cities it surveyed in 1997.[105] In central city areas with high concentrations of welfare recipients like New York, Detroit, and Los Angeles, the jobless rate is, in part, a reflection of the transportation problem.[106] In March 1997, when the official national unemployment rate was 5.2%, two low-income counties in New York City, the Bronx and Kings County, had unemployment rates of 12.6 and 11.4, respectively, over twice the national average. At then-current rates of job expansion in New York City, it was estimated in 1996 that it would take 21 years for all adults on public assistance to be absorbed into the economy, *even if every newly available job went to a welfare recipient.*[107] But large cities are not the only ones with steep unemployment rates despite a strong economy. A 1999 study by the Department of Housing and Urban Development found unacceptably high rates of unemployment (50% or more above the national average) in one in six central cities throughout the nation, most of them small- or mid-sized cities.[108]

Central cities are not the only places with few jobs. Many rural areas, such as the Mississippi Delta, Appalachia, the "colonias" on the Texas–Mexico border, and Indian reservations have long experienced extraordinarily high rates of unemployment.[109] In North Dakota, with the nation's lowest unemployment rate—1.9% in January 1997—unemployment for the Lakota Sioux on the Standing Rock Reservation was 75%.[110] The Transportation Equity Act of the 21st Century (TEA-21), passed in 1998, authorized $150 million a year for 5 years to provide transportation grants to cities and rural areas to enable low-income people, including those leaving welfare for work, to get to their jobs. However, if jobs remain scarce in rural

areas covering large distances, it remains to be seen how much
this will help.[111]

Job Creation: The Elusive Elixir

In designing welfare repeal, policy planners claimed that jobs
for all the welfare recipients who will need them will be found in
an expanding private economy, in currently available jobs in local, state, or federal government, or in jobs that will miraculously
be created by the nonprofit sector. No plans have been made for
federal government job creation on anything like the scale that
may be needed. Clinton evidently felt this was important when he
began his administration, but he later dropped it and proceeded
with the time limits.

THE PRIVATE SECTOR AND TAX INCENTIVES

While there is some indication that the private sector may be
more open to hiring welfare recipients than in the past,[112] businesses have been notoriously reluctant to hire welfare recipients
and have had to be prodded through government incentives. A really
tight economy is the key to changing this. Two types of federal
tax credits are currently offered to businesses to hire welfare
recipients. The Work Opportunity Tax Credit provides 35% of up
to $6,000 in "qualified first year wages" for employers hiring and
retaining individuals in seven target low-income groups. The second,
adopted after passage of the PRWORA, is the Welfare-to-Work
tax credit (50% of the first $10,000 paid to "hard-core" welfare
recipients, i.e., those who have been on the rolls 18 months or
longer). Some states are also using their own tax credits and payroll
subsidies as business incentives, but a GAO study showed that
this was not a popular state strategy. States feel such subsidies
are too expensive and difficult to negotiate.[113] Moreover, the Congressional Budget Office said that the wage subsidy could end up
costing the government more, since people who have subsidized
jobs collect public assistance in that form longer than those who
simply receive welfare checks.[114]

If past experience with tax incentives is any lesson, we cannot
expect them to be panaceas. Critics of the former tax-incentive
program—the Targeted Jobs Tax Credit—which allowed businesses
much freer rein in determining which low-income workers they

would hire, concluded that it had done little to boost the employment of disadvantaged workers. But there has been even less
enthusiasm from business for programs that target hiring at the
most hard-to-employ populations,[115] although this could change in
a really tight labor market, as it did during World War II, when
there was a shortage of civilian labor and businesses were willing
to provide on-the-job training.

Some high-turnover, low-wage industries, however, may welcome tax breaks and wage subsidies. Phil Wilayto describes how
this bit of corporate welfare works:

> Hire a W-2 worker [a welfare-to-work participant in Wisconsin's
> welfare reform program] and you get a tax credit of up to $2,100
> and a payroll subsidy of up to $300. [Since the average hourly
> wage for W-2 workers is $5.79 an hour] $5.79-an-hour times 40
> hours a week comes out to $1019.04 for the average month. But
> figure in the $300 monthly subsidy and the monthly cost to the
> boss drops to $719.04 or an average of $4.08-an-hour. So the
> cost of the worker's wages to the boss is less than the minimum
> wage. Now figure in the tax credit—up to $2,100 per worker—
> and the pot really starts to smell sweet. And remember, this is
> if the W-2 worker has a "real" job. If they've been assigned to
> the company under the guise of "community service," then they're
> just working for their welfare check. That means the employer
> got someone to work for them [sic] for free. And this is all in
> a county with one of the lowest unemployment rates in the state,
> where the bosses are crying for new workers.[116]

Despite their obvious advantages, businesses appear to have
been only moderately responsive to government incentives. In May
1998, the White House announced that 5,000 businesses had hired
a total of 135,000 welfare recipients. Only 70% of those jobs, however,
were full-time or paid health benefits; and in the press conference
extolling the great success of the program, the president of the
Welfare-to-Work Partnership acknowledged that they had probably
creamed those who were already job-ready.[117]

STATE AND LOCAL GOVERNMENT JOB CREATION: WHAT ARE THE PROSPECTS?

As our history has shown, publicly funded jobs programs have
been fairly rare in American history, and when adopted, they have
been criticized by the business community, often unfairly, as "make

work" jobs or as government's attempt to take over the preroga-
tives of the private sector.[118] Clifford Johnson, of the Center on
Budget and Policy Priorities, pointed out that "a great irony and
dilemma underpin American social policy in the 1990s. We extol
the virtues of work and simultaneously reject attempts to create
jobs through public means when work is not otherwise available."[119]
Nevertheless, if real welfare reform is to succeed, publicly funded
jobs will have to be part of the equation.

States and cities have been reluctant to provide publicly funded
jobs, thinking them too costly. And as Chapter 3 showed, this has
also been a deterrent to federal job provision as well. However,
properly run, publicly funded jobs programs can provide important employment experience and training for welfare recipients
with low levels of job readiness and for those who live in areas
where jobs in the private sector are scarce. Because they pay a
wage, they enable workers to gain access to employment-related
benefits that can substantially increase their present and future
incomes. Moreover, publicly funded jobs can provide important
social services, help economic development efforts in low-income
areas, and, during economic downturns, serve as an economic stimulus.

Since welfare repeal, the idea of publicly funded jobs has begun
to make something of a comeback.[120] The Center on Budget and
Policy Priorities devoted some research and advocacy to the effort to promote such programs, and the National League of Cities
sent out a "how-to" on publicly funded jobs to its member cities.[121] In addition to TANF, two federal programs now offer states
and cities some incentives to develop these programs. The first is
the Welfare-to-Work program initiated by the Clinton administration and included in the Balanced Budget Act of 1997. This turns
over a total of $3 billion in Welfare-to-Work grants to localities
where there is high unemployment and welfare use, requiring that
states spend it on the hardest to employ.[122] The Welfare-to-Work
grants are a tacit recognition that the job gap for undereducated,
unskilled people is one of the major obstacles to genuine welfare
reform. The second program is the Workforce Investment Act of
1998 (WIA), which replaced the Job Training Partnership Act (JTPA)
as the main federal employment training program in July 2000.
Under JTPA, cities could not use the funds for subsidized wage
programs, but WIA funds may be so used.[123]

With the additional Welfare-to-Work grants, a number of states
and cities are initiating short-term public job-creation programs,

and many more localities are being pressured by advocacy groups to create them. Washington State, Vermont, Philadelphia, Detroit, Minneapolis, Athens, Ohio, and Seattle are among the localities initiating such programs.[124] Although the current initiatives are still small, they are a significant beginning that should be built upon.

Initially, however, publicly funded jobs that include the requisites to make them work—training and education for participants, support services for both workers and employers, adequate supervision, job placement when the public jobs end, etc.—are costly, and in order to qualify for the bulk of the federal Welfare-to-Work grants, states will have to exceed the maintenance of effort they must show to qualify for TANF funds.[125] Thus, in order to get the federal money, states must spend more of their own money. However, most state governments have been in a downsizing mood, unwilling to either use their surpluses or add to the taxes that would have to be raised to create more jobs. Thus, it remains to be seen how far these new incentives will go in creating new jobs for welfare recipients. When asked by the U.S. Conference of Mayors to rate their capacity to create community-service jobs on a scale of one (poor) to five (most positive), officials in the 34 cities surveyed in 1997 produced a rating of 3.5—and this was at a time of low overall unemployment and a booming economy.[126]

WORKING ONE'S WAY OUT OF POVERTY?

Even if enough jobs were available, this would not guarantee freedom from poverty. Jobs must pay a "living wage" and offer benefits that enable families to become self-sufficient. Since the majority of welfare recipients have low levels of skill and education, they will be going to work in the lower end of the labor market. Reports from several states indicate an increase in earnings for welfare recipients who enter the labor market—thanks to some continuing, although temporary, subsidies as well as food stamps and the Earned Income Tax Credit.[127] However, since welfare payments have been below the poverty line in every state and people going to work incur increased expenses for transportation, clothing, child care, and the like, an increase in earnings does not tell us too much.

Most poor, working families have few income supports beyond the Earned Income Tax Credit (EITC) and food stamps, and, as we pointed out earlier, many of them are unaware that they can collect

these benefits. When the transitional welfare-to-work subsidies are
no longer available, will such families no longer need government
help? Although pay for workers at the lower end rose between 1996
and 2000—thanks to a buoyant economy, rising demand, and increases
in the minimum wage—this upturn was regionally uneven, still
moderate, and came after 20 years of declining wages. According
to most surveys, the majority of welfare recipients entering the
job market are making wages that are just slightly above the minimum
wage, but below the federal poverty level for families that work
full-time, year-round. While the stock market, adjusted for inflation,
has gone up by over 150% since 1968, the purchasing power of
the minimum wage has fallen by 30%.[128] In 1999, the minimum
wage for a full-time, 40-hour week paid only 80.6% of the poverty
level ($13,290) for a family of three and only 63% of the poverty
level for a family of four ($17,029).[129] Its real value was even lower
in 2000.

The EITC has been shown to be the most effective antipoverty
program for working families with children. It raised more children out of poverty in 1996 than all other government programs
combined, reducing childhood poverty from 22.3 to 19.1%.[130] (This
reduction of 14%, however, may say more about the meagerness
of the American welfare state than about the antipoverty effects
of the EITC.) Unlike traditional public assistance, the EITC provides less money to the very poor than to families in the maximum
range, and it offers nothing to those who have no earnings the entire
year. Further, as more families become eligible for the EITC, it
could face the same kinds of political barriers as other low-income projects have encountered, even though it is work-depen-
dent and lacks the stigma attached to pure "relief."

Moreover, there is still a question as to whether the EITC will
be enough to compensate for the increased expenses welfare-to-
work recipients have when they leave the rolls—not only rent, child
care, work attire, transportation, but also state or local taxes.[131]
An important study commissioned by Wider Opportunities for Women
calculates a "Self-Sufficiency Standard" with which to measure
the adequacy of wage income alone to meet the basic needs of
differing types of families living in various regions of the country
in 1999.[132] Using this standard—a more useful one than the notoriously low federal "poverty level"—researchers found that a mother
with one pre-school child living in the District of Columbia would
have to make at least $16.06 per hour ($2,827 per month) to meet

the basic needs of her family. If she had two children, one preschooler and one school-age, she would need to earn almost \$22.69 per hour. Housing and child care are the greatest expenses of working families with children, accounting for more than one-half their incomes.[133]

The first comprehensive study of Wisconsin's W-2 Program— the program that in many ways had been a model for the nation— may give us some clue as to the ability of families leaving welfare for work to achieve self-sufficiency. The study was conducted after 75% of those on the rolls had left. Presumably, these were the most employable. Although 62% were working at the time of the survey, and 83% had worked some time in recent months, 47% reported that they had difficulty paying for utilities, 37% for housing, and 32% for food. Indeed, families leaving welfare were almost 50% more likely to have no way of paying for groceries than when they were on welfare.[134] Another study estimated that for 40% of the welfare families in Wisconsin who leave the rolls for work, child-care costs could amount to more than one-half their earnings at a wage of \$6 an hour.[135]

Wisconsin's experience is not unique. Analysis of figures from other state studies conducted during the first 2 years of welfare "reform" show that by March 1998, only 8% of the previous year's recipients who left welfare for work had jobs paying weekly wages above the three-person poverty line, and the proportion with weekly wages *below three-quarters* of the poverty line more than doubled in 1 year—from 6% to 14.5%. Moreover, 40–50% of the welfare-to-work population in a nine-state study did not have jobs at the time of the study, and many families leaving welfare reported struggling to get food, shelter, or needed medical care.[136] Surveys of people living in homeless shelters found that between 10–20% were homeless because of being cut off from government benefits.[137] Economists at the University of Oregon concluded that their state's welfare program may actually provide a disincentive for welfare recipients who want to advance to higher wage levels in their new jobs. When welfare moms get raises, they actually lose money because of reductions in food stamps and rent subsidies and tax credits that turn into tax liabilities.[138] In short, many are suffering even more hardships than they were before.

The hardships faced by welfare-to-work recipients reflect four facts about the American economy in the late twentieth and early twenty-first centuries that most mainstream accounts of the economy obscure: first, the increasingly segmented nature of the contemporary labor market and the growing wage disparity between those at the high end and those in the middle and lower end—the largest gaps at any time since the Great Depression;[139] second, the loss of career ladders that in earlier times enabled workers to move between sectors;[140] third, the failure of wages, in general, to keep up with the growth in productivity;[141] and fourth, a deterioration in job security during the 1990s with the increasingly contingent nature of work (in 1997 constituting somewhere between 5 and 33% of all jobs, depending on how "contingent" work is defined).[142]

In the "booming" economy of 1999, with the lowest unemployment rate in nearly 30 years, just over one in four full-time workers (26.8%) 16 years and older earned poverty-level wages.[143] About one in ten households or more than 30 million people reported food insecurity in 2000, leading researchers at the Tufts University Center on Hunger, Poverty, and Nutrition Policy to conclude that "the U.S. has entered a new era, in which a strong economy is insufficient in reducing the number of hungry American families."[144] Given what researchers are discovering about the links between cognitive development and nutritional intake, such a finding should be terribly alarming to our policymakers.[145] If ethical concerns bear no weight, they should at least be concerned about what this implies for the competitiveness of the nation's workforce.

Younger families and workers, as well as new job entrants, are most at risk. They start out poorer than their parents did, and their income gains are smaller.[146] The worst declines in wages over the 1990s were for entry-level jobs, even for college graduates.[147] Two studies, using 1996 Census data, found that children of the working poor (63% of the one in five poor children) were the fastest-growing segment of the population of children living in poverty.[148] This segment grew at a faster rate even than those collecting welfare—indicating what may be in store for many of those families who "graduate" from welfare to so-called independence—an independence that can mean low income and continuous job insecurity.

Contrary to the assumption that welfare recipients do not "work," most welfare recipients cycle in and out of the labor market because the jobs they get pay less than the package of benefits (cash assistance, food stamps, Medicaid, etc.) that comes with welfare and are often insecure. According to Kathryn Edin and Laura Lein, many other welfare recipients work at underground jobs but do not report their incomes, knowing that to do so would push them further into poverty because their welfare checks would be reduced or withdrawn altogether.[149]

In addition to poverty-level wages or below, the low-wage sector is notorious for its lack of work-related benefits. The share of workers covered by employer-provided health care plans dropped 7% between 1979 and 1993.[150] Although the robust economy reversed the decline, in 1999, 15.5% of the population, or 42.6 million, were still without any insurance.[151]

Despite good economic times, even this low-wage labor market is not infinitely expandable. Economist Harry Holzer has shown that only 5–10% of jobs in central city areas where most welfare recipients live require few cognitive skills or work credentials.[152] Researchers have not come to any firm conclusion on whether recent immigrants take jobs away from native born people, especially blacks and native born Hispanics.[153] Forcing more welfare recipients into limited low-wage markets—especially those in central cities—may create more unemployment, especially in economic downturns. Noted economist, Robert Solow, has speculated that making welfare recipients work may create some more jobs, as employers will be able to purchase more, less-skilled (i.e., less productive) workers for the price of fewer, more-skilled workers. But it would still mean lower overall wages and more job insecurity for those on the lower rungs of the labor force.[154]

A recession could quickly wipe out the recent wage gains of low-income workers. However, even without a recession, if no pool of net new jobs is created, the entrance of millions of welfare recipients into the labor market could lower wages for the bottom one-third of the workforce.[155] Indeed, the construction of a large army of super-low wage workers and a reserve army of the unemployed may be one of the reasons for the passage of the PRWORA. One does not have to be a believer in conspiracies to see the connections between the corporate electoral campaign contributions and the right-wing think tanks that created the policy climate for welfare repeal.[156]

In addition to insufficient wages and benefits, the low-wage labor market provides little job security, and no opportunities for upward mobility.[157] In 1996, the national unemployment rate was about 5.5%, but for workers with less than a high school education (about one-half of all single mothers on welfare), the rate was three and four times higher.[158] A survey of welfare recipients who had been hired through the president's Welfare-to-Work Partnership program found higher rates of retention than for other entry-level workers,[159] but other studies of those who have moved from welfare to work show significant job loss.[160]

The Limits of Private Charity

Conservative welfare reformers, eager to reduce a socially committed government, hold that "privatizing compassion" would both solve government budget problems and set nonprofit organizations on a more productive course. Their voices have been magnified by a public relations campaign funded by foundations such as the Pew Charitable Trusts and the Bradley Foundation (the foundation that funded *The Bell Curve*).[161] Republican architects of PRWORA succeeded in getting written into the bill a "Charitable Choice" option (Section 104) that remained largely unnoticed until the Bush administration made Charitable Choice the centerpiece of its approach to treating the most intractable problems of poverty. Charitable Choice would allow community organizations, including those that are "faith-based," to contract for federal money to provide services to poor people without having to deny the explicit religious character of their organization. Until Charitable Choice, religious organizations that provided social services to the poor had to keep the provision of these services separate from their religious activities. For example, the Roman Catholic Church set up a separate legal entity, Catholic Charities, that provided services on a nonsectarian basis. Under the Bush plan, however, such restrictions that seek to protect the separation of church and state will be reduced. In addition, the Bush administration hopes to increase individual giving to private charities by increasing charitable tax deductions.[162] To administer the funding of these new "armies of compassion," as he calls them, Bush created a new White House office of Community and Faith-based Initiatives and new offices in each of the Cabinet departments that operate social programs.

There is no doubt that many religious organizations have been successful in treating some of the social problems of the poor. Although the Bush administration insists that "government cannot be replaced by charities," it is clear that it expects the nonprofit sector to do much more of the work.[163] Many churches in poverty-stricken neighborhoods may see Charitable Choice as a windfall, but it is unrealistic to think that this sector will be able to pick up the slack. More than 46 religious organizations, such as the National Conference of Catholic Bishops and the American Friends Service Committee have argued that placing more burdens on them would simply overwhelm their resources. Not only do they not have the infrastructure to hire a great many workers, but they would probably have to become impersonal and bureaucratic like the welfare departments they are replacing to handle this volume of work.[164]

To begin with, the PRWORA cut the Social Service Block Grant by 15%.[165] The reductions in entitlements and other low-income programs under the new welfare law will average $15.1 billion per year over 7 years, yet all giving to human service charities nationally amounted to only $12.2 billion in 1996, and most of it went for disaster relief.[166] Welfare repeal cut an average of $4 billion from the food-stamp program for the next 6 years, yet the total value of all food in the country's food banks is about $1 billion a year.[167] According to Richard Steinburg, professor of economics and philanthropy at Indiana University, each one-dollar cut in government aid to the poor is made up by no more than 35 cents or less from private charities.[168]

With cuts in the food-stamp budget and time limits kicking in, private charities and nonprofits are struggling to hold the shredding safety net together, and they are not having an easy time. In 1992, in the midst of a recession, the U.S. Conference of Mayors reported that 21% of requests for emergency food assistance in 29 cities it surveyed went unmet due to insufficient resources. In 1999, in the midst of a recovery, the Mayors' Conference reported the same percentage of unmet requests.[169] Second Harvest, the nation's largest distributor of donated food to emergency food providers, projected a shortfall from 1997 to 2002 of 24.558 billion tons of food or the equivalent of three meals a day for 3.24 million low-income people for an entire year. To make up for this loss, they estimated they would have to expand their collection and distribution activities by more than 425% over their 1995 capacity and maintain this expanded level throughout the 6-year period. Yet, despite this quantum leap in demand, the companies that donate food are now donating less than they were, in part because of streamlined business methods that result in less leftover food.[170]

It should be noted that charities that serve the poor have never been completely self-sufficient. Many have been heavily reliant on government subsidies, which have been extensively reduced. While some of the social services block grant funds that states are allowed to divert from cash assistance to welfare recipients will flow to churches and private charities, and while increased tax deductions for charitable giving may offer some help, private charities are likely to be stretched to the breaking point by welfare graduates who no longer have a safety net when circumstances get tight, and they are certainly not going to be able to provide the jobs that will be needed during economic downturns.

There has been, of course, a long and impressive tradition of self-help among economically oppressed groups, particularly African–Americans, especially before there was a federal welfare program. Large African–American congregations are most likely to seek public money, but much of the African–American community in poverty-stricken areas today is serviced by small, store-front churches that lack the financial, infrastructural, and administrative capacity to take on the role of social-service providers for large numbers of people for an indeterminate length of time. William Julius Wilson and others have argued that in leaving inner-city neighborhoods, black middle- and stable working-class families may have irretrievably altered the possibilities for recreating this self-help tradition.[171] There is concern among leaders of black civil society over their capacity to meet the multidimensional needs of the people in crisis in their communities.[172] Clinton was told as much when he put in a well-publicized appearance in February 1997 at the Riverside Church in New York City to plead for church and black business help for the poor. Earl Graves, CEO of *Black Enterprise* magazine, said to loud applause:

> The fact of the matter is that black businesses and the black church are doing more than their fair share in picking up the slack in the wake of more than a decade of cuts in services to the urban poor by Federal, state and local governments. It is unrealistic and unfair to expect the private sector in general—and black businesses in particular—to sacrifice profit margins in order to do the government's job.[173]

In addition to the inadequate resources that exist in the nonprofit world, there are two other problems with relying on religious organizations to deliver services to the poor. Under Charitable Choice, religious organizations that provide social services are not supposed to use public funds for sectarian worship, instruction, or proselytization among the subjects of their charity, and welfare clients are allowed to request alternate providers if they choose. But critics say it is not possible to ensure that religious coercion will not happen. This is not so likely to be the case with mainstream liberal denominations, but it is quite likely with the Religious Right and other evangelical churches that see their mission as winning new converts to the faith. Moreover, the very reason some of these programs—such as drug rehabilitation—seem to work is precisely because of the religious element in the program. In addition, religious organizations have been exempt from the civil rights laws that apply to secular organizations that receive government money. Will they now be allowed to violate such laws if they require a religious loyalty oath of their employees? And how will the government pick and choose among religious applicants for government grants? Will it be accused of supporting some religious groups and denying others? A number of potential constitutional problems attend the implementation of this provision.[174]

Another set of problems lies in the potential for conflict between the policies of the state and the ethical norms of religious or charitable organizations. In New York City, for example, a coalition of more than 70 nonprofits, spearheaded by two of the city's best-known churches, refused to hire New York City's workfare participants. Critical of the punitive way in which the city treats its welfare-to-work participants, they feared that the City was using the program to displace unionized workers.[175] Maryland encountered similar resistance when it tried to get religious organizations to administer noncash assistance to families who had been sanctioned for noncompliance with program requirements. Some of these organizations were concerned that the state was trying to pass off to religious organizations its obligation to poor families; others feared a church-state conflict and problems with liability.[176] And now that Charitable Choice has become institutionalized, some religious organizations fear that too much dependence on the public trough may curtail their ability to be prophetic critics of the government whenever it violates their religio/ethical principles.

Workfare: Work without Fairness

Given the political opposition and institutional restraints on government investment in genuine job creation, a number of states and cities have responded to the challenge to move their welfare caseloads from welfare to work by resorting to one or both of two expedients: changing eligibility rules and shifting funding to deter potential clients from applying for welfare or to make it harder for them to remain on it; and putting welfare recipients to work in

workfare programs. As we have seen, the law requiring states to
move increasing percentages of their caseloads into work activity
provides the states with a convenient loophole. Their work participation rates can be reduced if they reduce their caseloads below
the 1995 average. But the law does not stipulate *how* they are to
reduce their caseloads. Alhough technically states are not supposed
to receive credit for reductions caused by eligibility rule changes,
it is hard to tell if this is happening, and many states have dropped
people from the rolls through changes in eligibility rules, funding
cuts, etc., thus reducing their work-participation rates. In antici-
pation of the end of the welfare entitlement, most states had already significantly reduced their rolls but had not been required
to verify if those leaving the rolls had found jobs. The expanding
economy absorbed some of these people, but there could be many
who have simply fallen into the abyss of homelessness or the
underground economy, or will do so with the inevitable downturn.

The other expedient being used by some states and city governments—especially those like New York City with large welfare
caseloads—is a form of forced labor euphemistically called "workfare"
or sometimes, "Community Work Experience Programs." Although
loosely used, the term *workfare* refers to any program in which
welfare recipients work for the direct receipt of their benefits.[177]
The federal law is unclear about whether such workers are "employees." Due to this lack of clarity, workers in many such programs have been working off their welfare checks by engaging in
activities that are not defined as a real "jobs."[178]

Much workfare is created by state and city governments as a
way of both fulfilling the work-participation requirement of the
federal law and reducing the costs of state or city government.
Eager to reduce taxes, states and municipalities have naturally not
been anxious to enforce federal employment guidelines and have
thus carved workfare slots out of jobs held by retiring workers or
those whose hours and wages have been cut.[179] Workfare participants have been engaged in raking parks, collecting garbage, serving
as day-care or preschool aides, as bus monitors or clerks in hospitals or government offices, or taking care of the children of other
welfare recipients. Although a coalition of unions, civil rights, religious, and grassroots advocacy groups lobbied Congress to recognize
basic federal employment protection for workfare participants and
the Department of Labor (DOL) issued guidelines to this effect,
several states and municipalities balked at enforcing the DOL's

guidelines, forcing advocates to go to court, not always success-fully.[180] The regulations that took effect in October 1999 finally required all federal worker protection laws to apply to TANF recipients.[181]

But there are still some holes in the DOL guidelines. They do not state an opinion about legal protections that fall outside their jurisdiction, such as the right to organize under the National Labor Relations Act or to claim workers' compensation under state employment laws. This is especially troubling since many of these jobs fail to provide adequate health and safety protections.[182] Moreover, the 1997 Taxpayer Relief Act prohibits workfare workers from being eligible for the federal EITC. Although advocates are pushing to have them qualify for the EITC, there is talk that this would make welfare a more desirable alternative to work in the low-wage labor market (since welfare recipients would continue to get child-care and health-care subsidies) and thus discourage welfare recipients from moving off welfare. And because they are required to work less than a 40-hour week to work off their benefits, workfare participants fail to meet the minimum hours standard for making use of the Family and Medical Leave Act.

Unlike AFDC, which mandated that the number of hours required of workfare participants be equal to the size of the welfare grant divided by the minimum wage, TANF provided no such minimum-wage protection. Some of the worst abuses of workfare will be challenged in the courts or changed because of lobbying by unions and other advocates of the poor. Some concessions to union and public pressure were reflected in the Balanced Budget Act of 1997. States must now pay welfare enrollees in workfare program benefits at least equal to the minimum wage,[183] although California continued to violate this federal directive.[184] Nevertheless, workfare is a far cry from a genuine public job-creation program.

The rationale behind workfare is that welfare recipients who have been out of the labor market or who have never worked before need a period of transition into the workplace—a time when they can learn to practice the social attitudes and disciplinary skills associated with the workplace. Presumably, after a period of such apprenticeship, welfare recipients would be ready to be hired as permanent workers by the agencies in which they performed their service or by private firms. But a study by the Hunger Action Network of New York State in 1995 and an investigation by the *New York Times* in the spring of 1998 found little evidence that workfare enhanced the employability of its participants.[185] Rather, it appears to be a form of forced labor. Stanley Hill, former head of New York City's largest municipal union, labeled it "slavery."[186]

Although workfare is not a new program, its scope is unprecedented. A preliminary survey of 30 states by the Welfare Law Center in the winter of 1997 showed workfare programs operating in at least one-half of these states.[187] While most states see workfare as a last resort, preferring to get welfare clients off the rolls and into real jobs as quickly as possible, it could become the major means for moving welfare recipients into work activity in the event of a recession.[188]

Displacement is becoming one of the top concerns of organized labor. While there is as yet no solid research that measures the displacement effects, anecdotal evidence from different parts of the country has been accumulating. In New York City, where the potential welfare caseload that could be put to work is equal in size to the entire municipal workforce, the *New York Times* found that about 34,000 former welfare recipients were taking jobs formerly held by Parks Department employees, city hospital workers, and Teamsters in the building trades. This was after the City had reduced municipal payrolls by 20,000. According to the *Times*, "these unheralded workers (WEP participants) do much of the grunt work that makes the city run."[189] Yet if they are of such value, why not make them bona fide jobs?

Summary: The Uncertain Future of Welfare-to-Work

The Personal Responsibility and Work Opportunity Reconciliation Act was passed during a period of strong economic growth and tight labor markets, and economic indicators became increasingly better during the first 3 years of its implementation. It is not surprising, therefore, that preliminary studies conducted during these first years of "reform" showed a significant number of welfare recipients entering the labor market. With rapidly decreasing welfare rolls and budget surpluses, most states are providing services to "make work pay," that is, to make welfare less financially attractive than work. But the law's erroneous assumptions about both the capacity of the labor market to absorb everyone expected to enter it, as well as its ability to provide a way out of poverty for undereducated and unskilled workers, many with multiple barriers to employment, belie the optimism of the law's architects.

The "tough love" approach of the PRWORA may have given some welfare recipients the push they needed to enter the labor force, develop self-discipline, and begin the process of skill development that will lead to higher pay. But for many others, the harsh new rules and time limits have meant further misery and deepening poverty. Welfare rolls have dropped, but significant numbers of welfare graduates are not becoming self-sufficient. Indeed, dependence on private charity in the form of food banks, soup kitchens, and homeless shelters appears to have increased. Moreover, turning authority for designing welfare programs over to the states has meant not only greater experimentation, but greater abuse and the opportunity for profit-making corporations to feed at the poverty trough. If all of this has been happening in a time of strong economic growth, what will happen during a recession?

There may however be at least one silver lining to the new emphasis on work. Several states and cities are now realizing that it is not just enough to push welfare recipients into a labor market that is unable to absorb them. Public job creation is at least beginning to be discussed as an alternative, and several areas of the country are experimenting with it. Moreover, a strong grassroots movement for a "living wage" has arisen in many areas of the country. As more welfare recipients face time limits with no significant job prospects, a new attention to the incapacity of the private labor market to provide a way out of poverty could be the result.

CHAPTER 9

Washington's New Poor Law: Part II

he stated premise of welfare reform is that economic self-sufficiency can be achieved through employment. This requires not only that there are enough good jobs but that the new workers are equipped to get and hold them. As previously noted, at any one time the majority of the welfare caseload consisted of long-time recipients. To the writers of the PRWORA, this demonstrated that welfare clients had life too easy, would not make the effort to get a job, and therefore needed a push. Yet, as noted in Chapter 1, several studies refute this assumption, demonstrating that a majority of welfare mothers is substantially related to the labor market. These studies indicate that approximately 10–20% of welfare mothers fit the stereotype.[2]

If most welfare mothers were substantially related to the labor market yet could not achieve economic independence, either the labor market lacked sufficient jobs at livable wages to employ all who needed them, or welfare recipients faced serious human-resource deficits with regard to preparation for and continuation in the higher-wage labor market. In fact, both impediments operate synergistically to keep people poor and therefore in need of government support. Chapter 8 argued that there may not be enough good, let alone bad, jobs for all of those who are now expected to work. The first part of this chapter examines the other end of the welfare-to-work equation: the barriers to employment faced by welfare recipients with regard to education and training, disabilities, the need for child care and other supportive services on the one hand, and the commitment of welfare reformers to meet these needs on the other. The last part of the chapter examines the combined effects of welfare "reform" with cuts in other safety-net programs that the poor and near-poor rely on to survive, exploring the effect that these have already had on vulnerable populations even during a period of economic growth. The prospects for periods of recession and of more typical labor-market conditions are thus implied.

Education and Training: Enormous Needs, Inadequate Provision

Hard evidence of what skills and educational levels are required for jobs at the lower end of the labor market is difficult to produce, because they often depend on other variables like the tightness of the local labor market. Nevertheless, for a welfare-to-work program to be successful in leading to self-sufficiency, especially for those with one or more barriers to work, some estimate of what employers require is needed. Jobs for the Future, a research and advocacy organization, gathered evidence about the skills employers expect from entry-level workers, identifying two tiers of entry-level jobs: those that require only the most basic work-related "soft skills," such as work discipline and the ability to take direction from a supervisor; and jobs requiring literacy, technical skills, communication, and/or problem-solving. Skills needed to advance beyond entry-level—that is, a job that pays above the poverty level—were identified as analytical and "navigational" skills. However, there is evidence, say the researchers, "that employers are steadily raising the 'hurdle bar' into the low end of the labor market as the use of computers, team approaches to work organization, and customer service become increasingly important."[3]

If information about specific skills and educational levels needed for successful entry into the labor market is hard to come by, there is universal agreement that higher earnings are generally a function of higher levels of education and training.[4] Yet, only a little over one-half of all first-time recipients of AFDC in 1996 had high school diplomas, and about 90% had no more than that. A 1991 Department of Labor report estimated that 20–29% of economically disadvantaged adults were functionally illiterate,[6] while a study in Washington State showed that 36% of the caseload had learning disabilities that had never been remediated.[7] Obviously, if entry into the labor market for welfare mothers is to be the road to self-sufficiency, a substantial level of support for education and training needs to be made; this means education not only at the point of workforce entry, but from kindergarten on up.

The PRWORA requires mothers under the age of 18 to attend high school or an alternative educational or training program in order to collect welfare, but it includes other baffling restrictions on activities needed to prepare people for economically productive work. According to Mark Greenberg, senior staff attorney with the Center for Law and Social Policy, policymakers' conclusion that education and training do not pay off may be based on a misreading of the random assignment research of the early 1990s. This led many states and policymakers to conclude that job search programs are more effective than education and training in leading to rapid connection to jobs.[8]

TANF funds for job search and job readiness assistance are capped at only 6 weeks, and no more than 4 weeks can be consecutive. While this does not restrict states from doing more with their own money, it sends an important signal to states that may discourage them from going further. In addition, the Balanced Budget Act of 1997, which modified the PRWORA, stipulates that no more than 30% of all families on state welfare rolls may count toward the work-participation rate required for TANF funds by participating in vocational education. The 30% cap also pertains to parents under age 20 who are engaged in education directly related to employment and who are completing high school or its equivalent.

Unlike the Family Support Act, which set no restrictions on vocational educational training, the PRWORA limits TANF funding for this purpose to 1 year. Yet most good training programs in community and technical colleges are 2-year programs. Maurice Emsellem, attorney for the National Employment Law Project, has pointed out that basic education and training activities, such as the General Equivalency Diploma (G.E.D.) and English-as-a-Second-Language programs, no longer automatically count toward a state's work participation rate.[9] If they so choose, states can make these programs less available to welfare recipients. Indeed, in a GAO study conducted 2 years after passage of welfare repeal, most states appeared to be emphasizing rapid job placement over education and training.[10] Chapter 6 pointed out how earlier welfare "reform"— the WIN program—followed a similar pattern.

Yet if the government is unwilling to invest in the education and training of welfare recipients, who will? In at least two employer surveys conducted in the Midwest, employers were found to have little interest in providing training to people who lacked basic skills.

While they were receptive to ideas about increasing the quality and effectiveness of learning at work, it had to be with minimal time and expense and be related to the "bottom line."[11]

In their effort to get family heads into the labor market as quickly as possible, authors of the PRWORA excluded higher education as an activity that can count toward the work requirement under TANF. Policymakers assumed that people with the skills for postsecondary education typically have the ability to find employment. For such people, they concluded, postsecondary education should come after employment, not before.[12] In an era when almost every decent-paying job requires a college education or beyond and where research has shown higher education to be the most impressive contributor to higher employment and earnings among single mothers on welfare,[13] this omission would appear to be counterproductive to the authors' alleged interest in self-sufficiency.

It takes enormous energy and self-discipline for a poor, single mother to take care of her children and keep up with a course of study. If these women are now required to add up to 35 hours of work outside the home to their already stressful schedules, they may well be forced to sacrifice their education and even their children's care. Charisse Texeira, the 34-year-old mother of a toddler and an "A" student at Rockland Community College in New York state, was one of some 700,000 higher education students nationwide who were on welfare when the law went into effect. Texeira, who had expected to get both her high school diploma and an associate's degree in the same program, was devastated when her caseworker told her she would have to take any minimum wage job the county wanted to give her. "How can I work 35 hours a week, go to school, and take care of my daughter?" she asked.[14] For responsible parents like Texeira, who are doing what society expects of them to better their condition, the new law is cruel.

But the law is even harder on women who are not only poor, but struggling with addiction, depression, or disability. Sonia Roberts, a 25-year-old North Philadelphia mother of three who grew up amid alcohol and drugs but had managed to earn 62 credits toward an associate's degree, feared that the 20 hour-a-week work requirement imposed by Pennsylvania would force her to leave school. When interviewed by a *Philadelphia Inquirer* reporter in April 1999, Roberts was taking required courses that met every afternoon for several hours. Because of this, she had to find a night job. On such a schedule, she got to see her children for barely an hour a day. She also had to find child care for children of three different ages at off hours.[15]

Not only will the mandated quotas for moving welfare recipients into work or workfare force individuals to make difficult choices, but the choices themselves could well dry up. Lower student enrollments may force states to curtail the programs they had developed over the past decade to meet the needs of students like Texeira and Roberts. As the PRWORA went into effect, community colleges across the country braced themselves for falling enrollments. "We're very concerned," said David Baime of the American Association of Community Colleges. "The welfare changes are resulting in enrollment drops. These students don't have the time and wherewithal to work, raise children, and handle course work all at once."[16] States like New York and California with large numbers of higher education students on welfare have felt the effect of this ruling most severely. At the City University of New York, where 10% of the student body was on welfare, enrollment of welfare students dropped 17% after Mayor Rudolph Giuliani introduced new work requirements for welfare recipients.[17]

Final regulations issued by the Department of Health and Human Services in April 1999 allow states some flexibility in providing for higher education and encourage them to do so.[18] For example, the regulations do not further define each of the 12 categories of activities that count as "work experience," allowing states to interpret them liberally. They also allow states to count their caseload reductions as part of their state work participation rate, thus making it possible for some or all of those remaining on the rolls to participate in noncountable activities like higher education.

Making use of the flexibility offered by the regulations, several states have developed creative ways to get around the impasse. Some have found ways of interpreting higher education as an activity that serves as a "work requirement." Kentucky, for example, allows postsecondary education to count as work by interpreting it as "vocational training."[19] Other states count it if combined with some work.[20] The University of California stood to lose $300 million in revenues generated by welfare students[21] before the state began allowing time spent in class, labs, and/or internships to count toward the weekly work requirement of 32 hours.[22]

Other states like Maine have dedicated separate state funds to higher education programs that do not have the work requirements and time limits imposed by TANF and are encouraging community colleges and universities to develop work-study programs for welfare recipients so that they can fulfill their work requirements on campus.[23] But here is another hitch. Community colleges, where the bulk of the TANF students are to be found, receive only 15% of federal work-study money despite enrolling 40% of all those in higher education.[24] Thus, if such a program is to work, states will have to commit more money for this purpose out of their treasuries. With some tobacco money and unused surpluses, states appear to be more open to doing this, but come a recession, free schooling and supportive services for welfare recipients may be among the first things to go.

Child Care: A Major Barrier to Employment and Self-Sufficiency

Another impediment to economically productive work for welfare mothers is the lack of adequate child care. About two-thirds of AFDC recipients in 1996 were children. In 1994, 46% of AFDC families had children under the age of 5.[25] Thus, almost one-half of all welfare families need child care (not to mention after-school care) if their parents are to be employed. While funds were too low, the old law at least guaranteed child-care assistance for families on welfare and 1 year for those "transitioning off." The new law provides no such guarantee. It consolidates four federal child-care programs—one for those on welfare, another for those transitioning off, a third for low-income families at-risk of welfare dependency, and a fourth that provided funds to increase the overall quality and supply of child care—into a new block grant called the Child Care and Development Fund.

The Child Care block grant included an increase of $4 billion over 6 years. However, the Congressional Budget Office estimated that the law provides $1.4 billion less than what will be needed over that time, even if all the states were to put up the matching funds necessary to get the federal money.[26] Although many states have increased their own spending in order to draw down federal matching funds and are using surplus money from their greatly reduced welfare rolls, according to some researchers the money may not be adequate to serve all the families that meet the eligibility criteria. Even states that have transferred large amounts of TANF funding to child care continued to have enormous unmet needs.[27] The U.S. Department of Health and Human Services estimated that only 1 in 10 potentially eligible low-income families actually gets the child-care assistance it needs.[28] Of cities surveyed by the U.S. Conference of Mayors in 1997, 71% reported that the average costs for full-day, center-based child care were not being met, and 62% reported that it did not cover the average current cost for full-day, home-based care.[29] In 1998, New York City lacked child care for 61% of the children whose mothers were supposed to be participating in workfare that year.[30]

Before welfare repeal, two-thirds of the 1.5 million children in federally subsidized child care were from working poor families. Only 4% of total child-care funds are set aside to improve the quality and expand the supply of child care. As more welfare recipients are forced to go to work, they will compete with these working poor families for the day-care slots available. Child-care advocates are concerned that what happened in Wisconsin's Milwaukee County (the state with the fastest exodus of welfare recipients into the labor market and one of the most generous sets of transitional subsidies) might happen elsewhere. Although the state increased its child-care expenses and included nonwelfare working families in the subsidies, very few nonwelfare families actually received the subsidies.[31] With no guarantee of child care for families not on public assistance, welfare recipients who exhaust their time limits may also face a child-care crisis.[32]

Neither the history of state support for child care nor current state efforts to respond to the crisis offer much basis for hope. A Children's Defense Fund analysis of state efforts to support child care in 1994 showed that as many as 20 states forfeited a proportion of the federal funds available for child care by failing to put up the matching funds.[33] Even in the states with the highest commitment to child care, the amounts allocated were inadequate to the need, and all states placed early care and education low on their priorities.[34]

Beyond the quantitative problem, there is also the question of quality. Many states are solving the child-care crisis by paying some TANF mothers to care for other recipients' children in their own homes, thus combining the work requirement with the child-care provision. While some states provide training, licensing, and supervision of such "family day-care providers," many have found it expedient to pay for informal arrangements in which a relative, friend, or neighbor agrees to take care of the children. A quarter of the children in government-financed child care in New York City are already cared for under such informal arrangements. The City has no quality control, safety oversight, or basic information about the people being paid to care for these children. A 1995 study of unregulated care in four cities found that only 9% of the households examined provided what was rated as "good quality care." More than one-third of the care was determined to have adversely affected the children's developmental progress.[35] A certain percentage of these informal arrangements may represent welfare clients' choice. However, with the lack of formal day care at times that fit workers' schedules, low state subsidies that make it impossible to purchase day care from formal providers, or ignorance about the availability of the service or care, day-care advocates fear that as the need expands, more states may resort to such informal arrangements. One reason is that the latter cost about one-third as much as formal day-care centers and about one-half of what states pay to licensed, family providers.[36]

Other welfare recipients are being put to work in private child-care agencies, but at those that usually pay the lowest wages and provide little or no training. The Center for the Child Care Work Force found that fewer than one-half the centers that hire welfare recipients offer on-site training, and only one in five offers the kind of college-credit training required for the better-paying child care jobs.[37]

The Uncertain Future of Child Support

In theory, child support from noncustodial parents is supposed to compensate for the increased financial insecurity of single mothers, but the record of such collection is poor. More than $34 billion in potential child-support income goes unpaid each year, and almost two-thirds of single mothers receive no assistance.[38] There are large differences among single-parent families with respect to child support. For example, in 1993, only 44% of children in families of never-married parents receive child-support payments, compared to 73% with divorced parents.[39] Much less likely to have married than their white counterparts, black and Hispanic single mothers are also less likely to get child support, and when they do get it, they are more likely to get less than white parents.[40]

Welfare "reform" has tried to alleviate the problem to both the state and the single-parent families. Under the PRWORA, jointly funded, federal-state, child-support agencies are supposed to help collect this support, both for families on public assistance and for others who ask for help. While streamlined procedures for collecting this money have increased the collections, it must be recognized that the poor economic prospects of many fathers has a great deal to do with their absence from the home. While states and private agencies have begun new programs to address this need, a study of such programs for fathers undertaken during the last period of welfare reform showed little promise of success.[41] Since such programs typically offer counseling and training but do little to provide family-supporting jobs or to increase the minimum wage, only changes in the overall labor market are likely to solve the problem.

Support for the view that some noncustodial fathers are unable to pay or able to pay very little comes from the record of Sweden's program of "advance maintenance." This is a policy of paying through government funds an amount thought necessary for a child's support and collecting the amount from noncustodial parents that they are considered able to pay. The program is available in France, Germany, and the Netherlands, in addition to Sweden. Although the Swedish government recovers over 80% of support obligations, these collections meet only somewhat over one-third of the amounts paid out as advance maintenance. As Marguerite Rosenthal has observed, "the maintenance advance is really serving as a supplementary grant to the custodial parent and her children."[42] The difference between this approach and the U.S. grant to single parents with income deficiencies—Aid to Families with Dependent Children or its successor, Temporary Assistance to Needy Families—is profound. The former treats the government grant as child support and the latter, as welfare.

Welfare Caseloads: A Mirror of Public Neglect

As the most work-ready welfare recipients move into the labor force, states may be left with a group of recipients with multiple barriers to work whose problems will require much more attention and support. Some of these may still be on the rolls, while others may have been dropped for rules violations, but in either case, states will confront much more intractable problems than any of them was willing to acknowledge in the first heady days of welfare "reform." A study by the Kaiser Foundation found that 30%

of the welfare caseload is composed of women who are caring for disabled children or are themselves disabled.[43] A Michigan study showed that welfare recipients were twice as likely as the general population to report physical limitations and four to five times more likely to report having suffered severe domestic abuse during the past year than women in national averages.[44] The California Senate estimated that 15% of its caseload required mental health treatment, 25% needed treatment for substance abuse, and 20% needed help to deal with domestic violence.[45] A two-county study in Oregon found that 70% of applicants for a JOBS program (under AFDC) had alcohol or drug problems, 60% had been or were being physically or sexually abused, 50% had mental health problems, and 35% had spent time in jail.[46] Although drug abuse has remained flat since 1992, except among teenagers, an estimated 13 million Americans in 1996 were illicit drug users. Yet in 1995, the states were able to provide treatment to only 340,000 persons with serious substance abuse problems.[47]

While there is no definitive national estimate of the prevalence of domestic violence among welfare recipients, five major research studies found that between 20% and 30% of welfare recipients are current victims of domestic violence and more could be past victims, bringing totals to as much as 75%.[48] The new welfare law (PRWORA) gave states the option of exempting battered women from the work requirements, and by 1999 at least three-fifths of them had adopted this option. But there was some evidence that far fewer battered women were being identified by the states than might actually exist in the welfare population. Many women who work with victims fear that some states may not exercise this option or may have trouble implementing it.[49] The effects of domestic violence can make it difficult for some battered women to get or maintain employment or to advance in their jobs.[50] Moreover, battered women need a lengthy period of time to heal from the emotional and physical scars of battering that the time limits in some states may not honor.[51] In addition, since the welfare law requires single mothers to cooperate in establishing the paternity of their children or risk financial penalty, obeying the law could subject abuse victims to more of the same.

The GAO recognized that even with more extensive supports, there may be people with such severe problems that they cannot work.[52] The Michigan study just cited estimated that as the number of "barriers" to work (i.e., physical or mental disability, lack of child care, a poor education) increase, the likelihood of a woman's finding at least half-time work decreases. Only 15% of the respondents in their sample reported no barriers to work, while one-quarter of the women had four or more.[53] If the estimates of the problem gathered from several regions are any indication, the numbers of such cases could exceed the 20% states are allowed to exempt from the federal time limit. In addition, as the GAO pointed out, there may be children at risk of negative outcomes because their parents fail to comply with the program requirements.

Finally, in all of the policy discussions on welfare reform, little attention has been paid to the increasing numbers of persons who are raising their grandchildren. As more mothers are forced into the labor market, more children are being left in the care of either the child-welfare agency or relatives, often grandmothers. Critics of the welfare system now claim that some welfare mothers may have found a new way to beat the system—by abandoning their children to relatives, or pretending to do so, since in many states grandmothers may be able to collect kinship child-care payments. Nationwide, about 1.4 million children in early 1999 were being reared by grandparents, representing a 52% increase since 1990. About one-half of these children were with a grandmother only, and 57% of the grandmothers had incomes below the poverty line.[54]

What research is available on grandparent-headed families is usually in large-scale survey form, leaving unanswered questions about the quality of care and its effects not only on children but on the caregivers.[55] But as reports from Wisconsin, the first state to cut its welfare loads by 91% indicate, the burden on grandmothers may be growing worse. In some cases, children placed with grandparents may be in more stable homes than the ones they left, but the burden on too many of these women—older, often in ill-health, and exhausted from a lifetime of child-rearing themselves—is cause for concern. Tulsa County, Oklahoma, reported that the county family homeless shelter was seeing many elderly individuals who are taking care of their grandchildren because their children cannot meet the state's new requirements.[56]

In summary, many welfare recipients confront a host of interrelated personal problems that require a multipronged and probably extended response. The question for our society is: What is our specific obligation to those who cannot help themselves, who have been debilitated by social disadvantage to the point where they are not self-supporting, or for whom there are insufficient jobs at decent wages?

With the TANF surpluses derived from drastically reduced welfare rolls, many states have increased both their welfare grants and their social services for those still on the rolls, as well as services for the working poor. Several other states, however, appear to have answered the question with the prescription: sink or swim. For example, Idaho and Wyoming have let their surpluses gather dust in Washington, even as they have reduced their safety nets. New York and Minnesota have simply traded their surpluses for services they used to pay for out of state funds, instead of using the surplus to create more services.[57] Some states have been placing disabled mothers in workfare programs, making it even more difficult for them to care for their families.[58] Some have been terminating welfare payments to persons who, because of their drug addictions, cannot find or hold on to jobs, yet these states have not been providing them with the rehabilitation programs they need to kick the habit. South Carolina even imprisoned a woman for endangering the life of her fetus at a time when no drug rehabilitation programs were available in the entire state.

Medicaid Losses: The Law of
Unintended Consequences

During the congressional debate over welfare, neither the authors of the TANF law nor its legislative critics paid much attention to the law of unintended consequences. The law's drafters provided that the children of those no longer eligible for welfare could continue to receive Medicaid if their financial circumstances warranted it, but as we mentioned in Chapter 8, the Medicaid rolls have declined along with the welfare rolls.[59] The first comprehensive study of this trend, conducted by Families USA, revealed that an estimated 1.25 million people—62% of them children and most of them still eligible—lost Medicaid coverage between 1995 and 1997.[60] While some of this drop may be attributable to the improved economy, health-care officials fear that most of it is due to other factors related to the way in which families leave the welfare rolls or are diverted from them in the first place. Some low-income families may be forgoing both welfare and Medicaid because new work regulations make it harder to combine a relief check with the off-the-book earnings that have long been a common method of survival for welfare mothers.[61] But many welfare departments were not informing clients that they were eligible for other benefits like

Medicaid, food stamps, and the EITC when they left the rolls or were diverted from them.

Alarmed by reports about the loss of Medicaid, the Clinton administration urged states to simplify their procedures and to educate the low-income public on the issue.[62] In addition, the 1997 budget agreement created a new Children's Health Insurance Program (CHIP) that gives states roughly $4 billion a year for the next 10 years to expand their health coverage for children in families with incomes of up to 200% of the federal poverty line.[63] Since most families who leave the rolls for work get jobs without medical benefits or make too little to afford the plans that are offered, it is important that states adopt the CHIP program and make it as widely available as possible.

The Synergistic Effects of Welfare Repeal and Cuts in Other Safety-Net Programs

In addition to the 5-year time limit on welfare created by the PRWORA, the law made large cuts in the food-stamp program, medical aid to low-income legal immigrants and disabled children, low-income housing, child nutrition programs, and various other social services for the poor. Since the poor often depend on a variety of government programs for their survival, no attempt to assess the effects of welfare repeal would be complete without calling attention to the scope and significance of the cuts in these other programs.

States may use the surplus money they have accrued in the TANF budget (because of rapidly declining enrollments) to fund other types of programs for the poor, but they cannot count on the federal government to fund such activities at the level of the past. As of this writing, states did not appear to be too concerned about the federal cuts because of the TANF surpluses and declining enrollments. However, in a recession, that lack of concern could quickly change.

More than 93% of the budget reductions in entitlements during the 104th Congress came from programs for low-income people, even though such programs represented only 23% of all entitlement spending. Nondefense discretionary programs for the poor (i.e., nonentitlements that include Head Start, WIC, and low-income housing subsidies) sustained cuts of more than 10%, while appropriations for other nondefense discretionary programs were reduced by only 5%. According to the Center on Budget and Policy Priorities, these figures are even conservative. They fail to include reductions in programs not classified as low-income but which affect low-income people, and they do not include changes in tax benefits that redistribute income to the highest 5 and 1% of income earners. Taking these into account raises the burden of the deficit reduction borne by low-income households to 95% of all budget reductions.[64]

While some funding for low-income programs was restored in the 1997 budget agreement, the losses are still substantial. In a telling indication of our government's priorities, the Clinton administration's proposed fiscal year 2000 budget contained a request for military spending that outweighed all categories of civilian discretionary spending combined.[65] And when extra money was needed to fund the air war in Yugoslavia, the government had no trouble in coming up with the extra. Moreover, the federal cuts are not the only ones. States, counties, and cities across the country have been following the lead of the federal government.

THE EFFECTS OF CUTS IN FEEDING PROGRAMS

The single largest set of reductions has been in the food-stamp program. These include downward adjustments in the budget plan used to calculate food-stamp awards, elimination of benefits to many legal immigrants, time-limits for able-bodied adults without dependents, and changes in eligibility and income criteria for families.[66]

As the legislation moved toward implementation, analysts found that the food-stamp reductions were likely to have far harsher consequences for childless adults than many had at first thought.[67] The Congressional Budget Office estimated that in an average month, nearly one-half million jobless individuals—most of whom were willing to work and one-third of whom were over 40—would be denied food stamps under this provision because they failed to live in an exempt area (an area where unemployment is high and state officials have applied for and been granted a waiver on the time limits). According to the USDA, among those likely to be affected, the average income was only 28% of the federal poverty level. Analysts at the Center on Budget and Policy Priorities pointed out that this new provision marks the first time in the history of the program that individuals are being terminated because no work is available, not because these individuals have refused to work.[68]

Since passage of the PRWORA, some states have applied for waivers, claiming that they had neither the jobs nor the job-preparation programs that would allow recipients to remain eligible for food stamps. In addition, the Clinton administration, backed by both Republican and Democratic governors and advocates for immigrants and the poor, succeeded in restoring food stamps for some 250,000 elderly and disabled legal immigrants who were in the country at the time the bill was passed—although other legal immigrants are still denied.[69] It should be noted that the PRWORA cut the Child- and Adult-Care Feeding Program that helps pay for meals to low-income people, as well as the Summer Food Program that takes the place in some localities of free and reduced-price meals during the school year.[70]

CUTS IN DISABILITY AND MEDICAL CARE

Seeking to reduce taxes on the wealthy while also reducing the deficit, conservative Republicans chose the most politically vulnerable population groups to bear the burden of budget reductions. The PRWORA eliminated SSI benefits for thousands of low-income disabled children who failed to fit new, stricter definitions of disability. A spokesman for the Social Security Administration estimated that between 100,000 and 200,000 children—or 10–20% of all children on the rolls—would eventually lose their benefits.[71] Such children could also lose their automatic eligibility for Medicaid because of these new restrictions.[72]

With a few exceptions, the PRWORA eliminated SSI benefits for low-income elderly and disabled legal immigrants. It also eliminated Medicaid coverage for the first 5 years to legal immigrants who entered the country after the law was signed. States have the option of continuing this ban for a longer period and of denying Medicaid (but not CHIP) to legal immigrants already living in the United States when the law was signed. Eligibility for SSI for immigrants residing in the country when the law was passed is restricted to those who were receiving SSI at the time of welfare reform and those who qualify now or in the future on the basis of disability only.[73]

In budget negotiations with Congress in 1997, the administration succeeded in restoring some of the funds that PRWORA had denied to legal immigrants and in giving states the option of purchasing food stamps for legal immigrants who had been denied federal eligibility. The president and Congress acceded to pressure not only from immigrant groups, who began to demonstrate a newfound political militancy, but from Republican lawmakers in states and cities with large immigrant populations. New York's mayor, Rudolph Giuliani, whose workfare program has been justly criticized for its harshness, championed immigrant benefits, warning that cuts to immigrants would have severe impacts on city budgets like his own.

Left without protection, however, are legal immigrants now in need of low-income assistance who were not eligible at the time PRWORA was enacted, legal immigrants who arrived since the bill was signed, elderly immigrants who do not have a sufficiently severe disability to meet the SSI disability test, undocumented aliens, and thousands of disabled children.[74]

While the budget negotiations of 1997 restored some measure of justice and compassion, the very fact that such cuts were written into the legislation in the first place caused anguish for thousands of immigrants and disabled children and their families, perhaps permanently shaking their sense of security. As early as November 1996, letters went out to the parents of 260,000 disabled children telling them that they could lose their SSI coverage, and in February 1997, legal immigrants were similarly informed. With receipt of the letters came reports to charities and churches of potential suicides among the poor elderly, who were fearful of becoming a burden on their children and grandchildren.[75] Confused about the law, some nursing homes began mistakenly to deny admission to elderly legal immigrants who had been given the reprieve by President Clinton and to deny care to current residents. Others found it easier to refuse all legal immigrants. "It's heartbreaking," Sheryl Geminder, director of admissions at the Sephardic Home for the Aged in Brooklyn, told the *New York Times*, "but we're all too terrified to admit anybody who is not a citizen."[76]

The effects of denying aid to the sick elderly and to disabled children are not limited to those groups. They are often thrown back upon the care of their families, many of whom are already impoverished or hard-pressed. Even family members who are not poor could be driven over the edge by the burden of having to pay for the care of a sick elderly relative or child or to be forced to provide the care themselves. A legal immigrant who testified at a hearing on welfare reform in suburban Westchester County, New

York, told public officials that if her mother, who had Alzheimer's disease, were to lose her Supplemental Security Income, she (the daughter) would have to quit her job to take care of her. This would leave her without an income, and she could end up on welfare herself. Another who testified was caring for her 24-year-old, severely retarded son. Mistakenly or not, she had just been told by her caseworker that she would lose the benefits that enabled her to pay for his care.[77] Those who tout the merits of "family values" have curiously ignored the devastating effects of these policies on family care and stability.

Such cuts are increasing the demand on the already strapped resources of churches and private charitable groups and could result in increases in epidemic diseases, if people go untreated. In addition, those too sick to be cared for by relatives will end up in the acute care beds of hospitals, and patients who need those beds may be spending more time in the emergency room.

Denying aid to immigrants will also increase the incidence of a disturbing trend in recent years—the surveillance of and discrimination against people with heavy accents and foreign names. The refusal of some nursing homes to admit or provide care for all immigrants is indicative of the problem. Faced with new penalties for violating the federal law, it is not inconceivable that state welfare officials and employers could engage in unconstitutional, unannounced visits to homes or invasive questioning of welfare recipients, require the fingerprinting of all who apply for welfare, and the like.

Cuts in other safety-net programs will exacerbate the hardships for millions of families and individuals. As part of the PRWORA, Congress cut 15% or $420 million from the $2.8 billion it distributes annually to the states under the Social Services Block Grant. States use this money for multiple purposes, such as paying for shelters and day care, rehabilitating juvenile criminals, rescuing children from parental abuse, and providing home-care services for the elderly. States can transfer some TANF funds to the Social Services Block Grant, and, with reduced welfare caseloads and increased state revenues, many are currently weathering the cuts. But when the effect of welfare repeal really sets in, they will have less money to work with than they had before PRWORA. How will they decide between continuing home care for elderly and disabled people and nutrition programs or protective services for children?

THE DWINDLING STOCK OF AFFORDABLE HOUSING

Low-income housing programs have also taken a beating. Diminished spending on housing began in the 1970s, but the Reagan administration dealt a deadly blow to affordable housing when it reduced the low-income housing budget by 75%, even as poverty was rising.[78] Further reductions in housing appropriations over the last few years have grown to crisis proportions. Clinton proposed an increase of 50,000 Section 8 housing vouchers to help families transitioning off welfare pay for rent in the private market.[79] However, this is a drop in the bucket compared with the 5.3 million households in 1995 that faced a crisis of unaffordable rents and substandard living conditions.[80] This was the largest shortage on record.[81] The problem is no longer largely limited to the cities or to persons on welfare. About one-seventh of all families who rent have incomes of less than 50% of the area median. More than three of five of these poor renters (not limited to welfare recipients) spend at least one-half their income on rent and utilities. The National Low-Income Housing Coalition pointed out that in 2000, employees earning the minimum wage could not afford to rent even a "modest," two-bedroom apartment in any county in the nation.[82]

There has long been criticism that the very poor were too concentrated in public housing, causing housing projects to become warrens of crime and squalor. To remedy this, the Department of Housing and Urban Development has begun a program to tear down 100,000 apartments in high-rise buildings around the country to make room for a variety of low-rise alternatives and mixed-income housing. This is a laudable goal, but if the experience of Chicago is any example, the plight of the poor could be made even worse. The city planned to tear down 8 of the 23 buildings in the infamous Cabrini Green housing project to erect condominiums, town houses, and schools. A lawyer for the Cabrini Green tenants said the plan "has all the earmarks of the American nightmare, an old fashioned land-grab" that amounts to "ethnic cleansing." The plan means a net loss of 1,000 apartments for low-income, predominantly African–American, people. Many residents of Cabrini Green feared the entire apartment complex would eventually be demolished.[83]

Children and families are the fastest growing subset of the homeless, representing at least 40% of the estimated 400,000 homeless in 1996.[84] As homelessness has grown, public attitudes have hardened.

Cities have become more restrictive and punitive in their policies, enacting ordinances against panhandling, restricting the movement of homeless people, and engaging in police sweeps and the razing of shantytowns.[85] New York's Governor Pataki even proposed to charge homeless people rent for staying in public shelters if the state determined that they had personal assets, jobs, or other sources of income beyond basic welfare grants.[86] Mary Brosnahan, executive director of the Coalition for the Homeless, pointed out: "People who are gainfully employed [as many of the homeless are] should be . . . encouraged to save money for security deposits and first and last month's rents [in the private market]. We should try to marshal resources to get people out of this hideous system rather than punishing them."[87]

Direct cuts in the safety-net programs will be augmented by the indirect assault Congress, the states, and even the private sector have been simultaneously making on a system of programs and subsidies that redistribute income downward. This intricate redistributive network includes public-school systems, open-admissions, and affirmative-action programs in colleges and workplaces,[88] Social Security, Medicare and the like. It serves as a kind of social and political glue, holding a diverse society together and providing a measure of social and economic fairness that is critical to the survival of democracy. Both federal and state governments now seem more willing to allow the wealthier to opt out of such systems under the guise of providing individuals with more "choice" (as they propose to do in allowing people to use their Social Security checks to invest in the stock market or to use an education voucher to pay for private schooling). Recent changes in Medicare have also fragmented what was formerly a single insurance pool that spread risks among the full population. While Medicare patients are now offered "choice" among competing health plans, Medicaid's obligation to cover Medicare copayments for the poor elderly has been limited. If such changes continue, health and education for the poorest will suffer even more than at present, and the sociopolitical fabric of the society could be torn, along with the safety net.

Finally, since the new welfare rules and funding levels affect different groups of people with different needs, the combined effects of various restrictions could have devastating impacts on particular households. For example, grandparents could be cut off of SSI while children and other adults in the household lose welfare and food stamps.

The Discriminatory Impact of Welfare Repeal

In exacerbating the suffering of those at the bottom, the PRWORA creates several new castes with complex rules for who should and should not get certain government benefits or be singled out for special coercion. While the rules governing aid to immigrants have always been complex, the new law creates several new categories of "deserving" and "undeserving" immigrants. For example, "qualified aliens" (permanent residents, refugees, asylees and certain others granted conditional entry) are deserving of some government help. "Nonqualified" aliens (undocumented immigrants and those in PRUCOL [permanently residing under color of law] status) are undeserving. After PRWORA, there is also a new distinction between qualified legal immigrants who were in the U.S. before the law was signed (deserving of some benefits), and legal immigrants who arrived later (undeserving).

Within the TANF, SSI, and housing-assistance programs, the law requires state and federal authorities to notify the Immigration and Naturalization Service at least quarterly of known illegal immigrants and to implement new verification systems; and it forbids federal, state or local laws from prohibiting these surveillance and reporting requirements.[89] Since the vast majority of welfare use among immigrants is for the elderly and disabled, these new restrictions represent crackdowns on the most vulnerable parts of the population. According to the Welfare Information Network, the costs to states and communities of these changes, not to mention the individuals and families themselves—in humanitarian, public health and safety, economic, political, and fiscal terms—could be quite large.[90]

Although the majority of those who have collected welfare in the past have been white, minority groups—particularly African–Americans, Hispanics, and Native Americans—have been disproportionately represented on the welfare rolls and among the working poor. The combined impact of welfare repeal and cuts in other low-income programs can be expected to further impoverish these groups. Two years into welfare repeal, the *New York Times* reported that whites were leaving the welfare rolls much faster than blacks or Hispanics, pushing the minority share of the caseload to the highest level on record—twice that of whites. In addition, the remaining caseload is largely urban and concentrated in inner cities where there are fewer jobs than in the suburbs.[91]

Given the nation's historic pattern of racial discrimination and the differential impact on racial minorities of the macroeconomic changes we discussed earlier, it should come as no surprise that the welfare rolls are now dominated by people of color. Yet, according to the *Times*, "most officials reacted with surprise when presented with the figures." This racial/ethnic skewing of the welfare rolls can lead to the further scapegoating of welfare recipients as it has in the past, when the perception, if not the reality, was that welfare was a "black program." While some African–American leaders interviewed by the *Times* dismissed the possibility of racial backlash, they were speaking during a time of economic growth and low unemployment. Should the economy sour, the potential for increased hostility is there, and, as representative Donald Payne (D-N.J.) observed, "wedge issue politicians always use welfare as an issue."[92]

It hardly needs mentioning that the new welfare law is also disproportionately harsh on poor women, who make up 90% of the adults affected by welfare repeal. The new poor law intensifies the stigmatization of poor, single mothers that was historically a part of the poor relief experience.[93] Gwendolyn Mink has provided a spirited argument that poor women constitute a "separate caste, subject to a separate system of law" that "penalizes their moral choices, prescribes intimate associations that may be unwanted . . . infringes rights regarded as fundamental to the personhood of all other citizens," and forces them into a regimen of prescribed work that no other mothers with young children are required *by law* to undergo.[94]

Poor women seemed to be the ghosts haunting the welfare debate. Even the staunchest congressional and media critics of the PRWORA, including many congressional feminists, failed to recognize the ways in which the bill blames these women for poverty and "welfare dependency" and punishes them for being poor.[95] When critics of the bill wanted to describe the potential tragedies that lay ahead if the bill were to be implemented, they were inevitably couched in terms of what the bill would do to immigrants or to children, as if at least one-half or more of the immigrants who would suffer from the bill were not women. *Time* magazine's comment was typical: "Neither governors nor Congress is likely to tolerate more malnourished or neglected children."[96] Some editors, however, made the underlying prejudice against poor women more explicit. Said the *Washington Post*, "The central issue in reforming [welfare] has been the same for years. How do you increase the pressure on welfare mothers to go to work while continuing to support their children if they fail?"[97]

In the surreal thinking associated with welfare repeal, poor women exist in a kind of social vacuum. They are not immigrants, elderly, sick, disabled, caring for elderly or disabled family members, victims of spousal or partner abuse, discriminated against in the workplace, or weighed down with the daily struggle of rearing children in rat-, roach-, and drug-infested neighborhoods with too little money to make it through the month. Before welfare "reform" was enacted, Christopher Jencks and Kathryn Edin had pointed out that a significant minority of the population, even if they "played by all the rules," could not afford to have children without government help. (The recently enacted child tax credits recognize this reality, even for the middle class.) "Are we to assume," ask Jencks and Edin, "that the losers in this lottery have no right to bear children at all? And, if not, are we really prepared to enforce this principle and all of its implications?"[98] The answer of welfare "reformers" seems to be a Malthusian yes.

Even as the White House convened a conference on Early Child Development, which stressed the importance of close parental contact for healthy child development, and Clinton's advisers were calling for tax incentives so parents could stay home with their young children, federal and state welfare reformers were coercing poor mothers into spending long hours away from their children. Many poor parents were also being denied aid for rule infractions, such as missing work to care for a sick child or because they could not find child care.[99] Evidently, in the minds of these welfare "reformers," poor children are somehow unaffected if their parents are forced to work without adequate support or are denied welfare because their time limits have expired.

The Politics of Welfare Reform

Peter Edelman, an assistant secretary in the Department of Health and Human Services, called Clinton's signing of the new poor law "the worst thing Bill Clinton has done,"[100] conceding that in an election year, no one, himself included, had wanted to call him on it.[101] If liberals like Edelman were perhaps compromised by their proximity to the White House, there had been ample evidence out in the trenches that the PRWORA's approach to welfare reform, with its strict time limits, work requirements, and weak focus on

education, would not work, and Clinton had known this. He had
come to Washington having boasted that he had "grown the economy"
in Arkansas with his job-training and job-creation programs. But
as Robert Scheer pointed out, in some of the poorest counties in
Arkansas where the greatest efforts were made, the only jobs that
resulted were either part-time jobs in fast food outlets or in the
growing prison system. As the president of a local Chamber of
Commerce admitted, the real problem was that "we don't have a
national jobs and relocation policy."[102]

The 5-year budget reduction agreement Clinton negotiated with
congressional Republicans in May 1997 added money for five
significant social programs in addition to the Welfare-to-Work grants.
On balance, however, it was a victory for the Republicans, who
boasted in an internal memorandum that they had scaled back "the
President's insatiable appetite for more government spending programs."[103] Funding for all but one either terminates or declines
after a few years. In contrast, tax relief for the nation's richest
people escalates with time. The Center on Budget and Policy Priorities
has pointed out that by the year 2007, tax relief for the top 5%
and 1% of the population *will cost almost twice as much as all of
the social programs combined.*[104]

Since these budgets were based on the dubious assumption
that the economy would continue to grow at its then current rate,
it takes little imagination to see that with such substantial revenue
losses, further social spending cuts might be needed down the line.
If so, they may have to come out of the entitlement programs that
the middle class has come to depend on. Even as we write, there
has been a growing chorus of policy pundits advocating the privatizing of Social Security, public education, and other pieces of
the diminishing welfare state that serve all citizens.

Summary: The New (Old) War on the Poor

Our examination of the assumptions upon which the new Poor
Law is based, the preliminary experience with some of its provisions that were incorporated in state waiver programs, and the
first 2–3 years of the law's implementation reveal serious problems with a piece of legislation that was supposed to create strong,
self-supporting families. Among the problems surveyed in Chapters 8 and 9 are: the inadequacy of the low-wage labor market into
which recipients are being thrust; the punitive and often cruel

regulations adopted by many states; the potential for abuse that lurks in the privatization of welfare services; the law's weak commitment to education, training, and rehabilitation; the lack of adequate supportive services for families transitioning from welfare to work, especially child care and education; the synergistic effect of welfare repeal and cuts in other safety net programs; and the discriminatory impact of the law on immigrants, people of color, and women.

All of this amounts to a new war on the poor, masked initially by the strong economy and the official perception that when welfare recipients leave the rolls for work, they are on the road to self-sufficiency. Although most advocacy groups believe the fight for genuine welfare reform at the national level is a lost cause, we caution against such an attitude. We believe that effective welfare reform can only happen on a national level, and in Chapter 10, we outline both a new national plan for really reforming welfare and some strategies that could move the nation in that direction.

CHAPTER 10

 ⊙━━━✠✠✠✠✠✠━━⊙

Real Welfare Reform:
The Roads Not Taken

T he lowest unemployment rates in 30 years delayed the full
impact of Washington's New Poor Law. However, the economy
that eased the transition from welfare to work and that would
have reduced the relief rolls without PRWORA will certainly not
hold. Political leaders have not committed themselves to keeping
unemployment low—much less pushing it down still further to real
full employment. Thus, when the next recession comes, it will visit
its hardships on a nation that no longer maintains even a partial
entitlement to welfare—a nation whose leaders have so consistently
bad-mouthed government that it will be difficult to employ the macroeconomic solutions that have proven effective in past recessions.[1]
Expiring time limits will leave many of the poor without either
welfare or work. While welfare reform may have given some single
mothers the nudge they needed to enter or return to the labor market,
the repeal of AFDC portends greater insecurity, poverty, and privation for many families and children who are already economically disadvantaged.

Although preliminary studies from several states indicate that
substantial proportions of the welfare caseload found work, many
were employed in jobs that paid annual wages less than the federal poverty level for a family of three and that lacked paid vacations, sick leave, and health and retirement benefits. In nearly every
state, the majority of poor families have one or more adults who
are employed and thus experiencing "poverty despite work."[2] In
1999, notwithstanding the prolonged economic boom and rising
real wages for at least 5 years, over one-fourth of all U.S. workers, one-third of women, two-fifths of black women , and just over
half of Hispanic women earned poverty-level wages.[3] In view of

266

the fact that many AFDC recipients worked in order to supplement their grants, it may be conjectured that some who leave the rolls must now exist on wages alone. Further, by increasing the number of job seekers, welfare "repeal" could have a depressing effect on the wages of low-income workers or could have kept them from rising more than they have in an economic boom.[4] Tight labor markets are not universal, and it is unlikely that the jobs many welfare leavers get will lead to upward mobility or permanent attachment to the work force.

Although dramatic roll reductions enabled federal and state officials to brag about welfare reform's "success," the states' increased penalties for failure to conform to the new rules, their greater use of diversion policies, and their initial failure, in most cases, to track welfare recipients who leave the rolls mean that a substantial proportion of the caseload may fall between cracks—neither counted as working nor on welfare. Indeed, reports from food pantries, soup kitchens, and homeless shelters seem to confirm this trend. Also consistent with these reports is early research that found most states implementing policies that made families worse off than under the old, much-maligned welfare system.

Welfare repeal seems to result in other harmful effects on the poor: reductions in the numbers of families receiving Medicaid and food stamps, even though they are eligible; loss of benefits for many legal immigrants and disabled children; welfare mothers forced to drop out of college and other educational and training programs; inadequate and sometimes dangerous day care; and further racial/ethnic skewing of the welfare rolls.

While the latter part of this book analyzed these effects of Washington's New Poor Law, the first part plumbed the reasons for welfare repeal. Our analysis identified the basic characteristics of AFDC that contributed to its vulnerability throughout its 60-year history. We also pointed out some changing conditions that weakened the program. And history also revealed failed opportunities for welfare reform that further damaged its image and reduced public support. Finally, there were some immediate conditions that brought Title IV of the Social Security Act to the chopping block in the summer of 1996. Following a summary of these reasons for repeal, this chapter considers the functions of AFDC in the light of our findings, that is, the extent to which it serves patriarchy, racism, capitalism, or all three. We conclude with a proposal for real reform. The centerpiece of this reform is a policy absent throughout the history of AFDC, which is living-wage jobs for all or an *entitle-ment* to work. Between 1950 and 1996, the United States had a partial entitlement to welfare,[5] but, paradoxically, in view of American worship of the work ethic, the U.S. never had an entitlement to work. We need both an entitlement to work and restoration of an entitlement to welfare. In this final chapter, we look at the reasons why full employment or an entitlement to work has continued to elude us and whether it is possible to create the mass movement that would be necessary for its enactment.

Reasons for Repeal

The Missing Entitlement

The labor market in which AFDC operated throughout nearly all its history and the pervasive denial of the conditions that consistently afflicted millions of workers contributed mightily to its vulnerability. This was the case when mothers were considered nurturers and categorized as unemployable, and it became even more so when their role expectations changed.

Although relief rolls expand in response to a number of factors, and indeed did so in the 1960s when unemployment rates were falling, the chronic problems of unemployment, involuntary part-time employment, and low wages that are detailed throughout this book contributed to the size of AFDC caseloads. Growth in a program that does not directly benefit those who pay for it tends to cause resentment among taxpayers and to increase its political liability. High rates of unemployment among African–American men and women made their families disproportionately dependent on AFDC and burdened the program with another source of unpopularity—racial prejudice.

Unpopularity and resentment of welfare are aggravated when the structural roots of economic dependency are denied or downplayed and the individual factors magnified. Official unemployment rates that conceal "the underbelly" of the U.S. economy shape the public's perception that the labor market can absorb all who merely make themselves available for work. As explained in Chapter 8, most of the unemployed and underemployed are uncounted: those who are forced to work part-time, who become too discouraged to continue to look for a job, who are in prison, often for reasons related to unemployment, and who, like many women, earn so little that their families are hungry without income supplements.[6] Nor does the public recognize that increases in unemployment are often deliberate government policies undertaken to prevent inflation. It follows that those who become unemployed and underemployed as a result of these policies are, in effect, sacrificed on the altar of price stability. With the problem all but denied, minimized, undercounted, or misdiagnosed, those who suffer are seen as perpetrators—malingering rather than unfortunate. And public policy that forces them to work by restricting and ultimately denying them relief carries the name of reform rather than repression. The official denial of chronic underemployment and unemployment in the U.S. labor market carried heavy political consequences for the unemployed and their families.

The architects of the Social Security Act, who were members of the administration's Committee on Economic Security and among Roosevelt's closest advisors, doubted that the economy could ever absorb all of the unemployed. They recommended that public employment projects "be recognized as a permanent policy of the government and not merely as an emergency measure."[7] As this book has demonstrated, their doubts were justified, but their recommendations went unheeded. Except for war time, the U.S. labor market has been characterized by chronic unemployment and underemployment. Unemployment was relatively low in the late 1990s. Even so, in 1998, when the national unemployment rate was 4.5%, 74 cities and 300 counties had rates of 9% or higher.[8] And according to the U.S. Department of Housing and Urban Development, one in six U.S. cities had chronically high unemployment rates despite the general decline in unemployment.[9] People of color have suffered disproportionately from labor-market disadvantages, but it is important to recognize that the great majority of the unemployed always were, and still are, white.

Very large work programs were established during the Great Depression and discontinued during World War II. President Roosevelt talked to his close associates about a permanent job program for the unemployed who exhausted their unemployment insurance benefits and could not find work, and he evidently worked out some of the details with Harry Hopkins and Frances Perkins. They did not, however, translate their plans for a permanent, standby public employment program into a legislative proposal.[10]

Toward the end of the war, Roosevelt called for an Economic Bill of Rights that began with the "right to a useful and remunerative

job in the industries or shops or farms or mines in the nation."[11]
But despite the demonstrated benefits of wartime unemployment
in the 1–2% range, less than one-half the rates that are presently
considered low, a determined opposition of agrarian and business
interests defeated full employment in the postwar years. Among
the many consequences of virtual full employment in the war years
was a drop in ADC caseloads—despite factors that would otherwise
have caused the rolls to expand (more states signed on, benefits
levels rose, etc.). Instead of adopting a policy of jobs for all, Congress
passed an employment bill with no such guarantees. Despite favorable
public opinion, there was no mass movement for full employment
strong enough to counter a determined minority that was able to
exercise veto power in our divided national government. One reason
is that a number of conditions and public policies prevented large-
scale unemployment from appearing in the immediate postwar years.

After the Korean War, unemployment rose and became increasingly
serious for young workers and for black men and women who were
shut out of the growth industry—white-collar work—by discrimination. The consequences of federal failure to provide work for
the unemployed on a permanent basis, which had been masked during
the two wars, became apparent to some economists and some members
of the legislative and executive branches of government from the
mid-1950s on. Yet, it was largely neglected by both economic and
social policies.

Jobs for all was a stated goal of civil-rights leaders. Yet, full
employment was not the issue over which the historic battles of
the movement were fought. In the 1960s, freedom or civil rights
came first. In this decade of great social movements, there was
no mass mobilization for full employment. Perhaps Martin Luther
King was moving in that direction; he had begun to emphasize
economic as well as civil rights, but the assassin's bullet left that
prospect in the realm of speculation. King's untimely assassination stilled an important voice for jobs, just as Roosevelt's death
two decades earlier had robbed full employment of potentially its
most effective advocate.

Efforts to create public employment and to gain passage of
full employment during the high unemployment years of the 1970s
were either short-lived or unsuccessful. The Comprehensive
Employment and Training Act (CETA) was the first, large-scale
public employment program since the Great Depression and, like
its predecessors, unfairly maligned, despite its accomplishments

for the jobless and its services to communities. Changes in its structure increased its vulnerability. Whereas the New Deal work programs were terminated as the war economy was conquering unemployment, Ronald Reagan terminated the CETA program in the early 1980s, even as federal policies were creating more unemployment. The Humphrey Hawkins Full Employment and Balanced Growth Act of 1978 was no more likely to give everyone the right to practice the work ethic than the watered-down Employment Act of 1946. The *entitlement to work* was to remain a missing entitlement. Yet, as unemployment worsened, the effort to push more poor women into the labor market increased.

THE SINGLE-PARENT FOCUS

At the time the Social Security Act was being considered, the champions of assistance for dependent children advocated a program that would achieve the goal that had eluded the state mothers' aid programs: freeing single mothers from the breadwinning role. Concerned with the welfare of children, the leaders of the Children's Bureau, who designed the program that became ADC, nonetheless confined their proposals to single-parent families under the assumption that employable males would be assured jobs—an assumption that proved to be wrong. Their approach to child welfare carried on the maternalist tradition of protecting women, rather than encouraging and supporting their economic independence or giving them a choice between full-time nurturing and employment. This policy was at the same time compatible with the drive to discourage women's employment during the Great Depression, when jobs were in such short supply. Even so, conservatives, particularly representatives of southern agricultural interests, saw to it that the program would offer no competition to low wages and no deterrent to women's employment when they were needed in the fields. Many men—the welfare fathers—were short-changed in both employment and assistance policies. Either in occupations not covered by unemployment insurance or suffering chronic unemployment or underemployment, millions of these men never established a firm foothold in the labor market.

State general-assistance programs, the shaky and often nonexistent safety net for nearly all two-parent families, were, if available, nearly always meager, affording little relief to the victims of a chronically loose labor market. Thus, men with marginal connections to the labor force recognized that their families might be better off economically if they were out of the home. Or deprived of an important family role, they ceased to be part of their families and sought escape from uselessness and humiliation. Interestingly, recent research has shown a relationship between men's detachment from the occupational community and detachment from the family in some European countries.[12]

Labor-market disadvantages of both men and women are important contributors to the economic strains that break marriages or keep them from forming in the first place. Examining labor-market issues over time, William Julius Wilson and his colleagues demonstrated that rising rates of African–American single parenthood were related to the increase of unemployment among black males.[13] In addition, the formidable labor-market disadvantages of women, particularly women of color, are critical not only to single mothers' need for assistance but to economic sufficiency in two-parent families. Many middle-income families feel they need two incomes, and that is even more the reality for low-wage couples.

President Truman's proposal to provide aid to all those in need rather than to confine federally assisted relief to particular categories of the poor might have reduced the growth of poor single-parent households. Like the proposed welfare reforms of his successors, Presidents Nixon and Carter, Truman's would not only have removed incentives for desertion but strengthened family assistance politically, leaving it less vulnerable to the kind of attack on single mothers and women of color that grew in intensity in the 1980s and 1990s and culminated in repeal.

ANTIPOVERTY POLICIES

The nation had another chance to address economic disadvantage. Mounting many commendable programs, Lyndon Johnson's war on poverty aimed for a "great society" with flawed strategies and limited resources. "Economic opportunity," the watchword of the antipoverty program, was not defined as employment opportunity. The chronic unemployment and underemployment of the urban ghettos—30% even when overall unemployment rates were dipping to 3.5%—were, in time, documented by Congress and the Department of Labor. The secretary of labor, Willard Wirtz, advocated for job creation at the Cabinet level, and Robert Kennedy recognized that no government program addressed the crisis of black unemployment. Lyndon Johnson resisted job creation because it was an expensive strategy that also might have cost him the business and other conservative support that he sought for his antipoverty program.

Ironically, the antipoverty program stimulated a welfare explosion. Fearful of civil disorder, local agencies yielded to pressure from welfare recipients and their advocates, adding to the rolls eligible families who had been denied assistance in earlier decades. The War on Poverty, through its Community Action Program, came to focus on welfare rights, and advocacy for the poor was largely for income support instead of work. Indeed, welfare advocates were to continue this one-sided approach to economic justice until welfare repeal forced them to give more consideration to job creation.

The Johnson administration, which had declared itself for a "hand-up" instead of "handout," was disinclined to interpret the welfare explosion as a victory for its antipoverty policies, even though its community-action programs encouraged the welfare explosion. Nor did political leaders interpret the rise in relief as a response to long-neglected need. From the executive branch itself came a different explanation: the breakdown of the Negro family. As black recipience increased and AFDC became larger and more expensive, it became more vulnerable, particularly to a developing white backlash that was fueled by the perception that federal programs were rewarding blacks for rioting and by the stereotype that blacks are less committed to the work ethic than whites.

In the first 25 years of ADC, states had been the instruments of restrictive and racially exclusive welfare policies, often countenanced and unrestrained by Washington. Now official federal policy turned in this direction. Indeed, welfare "reform" began in the late 1960s when AFDC began to serve a larger proportion of those in need, especially a larger proportion of people of color. The 1967 welfare "freeze," a thinly disguised attack on black recipients, was an attempt to punish welfare mothers for out-of-wedlock births, but it was also an attempt to cut back relief. To attack the sexual behavior of black recipients was a better strategy in a time of gathering backlash than to own up to class-based reasons for cutting back the program that had expanded so greatly. Yet, just a few years later, class factors were clearly at work in the opposition of southern legislators to even a modest income guarantee because it threatened their cheap labor supply—the women and men who ironed other people's shirts or pushed wheelbarrows.

RIGHT-WING RESURGENCE

Following the 1964 rout of Republican Barry Goldwater, conservatives rebounded with strategies for winning back the political and economic commanding heights. Their strategy included well-financed ideological campaigns that, among other things, provided the rationale for restrictive welfare "reform." The media reinforced popular stereotypes about the poor and portrayed welfare as a black program. Reconstructing the poor, neoconservative academics and pundits gave scientific credibility to individualistic interpretations of poverty in a manner reminiscent of that use of similar pseudoscience, Social Darwinism, in the nineteenth century. In so doing, they provided a rationale for rampant inequality and hands-off government. Welfare dependency and allegedly abundant and easy-to-get assistance became the root of U.S. social and economic problems instead of a symptom of poverty, unemployment, declining wages, and the institutionalized racism and sexism that were still endemic. What was at core an underemployed working class came to be labeled a dangerous and deviant "underclass."

Resurgent conservatism also orchestrated the response of economic and political elites to the temporary loss of American economic hegemony in the 1970s and to the new phenomenon of stagflation. With the election of Ronald Reagan, the ideas promulgated by conservatives became official policy. Reaganomics featured a tripartite effort to reduce inflation and discipline labor through weakening collective bargaining rights, reducing social-welfare benefits, and increasing unemployment. Washington not only failed to protect workers against worsening labor market conditions but consciously pursued policies that created or exacerbated those conditions.

FAILURE TO ENACT REFORM

The unsuccessful reform proposals of two administrations during the 1970s also served to discredit AFDC. Presidents Nixon and Carter found that their promises to clean up the "welfare mess" were popular campaign rhetoric. Both presidents abetted negative perceptions of welfare, and neither really pushed hard for his proposed reforms. Both failed campaigns reinforced perceptions of an on-going "crisis" in welfare.

Had either the Nixon or Carter plan been enacted, the working poor, including many more whites, would have been added to the rolls, making the program larger, but sheltered from the racial backlash. If the program had expanded over the years, it could have blurred that false dichotomy between the welfare and the working poor that undermines solidarity in the working class and weakens it politically. The primarily black and northern constituency of the National Welfare Rights Organization did not stand to benefit initially from the modest guarantees of Nixon's Family Assistance Plan (FAP). So NWRO expended a great deal of energy to "Zap FAP," which might have been a political advantage to its constituency. In any case, the fight to zap FAP sapped NWRO.

Except for a brief, anomalous period when welfare advocacy was encouraged by public policies and social movements that spurred "rights consciousness," welfare mothers were a politically iso-lated and weak group without the resources to defend their inter-ests against retrenchment, particularly in the climate of the 1980s and 1990s. They had not been an organized constituency at the time when ADC was enacted and were not when it was repealed. Paul Pierson hypothesizes that welfare states are hard to retrench because social welfare programs create vested interests or con-stituents who resist the loss of their benefits, but he also recog-nizes that means-tested programs with marginalized beneficiaries have to rely primarily on public-interest groups and providers.[14] In the case of AFDC, these, as we discuss shortly, were weak or nonsupportive.

BUDGETARY "CRISIS"

Considered a deliberate effort to undermine social spending by some respected observers, burgeoning budgetary deficits formed a critical context for welfare repeal. Tax cuts robbed the federal treasury of revenues, steep rises in military spending contributed to deficits, and high levels of unemployment cost the treasury in both revenues and outlays. To continue, much less increase, spending for social programs became fiscally irresponsible. Saving taxpayers' money is always a popular, if not primary, rationale for cutting back relief or discouraging reform. The immediate death blow that California's Proposition 13 dealt to Carter's proposal for welfare reform is a case in point. Certainly, the national budget "crisis" was a particularly potent weapon for cutback.

CHANGING ROLES OF WOMEN

As increasing numbers of women joined the labor force, it became harder to justify government income support for those who did not work outside the home. This was the case even though many employed women worked part-time and would have been hard pressed to support their families, particularly at the low wages that welfare mothers could command. Welfare "reform" broke with the maternalist tradition but without the assurance of jobs, living wages, or adequate care for children. Just as earlier welfare reform assured that men would be entirely dependent on the sale of their labor, so the loss of their entitlement to welfare has moved women closer to commodification.[15] Thus, while industrial society commodified men, postindustrial society is now commodifying women, who must sell their labor in order to support themselves and their children. However inadequately and grudgingly, mothers' aid and AFDC had compensated the family or "reproductive" work of some mothers.[16] Furthermore, both mothers' aid and AFDC had recognized that the care of children in the home was "work."

WEAK OR HALF-HEARTED ALLIES

Deprived of its more progressive elements by the postwar purges and further weakened by recent assaults of business and government, the American labor movement claimed the allegiance of only one-half the proportion of the work force that belonged to unions in its heyday. Thus, the labor movement had neither the inclination nor the clout to mount a strong defense of welfare or women and children. Moreover, labor's decline and turn toward the political center deprived the Democratic party itself of progressive strength. The strong working-class parties that are associated with the development and flowering of welfare states in some other countries are not a feature of the political landscape of the United States.

Those who administer government programs often develop an interest in their continuation and expansion. Although some Clinton appointees to the Department of Health and Human Services were considered liberals on the issue of welfare reform, they were constrained from speaking out by their loyalty to the president who had appointed them, their fear of undercutting a Democratic president at a time of Republican triumph, and by their hope that the bill that was passed might somehow be amended afterward. Although some of these officials eventually resigned in protest, they had, during their tenures, approved waivers that permitted states to initiate some of the harsh measures that later became part of the new poor law.

Other potential allies with middle-class constituencies, like the women's or civil-rights movements, did not make defense of public assistance a major priority. Neither were they inclined to invest substantial resources in that struggle for a sufficient amount of time. The women's movement, at best inconsistent in its support of poor women, had viewed women's employment outside the home as liberation. The movement had not resolved the question of how women's work in the home should be valued or compensated.

For their part, advocates for the poor lobbied, and some attempted to mobilize other defenders, but they lacked strong, organized constituencies. Moreover, most of these advocates, particularly after the 1970s, focused narrowly on welfare rather than on employment opportunities and job creation as well, and that reduced their appeal and their support. Indeed, neither advocates nor policymakers based their prescriptions on the actual preferences of the poor, that is, what combinations of work or welfare they favored and under what conditions.

ADC would not have been enacted without the coattails of two popular movements that arose on behalf of the elderly and the unemployed in response to economic crisis in the 1930s. The elderly remain a powerful force and are better able to defend the old-age programs against attack than welfare mothers. The assault on AFDC, although part of the same neoconservative trend, peaked at a different time from the effort to undermine and privatize social security. The effect, if not the intention of the attackers, was to divide the beneficiaries of these two social programs. Thus, neither the elderly nor the other advocates of social security provided protective cover for mothers and children in the years preceding welfare repeal.

"NIXON IN CHINA"

Bill Clinton was not the first candidate to exploit the welfare issue in a presidential campaign. As noted, two moderates, Nixon and Carter, found it a crowd pleaser. However, once in office, both proposed mildly reformist schemes that were opposed, not welcomed, by conservatives. Clinton's pledge to "end welfare as we know it" set up powerful expectations and was followed by his radical proposal of time limits on the receipt of welfare—a change that contravened 60 years of federal welfare policies and opened the door to the loss of entitlement. Having made the promise that became a popular slogan, Clinton was unable to resist signing a welfare "reform" bill during his campaign for reelection, even one that he had first vetoed and claimed to dislike. Support of time limits and work requirements for mothers of young children were firsts for a Democrat in the White House, handing the antiwelfare Republicans a gift.

The waiver process, first stepped up under Bush but greatly accelerated under Clinton, put radical welfare reforms in place in many states, thereby paving the road to repeal. It is unlikely that a Republican could have gotten away with these waivers or with signing an end to entitlement— any more than a Democrat could have opened up China. As popular as he was, even Ronald Reagan did not go nearly that far, although his antiwelfare rhetoric and workfare initiatives abetted welfare "reform."

To some extent, the nomination of a Democrat who had led a drive for a more centrist position in the Party was a sign that a ruling elite had changed its mind. On the other hand, Democrats in the White House have tended to be centrists who lean Left or Right, depending on what pushes them. Economic collapse in the 1930s and disruptive mass movements in good times like the 1960s have moved them to progressive reforms, albeit far short of the demands of protest groups. Neither was present in the 1990s. In conservative times, a Democrat like Clinton may find it politically prudent to coopt a conservative or Republican agenda in contrast to other moderate Democrats like Roosevelt, Kennedy, and Johnson, who were pushed to the Left. Thus, in 1996, the putative heir to the New Deal declared that "the era of big government is over,"[17] which brings us to a second immediate antecedent of welfare repeal.

CONSERVATIVE CONGRESSIONAL VICTORY

In the midterm election of 1994, Democrats surrendered both houses of Congress—the House of Representatives for the first time in nearly 50 years. The conservative victory was achieved with low voter turnout, reflecting malaise over an economy that was just beginning to recover, over continuing real-wage decline, and perhaps also disappointment with the "New Democrat" who was unable to make good on promises like "growing the economy" or health-care reform. Having failed in their initial attempts to downsize government by substantially reducing the giant Social Security program, Conservatives turned their axes to the smaller but more vulnerable means-tested programs, especially one of the least popular—AFDC. (They did, of course, renew a battle against Social Security that is still going on.) Advocates for the poor, who had been defending low-income programs with some success in the 1980s, found themselves in a new and hostile environment. Rational persuasion no longer worked; friendly congressional ears, long attuned to the sounds of advocates and social-welfare bureaucrats, were gone or were no longer in command. Although AFDC recipients had been organized 30 years earlier with the aid of government and private funding, they were no longer an organized constituency, and thus support among recipients for the program was not strong. There was better political support for food and nutrition programs that benefit normally conservative providers as well as recipients.

RACE, GENDER, CLASS

Disentangling the influence on public relief of racism, sexism, and capitalism is complicated by the fact that welfare policy often fell short of its stated objectives, leaving the observer to ask what was really intended. As noted, when ADC was enacted, its advocates in the Children's Bureau and the New Dealers who framed the legislation espoused the maternalist goal of freeing single mothers from the breadwinning role so that they could assume the primary woman's role of nurturing the young. In its early years, ADC fell far short of its advocates' goal of relieving single mothers from breadwinning, but it nonetheless freed some women from wage labor or met maternalist goals for a portion of the population in need. Even so, the majority of single mothers were either excluded from relief or obliged by very low benefits to work on or off the books.

Feminist writers hold that public relief has supported the family ethic that extols marriage and the two-parent family.[18] However, throughout its history, ADC/AFDC largely excluded the "normative" family and poor women who presumably conformed to prescribed sexual roles. In the 1960s, a few two-parent families with an unemployed father became eligible, but the relief explosion was overwhelmingly composed of single-parent families who had been excluded by previous policies. Some money probably trickled down to men. When, for example, "man-in-the-house" rules were struck down by the Supreme Court, their families got on welfare and perhaps shared relief benefits with them, being able to do so more easily, not only because coverage was expanded, but because allowances increased in the 1960s.[19] With the explosion of the welfare rolls in those years, AFDC came closer to meeting maternalist goals. From a patriarchal perspective, this meant government was making it possible for more women to live without men. As those who have developed the concept of state patriarchy have pointed out, women became more dependent on government but less dependent on individual men.[20] A drive for welfare "reform" followed immediately upon the heels of the welfare explosion.

Was the opening gun in welfare "reform," the attempted "freeze" and imposition of work requirements for mothers for the first time in ADC history, an attempt primarily to trim rolls that had become too large? Was it intended to loosen the tightest labor market in more than a decade? Or, since illegitimacy was a target, were gender and race major factors in the attack? And what about cutting costs? Cutting back relief is always a relief to taxpayers, notwithstanding their willingness to pay for other forms of welfare like a savings and loan bailout or giveaways to defense contractors. Later, of course, cutbacks were associated with rolling back big government. Perhaps all of these were at play.

It took 30 years to carry out welfare "reform" and to repeal AFDC. The rhetoric of welfare "reform," as we have observed, was often racial and often patriarchal, and the victims of welfare repeal were overwhelmingly single women and their children, disproportionately people of color. Welfare "reformers" treated single parenthood as the root of most social problems, if not of all evil. Since the program was perceived as a "black" program or for people of color, an attack on welfare was also a form of lashing back at blacks. This perception, of its being a black program, however inaccurate, helps to explain why removing life supports from women and children was so easily countenanced by the public. It is always easier to conduct class warfare if that class is disproportionately composed of denigrated minorities. But how much did policymakers care that lower-class women were able to live without men or outside a family ethic that may not even be normative for the middle class? Regardless of the rhetoric of reform and its appeal to various segments of the polity, the bottom line is strict work requirements and lifetime limits on the receipt of relief. In a clear reversal of maternalist values, any job at any wage is preferable to family care, even of the very young or very frail. In this way, the low-wage labor market is swollen with exiles from relief.

If the public relief system has regulated single mothers and excluded married mothers, how has it treated men of the same class or race as many women on welfare? Unemployed, underemployed, out of the labor force, they have had little or no access either to regulatory relief or to nonregulatory social-welfare programs like Social Security. If regulatory relief has been the lot of women who fail to conform to the traditional family ethic, what about the men who, lacking economic opportunities, are unable to conform to the work ethic and have little or no recourse to relief? The swelling population of U.S. prisons and their racial composition bear witness to a control of poor men, especially men of color, that is considerably more coercive than AFDC.

Welfare "reform," it has been argued, is a response to the issue of "less eligibility," which as pointed out in Chapter 1 (see p. 7), is the effort to make relief less desirable than the lowest wage.[21] Less eligibility, it is said, was threatened by the combination of wider coverage and higher benefits in relief, on the one hand, and declining wages, on the other. However, wages were relatively high when welfare "reform" began, and so was the minimum wage. Both the wage decline that began after 1973 and welfare "reform" were part of a strategy in which government aided business in reducing the prospects and power of labor.

As AFDC was withering under intense attack, another public-assistance program was growing up alongside it, one that serves capital and provides support to both single-parent and married-couple families. If reduced benefits, stricter work requirements, and lifetime limits on receipt of assistance are the stick, the Earned Income Tax Credit is the carrot of welfare "reform." If a parent(s) is employed but does not earn enough for the family to escape poverty, she, he, or they will get an income supplement. Because all but a small proportion of EITC expenditures are treated as direct outlays in the federal budget, it is in important respects a public-assistance program. However, it is no substitute for conventional welfare programs or the negative income tax because it pays nothing to those who do not work and provides tiny subsidies to those with very low earnings.

The growth of the EITC, which exceeds federal expenditures for the AFDC successor TANF and which continued to increase in a time of budgetary constraint, suggests that saving taxpayers' money or shrinking government may not be the primary force in welfare "reform." The EITC encourages the work ethic by making work pay more, and it has fewer of the disincentives of earlier wage supplementation programs that reduced allowances in direct proportion to earnings.[22] The EITC expands the cheap labor supply and relieves low-wage employers of the responsibility for paying a living wage. Congress is willing to pay for welfare that has these class functions. Nor did policymakers seem troubled by the fact that the EITC enables single mothers, including women of color, to remain independent of men or to deviate from the norm of the family ethic.

As the EITC grew in size and perhaps because welfare repeal was enforcing the work ethic, some congressional conservatives began to view the EITC as a welfare program and to subject it to some of the traditional attacks on relief.[23] However, neither gender nor race has played a part in these attacks. Thus far, the EITC has escaped the budget cutters' axe. Even if the stick has made the carrot of welfare reform less necessary, the EITC, unlike AFDC, has an important political asset: beneficiaries higher on the class ladder than the poor (i.e., employers). And both the EITC and TANF expand the army of poorly educated women and men for the service jobs in the postindustrial economy.

Real Reform: An Entitlement to Work and to Welfare

A nation with abundant resources and a commitment to economic rights for all its people should either provide opportunities for them to earn a decent living, some form of income support, or a combination of the two. As Martin Luther King put it, "We must create full employment or we must create incomes."[24] Although the United States possesses abundant resources, it lacks the political will to provide either.

Current welfare "reform" emphasizes work over welfare. Yet "welfare reform," as established by the misnamed Personal Responsibility and Work Opportunity Reconciliation Act of 1996, neither assured work opportunities nor welfare. The amount of money that Congress appropriated for job creation a year later, while a welcome sign, provides work opportunities for only a small proportion of the 1 million persons who are likely to be pushed into the labor market as a result of this "reform." There are several other federal funding streams for job creation programs in a number of cities.[25] However, these programs still amount to "a drop in the bucket" according to one of the most active advocates and knowledgeable observers of this offshoot of welfare "reform."[26] Yet to be enacted is the modification of PRWORA that would reduce one of its most repressive features: the assurance that no one, regardless of time limits, would be removed from the rolls unless a job is available or created.[27] Although hardly real welfare "reform," this should be a *sine qua non* for *welfare repair*, an important small step toward reentitlement.

The assurance of jobs at living wages for all men and women is preferable to welfare as a primary strategy for ending the poverty of persons who are neither elderly, disabled, nor performing vital work in the home, such as caring for very young or infirm family members.[28] To begin with, a work entitlement would reform welfare and would also meet the needs and improve the well-being of a much larger proportion of the population than is on welfare. The advantages of a work strategy, however, are not just quantitative. A work strategy meets two basic human needs whereas, for those not providing family care, a welfare strategy meets only one of these. Human beings have a need for income sufficiency or adequate material resources and a need, as well, to be productive, contributing members of their communities or societies. The first of these can be achieved by income support, but the second cannot, unless an individual is fully occupied in family care or volunteer work. In the words of William Beveridge, the principal architect of both the welfare state and full employment in postwar Britain: "Idleness is not the same as Want; it is a positive, separate evil from which men [sic] do not escape by having an income."[29] Beveridge believed that unemployment is a "personal catastrophe" because "a person who cannot sell his labour is in effect told that he is of no use"[30] More concerned about the pain of the unemployed individual than the inconvenience that a tight labor market causes employers, Beveridge defined full employment as more vacant jobs at good wages than unemployed men. Full employment was not merely a low rate of unemployment.

A generation later, Martin Luther King, Jr., moved by the severe joblessness that was debilitating not only his people but many others as well, similarly recognized the "personal catastrophe" of unemployment:

> In our society it is murder, psychologically, to deprive a man [sic] of a job or an income. You are in substance saying to that man that he has no right to exist. You are in a real way depriving him of life, liberty, and the pursuit of happiness, denying in his case the very creed of his society.[31]

The world community, at least in principle, has acknowledged this life-denying impact of unemployment. The United Nations Charter and the Universal Declaration of Human Rights, as well as subsequent international agreements like the Covenant on Economic, Social and Cultural Rights, recognize that work is essential to human life and social development and that to deprive human beings of work is to deprive them of a basic human right. In its prescriptions for the employment practices among its signatories, the U.N. Charter is unambiguous. Articles 55 and 56 of Chapter IX pledge member states to action in support of full employment and higher standards of living. According to the Universal Declaration: "Everyone has the right to work, to free choice of employment, to just and favorable conditions of work and to protection against unemployment."[32]

The Beveridge model and, especially, the full employment model pursued for over 60 years in Sweden combined expansive economic and social policies. In both of these conceptions, the welfare state is a full-employment state. Under conditions of full employment, there are fewer individuals and families in need of government assistance, particularly benefits directly and indirectly related to the cost of unemployment. More money flows into state coffers when more people are employed. At the same time, a strong welfare state creates jobs, for example, in child, home, and health care. A full employment state might truly end "welfare as we know it" and develop, instead, quality services and benefits for all, certainly not confining them inequitably to persons who are on welfare or "transitioning" off it. In short, full employment and the welfare state are partners in the pursuit of economic justice.

With full employment, governments find it easier to finance universal-benefit programs, such as paid parental leave, subsidized child care, health insurance, and children's allowances. European countries built welfare states while they were concurrently pursuing policies of full employment, and now that this goal has been abandoned, the welfare state is burdened by the combination of reduced revenues and the costs of unemployment.[33] The succeeding pages discuss employment as a primary strategy for social welfare. They point out some desirable attributes of full employment, consider the drawbacks that have been attributed to it, and identify some issues of feasibility.

Social Respect

Is emphasizing the role of work simply a reflection of an outdated order or is it a cultural lag, as some social theorists would have it?[34] German economist Jörg Huffschmid has this to say of his country: "It is not just the basic institutions and processes of German society that operate on an assumption that people gain their livelihoods by paid labour. People themselves seek social recognition and individual identity in paid work, even though they place increasing value on the quality of that work."[35] As important as work is to German society, work is perhaps even more important to the social recognition and individual identity of people in the United States.

Another argument for a jobs strategy is that respected and more adequate income support usually comes in the form of occupational welfare, based on income, taxes on earnings or "contributions," and job tenure. This has undoubtedly been a strength of the Earned Income Tax Credit. In the United States, particularly, benefits not directly connected with employment have never been a socially respected alternative to employment for people of working age. We need not approve of this (our own advocacy of welfare rights predates the Welfare Rights Movement), but it is a fact that should be considered in choosing a primary strategy for reducing poverty and inequality. Aid to Families with Dependent Children was an entitlement in the sense of being legally available to all who met its eligibility criteria, but that did not mean that recipients were considered entitled or deserving in the broader sense of the terms.

Time for Family, Community, and Leisure

To favor a jobs strategy is not to stand for all work and no play or for a workhouse state. Reductions in standard work time can create jobs or redistribute available work, increase productivity,[36] and afford more time for family, community, leisure, and learning. Owing primarily to lower wages and job insecurity, trends in the recent past were in the opposite direction. Barry Bluestone and Stephen Rose, who examined several sets of data, both cross-sectional and longitudinal, found a modest increase in work-time for the labor force as a whole over a recent, 20-year period, a figure that includes a slight reduction in men's, but a large increase in women's, hours. During the 1980s, a substantial minority of prime-age workers were "overworked and underemployed," experiencing at least 1 year of substantial overtime (average work week of 46 hours or more) and 1 year of significant underemployment (average of less than 35 hours), which the authors interpret as feasting before anticipated famine. Dual-worker families have substantially increased their combined hours of work.[37]

Since some men and women are starved for time while the unemployed and underemployed have too much time on their hands, there is a need to share available work. Such sharing is a way of redistributing income and the opportunity to take part in economic activity as well. Changes in the labor laws could decrease employers' incentives for overtime and could also reduce standard work time.[38] Such measures can create more jobs, although they should be taken in conjunction with stimulative monetary and fiscal policies, including government job creation. In Germany, where the latter policies have not accompanied it, reduction of the work week by about 2 hours did, nonetheless, decrease the unemployment effects of austerity measures.[39] However, until wages rise in the United States, such reduced work-time policies will probably be unaffordable and unacceptable to many workers. Low wages thus retard measures that would provide more leisure time and more work sharing.

Advantages for Women

When it was conceptualized in the 1940s, full employment was a gendered issue and had to be updated to fit contemporary realities.[40] Gender-free full employment requires that the workplace, work-time, indeed the very definitions of work be friendlier to women and families, both single- and two-parent. Universal child care is critical to full employment for men and women and is, at the same time, a source of jobs. The greater likelihood of mothers of young children working outside the home and of other family caregivers doing so are two factors that have contributed to the gain of nearly 400,000 jobs in private-sector, day-care centers in recent decades.[41]

The welfare state should offer, and in most other developed countries does offer, another option that reduces the need for job creation. Certain forms of family care (of the very young and the mentally or physically disabled or infirm) are compensated through paid family leave, thereby implying that they are productive work. Such a policy would seem particularly appropriate in an economy where, even with relatively low unemployment rates, millions of people are disadvantaged, either by unemployment, low wages, or a combination of the two. Yet, the sexist convention of treating vital work in the home as nonwork, uncompensated unless done by nonfamily members, persists. With welfare "reform," public policy has become even less willing to define family care—nearly always performed by women—as work. Indeed, with its commodification of women, welfare "reform" has meant an obsession with driving into the labor market even those who are mentally fragile or caring for disabled family members.[42]

A notable departure from this narrow and sexist definition of work is the "Immodest Proposal" of the Women's Committee of 100, a group of feminist academics, professionals, and activists who, in preparation for the "abolition, renewal, or replacement" of TANF when it sunsets in 2002, recommend policies that "recognize and reward the work of caring for dependents" through some form of caregiver's allowance.[43] The Committee also puts forth proposals for "transforming wage work," including a living wage, effective protection of the right to unionize, comparable worth, and affirmative action—everything but the critical entitlement to work or government assurance of a job for all who want one.

FULL EMPLOYMENT AND RACE

African–Americans, as this book repeatedly shows, have much to gain from full employment and much to lose from high employment. In Chapter 3, we cited the prescient observation of NAACP board member Judge William H. Hastie: "The Negro has the most to lose if the objectives [of the Murray-Wagner full employment bill of 1945] are not achieved. The fact must be brought home to minority groups that they will never be able to make progress unless there are adequate jobs for people." Repeatedly, this book has borne witness to how chronic unemployment and underemployment of black women and men have undermined not only themselves but their families and communities.

In Chapter 1, we called attention to the fact that when unemployment declined in some metropolitan areas in the 1980s, economically disadvantaged young men, especially African–Americans, were the big gainers, and we reported similarly promising consequences of tight labor markets for women and minorities during the second half of the 1990s. During that economic expansion, tight labor markets meant employment and wage gains for young men with less than a college education, the group including the fathers of many women and children on welfare. Among men with less than college educations, moreover, wage gains for blacks were double those of whites. Between 1992 and 1998, real wages of young, noncollege-educated white men rose by 5%, compared to 10% for blacks in the same age and educational groups. The impact of tight labor markets on wages is dramatically demonstrated when areas with high and low unemployment are compared. In areas with unemployment rates below 4% throughout the entire expansion, real wages for young, noncollege-educated black men increased by 11%, while in areas where unemployment remained above 7%, their real wages declined by 5%.[44]

HEALTH AND EMPLOYMENT

Much research reveals that unemployment is bad for our health. M. Harvey Brenner, who has done important work on the relationship between unemployment and health, writes that "a vast epidemiological literature has . . . accumulated on the significant and consistent relationship between unemployment and elevated morbidity and mortality rates."[45] Brenner's work and the other studies he reviews include both physical and mental health. Three Canadian medical specialists, Jin, Shah, and Svoboda, reviewed 46 articles describing studies during the 1980s and 1990s, including a number by Brenner, and concluded that "the evidence strongly supports an association between unemployment and a greater risk of morbidity (physical or mental illness or use of health-care services), both at the population and individual levels, and a greater risk of mortality at the population level."[46] While the relationship is a complex one, Jin and his colleagues found that the direction of causation from unemployment to illness is greater than the converse, that is, illness causing unemployment.[47] A recent British study of 6,000 individuals, not included in the Canadian review, concluded that unemployed women and men experience significantly more mental stress than their employed counterparts.[48] However, none of this research, including the review by Jin et al., and, by inference, the studies themselves—distinguished between economic and social factors, that is, income loss and loss of employment or the work role.

THE PROBLEM OF BAD JOBS

Those who favor a jobs strategy should nonetheless acknowledge that many jobs are routine, risky, and, to put it mildly, unpleasant. And the extension of mass production known as "lean production," deemed "a system of brutal work intensification," is increasing the stress of workers and resulting in more job-related injury and illness.[49] Yet, economic rewards and social arrangements may be as important in evaluating a job as the task itself. The missing ingredient may well be labor power and organization that lead to better pay and working conditions as well as social and self-respect. Work in the steel industry was hardly desirable in the early years of this century, but worker organization and changes in power relations made it a well-paid, blue-collar job, the loss of which has reduced living standards for many working-class people. In the service sector, good pay, benefits, and smart uniforms make the job of flight attendant, essentially serving meals to passengers, both desirable and respected.[50] Here, too, as in the heyday of the steel industry, there is a strong union.

The importance of labor's power in improving the quality and rewards of some jobs shows that there is a clear need for a revitalized labor movement in a full-employment strategy, one that can contribute its strength to the struggle to make bad jobs better. Many such jobs are vital services for the young, the frail, and the dying. They are badly paid but good work. A promising development is the unionization of 74,000 public health-care workers in Los Angeles County in 1999. The largest organizing victory since the United Auto Workers' win at General Motors in 1937, this gain for the labor movement is likely to enhance the quality of services as well as improve the wages of home-care aides.[51]

In her history of a civil-rights struggle in a Southern county, Melissa Fay Greene gives several examples of how economic or social factors influence workers' perceptions of their jobs. Although field labor was hard, sometimes dizzying work, it was "not that farming itself demeaned the people, but the economics of the sharecropping arrangement. . . ." Working long hours in furnace heat, a black worker did not shy away from "arduous exertion"; what galled him was the segregated water fountains, one white with refrigerated cold water and one black with warm tap water.[52] Doctoring and nursing, to point in still another direction, are esteemed occupations that are sometimes, as in the case of infectious diseases, hazardous, and in their contacts with blood, guts, and excrement, often unclean.

IS FULL EMPLOYMENT FEASIBLE? OLD AND NEW OBSTACLES

Those who have spent many years and much of their professional careers studying employment and unemployment here and abroad remain convinced of its feasibility as well as its desirability.[53] At the same time, it would be foolish not to recognize the formidable obstacles that full employment faces. Huffschmid, a distinguished German economist, reminds us that unemployment has always been an outgrowth of the unregulated competition and drive for profit maximization that is characteristic of capitalist markets; only during the extraordinary periods of war or postwar reconstruction has it largely, but only temporarily, disappeared.[54] That, of course, is true of most countries but not of all.[55]

The rapid advance of technology and the globalization of the economy only make the achievement of jobs for all at living wages more difficult. Yet, neither new nor old forces destroy the rationality and feasibility of full employment.[56] It is true that new technologies have permitted new forms of management and control. It is easy, however, to overlook the fact that the way in which new technologies have been implemented, the more competitive environment in which some firms are operating, and globalization have all been abetted by the ideological campaigns and political decisions that have been identified in earlier chapters of this book, namely, loosened labor markets, deregulation, and international trade agreements that exclude workers' rights.

Competitive exigencies are accepted rationales for downsizing, but, as Paul Osterman has shown, layoffs were less likely to result from firms' poor performance in the early 1990s than 20 years earlier. Osterman sees this as an example of the change in business norms since the 1980s, another being the fact that a 1938 Supreme Court decision permitting permanent replacement of strikers was not implemented for 40 years following the decision.[57] It is important to recognize the ideological and political forces that led to these changes in business norms and practices and to the antiworker government policies that support them.

In December 1999, tens of thousands of protesters, from unionists to defenders of endangered species, demonstrated in Seattle, Washington, against what one of the organizers called "the secretive, undemocratic institutions that undermine critical health, labor, safety and environmental standards throughout the world."[58] The protest that led to the collapse of the World Trade Organization (WTO) negotiations in Seattle could be the beginning of what must be a long political struggle to win back some modicum of citizen control over economic policy. At the same time, it is important to keep in mind what this book has also shown—that the U.S. never pursued or achieved full employment in the postwar period and that millions of Americans were consigned to unemployment, underemployment, and, particularly for employable men, a shaky and often nonexistent safety net. In other words, economic justice demands much more than tearing down the neoliberal edifice erected in the last quarter century.

TECHNOLOGY AND JOBS

Will technology eat up jobs or put an end to work? The convergence of advances in computer and communications technology will cause, at the very least, dislocation of many workers, even if it does ultimately generate more jobs. To take advantage of such employment requires upgrading the education of our population, not only because education is important in itself, but for occupational reasons as well, providing we take other necessary measures for direct and indirect job creation. Here, too, welfare "reform" is poor public policy, for enrollment in postsecondary education is made much more difficult by the requirement that welfare recipients engage in work activities. Moreover, the new law imposes limits on enrollment in basic education and training and reduces the proportion of state caseloads that can be offered this option.[59] These policies not only maintain an undereducated postindustrial reserve army of women who are unable to work anywhere else except in low-wage service jobs, but they also expose the hypocrisy of politicians who claim to favor educational upgrading.

In discussing education and training, however, it is important to point out that the number of low-skill jobs has held steady in the last decade or so, and that workers have upgraded their education and skills but have not been rewarded for their productivity with higher wages.[60] One reason is increased competition at the bottom from newcomers, high-skill workers who have lost their jobs, and trimming of the welfare rolls. Here, too, welfare "reform" exacerbates rather than eases a problem. Another reason is the failure of government to protect bargaining rights and other labor-market institutions. According to the U.S. Department of Labor, the near future will be one in which low-skill jobs continue to increase, even though occupations requiring at least an associate's degree are likely to grow faster. In fact, 18 of the 30 occupations with the largest projected job growth between 1996 and 2006 are cashiers, salespersons, retail workers, truck drivers, home health aides, and others that require not a Ph.D. or even an A.A. degree, but short-term, on-the-job training.[61] Our immediate task is to make sure that all jobs in the economy pay livable wages and provide vital benefits like health care.

DOES GLOBALIZATION MAKE FULL EMPLOYMENT IMPOSSIBLE?

Globalization is nearly a household word, and imprecise as the term is, many observers take for granted that it is a fitting description of the world economy. As Linda Weiss points out, "the notion of a 'global' economy, dominated by stateless corporations and borderless finance, has captured the imagination of countless commentators. . . . In this view, not only the sovereignty of nation-states but the very idea of a 'national' economy and the capacity of central governments to manage it are being undermined."[62] Lester Thurow is one economist who throws up his hands, declaring: "The era of national regulation of business is simply over," and "world regulation is not about to replace national regulation."[63] Yet, evidence that "most 'MNCs' [multinational corporations] are 'national' firms which operate internationally while retaining a home base"[64] suggests that multinationals may be subject to national regulation.

The effect of the international economy on employment and wages is a complex one on which there is a range of opinions. On the one hand, Adrian Wood argues that expansion and changing patterns of trade between the developed countries of the North and the developing countries of the South have hurt unskilled workers in the North, reducing their wages and destroying their jobs.[65] Wood believes that northern governments must take action to solve this problem with policies such as expanding the supply of skilled workers through education and training, creating more unskilled jobs on projects to improve infrastructures, creating jobs in maintenance or community work, and supplementing the incomes of low-wage workers. The U.S., of course, does the latter through the Earned Income Tax Credit, but the former would use tax money to subsidize jobs that are in the public interest and would be a hedge against recession.

Paul Krugman and Robert Lawrence provide evidence that "international trade has had little net impact on the size of the manufacturing sector. . . ."[66] The United States, say Krugman and Lawrence, continues to buy the bulk of its imports not from developing countries with cheaper labor, but from other advanced countries whose workers have similar skills and wages. The share of manufacturing in the Gross Domestic Product has declined partly because goods have become relatively cheaper, and, consequently, U.S. residents are spending a smaller fraction of their incomes on them. Also taking a position that downplays the job-destroying effects of imports and of relocation of production to developing countries, the International Labour Organization emphasizes that foreign direct investment is not a one-way process and that it generates benefits to the capital-exporting country.[67]

There has long been tension between what Heilbroner aptly calls "the border-blind view of merchantdom and the border-bound view of dukedom,"[68] but technological advances in transportation and communications have given "merchants" an advantage in their quest for higher profits and stock prices. And nation states and labor, being less mobile, have lost power as a result of what is really *increased* internationalization of capital rather than an altogether new phenomenon.

How different is the current situation from earlier world trade? In his position as chief economist for the World Bank, Lawrence Summers ventured an answer:

FDI [foreign direct investment or multinational business] has
always existed and many of the world's largest firms have been
transnational from birth. The "globalization" of production has
happened, sure, but has the telecommunications revolution really
had a major impact? I would guess the invention of relatively
simple things, like steamship transport, did more for world trade
than digitalized data transmission through fiber optic cables. How
exactly has the nature of manufacturing been "fundamentally
altered?" Aren't people just incrementally better at doing things
they've always done, like locating production in the lowest cost
location for delivery to markets (now "globalization of production"),
like managing inventories in a least cost way (now "just-in-time
inventory management"), like choosing the appropriate level of
vertical integration depending on the production process (now
"critical buyer-seller links"), like matching production to demand
(now "short product cycles"). Is a "revolution" really the appropriate
metaphor for these changes?[69]

Linda Weiss' research has led her to reject the term *globalization* and to conclude that the powerlessness of the nation-state has
been exaggerated. Perhaps the most compelling reason for her conclusion is that states differ considerably in their ability to coordinate industrial restructuring to meet the changes in international
competition. We agree with Weiss that a function of this myth of
state powerlessness is to rationalize policies of retrenchment by claiming
they are responses to global trends that are beyond national control.[70] Powerlessness seems especially exaggerated in the case of
the U.S. A nation responsible for one-fourth of the economic activity on earth—$6.3 trillion out of a total world output of $23 trillion—is not exactly without options.[71] It could, for example, enact
"stay or pay" policies that tax companies for some of the costs of
unemployment and economic losses suffered by communities when
they leave, and it could certainly reverse policies that abet business flight, such as tax incentives for companies that go abroad rather
than continue to conduct their businesses in the United States.[72]

Consumers can boycott employers who destroy communities
on which they have depended or who sell goods produced in
sweatshops in the U.S. or abroad in violation of the labor laws
for which earlier generations struggled. Students in the United States,
in a revival of the "ethical consumption" principles of the Progressive era in the early decades of the twentieth century, are once
again leading the way: protesting the purchase by their colleges
and universities of supplies made in sweatshops.

Another approach would be to oppose, amend, restructure, or repeal agreements like North American Free Trade Agreement (NAFTA) and WTO that permit "downward harmonization" or violation of hard-won economic rights. With countervailing pressure from citizens, government would be less free, either to aid business flight directly or to put its hands behind its back in new forms of pro-business laissez-faire. Ultimately, politicians must respond to aroused electorates as the Seattle statement of WTO-supporter Bill Clinton suggests: "I think it is imperative that the WTO become more open and accessible. . . . If the WTO expects to have public support grow for our endeavors, the public must see and hear, and in a very real sense, actually join in the deliberations."[73]

MONETARY POLICY

There is a very potent instrument for job destruction that is related neither to technology nor globalization and that is clearly in the hands of government. For a number of years, the Federal Reserve Board would not allow unemployment to go below 6%, and it took preemptive strikes against phantom inflation by raising interest rates, increasing unemployment, and driving up the costs of borrowing at all levels of government. In fall 2000, with evidence that the economy had "shifted into a lower gear," the Fed, citing low unemployment and high energy prices, was not yet ready to proclaim that inflation no longer threatened. Indeed, the Fed imposed six rate increases, totaling 1.75 percentage points, between June 1999 and May 2000.[74]

It is important to recognize that these policies of the Fed violate federal law. The Humphrey-Hawkins Full Employment and Balanced Growth Act of 1978 requires the Federal Reserve Board to give higher priority to the prevention of unemployment than to the prevention of inflation. The Fed's policy, however, has been just the opposite. Excessive fear of inflation is not new. Even at the bottom of the Great Depression, the Federal Reserve Board was more worried about inflation than unemployment.[75] Responding to these fears, President Roosevelt cut federal spending sharply; the result was job loss for 2 million people and the "depression within a depression."[76] Bringing the Federal Reserve under direct democratic control by not allowing Congress and the president to pass the buck for 4-year intervals, or the length of the chairperson's term, has to be a top

priority of those who advocate jobs for all. This does not mean
making it a captive of whatever political winds are blowing in
Congress or the White House at the time. It does mean that the
Federal Reserve Board should make its procedures transparent
and hold its decision-makers accountable to the public and to
a publicly supported, full-employment policy. Perhaps, then, the
Federal Reserve could be a government force for job creation
rather than job destruction.

Ruling economic dogma has provided a rationale for policies
of the Federal Reserve Board that disemploy workers in the name
of inflation control but serve primarily the interests of bondhold-
ers (who fear that inflation will erode the value of their holdings).
Adherents of this dogma warned that efforts to push joblessness
below a so-called "natural rate" of inflation would set off accelerating inflation by pushing up wages. But lower unemployment
rates in the 1990s—below the once-fateful 5%, or "natural," levels— have dealt this pseudoscientific law a serious, if not yet fatal,
blow. Well before this recent dip in unemployment rates, Robert
Eisner, a past president of the American Economic Association,
maintained that this NAIRU or "nonaccelerating-inflation rate of
unemployment" did not hold up empirically. Even using a conventional model to estimate the NAIRU, Eisner found that "there is
no basis for the conclusion that low unemployment rates threaten
permanently accelerating inflation."[77] Further, Eisner's research
found that lowering unemployment below the Nonaccelerating
Inflation Rate of Unemployment might actually reduce inflation.
Nobel laureate in economics William Vickrey called the "natural" rate of unemployment "one of the most vicious euphemisms
ever coined."[78]

Even if inflation is not a current problem, it is important, in
view of the severe political consequences of the fear of inflation,
to point out that countries committed to full employment have employed means of maintaining price stability other than the principal U.S. method of increasing unemployment. These include the
development of mechanisms for achieving tripartite cooperation
among business, labor, and government; labor market policies to
promote efficiency, such as extensive training targeted to present
and future employment needs; mobility grants to enable workers
to take jobs in areas with more job openings; efficient employment services that reduce the time it takes to fill job vacancies;
and the selective use of domestic credit controls to slow down

economic expansion (e.g., in an overheated sector of the economy like housing).[79] Other measures that have been proposed include anti-inflation tax incentives.[80]

FISCAL POLICY

In achieving full employment, fiscal policy has an important role to play. Public investment, expansion of the welfare state, and direct government job creation all stimulate the economy, increase jobs, and increase productivity and/or the quality of life. According to research by David Aschauer, subsequently corroborated by other investigators, a dollar spent for public investment raised gross national product by two to five times the amount of a dollar of private investment.[81] Spending for education, infrastructure, civilian research and development, and housing construction is more labor intensive than equivalent military spending and could do much to improve the functioning of our economy. It would clearly create jobs. Until we have solved the shortage of affordable housing, for example, is it time to think about the "end of work"? The nation uses fiscal policy in the form of tax expenditures to subsidize home ownership, thereby stimulating employment in the industries that supply housing for the middle and upper classes, but fiscal policy is much less expansive, and has become even less so, in the sphere of housing for lower-income groups.[82]

Some of the economic functions of the welfare state have been discussed. The weaker the safety net the more workers are forced into the low-wage, low-productivity sector and the more likely are such jobs to remain "bad jobs." Sir John Eatwell is one economist who views such jobs as "disguised unemployment."[83] An estimated 16.7 million people who worked full-time, year-round, in 1999 had earnings low enough to be considered "disguised unemployment."[84] The social wage is supposed to complement or substitute for the economic wage. In the last few decades, both were in decline. At about the same time that average AFDC benefits for 3-person families were falling nearly 45% in constant dollars (between 1975 and 1996), average real wages in nonsupervisory private production were decreasing by 13.1% (between 1973 and 1996), and weekly earnings were dropping by 18.9%.[85] In 1999, average real wages were still about 5% (4.8%) below the 1973 level, and real weekly earnings 11.0% below. While median female wages were up 11.7% between 1973 and 1999, men's fell 8.3%.[86]

As we have already suggested, welfare "reform" in this postindustrial era recalls similar policies in England at the height of the industrial revolution. "At the very time when society was imposing unprecedented strains on the mass of its members," wrote two historians who commented on England's poor law reform in 1834, "the concept of the need of the individual for group support was being lost."[87] This is similar to a contemporary observation by an official of the prestigious Council on Foreign Relations: "Just when workers are most in need of the nation state as a buffer from the world economy, it is abandoning them."[88]

GOVERNMENT JOB CREATION: MUCH WORK TO BE DONE

Direct job creation is a necessary component of stimulative fiscal policies. We have talked about the advantages to the individual and family of an entitlement to work. What about the returns to society? There is much work that is left undone in our society largely because the private sector has not found a way to make it profitable. Child and elder care, universal health care, low- and moderate-income housing, mass transit, environmental cleanup, school construction and repair, education, recreation, cultural preservation, and infrastructure repair all remain at vastly inadequate levels relative to need. A fully employed society would meet these needs, and in so doing, would contribute to the mitigation of almost every social problem that confronts us as a society: crime, drug and alcohol addiction, domestic violence, poverty, and malnutrition, and the host of problems that result from poor or no health care. Jobs for people employed in dealing with these social problems would be reduced, but far better that people be employed in preventing problems than in cleaning them up, or as in the case of prisons, shoving them out of sight.

A public employment program that provides employment for all those who seek gainful work but are unable to find it in the private sector would establish, in effect, an entitlement to work. Compared to fiscal policies like tax cuts or general increases in government spending that would drive down overall unemployment rates, direct job creation can be targeted to areas where jobs are needed and is therefore more efficient and less inflationary. The record of federal job creation programs is a positive one that conflicts sharply with the efforts by opponents to discredit them. Economist Nancy Rose concludes her informative,

and by no means uncritical study of relief programs during the
Great Depression with a call to bring back large-scale voluntary
work programs.[89]

Philip Harvey has made a cogent argument for a government-
guaranteed jobs program for all employable persons of working
age in the United States.[90] Harvey anticipates that the program he
proposes, because of the increased tax revenues and reductions of
certain types of income support, would not increase the long-term
tax burden and, in effect, would be self-financing. However, it would
entail start-up costs. Raymond Majewski and Edward J. Nell have
designed an "Employer of Last Resort Program" that would: create employment for those unable to find jobs in the private sector;
help to stabilize employment and output in the private sector; stabilize
wages; improve the skills of the workers involved; and avoid inflation by reducing the stimulus provided by the program as the
economy approaches full employment.[91]

There are important economic reasons to pursue a policy of
full employment, but they are seldom mentioned, even by
progressives. Unemployment, as Robert Eisner put it, literally
means the nation is throwing away potential output.[92] Not only
does unemployment destroy many of the unemployed, but jobless workers and unused capacity cannot build urban transit systems or housing, nor can they meet the human-service needs of
our nation. Full employment, in contrast, expands output. Unemployment is costly, while full employment can bring us closer to
the good society.

Mainstream economics has been concerned with the inefficiency
of equality or its presumably negative effect on incentives.[93] Other
economists, however, point to the inefficiency of inequality in the
form of crime, family violence, and illness.[94] Unemployment is
another form of waste, both of individuals and of societal resources.
If unemployment had been 4% in 1994, the unrealized, interim
goal of the Humphrey–Hawkins Full Employment and Balanced
Growth Act of 1978, instead of the actual rate of 6.1%, the United
States would have produced roughly $280 billion in additional
goods and services that year.[95]

Is Jobs for All Politically Possible?

A rich society like the United States can create jobs, and it
can also hold down inflation other than by causing unemployment.[96]

Yet, this is only possible if interventionist, democratic government, itself deeply wounded by near treasonous, conservative assault for a quarter of a century, gains control over the capitalist economy. Contrary to the laissez-faire creed, capitalism in the United States has functioned very well during brief periods of very low unemployment when waging war temporarily removed inhibitions against government spending. Government intervention in the 1930s did not conquer unemployment because it always fell short of the necessary fiscal stimulus. It did save capitalism, however, from its own collapse.[97]

The principal barriers to full employment, then, are political, not economic or technical.[98] Joel Blau has put his finger on the political problem: "The obstacle to it arises from the distinct shift of power that full employment represents."[99] As we have pointed out in earlier chapters, brief holidays of full employment have not been unkind to the "haves," even though they have disproportionately aided the "have-nots." Nonetheless, elites have feared both inflation and inflated worker power. Both advocates and opponents know that full employment at decent wages would change the character of capitalism.

The task, then, is to overcome the small but economically and politically powerful opposition and to bring capitalism under democratic control. But this entails a long, hard struggle for the public mind and the mobilization of massive public support, a struggle that is made all the more difficult by the widening income gap between those at the top and other income groups. This increasing inequality is itself a grave threat to democratic government. On the other hand, the reduced job security and higher rates of turnover that are characteristic of the emerging labor market could make the clientele for full employment far wider than the traditionally at-risk population.

THE ELUSIVE MOVEMENT FOR FULL EMPLOYMENT

Full employment is thoroughly consonant with mainstream American values. Why, then, has there been no full-employment movement? Does that suggest it is impossible to create one? Before World War II had overcome some technical barriers by demonstrating that Keynesian methods could create jobs for all who seek them, such a goal would have seemed utopian. In the 1930s, mass unemployment created a potential constituency for full employment, but movement building was around creating temporary jobs for the unemployed or compensating them for unemployment. (For a few years in the early 1940s, the U.S. achieved full employment, but only as a by-product of war.)

In the mid-1940s, full employment nearly prevailed. The Senate passed a full-employment bill, and the president favored and would have signed it. It could be argued that our divided governmental structure gave veto power to one House of Congress that exercised it on behalf of the business interests that opposed full employment, but that probably would not have happened if there had been widespread, organized support for the bill. And the reason there was too little is that public policies, propaganda, and circumstance—accumulated savings, pent-up consumer demand, purging women from the labor market, and the G.I. Bill—prevented the reemergence of massive unemployment in the immediate aftermath of demobilization.

What about the 1960s? Jobs and freedom were both in the air. But the first priority was to obtain for low- and middle-income African–Americans the basic civil and political rights that everyone else in the society enjoyed. The Johnson administration chose an expansionary fiscal policy, a tax cut, that did increase jobs and reduce unemployment, but it refused to address the serious unemployment and underemployment in the ghettos by creating jobs where they were needed most. This was a time, like the present, when consciousness of chronic unemployment was being buried by low official unemployment statistics. Whether charismatic leadership committed to the right to employment could have mobilized a jobs-for-all movement remains unanswered.

The return of high, if not depression-level, unemployment in the 1970s brought forth both a substantial job-creation program and serious consideration of a full-employment bill. Congressional initiatives were supported by liberal and labor organizations but without any mobilization of the unemployed or underemployed. In the absence of such pressure from the bottom, real job guarantees were gutted by political and labor leaders with impunity. Meantime inflation was rising, and with fear of it fanned by conservatives, the public countenanced both the termination of CETA and violation of the Humphrey-Hawkins Full Employment and Balanced Growth Act. At the time, an important, powerful constituency for CETA, state and local governments lost interest in it because revenue sharing served a function CETA had previously filled.

A serious obstacle to building a full-employment movement is the problem of identifying a constituency, those who see themselves as beneficiaries of such a program. People who are unemployed are, of course, potential beneficiaries, but they may not define themselves as permanently in need of a job and may instead consider temporary income support or compensation their need. Those who are chronically unemployed or marginally employed may be difficult to identify and organize, although they may well recognize their condition is not temporary. The working- and middle-class people who suffer job insecurity and fear downsizing and the loss of occupational benefits and pay through various temporary and contingent-work relationships are also potential beneficiaries, but they may not see full employment as the solution. Low wages and unequal pay for women and minorities are forms of underemployment, and so advocacy of pay equity and living wages is potentially part of a full-employment movement. Indeed, the goal of full-employment transcends simply a job for all. It calls for a living-wage job, benefits like child and health care, and an expanded definition of work to include vital care in the home, hence income support for people so employed.

Much may depend on whether the labor movement defines itself as a beneficiary of full employment: whether it recognizes that tight labor markets aid organizing and increase strength at the bargaining table regardless of how many of their members are jobless. The AFL-CIO's "America-Needs-a-Raise" campaign in the mid-1990s was an example of labor's defining its interests broadly, for increasing the minimum wage would not directly benefit union members, all of whom are paid more. Unless powerful organizations and masses of people can be persuaded to regard themselves as beneficiaries, advocacy for full employment will continue to be confined largely to public-interest groups. As such, it is unlikely to succeed.

THE POLITICS OF WELFARE REPAIR

By turning welfare into a block grant and giving states wide authority in the design of programs, the architects of the PRWORA have made it harder, but not impossible, to mount a national movement for genuine welfare reform. Despite the formidable obstacles to building a full-employment movement, the repeal of welfare has had the unanticipated consequence of turning many welfare advocates into jobs advocates or at least champions of job creation for welfare recipients whose benefits expire. Such attention to the deficiencies of the labor market is rare in prosperous times. The repeal of AFDC has also stimulated a "resurgence of organizing around income security issues."[100]

However, advocates of the poor, as well as organizations of the poor themselves, have had to redirect their strategies and tactics from the national to the local, county, and state levels. This transition has required a whole new learning process and the establishment of new coalitions, communications networks, and policy foci. The Center for Community Change, an advocacy and funding organization, has described the difficulties:

> Few [grassroots, low-income organizing groups] had a statewide presence or relationships with state policymakers. State-level advocacy and policy groups that did have this access were overwhelmed by the deluge of new options facing states. These groups could not respond to all of them immediately or comprehensively. The problem was compounded by the fact that, at precisely the moment welfare reform was enacted, the capacity of states' primary sources of policy expertise on safety net programs—legal services organizations—was reduced by federal budget cuts and restrictions on their activities.[101]

Another difficulty faced by those trying to repair welfare stems from the history of liberal funding for social change. As noted earlier in this book, liberal foundations tended to fund discrete grassroots organizing efforts, but not networking and policy development linked to grassroots efforts. Thus, few grassroots groups were in touch with policy organizations that could provide training, guidance on strategy and tactics, legislation, and analyses of current policy. And policy organizations, no matter how astute their analyses and prescriptions, were politically ineffective without a low-income constituency from which they could learn and a grassroots organizing base that could turn their proposals into political demands. Another problem facing those attempting to organize for reform was the lack of communications linkages among grassroots groups that would enable them to learn from each other's experiences and develop the sense of a "national" movement.

PRWORA's devolution of responsibility for welfare was partly an effort to dissipate the efforts of advocates for the poor. However, the Internet has helped to overcome this obstacle. It has been a tremendous boon to renewed organizing and education on the issues confronting those seeking to repair welfare. The Welfare Law Center, for example, has established a Low-Income Networking and Communications (LINC) Project to promote computer-based communications among low-income groups. With funding and technical expertise from the Welfare Law Center, dozens of grassroots groups have developed their own websites and have begun to learn from each other and, where possible, to coordinate their actions. In addition, training programs and technical assistance have been easier to disseminate as have examples of best practices.

A new sophistication about the systemic nature of the beast that confronts them is now part of the consciousness of many low-income groups. For example, the website that contains links to grassroots groups across the United States also contains links to people fighting similar struggles in many other parts of the world.[102] One example of the way in which knowledge of the systemic nature of poverty is being communicated can be found on the website of the Kensington Welfare Rights Union of Pennsylvania. Once an isolated grassroots organization, the Kensington group coordinated a 10-day march from Philadelphia to the United Nations in June 1997 of poor and homeless families from many parts of the U.S. who, using the international human rights documents that have become part of international law, charged the United States with violating the economic human rights of its people. In June 1998, it sponsored a "New Freedom Bus" that crossed the country gathering stories of economic human rights violations and held a Human Rights Tribunal at the end of the tour whose documentation was transferred to the United Nations. In October 1999, the group planned a "March of the Americas" to demonstrate the links between poor people across the Western hemisphere. Its "call" to action reflects the group's understanding of the systemic roots of poverty:

> As the economy globalizes, the struggle of the poor must be an international struggle. For too long, our common enemy has attempted to divide the poor in different countries. Now if we do not globalize from below to reclaim our world, and our economic human rights, we will die.[103]

Actions like these have not changed many minds in Washington, and the appointment as HHS secretary of Tommy Thompson, author of Wisconsin's infamous W-2, is a clear signal that the Executive Branch under George W. Bush will, if anything, be harder to move. Nonetheless, grassroots initiatives like Kensington's have begun to raise consciousness at the local and state levels and have contributed to some incremental changes in several states' welfare-to-work programs.

Another benefit of the Internet has been the establishment of a sophisticated monitoring network known as the National Welfare Monitoring and Advocacy Partnership (NWMAP). It is made up of organizers, advocates, service providers, and researchers from across the United States.[104] To help groups get around the new difficulties posed by trying to monitor and analyze the impacts of 50 different state welfare programs, the NWMAP has devised a survey instrument to assess and document both positive and negative impacts, as well as to communicate the results to policymakers, the media, and the general public. The Center for Responsive Philanthropy described the outcome: With this instrument, low-income groups "have used surveys created and tabulated on inexpensive PC database programs to mobilize poor people, create policy initiatives, and build a public profile."[105] Thus, within just 3 years of welfare repeal and despite the failure of states to document what happened to those who left the welfare rolls, a reliable body of information has been amassed by grassroots organizers and sympathetic providers.

The Internet has also facilitated the sharing of sophisticated analyses of economic issues relevant to welfare reform from research organizations like the Center on Budget and Policy Priorities and dozens of similar institutes and foundations. These analyses have helped shape the demands that local organizers make on their states, cities, and counties. This monitoring and research effort has been extremely important in exposing a fact that the establishment has long tried to hide—that there are not enough family-supporting jobs for all who will be expected to get them.

Ironically, although not unexpectedly, a major benefit of welfare repeal may be the renewed attention that is now being paid to the structure of the labor market. Increasingly, groups interested in protecting the welfare poor from abuse are pointing out that few of the jobs welfare recipients get pay wages above the poverty line or provide benefits. A focus on the deficiencies of the labor market in a time of low unemployment is unusual and an unanticipated consequence of welfare repeal.

There has also been renewed emphasis on raising the national minimum wage, with advocacy groups pointing out that the minimum wage has failed to keep up with inflation. Exposure to the realities of the low-wage labor market had also spurred the development of "living-wage" campaigns in more than 40 cities and counties in 17 states and "first source" hiring legislation in more than 30 local jurisdictions across the country by fall 1999.[106] ACORN (Association of Communities Organized for Reform Now), a multistate grassroots organization of poor and moderate-income people that began in the 1970s as an offshoot of the National Welfare Rights Movement, is one of the organizations that has been spearheading these campaigns. "Living-wage" campaigns are aimed at passing legislation that requires businesses getting contracts, tax abatements, or other subsidies from city, county, or state governments to pay a "living wage," usually at the 4-person poverty level or above. Increasingly, living-wage campaigns are proposing other community standards such as paid vacations, health insurance, public disclosure, community advisory boards, language that supports union organizing, and even environmental standards.[107] Significantly, *New York Times* economics analyst Louis Uchitelle refers to the living-wage campaigns as a "movement."[108]

Because their goals are wider than welfare or workfare, living-wage campaigns have been successful in drawing together diverse groups like organized labor, welfare advocates and recipients, civil-rights organizations, and religious groups, thus overcoming the divide-and-conquer difficulties of earlier efforts to reform welfare. They have also demonstrated that the dire predictions of economic conservatives—that raising the wage will result in more unemployment, inflation, or runaway jobs—have not happened. In fact, it has had a generally positive economic impact on the city or state.[109]

First Source hiring agreements are more narrowly targeted to combating both job discrimination and the paucity of jobs in areas where welfare recipients live. They require employers getting benefits or contracts from cities to agree to consider applicants from a specified pool of job-seekers, usually low-income, minority, or otherwise disadvantaged persons from particular neighborhoods, before opening the search to a wider pool. The establishment of community hiring halls has been recommended to back up First Source agreements.[110] Although they cannot address the lack of living-wage jobs, first source hiring campaigns and employment linkage programs that seek to connect disadvantaged job-seekers to local employers have some advantages. They can teach those who campaign for them how local and state power structures work and how fiscal and zoning policies can be used to direct finances and opportunities to areas where they are most needed. First source campaigns can thus create a more informed advocacy community.

Another result of welfare repeal is, as pointed out in Chapter 8, new attention to public job creation. While still limited, at least two states and dozens of communities across the country have begun public job-creation programs. The fact that the National League of Cities has sent out a "how to" on public job creation is a significant indication of the extent to which a systemic understanding of poverty has begun to penetrate a heretofore impervious policy establishment. The Department of Labor's job-vacancy surveys, now underway in six localities around the country, are likely to provide new grist for advocates pushing for public job creation.

Workfare abuses have stimulated union organizing among workfare clients. Spearheaded by ACORN and by union locals and some central labor councils, and joined by religious and community groups, several efforts to organize those who are working off their welfare checks are underway. Coupled with a new militancy among organized labor, such efforts hold the potential for ending the division between the welfare poor and the rest of the working class that has long haunted the nation's new poor-law reform efforts.

Other efforts to repair welfare's shortcomings are aimed at the human resource side of welfare-to-work. As time limits begin to kick in, there is increasing recognition of the fact that the supportive services needed not only to prepare welfare recipients for the workplace but also to sustain them in it are far from adequate. Grassroots groups have been advocating for, and have won, increased child-care funding and additional day-care programs; they put pressure on President Clinton to develop a national health-care program for all needy children; and they have been using loopholes in the language of the PRWORA and flexible federal regulations to make it possible for welfare recipients to continue to get the higher education and longer vocational education and training they need and to extend benefits to some groups of immigrants who were cut off by the PRWORA. A national network of legal teams, foremost among them the Welfare Law Center, has won court edicts that have reversed many of the abuses of which state TANF programs have already been found guilty. Perhaps the most far-reaching and, according to the *New York Times*, "certainly one of the most surprising and possibly one of the most consequential constitutional developments in years," was the stunning 7-2 decision of the United States Supreme Court that bars states from paying lower welfare benefits to those families who have lived in the state for less than 1 year.[111]

The Building Blocks for a Full-Employment Movement

While the intensified energy demonstrated by welfare clients and their advocates is heartening, a full-employment movement will take much more than welfare repair. The following list provides a set of building blocks for such a movement.

DEVELOP A SOPHISTICATED MONITORING, EDUCATION, AND MEDIA STRATEGY

The development of such a strategy will expose the economic myths that have long supported public disdain for welfare recipients and a studied indifference to the underside of the American economy.

Since many of the potential constituency for full employment do not know that they suffer from various forms of joblessness, an important step toward political mobilization is to help them recognize the magnitude of the problem and that they are part of it. As we have emphasized, official statistics, which greatly underestimate the extent of true joblessness, contribute to the erroneous impression that there are enough jobs for anyone who wants to work. Very soon after enactment of the Personal Responsibility and Work Reconciliation Act of 1996, the *New York Times* wrote that it is "virtually impossible for New York City to move hundreds of thousands of New Yorkers from public assistance onto full time jobs over the next few years."[112] Indeed, at the current rate of job growth, the *Times* reported, it would take 21 years for all adults on public assistance to be absorbed into the economy, even if every available job went to welfare recipients. Such facts were not widely recognized in the years preceding enactment of welfare "reform." Official denial of the extent of unemployment is one reason why it has been possible for welfare "reform" to impose strict work requirements and to set lifetime limits on receipt of public assistance.

In the past, interest in job creation or full employment peaked during depression, when fear of its return was heightened, or during times of severe recession. In better times, interest in job creation has waned, until PRWORA turned the spotlight on labor-market deficiencies. As more benefits expire, PRWORA may help to convince the public that the problem is chronic and that it is not only the lack of good jobs but not enough jobs of any kind. One means of proving this is through adopting an official measure of unemployment that includes underemployment and disguised unemployment in the form of low wages. Inaugurating and publicizing the results of national job-vacancy surveys (see Chapter 8) would also arouse public concern over unemployment. If the problem is no longer perceived as temporary and confined to downturns, permanent solutions may be sought.

Those who profit from unemployment and from the higher interest rates that disemploy workers are clearly powerful. One manifestation of their power is to persuade citizens that the policies that create unemployment and underemployment serve the general interest, not just the interests of the highest economic strata. A critical task for those who advocate full employment, then, is to dispel myths like that of a "natural" rate of unemployment and to depict the real costs of unemployment for the entire society—in poor health, family instability, crime, and wasted resources.

Demonstrating that the problem of unemployment is not only widespread, but serious can help to increase its political feasibility. Unemployment must be shown to be a primary problem, one that causes any number of lesser, that is, secondary or tertiary, problems.[113] In this regard, it is necessary to deconstruct the official unemployment rates to show that they conceal more unemployment and underemployment than they reveal.

PUBLICIZE THE BENEFITS OF FULL EMPLOYMENT

One lesson from our history of welfare reform is to avoid strategies that pit the working poor against those who currently collect welfare. Organizing strategies need to employ demands that benefit more than single mothers on welfare. Our history shows that both men and women have suffered exclusion from the labor market and constraints on relief. Strategies targeted to the most politically powerless become easy targets for budget cutters, especially when the economy turns down and policymakers need a scapegoat.

In some ways, the new focus on work, as opposed to income support, may make it easier to avoid the dichotomy that was built into the very structure of the legislation that established ADC/AFDC. Since welfare recipients are now expected to become members of the working class, the old stereotype of the "welfare queen" or drone may be losing its punch. The former drones are becoming the deserving poor.

The political feasibility of full employment can be strengthened by showing that it benefits not just the unemployed but the
entire society. Although it has start-up costs, these are affordable
in a nation that is much richer and that has a much smaller debt
in proportion to its resources than in 1944 when Franklin Roosevelt
called for an Economic Bill of Rights. In the long run, however,
there is a net gain to society. A program of full employment would
increase tax revenues, expand the national product, and reduce
the enormous social and economic costs of joblessness.

Advocates of jobs for all also need to persuade the myriad
organizations that advocate for workers' rights, welfare rights,
the equality of women, ethnic and racial minorities, world peace
and nuclear disarmament, and environmental sustainability that
the struggle for full employment has the potential for uniting the
liberal-left movements that share similar purposes but often lack
coherent and common strategies. The agendas of all these movements would be advanced by a policy of full employment, and
every major social problem would be easier to solve.

Focus Reform Efforts on the Structure of the Labor Market

Even as we work to repair the damage that poverty may have
done to the individual, for example, through education, training,
and rehabilitation programs, efforts to repair welfare should focus on the quantity and quality of jobs and the supportive services
needed to make a jobs strategy work. The history of the failed
Family Support Act has demonstrated that concentrating on human resource development without an adequate supply of jobs at
family-supporting wages that are in areas accessible to former welfare
recipients is bound to fail to make real economic independence
possible. Thus, education and training must be linked to guarantees of jobs and public job creation if there are not enough available in the local labor market.

Articulate a Vision

Finally, movements need dreams to inspire and direct their efforts.
Advocates of jobs for all need to put forth an inspiring vision of
the just, decent society in which the highest priority is assigned
to meeting human needs, to preserving our connection with the
natural world, to supporting community, social and economic equality,

and our individual and human potential. One such vision might go like this:

> Imagine a society in which all people able to work have jobs that enable them to earn a living adequate for health and well-being.
>
> Imagine a society in which everyone has the legally enforceable right to a clean, healthy environment and to safe, nutritious food.
>
> Imagine a society in which everyone has access to safe, affordable housing, and no one need be homeless.
>
> Imagine a society where no one has to fear the loss of adequate income in old age.
>
> Imagine a society in which recession and periodic loss of job and income no longer threaten.
>
> Imagine a society in which the parents of young children and those taking care of the sick and elderly are given adequate time to care for their loved ones without loss to their incomes or loss of opportunities for advancement in the workplace.
>
> Imagine a society in which everyone has the right to competent health care, regardless of ability to pay.
>
> Imagine a society in which higher education and opportunities for lifelong learning are available to all.
>
> Imagine a society in which everyone has adequate time for familiy life, civic activities, and the arts and culture.
>
> Imagine a society in which racial, gender, and cultural animosities are reduced, and people feel safe in their homes and streets.

Jobs for all at decent wages is the centerpiece of this vision. Former chief economist of the World Bank, Joseph Stiglitz, has written: "There is no safety net that can fully replace the security provided by an economy running at full employment."[114] We believe that to be true, but we favor an entitlement to social welfare as well as to work. A social welfare entitlement includes essential services for families and workers and adequate income support for those who are disabled, retired, engaged in vital work in the home, or earning too little to support themselves and their families. Entitlements to both work and social welfare would be a true millennium—a world free from unemployment, extreme inequality, and economic ruin. The first steps toward that goal are to block reauthorization of PRWORA, Washington's New Poor Law, and to advocate the creation of jobs for all welfare recipients not occupied in full-time family care.

We acknowledge that our vision is more distant since George W. Bush took office. Although Bush took the presidency after a close and bitterly contested election, he and his team act as if they won a mandate to march swiftly to the Right of his campaign rhetoric. In office, that rhetoric, "compassionate conservatism," translates into tax cuts that benefit the rich and rob the Treasury of funds for vital services. It could also mean a military build-up and a new, deregulation drive cruelly indifferent to the natural and social environments. If the administration's controversial Free Trade Area of the Americas treaty is adopted, services in social welfare, health care, and education could be turned over to the private sector, thus jeopardizing more of the welfare state.

In their arrogance, Bush and his cohorts may be exposing the wide gap between their militant conservatism and the economic interests of most Americans. They have betrayed their constituency in the heartland by proposing cuts in agricultural subsidies, and they have also retracted campaign promises to environmentalists. Could the naked elitism of this barely elected administration— dubbed "court-appointed" by some of its detractors—produce a countermobilization? Arrogance has already cost it the Senate.

Who are the likely partners to such a mobilization? The alliance could include members of the depleted industrial workforce, the poorly paid ranks of a service sector expanded by welfare "reform" and becoming better organized, and betrayed quarters of the agricultural sector. Poor women, minorities, and the organizations they represent have high stakes in such a mobilization. "Turtles and teamsters," as the Seattle alliance of conservationists and unionists was called, could continue to work together and contribute to a progressive mobilization. They could be joined by students who have begun to support workers' struggles for economic justice. Workers have had a taste of low unemployment in recent years. That memory could increase their appetite for political protest if markets contract and social welfare provides less protection than in earlier recessions.

The history of the twentieth century teaches us that social movements are a requisite for social reform. Social movements, whether nascent or reborn, exist. The question is whether they can coalesce around the common cause that would make all of their goals easier to achieve. The readers of this book should have no doubt about what roads we believe reform should take.

Notes

CHAPTER 1
WASHINGTON'S NEW POOR LAW AND WELFARE REPEAL: INTRODUCTION AND OVERVIEW

1. "Social Security Bill Is Signed—Gives Pension to Aged, Jobless," *New York Times*, 15 August 1935, 4.

2. Francis X. Clines, "Clinton Signs Bill Cutting Welfare: States in New Role," *New York Times*, 23 August 1996, A1.

3. David A. Super, Sharon Parrott, Susan Steinmetz, and Cindy Mann, *The New Welfare Law* (Washington, D.C.: Center on Budget and Policy Priorities, 1996), 1. The authors used estimates of the Congressional Budget Office. The cost savings from the immigrant restriction in PRWORA, as enacted in August 1996, were expected to account for almost one-half of total savings. Ruth Gordner, "Immigrant Families and Welfare Reform: A Background Briefing Report," Washington, D.C., Family Impact Seminar, 24 October 1997, 2. A year later in the Balanced Budget Act of 1997, negotiated between Congress and the president, an additional $3 billion was added for welfare-to-work programs.

4. U.S. Congress, Public Law 104–193, *Personal Responsibility and Work Opportunity Reconciliation Act of 1996* (PRWORA), sec. 401(b).

5. U.S. Congress, Congressional Budget Office, *The Economic and Budget Outlook: Fiscal Years 1997–2006* (Washington D.C.: U.S. Government Printing Office, May 1996), table 2.6, 46; table E-2, 134; table E-3, 135; table E-10, 142.

6. U.S. Department of Labor, Bureau of Labor Statistics, Comparative Real Gross Domestic Product Per Capita and Per

313

Employed Person, Fourteen Countries, 1960–1996, Washington D.C., unpublished data, February 1998, table 1. In 1993, Germany, France, Sweden, and the United Kingdom, all with less income per capita, spent from 23–38% of their gross domestic products on social expenditures, compared to 15% in the United States. Organization for Economic and Cultural Development, *OECD Social Expenditure Database* [Paris: OECD, 1996], table 1, 22.

The top one-fifth of all families grabbed 94% of national income gains of $583 billion inflation-adjusted dollars between 1977 and 1989, while the richest 1%, with average 1989 incomes of $559,000, got 60%. Sylvia Nasar, "The 1980s: A Very Good Time for the Very Rich," *New York Times,* 5 March 1992, A1, D24.

Past President of the American Economic Association Robert Eisner compared the post-World War II debt with that of the mid-1990s in "Why the Deficit Isn't All Bad: Balancing Our Deficit Thinking," *The Nation* 261 (11 December 1995), 743–745. For the 1996 debt held by the public, see U.S. Congress, Congressional Budget Office, *An Analysis of the President's Budgetary Proposals for Fiscal Year 1998* (Washington, D.C.: U.S. Government Printing Office, March 1997), table A-3, 51.

7.   U.S. House of Representatives, Committee on Ways and Means, *1996 Green Book: Background Material and Data on Programs within the Jurisdiction of the Committee on Ways and Means* (Washington, D.C.: Government Printing Office, 1996), table 8-1, 437–438.

8.   Calculated from ibid., table 8-25, 467.

9.   Ibid., table 8-28, 473. In 1994, 41% of all families with children had one child, 38% had two, and 6% had more than three. Steve W. Rawlings and Arlene Saluter, *Household and Family Characteristics,* U.S. Bureau of the Census, Current Population Reports, Series P20-483 (Washington, D.C.: U.S. Government Printing Office, 1995), table 1, 1.

10.   Mark R. Rank and Li-Chen Cheng, "Welfare Use across Generations: How Important Are the Ties That Bind?" *Journal of Marriage and the Family* 57 (August 1995), 678. Rank and Cheng base their findings on a large, representative sample

of American households. When they considered individuals who received welfare for 4 or more of the 6 years preceding the study, Rank and Cheng found that 69% said their parents never used welfare, 16% used it sometimes, and 15% used it frequently. See also *Welfare Myths: Fact or Fiction? Exploring the Truth about Welfare* (New York: Welfare Law Center, 1996), 8.

11.   LaDonna Ann Pavetti, "Who Is Affected by Time Limits?" in Isabel A. Sawhill, ed., *Welfare Reform: An Analysis of the Issues* (Washington, D.C.: Urban Institute Press, 1995), 32; Mary Jo Bane and David Ellwood, *Welfare Realities—From Rhetoric to Reform* (Cambridge, Mass.: Harvard University Press, 1994), 39; and Kathleen Mullan Harris, "Work and Welfare among Single Mothers in Poverty," *American Journal of Sociology* 99 (September 1993), 317-352.

12.   Irwin Garfinkel and Sara S. McLanahan, *Single Mothers and Their Children: A New American Dilemma* (Washington, D.C.: Urban Institute Press, 1986), 38. Garfinkel and McLanahan base their conclusions on a review of the literature, including unpublished papers and reports.

13.   While benefits were dropping 37%, the proportion of single-mother families was rising nearly 50%. Single-mother families were 16.3% of all families with children in 1975, and 23.8% in 1995, an increase of 46%. See Eleanor Baugher and Leatha Lamison-White, *Poverty in the United States: 1995,* U.S. Bureau of the Census, Current Population Reports, Series P60-194 (Washington, D.C.: U.S. Government Printing Office, 1996), table C-3, C-8-C-9. For discussion of several studies that relate teenage pregnancy to poverty, see Richard A. Weatherley, "Teenage Pregnancy, Professional Agendas and Problem Definitions," *Journal of Sociology & Social Welfare* 14 (1987), 5-35.

      For the relationship between unemployment and single parenthood, see William J. Wilson, *The Truly Disadvantaged: The Inner City, the Underclass, and Public Policy* (Chicago: University of Chicago Press, 1987). Teenage pregnancy rates in the Netherlands, France, Sweden, and the United Kingdom ranged in this order from 8 to 33 per 1,000 females aged 15-19, compared to 61 per 1,000 in the United States. See Kristin A. Moore, Nancy O. Snyder, and Dana Glei, *Facts at a Glance*

(Washington, D.C.: Child Trends, Inc., 1995). In the mid-1980s, government income transfers reduced the poverty of single parents by 90% in the Netherlands, 81% in Sweden, 75% in the U.K., 59% in France, and 34% in Germany, compared to only 5% in the U.S. See Timothy M. Smeeding and Lee Rainwater, "Cross-National Trends in Income Poverty and Dependency: The Evidence for Young Adults in the Eighties," The Luxembourg Income Study, Working Paper No. 67 (Syracuse, N.Y.: Syracuse University, August 1991), table 7.

14.   Roberta Spalter-Roth, Beverly Burr, Heidi Hartmann, and Lois Shaw, *Welfare That Works: The Working Lives of AFDC Recipients* (Washington, D.C.: Institute for Women's Policy Research, 1995). This study was based on the labor-force activity of a nationally representative sample of single welfare mothers over a 2-year period. In another study, interviews of a nonrandom sample of 214 "welfare-reliant" mothers in four cities found that between 36% and 60% supplemented their benefits with work (most of them engaged in unreported work in the formal sector with some doing unreported work, underground work, or a combination of these activities), and 65% had been employed in the formal sector within the previous 5 years. Kathryn Edin and Laura Lein, "Work, Welfare and Single Mothers' Economic Strategies," *American Sociological Review* 61 (February 1996), 253-266. Mark Robert Rank, who combined qualitative and quantitative research methods in a study of welfare recipients in Wisconsin, found that "virtually every welfare recipient interviewed in this study had a background of employed work." See *Living on the Edge:The Realities of Welfare in America* (New York: Columbia University Press, 1994), 114.

15.   U.S. Bureau of Labor Statistics, News, U.S. Department of Labor 9732, Washington, D.C., 7 February 1997, tables A1, A3, A9. For job vacancies, see Employment and Training Institute, University of Wisconsin/Milwaukee, *Survey of Job Openings in the Milwaukee Metropolitan Area* (biannual); and Harry Holzer, *Unemployment, Vacancies and Local Labor Markets* (Kalamazoo, Mich.: Upjohn Institute, 1989). For a study of job vacancies in Harlem, see Katherine S. Newman and Chauncy Lennon, *Finding Work in the Inner City: How Hard Is It Now? How Hard Will It Be for AFDC Recipients?* (New York: Columbia University Press, 1995).

16. Gregory DeFreitas, "Fear of Foreigners: Immigrants as Scape-
      goats for Domestic Woes," in Randy P. Albelda, ed. et al.,
      Real World Micro, 8th ed. (Somerville, Mass.: *Dollars and
      Sense,* 1999), 79. DeFreitas, an economist, has done exten-
      sive research and reviews of the literature on immigration.

17. Gordner, op. cit., 7 (see note 3). The author cites as sources
      for her section on "Immigrants' Effects on Private and Public
      Sectors": Alexander P. Morse, *America's Newcomers: An
      Immigrant Policy Handbook* (Washington, D.C.: National
      Conference of State Legislatures, State and Local Coalition
      on Immigration, Immigrant Policy Project, 1994); Michael
      Fix and Jeffrey S. Passel, *Immigration and Immigrants: Setting
      the Record Straight* (Washington, D.C., Urban Institute, 1994);
      Michael Fix and Wendy Zimmerman, *Immigrant Families and
      Public Policy: A Deepening Divide* (Washington, D.C.: Urban
      Institute, 1995); and U.S. Congress, Congressional Budget
      Office, *Immigration and Welfare Reform* (Washington, D.C.,
      1996). An Urban Institute "News and Info" release ("Setting
      the Record Straight on Immigration and Immigrants,"
      [Washington, D.C., Urban Institute, 24, May 1994]), based
      on the Fix and Zimmerman study, reports that "public
      assistance use among nonrefugee immigrants of working age
      (15-64) . . . is low and falls below that of natives." "Use
      of welfare by illegal immigrants is undetectably low." Further,
      public sector costs and benefits of immigrants vary by level
      of government; the federal government is a net gainer; the
      impacts vary by state; and at the local level, costs of immigrants,
      heavily influenced by expenses of educating immigrant children,
      exceed the taxes they pay. (This finding suggests the federal
      government should provide tax relief to burdened localities
      rather than the present policy of reducing federal responsibility.)
      After statistical analysis of data from the 1980 census, Gregory
      DeFreitas found that in the 79 metropolitan areas with
      populations over 500,000 immigrants were typically less likely
      than native-born persons to receive welfare benefits or other
      government transfers. See his *Inequality at Work: Hispanics
      in the US Labor Force* (New York: Oxford University Press,
      1991), 418-428. In another review of the evidence, DeFreitas
      found that refugees, particularly from Cambodia, Laos, and
      Vietnam, had high AFDC recipiency rates and that elderly
      persons entering after 1980 were disproportionately dependent

on Supplemental Security Income largely because they lacked sufficient U.S. work experience to qualify for social security. Mexican immigrants, many of them undocumented, were much less likely to get public assistance than natives. See Gregory DeFreitas, "Immigration, Inequality, and Policy Alternatives," in Dean Baker, Gerald Epstein, and Robert Pollin, eds., *Globalization and Progressive Economic Policy* (Cambridge: Cambridge University Press, 1998), 347-349.

18.   U.S. House of Representatives, op. cit., 474 (see note 7).

19.   Leatha Lamison-White, *Poverty in the United States: 1996*, U.S. Bureau of the Census, Current Population Reports, Series P60-198 (Washington, D.C.: U.S. Government Printing Office, 1997), table C-3, C-8-C-13.

20.   U.S. Bureau of the Census, *Poverty in the United States: 1992*, Current Population Reports, Series P60-185 (Washington, D.C.: U.S. Government Printing Office, 1993), table 11, 70-73.

21.   Murry Edelman, *Constructing the Political Spectacle* (Chicago: University of Chicago Press, 1988), 18.

22.   James K. Galbraith, *Created Unequal: The Crisis in American Pay* (New York: The Free Press, 1998), 4-5.

23.   Notable among these was a publication of the Center on Social Welfare Policy and Law (now Welfare Law Center), op. cit. (see note 10). See also Mimi Abramovitz and Fred Newdom, *Challenging the Myths of Welfare Reform,* rev. ed. (New York: Bertha Capen Reynolds Society, 1994).

24.   For a discussion of this form of policy feedback, see Paul Pierson, *Dismantling the Welfare State? Reagan, Thatcher, and the Politics of Retrenchment* (Cambridge, England: Cambridge University Press, 1994), 39-50. Pierson refers to a study by Anna Shola Orloff and Theda Skocpol that found that perceived corruption in administration of Civil War pensions led middle-class reformers and, in turn, policymakers to oppose extending pensions to the general population. See their "Why Not Equal Protection? Explaining the Politics of Social Spending in Britain, 1900–1911, and the United States, 1880s–1920s," *American Sociological Review* 49 (1984), 726-750.

25.   Richard Hofstadter, *The Age of Reform* (New York: Vintage Books, 1955).

26.   Paul Slack, *Poverty & Policy in Tudor & Stuart England* (London: Longman, 1988), 28-29. The English statute of 1576 tacitly acknowledges the want of unemployment by ordering that "a competent store and stock of wool, hemp, flax, iron, or other stuff" be provided by the towns and cities "so that poor and needy persons being willing to work may be set on work." *An Acte for the Setting of the Poore on Worke, and for the Avoyding of Ydlenes,* 18 Elizabeth (1576) (England), Chapter III, Sec. IV. And the Statutes of 1598 and 1601 authorized such setting to work of the unemployed. But work relief was not forthcoming, and, according to Slack, parish authorities were more likely to provide them with cash supplements than with employment.

27.   Philip Harvey, "Combating Joblessness: An Analysis of the Principal Strategies That Have Influenced the Development of American Employment and Social Welfare Law during the Twentieth Century," unpublished paper, Rutgers School of Law, Camden, N.J., 1999. See also his "Joblessness and the Law before the New Deal," *Georgetown Journal of Poverty Law and Policy* 6 (1999), 1-41.

28.   See, e.g., Marc Blaug, "The Myth of the Old Poor Law and the Making of the New," *Journal of Economic History* 23 (June 1963), 151-184; and George R. Boyer, "The Old Poor Law and the Agricultural Labor Market in Southern England: An Empirical Analysis," *Journal of Economic History* 46 (March 1986), 113-135. Blaug's focus is on the allowance as a means of preventing hunger, and Boyer emphasizes that allowances were more generous, not where need was greater, but where laborers were closer to London and where cottage industry was less available to supplement the incomes of poor laborers.

29.   Quoted in Sidney Webb and Beatrice Webb, *English Poor Law History,* 2 vols. (London: Longmans, Green and Co., 1929), 1, 62. According to G. M. Trevelyan, the Speenhamland system was "a fatal policy, for it encouraged farmers to keep down wages." *A Shortened History of England* (Hammondsworth, England: Penguin Books, 1942), 457.

30. According to a careful examination of surveys of poor-relief practices in English parishes, unemployed men were the targets of the 1834 reform, whereas reforms later in the century were directed against all classes of paupers. Karel Williams, *From Pauperism to Poverty* (London: Routledge & Kegan Paul, 1981), 6.

31. Ibid., 6 and passim; Webb and Webb, op. cit., 2, 1038-1039 (see note 29). See also Blanche D. Coll, *Perspectives in Public Welfare* (Washington, D.C.: U.S. Government Printing Office, 1973), 41-45.

32. Coll, ibid., 40-45.

33. For discussions of charity organization, see esp. Michael B. Katz, *In the Shadow of the Poorhouse: A Social History of Welfare in America* (New York: Basic Books, 1986), 58-84; Roy Lubove, *The Professional Altruist: The Emergence of Social Work as a Career,* 1880–1930 (Cambridge, Mass.: Harvard University Press, 1965), 1-21; and Frank Dekker Watson, *The Charity Organization Movement in the United States: A Study in American Philanthropy* (New York: Macmillan, 1922).

34. According to historian Raymond A. Mohl, "the most significant development in public welfare during the period [1870–1900] lay in the abandonment of outdoor relief by most of the nation's largest cities." Mohl points out that COS leaders castigated public assistance and in many cities led the successful drive against public outdoor relief. See his "The Abolition of Public Outdoor Relief, 1870–1900," in Walter I. Trattner, ed., *Social Welfare or Social Control: Some Historical Reflections on Regulating the Poor* (Knoxville, University of Tennessee Press, 1983), 43-44.

35. Mrs. Charles Russell Lowell, "The Economic and Moral Effects of Public Outdoor Relief," *Proceedings of the National Conference of Charities and Correction at the Seventeenth Annual Session,* held in Baltimore, Md., May 14–21, 1890 (Boston: Geo. H. Ellis, 1890), 85.

36. One representative of voluntary charity who joined the campaign to restore public outdoor relief to widows and their families in the second decade of the twentieth century al-

luded to a choice between "the barbarous, merciless, break-
ing up of good families and the lawful intervention of the
State." Mrs. William Eisenstein, "Pensions for Widowed
Mothers as a Means of Securing for Dependent Children the
Benefits of Home Training and Influence," in Eleventh New
York State Conference of Charities and Correction, Proceedings,
Rochester, N.Y., November 15–17, 1911 (Albany, N.Y.: J.
B. Lyon Company, 1911), 229, cited by David M. Schneider
and Albert Deutsch, *Public Welfare in New York State, 1867–
1940* (Chicago: University of Chicago Press, 1941), 185.

37. Katz, op. cit., 18 (see note 33).

38. Abbott further stated that "in spite of many amendments,
the general principles of the old statutes have been very little
changed. They were written for a parochial society, and they
were written for a less democratic period of society." See
her "Abolish the Poor Laws," *Social Service Review* 8 (March
1934), 1.

39. For a comparison of the poor laws and PRWORA, see William P. Quigley, "Dismantling the Welfare State: Welfare
Reform and Beyond," *Stanford Law & Policy Review* 9 (Winter
1998), 101-103.

40. Josephine Chapin Brown, *Public Relief, 1929–1939* (New
York: Henry Holt and Co., 1940), 9-10. In 4 of the 14 states
that denied the right to vote, the restrictions applied only to
pauper inmates of poorhouses. In 30 states, the word pauper was used in the legal title of the statute, in the text of
the statute, and often also in a section head (Abbott, op. cit.,
2 [see note 38]).

41. PRWORA, ibid., sec. 101 (see note 4).

42. For examples of Conservative attacks on welfare, see, e.g.,
George Gilder, *Wealth and Poverty* (New York: Basic Books,
1981); Charles Murray, *Losing Ground: American Social Policy,
1950–1980* (New York: Basic Books, 1984); and Lawrence
Mead, *Beyond Entitlement: The Social Obligations of Citizenship* (New York: The Free Press, 1986). The works of
these writers are reviewed in Chapter 5.

43. For examples of the liberal approach, see: John D. Kasarda,
"Urban Change and Minority Opportunities," in Paul Peterson,

ed., *The New Urban Reality* (Washington, D.C.: Brookings Institution, 1985); and John D. Kasarda, "Jobs, Migration, and Emerging Urban Mismatches," in Michel G. H. McGeary and Laurence E. Lynn, Jr., eds., *Welfare Policy for the 1990s* (Cambridge, Mass.: Harvard University Press, 1989), 70-102. See also Thomas J. Sugrue, "The Structures of Urban Poverty: The Reorganization of Space and Work in Three Periods of American History," in Michael B. Katz, ed., *The Urban "Underclass" Debate: Views from History* (Princeton, N.J.: Princeton University Press, 1993), 114-115.

44.   Neoclassical development theory came into vogue after World War II as a way of explaining why poor countries ("underdeveloped") primarily in the southern zone of the world were not so industrially or technologically advanced ("developed") as those in the north. Variants of this theory were developed in the fields of sociology, economics, and political science by such theorists as Talcott Parsons (sociology), W. W. Rostow (economics), and Gabriel Almond (political science). What all the variants had in common was the assumption that the countries of the so-called "Third World" were deficient in cultural rationality, values, technical prowess, etc., and that they needed to follow the development path laid down by the First World nations. According to critics of development theory, the theory ignored questions of unequal power and the effects of global capitalist relations of production (colonialism, imperialism) on the poverty that they witnessed. It was a rationale for continued First World domination of the rest of the world and the West's answer to the attraction of communism among the decolonizing nations of the south. For an explanation and critiques of neoclassical development theory, see: "Development and Underdevelopment," in *The Oxford Companion to Politics of the World* (Oxford: Oxford University Press, 1993), 239-243; and Wolfgang Sachs, ed., *The Development Dictionary* (London: Zed Books Ltd., 1992).

45.   Peter Steinfels, *The Neoconservatives: The Men Who Are Changing America's Politics* (New York: Simon & Schuster, 1979), 144. For an example of Moynihan's calling attention to black, male unemployment but avoiding either a critique of the labor market or a call for job creation, see the document known as "The Moynihan Report": U.S. Department of

Labor, Office of Policy Planning and Research, *The Negro Family: The Case for National Action* (Washington, D.C.: Author, March 1965).

46. Frances Fox Piven and Richard A. Cloward, *Regulating the Poor: The Functions of Public Welfare* (New York: Vintage Books, 1971), 342. In an updated edition of this book (1993, 399), Piven and Cloward write: "*the explosion of the rolls is the true reform*" (their emphasis).

47. Frances Fox Piven and Richard A. Cloward, "The Origins of the Contemporary Relief Debate," in Fred Block, Richard A. Cloward, Barbara Ehrenreich, and Frances Fox Piven, *The Mean Season: The Attack on the Welfare State* (New York: Pantheon Books, 1987).

48. Fred Block, Richard A. Cloward, Barbara Ehrenreich, and Frances Fox Piven, "The Trouble with Full Employment," *The Nation*, 17 March 1986, 694-697.

49. For Mimi Abramovitz's position on the function of relief for women, see *Regulating the Lives of Women: Social Welfare Policy from Colonial Times to the Present,* rev. ed. (Boston: South End Press, 1996). For her defense of welfare, see Abramovitz and Newdom, op. cit. (see note 23).

50. Block et al., op. cit. (see note 48). See Jeremy Rifkin; *The End of Work: The Decline of the Global Labor Force and the Dawn of the Post-Market Era* (New York: G. P. Putnam's Sons, 1995); and Stanley Aronowitz and William DiFazio, *The Jobless Future* (Minneapolis, Mich.: University of Minnesota Press, 1994).

51. For documentation of their consistent espousal of both economic and civil rights, see Dona Cooper Hamilton and Charles V. Hamilton, *The Dual Agenda: Race and Social Welfare Policies of Civil Rights Organizations* (New York: Columbia University Press, 1997).

52. See, e.g., Ellen Schrecker, *Many Are the Crimes: McCarthyism in America* (New York and Boston: Little, Brown and Co, 1998).

53. Although widely used, the term *underclass* has come under intense scrutiny from a number of progressive scholars who criticize its imprecision and see in its use a dangerous political

agenda. For the underclass debate, see: Michael B. Katz, ed., op. cit. (see note 43); Herbert J. Gans, "Deconstructing the Underclass: The Term's Dangers as a Planning Concept," *Journal of the American Planning Association* 56 (Summer 1990), 271-277; and Walter W. Stafford and Joyce Ladner, "Political Dimensions of the Underclass Concept," in Herbert J. Gans, ed., *Sociology and Critical American Issues* (Newbury Park, Calif.: Sage Publications, 1991), 138-155.

54. Jacqueline Jones, *The Dispossessed: America's Underclass from the Civil War to the Present* (New York: Basic Books, 1992). See also her *American Work: Four Centuries of Black and White Labor* (New York: W.W. Norton, 1998).

55. Kathryn Edin and Laura Lein, *Making Ends Meet: How Welfare Mothers Survive Welfare and Low-Wage Work* (New York: Russell Sage Foundation, 1997).

56. Rank, op. cit., 172 (see note 14).

57. For an overview of job vacancy studies and their results, see Philip Harvey, "How Many Jobs Are There? The Need for a National Job Vacancy Survey," *Uncommon Sense* 15 (New York: National Jobs for All Coalition, March 2000).

58. See, e.g., Rachel L. Swarms, "4,000 Hearts Full of Hope Line Up for 700 Jobs," *New York Times,* 19 March 1997, A1, B4.

59. Richard B. Freeman, "Employment and Earnings of Disadvantaged Young Men in a Labor Shortage Economy," in Christopher Jencks and Paul E. Paterson, eds., *The Urban Underclass* (Washington, D.C.: Brookings Institution, 1991), 103-121.

60. Paul Osterman, "Gains from Growth? The Impact of Full Employment on Poverty in Boston," in ibid., 130.

61. William Julius Wilson, *When Work Disappears: The World of the Urban Poor* (New York: Vintage Books, 1996), compares the "jobless ghetto" of the early 1990s "in which a substantial majority of individual adults were either unemployed or had dropped out of the labor force altogether" with black ghettos, circa 1950–1960, in which well over 60% were employed (p. 19).

62. Ibid., 145.

63. "Faced with a shortage of trades workers to meet the voracious demand for construction in the United States, desperate builders and eager unions have begun aggressive campaigns to court new workers, attracting women and members of racial minorities to the traditional bastion of white men, a world where a coveted union card was handed from father to son. The Chicago-area carpenters union is investing $15,000 a year in each trainee in its apprenticeship program and last December opened a $3.5 million training center in a poverty-scarred neighborhood on the city's South Side." Dirk Johnson, "Facing Shortage, Builders and Labor Court Workers," *New York Times*, 13 March 1999, A1. See also, Sylvia Nasar, "More Groups Are Sharing in Job Growth: Blacks and Teen-Agers Showed Gains in April," *New York Times*, 8 May 1999, C1, C14.

64. For a discussion of such labor-market policies in a scheme for full employment, see Helen Ginsburg, *Full Employment and Public Policy: The United States and Sweden* (Lexington, Mass.: Lexington Books, 1983), chap. 6.

65. See, e.g., Rudolf Meidner, "The Swedish Model in an Era of Mass Unemployment," *Economic and Industrial Democracy* 18 (February 1997), 87-98.

66. Staughton Lynd ("A Jobs Program for the '90s," *Social Policy* 25 [Fall 1994], 22-35) reports a potential in Youngstown, Ohio, for creating approximately 2,700 jobs to meet needs in house repair and rehabilitation and day care. A survey undertaken by academics and community activists in Long Island found that to deal with deficiencies in affordable housing, the environment, education and health care, and mass transportation, sufficient jobs could be created to offset unemployment caused by military cutbacks in the island's defense-dependent economy. See Long Island Alliance for Peaceful Alternatives, *Reinvestment in Long Island* (Garden City, N.Y.: Author, March 1993). A report on public employment to meet community needs identifies five major areas of tasks that have been performed by participants in past and current job-creation initiatives: construction, environmental protection, community services, public health, and education/child care. Clifford M. Johnson and Alex Goldenberg, *Work to Be Done:*

Designing Publicly-Funded Jobs to Meet Community Needs (Washington, D.C.: Center on Budget and Policy Priorities, September 1999).

67. Frances Perkins, *The Roosevelt I Knew* (New York: Viking, 1946), 190.

68. Nancy Rose, *Workfare or Fair Work: Women, Welfare, and Government Work Programs* (New Brunswick, N.J.: Rutgers University Press, 1995), 3.

69. Ibid., 114-115.

70. Feminists lobbied successfully for the Family Violence Option (FVO), an amendment to PRWORA that gives states the option to exempt battered women from revealing the identities of abusive fathers of their children if complying with these requirements would put them at risk and to provide opportunities for victims of domestic violence to obtain counseling, safety planning, and other needed services before seeking work. By 1999, most states had either adopted the FVO or were making plans to do so, but there are problems in FVO implementation, particularly in making TANF recipients aware of the benefits of disclosure. See Jody Raphael and Sheila Haennicke, *Keeping Battered Women Safe through the Welfare-to-Work Journey: Report on the Implementation of Policies for Battered Women in State Temporary Assistance to Needy Families (TANF) Programs* (Chicago: Taylor Institute, September 1999).

71. See, e.g., Abramovitz, op. cit. (see note 49); and Linda Gordon, *Pitied But Not Entitled: Single Mothers and the History of Welfare 1890–1935* (New York: The Free Press, 1994).

72. Winifred Bell, *Aid to Dependent Children* (New York: Columbia University Press, 1965).

73. Frances Fox Piven and Richard A. Cloward, "Welfare Doesn't Shore Up Traditional Family Roles: A Reply to Linda Gordon," *Social Research* 55 (Winter 1988), 642-643.

74. PRWORA, op. cit., sec. 101 (see note 4).

75. Michael Katz, "Reframing the Debate," in Katz, op. cit., 454-455 (see note 43).

76. John L. Hammond and Barbara Hammond, *The Village Labourer, 1760–1832: A Study in the Government of England before the Reform Bill* (London: Longmans, Green, and Co., 1948), 148.

77. Maternalist policies also included not only measures like mothers' pensions, but legislation to protect women in the labor market through minimum wages and maximum working hours. The latter, by protecting their health, supported their child-bearing and nurturing roles. See. e.g., Theda Skocpol with Gretchen Ritter, "Gender and the Origins of Modern Social Policies in Britain and the United States," in Theda Skocpol, ed., *Social Policy in the United States* (Princeton, N.J.: Princeton University Press, 1995), 72-135.

78. President Richard Nixon used the term *workfare* during his presidential campaign in 1968 and in introducing his Family Assistance Plan in 1969, but he meant that work was to pay more than welfare and that recipients would be required to accept work or training (although their children would continue to receive benefits even if they failed to comply). See Vincent J. Burke and Vee Burke, *Nixon's Good Deed: Welfare Reform* (New York: Columbia University Press, 1974), esp. 110-112. The practice of requiring recipients to work off their benefits began to be implemented under Ronald Reagan and his successors in the Oval Office.

79. U.S. Department of Health and Human Services, Administration for Children and Families, Press Release, "State Welfare Demonstrations," 7 October 1996. Waivers of 34 of the 43 included reductions of benefits for failure to comply with one or more requirements; 14 would provide no additional benefits for a child conceived while the mother is on welfare; 19 imposed time limits shorter than 5 years; and only 1 included any progressive job generation.

80. Schlesinger observes that "historically it has not been local government that has served as the protector of the powerless in the United States; it has been the national government." See Arthur J. Schlesinger, Jr., *The Cycles of American History* (Boston: Houghton Mifflin, 1986), 242.

81. Mimi Abramovitz (op. cit. [see note 49]), and Dorothy C. Miller, *Women and Social Welfare: A Feminist Analysis* (New

York: Greenwood Press, 1990) take the family-ethic position whereas Piven and Cloward (ibid. and op. cit., [see note 46] take the work-ethic position. Linda Gordon, noting that a version of her arguments had been made by Abramovitz, writes that "promoting the family-wage system is a better overall explanation of the social-control functions of the welfare state than has been previously offered" ("What Does Welfare Regulate?" *Social Research* 55 [Winter 1988], 609-630).

82. See, e.g., Helen Ginsburg, op. cit. (see note 64); Margaret G. Rosenthal, "Sweden: Promise and Paradox," in Gertrude Schaffner Goldberg and Eleanor Kremen, eds., *The Feminization of Poverty: Only in America?* (New York: Praeger, 1990). In the late 1980s, when Swedish unemployment rates were below 3% and women's labor force participation rates were over 75%, 29.1% of Swedish single parents were poor without income transfers; their poverty was reduced 81.1% by welfare state programs, bringing the rate down to 5.5%. See Timothy M. Smeeding and Lee Rainwater, op. cit., table 7 (see note 13).

83. In the Netherlands, when unemployment stood at 10.3% (1986), income transfers reduced single-parent poverty by 93%, leaving a poverty rate of 5.5% (1987). See Smeeding and Rainwater, ibid.

84. Jörg Huffschmid points out that between 1980 and 1990, Germany was an economic success, its share of world exports rose almost 14%, and the profit rate of German corporations was up more than one-third. But in the same decade, the number of unemployed and the number of poor people more than doubled. Jörg Huffschmid, "Economic Policy for Full Employment: Proposals for Germany," *Economic and Industrial Democracy* 18 (January 1997), 67-86.

CHAPTER 2
AID TO DEPENDENT CHILDREN IS BORN

1. Franklin D. Roosevelt, Annual Message to the Congress, 4 January 1935, *The Public Papers and Addresses of Franklin Delano Roosevelt,* 6 vols. (New York: Random House, 1938), 4, 19.

2.   Ibid., 20.

3.   Committee on Economic Security, *The Report of the Committee on Economic Security of 1935, 50th Anniversary Edition* (Washington, D.C.: National Conference on Social Welfare, 1985), 8-9. On 29 June 1934, President Roosevelt appointed the Committee on Economic Security to study the problems relating to economic security and to make recommendations for legislation. The committee consisted of the Secretaries of Labor (the chairperson), Treasury, and Agriculture, the Attorney General, and the Federal Emergency Relief Administrator. Secretary of Labor and Chair of the Committee on Economic Security Frances Perkins stated: "More important than all social-insurance devices together is employment." Quoted in Arthur Schlesinger, Jr., *The Coming of the New Deal* (Boston: Houghton Mifflin, 1958), 304.

4.   The program is referred to as Aid to Dependent Children or ADC in discussions pertaining to the years 1935–1962, when it became Aid to Families with Dependent Children or AFDC as a result of Public Law 87-543, the Public Welfare Amendments of 1962. Evidently, a public-assistance program for dependent children was not part of the original objectives of Roosevelt, Perkins, and Harry Hopkins, the federal emergency relief administrator. See Wilbur J. Cohen, "The Social Security Act of 1935: Reflections Fifty Years Later," in Committee on Economic Security, ibid., 8.

5.   In 1972, the two programs for the adult, unemployable poor, Old Age Assistance and Aid to the Blind, plus a third, Aid to the Permanently and Totally Disabled (added as part of the 1950 Amendments to the Social Security Act) were combined into a single, all-federal program, Supplemental Security Income. AFDC remained a federal-state program until its repeal in August 1996.

6.   U.S. House of Representatives, Committee on Ways and Means, *Hearings on H.R. 4120: A Bill to Alleviate the Hazards of Old Age, Unemployment, Illness, and Dependency . . ., 74th Cong., 1st sess.* (Washington, D.C.: U.S. Government Printing Office, 1935), 159 (hereafter House Hearings).

7.   Based on his extensive study of Eisenhower, including the documentary record, Robert Griffith concluded that "Eisenhower

was . . . committed to at least maintaining the modest social
welfare programs that had emerged from the New Deal." For
example, he told the Western Governors' Conference in 1952
that "social gains" were no longer an issue but a necessary
"floor that covers the pit of disaster." See Robert Griffith,
"Dwight D. Eisenhower and the Corporate Commonwealth,"
American Historical Review 87 (February 1982), 102.

8.   "Twenty years earlier," writes Linda Gordon, "there had been
      an agitation for mothers' pensions. Not even a ripple of such
      a campaign was evident in the 1930s." Linda Gordon, *Pitied
      but Not Entitled: Single Mothers and the History of Welfare
      1890–1935* (New York: The Free Press, 1994), 212.

9.   See, e.g., Walter Trattner, *From Poor Law to Welfare State:
      A History of Social Welfare in America,* 5th ed. (New York:
      The Free Press, 1994), 182, 216-217.

10.   Ibid., 218.

11.   Perhaps the leading authority on relief in the 1930s,
      Josephine Brown, who personally favored a different and
      more liberal approach than that proposed by the CES, wrote
      that "a recommendation for assistance to dependent children
      was included in the report [of the CES] at the instance
      of the Federal Children's Bureau." Josephine Chapin Brown,
      Public Relief, 1929–1939 (New York: Henry Holt and Co.,
      1940), 301.

12.   For a discussion of the restrictive poor laws preceding the
      mothers'-aid reforms, see Raymond A. Mohl, "The Aboli-
      tion of Public Outdoor Relief, 1870–1900: A Critique of the
      Piven and Cloward Thesis," in Walter I. Trattner, ed., *So-
      cial Welfare or Social Control? Some Historical Reflections
      on Regulating the Poor* (Knoxville, Tenn.: University of Ten-
      nessee Press, 1983); and Brown, ibid., 26-27.

13.   According to the Proceedings of the White House Confer-
      ence, there were known to be 93,000 children in institutions
      and many additional thousands in foster or boarding homes.
      *Proceedings of Conference on the Care of Dependent Chil-
      dren* (Washington D.C.: U.S. Government Printing Office,
      1909), 9-14, in Ralph E. Pumphrey and Muriel W. Pumphrey,
      eds., *The Heritage of American Social Work: Readings in*

Its Philosophical and Institutional Development (New York: Columbia University Press, 1961), 327.

14. Ibid.

15. Brown, op. cit., 26-27 (see note 11).

16. Committee on Economic Security, op. cit., 36 (see note 3).

17. The Bureau's 1933 report, *Mothers Aid, 1931,* Children's Bureau Publication No. 109 (Washington, D.C.: U.S. Government Printing Office, 1933) indicated that the failure of the program was due to inadequate coverage and lack of funding; the conclusion was that leaving the programs to the states alone was a mistake. Cited in Edwin Amenta, *Bold Relief: Institutional Politics and the Origins of Modern American Social Policy* (Princeton, N.J.: Princeton University Press, 1998), 96.

18. U.S. Committee on Economic Security, *Social Security in America: The Factual Background of the Social Security Act as Summarized from the Staff Reports to the Committee on Economic Security,* Social Security Board Pub. No. 20 (Washington, D.C., 1937), 229-230. The section of the report on "Security for Children" was prepared by Lenroot and Eliot.

19. Eric F. Goldman, *Rendezvous with Destiny* (New York: Alfred A. Knopf, 1953), 320-321.

20. It is true that Hoover departed somewhat from his laissez-faire predilections and pronouncements by devising numerous government aids to recovery. Economic historian Broadus Mitchell cites examples of Hoover's governmental activism but nonetheless concludes that: "Hoover never grasped the magnitude of the problem or summoned resources to meet it." See Broadus Mitchell, *Depression Decade: From New Era through New Deal, 1929–1941, vol. IX, The Economic History of the United States* (New York: Holt, Rinehart and Winston, 1947), 405.

21. Herbert Hoover, *The Memoirs of Herbert Hoover: The Great Depression, 1929–1941* (New York: Macmillan, 1952), 56, 174.

22. Ibid., 152, 155.

23. Arthur M. Schlesinger, Jr., *The Crisis of the Old Order, 1919–1933* (Boston: Houghton Mifflin, 1957), 250.

24. Dorothy Kahn, Statement before U.S. Senate, Subcommittee of the Committee on Manufactures, 28 December 1931, *Unemployment Relief,* 72d Congress, First sess., S. 174 and S. 262, in Pumphrey and Pumphrey, op. cit., 410 (see note 13).

25. Schlesinger, op. cit., 250 (see note 23).

26. Frances Perkins, *The Roosevelt I Knew* (New York: Viking, 1946), 182.

27. Schlesinger, op. cit., 3 (see note 3).

28. Ibid., 301.

29. Frances Fox Piven and Richard A. Cloward *(Regulating the Poor: The Functions of Public Welfare,* updated ed. [New York: Vintage Books, 1993], 74) write that FERA "broke all precedents in American relief-giving." In a number of respects, which we point to below, this is true. However, FERA did work through state relief administrations in both its direct- and work-relief programs. See Arthur E. Burns and Edward A. Williams, *Federal Work, Security and Relief Programs,* Research Monograph XXIV, Federal Works Agency and Work Projects Administration (Washington, D.C.: U.S. Government Printing Office, 1941), 37. Thus, the extent to which its regulations, e.g., prohibitions against racial, religious, and political discrimination, could be enforced was limited.

30. Burns and Williams, ibid., 50. In some states, notably those below the Mason-Dixon Line, the federal government was providing 95–99% of all relief prior to the passage of the SSA. See Edith Abbott, *Public Assistance,* 3 vols. (Chicago: University of Chicago Press, 1940), 3, 763.

31. U.S. Committee on Economic Security, op. cit., 241 (see note 18).

32. Burns and Williams, op. cit., 26-27 (see note 29).

33. U.S. Senate, Committee on Finance, Statement of Dorothy Kahn, *Hearings before the Committee on Finance, United States Senate, Seventy-Fourth Congress, First Session on S. 1130, A Bill to Alleviate the Hazards of Old Age, Unemployment, Illness, and Dependency, to Establish a Social Insurance Board*

in the Department of Labor, to Raise Revenue, and for Other Purposes (Washington, D.C.: U.S. Government Printing Office, 1935, 652 [hereafter Senate Hearings]). Some would also argue that the payment of benefits in cash so that recipients were free to spend it just as they did their wages was an important FERA advance. Since relief had usually been provided in-kind—as food and fuel or in the poorhouse (indoor relief), FERA official Josephine Chapin Brown (op. cit., 230 [see note 11]) considered this "a marked reversal of past practice." However, Rule No. 3 of FERA authorized local relief agencies to provide orders, allowances, or their cash equivalents for housing shelter, fuel, household supplies, clothing, and medicine. In fact, food could be provided directly, in addition to the other prescribed ways. See Burns and Williams, op. cit., 26 (see note 29).

34. "Those receiving direct relief included many unemployable persons . . . as well as many employables for whom work relief could not be found." Burns and Williams, ibid., 41.

35. The exception was the very small mothers'-aid programs.

36. Robert Sherwood, *Roosevelt and Hopkins* (New York: Harper & Brothers, 1948), 65.

37. Schlesinger, op. cit., 385, 396 (see note 3). For discussion of the militancy of both the "largest movement of the unemployed this country has known" and of the industrial-workers' movement, see Frances Fox Piven and Richard A. Cloward, *Poor People's Movements: Why They Succeed, How They Fail* (New York: Pantheon Books, 1977), 41-76, 107-147. Edwin Amenta and Sunita Parikh have argued that the strike volume or number of "man days" idle as a percentage of all private nonfarm working time was less in the New Deal years than during the war and immediate postwar periods, but that labor militancy did not lead to significant reforms in the latter period. However, that does not mean that in the earlier period, when this labor strife was occurring, it did not seem threatening or unprecedented. Nor does strike volume measure the bitterness or intensity of the conflicts. Labor militancy was, moreover, only one of the factors threatening social peace and political legitimacy or creating pressure for reform. See Edwin Amenta and Sunita

Parikh, "Capitalists Did Not Want the Social Security Act:
A Critique of the 'Capitalist Dominance' Thesis," *American Sociological Review* 56 (1991), 124-129.

38. Roosevelt liked to tell a story that helped to explain business ingratitude to the New Deal. A man with a silk hat who did not know how to swim fell off a pier. A friend rescued him, but his silk hat floated away. At the time he was grateful to his friend for saving his life, but a few years later, he berated his friend because his silk hat was lost. Recounted in James MacGregor Burns, *The Crosswinds of Freedom: From Roosevelt to Reagan—America in the Last Half Century* (New York: Vintage Books, 1990), 41.

39. William E. Leuchtenburg, *Franklin D. Roosevelt and the New Deal, 1932–1940* (New York: Harper, 1963), 92.

40. "An Open Break Develops," *New York Times,* 3 May 1935, 1.

41. Edwin E. Witte, *The Development of the Social Security Act* (Madison, Wisc.: The University of Wisconsin Press, 1962), 94. They were willing to give unemployment insurance a try and favored the assistance provisions. One of their absent colleagues was also a dissenter. The Ways and Means Committee had jurisdiction of the bill in Congress and held hearings on it.

42. Jill S. Quadagno, "Welfare Capitalism and the Social Security Act of 1935," *American Sociological Review* 49 (October 1984), 632-647. A more recent study by a Canadian scholar, Colin Gordon, also points to resistance on the part of small firms and southern political and economic interests to socialization or nationalization of the costs of industrial welfare but emphasizes that representatives of the monopoly sector saw the act as serving its goals and were prime movers in its passage. Gordon, however, virtually ignores the tremendous influence of popular protest, especially the Townsend Movement discussed below. See Colin Gordon, *New Deals: Business, Labor, and Politics in America, 1920–1935* (Cambridge: Cambridge University Press, 1994), 240-279. For a debate over whether and which sectors of business favored the Social Security Act, see J. Craig Jenkins and Barbara G. Brents, "Social Protest, Hegemonic Competition and Social

Reform: A Political Struggle Interpretation of the Origins
of the American Welfare State," *American Sociological Review*
54 (December 1989), 891-909; Amenta and Parikh, op. cit.,
(see note 37); and J. Craig Jenkins and Barbara Brents,
"Capitalists and Social Security: What Did They Really Want?"
American Sociological Review 56 (1991), 129-132.

43. For this point, see David Plotke, *Building a Democratic Political
Order: Reshaping American Liberalism in the 1930s and 1940s*
(New York: Cambridge University Press, 1996), 91, 101-107.

44. See, e.g., Leuchtenburg, op. cit., 143-150 (see note 39).

45. For the influence of the AALL on the development of social
insurance in the United States and on the Social Security
Act, see Roy Lubove, *The Struggle for Social Security, 1900–
1935* (Cambridge, Mass.: Harvard University Press, 1968).

46. Edith Abbott, "Don't Do It, Mr. Hopkins?" *The Nation,* 9
January 1935, and "Federal Relief—Sold Down the River,"
The Nation, 18 March 1936, reprinted in Abbott, op. cit., 3,
758-764 (see note 30).

47. For treatment of these alternative, more radical approaches to
social provision, see Leuchtenburg, op. cit., 95-106, 132 (see
note 39); and James MacGregor Burns, *Roosevelt: The Lion
and the Fox* (New York: Harcourt Brace, 1956), 210-215.

48. "Press Comment on Social Security Plan," *New York Times,*
19 January 1935, 2. *Times* columnist Arthur Krock observed
that if senators and representatives were correctly reporting
the feeling of their districts and testimony of their corre-
spondence, "the defeat or extreme dilution of the Roosevelt
proposals will mean the ascendancy of the ideas of Huey L.
Long, Doctor Townsend, or both." Arthur Krock, "In Washington: Roosevelt, Long, or Townsend," *New York Times,*
18 January 1935, 22. Similarly, Frank Bane, first head of
the Social Security board, later reminisced, "we had two great
allies that were helping us put Social Security legislation
through. They were far more important, I think, on the Hill,
than any of us were [*sic*]. These two were a gentlemen by
the name of Dr. Townsend, and the second one by the name
of Huey Long." "The Reminiscences of Frank Bane" (1963),
Oral History Collection of Columbia University, 24, cited

by Gordon, op. cit., 229 (see note 8).

49. Perkins, op. cit., 278-279 (see note 26).

50. "President Fights for Job Insurance," *New York Times,* 13 April 1935, 7. Dr. Francis Townsend's plan was for the federal government to provide a pension of $200 a month for persons over the age of 60, providing they left the labor market and spent the money. In April 1935, Dr. Townsend claimed that there were 3,000 Townsend clubs, ranging in size from 100 to 5,000 members after only 4 or 5 months of efforts to form clubs, and that the organization had collected between 20 and 30 million signatures on pensions. "Social Security: But Not by Townsend," *New York Times,* 22 April 1935, sec. 4, 1. Congressman Ernest Lundeen's bill, which became the focus of radical demands, called for providing unemployment benefits at prevailing wages for all workers, the program to be administered by commissions composed of rank-and-file members of workers' and farmers' organizations. Schlesinger, op. cit., 295-296 (see note 3) (Lundeen). See also Leuchtenburg, op. cit., 132 (see note 39) (Lundeen).

51. Leuchtenburg, ibid., 244-251.

52. Wagner observed in 1935 that his proposed legislation for a nationwide public employment exchange in 1928 was met with "the chill of public indifference" and that he got "no general support" in 1931 for legislation similar to the provision for unemployment insurance in the Economic Security Bill. "If one contrasts the Economic Security Bill with the public apathy toward the unfortunate that predominated a few years ago," Wagner observed, "he finds it hard to realize that he is still living in the same world." "Wagner Statement on Bill's Objectives," *New York Times,* 18 January 1935, 16.

53. Anne O'Hare McCormick, *The World at Home: Selections from the Writings of Anne O'Hare McCormick,* M.T. Sheehan, ed. (New York: Knopf, 1956), cited by Elmer E. Cornwell, Jr., *Presidential Leadership of Public Opinion* (Bloomington, Ind.: University of Indiana Press, 1965), 118.

54. Oswald Garrison Villard, "Issues and Men: The President and the Dying Congress," *The Nation,* 27 June 1934, 728, cited by Cornwell, ibid.

55. Ibid.

56. Cited in ibid., 119.

57. Perkins, op. cit., 278-279 (see note 26).

58. Jean Taft Douglas Bandler, "Family Issues in Social Policy: An Analysis of Social Security" (D.S.W. diss., Columbia University, 1975), 195.

59. Brown, op. cit., 26-28 (see note 11). In her testimony on the Economic Security Act, Lenroot pointed out that 20 states had mandatory laws, 29 had permissive laws, and 3 had none at all (House Hearings, op. cit., 264 [see note 6]. (The Territories and the District of Columbia were included.) Even where the laws were mandatory, some counties, owing to the press of the Great Depression, had not carried out the mandatory provisions of the state laws. Later Lenroot wrote that less than one-half of the local units authorized to grant mothers'aid was actually doing so. See Katharine F. Lenroot, "The Children's Titles in the Social Security Act," *Children* 7 (July–August 1960), 128.

60. Mark Leff, "The Mothers'-Pension Movement in the Progressive Era," *Social Service Review* 47 (1973), 413-414.

61. U.S. Congress, Public Law 74-271, 4 August 1935, Title IV, sec. 402(a) (hereafter Social Security Act).

62. Committee on Economic Security, op. cit., 36 (see note 3).

63. See, e.g., Bandler, op. cit., 199 (see note 58).

64. U.S. Department of Labor, Children's Bureau, *Mothers' Aid, 1931.* Children's Bureau Publication No. 220 (Washington, D.C.: U.S. Government Printing Office, 1933), cited by Leff, op. cit, 414 (see note 60). See also, U.S. Committee on Economic Security, op. cit., 234 (see note 18). Unmarried mothers were legally eligible in the state of Michigan, but a 1934 study found them to be less than 2% of the caseload. Michigan State Welfare Department, *Mothers' Aid in Michigan* (Lansing: the Department, 1934), 4, cited by Winifred Bell, *Aid to Dependent Children* (New York: Columbia University Press, 1965), 9.

65. House Hearings, op. cit., 268 (see note 6).

66.   Ibid., 364.

67.   Ibid., 267.

68.   Social Security Act, op. cit., Title IV, sec. 406(a) (see note 61).

69.   Gerard D. Reilly, who served on the legal staff of the Department of Labor from 1934–1941, wrote that "[Perkins] felt the Children's Bureau let her down on the provision for aid to mothers with dependent children. She maintained that she always thought a dependent mother was a widow with small children or one whose husband had been disabled in an industrial accident or one who had married a ne'er-do-well who had deserted her or hit the bottle. She said it never occurred to her, in view of the fact that she'd been active in drives for the homes that took care of mothers with illegitimate children, that these mothers would be called 'dependent' in the new legislation. She blamed the huge illegitimacy rates among blacks on aid for mothers with dependent children." Gerard D. Reilly, "Madame Secretary," in Katie Louchheim, ed., *The Making of the New Deal: The Insiders Speak* (Cambridge: Harvard University Press, 1983), 175.

      More than a decade earlier, Lenroot had supported the extension of mothers' aid to unwed mothers. Like others in the social services, Lenroot and her colleagues favored careful supervision of these and other single-mother families by social agencies but did not assume that mothers' marital status should automatically disqualify them form outdoor relief, nor that children should be separated from their parents except for urgent reasons. Katharine Lenroot and Emma O. Lundberg, *Illegitimacy as a Child Welfare Problem,* Children's Bureau Pub. No. 75 (Washington, D.C.: U.S. Government Printing Office, 1921), 67, cited by Marguerite G. Rosenthal, "Social Policy for Delinquent Children: Delinquency Activities of the U.S. Children's Bureau, 1912–1940" (Ph.D. diss., State University of New Jersery, 1982), 142-144.

70.   Brown, op. cit., 301 (see note 11).

71.   See, e.g., House Hearings, op. cit., 202 (see note 6).

72.   Ibid., Title IV, sec. 406(b).

73. Michael B. Katz, *In the Shadow of the Poorhouse: A Social History of Welfare in America* (New York: Basic Books, 1986).

74. See note 33.

75. Gordon, op. cit., 9 (see note 8). See also Bell, op. cit., 16-17 (see note 64); June Axinn and Herman Levin, *Social Welfare: A History of the American Response to Need,* 4th ed. (New York: Longman, 1997), 143; and Mimi Abramovitz, *Regulating the Lives of Women: Social Welfare Policy from Colonial Times to the Present* (Boston: South End Press, 1988), 204-205. Abramovitz, however, believes that mothers' pensions enabled many women to avoid the worst jobs.

76. Stephanie Coontz, *The Way We Never Were* (New York: Basic Books, 1992), 137.

77. House Hearings, op. cit., sec. 204(c) (see note 6).

78. Cohen, op. cit., 8 (see note 4). See also Schlesinger, op. cit., 313 (see note 3).

79. See, e.g., Byrd's questioning of Edwin Witte, the executive director of the Committee on Economic Security. Senate Hearings, op. cit., 69 (see note 33). Byrd's remarks were addressed to Old Age Assistance, but he was well aware that "the same provision applies to dependent children. . . ." (p. 579).

80. House Hearings, op. cit., 974 (see note 6). The "reasonable subsistence" language was also troubling because it was feared that a state would be forced by the federal statute to spend more than it wanted or could afford (pp. 974-978).

81. Lee J. Alston and Joseph P. Ferrie, "Labor Costs, Paternalism, and Loyalty in Southern Agriculture: A Constraint on the Growth of the Welfare State," *Journal of Economic History* 45 (March 1985), 95-117.

82. Witte, op. cit., 143-144 (see note 41).

83. *Report of the U.S. Advisory Council on Public Assistance, Containing Findings and Recommendations (Senate, 86th Congress, 2nd sess., Doc. No. 93)* (Washington, D.C.: U.S. Government Printing Office, 1960), 14 (hereafter Advisory Council on Public Assistance). For a discussion of state need standards, see Carmen D. Solomon, "Need and Payment Levels

in the Program of Aid to Families with Dependent Children (AFDC): Legislative History and Current State Practices," Report No. 81-149 EPW (Washington, D.C.: Congressional Research Service, 18 September 1981).

84. Social Security Act, op. cit., Title I, sec. 8(a); Title IV, sec. 403(a); (see note 61).

85. "AFDC: History of Provisions," *Social Security Bulletin, Annual Statistical Supplement,* 1996, 128.

86. "The Text of President's Message to Congress Proposing Broader Social Security," *New York Times,* 25 May 1948, 23. For congressional reactions to the president's proposals, see Arthur J. Altmeyer, *The Formative Years of Social Security* (Madison, Wisc.: University of Wisconsin Press, 1966), 173-184.

87. "AFDC: History of Provisions," op. cit., 129 (see note 85).

88. Witte, op. cit., 164 (see note 41). Witte's testimony before Congress, like the Report of the Committee on Economic Security (see note 3), pointed out that the proposed program was not really for mothers' pensions but aid for children deprived of fathers' support. House Hearings, op. cit., 161 (see note 6).

89. Cohen, op. cit., 8 (see note 4).

90. National Resources Planning Board, Committee on Long-Range Work and Relief Policies, *Security, Work, and Relief Policies* (Washington, D.C.: U.S. Government Printing Office, 1942), 198.

91. Altmeyer, op. cit., 174 (see note 86); Wilbur J. Cohen and Robert J. Myers, "Social Security Act Amendments of 1950: A Summary and Legislative History," *Social Security Bulletin* 13 (October 1950), 5.

92. Kathryn D. Goodwin, "Twenty-five Years of Public Assistance," *Social Security Bulletin* 23 (August 1960), 36.

93. Jacqueline Jones, *Labor of Love, Labor of Sorrow: Black Women, Work, and the Family from Slavery to the Present* (New York: Basic Books, 1985), 224-225.

94. Mary S. Labaree, "Unmarried Parenthood under the Social Security Act," *Proceedings of the National Conference of Social Work, 1939* (New York: Columbia University Press, 1939), 454. Labaree was Field Consultant in Child Welfare, Child Welfare Division, Children's Bureau, U.S. Department of Labor. Labaree does not specify the region of the country from which these examples were drawn.

95. Gordon W. Blackwell and Raymond F. Gould, *Future Citizens All* (Chicago: American Public Welfare Association, 1952), 16.

96. Advisory Council on Public Assistance, op. cit., 56 (see note 83).

97. Kathryn Edin and Laura Lein, *Making Ends Meet: How Single Mothers Survive Welfare and Low-Wage Work* (New York: Russell Sage Foundation, 1997).

98. "AFDC: History of Provisions," op. cit., 131 (see note 85).

99. U.S. Manpower Administration, *Barriers to Employment of the Disadvantaged, 1968; Manpower Report to the President* (Washington, D.C.: U.S. Government Printing Office, 1968), 98, cited by Piven and Cloward, op. cit., 128 (see note 29).

100. Adam Smith, *An Inquiry into the Nature & Causes of the Wealth of Nations,* 5th ed. (New York: Random House, Inc., 1937), 141.

101. Social Security Act, op. cit., Title IV, sec. 402(b) (see note 61).

102. Axinn and Levin, op. cit., 235 (see note 75).

103. Altmeyer, op. cit., 174 (see note 86) for rejection of the Truman proposal.

104. Advisory Council on Public Assistance, op. cit., 13 (see note 83).

105. *Report of the National Advisory Commission on Civil Disorders* (Washington, D.C.: National Advisory Commission on Civil Disorders, 1 March 1968), 253.

106. Paul A. Levy, "The Durability of Supreme Court Welfare Reforms of the 1960s," *Social Service Review* 67 (1992), 223, citing Center on Social Welfare Policy and Law, *Materials on Welfare Law* (New York: Center on Social Welfare Policy and Law, 1972), 1, 4-29.

107. Phyllis R. Osborn, "Aid to Dependent Children—Realities and Possibilities," *Social Service Review* 28 (1954), 164, citing Social Security Act, as amended, 1950, Title IV, sec. 40.

108. House Hearings, op. cit., 496 (see note 6).

109. Bell (op. cit., 46 [see note 64]) cites Federal Security Agency, Social Security Board, Bureau of Public Assistance, File No 623.1/03, 4 October 1943.

110. Ibid., 107, citing Arkansas Department of Public Welfare, *Annual Report,* 1953 through 1960 (Little Rock: The Department), relevant years, table entitled "Reasons for Closing ADC Cases."

111. Osborn, op. cit., 165 (see note 107).

112. Piven and Cloward, op. cit., 124-125; 141; 143 (see note 29).

113. U.S. Department of Labor, Children's Bureau, *Mothers' Aid, 1931,* Children's Bureau Publication No. 220 (Washington, D.C.: U.S. Government Printing Office, 1933), 13, 26-27, cited in Leff, op. cit., 414 (see note 60).

114. Richard Sterner, *The Negro's Share: A Study of Income, Consumption, Housing, and Public Assistance* (New York: Harper and Brothers, 1943), 138, cited by Nancy H. Cauthen and Edwin Amenta, "Not for Widows Only: Institutional Politics and the Formative Years of Aid to Dependent Children," *American Sociological Review* 61 (1996), 433.

115. Gordon, op. cit., 38 (see note 8).

116. U.S. Department of Labor, Children's Bureau, *Laws Relating to "Mothers' Pensions" in the United States, Denmark, and New Zealand,* Children's Bureau Publication No. 7 (Washington, D.C.: U.S. Government Printing Office, 1914), 22, cited by Leff, op. cit., 401 (see note 60).

117. Bell, op. cit., 29 (see note 64).

118. Paul A. Levy, op. cit., 227 (see note 106), citing House of Representatives Report No. 615, 75th Cong., 1st sess. 24 (1935); Senate Report No. 628, 74th Cong, 1st sess. 36 (1934). See also Bell, ibid., 29.

119. Bell (ibid., 20) reviews evidence regarding the support of the Children's Bureau for this policy. The report of Lenroot and Eliot simply reveals the existence of suitable homes policies in the mothers'-aid programs when it alludes to the fact that many families receiving emergency relief would be technically eligible for the mothers'-aid programs. However, it was not known "how many would be found to measure up to policies established with reference to the character of the mother and her competency to give proper care to her children." U.S. Committee on Economic Security, op. cit., 239-240 (see note 18).

120. Bell (ibid., 29-33) refers to a model act prepared by the Child Welfare League of America and to statements of the Social Security Board and the Federal Bureau of Public Assistance.

121. James T. Patterson, *America's Struggle against Poverty, 1900–1980* (Cambridge, Mass.: Harvard University Press, 1981), 69.

122. Bell, op. cit., 31 (see note 64)

123. Discussion of the Florida action draws on Bell's research, ibid., 126-136.

124. See ibid., 137-148.

125. "Louisiana Drops 23,000 Children on Relief Rolls as Illegitimates," *New York Times,* 28 August 1960, 62.

126. The National Urban League, in calling on the American Red Cross and the federal government to aid the children dropped from the Louisiana rolls, pointed out that 95% of the affected families were Negroes. The League charged that the legislation was a "political reprisal aimed at intimidation of colored citizens seeking constitutional rights to ballot box and education." "Louisiana Action Hit," *New York Times,* 30 August 1960, 25.

127. "Flemming Bars Cut in Louisiana Aid: New Rule Is Urged," *New York Times,*" 18 January 1961, 28.

128. "The Child Comes First," *New York Times*, 21 January 1961,
     20. The *Times* editorial also observed that "a home does not
     necessarily, automatically, invariably become 'unsuitable'
     because it has in it a child born out of wedlock." Although
     it had published several news items that gave evidence of
     the racial intent and impact of the Louisiana legislation, the
     Times editorial did not call attention to its anti-Negro bias.

129. Ibid.

130. Winifred Bell, *Rejected Families: A Study of "Suitable Home"
     Policies in Aid to Dependent Children* (unpublished D.S.W.
     diss., Columbia University, 1964), chapter 6, cited by Charles
     E. Gilbert, "Policy-Making in Public Welfare: The 1962 Amend-
     ments," *Political Science Quarterly* 81 (1966), 206.

131. Piven and Cloward, op. cit., 127, 136 (see note 29).

132. Advisory Council on Public Assistance, op. cit., 12 (see
     note 83).

133. U.S. Congress, Public Law 104-193, *Personal Responsibility
     and Work Opportunity Reconciliation Act of 1996,* Sec. 101.

134. For the proportion of widowed and nonwidowed families see
     1937–1938 Advisory Council or Social Security, Final Re-
     port, reprinted in Committee on Economic Security, op. cit.,
     18 (see note 3). Only 3.5% of children receiving ADC ben-
     efits during fiscal year 1937–1938 were living with unmar-
     ried mothers; five of the 30 states reporting accepted no children
     born out of wedlock, and 11 others, fewer than 50 each. How-
     ever, in presenting these data, Mary Labaree of the Children's
     Bureau observed that "this low percentage may be due to
     the slow process of change from mothers'-aid statutes with
     restrictive clauses to more liberal statutes." See Labaree, op.
     cit, 447 (see note 94).

135. Abramovitz, op. cit., 265 (see note 75).

136. Elizabeth Alling and Agnes Leisy, "Aid to Dependent Children
     in the Postwar Years," *Social Security Bulletin* 13 (1950), 6.

137. Osborn., op. cit., 161 (see note 107).

138. Alling and Leisy, op. cit., 4 (see note 136).

139. Ibid., 5.

140. Blackwell and Gould, op. cit., 21 (see note 95).

141. Ibid., 162. In the middle 1960s, when fathers' deaths were an even less frequent cause of single motherhood, social-policy analyst Alvin Schorr proposed a program of Fatherless Child Insurance to cover not only fathers' deaths but the more prevalent risk to income security—"social orphaning." See Alvin L. Schorr, *Poor Kids* (New York: Basic Books, 1966).

142. Goodwin, op. cit., 37 (see note 92).

143. Osborn, op. cit., 160 (see note 107).

144. Ibid., 172.

145. Axinn and Levin, op. cit., 234-236 (see note 75); see also, Trattner, op. cit., 282 (see note 9). Griffith (op. cit. [see note 7]), in his careful review of Eisenhower's philosophy of government, points out that he sought to limit the New Deal or federal state, and although Griffith does not allude to intergovernmental relations in the field of social welfare, this would imply wider latitude for the states.

146. Osborn, op. cit., 156 (see note 107). The 1939 amendments to the Social Security Act required that state ADC plans provide safeguards restricting the use or disclosure of information on applicants or recipients to purposes directly connected with plan administration. "AFDC: History of Provisions," op. cit. (see note 87). This meant that local agencies were no longer permitted to publish in the newspaper lists of the families receiving ADC and the amounts of their grants.

147. Axinn and Levin, op. cit., 235 (see note 75).

148. Trattner, op. cit., 282 (see note 9); Axinn and Levin, ibid., 235.

149. Warren Weaver, Jr., "Governor Scores Newburgh's Code," *New York Tiimes*, 14 July 1961, 20; see also, Foster Hailey, "Newburgh Rules Become Effective," *New York Times,* 16 July 1961, 48.

150. "Newburgh," *Wall Street Journal*, 10 July 1961, 105, cited by Irwin Garfinkel and Sarah S. McLanahan, *Single Mothers and Their Children: A New American Dilemma* (Washington,

D.C.: The Urban Institute Press, 1986), 106. For Goldwater's endorsement, see "Goldwater Hails Newburgh Plan as Ideal for All Cities," *New York Times*, 19 July 1961, 27.

151. Axinn and Levin, op. cit., 234-236 (see note 75); Osborn (op. cit., 163. [see note 107]) makes the point that in earlier years (by which she appears to mean the early 1940s) there had been no ADC programs in Connecticut, Illinois, Iowa, Kentucky, Mississippi, South Dakota, Texas, Alaska, Puerto Rico, and the Virgin Islands. If those states are excluded, the increase in the number of children receiving ADC between 1940 and 1953 was 46.5%, compared to a 29% increase in the population under 18 years of age. This is instead of 79.8% when the additions from the new states are counted.

152. Piven and Cloward, op. cit., 191 (see note 29). The authors point out that the pattern in the 1960s was the reverse, with growth in the caseload being a much more important factor than increase in benefits.

153. Osborn, op. cit., 159 (see note 107) reveals that the actual increase in purchasing power of ADC payments from June 1945 to October 1952 was $2.62 per child, while the dollar amount was $12.

154. Axinn and Levin, op. cit., 234 (see note 75).

155. *Temporary Unemployment Compensation and Aid to Dependent Children of Unemployed Parents,* Hearings before the House Ways and Means Committee, 87th Cong., 1st sess. (15 February 1961), 103, cited in James L. Sundquist, *Politics and Policy: The Eisenhower, Kennedy, and Johnson Years* (Washington, D.C.: The Brookings Institution, 1968), 126.

156. In 1940, for example, the National Resources Planning Board reported that owing to absence of federal funds and adequate financial provision, there was in most states a denial of aid to some needy general assistance recipients. National Resources Planning Board, op. cit., 199-202 (see note 90).

157. Burns and Williams, op. cit., 111 (see note 29).

158. Advisory Council on Public Assistance, op. cit., 10 (see note 83).

159. Goodwin, op. cit., 35 (see note 92).

160. In his Message to Congress (*New York Times*, 25 May 1948, 23), President Truman had written that "federal grants to states under the present Act may be used only for three groups," but that "other persons in equal need do not share in these funds." The National Resources Planning Board (op. cit., 526 [see note 90]) recommended a federal grant for general public assistance in view of the financial incapacity of the states for handling this function. Altmeyer (op. cit., 174, 183-184 [see note 86]) reports that the Ways and Means Committee of the House of Representatives rejected the administration's proposal to extend federal matching to include public assistance to all needy individuals, regardless of category, and that the proposal was not restored in subsequent actions by either house of Congress.

161. Altmeyer, ibid., 187. Altmeyer considered the Old Age and Survivors' Insurance amendments impressive.

162. Eileen Boris and Peter Bardaglio view the welfare state as a form of patriarchy in which women have shifted their economic dependence from their husbands or family patriarchs to the state. See their "Transformation of Patriarchy: The Historical Role of the State," in Irene Diamonnd, ed., *Politics and Public Policy* (New York: Longman, Green, 1983).

163. Plotke, op. cit., 348 (see note 43).

164. For both of these points, see Edward Berkowitz and Kim McQuaid, *Creating the Welfare State: The Political Economy of Twentieth Century Reform,* 2nd ed. (New York: Praeger, 1988). The authors point out that Roosevelt thought it was easy to liberalize an existing program but not to create a new one (p. 112). The bureaucrats on the Social Security Board, they point out, began to circulate their own proposals tailored to specific interest groups, e.g., health care for the elderly (p. 149). On Disability Insurance, which passed the Senate by one vote in 1956, and with a threat of a presidential veto, Wilbur Cohen had coached Senator Walter George who led the fight (p. 153). These examples pertain to health care and disability insurance, but there were gains in public assistance as well. Truman's biographer, Alonzo Hamby, devotes

a chapter to "The Trials of Liberalism in a Conservative Age."
See his *Man of the People: A Life of Harry S. Truman* (New
York: Oxford University Press, 1995), 361-386.

CHAPTER 3
WELFARE LAW AND LABOR LAW:
THE FORMATIVE YEARS

1. For work on the relationship between the economic pros-
    pects of males and single parenthood, see, e.g., William Julius
    Wilson with Kathryn Neckerman, *The Truly Disadvantaged*
    (Chicago: The University of Chicago Press, 1987), 63-92;
    William Julius Wilson, *When Work Disappears: The World
    of the New Urban Poor* (New York: Vintage Books, 1996),
    87-110; and Kenneth B. Clark, "Sex, Status, and Underem-
    ployment of the Negro Male," in Arthur M. Ross and Herbert
    Hill, eds., *Employment, Race, and Poverty: A Critical Study
    of the Disadvantaged Status of Negro Workers from 1865 to
    1965* (New York: Harcourt, Brace & World, 1967).

2. Harry L. Hopkins, *Spending to Save: The Complete Story of
    Relief* (New York: W. W. Norton, 1936), 182. According to
    one Hopkins' biographer, he expected the Works Progress
    Administration (WPA) to be a permanent agency. See George
    McJimsey, *Harry Hopkins: Ally of the Poor and Defender
    of Democracy* (Cambridge, Mass.: Harvard University Press,
    1987), 114. Another Hopkins biographer writes: "And it was
    clear to everyone both PWA and WPA would be around for
    a good long time to come." Henry H. Adams, *Harry Hopkins:
    A Biography* (New York: G. P. Putnam & Sons, 1977), 88.

3. Frances Perkins, *The Roosevelt I Knew* (New York: Viking,
    1946), 188-189.

4. See June Hopkins, *Harry Hopkins: Sudden Hero, Brash
    Reformer* (New York: St. Martin's Press, 1999), 184, 189.
    Hopkins persuaded President Roosevelt for a time, but bud-
    get director, Daniel W. Bell, convinced Roosevelt to sepa-
    rate work assurance from the Economic Security Bill. Hopkins
    cites Edwin E. Witte (*The Development of the Social Secu-
    rity Act* [Madison, Wisc.: University of Wisconsin, 1962],
    44) for this point.

5.   Irving Bernstein, *A Caring Society: The New Deal, the Worker, and the Great Depression* (Boston: Houghton Mifflin, 1985), 149. Bernstein holds that a permanent public works-public employment policy would have meant long-term budgeting and consequently a favorable impact on the economy and larger projects, but this was politically dangerous because it would have admitted that the New Deal had failed to revive the private economy. The Republicans would certainly have used this admission against the Roosevelt administration in the 1936 presidential election (p. 77). June Hopkins considers the WPA a "compromise . . . an alternative to a permanent program of government jobs. Ibid., 188.

6.   Arthur J. Altmeyer, *The Formative Years of Social Security* (Madison, Wisc.: University of Wisconsin Press, 1966), 12-13.

7.   Ibid., 93.

8.   Peter Bachrach, "The Right to Work: Emergence of the Idea in the United States," *Social Service Review* 26 (1952), 154.

9.   In 1938, when the number unemployed was 10.4 million, the WPA provided work for 3.3 million, or nearly one-third. See Nancy E. Rose, *Put to Work: Relief Programs in the Great Depression* (New York: Monthly Review Press, 1994), 19, 96.

10.   William E. Leuchtenburg, *Franklin D. Roosevelt and the New Deal, 1932-1940* (New York: Harper, 1963), 130. According to the National Resources Planning Board, the highest proportion of the unemployed served by the WPA was 39.1% in October 1936. The annual ratio declined steadily from 33.5% in 1936 to 26.5% in 1939. U.S. National Resources Planning Board, Committee on Long-Range Work and Relief Policies, *Security, Work, and Relief Policies* (Washington, D.C.: U.S. Government Printing Office, 1942), 236.

11.   Arthur E. Burns and Edward A. Williams, *Federal Work, Security, and Relief Programs*, Research Monograph XXIV, Federal Works Agency and Work Projects Administration (Washington, D.C.: U.S. Government Printing Office, 1941), 74. After 1935, the federal work programs were, in addition to the WPA, the Civilian Conservation Corps (CCC), which employed young men and veterans on conservation projects; the National Youth Administration (NYA), for in-school and

out-of-school young persons aged 18–24; the Farm Security Administration, which made loans to low-income farm families; and the Public Works Administration (PWA), for the dual purpose of providing employment and state and local public construction.

12. Ibid., 126.

13. Rose, op. cit., 76-77 (see note 9). See also Bernstein, op. cit., 74 (see note 5). In 1937, Roosevelt's fear of inflation led him to cut back the WPA drastically, thus contributing to a severe recession within the Depression. See Leuchtenburg, op. cit., 244-250 (see note 10).

14. For example, Governor Eugene Talmadge of Georgia sent a letter to President Roosevelt from a farmer who wrote: "I wouldn't plow nobody's mule from sunrise to sunset for 50 cents per day when I could get $1.30 for pretending to work on a DITCH." See Arthur M. Schlesinger, Jr., *The Coming of the New Deal* (Boston: Houghton Mifflin, 1958), 274.

15. Philip Harvery points out that the CWA was the most ambitious of the New Deal public employment programs, employing the largest workforce, paying the highest wages, and the only one not to require a means test to establish eligibility. See his *Securing the Right to Employment: Social Welfare Policy and the Unemployed in the United States* (Princeton, N.J.: Princeton University Press, 1989), 99.

16. Bachrach, op. cit., 154 (see note 8). Conservative congressmen expressed fear that if CWA were to continue, the 4 million persons employed by CWA would demand that government jobs be made permanent, and the rest of the unemployed would pressure the government for an expansion of the program. Bachrach (p. 154) cites Robert Sherwood (*Roosevelt and Hopkins* [New York: Harper & Brothers, 1948], 56), who states that Roosevelt found this argument persuasive. Leuchtenburg (op. cit., 122 [see note 10]) reports that FDR was alarmed at how much CWA was costing.

17. "Proceedings of the National Emergency Council, 19 December 1933–18 April 1936," microfilm, Franklin Delano Roosevelt Library, Hyde Park, N.Y., session of 23 January 1934, cited by Leuchtenburg, op. cit., 122 (see note 10).

18. For a discussion of opposition to the CWA, see Harvey, op. cit., 99-106 (see note 15); and Bonnie Fox Schwartz, *The Civil Works Administration, 1933-1934* (Princeton, N.J.: Princeton University Press, 1984), 214-220.

19. Edwin Amenta, *Bold Relief: Institutional Politics and the Origins of Modern American Social Policy* (Princeton, N.J.: Princeton University Press, 1998), 199; Edward Berkowitz and Kim McQuaid, *Creating the Welfare State: The Political Economy of Twentieth Century Reform* (New York: Praeger, 1980), 121.

20. Rose, op. cit., 114 (see note 9).

21. Theda Skocpol, "'Brother, Can You Spare a Job?' Work and Welfare in the U.S.," in Theda Skocpol, *Social Policy in the United States: Future Possibilities in Historical Perspective* (Princeton, N.J.: Princeton University Press, 1995), 240-244.

22. Nancy E. Rose, *Workfare or Fair Work: Women, Welfare, and Government Work Programs* (New Brunswick, N.J.: Rutgers University Press, 1995), 31.

23. Bernstein, op. cit., 291 (see note 5).

24. Ibid., 290. Bernstein also considers that "the fundamental problem during the thirties was that equal rights for women was simply not a significant political issue" (p. 292).

25. Alice Kessler-Harris, *Out to Work: A History of Wage-Earning Women in the United States* (New York: Oxford University Press, 1982), 263.

26. Burns and Williams, op. cit., 62 (see note 11). In 1938, the lowest pay for unskilled workers was raised to $26 a month.

27. According to one report, unskilled black workers made only $.65 a day. Dona Cooper Hamilton and Charles V. Hamilton, *The Dual Agenda: The African–American Struggle for Civil and Economic Equality* (New York: Columbia University Press, 1997), 24. Leuchtenburg (op. cit., 187 [see note 10]) points out that unlike the Civilian Conservation Corps (CCC), WPA had no quotas for blacks.

28. Bernstein, op. cit., 294 (see note 5).

29.   Ibid., 291. At the insistence of Eleanor Roosevelt, 86 CCC camps for women were established, but they only served 6,400 enrollees. The female enrollment in PWA was 7%.

30.   Rose, op. cit., 101 (see note 9). During the Great Depression, popular opinion held that jobs were reserved for providers; they were not regarded as rights for everyone who wanted to work. This typically meant that married men had top priority, although providers could also include widows, single women, and married women with unemployed or disabled husbands. On this point, see Alice Kessler-Harris, *A Woman's Wage* (Lexington, Ky.: University Press of Kentucky, 1990), 71.

31.   Bernstein, op. cit., 295 (see note 5).

32.   Hamilton and Hamilton emphasize the "legacy of the two-tier system" for African–Americans: "Plagued by racial discrimination and other economic disadvantages, African–Americans have continually had to push for job-creation programs that would permit them to earn and contribute to social insurance protections." See Hamilton and Hamilton, op, cit., 261 and passim (see note 27).

33.   *Employment and Earnings* 19 (February 1973), table A-1, 27.

34.   Kessler-Harris (op. cit., 276-278 [see note 25]) argues that 3 million women, in addition to the approximately 11 million, were in the labor force in 1940 but unemployed, and that approximately 1 million more were discouraged workers who were not counted as in the labor force but would have worked if jobs were available. The increase in labor-force participation then was from 15 million to 19.5 million, an increase of 43% rather than 80.5%. Also, she holds, the population increase needs to be factored in, thus bringing down still further the number who might not otherwise have entered the labor force without the war. Despite the publicity given to women workers with young children, older, married women contributed most of the increase.

35.   Stephanie Coontz, *The Way We Never Were* (New York: Basic Books, 1992), 159.

36. James MacGregor Burns, *The Crosswinds of Freedom: From Roosevelt to Reagan* (New York: Vintage Books, 1989), 188.

37. Elizabeth Allison and Agnes Leisy, *Social Security Bulletin* 13 (August 1950), 4.

38. June Axinn and Herman Levin, *Social Welfare: A History of the American Response to Need*, 4th ed. (New York: Longman, 1997), 228-229; August Meier and Elliott Rudwick, *From Plantation to Ghetto*, 3rd ed. (New York: Hill and Wang, 1976), 268.

39. Arthur M. Ross, "The Negro's Position in the Labor Market," in Ross and Hill, op. cit., 17 (see note 1).

40. Kessler-Harris, op. cit., 279 (see note 25).

41. Burns, op. cit., 184 (see note 36).

42. Axinn and Levin, op. cit., 227 (see note 38).

43. Ibid., 228.

44. Gordon W. Blackwell and Raymond F. Gould, *Future Citizens All* (Chicago: American Public Welfare Association, 1952), 7, 10-11.

45. Allison and Leisy, op. cit., 4 (see note 37); Blackwell and Gould, ibid., 10.

46. Donald E. Spritzer, *Senator James E. Murray and the Limits of Post-New Deal Liberalism* (New York: Garland Publishing, 1985), Chapter V. The bill was referred to as the Murray Full-Employment Bill and as the Murray-Wagner Full-Employment Bill.

47. U.S. Congress, Senate, Subcommittee of the Committee on Banking and Currency, *Full Employment Act of 1945, Hearings . . . on S. 380*, 30 July–1 September 1945, 9-22, cited in ibid., 111.

48. A 1944 poll reported in *Fortune* found two-thirds of the respondents answering in the affirmative to this question: "Do you think the federal government should provide jobs for everyone able and willing to work, but who cannot get a job in private employment?" Stephen Kemp Bailey, *Congress Makes*

a Law: The Story behind the Employment Act of 1945 (New York: Columbia University Press, 1950), 8.

49.   The National Resources Planning Board believed "that it should be the declared policy of the U.S. Government . . . to under- write full employment for the employables. . . ." U.S. National Resources Planning Board, *National Resources Development: Report for 1943, Part. 1. Post-War Plan and Program* (Wash- ington, D.C.: U.S. Government Printing Office, January 1943), 3. See also, National Resources Planning Board (op. cit., 1 [see note 10]) in which it is stated that the order of social provision should be: (1) "work for all who are able and willing to work"; (2) social insurance for those whose work is inter- rupted; (3) public assistance for those individuals and families not covered by social insurance; and (4) public provision of services essential to the health, education, and welfare of the population where these are not available. The National Resources Planning Board (NRPB) was a nonadminstrative agency located in the Executive Office of the President that was instructed by Roosevelt to formulate national social and economic policies for the postwar period. The Committee on Long-Range Work and Relief Policies was given the task of surveying work and income-maintenance programs and of designing ways to restructure them. The proposals of the com- mittee formed the basis for important progressive congressional bills and presidential pronouncements in the 1940s.

50.   Leuchtenburg, op. cit., 347 (see note 10).

51.   Franklin Delano Roosevelt, *The Public Papers and Addresses of Franklin Delano Roosevelt, 1944-45,* 13 vols., Samuel I. Rosenman, comp. (New York: Russell & Russell, 1950), 13, 41. The Economic Bill of Rights was proposed in *National Resources Development: Report for 1943*, op. cit., 3 (see note 49).

52.   Bailey, op. cit., 237 (see note 48).

53.   Ibid., 42. In a speech in San Francisco, Dewey stated, "if at any time there are not sufficient jobs in private enterprise to go around, the government can and must create job op- portunities for all in this country of ours." Bailey cites the *New York Times*, 22 September 1944, 10. Bachrach, how- ever, citing another speech of Dewey, holds that he was only

willing for government to create jobs in an atmosphere in which business felt free to grow and flourish. *New York Times*, 31 October 1944, cited by Bachrach, op. cit., 160 (see note 8). Roosevelt, on the other hand, thought business would have to adjust to job-creation programs if these were not pleasing. *New York Times*, 29 October 1944, 34, cited in ibid.

54. Bailey, op. cit., 161 (see note 48).

55. Spritzer (op. cit., 111 [see note 46]) holds that Truman was influenced by dire predictions such as the warning of the Office of War Mobilization and Reconversion that unemployment could reach 8 million the following spring. Truman asked Senator Robert Wagner of New York to interrupt his vacation in order to reconvene hearings on the full-employment bill of which he was a major sponsor. See also Heinz Eulau, Mordecai Ezekiel, Alvin H. Hansen, James Loeb, Jr., and George Soule, "The Road to Freedom: Full Employment," *The New Republic,* 24 September 1945: Special Section, Part Two, 412.

56. Eulau et al., ibid.

57. For this point, see, G. William Domhoff, *The Power Elite and the State: How Policy Is Made in America* (New York: Aldine de Gruyter, 1990), 198-199.

58. Ibid.

59. Report on meeting of national organizations on Full Employment bill, Thursday, 25 July 1945 (NAACP Papers, Group II, A-111), cited by Hamilton and Hamilton, op. cit., 68 (see note 27). In the Special Section of the *New Republic* on full employment, the NAACP placed an ad entitled, "Full Employment Can Prevent Riots." Included were excerpts from Senate testimony of the NAACP Secretary Walter White: "We want white Americans to have jobs because if they do they will not be tempted to gang up on Negroes who have employment. We want Negroes to have their full and fair share of the jobs that are available so that they can live like decent human beings, free from resentment because their color alone deprives them of employment." *The New Republic*, 24 September 1945, 411.

60.   Alonzo Hamby, *Man of the People: A Life of Harry S. Truman*
       (New York: Oxford University Press, 1995), 366.

61.   U.S. Congress, Senate, 79th Cong., 1st sess., *Full Employ-
       ment Act of 1945,* S. 380.

62.   According to Bailey, "the Bill's terminal reliance upon a pro-
       gram of federal investment and expenditure" bears the mark
       of Keynsian theory, and the same is true of the idea that the
       federal budget should be used to contribute to a larger con-
       text of the national economy. Bailey, op. cit., 15, 25 (see
       note 48).

63.   See Spritzer, op. cit., 112-113 (see note 46).

64.   Bailey, op. cit., 122 (see note 48).

65.   Ibid., 128.

66.   Ibid., 130-148.

67.   Eulau et al., op. cit., 395 (see note 55).

68.   U.S. Congress, Public Law 304, *Employment Act of 1946,*
       79th Cong., 2d sess., sec. 2. For a discussion of the full,
       employment issue, see Helen Ginsburg, *Full Employment and
       Public Policy: The United States and Sweden* (Lexington,
       Mass.: Lexington Books, 1983), 3-19.

69.   Bailey (op. cit., 127 [see note 48]) attributes this statement
       to Senator Glen Taylor of Idaho.

70.   The House Conference Report on S. 380, 79th Cong., 2d sess.,
       sec. 2, cited by Ginsburg, op. cit., 16-17 (see note 68). The
       conference report also rejected the term "full employment"
       and substituted "maximum employment" as the objective.

71.   Spritzer, relying on extensive evidence, reports that when
       the bill seemed in serious trouble, Truman conferred with
       leading Democrats on the conservative House Committee
       on Expenditures in the Executive Departments, who agreed
       to report a watered-down bill if the president did not insist
       on the Senate version, but that "beyond this, the President
       left the matter entirely up to Congress." Later Spritzer
       concludes that "it was the most that could be gained from
       a conservative Congress and a President who never was

committed to Keynsian goals"(Spritzer, op. cit., 114-115
[see note 46]). On the other hand, Alonzo Hamby, author
of a number of scholarly works on Truman, his presidency,
and the Fair Deal, observes that Truman saw his support of
the bill as an asset in his relationship with the liberal-labor
forces, "took the bill seriously, spoke out vigorously for it
and personally lobbied key legislators." To get it through
Congress, he appointed a cabinet committee chaired by
Treasury Secretary Fred Vinson. Hamby, op. cit., 366 (see
note 60). Observing relationships between Truman and
Congress, Neustadt points out that "President Truman never
did command a 'safe' working majority of the rank and file
in either House of Congress" and that "his 'honeymoon'
did not outlast the war." Moreover, particularly later in his
administration,Truman made bipartisan support for his foreign
policy a priority and often lost on domestic initiatives the
very Republicans who were the mainstays of the bipartisan
foreign policy. See Richard E. Neustadt, "Congress and the
Fair Deal," *Public Policy* 5 (1954), 351-381.

72. Bailey, op. cit., 80 (see note 48).

73. Ibid., 82.

74. Ibid., 179-181.

75. According to social-welfare historians June Axinn and Herman
Levin (op. cit., 231 [see note 38]), this was the "major social
legislation of the war and immediate postwar years."

76. "Against the women who wanted to work, traditionalists directed
a stream of vituperation in the immediate postwar years. Family
life depended on their staying at home, so it was morally
wrong for such women to seek jobs." See Kessler-Harris, op.
cit., 296 (see note 25). See also Rosalyn Baxandall, Linda
Gordon, and Susan Reverby, eds., *America's Working Women:
A Documentary History—1600 to the Present* (New York:
Random House, 1976), 280-298. The editors write, "educators,
social workers, psychologists, and journalists tried to convince
women that their place was in the home rearing children and
not in the paid labor force. On the one hand, the system could
not provide full employment; on the other hand, continued
industrial profits required, with the diminution of military

spending, an expansion in the consumption of household durable goods. An emphasis on 'homemaking' encouraged women to buy" (pp. 282-283).

77.   Ginsburg, op. cit., 15 (see note 68).

78.   Bailey (op. cit., 180 [see note 48]) reports that during the period of House consideration, a Michigan representative cited letters and newspaper articles on the subject of the shortage of labor, and two of the southern Democrats opposing the more liberal version of the legislation had almost no opposition to their actions from their districts.

79.   Spritzer, op. cit., 113 (see note 46).

80.   Neustadt, op. cit., 359 (see note 71).

81.   *Employment and Earnings,* op. cit., 27 (see note 33).

82.   U.S. Congress, Congressional Budget Office, *Defense Spending and the Economy* (Washington, D.C.: U.S. Government Printing Office, February 1983), table 1, 3.

83.   For the long-term effects of military spending on the nation's economy, see, e.g., Robert de Grasse, *Military Expansion, Economic Decline: The Impact of Military Spending on U.S. Economic Performance* (Armonk, N.Y.: M. E. Sharpe, 1983); and Seymour Melman, *The Permanent War Economy* (New York: Simon & Schuster, 1974).

84.   Ross, "The Negro in the American Economy," in Ross and Hill, op. cit., 18 (see note 1). On the labor-market position of Negroes, see also Charles C. Killingsworth, "Negroes in a Changing Labor Market," in Ross and Hill.

85.   U.S. Department of Labor, *Manpower Report of the President*, March 1965 (Washington, D.C.: U.S. Government Printing Office, 1965), table A-11, 204.

86.   *Report of the National Advisory Commission on Civil Disorders* (Washington, D.C.: National Advisory Commission on Civil Disorders, 1 March 1968), 117.

87.   Quoted by Clark, op. cit., 139 (see note 1). Secretary Hodges was addressing the Equal Opportunity Day Dinner of the National Urban League, 19 November 1963.

88. On these conditions, see Helen Ginsburg, *Unemployment, Subemployment, and Public Policy* (New York: New York University School of Social Work, Center for Studies in Income Maintenance Policy, 1975), 66-67.

89. Ginsburg, op. cit., table 2-5, 40 (see note 68).

90. Whereas the drop was 19.8% and 16.8% for nonwhite males and females, respectively, it was 13.3% and 2.8% for whites. *Manpower Report of the President*, 1965, table A-4, 196 (see note 85). Ross (op. cit., 22 [see note 39]) recognizes that the movement out of the labor force is partly explained by the growing popularity of higher education but points out that this does not explain why Negro youth had left the labor market to a much greater extent than their white counterparts.

91. Clark, op. cit., 147 (see note 1).

92. Ibid.

93. Barbara Bergmann's figures show a gain of about 17%, comparable to that of each of the succeeding decades. Barbara R. Bergmann, *The Economic Emergence of Women* (New York: Basic Books, 1986), 21.

94. Eveline M. Burns, *Social Security and Public Policy* (New York: McGraw Hill Book Co., Inc., 1956), 89. Edwin Amenta (op. cit., 229 [see note 19]) sees the purpose of ADC becoming less clear as the labor-force participation of women increased in the postwar period.

95. U.S. Department of Labor, Bureau of Labor Statistics, *Labor Force Statistics Derived from the Current Population Survey, 1948-87*, Bulletin 2307 (Washington, D.C.: U.S. Government Printing Office, 1988), table C-14, 805.

96. *Manpower Report of the President*, 1965, op. cit., table A-13, 206 (see note 85).

97. Calculated from Ross, op. cit., table 7, 32 (see note 84).

98. Blackwell and Gould, op. cit., 10 (see note 44); M. Elaine Burgess and Daniel O. Price, *An American Dependency Challenge* (Chicago: American Public Welfare Association, 1963), 191. The figures are from the U.S. Bureau of Public Assistance. Also accounting for some of the growth in caseloads

and expenditures were extensions of Aid to Dependent Children to additional jurisdictions, federal financial participation in allowances for adults caring for an ADC child, eligibility of new categories of adult caretakers (nieces and nephews), and a rise in the maximum monthly amount of assistance for which federal funds were available. See Burgess and Price, 191-194.

99. Allison and Leisy, op. cit., 12 (see note 37).

100. James L. Sundquist, *Politics and Policy: The Eisenhower, Kennedy, and Johnson Years* (Washington, D.C.: The Brookings Institution, 1968), 126. Sundquist points to a statement from the *Report of the Advisory Council on Public Assistance*, S. Doc. 93, 86th Cong., 2nd sess. (28 March 1960), 12: "There are instances of fathers who are unemployed and desert because they see no other way to get their hungry children fed."

101. James T. Patterson, *America's Struggle against Poverty 1900- 1980* (Cambridge, Mass.: Harvard University Press, 1981), 86.

102. Sundquist (op. cit., 442 [see note 100]) gives as evidence election surveys of the Survey Research Center, No. 431, September–November 1958, and No. 440, September–November 1960.

103. For a discussion of "the area development deadlock" or the 6 years of debate over the measure, see ibid., 60-73.

CHAPTER 4
EXPANDING ECONOMY AND EXPLODING RELIEF ROLLS

1.   Gilbert Y. Steiner, *The State of Welfare* (Washington, D.C.: The Brookings Institution, 1971), 32. Steiner commented on a *New York Times* editorial, 3 January 1969, which stated that "the welfare rolls have a life of their own outside the metropolitan job market." In discussing the "manpower program for welfare recipients," known as the Work Incentive Program, the 1974 *Manpower Report of the President* explained that "behind it was [*sic*] attempts by both the executive and legislative branches to deal with the anomaly of 'a rapidly accelerating rise in the numbers of children and adults receiving assistance under the federally funded program of Aid to Families with Dependent Children (AFDC), coincident with

generally high and rising employment'. . . ." U.S. Department of Labor, *Manpower Report of the President* (Washington, D.C.: U.S. Government Printing Office, 1974), 131. The quotation is from *Manpower Report of the President* (Washington, D.C.: U.S. Government Printing Office, 1970), 148.

2.   The total number of ADC recipients was less in 1945 than in 1940, even though the program expanded to new jurisdictions during those years. *Social Security Bulletin: Annual Statistical Supplement 1996*, table 9.G1, 357 (hereafter, *Annual Statistical Supplement, 1996*). The ADC caseload fell from 2.233 million in 1950 (5.3% unemployment), to 1.941 million in 1953 (2.9% unemployment). *Social Security Bulletin: Annual Statistical Supplement 1974*, table 153, 173.

According to the National Advisory Commission on Civil Disorders (*Report of the National Advisory Commission on Civil Disorders* [Washington, D.C., 1 March 1968], 128), the number of ADC recipients had risen and fallen with the unemployment rates of black males from the postwar years until the early 1960s. Henry Aaron is one expert who considers that neither the growth of single-mother families nor the AFDC caseload can be correlated with non-white males or total unemployment. See his review of Moynihan's *The Politics of a Guaranteed Income, Yale Law Journal* 82 (1973), 1725.

3.   President Kennedy's first executive order, issued the day after his inauguration, directed the secretary of agriculture, Orville L. Freeman, to double the rations of surplus foods provided by the federal government to 4 million needy persons across the nation. Kennedy called for a larger variety of foodstuffs and about double the volume of the present rations, which then provided for only 35% of a "subsistence diet." *New York Times*, 22 January 1961, 1.

4.   Charles E. Gilbert, "Policy-Making in Public Welfare: The 1962 Amendments," *Political Science Quarterly* 81 (June 1966), 203.

5.   See also James G. Patterson, *America's Struggle against Poverty 1900–1980* (Cambridge, Mass.: Harvard University Press, 1981), 131.

6.   Report of the Ad Hoc Committee on Public Welfare to the
     Secretary of Health, Education, and Welfare, September 1961,
     in Hearings on H.R. 10032, Public Welfare Amendments of
     1962, 87th Cong., 2nd sess., February 7, 9, and 13, 1962,
     78, cited by June Axinn and Herman Levin, *Social Welfare:
     A History of the American Response to Need,* 4th ed. (New
     York: Longman, 1997), 238.

7.   "Text of President's Message to Congress Seeking Reforms
     in Welfare," *New York Times,* 2 February 1962, 10.

8.   U.S. Department of Labor, *Manpower Report of the Presi-
     dent,* March 1965 (Washington, D.C.: U.S. Government Printing
     Office, 1965), table A1, 193; table A11, 204.

9.   *Annual Statistical Supplement, 1996,* table 9.G1, 367 (see
     note 2).

10. Bertram M. Beck, "Casework as a Method: A Reassessment,"
     Social Work Forum (New York, 1964), cited by Gilbert, op.
     cit., 199 (see note 4). Bertram Beck was then associate ex-
     ecutive director of the National Association of Social Workers.

11. Kennedy, op. cit. (see note 7).

12. HEW Secretary Ribicoff took other steps in this direction
     by allowing states, if they chose, not to deduct earnings of
     ADC recipients that were used for the education of their children
     and similarly to allow youngsters on welfare to keep money
     that they needed for educational and training purposes. *New
     York Times,* 30 January 1962, 1, 13.

13. *Annual Statistical Supplement, 1996,* table 9.G1 (see note 2).

14. See, e.g., Steiner, op. cit., 37–40 (see note 1).

15. Edward J. Mullen, Robert M. Chazin, and David M. Feldstein,
     *Preventing Chronic Dependency: An Evaluation of Public-
     Private Collaborative Intervention with First-Time Public
     Assistance Families* (New York: Community Service Soci-
     ety of New York, 1970). The disappointing outcome of this
     research was one reason, along with mounting evidence that
     social casework had little effect on poverty, why the social-
     service organization that conducted the experiment decided
     soon after to discontinue 123 years of family casework and
     individual counseling and to concentrate instead on work-

ing directly with local community groups to reduce their social disadvantages. See Gertrude S. Goldberg, "New Directions for the Community Service Society of New York: A Study of Organizational Change," *Social Service Review* 54 (June 1980), 184–219.

16.   Winifred Bell, "AFDC: Symptom and Potential," in Alvin L. Schorr, ed., *Jubilee for Our Time* (New York: Columbia University Press, 1974), 235.

17.   Ibid.

18.   U.S. House of Representatives, Committee on Ways and Means, *1996 Green Book: Background Material and Data on Programs within the Jurisdiction of the Committee on Ways and Means* (Washington, D.C.: U.S. Government Printing Office, 1996), table 8–25, 467 (hereafter *Green Book*). In the mid-1990s, the figure was still only 6.9%.

19.   Sar A. Levitan and Robert Taggart, *The Promise of Greatness: Social Programs of the Last Decade and Their Major Achievements* (Cambridge, Mass.: Harvard University Press, 1976), 50.

20.   The Work Experience and Training (WET) program, serving the same purpose as CWT but with 100% federal funding, was established under Title V of the Economic Opportunity Act. Not surprisingly, WET drove out its predecessor. However, in 3 years, 133,000 welfare recipients had enrolled in WET, of whom 22,000 had found jobs and 70,000 were in training. See Steiner, op. cit., 44 (see note 1). Levitan and Taggart (ibid., 50-51) write that three out of every four participants in WET departed without completing their assignments, only one-fifth of them to take a job, and among completers, less than one-half obtained employment immediately.

21.   Patterson, op. cit., 165 (see note 5). Reference is to a 1974 RAND study.

22.   Steiner, op. cit., 213 (see note 1).

23.   Levitan and Taggart, op. cit., 67 (see note 19). The program was state-operated and directed when it was revived, and as a result, many states adopted restrictive eligiblity and benefit standards; others refused to implement it. Ibid., 66–67.

24. Ibid.

25. Sar A. Levitan, *Programs in Aid of the Poor*, 5th ed. (Baltimore: The Johns Hopkins University Press, 1985), 80.

26. Patterson, op. cit., 163 (see note 5).

27. Steiner, op. cit., 236 (see note 1).

28. President's Commission for a National Agenda for the Eighties, *Government and the Advancement of Social Justice: Health, Welfare, and Civil Rights in the Eighties* (Washington, D.C., Author, 1980), 60, cited by Patterson, op. cit., 168 (see note 5).

29. Levitan and Taggart, op. cit., 15 (see note 19).

30. Ibid., 169.

31. Rosemary Stevens, *Welfare Medicine in America: The Case of Medicaid* (New York: The Free Press, 1974), p. 131, cited by Bruce S. Jansson, *The Reluctant Welfare State*: *American Social Welfare Policies, Past, Present, and Future*, 3rd ed. (Pacific Grove, Calif.: Brooks/Cole Publishing Company, 1997), 217.

32. Steiner, op. cit., 148 (see note 1).

33. Ibid.

34. Levitan and Taggart, op. cit., 101 (see note 19).

35. U.S. Department of Labor, Bureau of Labor Statistics, *Labor Force Statistics Derived from the Current Population Survey, 1948–87*, Bulletin 2307 (Washington, D.C.: U.S. Government Printing Office, 1988), table A31, 489.

36. Ibid., table A24, 405.

37. Helen Ginsburg, *Full Employment and Public Policy: The United States and Sweden* (Lexington, Mass.: Lexington Books, 1983), table 2-4, 37.

38. Ibid., table 2-5, 40.

39. John C. Donovan, *The Politics of Poverty* (New York: Pegasus, 1967), 22.

40. Helen Ginsburg, *Unemployment, Subemployment, and Public Policy* (New York: Center for Studies in Income Maintenance Policy, New York University School of Social Work, 1975), 94. Ginsburg's discussion draws on the following sources: William Spring, "Underemployment: The Measure We Refuse to Take," *New Generation* 53 (Winter 1971), 1-25 (publication of the National Committee for the Employment of Youth, New York City) for background on the development of the original subemployment index inspired by Labor Secretary Willard Wirtz; U.S. Department of Labor, *A Sharper Look at Unemployment in U.S. Cities and Slums* (Washington, D.C.: U.S. Government Printing Office, 1967) for details of the 1966 survey; and U.S. Senate, Committee on Labor and Public Welfare, Subcommittee on Employment, Manpower and Poverty, *Comprehensive Manpower Reform, Hearings*, Pt. 5, 92nd Congress, 2nd sess. (Washington, D.C.: U.S., Government Printing Office, 1972), 2276, 2280, for discussion of a similar survey conducted as part of the 1970 Census.

41. Mollie Orshansky, "Counting the Poor: Another Look at the Poverty Profile," *Social Security Bulletin* 28 (January 1965), 7.

42. William Spring, Bennett Harrison, and Thomas Vietorisz, "Crisis of the Underemployed: In Much of the Inner City 60% Don't Earn Enough for a Decent Standard of Living," *New York Times Magazine*, 5 November 1972, 44, 46ff.

43. Ginsburg, op. cit., 95 (see note 40).

44. Patterson, op. cit., 178 (see note 5), on the California and New York share in the rise of relief.

45. Spring, Harrison, and Vietorisz, op. cit., 51 (see note 42).

46. William Julius Wilson, *The Truly Disadvantaged: The Inner City, the Underclass, and Public Policy* (Chicago: University of Chicago Press, 1987), 83-100.

47. Judith Blake and Jorge H. del Pinal, "The Childlessness Option: Recent American Views of Nonparenthood," in Gerry Hendershot and Paul Placek, eds., *Predicting Fertility: Demographic Studies of Birth Expectation* (Lexington, Mass.: Lexington Books, 1981). Blake and del Pinal found that reproduction is likely to be most valued when alternative means

of achieving a more secure and recognized social role are
most limited.

48.   Sheldon Danziger, George Jakubson, Saul Schwartz, and Eugene
       Smolensky, "Work and Welfare as Determinants of Female
       Poverty and Household Headship," *Quarterly Journal of Eco-
       nomics* 97 (August 1982), 519–534.

49.   The Twentieth Century Fund Task Force on Employment Prob-
       lems of Black Youth, *The Job Crisis for Black Youth* (New
       York: Praeger Publishers, 1971), 91.

50.   Ibid.

51.   Ibid., 90-91.

52.   Ibid., 92.

53.   Ibid., 90.

54.   Calculated from Bureau of Labor Statistics, op. cit., table
       A24, 404, 428 (see note 35).

55.   U.S. Department of Health, Education, and Welfare, Wel-
       fare Administration, Bureau of Family Services, Division
       of Program Statistics and Analysis, *Characteristics of Families
       Receiving Aid to Families with Dependent Children*, November-
       December 1961, Washington, D.C., April 1963, table 3; U.S.
       Department of Health, Education and Welfare, Social and
       Rehabilitation Service, National Center for Social Statistics,
       *Findings of the 1967 AFDC Study: Data by State and Cen-
       sus Division*, Washington, D.C., July 1970, table 2.

56.   *The Affluent Society* (Boston: Houghton Mifflin, 1958) is
       the title of a widely quoted book by economist John Ken-
       neth Galbraith. In it, Galbraith, regarded as a liberal, em-
       phasized the disparity between the abundance of privately
       produced goods and public poverty, that is, the "shortages
       and shortcomings" of municipal services, air and water pol-
       lution, and the like (p. 250). Poverty was of two types, "case
       poverty," which was related to some characteristic of those
       afflicted by it, and "insular poverty," largely the result of
       whole groups of people remaining in places with poor eco-
       nomic prospects (pp. 325-326). Clearly, poverty was un-
       derestimated by Galbraith.

57. Robert K. Merton, "The Sociology of Social Problems," in Robert K. Merton and Robert A. Nisbet, eds., *Contemporary Social Problems*, 4th ed. (New York: Harcourt Brace, 1976).

58. Patterson, op. cit., 179 (see note 5). Patterson does not provide evidence regarding the rise in participation rates. It should be noted that AFDC eligibility rules, such as the very stringent criteria for two-parent families, and low benefit levels continued to exclude large numbers of poor children. Thus, in 1970, AFDC child recipients were 58.5% of children in poverty. The proportion rose to 80.5% in 1973 but dropped to 63.2% in 1980. In 1979, the first year for which figures are available, AFDC recipients were only 54.4% of the prewelfare poor population of families with children. (We can assume that the figure in 1970 was lower because the figure for percentage of poor children was 68.0%, compared to 58.5% in 1970. In fact, the two measures tend to rise and fall in tandem. *Green Book*, op. cit., table 8-27, 471 [see note 18].)

59. Frances Fox Piven and Richard A. Cloward, *Regulating the Poor: The Functions of Public Welfare*, updated ed. (New York: Vintage Books, 1993), 331-332, 334.

60. Daniel P. Moynihan, *The Politics of a Guaranteed Income: The Nixon Administration and the Family Assistance Plan* (New York: Random House, 1973), 81.

61. U.S. Department of Labor, Office of Policy Planning and Research, *The Negro Family: The Case for National Action* (Washington, D.C.: U.S. Department of Labor, March 1965), 5 (hereafter Moynihan Report).

62. Patterson, op. cit., 179 (see note 5).

63. Calculated from Joseph Dalaker and Mary Naifeh, *Poverty in the United States: 1997*, Current Population Reports, P60–201 (Washington, D.C.: U.S. Government Printing Office, 1998), table C-3, C-10.

64. Calculated from *Annual Statistical Supplement*, 1996, op. cit., table 9.G1 (see note 2).

65. Ibid.

66. Patterson (op. cit., 255 [see note 5]) cites a number of "sources focusing on the role of eligibility for AFDC."

67. *Green Book*, op. cit., table 8-1, 386 (see note 18). The average family size of AFDC recipients in 1970 was 4.0. The average benefit was $178 ($2,136 annual), and the 4-person poverty standard was $3,968.

68. The phrase is Patterson's. See James T. Patterson, *Great Expectations: The United States, 1945–1974* (New York: Oxford University Press, 1996), 673.

69. *March on Washington for Jobs and Freedom*, August 28, 1963, Organizing Manual No. 1, National Office, March on Washington for Jobs and Freedom, 170 West 30th Street, New York, N.Y. (n.d.), cited in Dona Cooper Hamilton and Charles V. Hamilton, *The Dual Agenda: Race and Social Welfare Policies of Civil Rights Organizations* (New York: Columbia University Press, 1997), 126.

70. Hamilton and Hamilton, ibid., 121-145.

71. "March on Washington for Jobs and Freedom," Lincoln Memorial Program, Washington, D.C., 28 August 1963. Two other demands included a "national minimum wage act that will give all Americans a decent standard of living" and "a broadened Fair Labor Standards Act to include all areas of employment which are presently excluded."

72. Martin Luther King, Jr., *Where Do We Go from Here: Chaos or Community?* (New York: Harper & Row, 1967), 163.

73. Katz refers to Shriver's linking the two at a symposium on integration in April 1964. See Michael B. Katz, *The Undeserving Poor: From the War on Welfare to the War on the Poor* (New York: Basic Books, 1989), 86. Katz also cites David Zarefsky (*President Johnson's War on Poverty* [Tuscaloosa, Ala.: University of Alabama Press, 1986], 44), who points out that the Economic Opportunity Act sometimes was regarded as but the logical counterpart of the Civil Rights Act that had just been passed in June.

74. The title of Guida West's history of the movement is *The National Welfare Rights Movement: The Social Protest of Poor Women* (New York: Praeger, 1981).

75. Lyndon B. Johnson, *Public Papers of the Presidents: Lyndon B. Johnson, 1963–64* (Washington, D.C.: U.S. Government Printing Office, 1965), 1:411, 480, 483; 2:989, 1360.

76. For example, Roosevelt, in writing of Harry Hopkin's task as federal emergency relief administrator, referred to "two important points of policy," one of which was that "work, rather than idleness on a dole, was preferred." Cited in Robert Sherwood, *Roosevelt and Hopkins: An Intimate History* (New York: Harper & Brothers, 1948), 44. In Chapter 1, we cited Roosevelt's statements in proposing the Social Security Act, namely, that relief "induces moral disintegration"; that "work must be found for the able-bodied but destitute workers"; that relief should be in the form of work because it "preserve[d] not only the bodies of the unemployed . . . but also their self-respect, their self-reliance and courage and determination"; and his declaration therefore that the federal government "must and shall quit this business of relief."

77. Adam Yarmolinsky, "The Beginnings of OEO," in James L. Sundquist, ed., *On Fighting Poverty* (New York: Basic Books, Inc., 1969), 36. Adam Yarmolinsky was deputy director of the President's Task Force on the War against Poverty in 1964.

78. Sanford Kravitz, "The Community Action Program—Past, Present, and Its Future?" in Sundquist, ibid., 65. Kravitz was associate director, Community Action Program, Research Demonstration, Training and Technical Assistance Projects Office of Economic Opportunity.

79. W. Willard Wirtz, memorandum to Honorable Theodore Sorenson, 23 January 1964, Sorensen Papers, Kennedy Library, cited by Katz, op. cit., 93 (see note 73). For further evidence of Wirtz' position, see Steiner, op. cit., 9 (see note 1); and Sundquist, ibid., 24.

80. "Poverty and Urban Policy: Conference Transcript of 1973 Group Discussion of the Kennedy Administration Urban Poverty Programs and Policies," Boston, Mass., John F. Kennedy Library, 286-288.

81. Ibid., 286-287.

82. Margaret Weir, "Innovation and Boundaries in American
     Employment Policy," *Political Science Quarterly* 107
     (1992), 255-258.

83. "Poverty and Urban Policy," op. cit., 287 (see note 80).
     For Senator Gaylord Nelson's proposals, see Margaret Weir,
     *Politics and Jobs: The Boundaries of Employment Policies
     in the United States* (Princeton, N.J.: Princeton University
     Press, 1992), 70.

84. "Poverty and Urban Policy," op. cit., 287-288 (see note 80);
     James L. Sundquist, Origins of the War on Poverty," in
     Sundquist, op. cit., 26-27 (see note 77). Patterson (op. cit.,
     141 [see note 5]) points out that Johnson did not want a pro-
     gram that would cost too much or force a rise in taxes.

85. During the New Deal, Johnson was the Texas state director
     of the National Youth Administration, which provided jobs
     for in-school youth. See Chapter 3, pp. 59-60, for a discus-
     sion of business opposition to New Deal work programs. Johnson
     engaged in a vigorous campaign to win support for the pro-
     gram, speaking at groups ranging "from the Daughters of the
     American Revolution to the Socialist Party, from the Busi-
     ness Council to the AFL-CIO." (Memorandum from Horace
     Busby to the President, 14 January 1964, cited by Doris Kearns,
     Lyndon Johnson and the American Dream [New York: Harper
     Row, 1976], 412). Zarefsky (op. cit., 26 [see note 73]) notes
     that LBJ "enlisted the support of influential businessmen who
     spoke in behalf of the program."

86. Judith Russell, "The Making of American Antipoverty Policy:
     The Other War on Poverty" (Ph.D. diss., Columbia Univer-
     sity, 1992), 22. The phrase, "early on," is important; several
     years later, antipoverty director Shriver and Robert Kennedy
     recognized the significance of unemployment.

87. Ibid., 67-68, 102.

88. Ibid., 22-23.

89. Ginsburg (op. cit., 49-50 [see note 37]) writes that initially
     MDTA focused on retraining experienced, predominantly white
     workers who were displaced by technological change, but
     that as overall unemployment declined in the 1960s, espe-

cially among white, male family heads, the emphasis shifted to those lacking experience and skills. According to Sar Levitan, the limited data then available suggest that the programs enacted prior to the antipoverty program, such as MDTA and the Area Redevelopment Act, were helping very small numbers of the poor. Sar A. Levitan, *The Great Society's Poor Law: A New Approach to Poverty* (Baltimore, Md.: Johns Hopkins Press, 1969), 14.

90. Levitan and Taggart, op. cit., 134-136 (see note 19). For discussion of the development of manpower policy to handle the problem of structural unemployment and the Keynsian structuralist controversy, see Gary Mucciaroni, *The Political Failure of Employment Policy, 1945–1982* (Pittsburgh: University of Pittsburgh Press, 1990), 40-45; and Weir, op. cit., 67-73 (see note 83).

91. Zarefsky, op. cit., 100 (see note 73).

92. Robert F. Kennedy, *Congressional Record* 112 (3 October 1966), 24795, cited by Zarefsky, ibid., 100-101.

93. U.S. Congress, Public Law 88-452, 20 August 1964, *The War on Poverty, The Economic Opportunity Act of 1964*, Title II, Sec. 202(a).

94. Among the emphases of MFY's community programs were: (1) increasing the ability of local residents to participate in and influence the social and political life of their community; (2) dramatizing community needs and mobilizing public action to deal with those needs; (3) increasing institutional responsiveness to lower-class needs by improving communication between disadvantaged people and appropriate community institutions; and (4) improving the competence of local leaders to deal with grievances and to defend their constituents' rights and privileges. Mobilization for Youth, *A Proposal for the Prevention of Delinquency by Expanding Opportunities,* 2nd ed. (New York: Author, 1962), 132-133.

Donovan (op. cit., 32 [see note 39]) writes that "the idea [of community action] came from the President's Committee on Juvenile Delinquency." His major source is Brian Smith ("The Role of the Poor in the Poverty Program: The Origin and Development of Maximum Feasible Participation" [Master's thesis, Department of Public Law and Government, Columbia University, 1966]), who, Donovan (p. 44) is convinced, is accurate. For a discussion of the role played by the Ford Foundation and the President's Committee on Juvenile Delinquency in the origins of community action, see Peter Marris and Martin Rein, *Dilemmas of Social Reform: Poverty and Community Action in the United States* (New York: Atherton Press, 1969), esp. 732. Grants of the PCJD and the foundation tended to converge in some cities. Yarmolinsky (op. cit. 48-49 [see note 77]) recalls that at one of the first brainstorming sessions about community action, Richard Boone, active with both the demonstration programs of the Ford Foundation and the PCJD, cautioned against planning among organizations without involving the poor.

95.   Hearings before the Subcommittee on the War on Poverty Program: The Economic Opportunity Act of 1964, Part I, 1964, 305, cited in Donovan, op. cit., 35 (see note 39).

96.   Kravitz (op. cit., 63 [see note 78]) points out that "[some] writers tracing the development of the maximum-feasible-participation issue cite its congruence with the civil rights issue." Kravitz quotes an unpublished paper (mimeo) by David Grossman written in 1966: "The civil rights movement carried with it overtones of participatory democracy that had been dormant in much of American life for decades."

97.   Katz (op. cit., 100 [see note 73]) draws on Adam Yarmolinsky's discussion in "Poverty and Urban Policy" (op. cit. [see note 80]).

98.   Piven and Cloward (op. cit, 256-260 [see note 59]) view the PCJD, the CAPs, the Community Mental Health Centers Act of 1963, and Title I of the Demonstration Cities and Metropolitan Development Act as ostensibly dealing with different social problems but all operating similarly—all targeted to the inner city, all channeling some portion of funds to new organizations in the ghettos and circumventing existing municipal agencies, and, most important, all making service agencies of local government the targets of reform. Kravitz (op. cit., 66 [see note 78]), for example, viewed Model Cities as "a new version of community action."

99.   Levitan and Taggart, op. cit., 175 (see note 19).

100. Patterson, op. cit., 153 (see note 5).

101. Ibid.

102. Paul A. Levy, "The Durability of Supreme Court Welfare Reforms of the 1960s," *Social Service Review* 66 (June 1992), 217.

103. Ibid., 219, 224.

104. Calculated from *Annual Statistical Supplement, 1996,* op. cit., table 9.G1 (see note 2) for growth in relief rolls.

105. Piven and Cloward, op. cit., 248 (see note 59).

106. U.S. Department of Health, Education, and Welfare, *The Administration of Aid to Families with Dependent Children in New York City,* November 1968–February 1969 (Washington, D.C.: The Department), 48-49, cited by Piven and Cloward, ibid., 289.

107. Susan Handley Hertz, who studied the welfare-rights movement in the State of Minnesota, wrote that NWRO was the "most visible" of a set of loosely interlocking local and national organizations of welfare mothers that had emerged across the country by 1970." See *The Welfare Mothers Movement: A Decade of Change for Poor Women?* (Lanham, Md.: University Press of America, 1981), 1, 174. According to one estimate, NWRO's membership was 85% black, 10% white, and 5% Latina in 1972. George T. Martin, Jr., "The Emergence and Development of a Social Movement Organization among the Underclass: A Case Study of the National Welfare Rights Organization" (Ph.D. diss., Department of Sociology, University of Chicago, 1972), 2, cited by Frances Fox Piven and Richard A. Cloward, *Poor People's Movements: Why They Succeed, How They Fail* (New York: Pantheon Books, 1977), 317.

108. In 1969, blacks were 45.2% of AFDC parents. *Green Book,* op. cit., table 8-28 (see note 18).

109. West, op. cit., 129 (see note 74).

110. Ibid.

111. Piven and Cloward, op. cit., 293 (see note 107).

112. Ibid., 297-301 (individual grievances); 301-305 (collective grievances).

113. West, op. cit., 292 (see note 74).

114. Ibid., 295. West points to Steiner's (op. cit., 298 [see note 1]) figures for New York City where special grants increased from $3.08 million in April 1967, before the NWRO drive began, to $11.57 million in May of the following year.

115. Steiner, ibid., 283.

116. Piven and Cloward, op. cit., 309 (see note 107). West (op. cit., 51-52 [see note 74]) writes that NWRO claimed 800 groups in 50 states.

117. Steiner, op. cit., 310 (see note 1). See also, West, ibid., 50-51.

118. West, ibid., 28-36, 367. The largest source of private funds was white Protestant churches.

119. Steiner, op. cit., 293 (see note 1). The Philadelphia Welfare Rights Organization charged that one cannot "take government money and stay free."

120. Mildred Calvert, "Welfare Rights and the Welfare System," in *Welfare Mothers Speak Out* (New York: W. W. Norton, 1972), 25-26, 27, 30. Mrs. Calvert was chairman, Northside Welfare Rights Organization, and secretary, Milwaukee County Welfare Rights Organization.

121. Betty Niedzwiecki, "At War with the War on Poverty," in ibid., 40. Mrs. Niedzwiecki was chairman, MOM's Welfare Rights Organization, and editor, Milwaukee County Welfare Rights Organization Newsletter.

122. Roxanne Jones, cited in "Welfare Mythology," in ibid., 85. Mrs. Jones is identified as from Philadelphia.

123. Richard Polenberg, *One Nation Divisible: Class, Race, and Ethnicity in the United States since 1938* (New York: Penguin Books, 1980), 193.

124. *Report of the National Advisory Commission on Civil Disorders*, op. cit., 20-61 (see note 2).

125. James MacGregor Burns, *The Crosswinds of Freedom: From Roosevelt to Reagan—America in the Last Half Century* (New York: Vintage Books, 1989), 566.

126. Arthur M. Schlesinger, Jr., *A Thousand Days: John F. Kennedy in the White House* (Boston: Houghton Mifflin, 1965), 1011.

127. Ibid., 1009.

128. Ibid., 1006-1007.

129. *Report of the National Advisory Commission on Civil Disorders,* op. cit., 19 (see note 2).

130. Schlesinger, op. cit., 966 (see note 126).

131. Yarmolinsky ("Poverty and Urban Policy," op. cit., 193 [see note 80]) declared that the Kennedy administration's stance on civil rights had "no concern whatsoever about holding the black vote, about an upsurge of revolt of the masses."

132. Poverty and Urban Policy, ibid., 161.

133. Polenberg, op. cit., 189 (see note 123). "When its efforts to cancel an August [1963] march on Washington failed, the administration ensured that the speeches were moderate in tone and, in effect, converted the demonstration from a protest against federal inaction into a rally in favor of its own civil rights bill."

134. Cloward was research director of Mobilization for Youth, and his and Lloyd Ohlin's theory of delinquency was the intellectual basis for MFY's approach to juvenile delinquency. He called attention to the March on Washington, the bombings of 1963, and to the administration's response to "forces within the Democratic party that were being activated and radicalized . . . by the civil rights movement and by the insurgency that was beginning to take form in the cities." "Poverty and Urban Policy," op. cit., 160 (see note 80).

135. "Poverty and Urban Policy," ibid., 392, 395.

136. James W. Button, *Black Violence: The Political Impact of the 1960s Riots* (Princeton, N.J.: Princeton University Press, 1978), 26. Button also calls attention to the greater ease of organizing programs in urban ghettos, as opposed to rural

areas. By 1967, the Office of Economic Opportunity reported that 57% of the persons involved in the antipoverty programs in the previous year were nonwhite.

137. Schlesinger, op. cit., 930 (see note 126). Button (ibid., 26) points out that by 1960, more than one-third of all blacks in the country were concentrated in nine key presidential election states and that this increased the leverage of the black vote on presidential politics.

138. "Poverty and Urban Policy," op. cit., 167-168 (see note 80).

139. Piven and Cloward (op. cit., 256-279 [see note 59]) identify "the federal strategy in the cities," pointing out the "urban bias" of the poverty program, the concentration of funds in the nation's 10 largest cities, the decision to create new, local agencies rather than to reform existing services, and the staffing and control of the new agencies by African–Americans. "Through both neighborhood and citywide structures . . . the national administration revived the traditional processes of urban politics: offering jobs and services to build party loyalty"(p. 261).

140. Zarefsky, op. cit., 27 (see note 73).

141. Button, op. cit., 158 (see note 136).

142. Ibid.

143. Alvin Schorr's 1966 book contains a full discussion of the guaranteed income, negative income tax, and family allowance. Alvin L. Schorr, *Poor Kids* (New York: Basic Books, 1966), 129-165. See also Robert Theobald, *Free Men and Free Markets* (New York: C. M. Potter, 1963). New income-maintenance strategies boosting AFDC benefits were out of bounds for antipoverty planners because of the difficulty of getting Congressional approval. See Weir, op. cit., 68 (see note 83).

144. Moynihan, op. cit., 132 (see note 60.)

145. The Urban Coalition was founded in 1967 in response to contemporaneous urban riots. Included in the Coalition were business executives like the chairman of the board of Time, Inc., representatives of the AFL-CIO, the head of the Na-

tional Council of Churches, the secretary of the Leadership Conference on Civil Rights, and the mayor of Pittsburgh. Moynihan (ibid., 278 [see note 60]) writes that "business had been shaken by the rioting, its presumed interests threatened, but, just as importantly, a civic conscience had been aroused." The theory was that communication and cooperation had broken down among power centers and interest groups of the metropolis. The idea was to collect enough power and resources in one place to act in ways that would respond to the perceived needs of minority communities.

146. George Gallup, *The Gallup Poll,* vol. 3, 1959–1971 (New York, 1972), 1919-1921, cited by Patterson, op. cit., 109 (see note 5). Kallen and Miller, who studied a sample of 600 black and white women living in Baltimore, found that both groups agreed that able-bodied men and women should work and sexual misbehavior (out-of-wedlock births) should not be supported by welfare. David J. Kallen and Dorothy Miller, "Public Attitudes toward Welfare," *Social Work* 16 (July 1971), 83-90.

147. Joe R. Feagin, *Subordinating the Poor: Welfare and American Beliefs* (Englewood Cliffs, N.J.: Prentice-Hall, 1975), 103.

148. Ibid., 97.

149. Charles Frankel, "Obstacles to Human Welfare," *Social Welfare Forum, 1961* (New York: Columbia University Press, 1961), 273.

150. Dalaker and Naifeh, op. cit., table C-1, C-2 (see note 63).

151. West, op. cit., 93 (see note 74).

CHAPTER 5
SETTING THE STAGE FOR WELFARE "REFORM," 1967–1980

1. Robert Kuttner, *The End of Laissez-Faire: National Purpose and the Global Economy after the Cold War* (New York: Alfred A. Knopf, 1991), 58.

2. In the war year of 1969, when unemployment fell to 3.5%, Washington's military expenditures amounted to 8.6% of GNP.

Other countries with lower levels of military spending, however, achieved higher levels of employment. Helen Ginsburg, *Full Employment and Public Policy: The United States and Sweden* (Lexington, Mass.: Lexington Books), 1983, 22. For the harmful effects of military spending, see Seymour Melman, *The Permanent War Economy* (New York: Simon & Schuster, 1974); *What Else Is There to Do?* A Report to the National Commission for Economic Conversion and Disarmament (Washington, D.C.: National Commission for Economic Conversion and Disarmament, October 1993).

3.   Kuttner, op. cit. (see note 1), 58. Other accounts of this period can be found in: Samir Amin, *Maldevelopment: Anatomy of a Global Failure* (London: United Nations University Press, 1990); Richard J. Barnet and John Cavanagh, *Global Dreams: Imperial Corporations and the New World Order* (New York: Simon & Schuster, 1994); Stephen Gill and David Law, *The Global Political Economy: Perspectives, Problems and Policies* (Baltimore: The Johns Hopkins University Press, 1988); William Greider, *One World, Ready or Not: The Manic Logic of Global Capitalism* (New York: Simon & Schuster, 1997); Arthur MacEwen, *Debt and Disorder: International Economic Instability and U.S. Imperial Decline* (New York: Monthly Review Press, 1990); Arthur MacEwen and William K. Tabb, eds., *Instability and Change in the World Economy* (New York: Monthly Review Press, 1989).

4.   Stagflation was perplexing because in the 1960s, the so-called Phillips Curve (named for A. W. Phillips, who, in the late 1950s, assessed the relationship between wages and unemployment in England over a 100-year period) came to dominate economic thinking. The Phillips Curve (in the original article) was a presumed inverse relationship between unemployment and wages but soon was popularized as a trade-off between unemployment and prices. (See: A. W. Phillips, "The Relationship between Unemployment and the Rate of Change of Money Wage Rates in the United Kingdom, 1861–1957," *Economica,* November 1958.) Higher unemployment would cause inflation to be lower, and lower unemployment could be achieved with lower inflation. With stagflation, however, higher unemployment did not reduce inflation. The perplexity was also due to the popular interpretation of Keynesian

theory as supposing that inflation was not a problem until full employment was reached. Then increasing demand would be inflationary if output could not increase. However, some economists have pointed out that Keynes, in his earlier writings, recognized that inflationary bottlenecks could be encountered before reaching full employment, and policies would have to be devised to counter them.

5.   Although "full employment" as we define it had never been the goal of policymakers in the United States after the defeat of the Full Employment Bill of 1945, liberal policymakers for most of the post-war period maintained what they considered full employment (i.e., an employment level that did not trigger inflation) as a major policy goal. Margaret Weir, however, points out that the concept of full employment employed by U.S. policymakers was narrow and limited by ideological and institutional boundaries in comparison to that of their European counterparts. Margaret Weir, *Politics and Jobs: The Boundaries of Employment Policy in the United States* (Princeton: Princeton University Press, 1992).

6.   Writing in the early 1980s, economist Helen Ginsburg observed the change in economic priorities that had occurred: "It has since become commonplace to see open advocacy of the use of economic policy to increase unemployment and to help hasten the advent of recessions. . . . " Helen Ginsburg, *Full Employment and Public Policy: The United States and Sweden* (Lexington, Mass.: Lexington Books), 24.

7.   Gerald Epstein, "Domestic Stagflation and Monetary Policy: The Federal Reserve and the Hidden Election," in Thomas Ferguson and Joel Rogers, eds., *The Hidden Election: Politics and Economics in the 1980s Presidential Campaign* (New York: Pantheon Books, 1981), 174.

8.   The growth rate in the real after-tax corporate profit declined from 2.8% a year between 1959 and 1969 to 1.6% for 1968 and 1979. But stock prices took an even sharper dip, declining by 50% between 1968 and 1978, the poorest ever 10-year period for stocks, including even the Great Depression. This poor performance harmed the wealth of stockholders and the ability of corporations to raise funds for investment. William C. Brainard, John B. Shoven, and Laurence Weiss,

"The Financial Valuation of the Return to Capital," *Brookings Papers on Economic Activity* 2 (1980), 453-511, cited in Epstein, ibid., note, 83, 192-193.

9.   Marc Allan Eisner, *The State in the American Political Economy* (Englewood Cliffs, N.J.: Prentice-Hall, 1995), 266.

10.   For extensive discussions of the way in which Keynesian theory was employed by U.S. policymakers and of the debates within the economic policy establishment, see Gary Mucciaroni, *The Political Failure of Employment Policy, 1945-1982* (Pittsburgh: University of Pittsburgh Press, 1992), Chapter 1; and Weir, op. cit., 27-61 (see note 5).

11.   Monetarists, like Friedman, believe the money supply should not be expanded in relationship to growth but that a fixed amount of growth in money should be the aim—independent of judgment about the economy's needs.

12.   William Greider has observed that "the awkward little secret of the American system was that modern recessions did not flow ineluctably from mysterious natural forces in the business cycle. Recessions were induced by the federal government . . . the Federal Reserve's decision to force up interest rates to an abnormal level." William Greider, *Secrets of the Temple: How the Federal Reserve Runs the Country* (New York: Touchstone/Simon & Schuster, 1987), 393.

13.   Pushing real interest rates up strengthened the U.S. dollar and hence made U.S. exports much more expensive. That led to declining exports and was an important part of the loss of U.S. industry jobs at that time.

14.   Secretary of the Treasury John Connolly gave "an unusually candid interpretation" in 1972 before the Joint Economic Committee of Congress in which he said: "It is significant that compared to the 5.9 percent rate for total employment, about 17 percent was the rate for young people and about 10 percent was the rate for blacks. If you take the unemployment rate of male adults, heads of families, you get down to an unemployment figure of 3 percent. So we can't be carried away by an unemployment figure of say, 6 percent." Connolly, *1972 Economic Report of the President, Hearings*, pt. 2, 323, cited in Ginsburg, op. cit., 33 (see note 6).

15. Greider, op. cit., 135-138 (see note 12). Many politicians, including the president at the time, Jimmy Carter, did not fully understand how monetary policy worked. Other politicians who did understand, however, were averse to explaining it because it violated their adherence to the ideology of free markets.

16. An economist at the University of Southern California and later Pepperdine University, Arthur B. Laffer, developed a theory about the relationship between taxes and government revenues known as the "Laffer Curve." His hypothesis asserts, on the basis of a mathematical model, that after a point, raising tax rates results in reduced government revenues and that reducing taxes will result in increased government revenues. Laffer's theories were taken up with enthusiasm by the Reagan administration. For an explanation and critique of both Friedman's and Laffer's theories, see Thomas Karier, *Great Experiments in American Economic Policy: From Kennedy to Reagan* (New York: Praeger, 1997).

17. In reality, the rising costs of labor and government transfers that supply-siders complained of were due to the inflation caused by the unregulated international currency market, the OPEC oil price hikes, and the Fed's deliberate policy of tightening credit. Kuttner, op. cit., 78 (see note 1).

18. Leonard Silk and David Vogel, *Ethics and Profits* (New York: Simon & Schuster, 1976); Samuel Huntington, "The United States," in *The Crisis of Democracy: Report on the Governability of Democracies to the Trilateral Commission* (New York: New York University Press, 1975); and Frances Fox Piven and Richard A. Cloward, *Regulating the Poor: The Functions of Public Welfare*, updated edition (New York: Vintage Books, 1993), 359.

19. William E. Simon, *A Time for Truth* (New York: Reader's Digest Press/McGraw Hill, 1978), 13.

20. Huntington, op. cit., 79 (see note 18).

21. Sheila D. Collins, *The Rainbow Challenge: The Jackson Campaign and the Future of U.S. Politics* (New York: Monthly Review Press, 1987), 52-59; Thomas Byrnes Edsall, *The New Politics of Inequality* (New York: W.W. Norton & Co., 1984),

113. Edsall points out that the rate of decline in public confidence in the business community, as measured by public opinion polls, was sharper during this period than for any other major institution.

22.   Edsall, ibid., 107-140.

23.   William Greider, *Who Will Tell the People? The Betrayal of American Democracy* (Touchstone/Simon & Schuster, 1992), 48.

24.   Ibid.

25.   Edsall, op. cit., 120-140 (see note 21).

26.   Companies could write off their losses when they moved to nonunion locations and many nonunion states invested heavily in subsidies to new firms. Many companies that are essentially American-owned have incorporated abroad to avoid paying taxes to the U.S. government. For a thorough description of the way in which corporate tax policies have changed, see: Donald L. Barlett and James B. Steele, *America: Who Really Pays the Taxes?* (New York: Touchstone/Simon & Schuster, 1994).

27.   For analyses of the way in which the attack on welfare was a surrogate for the attempt to dismantle the entire welfare state, see Fred Block, Richard A. Cloward, Barbara Ehrenreich, and Frances Fox Piven, *The Mean Season: The Attack on the Welfare State* (New York: Pantheon Books, 1987); and Frances Fox Piven and Richard A. Cloward, *The New Class War: Reagan's Attack on the Welfare State and Its Consequences,* rev. expanded edition (New York: Pantheon, 1982).

28.   For a history of the "neoconservative movement, see Peter Steinfels, *The Neoconservatives: The Men Who Are Changing America's Politics* (New York: Simon & Schuster, 1979). According to Steinfels (p. 294) neoconservatism began as an antibody on the left. Many of its leading figures originally conceived of it that way and perhaps still do; it was a reaction to what they considered the destabilizing and excessive developments of the sixties, and when they had been quelled, it would once again be indistinguishable from mainstream liberalism." Among the key neoconservatives were sociologists like Daniel Patrick Moynihan, Peter Berger, and Nathan

Glazer; political scientist Samuel P. Huntington; literary figures like Irving Kristol, Norman Podhoretz, and Midge Decter, who edit the neoconservative journal *Commentary*; and religious writers like Robert Novak and Richard John Neuhaus.

29. "Part 2: The New Right and the American Way," *Searchlight*, October 1980, 3; Barbara Ehrenreich, "The New Right Attack on Social Welfare," in Block et al., op. cit., 161-195 (see note 27).

30. Public opinion polls show most Americans equating "welfare" with undeserved "dependence" on the public trough—and welfare recipients as those who flout shared American values of independence and hard work. But there is also strong support for helping the truly needy, and in recessionary periods, the public usually exhibits more sympathy for the poor. What the polls demonstrate is that the terms that are used influence the response. R. Kent Weaver, Robert Y. Shapiro, and Lawrence R. Jacobs, "The Polls—Trends: Welfare," *Public Opinion Quarterly* 59 (1995), 606-627. See also Fay Lomax Cook and Edith J. Barrett, *Support for the American Welfare State: The View of Congress and the Public* (New York: Columbia University Press, 1992), 62-64.

31. For an extensive discussion of the way in which poverty programs have been race-coded, see Jill Quadagno, *The Color of Welfare: How Racism Undermined the War on Poverty* (New York: Oxford University Press, 1994).

32. Martin Gilens, "'Race Coding' and White Opposition to Welfare," *American Political Science Review* 90 (September 1996), 593-604. Gilens argues that while Americans strongly support the welfare state, they are opposed to welfare because they think that most people who receive it are blacks and believe that African–Americans are less committed to the work ethic than other Americans. Martin Gilens, *Why Americans Hate Welfare: Race, Media, and the Politics of Antipoverty Policy* (Chicago: University of Chicago Press, 1999), 2.

33. See Dan T. Carter, *From George Wallace to Newt Gingrich: Race in the Conservative Counterrevolution, 1963-1994* (Baton Rouge, La.: Louisiana State University Press, 1996).

34. Gilens, *Why Americans Hate Welfare,* op. cit., 132 (see note 32). Gilens (p. 123) found that in 1969 and 1970, 52% of the poor people pictured in poverty and welfare stories were African–Americans, but in 1972 and 1973, blacks comprised 70% of the poor people pictured in stories indexed under poverty and 75% of those pictured in stories on welfare. "Overall," he states, "the sustained negative coverage of welfare during 1972-73 was accompanied by the highest proportions of blacks in newsmagazine images of the poor of any point during the entire forty-three year period examined."

35. Religious revival, which takes a political form—especially an evangelical Protestant form—has appeared periodically in American political life. It appears to be a response to "disruptive, large-scale secularizing changes in society and economy" which in other countries would produce traditional conservative or socialist parties. Walter Dean Burnham, "Appendix A: Social Stress and Political Response: Religion and the 1980 Election," in Ferguson and Rogers, op. cit., 137-140 (see note 7). Arthur Schlesinger, Jr., also points to periods in which private interest is seen as the means of social salvation. "These are times of 'privatization' (barbarous but useful word), of materialism, hedonism, and the overriding quest for personal gratification. Class and interest politics subside; cultural politics—ethnicity, religion, social status, morality—come to the fore." Arthur M. Schlesinger, Jr., *The Cycles of American History* (New York: Houghton Mifflin, 1986), 28.

36. "The American Underclass," *Time*, 29 August 1977, 14-15, cited in Michael B. Katz, "The Urban Underclass as a Metaphor of Social Transformation," in Michael B. Katz, ed., *The "Underclass" Debate: Views from History* (Princeton, N.J.: Princeton University Press, 1993), 4-5.

37. Katz's book, ibid., provides a very useful compendium of critiques and historical analysis of the debate over the underclass concept.

38. Between 1960 and 1987, single-mother families increased from 7.4% of all families with children to 19.7%. White, single-mother families increased from 6% in 1960 to 15.5%

in 1987, while black, single-mother families increased from 21.3% to 48.4%. Gertrude Schaffner Goldberg, "The United States: Feminization of Poverty amidst Plenty," in Gertrude Schaffner Goldberg and Eleanor Kremen, eds., *The Feminization of Poverty: Only in America?* (New York: Praeger, 1990), table 2.2, 37.

39. Andrew T. Miller, "Social Science, Social Policy, and the Heritage of African–American Families," in Katz, op. cit., 254-289 (see note 36).

40. For a description of the way in which the Religious Right reshaped the Republican party, see Haynes Johnson, *Sleepwalking through History: America in the Reagan Years* (New York: W. W. Norton, 1991), 193-214.

41. According to the Edsalls, the success of the Civil Rights movement in eliminating subsidies to segregated Christian schools ignited what had been a loose confederation of Christian school associations into a powerful political movement. Thomas Byrnes Edsall with Mary D. Edsall, *Chain Reaction: The Impact of Race, Rights, and Taxes on American Politics* (New York: W. W. Norton, 1992), 132-133.

42. The Economic Policy Institute points out that from the late 1970s on, before-tax inequality has been much greater than after-tax inequality, indicating that the main source of declining living standards and economic anxiety for the working and middle classes has been changes in the overall economy. Between 1965 and 1993, of 23 industrialized countries, the United States had the lowest increase in tax revenues as a percentage of GDP. Lawrence Mishel, Jared Bernstein, and John Schmitt, *The State of Working America 1996-97* (Armonk, N.Y.: M.E. Sharpe, 1996), 101-106. In 1985, total tax receipts as percentage of GDP were 29% in the U.S., compared to 33% in Canada, 38% in West Germany and the U.K., and 46% in France. See OECD, *OECD in Figures,* 1988 Edition (Paris: Author, 1988), 32-33.

43. George Gilder, *Wealth and Poverty* (New York: Basic Books, 1981), 73.

44. Ibid., 70

45. Daniel Patrick Moynihan, "The Negro Family: The Case for National Action," in Lee Rainwater and William L. Yancey, eds., *The Moynihan Report and the Politics of Controversy* (Cambridge, Mass.: M.I.T. Press, 1967).

46. Some feminists have argued that the patriarchal welfare state simply replaces the patriarchal family system. Unlike Gilder, however, they do not find acceptable the subordinate role to which both systems assign them. See Mimi Abramovitz, *Regulating the Lives of Women: Social Welfare Policy from Colonial Times to the Present*, rev. ed. (Boston: South End Press, 1996). Other feminists argue that although the welfare system had been coercive and patriarchal in many ways, still it enabled some women to achieve a measure of independence and to engage in collective struggles about their entitlements. For the arguments on both sides, see Linda Gordon, ed., *Women, the State, and Welfare* (Madison, Wisc.: University of Wisconsin Press, 1990).

47. Gilder, op. cit., 116 (see note 43).

48. Ibid., 111.

49. Ibid., 117.

50. Ibid., 126.

51. Ibid., 67

52. Charles Murray, *Losing Ground: American Social Policy, 1950-1980* (New York: Basic Books, 1984).

53. Murray, ibid., sets up a hypothetical case study to test this conclusion. Using a fictional couple, "Phyllis and Harold," he seeks to demonstrate that providing money to the poor creates a rational disincentive to engage in work and form stable families. By using typical welfare payments and living costs in the state of Pennsylvania, Murray attempted to show that in 1960, before the Great Society programs, it was more economically rational for the poor to get married, to stay off welfare, to defer having children, and to get low-paying jobs. After the 1960s, however, the welfare grant could be supplemented with food stamps, Medicaid, housing subsidies, and the like, making it more profitable to stay home and have kids than to work full time at a minimum-wage job.

It is also possible for Harold to live with Phyllis without getting married, to not work or work only occasionally, and have more disposable income.

54.   Ibid., 233-234.

55.   For a summary of the critique of Murray's work, see the following: Michael B. Katz, *The Undeserving Poor: From the War on Poverty to the War on Welfare* (New York: Pantheon Books, 1989), 153-156; Theodore R. Marmor, Jerry L. Mashaw, and Philip L. Harvey, *America's Misunderstood Welfare State: Persistent Myths, Enduring Realities* (New York: Basic Books, 1990),104-114; Robert Greenstein, "Losing Faith in *Losing Ground*," *The New Republic*, 25 March 1985, 12-17; David T. Ellwood, *Poor Support: Poverty in the American Family* (New York: Basic Books, 1988), 61; and Goldberg, op. cit., 38-41 (see note 38).

56.   Frances Fox Piven pointed out that Murray's argument was a repeat of arguments used by English social thinkers in 1834 to justify the repeal of poor relief. The results were increased desperation and reduced life expectancy. Frances Fox Piven, "From Workhouse to Workfare," *New York Times*, 1 August 1996, A27.

57.   Katz, op. cit., 55 (see note 55).

58.   Richard J. Herrnstein and Charles Murray, *The Bell Curve: Intelligence and Class Structure in American Life* (New York: The Free Press, 1996).

59.   For an analysis of the corporate and foundation connections for this right-wing assault on liberal values and institutions, see Phil Wilayto, *The Feeding Trough: The Bradley Foundation, "The Bell Curve" and the Real Story behind Wisconsin's National Model for Welfare Reform* (Milwaukee, Wisc.: A Job is a Right Campaign, 1997).

60.   Polls have consistently found that while a majority of the public thinks that government spends too much on welfare and that it is ineffective, support for government spending increases dramatically when the phrasing is changed to "assistance to the poor" or similar specific phrases connoting sympathetic recipients such as "poor children" and the

"homeless" or for job training and employment programs. Weaver, Shapiro, and Jacobs, op. cit., 606-627 (see note 30). For a more positive view of the welfare state in a survey taken in the late 1980s, see Cook and Barrett, op. cit. (see note 30).

61.   Katz, op. cit. (see note 55).

62.   Lawrence M. Mead, *Beyond Entitlement: The Social Obligations of Citizenship* (New York: The Free Press, 1986).

63.   Ibid., 1.

64.   Ibid., 68-69.

65.   Ibid., 84.

66.   Jason DeParle, "Learning Poverty Firsthand," *New York Times Magazine*, 27 April 1997, 35.

67.   Conservative social scientists Abigail and Stephan Thernstrom characterize this as one of the biggest losses in any election in this century. See their *America in Black and White: One Nation, Indivisible* (New York: Simon & Schuster, 1997), 75. Sundquist points out that Johnson's slip in approval rating (from the 56% to 69% range in October 1965 to the 31% to 49% range in September 1966) was across the board, including handling of civil rights (60% to 43%) and the war on poverty (60% to 41%). See James L. Sundquist, *Politics and Policy: The Eisenhower, Kennedy, and Johnson Years* (Washington, D.C.: The Brookings Institution, 1968), 497. Edsall and Edsall, citing the *Congressional Quarterly Almanac*, 1966 (Washington, D.C.: *Congressional Quarterly, 1967*, 1, 398), point out that all seven southern Democrats who lost House seats in 1966 were supporters of Johnson's Great Society. See their *Chain Reaction,* op. cit., 60 (see note 41).

68.   Edsall and Edsall, op. cit., 59 (see note 41), interpreting poll data cited by Sundquist, ibid., 499.

69.   Thernstrom and Thernstrom, op. cit. (see note 67), 176; Edsall and Edsall, (op. cit., 60 [see note 41]) call attention to the defeat of civil rights champion Senator Paul Douglas, who, in 1960, carried every white ward on the south side of the city, but 6 years later, lost six of eight of these white ethnic

enclaves that had been targeted by Martin Luther King's open-housing drive.

70. For a review of this evidence, see Gerald David Jaynes and Robin M. Williams, Jr., eds., *A Common Destiny: Blacks and American Society* (Washington, D.C.: National Academy Press, 1989), 118-122.

71. Angus Campbell and Howard Schuman, "Racial Attitudes in Fifteen American Cities," *Supplemental Studies for the National Advisory Commission on Civil Disorders* (Washington, D.C.: U.S. Government Printing Office, 1968), 38.

72. James Button, *Black Violence* (Princeton: Princeton University Press, 1978), 165.

73. "The Racial Attitudes of White Americans," in *The Politics of Protest*, vol. 3, Staff Report to the National Commission on the Causes and Prevention of Violence, prepared by Jerome Skolnick (Washington, D.C., 1969), 140-141.

74. The Council of Economic Advisors played a key role in shaping poverty policy during this period. Henry Aaron has noted that the most striking characteristic of their view of the poverty cycle was the absence of any mention of poverty's relationship to the economic system. Henry Aaron, *Politics and the Professors* (Washington, D.C.: Brookings Institution, 1978), 20, cited in Margaret Weir, "Innovation and Boundaries in American Employment Policy," *Political Science Quarterly* 107 (1992), 260.

75. According to Richard Polenberg, Nixon recognized that "the election results in 1968 (43.4% of the popular vote for Nixon, 13.5% for Wallace, and 44.1% for civil rights advocate, Hubert Humphrey) pointed unmistakably toward the importance of the white backlash vote" and "set out to win George Wallace's constituency with the ardor of a Don Juan." Richard Polenberg, *One Nation Divisible: Class, Race, and Ethnicity in the United States since 1938* (New York: Penguin, 1980), 222, 237-238.

76. Ibid., 221.

77. See Anna B. Mayer and Marguerite Rosenthal, "The Poor Get Poorer: Making the Family Impossible," in Alan Gartner,

Colin Greer, and Frank Riessman, eds., *What Nixon Is Doing to Us* (New York: Harper & Row, 1973).

78. For an extended analysis of this period of deindustrialization, see Bennett Harrison and Barry Bluestone, *The Great U-Turn: Corporate Restructuring and the Polarizing of America* (New York: Basic Books, 1990).

79. William Julius Wilson, *When Work Disappears: The World of the Urban Poor* (New York: Vintage Books, 1996). See also: Thomas J. Sugrue, "The Structures of Urban Poverty: The Reorganization of Space and Work in Three Periods of American History," in Katz, op. cit., 85-117 (see note 36); and Loic J. D. Wacquant and William Julius Wilson, "Poverty, Joblessness, and the Social Transformation of the Inner City," in Phoebe H. Cottingham and David T. Ellwood, eds., *Welfare Policy for the 1990s* (Cambridge, Mass.: Harvard University Press, 1989), 70-102.

80. U.S. Immigration & Naturalization Service, *Statistical Yearbook* (http://www.ins.usdoj.gov/stats), cited by Gregory DeFreitas, *In Real World Micro* (Boston: Southend Press, 1999).

81. Warren and Jeffrey Passel, "A Count of the Uncountable: Estimates of Undocumented Aliens Counted in the 1980 Census," *Demography* 24 (August 1987), 375-393, cited in Gregory DeFreitas, "Globalization and Progressive Economic Policy," in Dean Baker, Gerald Epstein, and Robert Pollin, eds., *Globalization and Progressive Economic Policy* (Cambridge: Cambridge University Press, 1998), 340. Press studies by academic demographers and the Census Bureau have refuted the "guesstimates" of the illegal population most often cited by the media and politicians, which were in the 8–12 million range (DeFreitas, 339).

82. Economist Vernon Briggs believes that the majority of immigrants must seek employment in declining sectors of goods-producing industries (agriculture and light manufacturing) or low-wage sectors of the expanding service sectors where they compete with poor native workers. Vernon M. Briggs, Jr., "The Changing Nature of the Workforce: The Influence of U.S. Immigration Policy" (Washington, D.C.: National Planning Association, December 1990), 10. David North, who

studies immigrants in Los Angeles' labor market, contends that the decline in pay in the secondary labor market is related to the high proportion of legal and illegal immigration. David S. North, "Enforcing the Minimum Wage and Employer Sanctions," *Annals of the American Academy of Political and Social Science* 534 (July 1994), 58-68. David Howell and Elizabeth Mueller have found significant support for negative earnings effects of recent immigrants on black male workers in the New York metropolitan area during the 1980s. David R. Howell and Elizabeth J. Mueller, "Immigration and Native-born Male Earnings: A Jobs-Level Analysis of the New York City Metropolitan Area Labor Market, 1980-90," unpublished paper, Robert J. Milano Graduate School, New School University, New York, N.Y., March 1998.

On the other hand, Gregory DeFreitas points out that studies of the entire labor market of specific cities like Los Angeles, Miami, and New York have found that increased immigration had no overall effect on the unemployment of native-born workers, and several national studies covering multiple cities have produced similar results. DeFreitas makes another important point, namely, that immigrants increase not only the supply but the demand for workers. In addition to spending their earnings in local markets, they have above-average self-employment rates and create new jobs through hiring employees and purchasing supplies for their businesses. Although he found insignificant wage effects for native white women, black men, and Hispanics, DeFreitas' research on the effects of Hispanic immigration on less-skilled native workers in the 79 largest metropolitan areas in the last half of the 1970s did identify one problem of some consequence for welfare "reform"—that there were significant, although small, negative effects for black women. See DeFreitas, op. cit., 340 (see note 81).

The conclusions of an expert panel convened by the National Research Council are similar to those of DeFreitas in their view that immigration is a modest factor, if any, in the labor-market conditions of recent decades, although De Freitas thinks this could change with millions of welfare recipients forced to find jobs in coming years. See James P. Smith and Barry Edmonston, eds., *The New Americans: Economic, Demographic and Fiscal Effects of Immigration* (Washington,

D.C.: National Academy Press, 1997), 7. For other studies, see Daniel S. Hamermesh and Frank D. Bean, eds., *Help or Hindrance? The Economic Implications of Immigration for African Americans* (New York: Russell Sage Foundation, 1998); Frank D. Bean and Stephanie Bell-Rose, eds., *Immigration and Opportunity: Race, Ethnicity, and Employment in the United States* (New York: Russell Sage Foundation, 1999).

83.   Greider, op. cit., 137-142 (see note 12).

84.   Source of calculations by Robert Lekachman is *Economic Report of the President,* January 1981, 236, 253, 255, 274, cited in Robert Lekachman, *Greed is not Enough: Reaganomics* (New York: Pantheon, 1982), 73.

85.   Michael H. Schuman, "Why do Progressive Foundations Give Too Little to Too Many?" *The Nation* (January 12/19, 1998), 13.

86.   Ideas championed by these think tanks include: the dangers of "Big Government" and a "permissive" welfare state, privatization, the end of affirmative action, the flat tax or no income tax, unfunded mandates, school vouchers, workfare, and free-trade agreements, 87. Schuman, op. cit., 11-15 (see note 85). Sarah Covington, *Moving a Public Policy Agenda: The Strategic Philanthropy of Conservative Foundations*, (Washington, D.C.: National Committee for Responsive Philanthropy, 1999).

87.   Schuman, op. cit., 11-15 (see note 85).

88.   For a detailed account of the transformation of the Democratic party during the 1970s, see Edsall, op. cit. (see note 21), 23-66. The transformation of the party, says Edsall, left it highly vulnerable to pressures from the business community, which had been organizing effectively since the early 1970s (p. 64).

89.   Arthur Schlesinger, Jr., called Carter, "the most conservative Democratic president since Grover Cleveland. From a longer perspective, the differences between Carter and Reagan will seem less consequential than the continuities" (op. cit., 33 [see note 35]).

90.   Edsall, op. cit., 75 (see note 21).

91. For accounts of the demise of New Deal liberalism and the rise of radical conservatism, see Edsall, ibid.; Grieder, op. cit. (see note 23); and Kevin Phillips, *The Politics of Rich and Poor: Wealth and the American Electorate in the Reagan Aftermath* (New York: Harper Perennial, 1990), 32-36.

CHAPTER 6
ENTER WELFARE "REFORM," 1967–1980

1. The number of families on AFDC more than doubled between 1967 and 1971. The yearly rise ranged from 15.9% (1967–1968) to 30.0% (1969–1970). The unemployment rates from 1966 to 1969 were the lowest since the Korean War. The caseload rose 3.1% between 1972 and 1973 and went up 8.2% between 1974 and 1975, when unemployment rose from 5.6 to 8.5%, the latter being the highest since 1941. Between 1975 and 1980, the years of stagflation, the rolls rose 6.2% (less than 1% between 1975 and 1979). For AFDC caseload, see *Social Security Bulletin: Annual Statistical Supplement, 1996,* Table 9.G1, 357 (hereafter *Annual Statistical Supplement*). For unemployment rates, U.S. Department of Labor, Bureau of Labor Statistics, *Labor Force Statistics Derived from the Current Population Survey, 1948-87,* Bulletin 2307 (Washington, D.C.: U.S. Government Printing Office, 1988), table A-31, 489.

2. Vincent J. Burke and Vee Burke, *Nixon's Good Deed: Welfare Reform* (New York: Columbia University Press, 1974), 164. Jill Quadagno cites New York State cutbacks of 8% in family allowances and eligibility tightening efforts and cutbacks in Illinois. See *The Color of Welfare: How Racism Undermined the War on Poverty* (New York: Oxford University Press, 1994), 121.

3. In constant dollars, average benefits dropped by 36% between 1971 and 1980. Calculated from *Annual Statistical Supplement*, op. cit., Table 9.G1, 357 (see note 1).

4. *Congressional Record*, vol. 113, pt. 17, 90 Cong., 1 sess. (1967), 23053, cited by Gilbert Y. Steiner, *The State of Welfare* (Washington, D.C.: The Brookings Institution, 1971), 46.

5. Theodore R. Marmor and Martin Rein, "Reforming 'the Welfare Mess': The Fate of the Family Assistance Plan, 1969-72," in Allan P. Sindler, ed., *Policy and Politics in America: Six Case Studies* (Boston: Little, Brown and Company, 1973), 11.

6. Daniel P. Moynihan (*The Politics of a Guaranteed Income* [New York: Random House, 1973], 359) quotes the statement made by President Lyndon Johnson when he signed the legislation on 2 January 1968.

7. Ibid. In 1965, 57.5% of the births to unmarried women were "blacks and others." The figure for 1970 was 56.1%. U.S. Department of Commerce, Bureau of the Census, *Statistical Abstract of the United States: 1980* (Washington, D.C.: U.S. Government Printing Office, 1980), No. 95, 66.

8. Joel F. Handler, *The Poverty of Welfare Reform* (New Haven, Conn.: Yale University Press, 1995), 57.

9. The "freeze" was also regarded by welfare advocates as a means of reducing benefits. Since HEW did not permit waiting lists in AFDC, states would have the option either to appropriate more money or to spread their funds further by reducing benefits. Steiner, op. cit., 47 (see note 4).

10. James T. Patterson, *America's Struggle against Poverty, 1900-1980* (Cambridge, Mass.: Harvard University Press, 1981), 175. See also Walter I. Trattner, *From Poor Law to Welfare State: A History of Social Welfare in America,* 4th ed. (New York: The Free Press, 1989), 295.

11. "Text of President's Message to Congress Seeking Reforms in Welfare," *New York Times,* 2 February 1962, 10.

12. June Axinn and Herman Levin, *Social Welfare: A History of the American Response to Need,* 4th ed. (New York: Longman, 1997), 246-247.

13. Steiner (op. cit., 59-60 [see note 4]) points out that the total day-care authorization for the first 3 years was $25 million, $8.8 million of which was actually appropriated.

14. Ibid., 51. See his discussion of daycare, 50-74.

15. Veto of the Economic Opportunity Amendments of 1971, 10 December 1971, in *Public Papers of the Presidents of the*

United States: Richard M. Nixon, 1971 (Washington, D.C.: U.S. Government Printing Office, 1972), 1178. Jill Quadagno (op. cit., 149-153 [see note 2]) argues that Nixon's veto of the child-care legislation was largely motivated by its driving up costs of welfare reform. Moreover, its advocates' insistence on allowing community-action groups to be prime sponsors of child-care programs would revive Johnson's antipoverty program. Quadagno also points out that Nixon's veto rationale was a "concession to right-wing proponents of family values." Supportive of this interpretation is the statement of Nixon's director of the Office of Child Development, Edward F. Zigler: that Nixon turned against the bill "because of the outpouring of mail from the evangelicals and far right" who didn't want women to work. See Carol Lawson, "For Architect of Child Care, Small Gains," *New York Times,* 22 June 1989, C12.

16. Patterson, op. cit., 175 (see note 10).

17. Steiner, op. cit., 73 (see note 4). Levitan and Taggart give similar results: One in 10 recipients enrolled, of whom less than one-fifth completed a course of training. One of 7 participants ended up being placed in jobs where they stayed for 90 days or more. See Sar A. Levitan and Robert Taggart, *The Promise of Greatness: Social Programs of the Last Decade and Their Major Achievements* (Cambridge, Mass.: Harvard University Press, 1976), 54.

18. Levitan and Taggart, ibid., 54.

19. Steiner, op. cit. 65-74 (see note 4); Levitan and Taggart, ibid., 54-55.

20. Bradley R. Schiller, "Lessons from WIN: A Manpower Evaluation," *Journal of Human Resources* 13 (Fall 1978), 515-516.

21. Trattner, op. cit., 313 (see note 10). Unemployment had risen to nearly 6% in 1971.

22. U.S. Department of Labor, *Manpower Report of the President, 1974* (Washington, D.C.: U.S. Government Printing Office, 1974), 140.

23. Ibid. The *Report* cites a study by Sar A. Levitan, Martin Rein, and David Marwick, *Work and Welfare Go Together* (Baltimore:

Johns Hopkins University Press, 1972, Policy Studies in Employment and Welfare, No. 13).

24.   William F. Henry and Guy H. Miles, *Developing a Model WIN Project for Rural Areas* (Minneapolis: North Star Research and Development Institute, January 1972), cited in Levitan et al., ibid., 40.

25.   Steiner, op. cit., 74 (see note 4).

26.   Advisory Council on Public Welfare, *Having the Power, We Have the Duty*: *Report to the Secretary of Health, Education, and Welfare* (Washington, D.C.: U.S. Government Printing Office, 1966). A summary of the Council's recommendations is found on pp. xii-xiv. Congress authorized the creation of the Advisory Council to review federally funded public-assistance and child-welfare services and to make recommendations for improvements. President Johnson appointed the Council in 1964.

27.   Ibid., xii.

28.   Steiner, op. cit., 109 (see note 4).

29.   Advisory Council, op. cit., xi (see note 26).

30.   Receipt of public assistance in prosperous Sweden grew from 3.5% of the population in 1964 to 6.3% in 1971, and in Great Britain from an already increased rate since 1950 of 5.5% in the mid-1960s to 8.4% in 1972. "The increases in British and Swedish rolls seem at least comparable to those in the United States and have brought with them little of the sense of impending social doom experienced in America." Martin Rein and Hugh Heclo, "What Welfare Crisis? A Comparison among the United States, Britain, and Sweden," *Public Interest* 33 (Fall 1973), 69-70.

31.   Advisory Council on Public Welfare, op. cit., 5 (see note 26).

32.   Ibid., xiii.

33.   *Report of the National Advisory Commission on Civil Disorders* (Washington, D.C.: Author, 1 March 1968), v (hereafter Kerner Commission).

34.   Ibid., 231.

35. Ibid., 232.

36. Ibid., 233-236.

37. Bureau of Labor Statistics, op. cit., table A-31, 489 (see note 1).

38. Kerner Commission, op. cit., 252 (see note 33).

39. Ibid., 255. The welfare recommendations for"overhauling" the present system of welfare are on pp. 254-256.

40. Ibid., 256.

41. The Kerner Commission (ibid.) observed that a "minimum standard of decent living" had long been called for by many groups and individuals, including the AFL-CIO, major executives of corporations, and many civil-rights and welfare organizations.

42. Moynihan, op. cit., 360 (see note 6).

43. President's Commission on Income Maintenance Programs, *Poverty Amid Plenty: The American Paradox* (Washington, D.C.: U.S. Government Printing Office, 1969), 7 (hereafter Heineman Commission).

44. Ibid., 6.

45. Ibid., 9.

46. See W. Joseph Heffernan, Jr., "The Failure of Welfare Reform: A Political Farce in Two Acts," Institute for Research on Poverty Discussion Papers (Madison, Wisc.: University of Wisconsin-Madison, 1974), 7. In his review of Moynihan's book, *The Politics of a Guaranteed Income*, Henry Aaron of the Brookings Institution takes exception with Moynihan's claim that the negative income tax was a conservative idea and credits liberal academics, Christopher Green, James Tobin, Joseph Pechman, and Peter Mieszkowski for development of the idea. See *Yale Law Journal* 82 (1973), 1725-1726.

47. Milton Friedman, "The Case for a Negative Income Tax," in Melvin R. Laird, ed., *Republican Papers* (Garden City, N.Y.: Anchor, 1968), cited by Burke and Burke, op. cit., 17-18 (see note 2).

48. Milton Friedman, *Capitalism and Freedom* (Chicago: University of Chicago Press, 1962/1982), 192.

49.   Christopher Green, *Negative Taxes and the Poverty Problem* (Washington, D.C.: Brookings Institution, 1967).

50.   Burke and Burke, op. cit., 18-21 (see note 2). The author of the plan was economist Joseph Kershaw, OEO's director of research, plans, programs, and evaluation. Reportedly, Sargent Shriver became an advocate of the NIT, recommending it to the president's budget director in a memorandum (Memorandum to Charles L. Schultze, budget bureau director, "National Anti-Poverty Plan," 25 October 1965, p. 8), cited in Burke and Burke, 19.

51.   The experiment in New Jersey was carried out by the University of Wisconsin's Institute for Research on Poverty. Steiner (op. cit., 96 [see note 4]) refers to it as "the most ambitious socioeconomic experiment ever undertaken in America without a base in legislation or executive order." See Neil Gilbert, Harry Specht, and Paul Terrell, *Dimensions of Social Welfare Policy*, 3rd ed. (Englewood Cliffs, N.J.: Prentice Hall, 1993), 76-77, for discussion of the results of the New Jersey experiments that found that the NIT did not seem to reduce work incentive. The later Seattle/Denver Income Maintenance Experiments "sharply contradicted" those findings after a longer period of study and a much larger sample. There is no evidence that the results of either experiment influenced federal policy. For the background on the New Jersey Graduated Work Experiments, see Burke and Burke, ibid., 21-22.

52.   "A Statement by Economists on Income Guarantees and Supplements" (n.d.). The originators were Professors John Kenneth Galbraith (Harvard), Paul Samuelson (MIT), Robert Lampman and Harold Watts (Wisconsin), and James Tobin (Yale). See Steiner, op. cit., 96 (see note 4).

53.   See, e.g., Robert Theobald, *Free Men and Free Markets* (New York: C. M. Potter, 1963). In his review of the NIT, Alvin L. Schorr (*Poor Kids* [New York: Basic Books, Inc., 1966], 130-131) observes that Theobald's proposal is "programmatically similar" to that of Friedman but that it has higher benefit levels and is designed to meet the problem of distributing national income.

54. Heineman Commission, op. cit., 7 (see note 43). Four members of the commission, either black persons or unionists, proposed higher guarantees (77-78, 86).

55. Heffernan, op. cit., 15 (see note 46).

56. Heineman Commission, op. cit., 59 (see note 43).

57. Ibid., 59-60.

58. Leonard Goodwin, *Do the Poor Want to Work? A Social-Psychological Study of Work Orientations* (Washington, D.C.: The Brookings Institution, 1972), 112.

59. Ibid., 113.

60. Heineman Commission, op. cit., 4 (see note 43).

61. Ibid.

62. Ibid.

63. Ibid., 7.

64. Burke and Burke, op. cit., 110 (see note 2).

65. Secretary of Health, Education, and Welfare Robert Finch, quoted in Moynihan, op. cit., 469 (see note 6). Nixon's chief of staff, H. R. Haldeman, described it as "a work-for-welfare program. It expanded Federal aid to the working poor, as well as the unemployed poor, but everyone who accepted aid also had to accept work or job training." In his diary entry for 14 July 1969, Haldeman wrote that it would be expensive to begin with, but gradually the incentive to get better jobs would take people off the welfare rolls. Or so we hoped." H. R. Haldeman, *The Haldeman Diaries: Inside the Nixon White House* (New York: G. P. Putnam's Sons, 1994), 71.

66. Nixon's 8 August 1969 television address introducing his Family Assistance Plan, cited in Moynihan, ibid., 224.

67. Burke and Burke, op. cit., 111 (see note 2); and Richard P. Nathan, "Family Assistance Plan: Workfare/Welfare," *New Republic*, 24 February 1973, 19.

68. Burke and Burke (ibid., 110-111) cite President Nixon's 1969 speech to the nation that announced the Family Assistance

Plan and explained what he meant by workfare. Haldeman (see note 65), however, used the phrase "work-for-welfare program."

69. Joel F. Handler and Yeheskel Hasenfeld, *The Moral Construction of Poverty: Welfare Reform in America* (Newbury Park, Calif.: Sage Publications, 1991), 147. Senator Russell Long, chair of the Senate Finance Committee, said FAP "looked like a reenactment of the work incentive program Congress wrote into law in 1967. . . . " (Moynihan, op. cit., 458 [see note 6].)

70. See, e.g., Marmor and Rein, op. cit., 16 (see note 5).

71. Marmor and Rein (ibid.) estimated that training funds would only accommodate 150,00 recipients out of 1.1 million required to register for work and provide child care to only 450,000 children.

72. Unless otherwise noted, descriptions of FAP are taken from "Welfare Reform Fact Sheet," prepared by the SocialSecurity Administration, August 1969, for general distribution, reprinted in Moynihan, op. cit., 229-235 (see note 6). Daniel P. Moynihan, who served as assistant for urban affairs and as executive secretary of the Urban Affairs Council in the Nixon administration, claims to have had major responsibilty for the development of FAP (p. 269).

73. In his report of that encounter, Nathan (op. cit., 20 [see note 67]) shows how a family aided under multiple social programs, each of which took a slice out of every additional dollar in earnings, could have faced a cumulative tax of well over 100%.

74. Heffernan, op. cit., 34 (see note 46).

75. Steiner, op. cit., 315 (see note 4).

76. U.S. House of Representatives, Committee on Ways and Means, *1996 Green Book: Background Material on Data and Programs within the Jurisdiction of the Committee on Ways and Means* (Washington, D.C.: U.S. Government Printing Office, 1996), table 8-28, 474.

77. Steiner, op. cit., 315 (see note 4).

78. This characterization of the Nixon proposals is by liberal social policy experts Theodore R. Marmor and Martin Rein, op. cit., 3 (see note 5). For more recent interpretations of Nixon's introduction of FAP, see Herbert S. Parmet, *Richard Nixon and His America* (Boston: Little, Brown and Company, 1990).

79. Rein and Heclo, op. cit., 61 (see note 30).

80. Moynihan, op. cit., 72-73 (see note 6).

81. On Moynihan's exaggerations and dubious use of statistical correlations, see Aaron, op. cit., 1729 (see note 46); and Joan Hoff-Wilson, "Outflanking the Liberals on Welfare," in Leon Friedman and William F. Levantrosser, eds., *Richard M. Nixon: Politician, President, Administrator* (New York: Greenwood Press, 1991), 89-91. Hoff-Wilson emphasizes that "underlying most of Moynihan's statistically based assumptions was the idea that a welfare crisis existed in New York City (and therefore would soon appear in the rest of the country)" (p. 90). On Moynihan's influence on the president, see Parmet, op. cit., 549 (see note 78); and Hoff-Wilson, 96.

82. Hoff-Wilson, ibid., 90.

83. Quadagno (op. cit., 123 [see note 2]) calls attention to Nixon's promises as a presidential candidate to rectify the just grievances of these "forgotten" Americans.

84. Ibid., 123-124.

85. Ibid., 124. Quadagno (pp. 124-125) points out that the Kerner Commission had reached a similar conclusion, and she also shows (p. 126) that training under FAP would be geared to males.

86. Ibid., 127-131.

87. Ibid., 97.

88. Moynihan, op. cit., 250-268 (see note 6); see also Burke and Burke, op. cit., 125-127 (see note 2).

89. Heineman Commission, op. cit., iii. (see note 43). In the preface to the commission's report, 12 November 1969, Heineman wrote: "We feel that the Family Assistance Program . . .

represents a major step forward towards meeting the needs that we have documented."

90. "By 1970, NWRO had begun to encourage liberals to join in political actions to defeat Nixon's FAP. Friends attending the NWRO conference that year were urged to 'Zap FAP.'" Guida West, *The National Welfare Rights Movement: The Social Protest of Poor Women* (New York: Praeger, 1981), 184.

91. Jeanette Washington, a NWRO leader from New York City, complained at a 1970 meeting with liberal groups: "The working poor would get money but they'd take it from us." Some welfare mothers also thought FAP threatened their "right" to refuse work out of the home, a right that had been established in most large northern cities where they had been designated as inappropriate for work assignments. Burke and Burke, op. cit., 150 (see note 2).

92. Johnnie Tillmon, "Welfare Is a Women's Issue," in Francine Klageburn, ed., *The First Ms. Reader* (New York: Warner Books, 1973), 57, 114, cited by West, op. cit., 312-313 (see note 90). Tillmon was correct about the elderly: SSI guaranteed them a cash grant of $140 a month, compared to $42 for a parent under FAP. For SSI benefits in 1974, see Levitan and Taggart, op. cit., 46 (see note 17). Regarding work standards, Piven and Cloward point out the bill provided that recipients could be compelled to work at jobs significantly below the minimum wage. Frances Fox Piven and Richard A. Cloward, *Poor People's Movements: Why They Succeed, How They Fail* (New York: Pantheon Books, 1977), 340.

93. Linda Gordon, "What Does Welfare Regulate?" *Social Research* 55 (Winter 1988), 625.

94. Dona Cooper Hamilton and Charles V. Hamilton, *The Dual Agenda: Race and Social Welfare Policies of Civil Rights Organizations* (New York: Columbia University Press, 1997), 191.

95. James T. Patterson, op. cit., 163-164 (see note 10).

96. Burke and Burke, op. cit., 147 (see note 2); Moynihan, op. cit., 378 (see note 6).

97. Moynihan, ibid., 378.

98. Burke and Burke (op. cit., 147 [see note 2]).

99. Senator Moynihan (op. cit., 465 [see note 6] cites a Senate speech of Long on FAP's work disincentives. Moynihan (p. 336) writes that "the term 'Black Brood Mares, Inc.,' was coined and ascribed to Russell B. Long, Democrat of Louisiana, majority whip and chairman of the Senate Finance Committee."

100. Lester M. Salamon, "The Stakes in the Rural South: Family Assistance," *New Republic*, 20 February 1971, 17-18.

101. The antipathy to expanding the rolls was shared by Long. For positions of Long, see Burke and Burke, op. cit., 177-178 (see note 2); and Moynihan, op. cit., 458-459, 523 (see note 6). Long said FAP was an "expansion of welfare to make 15 million people eligible . . . in addition to the 10 million now on the rolls" (Moynihan, p. 458). For Burns' positions, see Moynihan, 181-182; and Burke and Burke, 67.

102. Moynihan, ibid., 285-294. Paul Pierson points out that the NAM represents the more capital-intensive firms ("The Creeping Nationalization of Income Transfers in the United States, 1935-94," in Stephan Leibfried and Paul Pierson, eds., *European Social Policy: Between Integration and Fragmentation* [Washington, D.C.: Brookings Institution, 1995], 323).

103. Burke and Burke, op. cit. 134-135 (see note 2).

104. Piven and Cloward (op. cit., 336 [see note 92]) point to regressive features such as loss of procedural rights that recipients had won through protest and litigation in the 1960s, for example, a right to a hearing if terminated from the rolls. They also note that it would have required recipients to take jobs at less than the minimum wage.

105. Burke and Burke, op. cit., 178, 184-185 (see note 2).

106. Hamilton and Hamilton, op. cit., 179 (see note 94).

107. Ibid., 191.

108. Ibid., 192. Similarly, a group characterized by Richard Nathan (op. cit., 21 [see note 67]) as "theorists of income maintenance on the liberal side" were concerned that forcing black women to work in menial jobs, as housemaids for suburban whites, field

hands, and charwomen without opportunity for advancement "could produce a dangerous form of welfare servitude based on race." This, of course, was the opposite of what southern conservatives feared.

109. Burke and Burke, op. cit., 179 (see note 2). See also Moynihan (op. cit., 415 [see note 6]) reporting Republican Governor Nelson Rockefeller's favorable testimony on behalf of the National Governors' Conference.

110. "Nixon himself quickly tired of the struggle and refused to exert the pressure that might have secured passage of a modified bill. . . ." (Patterson, op. cit., 194-195 [see note 10); see also Trattner, op. cit., 308 (see note 10). Piven and Cloward (op. cit., 341 [see note 92]) assert that the opposition could have been overcome had Nixon persevered.

111. Haldeman, op. cit., 181 (see note 65).

112. Burke and Burke, op. cit., 184-185 [see note 2]). Labor Secretary James D. Hodgson and HEW Secretary Elliot Richardson are said to have pleaded with Nixon to deal with Ribicoff. Nineteen Republicans led by Senator Charles Percy also told him FAP would fail unless he compromised with Ribicoff and urged him to do so.

113. Ibid., 184.

114. Abe Ribicoff, "He Left at Half Time: The Politics of a Guaranteed Income by Daniel P. Moynihan," *New Republic,* 17 February 1973, 22.

115. Heffernan, op. cit., 22 (see note 46); Ribicoff, ibid., 26; and Parmet, op. cit., 559-560 (see note 78). According to John Erlichmann's Notes of Meetings with the President, 21 April 1972, Nixon said: "Flush it. . . . Blame it on the budget." Reported by Parmet, 559.

116. West, op. cit., 318 (see note 90).

117. Piven and Cloward (op. cit., 346-347 [see note 92]) hold that NWRO's influence over an important vote in the Senate Finance Committee was not so critical; had the vote gone the other way, opponents of FAP, like the Committee Chairman Senator Russell Long, would have staged a filibuster

for which there would have been insufficient votes for cloture. Piven and Cloward were evidently assuming the abdication of Nixon, who they thought could have overcome southern resistance.

118. Heffernan, op. cit., 121 (see note 46).

119. Moynihan, op. cit., 534 (see note 6). Liberals may have voted against FAP in a critical committee vote but, says Moynihan, were maneuvered into the position by the Southerners.

120. For Wiley's statement, West (op. cit., 318 [see note 90]) cites a memorandum of 12 October 1972 from Audrey Collom and John Kinney, "FAP is Not Dead: What Can We Do?" Collom was the staff assistant to the Chair of NWRO.

121. Ribicoff, op. cit. (see note 114). Heffernan (op. cit., 21 [see note 46]) considers this "approximately analogous to writing a definitive history of the Civil War just before the Battle of Gettysburg."

122. Burke and Burke, op. cit., 182 (see note 2).

123. Subtracting for his penchant for hyperbole, we can cite Moynihan's (op. cit., 75 [see note 6]) statement that both 1968 nominating conventions took place in "an atmosphere of siege, intrigue, even suspicion of subversion."

124. The 3-year legislative struggle at the national level "consumed NWRO's limited resources . . . , reduced ties with its local grass-roots base, exhausted its monies, antagonized some of its supporters and created internal friction between the national and local leadership" (West, op. cit., 375 [see note 90]). Piven and Cloward (op. cit., 343-344 [note 92]) counseled NWRO against lobbying at the federal level and urged it to "turn back to the streets and welfare centers, with the aged and the working poor as new targets."

125. Irwin Garfinkel and Sara S. McLanahan, *Single Mothers and Their Children: A New American Dilemma* (Washington, D.C.: The Urban Institute Press, 1986), 116. Pointing to early findings of the New Jersey experiments, which suggested that a guaranteed income did not reduce work efforts of recipients, Marmor and Rein (op. cit., 15 [see note 5]) write: "Thus the decision to require work and training tests was not sup-

ported by the best information then available, but rather by the belief that in order to win political support for FAP, the administration had to include in it sanctions as well as incentives."

126. Joseph Califano, *Governing America: An Insider's Report from the White House and the Cabinet* (New York: Simon and Schuster, 1981), 320-321.

127. See, e.g., Mark Blaug, "The Myth of the Old Poor Law and the Making of the New," *Journal of Economic History* 23 (1963), 151-184; and George R. Boyer, "The Old Poor Law and the Agricultural Labor Market in Southern England: An Empirical Analysis," *Journal of Economic History* 46 (March 1986), 113-135.

128. U.S. Congress, Congressional Budget Office, *The Administration's Welfare Reform Proposal: An Analysis of the Program for Better Jobs and Income* (Washington, D.C.: U.S. Government Printing Office, 1978), 16-17.

129. Patterson, op. cit., 206 (see note 10).

130. The Congressional Budget Office estimated that PBJI would add 3.5 million families to the welfare rolls (op. cit., 71 [see note 128]), would increase federal costs by $17.4 million, and reduce state and local expenditures by $3.4 million. Cumulative marginal tax rates would be high, for example, between 66 and 72%, for a single parent not expected to work, and 54% at about $6,000 earnings for a family of four with a member expected to work (p. 31).

131. Califano, op. cit., 322, 334-336, 344, 348 (see note 126).

132. Elizabeth Wickenden, "The Carter Welfare Reform Proposal— A Critical Analysis," *Washington Social Legislation Bulletin* (Child Welfare League of America) vol. 25, 26 September 1977.

133. The phrase, "veto coalition," is used by Paul Pierson, op. cit., 314-318 (see note 102).

134. Wickenden, op. cit., (see note 132). The proposal called for 1.4 million subsidized jobs, but these would replace 725,000 existing public service jobs under the Comprehensive Em-

ployment and Training Act, bringing the net job creation down to less than one-half the 1.4 million.

135. Center on Social Welfare Policy and Law, "Administration's Welfare Reform Plan," memorandum to welfare specialists, cited by West, op. cit., 149 (see note 90).

136. Steven R. Weisman, "Clash between Carter and Moynihan Slows Welfare Reform Plan," *New York Times*, 1 April 1979, 36.

137. Whereas FAP's cash guarantee, plus the value of food stamps, was 66% of the 1969 poverty threshold, PBJI's was 69% of the 1978 standard.

138. Toni Carabillo, "'Promises, Promises': A NOW Observer Assesses the Carter Presidency," *Do It NOW* 10 (September/October 1977), 13, cited in West, op. cit., 327 (see note 90). See also National Organization for Women, Inc., Testimony on Welfare Reform Submitted to the Subcommittee on Public Assistance of the Senate Finance Committee, Washington, D.C., 12 May 1978 (hereafter NOW).

139. NOW, ibid., 6.

140. Handler and Hasenfeld, op. cit., 163 (see note 69).

141. NOW, op. cit., 3-4 (see note 138).

142. Congressional Budget Office, op. cit., 31 (see note 128).

143. Axinn and Levin, op. cit, 284 (see note 12).

144. Califano, op. cit., 362 (see note 126).

145. Ibid., 364.

146. Ibid., 354.

147. Weisman, op. cit., 1, 36 (see note 136).

148. For an analysis of the SIME/DIME results, see Michael T. Hannan, Nancy B. Tuma, and Lyle P. Groenveld, "Income and Independence Effects on Marital Dissolution: Results from the Seattle and Denver Income-Maintenance Experiments, *American Journal of Sociology* 84 (1987), 611-633. The effect on marital disruption only seems to have occurred among families receiving the lowest level of benefits.

149. This section draws on Robert Cherry and Gertrude Schaffner Goldberg, "The Earned Income Tax Credit: What It Does and Doesn't Do," in Ron Baiman, Heather Boushey, and Dawn Saunders, eds., *Political Economy and Contemporary Capitalism: Radical Perspectives on Economic Theory and Policy* (Armonk, N.Y.: M. E. Sharpe, 2000). For examples of recent scholarly attention to the EITC, see: Jeffrey B. Liebman, "The Impact of the Earned Income Tax Credit on Incentives and Income Distribution," in James M. Poterba, ed., *Tax Policy and the Economy* (Cambridge, Mass.: M.I.T. Press, 1997); Martha N. Ozawa, "The Earned Income Tax Credit: Its Effect and Its Significance," *Social Service Review* 69 (December 1995), 563-582; John Karl Scholz, "Tax Policy and the Working Poor: The Earned Income Tax Credit," *Focus* 15 (Fall-Winter 1993-1994), 1-12; and Dennis L. Ventry, Jr., "The Collision of Tax and Welfare Politics: The Political History of the EITC," unpublished paper, University of California, Santa Barbara, undated.

150. U.S. Congress, Congressional Budget Office, *Reducing the Deficit: Spending and Revenue Options* (Washington, D.C.: Author, 1994), 200. Estimates for fiscal year 1997 were that the EITC would cost $25.7 billion, compared to $17.6 billion for combined expenditures of TANF and AFDC, which continued through part of the year. Estimates are from the Tax Analysis Division of the Congressional Budget Office (for EITC) and the Human Resources Cost Estimating Unit of the Congressional Budget Office (for AFDC/TANF), 8 August 1997. The AFDC/TANF estimate is based on a March 1997 estimate and may actually be high.

151. For discussion of Long's views and his leadership role in the enactment of the EITC, see Ventry, op. cit. (see note 149), 10-12. Policymakers wanted to ease the burden of Social Security payroll taxes that burdened lower wage workers.

152. Isaac Shapiro and Robert Greenstein, *Making Work Pay: The Unfinished Agenda* (Washington, D.C.: Center on Budget and Policy Priorities, 1993), 14-32; and Bradley R. Schiller, *The Economics of Poverty and Discrimination* (Englewood Cliffs, N.J.: Prentice-Hall, Inc., 1989), 105.

153. U.S. Bureau of the Census, *Workers with Low Earnings: 1964 to 1990*, Current Population Reports, Series P-60, No. 178 (Washington, D.C.: U.S. Government Printing Office, 1992), 2. Low annual earnings is defined as less than the poverty level for a 4-person family.

154. John Karl Scholz, op. cit., 2 (see note 149); and Sar A. Levitan, *Programs in Aid of the Poor*, 5th ed. (Baltimore: Johns Hopkins University Press, 1985), 51.

155. Russell Sykes, Memorandum to Partners in the EITC Coalition, Albany, N.Y., State Communities Aid Association, 8 June 1994.

156. Richard Perez-Peña, "Tax Credit Rise Urged for Poor in New York," *New York Times,* 2 March 1998, B4.

157. State Communities Aid Association, *The Earned Income Tax Credit: Extra Money for People Who Work* (Albany, N.Y.: Author, 1997).

158. Congressional Research Service, Library of Congress, *CRS Report for Congress: Cash and Noncash Benefits for Persons with Limited Income: Eligibility Rules, Recipient and Expenditure Data, FY 1996-FY 1998* (Washington, D.C., 15 December 1999), 67. The British social-welfare theorist, Richard Titmuss, described what the U.S. government calls "tax expenditures" as "fiscal welfare," and he used the term "iceberg phenomenon of social welfare" to suggest that these benefits are hidden from the budget process. "The Role of Redistribution in Social Policy," in Richard M. Titmuss, ed., *Commitment to Welfare* (New York: Pantheon Books, 1986).

159. See Ventry, op. cit. (see note 149), 26-30 for discussion of the expansion of the EITC. For work that shows that benefits that are seen as earned are a distinct political advantage, see Robert Greenstein, "Universal and Targeted Approaches to Relieving Poverty: An Alternative View," in Christopher Jencks and Paul E. Peterson, eds., *The Urban Underclass* (Washington, D.C.: The Urban Institute Press, 1991); and Fay Lomax Cook and Edith J. Barrett, *The American Welfare State: The Views of Congress and the Public* (New York: Columbia University Press, 1992).

160. Richard V. Burkhauser and Andrew J. Glenn, "Public Poli-
     cies for the Working Poor: The Earned Income Tax Credit
     versus Minimum Wage Legislation," unpublished paper,
     1993. Available from Employment Policy Institute, Wash-
     ington, D.C.

161. Rebecca M. Blank and Patricia Ruggles, "When Do Women
     Use AFDC and Food Stamps: The Dynamics of Eligibility
     versus Participation," photocopy, Washington, D.C., Urban
     Institute, 1993, cited in Scholz, op. cit., 4 (see note 149).

162. Shapiro and Greenstein, op. cit., 26-29 (see note 152).

163. Lynn M. Olson with Audrey Davis, "The Earned Income Tax
     Credit: Views from the Street Level," unpublished paper,
     March 1994. (Evanston, Ill.: Northwestern University, Cen-
     ter for Urban Affairs and Policy Research), WP-94-1.

164. See, e.g., Bruce D. Meyer and Dan T. Rosenbaum, "Welfare,
     the Earned Income Tax Credit, and the Labor Supply of Single
     Mothers," manuscript, 1998. (Evanston, Ill.: Northwestern
     University); and Liebman, op. cit. (see note 149).

165. For review of this evidence, see Robert Cherry, "Let's Have
     an Adequate Minimum Wage," *Uncommon Sense* 10, New
     York, National Jobs for All Coalition, June 1996. The esti-
     mates of job loss by opponents of minimum-wage hikes have
     been politically effective but greatly overestimated, and some
     recent evidence suggests there may not be any loss at all.
     For a study that showed no effect on Texas fast-food restau-
     rants after the minimum wage was increased to $4.25 an hour,
     see Lawrence Katz and Allan Krueger, "The Effects of the
     Minimum Wage on the Fast Food Industry," *Industrial and
     Labor Relations Review* 46 (October 1992), 6-21. Cherry also
     points out that with a higher minimum wage, some job loss
     does not harm workers, for they are able to work fewer weeks
     to obtain the same yearly income.

166. For a recent work that opposes minimum-wage increases on
     this and other grounds, see Daniel Shaviro, "The Minimum
     Wage, the Earned Income Tax Credit, and Optimal Subsidy
     Policy," *University of Chicago Law Review* 64 (Spring 1997),
     405-482. Cherry, ibid., points out that minimum-wage pro-
     ponents consider Department of Labor studies that find that

small proportions of minimum-wage hikes go to poor households are underestimates, for they include only workers paid
at an hourly rate. He cites Burkhauser and Glenn (op. cit.
[see note 160]) who found that if all workers whose pay was
below the minimum are included, including those not currently covered by the law, an estimated 33% of the minimum-wage increase would have gone to the working poor,
or about twice the estimate of the Labor Department, with
an additional 16% to the near poor.

167. Shapiro and Greenstein, op. cit., 11 (see note 152).

168. Minimum wage data are from the U.S. Department of La-
bor, Bureau of Labor Statistics, and the poverty standards
are from the U.S. Department of Commerce, Bureau of the
Census. See also Isaac Shapiro, *No Escape: The Minimum
Wage and Poverty* (Washington, D.C.: Center on Budget and
Policy Priorities, 1987), Appendix A, 19.

169. When AFDC was repealed, in August 1996, the year-round,
full-time earnings of a minimum-wage worker, plus the maximum credit of $3,556, was $12,396 or 98.7% of the 3-per-
son poverty standard. Later that year, the minumum wage
was raised, and the minimum wage and the EITC rose to
107.0% of the standard.

170. This, as Greenstein and Shapiro point out, does not mean
that the EITC provides more support to poor families than
other government programs such as TANF and food stamps,
but instead that a larger proportion of families receiving these
benefits have incomes further below the poverty line than
EITC recipients. Robert Greenstein and Isaac Shapiro, *New
Research Findings on the Effects of the Earned Income Tax
Credit* (Washington, D.C.: Center on Budget and Policy Priorities, 1998), 7-9.

171. Leatha Lamison-White, *Poverty in the United States: 1996*
U.S. Bureau of the Census, Current Population Reports, P60-
198 (Washington, D.C.: U.S. Government Printing Office,
1997), table C-3, C-8-C-9.

172. Perez-Peña, op. cit. (see note 156).

173. Liebman, op. cit. (see note 149).

174. *The Report of the Committee on Economic Security, 50th Anniversary Edition* (Washington, D.C.: National Conference on Social Welfare, 1985), 10.

175. Hamilton and Hamilton cite Congressional testimony of representatives of the National Association for the Advancement of Colored People and the National Urban League that estimated the proportions of Negro workers not covered by the social insurances as a result of the exclusion of these two occupations as one-half and two-thirds, respectively. Hamilton and Hamilton, op. cit., 30-31 (see note 94).

176. In her analysis of the politics of employment policy, Margaret Weir (*Politics and Jobs: The Boundaries of Employment Policy in the United States* [Princeton University Press, 1992], 139) sees the Humphrey-Hawkins bill as "a partisan measure, supported by the Democratic leadership to pressure the Republican executive and to provide a galvanizing issue in the upcoming presidential campaign."

177. Gary Mucciaroni, *The Political Failure of Employment Policy, 1945-1982* (Pittsburgh: University of Pittsburgh Press, 1990), 76.

178. See, e.g., Gertrude S. Goldberg, "New Nonprofessionals in the Human Services: An Overview," in Charles Grosser, William Henry, and James Kelly, eds., *Nonprofessionals in the Human Services* (San Francisco: Josey-Bass, 1969).

179. Arthur Pearl and Frank Riessman, *New Careers for the Poor* (Glencoe, Ill.: The Free Press, 1965).

180. Kerner Commission, op. cit., 234 (see note 33).

181. Mucciaroni, op. cit., 81 (see note 177).

182. Ibid., 81; and Helen Ginsburg, *Full Employment and Public Policy: The United States and Sweden* (Lexington, Mass.: Lexington Books, 1983), 50.

183. Sar A. Levitan and Frank Gallo, *Spending to Save: Expanding Employment Opportunities* (Washington, D.C.: Center for Social Policy Studies, George Washington University, 1992), 8; and Mucciaroni, op. cit., 83 (see note 177).

184. Weir, op. cit., 118 (see note 176); and Levitan and Gallo, ibid., 8.

185. Mucciaroni, op. cit., 168 (see note 177).

186. Ibid., 85-86.

187. Ibid., 168-169.

188. Philip Harvey points out that while econometric studies conducted early in the CETA program found that the substitution effect was large, later case study and survey research suggest that the econometric studies overstated the problem. See Philip Harvey, *Securing the Right to Employment: Social Welfare Policy and the Unemployed in the United States* (Princeton, N.J.: Princeton University Press, 1989), 80. Ginsburg points out that critics of CETA, like the Ford Council of Economic Advisors, consistently used the high estimates of substitution. See Helen Ginsburg, "Down and Out: Public Policies toward the Jobless and the Disabled, *Policy Studies Review* 4 (May 1985), 754. For the point about preserving rather than substituting for local services, see Nancy Rose, "Workfare vs. Fair Work: Public Job Creation," *Uncommon Sense* 17 (New York: National Jobs for All Coalition, May 1977).

189. Paul Bullock, *CETA at the Crossroads: Employment Policy and Politics* (Los Angeles: Institute of Industrial Relations, University of California), 115.

190. Mucciaroni, op. cit., 184 (see note 177).

191. Helen Ginsburg, op. cit., 753 (see note 188).

192. Levitan and Gallo (op. cit., 20 [see note 183]) report that two major, independent evaluations of CETA sponsored by the Labor Department concluded that "the overwhelming majority of public service employment activities appeared to be beneficial."

193. Bullock, op. cit., 55, and passim (see note 189); and Mucciaroni, op. cit., 185 (see note 177).

194. Mucciaroni (ibid., 168) points out that although CETA expenditures dropped from $8.9 billion in 1980 to $7.6 billion in 1981, they were still higher than during the Nixon and Ford years.

195. Cited by Harvey L. Schantz and Richard H. Schmidt, "The Evolution of Humphrey-Hawkins," *Policy Studies Journal* 8 (Winter 1979), 369.

196. Ginsburg, op. cit., 63 (see note 182).

197. Weir, op. cit., 134 (see note 176).

198. Ibid., 135.

199. Ibid., 136.

200. Ibid., 138.

201. Ginsburg, op. cit., 65 (see note 182).

202. Ibid.; Schantz and Schmidt, op. cit., 372 (see note 195). In later versions of the bill, interim unemployment targets were set: 3% in 18 months, later in 4 years, and finally adult employment to 3% and overall unemployment to 4% within 5 years.

203. Schantz and Schmidt, ibid., 374.

204. Mucciaroni, op. cit., 182 (see note 177).

205. The unemployment rate in 1982 was 9.7%. In January 1984, it was up to 11.4%, and the annual average was 9.6%. U.S. Department of Labor, op. cit., table A-31, 489 (see note 1).

206. Harvey, op. cit., 110 (see note 188).

207. Ginsburg, op. cit., 141 (see note 182).

208. Weir, op. cit., 136 (see note 176).

209. Melvyn Dubofsky, "Jimmy Carter and the End of the Politics of Productivity," in Gary M. Fin and Hugh Davis Graham, eds., *The Carter Presidency: Policy Choices in the Post-New Deal Era* (Lawrence, Kan.: University Press of Kansas, 1998), 103. See also, Ginsburg, op. cit., 141 (see note 182).

210. Ginsburg, ibid., 141.

211. Dubofsky, op. cit., 100 (see note 209).

212. Weir, op. cit., 138 (see note 176).

213. Ginsburg, op. cit., 142 (see note 182).

214. Schantz and Schmidt, op. cit., 371-372 (see note 195).

215. Ginsburg, op. cit., 140 (see note 182).

216. Weir, op. cit., 140 (see note 176).

217. Ginsburg, op. cit., 63 (see note 182).

218. In the last Johnson budget (1969), public assistance amounted to 1.3% of GDP, compared to 2.4% for the last Nixon budget (1974), an increase of 85%. *Social Security Bulletin, Annual Statistical Supplement, 1969,* table 1, 23; *Social Security Bulletin: Annual Statistical Supplement, 1974,* table 1, 39.

219. Under the Carter administration, public-assistance expenditures dropped from 2.9% of GDP in 1977 to 2.8% in 1981. *Social Security Bulletin, Annual Statistical Supplement, 1977-79,* table 1, 53; and Ann Kallman Bixby, "Public Social Welfare Expenditures, Fiscal Year 1991," *Social Security Bulletin* 57 (Spring 1994), table 2, 101.

220. U.S. Congress, Congressional Budget Office, *The Economic and Budget Outlook: Fiscal Years 1997-2006* (Washington, D.C.: U.S. Government Printing Office, 1996), table E-9, 141.

CHAPTER 7
THE FINAL ACT: WELFARE'S REPEAL

1. David A. Stockman, *The Triumph of Politics: Why the Reagan Revolution Failed* (New York: Harper & Row Publishers, 1986), 8.

2. Paul Pierson, *Dismantling the Welfare State? Reagan, Thatcher, and the Politics of Retrenchment* (Cambridge: Cambridge University Press, 1995), 116; Kevin Phillips, *The Politics of Rich and Poor: Wealth and the American Electorate in the Reagan Aftermath* (New York: Harper Perennial, 1990), 76-115.

3. Phillips, ibid., 76.

4. William Greider, "The Education of David Stockman," *Atlantic Monthly* (December 1981), 46.

5. Phillips, op cit., 82-83 (see note 2).

6. Michael B. Katz, *In the Shadow of the Poorhouse: A Social History of Welfare in America* (New York: Basic Books/ HarperCollins, 1986), 288.

7.   Phillips, op. cit., 84 (see note 2).

8.   Citizens for Tax Justice, *Corporate Income Taxes in the Reagan Years* (Washington, D.C.: Author, 1984).

9.   Robert S. McIntyre, *Inequality and the Federal Budget Deficit* (Washington, D.C.: Citizens for Tax Justice, September 1991), 12.

10. Phillips, op. cit., 78 (see note 2).

11. At various times in American history, corporations have lobbied for regulation, and consumer advocates have advocated deregulation. A minority of Democratic liberals during the Carter administration, along with consumer advocate, Ralph Nader, had lobbied for some deregulation as a means of breaking up monopolies. See Alan Stone, "State and Market: Economic Regulation and the Great Productivity Debate," in Thomas Ferguson and Joel Rogers, eds., *The Hidden Election: Politics and Economics in the 1980 Presidential Campaign* (New York: Pantheon Books, 1981), 237-247.

12. John Allen Poulos, "The S & L Tab," *New York Times*, 28 June 1991, A25; Robert Sherrill, "The Looting Decade: S & Ls, Big Banks and Other Triumphs of Capitalism," *The Nation,* 19 November 1990, 589.

13. Phillips, op. cit., 94-101 (see note 2).

14. Ibid., 108.

15. Ibid., 112-113.

16. Stockman, op. cit., 8 (see note 1).

17. Stockman quoted in Greider, op. cit., 27 (see note 4).

18. Stockman, op. cit., 181 (see note 1).

19. While cuts at the national level were severe, Pierson, op. cit., 118-119 (see note 2) attributes the steep reductions in AFDC to retrenchment at the state level where benefit levels are set. Advocates of the poor were not very well organized at this level, and benefits were not indexed to inflation, which made it easy for states to allow their purchasing power to erode. The interaction of AFDC benefits (a joint federal-state program) and food stamps (a federal program) gave states a

disincentive to raise welfare benefits, as that would reduce their food-stamp allotments; and finally, fear of becoming a "welfare magnet" deterred states from raising benefits.

20. In Chapter 6, we argued that making CETA for the poor alone was a political kiss of death.

21. The Extended Benefit program provided benefits to the unemployed beyond the normal cutoff point in times of recession. The virtual dismantling of this program in 1980 and 1981 substantially reduced the portion of the unemployed who got benefits during recessions from three-fourths and two-thirds during 2 years of severe recession in the mid-1970s to less than one-half during 1982 and 1983 when unemployment was nearly double-digit, and to one-third in the 3 subsequent recession years of the 1980s. Stephen A. Woodbury and M. A. Rubin, "The Duration of Benefits," in Christopher J. O'Leary and Stephen A. Wandner, eds., *Unemployment Insurance in the United States: Analysis of Policy Issues* (Kalamazoo, Mich.: J.W.E. Upjohn Institute for Employment Research, 1997); Isaac Shapiro and Marion E. Nichols, *Far from Fixed: Analysis of the Unemployment Insurance System* (Washington, D.C.: Center on Budget and Policy Priorities, 1992); and Pierson, op. cit., 119 (see note 2).

22. Congress of the United States, Congressional Budget Office, *An Analysis of the President's Budgetary Proposals for the Fiscal Year 1984* (Washington, D.C.: U.S. Government Printing Office, 1983), 89.

23. Memo from an officer of the Z. Smith Reynolds Foundation: "General Observations, Conservative Progress Briefing," 18-19 June, 1981. Memo in possession of Sheila Collins.

24. Katz, op. cit., 286 (see note 6). The appeal court noted that "far from raising questions of judicial interference in executive actions, this case presents the reverse constitutional problem: the executive branch defying the court and undermining what are perhaps the fundamental precepts of our constitutional system—the separation of powers and respect for the law." Associated Press, "U.S. Is Ordered to Pay Benefits to Many It Cut," *New York Times*, 23 February 1984, A14. See also Bob Wyrick and Patrick Owens, "The Disability Nightmare," *Newsday*, 20 March 1983, 6.

25. General Accounting Office, *An Evaluation of the 1981 AFDC Changes: Final Report* (July 1985), cited in U.S. Congress, Congressional Budget Office, *CBO Staff Memorandum: Forecasting AFDC Caseloads, with Emphasis on Economic Factors* (July 1993), 8, footnote 8.

26. Gertrude Schaffner Goldberg, *Government Money for Everyday People: A Guide to Income Support Programs,* 4th ed. (Needham Heights, Mass.: Ginn Press, 1991), 1. See footnote 4 for sources of estimates.

27. *Don't Stand There and Kill Us: A People's Report on AFDC,* prepared by Social Welfare Cluster, Social Services and Human Resources Department, National Urban League, May 1982, 26.

28. Pierson has suggested that one of the reasons why both the Reagan and Thatcher governments tried but failed to radically restructure means-tested programs was because the pain caused would have been too visible. "Cutbacks are facilitated when governments can somehow reduce their salience." Pierson, op. cit., 117, 126 (see note 2).

29. Stockman, op. cit., 204 (see note 1).

30. Later in the decade, certain universal entitlement programs, like Medicare, were somewhat reduced. Robert Greenstein, "Approaches to Relieving Poverty," in Christopher Jencks and Paul Peterson, eds., *The Urban Underclass* (Washington, D.C.: The Brookings Institution, 1991), 440.

31. Goldberg, op. cit. (see note 26) pointed out that during this time, falling real wages and demographic changes such as increased proportions of persons over the age of 65 and of families with a female householder and no husband present were increasing the need for social welfare.

32. Ibid.

33. Greider, op. cit., 35 (see note 4).

34. See, for example, Stephen P. Erie, Martin Rein, and B. Wiget, "Women and the Reagan Revolution: Thermidor for the Social Welfare Economy," in Irene Diamond, ed., *Families, Politics and Public Policies* (New York: Longman, Green, 1983), 94-119.

35. California's Community Work Experience Program (CWEP), initiated by Governor Reagan in 1972, was shut down in 1976. Out of some 70,000 welfare recipients deemed suitable for work, only 2,000 were actually placed in make-work jobs such as raking leaves, and only 400 graduated to "real" jobs. Robert Kuttner and Phyllis Freeman, "Women to the Workhouse: The Latest in Family Policy," *Working Papers* (November-December 1982), 18-19. Working Papers was published by the Trusteeship Institute, Cambridge, Mass., between 1981 and 1983. Paul Pierson puts the number even lower—at only 1,000 jobs at its peak. Pierson, op. cit., 123 (see note 2).

36. Pierson, ibid., 122-123.

37. Judith M. Gueron, *Reforming Welfare with Work*, occasional paper No. 2 (New York: Ford Foundation Project on Social Welfare and the American Future, 1987), 13.

38. Figures calculated by authors from Table 5.6, "AFDC Maximum Benefit in Constant 1996 Dollars for a Three-Person Family by State for Selected Dates," in *Aid to Families with Dependent Children: The Baseline* (Washington, D.C.: Office of Human Services Policy, Office of the Assistant Secretary for Planning and Evaluation, U.S. Department of Health and Human Services, June 1998), 79.

39. Robert D. Reischauer, "The Welfare Reform Legislation: Directions for the Future," in Phoebe H. Cottingham and David T. Ellwood, eds., *Welfare Policy for the 1990s* (Cambridge, Mass.: Harvard University Press, 1989), 10.

40. Ibid., p. 12, citing R. Y. Shapiro, K. D. Patterson, J. Russell, and J. T. Young, "The Polls: Public Assistance," *Public Opinion Quarterly* 51 (Spring 1987), 120-130. Cook and Barrett surveyed a random sample of adults in the late 1980s. Asking questions about Medicare, SSI, Social Security, Medicaid, Unemployment Insurance, AFDC, and food stamps, they found that despite the Reagan administration's relentless attacks on "big government," the welfare state in general was overwhelmingly supported by the American public. According to Barrett and Cook, the "most striking result is how few respondents believed benefits should be reduced for any of the programs. . . ." Although food stamps and AFDC enjoyed less support than

insurance and means-tested programs for the elderly, 85%
of respondents favored maintaining or increasing expenditures
for AFDC and 75% supported maintaining or expanding food
stamps. However, just over one-third of respondents said they
were willing to write a letter or sign a petition against AFDC
spending cuts, compared to about one-half for Medicaid and
over three-fifths for Social Security. Of course, poll support
and active support are two different things. Fay Lomax Cook
and Edith J. Barrett, *Support for the American Welfare State:
The Views of Congress and the Public* (New York: Columbia
University Press, 1992), 62, 64.

41.   Mark H. Greenberg, "Welfare Reform in an Uncertain Environment," paper presented at Planning a State/Local Welfare Strategy after the 104th Congress, organized by the Carnegie
Corporation-funded project, Confronting the New Politics
of Child and Family Policies in the United States, 9 February 1996 (Washington, D.C.: Center for Law and Social Policy,
1996), 6.

42.   States had the option, however, of making the child age option
1, instead of 3 years.

43.   *Comparison of Prior Law and the Personal Responsibility
and Work Opportunity Reconciliation Act of 1996 (P.L. 104-
193),* U.S. Government, Department of Health and Human
Services website (7 June 1998) http://aspe.os.dhhs.gov/hsp/
isp/reform.htm. See also L. Jerome Gallagher, Megan Gallagher,
Kevin Perese, Susan Schreiber, and Keith Watson, *One Year
after Federal Welfare Reform: A Description of State Temporary Assistance for Needy Families (TANF).* Decisions as
of October 1997 (Washington, D.C.: The Urban Institute, June
1998), 23-24.

44.   Thomas Downey, quoted in Howard Jacob Karger and David
Stoesz, "Welfare Reform: Maximum Feasible Exaggeration,"
Tikkun 4 (March/April 1989), 23.

45.   Felicia Kornbluh, "Subversive Potential, Coercive Intent: Women,
Work and Welfare in the '90s," *Social Policy* 21 (Spring 1991),
31; see also Greenberg, op. cit., 11 (see note 41).

46.   National Urban League, *A Case Study on the National Urban League's Policy Initiative on Welfare Reform and the*

Legislative Process (Washington, D.C.: Office of the Vice President for Washington Operations, National Urban League, December 1988), 15.

47. Karger and Stoesz, op. cit., 23 (see note 44).

48. Kornbluh, op. cit., 24 (see note 45).

49. Ibid. Prior to the law, only 27 states made welfare available to two-parent families.

50. In 1996, the last year of the AFDC program, only 6.6% of all AFDC families comprised two parents. Percentage calculated by authors from: *Aid to Families with Dependent Children: The Baseline*, table 2.1, "Trends in Total AFDC Enrollments, 1962-1996," 15; and table 2.6, "AFDC Unemployed Parent-Program Caseload by State, Selected Fiscal Years 1965-1996," op. cit., 26-27 (see note 38).

51. Karger and Stoesz, op. cit., 118 (see note 47).

52. Kornbluh., op. cit., 37 (see note 45).

53. Governor Bill Clinton and Governor Michael Castle, "The States and Welfare Reform," *Intergovernmental Perspectives* 17 (Spring 1991), 17.

54. Ibid., 18.

55. In his review of studies of state and local tax incentives meant to attract or retain businesses, Robert Lynch concludes that "the empirical evidence fails to support the ambitions of public officials to 'grow the economy' by shrinking the public sector and reducing taxes." In fact, the opposite is the case. Public spending on infrastructure and public services is a far more important contributor to business location than tax benefits. Robert G. Lynch, *Do State and Local Tax Incentives Work?* (Washington, D.C.: Economic Policy Institute, 1996). http://epn.org/epi/epi/eplync.html.

56. MDRC researchers found that most states did not even engage in workfare but instead in mandatory job search. Gueron, op. cit., 13-38 (note 37). See also Sar Levitan and Isaac Shapiro, "What's Missing in Welfare Reform?" *Challenge* 30 (July-August 1987), 41-48; Kenneth Jost, "Welfare Reform," *Congressional Quarterly Researcher*, 10 (April 1992), 324. The

only exception to the generally modest or inconsequential outcomes of welfare-to-work programs may have been the Child Assistance Program begun in several counties by New York State. An early assessment of this program in 1992 showed some progress in lifting the incomes of welfare mothers but only because it was nonpunitive and allowed them to keep a large proportion of their welfare grant even after getting a job. Kevin Sack, "Welfare Experiment Showing Signs of Success," *New York Times*, 11 June 1992, B1.

57.   James Riccio et al., *GAIN: Benefits, Costs and Three-Year Impacts of a Welfare-to-Work Program,* cited in U.S. General Accounting Office, *Welfare to Work: Current AFDC Program Not Sufficiently Focused on Employment,* GAO/HEHS-95-28, Report to the Chairman, Committee on Finance, U.S., Senate, Washington, D.C., December 1994, 19; and Theresa L. Amott and Jean Kluver, *ET: A Model for the Nation?* (Philadelphia: American Friends Service Committee, September 1986).

58.   Judith M. Gueron and Edward Pauly, *From Welfare to Work* (New York: Russell Sage Foundation, 1991). The authors note, however, that the study findings may not be generalizable to the current workfare debate, since the reviewed programs took place in a different political context. The General Accounting Office found that only a small percentage (11% in an average month) of welfare recipients from 1991 to 1993 were served by the JOBS program, and that the program's employment levels were weak. U.S. General Accounting Office, ibid., 2.

59.   U.S. General Accounting Office, *Welfare to Work: States Begin JOBS, but Fiscal and Other Problems May Impede Their Progress,* GAO/HRD-91-106, Washington, D.C., 27 September 1991.

60.   In 1992, 9.4 million people were counted as officially unemployed. This represented an official unemployment rate of 7.4%. Another 30.1 million were working part-time, and 6.2 million wanted jobs and did not have them. Adjusting for part-time employment, Dembo and Morehouse calculated the underemployment rate at 14.3%, almost double the official unemployment rate. David Dembo and Ward Morehouse, *The Underbelly of the U.S. Economy: Joblessness and the*

Pauperization of Work in America (New York: The Apex Press, 1993), 5.

61. Liz McNichol and Iris J. Lav, *Will States Maintain the Safety Net? Evidence from Bad Times and Good* (Washington, D.C.: Center on Budget and Policy Priorities, 28 February 1996), 2.

62. Greenberg, op. cit., 16 (see note 41).

63. Joel Handler, *The Poverty of Welfare Reform* (New Haven: Yale University Press, 1995), 65.

64. Lawrence Mishel and Jared Bernstein, *The State of Working America 1994-95* (Armonk, N.Y.: M.E. Sharpe, 1994), 207.

65. By early 1995, only 7% of single parents on AFDC were working full- or part-time, according to the Department of Health and Human Services. However, as we point out in Chapter 8, many may have been working at underground jobs to make ends meet. Meanwhile, the recession had increased the welfare rolls. Jeffrey L. Katz, "GOP Welfare Plan: Self-Help, and Leave It to the States," *Congressional Quarterly* 53 (25 February 1995), 614.

66. Telephone inverview with Sharon Daly, vice president for Social Policy, Catholic Charities USA, Washington, D.C., 30 July 1998.

67. Polls by the Wisconsin Policy Research Institute and the *Milwaukee Journal* showed 81% and 70% approval ratings for Learnfare. Kenneth Jost, op. cit., 325 (see note 56).

68. Transcript of Bush's State of the Union Message: "Let's Build on Our Strengths," *New York Times*, 29 January 1992, 17A.

69. Telephone interview with Mark H. Greenberg, senior staff attorney, Center for Law and Social Policy, Washington, D.C., 28 July 1998. According to Greenberg, heretofore welfare had been a low priority for Bush. After this, almost anything the states wanted to do was approved.

70. Between 1989 and 1991, the AFDC caseload rose 16%. Congressional Budget Office, "A Preliminary Analysis of Growing Caseloads in AFDC," CBO staff memorandum, December 1991. Mark Greenberg recalls that the CBO memorandum was influential because it suggested that the economy was

not the principal factor driving the caseload increase. It probably added to the perception that the system was out of control and needed fundamental change (telephone interview with Mark Greenberg, senior staff attorney, Center on Law and Social Policy, Washington, D.C., 4 August 1998). A subsequent (1993) CBO analysis of the rising caseload concluded that the economy had indeed been responsible for as much as 40% of the rise. About one-quarter was attributed to the recession and relatively weak economy that preceded and followed it, while another 15% could be explained by the weak demand in this recovery for low-wage service workers along with changes in immigration laws and Medicaid outreach initiatives. Congressional Budget Office, "Forecasting AFDC Caseloads with an Emphasis on Economic Factors," CBO staff memorandum, July 1993, Washington, D.C.

71.   In polls that gave respondents more options about the meaning of welfare "reform," there was no real support for the kinds of harsh proposals the Republicans had in mind and considerable support for a kinder and more balanced approach. In an extensive study of public attitudes toward welfare conducted in November 1993 by Peter D. Hart Research Associates and American Viewpoint (a Democratic and Republican firm, respectively), researchers found a conservative diagnosis about poverty and welfare (i.e., that it was caused by lack of individual effort more than circumstances) but no support for conservative prescriptions for reforming the system. Geoffrey Carin, Guy Molyneux, and Linda DiVall, *Public Attitudes toward Welfare Reform: A Summary of Key Research Findings* (Peter D. Hart Research Associates and American Viewpoint), 1993. In a Time/CNN poll taken in the second week of December 1994, 52% of the public, when asked if they thought welfare spending should be reduced, said, "yes," but the same percentage also said it would be unfair to end payments after 2 years to people who had no other sources of income, and 69% said the government should spend more money in the short run to train welfare recipients for jobs. A majority also favored cutting a variety of subsidies that went to upper income Americans. Richard Lacayo, "Down on the Downtrodden," *Time*, 19 December 1994, 30-34. See also Cook and Barrett, op. cit. (see note 40).

72. Using 1986 dollars, the value of the minimum wage in 1968 was $5.04, compared with $3.35 in 1986.

73. Michael J. Camasso, Carol Harvey, Radha Jahgannathan, and Mark Killingsworth, *A Report on the Impact of New Jersey's Family Development Program: Results from a Pre-Post Analysis of AFDC Case Heads from 1990-1996*, submitted to the USDHHS Administration for Children and Families and the Assistant Secretary for Planning and Evaluation (New Brunswick, N.J.: Rutgers University, December 1997).

74. Jason DeParle, "States' Eagerness to Experiment on Welfare Jars Administration," *New York Times*, 14 April 1994, A1.

75. Jason DeParle, "Despising Welfare, Pitying Its Young," *New York Times*, 18 December 1994, Sec. 4, 5.

76. Cecilia W. Dugger, "Iowa Plan Tries to Cut Off the Cash," *New York Times*, 7 April 1995, A1.

77. Jason DeParle, "The Sorrow and Surprises, after a Welfare Plan Ends," *New York Times*, 14 April 1992, A1.

78. Peter T. Kilborn, "Michigan Puts Poor to Work but Gains Appear Precarious," *New York Times*, 24 October 1995, A1.

79. Telephone interview with Clifford Johnson, senior fellow, Center on Budget and Policy Priorities, Washington D.C., 19 August 1998.

80. According to Patricia Reuss, only a handful of organizations—her own organization—NOW Legal Defense and Education Fund (NOWLDEF), NOW, and the Institute for Women's Policy Research —spoke out during the early stages of the welfare debate. By the time most got into the fray (after the 1994 Republican victory), it was too late. Telephone interview with Patricia Reuss, senior policy analyst, NOWLDEF, 21 July 1998. Deborah Weinstein, director of the Family Income Division of the Children's Defense Fund, stated that CDF had opposed all versions of welfare reform that included time limits. Memo from Deborah Weinstein, 3 December 1999.

81. Peter Edelman, " The Worst Thing Bill Clinton Has Done," *Atlantic Monthly*, March 1997, 44.

82.   Robert Sheer, "Trouble Still in Forest City," *The Nation*, 256 (22 March 1993), 370.

83.   Jason DeParle, "The Ellwoods and the Price of Reform," *New York Times Magazine*, 8 December 1996, 63 ff. Ellwood (p. 99), would later call President Clinton's use of the campaign phrase, "to end welfare as we know it," "vacuous and incendiary."

84.   Edelman, op. cit. (see note 81).

85.   DeParle, op. cit., 100 (see note 83).

86.   By the mid-1980s, the policy elite had concluded that only those deemed incapable of working—the elderly and the disabled—should be eligible to receive cash assistance. Sheldon Danziger, "Fighting Poverty and Reducing Welfare Dependency," in Cottingham and Ellwood, op. cit., 42 (see note 39).

87.   Mark H. Greenberg, senior staff attorney at the Center for Law and Social Policy, recalls that Health and Human Service administrators would try to negotiate with states, always with the knowledge that the White House would say, "yes." So they were negotiating with one hand tied behind their backs. Greenberg interview, op. cit. (see note 69).

88.   Quoted in Robert Pear, "A Welfare Revolution Hits Home, but Quietly," *New York Times*, 13 August 1995, Sec. 4, 1.

89.   Quoted in Peter T. Kilborn and Sam Howe Verhovek, "Clinton's Shift Ends Torturous Journey," *New York Times*, 2 August 1996, A18.

90.   Paul Leonard and Robert Greenstein, *Life under the Spending Caps: The Clinton Fiscal Year 1995 Budget* (Washington, D.C.: Center on Budget and Policy Priorities, April 1994). Under both the 1990 and 1993 budget acts, any action by Congress to increase an entitlement program or cut taxes would have to be "paid for" through an offsetting entitlement reduction or tax increase.

91.   Jason DeParle, "Clinton Sees Welfare Costing $6 Billion a Year," *New York Times*, 10 March 1994, A1; Jason DeParle, "A Draft Proposal on Welfare Raises Cabinet Concerns," *New York Times*, 23 March 1994, A1; Jason DeParle, "Welfare

Planners Struggle Over Final Sticking Points," *New York Times*, 31 March 1994, B6; and Jason DeParle, "Analysis Increases the Cost of Clinton's Welfare Plan," *New York Times*, 3 December 1994, A11.

92. In their study of voting patterns in the 1992 and 1994 elections, Ruy Teixeira and Joel Rogers challenge popular assumptions that the electorate has become more ideologically conservative. Rather, they conclude that the chief cause of voter volatility is declining living standards and the persistent failure of either party to successfully address the problem. The group that seems to swing back and forth between the Republican, Democratic, and independent candidates consists of non-college-educated, particularly white, voters for whom standards have declined most precipitously. See Ruy Teixeira and Joel Rogers, "Volatile Voters: Declining Living Standards and Non-College-Educated Whites" (Washington, D.C.: Economic Policy Institute, 1996), http://epn.org/epi/epruve.html.

93. With only 39% of the electorate voting, the Republicans were able to gain so much because they could rely on an organized army of Religious Right voters who were ideologically committed to the Republican cause. Those who might have voted for a viable opposition either stayed home or voted for "anyone but" the Democrats. Dozens of radio talk show hosts have also been credited with winning the election for the Republicans.

94. According to Peter Levine, a researcher at the Institute for Philosophy and Public Policy at the University of Maryland, compared to voters in 1992, 7% more voters in 1994 were wealthy, and 7% fewer working-class voters went to the polls. This was enough to tip the scales for the Republicans. Letter to the Editor, *New York Times*, 25 November 1994, A30. According to a *New York Times*/CBS News Poll, voters going into the 1994 election were more alienated and cynical about the political process than at any time since the late 1970s. Katharine Q. Seelye, "Voters Disgusted with Politicians as Election Nears," *New York Times*, 3 November 1994, A1; Seelye, "G.O.P. Freshmen Enter, Ready for Their Exits," *New York Times*, 11 December 1994, A34.

95.   Noam Chomsky, "Rollback Part I," *Z Magazine* 8 (January 1995), 20. According to Chomsky, pollsters found that the majority of those who voted in November 1994 also opposed one of the Contract's central components, defense increases, and 61% said that "spending for domestic programs should be increased."

96.   The Republicans' true agenda, which was not about democracy at all, but about complete market freedom for the corporation and punishment and coercion for the poor, is revealed in the kinds of authority that were retained by the federal government and those that were given to the states. For example, while states were to be given the freedom to experiment with eligibility criteria, work requirements, and even benefit levels for their welfare programs, they were mandated by the federal government to deny assistance to mothers under the age of 18, to children born after the parents applied for welfare, to most immigrants, and to families who sought to collect welfare after 5 years of being on it. In voting to turn the Special Supplemental Food Program for Women, Infants and Children (WIC) into a block grant, the Republicans rejected a proposal to require competitive bidding when a state buys infant formula. A major overhaul of the tort law system also federalized what had historically been a state function, making it almost impossible for nonwealthy consumers who had been harmed by some product to sue private companies for damages.

97.   For a particularly good assessment of the way in which the Republican Contract proposed to undermine the nation's environmental and health and safety regulations, see: *Breach of Faith: How the Contract's Fine Print Undermines America's Environmental Success* (New York: Natural Resources Defense Council, February 1995).

98.   One such voice was Robert Eisner, past president of the American Economic Association. See his "Why the Debt Isn't All Bad: Balancing Our Defit Thinking," *Uncommon Sense* 9 (New York: National Jobs for All Coalition, February 1996).

99.   Jason DeParle, "Newt's Endgame," *New York Times Magazine*, 28 January 1996, 39.

100. Technically, the Balanced Budget Amendment lost by two votes. The second "no" vote was cast by Senate majority leader Bob Dole, who changed his vote only so that he could, under Senate rules, bring back the proposal at a later date.

101. Robin Toner, "Tax Cut Edges Out Deficit as G.O.P.'s Guiding Tenet," *New York Times*, 3 April 1995, 1.

102. Center on Budget and Policy Priorities, *The New Fiscal Agenda: What Will It Mean and How Will It be Accomplished?* (Washington, D.C.: Center on Budget and Policy Priorities, January 1995), 5.

103. David Rosenbaum, "Chairman Proposes Redefining Tax Code," *New York Times*, 7 June 1995, A22.

104. Reuss, op. cit. (see note 80).

105. Telephone interviews with Mary Cooper, associate director, Washington Office, National Council of Churches of Christ, 3 July 1998; Sharon Daly, vice president for social policy, Catholic Charities USA, 30 July 1998; Mark Greenberg, senior staff attorney, Center for Law and Social Policy, 28 July 1998, 4 August 1998; Clifford Johnson, senior fellow, Center on Budget and Policy Priorities, 19 August 1998; Sharon Parrott, Center on Budget and Policy Priorities, 1 September 1998; Ellen Teller and Ellen Vollinger, Food Research and Action Center, 8 July 1998; Nanine Meiklejohn, legislative affairs specialist, American Federation of State, County and Municipal Employees, 4 September 1998; Jennifer Vasiloff, former executive director, Coalition on Human Needs, 27 July 1998; Deborah Weinstein, director of family income division, Children's Defense Fund, 31 August 1998; and Cynthia Woodside, government relations associate, National Association of Social Workers, 27 July 1998. All of these respondents are based in Washington, D.C.

106. Cynthia Woodside, ibid.

107. The term *manufacturing consent* is taken from a book by the same name. See Edward S. Herman and Noam Chomsky, *Manufacturing Consent: The Political Economy of the Mass Media* (New York: Pantheon Books, 1988).

108. Perhaps its ties to the Clinton administration (Hillary Rodham Clinton sat on the CDF's board and Peter Edelman, husband of CDF Director Marian Wright Edelman, served in the Executive Branch) effectively muzzled any strong political message coming from the rally. Or perhaps it was the timing. According to a former CDF staffer, the Stand for Children rally was already in motion in January 1996. The president had vetoed the Republican welfare bill, and it was not yet clear that it was going to come back. Marian Wright Edelman realized that CDF did not have enough grassroots capabilities. The loss of child care in 1990 and health reform had convinced her that something beyond the Washington beltway was needed. The rally, then, may have been an attempt to build the foundation for a very broad-based coalition in support of children. CDF feared that changing the agenda to a narrowly political one after it was clear that the president would repeal the entitlement to welfare would bring political calumny on the organization: that they could be accused of assembling people under false pretenses. Telephone interview with Clifford Johnson, op. cit. (see note 105), who was then director of programs and policies at CDF. Despite the lack of a clear political ultimatum, Deborah Weinstein reported that a number of the law's proponents interpreted the Stand for Children rally as being in opposition to the welfare bill anyway, since CDF's views on the subject were well known.

109. Elizabeth Wickenden, "The Carter Welfare Proposal—A Critical Analysis," *Washington Social Legislation Bulletin* 25 (26 September, 1977), 71. The *Washington Social Legislation Bulletin* is a publication of the Child Welfare League of America.

110. Robert Pear, "White House Says Young Will Suffer under G.O.P. Plan," *New York Times*, 30 December 1994, A1.

111. The Personal Responsibility Act did provide two "rainy day" funds intended to assist states in the event of unexpected increases in need, but both of these funds have been criticized as falling far short of what was previously available through entitlement programs. See Sharon Parrott, *Cash Assistance and Related Provisions in the Personal Responsibility Act (H.R. 4)* (Washington, D.C.: Center on Budget and Policy Priorities, 6 April 1995), 7-9.

112. The estimated loss to state and local governments of federal cutbacks was done by Fiscal Planning Services for the Center on Budget and Policy Priorities using Congressional Budget Office data published on 5 January 1995. The estimate was made using currently projected baselines for each year from 1996 to 2002 and was based on the assumption of a balanced budget by 2002, enactment of deep tax cuts, and the protection of Social Security and defense spending from budget cuts. Center on Budget and Policy Priorities, *Holding the Bag: The Effect on State and Local Governments of the Emerging Fiscal Agenda in the 104th Congress* (Washington, D.C.: Author, 31 January 1995).

113. Arthur M. Schlesinger, Jr., *The Cycles of American History* (Boston: Houghton-Mifflin, 1986), 248. Schlesinger points out that the real threats to individual liberty from big government come from agencies like the CIA, the FBI, and the Pentagon. These agencies are applauded by the people who would destroy the welfare state.

114. Dona Cooper Hamilton and Charles V. Hamilton, *The Dual Agenda: The African–American Struggle for Civil and Economic Equality* (New York: Columbia University Press, 1997), 231.

115. Goodling quoted in Jeffrey L. Katz, "GOP Welfare Plan: Self-Help and Leave It to the States," *Congressional Quarterly* 53 (25 February 1995), 616.

116. Robert Rector, quoted in Jeffrey L. Katz, "Key Members Seek to Expand State Role in Welfare Plan," *Congressional Quarterly* 53 (14 January 1995), 160. Malthus, who also wanted to "disclaim the *right* of the poor to support" [his emphasis], believed in "the strong obligation on every man to support his own children; the impropriety, and even immorality of marrying without a prospect of being able to do this. . . ." Thomas Robert Malthus, *An Essay on the Principle of Population*, vol. 3, 5th ed. (London: 1817), excerpted in Helen Ginsburg, ed., *Poverty, Economics and Society* (Boston: Little Brown & Co., 1972), 32.

117. "Researchers Dispute Contention that Welfare Is a Major Cause of Out-of-Wedlock Births," press release, University of

Michigan Research and Training Program on Poverty, the Underclass and Public Policy, 23 June 1994. The press release was signed by 79 prominent researchers in the fields of poverty, the labor market, and family structure.

118. The orphanage plan was found to be a nonwinner with the public. In a *New York Times*/CBS poll taken in the second week in December 1994, only 20% of the respondents were in favor of orphanages. DeParle, op. cit. (see note 75).

119. Among the major religious bodies opposed to the Republican welfare agenda were the National Conference of Catholic Bishops and the National Council of Churches of Christ (Protestant).

120. "The G.O.P. Assault on Welfare," *New York Times*, 25 December 1994, A30.

121. David Rosenbaum, "Clinton in Awkward Role in the Debate on Welfare," *New York Times*, 21 September 1995, B11.

122. Clinton is quoted in Jeffrey L. Katz, "Clinton's Changing Welfare Views," *Congressional Quarterly* 54 (27 July 1996), 2116.

123. Michael Wines, "The Social Engineers Let Welfare Go Unfixed," *New York Times*, 24 September 1995, sec. 4, 1.

124. Frank Rich, "Let 'Em Eat Vermeer," *New York Times*, 10 January 1995, A14.

125. Press release, Office of the Press Secretary, the White House, 9 January 1996.

126. The Senate bill differed from the House's in the following respects: It provided more funds for child care and included more active child-support enforcement measures; it would allow aid to children born while a mother was on welfare; it would allow undocumented aliens access to some child-nutrition programs; it would allow states to decide whether or not to deny Medicaid to legal immigrants; it would maintain federal control of the food-stamp program; and it would allow able-bodied 18–50-year-olds to receive food stamps for 4 months of every year, rather than 3 months in their lifetime, as the House version stipulated.

127. Jason DeParle, "The New Contract with America's Poor, *New York Times*, 28 July 1996, sec. 4, 1.

128. Robert Pear, "Senate Approves Sweeping Change in Welfare Policy," *New York Times*, 24 July 1996, A1.

129. Moynihan quoted in Peter T. Kilborn and Sam Howe Verhover, "Welfare Shift Ends Tortuous Journey." See also R.W. Apple, Jr., "His Battle Now Lost, Moynihan Still Cries Out," *New York Times*, 2 August 1996, A16.

130. See, e.g., Eric Foner, "From Civil War to Civil Rights: The First and Second Reconstructions," The Frank Tannenbaum Lecture, New York, 16 April 1997, The University Seminars at Columbia University.

131. Robert Pear, "Many Subtleties Shaped Members' Welfare Votes," *New York Times*, 14 August 1996, A22.

132. Ibid.

133. Ibid.

134. From numerous polls, Clinton was aware that "welfare reform" was one of the highest priorities among swing voters, yet he was getting less credit among voters for trying to change welfare than he did on almost any other issue. Todd S. Purdum, "Clinton in a Box as a Welfare Bill Edges Closer," *New York Times*, 26 July 1996, A1.

135. Robert Pear, "Senate Passes Welfare Measure Sending It for Clinton's Signature," *New York Times*, 2 August 1996, A16.

136. Among those who quit in protest were Peter Edelman, Mary Jo Bane, David Ellwood, and Wendell Primus.

137. Francis X. Clines, "Clinton Signs Bill Cutting Welfare: States in New Role," *New York Times*, 23 August 1996, A1.

138. Woodside interview, op. cit. (see note 105).

139. Daly, op. cit. (see note 105).

140. Cooper, op. cit. (see note 105).

141. Weinstein, op. cit. (see note 105).

142. This was a view expressed by Mark Greenberg, op. cit., 28 July 1998 (see note 105) and in a memo to authors on 17 August 1999.

143. Ibid.

144. Catholic Charities USA, *Transforming the Welfare System: A Position Paper of Catholic Charities USA* (Alexandria, Va.: Author, 1992). Sharon Daly, vice president for social policy of Catholic Charities USA, emphasized that while workfare is "indentured servitude" and mothers of preschool children should not be required to work, Catholic Charities USA was not against work requirements per se. Daly, op. cit. (see note 105).

145. *New York Times*, 8 August 1995, B7.

146. See Hamilton and Hamilton, op. cit. (see note 114).

147. The National Urban League adopted a formal policy position in 1984 calling for full employment with parity and offering specific recommendations for achieving this national goal. National Urban League, op. cit., 5 (see note 46). See also Suzanne Bergeron, Johanne Dixon, and Douglas G. Glasgow, "Welfare Reform: An Antipoverty Strategy," *Black Americans and Public Policy: Perspectives of the National Urban League* (Washington, D.C.: National Urban League, Inc., April 1988), 60.

148. The National Urban League, for example, has consistently lobbied at both state and national levels to challenge welfare as "workfare," to insist that welfare and general workforce development strategies be linked, to get state programs focused on the most needy cases, to oppose time limits without adequate safety nets or guaranteed public jobs, and to urge that community-based organizations be included in the planning and design of state welfare programs. National Urban League, op. cit., 18-22 (see note 46); Statement by Audrey Rowe, executive vice president, National Urban League, before the Senate Finance Committee, 29 March 1995; Letter to the president of the United States from Hugh B. Price, president, National Urban League, 7 March 1996; Letter to the Honorable Thomas A. Daschle, senate minority leader, United States Senate, from Audrey Rowe, executive vice president, National Urban League, 19 July 1996.

149. Letter to the president of the United States; Letter to the Honorable Thomas A. Daschle, ibid.

150. Arthur M. Schlesinger, Jr., op. cit., 252 (see note 113).

CHAPTER 8
WASHINGTON'S NEW POOR LAW: PART I

1.   Press briefing by Secretary of Health and Human Services Donna Shalala, CEO and President of the Welfare to Work Partnership Eli Segal, Deputy Assistant to the President for Domestic Policy Elena Kagan (Washington, D.C.: The White House Office of the Press Secretary, 27 May 1998). At the press briefing, the administration announced that a total of 135,000 former welfare recipients were now working at jobs they had obtained in the private sector through the president's Welfare-to-Work Partnership program—one in which businesses cooperate with states in placing and training welfare recipients. They also announced that the federal government had hired 4,800 former welfare recipients.

2.   How much of the welfare roll reductions were attributable to welfare-to-work programs, how much to diversion tactics (see note 26 below), and how much to the buoyant economy is still an open question. At least one early study made a strong case for roll reductions being attributable to the strong economy and not to states' welfare-to-work programs. See James P. Ziliak, David N. Figlio, Elizabeth E. Davis, and Laura S. Connolly, *Accounting for the Decline in AFDC Caseloads: Welfare Reform or Economic Growth?* Discussion Paper No. 1151-97 (Madison, Wisc.: Institute for Research on Poverty, November 1997). Available on the World Wide Web at: http://www.ssc.wisc.edu/irp/.

3.   U.S. Congress, Public Law 104-193, *Personal Responsibility and Work Opportunity Reconciliation Act of 1996*, Sec.401 (b). Hereafter PRWORA. The PRWORA does not compel states to cut off assistance after 5 years. Indeed, they can use their own money to continue to provide assistance if they so choose. However, the history of state support for the indigent, especially during economic downturns, does not provide much

hope that without a federal guarantee of funds most states would be more generous.

4.   See, e.g., Maurice Emsellem, *Welfare Reforming the Workplace: Key Concerns with the Work Requirements of the Personal Responsibility & Work Opportunity Reconciliation Act of 1996* (New York: National Employment Law Project, September 1996.)

5.   L. Jerome Gallagher, Megan Gallagher, Kevin Perese, Susan Schreiber, and Keith Watson, *One Year After Federal Welfare Reform: A Description of State Temporary Assistance for Needy Families (TANF) Decisions as of October 1997*, Occasional Paper No. 6 (Washington, D.C.: The Urban Institute, June 1998), 3-7, 12, 34.

6.   For a discussion of the difference between categorical grants-in-aid and block grants, see Neil Gilbert and Paul Terrell, *Dimensions of Social Welfare Policy*, 4th ed. (Boston: Allyn and Bacon, 1998), 220-229; and Sophie R. Dales, "Federal Grants to State and Local Governments, Fiscal Year 1975," *Social Security Bulletin* 39 (September 1976), 22.

7.   The Social Security Act of 1935, e.g., required that benefits for public assistance be in cash or "money payments" (rather than in-kind), thus ruling out the use of federal funds for institutional care, e.g., the poorhouse. It also limited the length of residence requirements, forbade the denial to welfare recipients of such rights as the franchise, and required states to grant opportunities for fair hearings for persons whose claims for assistance were denied. U.S. Congress, Public Law No. 271-74th Congress, *The Social Security Act*, 14 August 1935, Title I, sec. 2(a), (b), sec. 6; Title IV, sec. 402(a), (b), sec. 406; Title X, sec. 1002(a), (b).

8.   PRWORA, op. cit., Title IV, sec. 402 (see note 3).

9.   Pressure came from the White House and state and local officials who would have to pick up the bill for some of the cutbacks, and immigrant advocacy and community groups. Benefits were restored for elderly and disabled legal immigrants who were receiving benefits when the new welfare law was passed or who were living in the U.S. at the time and are or become disabled. See Ruth Gordner, *Immigrant*

Families and Welfare Reform: A Background Briefing Report (Washington, D.C.: Family Impact Seminar, 24 October 1997), 9.

10. Because only parents with children under 1 year of age are omitted from the work participation rate calculations, states have a financial incentive to set the exemption age at 1 year or less. Twenty-six states set the exemption age at 1 year, 2 states at 6 months, 12 states at 3 months and 5 states provide no exemption based on the age of the youngest child. Gallagher et al., op. cit., 25-28 (see note 5).

11. General Accounting Office, *Welfare Reform: States Are Restructuring Programs to Reduce Welfare Dependence*, Chapter Report GAO-HEHS-98-109, (Washington, D.C.: U.S. General Accounting Office, 17 June 1998), 30. Available at: U.S. General Accounting Office (1 September 1999), http://www.access.gpo.gov/su_docs/index.html.

12. "Ending Welfare as We Know It" was aired on public television on 5 June 1998.

13. In January 1996, combined benefits of AFDC and food stamps fell below the official U.S. poverty level ($12,320 for a family of three) in all 50 states; the median state provided benefits equal to 65% of the poverty level. U.S. House of Representatives, Committee on Ways and Means, *1996 Green Book: Background Material and Data on Programs within the Jurisdiction of the Committee on Ways and Means* (Washington, D.C.: U.S. Government Printing Office, 1996), table 8-12, 437-438.

14. The victory was the result of a welfare rights litigation campaign organized by the Center on Social Welfare Policy and Law (now the Welfare Law Center) that had its roots in the community-action programs and the work of social workers, lawyers, and clients at Mobilization for Youth, the New York City antidelinquency project on which they were based. See Paul A. Levy, "The Durability of Supreme Court Welfare Reforms of the 1960s," *Social Service Review* 66 (June 1992), 224-226. See also *Goldberg v. Kelly*, 90 S. Ct. 1011 (1970). While procedural rights to fair hearings had been won, the Court was still reluctant to recognize the welfare entitlement as a

"right" deserving of strict scrutiny and absolute protection by the courts. Following the ruling in *Dandrige v. Williams,* 90 S. Ct. 1153 (1970), the courts treated welfare benefits as "privileges" rather than "rights," which could be affected by laws for merely rational reasons rather than compelling ones. See Christopher E. Smith, *Courts and the Poor* (Chicago: Nelson-Hall Publishers, 1991), 115-116.

15. Smith, ibid., 226.

16. Memo from Mark Greenberg, 17 August 1999. In a survey of the due process rights of welfare recipients conducted by the Welfare Law Center 2 years into welfare "reform," the Center concluded that states appeared to be protecting the due process rights of applicants and clients to fair hearings, but the Center expressed alarm at the increasingly arbitrary way in which programs were being administered, making the need for hearings inevitable. They also reported deficiencies in the way procedural due process was being handled. See "Due Process and Fundamental Fairness in the Aftermath of Welfare Reform," *Welfare News* 3, no. 4, ISSN 1091-4064 (18 September 1998), 1-3. *Welfare News* is a publication of the Welfare Law Center, New York City.

17. "Law Firms Provide Invaluable Assistance in Welfare Law Center Cases," *Welfare News* 3, no. 2, ISSN 1091-4064 (30 June 1998), 1-4. The result of restricting legal services corporations from engaging in such litigation is that welfare advocates now have to seek the help of private firms.

18. National Governors' Association, "Governors Reflect on Welfare Reform's Second Year," press release, Washington, D.C., 28 July 1998.

19. Administration for Children and Families, Department of Health and Human Services, "Change in TANF Caseloads Since Enactment of New Welfare Law," available on DHHS website (19 September 2000) http://www.acf.dhhs.gov/news/stats/aug-dec.htm.

20. *Aid to Families with Dependent Children: The Baseline* (Washington, D.C.: Office of Human Services Policy, Office of the Assistant Secretary for Planning and Evaluation, U.S. Department of Health and Human Services, June 1998), 2.

21. States are required to collect three types of data: disaggregated case record data, that is, specific demographic and other information about each individual and family unit including those on relief and those who have left the program as well as data on the number of applications submitted and approved and the number of cases closed; aggregated data, which describes aspects of states' total caseloads; and financial data on both TANF and Maintenance of Effort-funded programs. States must provide these data to HHS on a quarterly basis. Liz Schott, Ed Lazere, Heidi Goldberg, and Eileen Sweeney, *Highlights of the Final TANF Regulations* (Washington, D.C.: Center on Budget and Policy Priorities, 29 April 1999), 19. Available at: Center on Budget and Policy Priorities (1 September 1999), http://www.cbpp.org/4-29-99wel.htm.

22. Administration for Children and Families, U.S. Department of Health and Human Services, *Characteristics and Financial Circumstances of TANF Recipients Fiscal Year 1999*, "Introduction," 1. Available (29 September 2000): http://www.acf.dhhs.gov/programs/opre/characteristics/fy99/analysis.htm. See also U.S. General Accounting Office, *Welfare Reform: States' Implementation Progress and Information on Former Recipients*. Statement of Cynthia M. Fagnoni, director of education, workforce, and income security issues, health, education, and human services division. Testimony before the Subcommittee on Human Resources, Committee on Ways and Means, House of Representatives, GAO/T-HEHS-99-116, 27 May 1999 (Washington, D.C.: U.S. General Accounting Office), 7; U.S. General Accounting Office, *Welfare Reform: Information on Former Recipients' Status* GAO/HEHS-99-48, April 1999 (Washington, D.C.: U.S. General Accounting Office), 4.

23. New York's Mayor Rudolph Guiliani refused to make welfare statistics available to researchers. Raymond Hernandez, "Most Dropped from Welfare Don't Get Jobs," *New York Times*, 23 March 1998, A1. Many states like Wisconsin would not release employers' quarterly wage reports that would have enabled researchers to determine how long welfare graduates actually stayed in the jobs that they found. According to John Pawaswert, director of the University of Wisconsin's Employment and Training Center, the reason is that governors do not want to

know whether people are keeping their jobs. "That's not the
goal of the program," he has said. "Cutting welfare rolls is."
Pawaswert, quoted in Abby Scher, "Thwarting Researchers,"
Dollars & Sense 221 (January/February 1999), 17. After the
Massachusetts welfare department learned that one in three
people leaving the rolls did not have a job, it stopped collecting
information on why people go off. Chris Tilly, "Beyond Patching
the Safety Net: A Welfare and Work Survival Strategy," *Dollars
& Sense*, 221 (January/February 1999), 36.

24.   For research on the causal dynamics of welfare roll reduc-
        tions, see Ziliak, et al., op. cit. (see note 2).

25.   Christoper D. Cook, "Plucking Workers: Tyson Foods Looks
        to the Welfare Rolls for a Captive Labor Force," *The Pro-
        gressive* 6, (August 1998), 28 ff.

26.   Thirty-six states impose partial sanctions (grant reductions
        by a percentage of the total grant or a flat amount) for ini-
        tial instances of noncompliance for some or all groups of
        families. In 15 of these states, partial sanctions are imposed
        for any instance of noncompliance. In the remaining states,
        a partial sanction is imposed initially, but after further non-
        compliance the sanction increases and the entire family is
        terminated from assistance. Thirty-six states impose full-family
        sanctions at some point during the sanction process, and one-
        half of these impose them immediately for any instance of
        noncompliance. "Sanctions for Noncompliance with Work Ac-
        tivities," State Policy Documentation Project, a joint project
        of the Center for Law and Social Policy and Center on Bud-
        get and Policy Priorities. Available (30 October 2000) on
        the Web at: http://www.spdp.org/tanf/sanctions. Advocates
        for the poor in New York City pointed out that two-thirds of
        all sanctions hearings resulted in reversals, indicating that
        the City was using such sanctions punitively, not, as it al-
        leged, to instill good work habits. See Vivian S. Toy, "Tough
        Welfare Rules Used as Way to Cut Welfare Rolls," *New York
        Times*, 15 April 1998, A1. A federal audit of New York City's
        welfare program sharply criticized the state for failing to
        monitor the City's program and found flagrant violations of
        the Food Stamp Act and other federal regulations. A review
        of 600 cases in two welfare offices found that city workers
        failed to make applications immediately available as required

by law, failed to screen families for emergency food needs, required the poor to search for jobs before receiving help, and cut off food stamps to needy families who were still eligible. See Rachel L. Swarns, "U.S. Audit Is Said to Criticize Guiliani's Strict Welfare Plan," *New York Times*, 20 January 1999, A1. In its comments on the proposed HHS TANF regulations, the Welfare Law Center also cited several instances of state sanction abuse. See *Comment on HHS Notice of Proposed Rulemaking on TANF Provision,* 18 February 1998. Available at: Welfare Law Center (1 September 1999), http://www.welfarelaw.org/.

27. Women with numerous barriers to employment, like serious health problems or substance abuse, may be more likely to be thrown off the rolls for violating the stricter work rules. Nina Bernstein, "Studies Dispute Some Assumptions on Welfare Overhaul," *New York Times*, 12 December 2000, A18. Three forms of diversion have been employed by the states to keep people from applying for TANF. Some states require applicants to engage in a job search before they can become eligible. Others provide only support services such as medical care, child care, and the like to persons determined to have short-term needs, while others make some payment to needy families either in the form of cash assistance or as a payment to vendors in return for the family's agreeing to be ineligible for welfare for some specified period of time. In several states, the period of ineligibility is for a lifetime. Gallagher et al., op. cit., 47 (see note 5). Deterrence can vary across states and within them. For example, a study of two county welfare offices in Alabama found sharp differences among them in how the application process is administered and thus the barriers clients faced in achieving eligibility. Jo M. Donohey, *Field Research on the Welfare Application Process in Two Alabama Counties* (Birmingham, Ala.: Alabama Poverty Project, June 1998). Available on the Web at: http://www.mindspring.com/~stanjj/jeff.html.

28. Cook, op. cit., 28-31 (see note 23). Interview with Jeanette Mott Oxford, director, ROWEL (Reform Organization for Welfare), St. Louis, Mo., 25 August 1998.

29. The Family Support Act did not require welfare recipients to engage in work or work-related activities if supportive services and staff were unavailable, and it exempted from

the work requirement persons who were ill, incapacitated, or aged as well as those living in remote areas and those with children under the age of 3 years (6 years if child care were not guaranteed by the state). However, states had the option of limiting the exemption to those with children younger than 1 year. The new law lowers the age-of-child exemption to 1 year and specifies that states must require recipients to engage in work activities either when the state determines they are ready or after 24 months of assistance, whichever occurs earlier. As of November 1997, 33 states had adopted the 24-month federal maximum, while 21 were requiring recipients to engage in work sooner, including 11 that required them to engage in work activities immediately upon application for welfare. The law leaves it up to the states to determine "hardship" cases. See GAO, op. cit., 35-39 (see note 11). See also Gallagher et al., op. cit., 25-28 (see note 5).

30.   Bruce N. Reed quoted, and participation data cited in: Robert Pear, "Most States Meet Work Requirement of Welfare Law, *New York Times*, 30 December 1998, A1. While the states appear to have exceeded their mandatory participation rate during the first 2 years, experts say it is uncertain whether they will be able to raise that rate to the mandated 50% rate by the year 2002. Participation rates for two-parent families lag behind. By 1997, 75% of these families were supposed to be participating. The rate was only 34% in 1997.

31.   GAO, *Welfare Reform: Information on Former Recipients' Status*, 6-17 (see note 22). See also: National Governors' Association, National Council of State Legislatures and American Public Welfare Association, *Tracking Recipients after They Leave Welfare: Summaries of State Follow-up Studies* (Washington, D.C.: National Governors' Association, July 1998); Jack Tweedie, Dana Reichert, and Matt O'Connor, *Tracking Recipients after They Leave Welfare* (Washington, D.C.: National Conference of State Legislatures, July 1999), 2-3, available at: National Conference of State Legislatures (5 September 1999), http://www.ncsl.org/statefed/welfare/leavers.htm. The states reporting data included Indiana, Iowa, Kentucky, Maryland, Michigan, Missouri, Montana, New Mexico, South Carolina, Tennessee, and Washington.

32. GAO, ibid., 16-17 (see note 22).

33. The GAO cautioned that assessing whether a family is better off after leaving welfare than when on it is a complex task. It depends on family size, whether or not the family receives child-support payments, whether others in the household have earnings, whether other kinds of noncash benefits are being supplied, what a family's work-related expenses amount to, and the effect of the EITC. Most of the preliminary studies did not include this kind of information. GAO, ibid., 20 (see note 22).

34. Alan Finder, "Some Private Efforts See Success in Job Hunt for Those on Welfare," *New York Times*, 16 June 1998, A1. Anu Rangarajan and Robert Wood, *Current and Former WFNJ Clients* (Princeton, N.J.: Mathematica, 2000. Available on the Web at http:/www.mathematica-mpr.com.

35. Most states were providing welfare-to-work participants with more services and increased earnings disregards. See: U.S. General Accounting Office, *Welfare Reform: Early Fiscal Effects of the TANF Block Grant*, AIMD-98-137 (Washington, D.C.: U.S. Government Printing Office, 18 August 1998). But eight studies analyzed by the GAO found that average quarterly earnings for former recipients were greater than the maximum annual amount of cash assistance and food stamps for a 3-person family in the states surveyed, but still below the meager federal poverty level. GAO, *Welfare Reform: Information on Former Recipients' Status*, 19 (see note 22).

36. See Sharon Parrott, *Welfare Recipients Who Find Jobs: What Do We Know about Their Employment and Earnings?* (Washington, D.C.: Center on Budget and Policy Priorities, 16 November 1998). Available at: Center on Budget and Policy Priorities (28 December 1998), http://www.cbpp.org/11-16-98wel.htm. This report includes studies of recipients who found jobs in California, Delaware, Florida, Georgia, Indiana, Maryland, Minnesota, Michigan, Ohio, Oregon, South Carolina, and Wisconsin. State data cited by the National Governors' Association from Indiana, Iowa, Kentucky, Maryland, Michigan, Missouri, Montana, New Mexico, South Carolina, Tennessee, and Washington showed that during the first 2 years of "reform," those who had left the rolls for

work were making an average of between \$5.50 and \$7 an hour, higher than the minimum wage but not enough to lift their families out of poverty. National Governors' Association, *Tracking Welfare Recipients*, 2 (see note 31). In three studies with reliable information on recipients' earnings analyzed by the GAO, the percentage of those who returned to welfare ranged from 19% after 3 months in Maryland to 30% after 15 months in Wisconsin. GAO, *Welfare Reform: Information on Former Recipients' Status*, 16 (see note 22).

37.   New York State Office of Temporary and Disability Assistance, "Local District and State Performance Measures," *Quarterly Report* 6 (January 1998), 11. The survey compared lists of people whose benefits ended during a given quarter of the year against records of wages that employers filed with the state in later quarters. The state's commissioner for the Office of Temporary and Disability Assistance cautioned that there was some disparity in employer reporting of wages from one quarter to another and that this could skew the results. He stated that the state intended to develop more precise ways of determining the fate of former welfare recipients. However, since less than one-third of the welfare dropouts showed earnings of \$100 or more per quarter in a period of high general employment, advocates for the poor felt fairly certain that their worst fears are being played out. Hernandez, op. cit. (see note 23).

38.   "Ending Welfare as We Know It" (see note 12).

39.   By March 1998, only 8% of the previous year's recipients had jobs paying weekly wages above the three-person poverty line, and the proportion with weekly wages below three-quarters of the poverty line surged upward from 6 to 14.5%. Moreover, many families who leave welfare are losing income entirely or not finding steady jobs. Arloc Sherman, Cheryl Amey, Barbara Duffield, Nancy Ebb, and Deborah Weinstein, *Welfare to What: Early Findings on Family Hardship and Well-Being* (Washington, D.C.: Children's Defense Fund and National Coalition for the Homeless, December 1998), 1. The Children's Defense Fund found that the number of children living in extreme poverty in 1997 was up by 426,000 from the previous year. Children's Defense Fund Press Release, "Extreme Child Poverty Rises by More than 400,000 in One

Year, New Analysis Shows," Washington, D.C., 22 August, 1999. Wendell Primus, Lynette Rawlings, Kathy Larin, and Kathryn Porter, *The Initial Impacts of Welfare Reform on the Incomes of Single Mother Families* (Washington, D.C.: Center on Budget and Policy Priorities, 22 August 1999), 3. The CBPP's study was based on census data, while the study by the Children's Defense Fund and Coalition for the Homeless was based on state follow-up studies conducted since implementation of the PRWORA.

40. *Implementing Welfare Reform in America's Cities* (Washington, D.C.: United States Conference of Mayors, November 1997), 47; *A Status Report on Hunger and Homelessness in America's Cities 1999* (Washington, D.C.: United States Conference of Mayors, December 1999); *Hunger and Homelessness in America's Cities 2000* (Washington, D.C.: United States Conference of Mayors, December 2000).

41. Between one-third and one-half (or more) of New York City's welfare leavers are unemployed, most report very modest or no income, and up to a majority have also been cut from food stamps and Medicaid. Requests for emergency food assistance in one study grew 36% between 1998 and 1999. Hundreds of thousands of requests for food went unmet, and 52% of the City's emergency feeding programs reported that welfare policies had increased hunger. *Downside: The Human Consequences of the Giuliani Administration's Welfare Caseload Cuts* (New York: Federation of Protestant Welfare Agencies, November 2000), 1, 8-9, available (6 February 2001) at: http://www.fpwa.org. Reports from particular counties with large numbers of welfare recipients report even higher measures of homelessness and food pantry use than national averages. Two years after welfare reform, Dane County, Wisconsin, reported a 32% rise in the number of families who had been turned away from the community's homeless shelters. Tulsa County, Oklahoma, reported that it was serving almost 50% more people in its food program as a result of federal food stamp changes. *Making Welfare Reform Work: A Report of the NACO Hearings on Welfare Reform Implementation* (Washington, D.C.: National Association of Counties, July 1997), 7. Congressman Tony Hall conducted a survey of 117 food banks across the country between 1998 and 1999.

He found that requests for assistance were up about 13% at 87% of the food banks. The reason behind the increased need was most often that those who were hungry were not earning a living wage because they had lost their welfare benefits or food stamps. Congressman Tony P. Hall, *Empty Shelves: 1999 Survey of U.S. Food Banks*. Available from the congressional office of Tony Hall (31 March 1999), http://www.house.gov/tonyhall/pr49.htm.

42. *Are States Improving the Lives of Poor Families? A Scale Measure of State Welfare Policies* (Medford, Mass.: Center on Hunger, Poverty, and Nutrition Policy, Tufts University, February 1998); *Paradox of our Times—Hunger in a Strong Economy* (Medford, Mass.: Center on Hunger, Poverty and Nutrition Policy, Tufts University, January 2000).

43. The Urban Institute cites falling welfare rolls as the "primary reason" why about half a million fewer adults and children nationwide participated in Medicaid in 1996, compared with 1995. Urban Institute, "Declining Welfare Rolls Fuel Drop in Medicaid: Employers are Major Source of Health Coverage for Low-Income People," press release, Washington, D.C., 18 May 1998. For additional data on Medicaid loss, see Families USA Foundation, *Losing Health Insurance: The Unintended Consequences of Welfare Reform*, publication no. 99-103 (Washington, D.C.: May 1999), available from Families USA (14 June 1999), http://www.familiesusa.org/unintend.pdf; Thomas Fraker et al., *Iowa's Limited Benefit Plan* (Washington, D.C.: Mathematica Policy Research, May 1997); David J. Fein, "The Indiana Welfare Reform Evaluation: Who Is On and Who is Off?" (Cambridge, Mass.: Abt Associates, September 1997); Kathleen A. Maloy, LaDonna A. Pavetti, Julie Darnell, and Peter Shin, "Diversion as a Work-Oriented Welfare Reform Strategy and Its Effect on Access to Medicaid: An Examination of the Experiences of Five Local Communities," A Report of the Findings of the Second Phase of the Research Funded by the Administration for Children and Families and the Assistant Secretary for Planning and Evaluation, U.S. Department of Health and Human Services, March 1999, available at George Washington University School of Public Health and Health Services, Center for Health Policy Research (16 July 1999), http://www.gwumc.edu/chpr/wr/new/welfrfrm.pdf.

The nation's food stamp rolls have dropped by one-third in 4 years. While some of this may be attributed to the low unemployment and growing economy, officials fear that it signals needy people's new hesitance to apply for benefits as a result of welfare "reform." It could also be caused by some states' refusal to inform those who apply for aid or who leave the rolls that they may still be eligible for food stamps. Evidence for this fear is found in reports of rising numbers seeking food from food pantries and soup kitchens. See Andrew C. Revkin, "A Plunge in Use of Food Stamps Causes Concern," *New York Times*, 25 February 1999, A1; Revkin, "Welfare Policies Alter the Face of Food Lines," *New York Times*, 26 February 1999, A1; Revkin, "As Need for Food Grows, Donations Steadily Drop, *New York Times*, 27 February 1999, A1. For data on food stamp participation, see National Governors' Association, *Tracking Recipients,* op. cit. (see note 31).

44. Robert Kuttner, "The Welfare Perplex," *New York Times*, 19 June 1994, E17.

45. Donohey, op. cit. (see note 27).

46. Timothy Egan, "As Idaho Booms, Prisons Fill and Spending on Poor Lags," *New York Times*, 16 April 1998, A1.

47. A study conducted on national welfare data from 1983 to 1994 confirms the likelihood of the "race-to-the-bottom" thesis. Researchers found that states tended to respond to the lowering of benefits in neighboring states by lowering their own benefits. There was a response in the other direction as well: States increased their benefits in response to increasing benefits in other states. But, significantly, the responsive increase in benefits was only at one-half the rate of the responsive decrease in benefits. David N. Figlio, Van W. Kolpin, and William E. Reid, *Asymmetric Policy Interaction among Subnational Governments: Do States Play Welfare Games?* Discussion paper 1154-1198 (Madison, Wisc.: Institute for Research on Poverty, 1998).

48. *Racing to the Bottom? Recent State Welfare Initiatives Present Cause for Concern* (Washington, D.C.: Center for Law and Social Policy, 21 February 1996).

49.   GAO, *Welfare Reform: States are Restructuring Programs,* op. cit., 89-92 (see note 11).

50.   Joe Sexton, "Welfare Reform, From the Inside Out," *New York Times,* 29 May 1997, B1.

51.   Wisconsin has spent heavily to make welfare-to-work pay off, even privatizing the program in Milwaukee County, "but despite the effort to import business-world efficiencies, many of those in the program describe their caseworkers as distant and distracted figures who neglect to return phone calls rather than the partners in self-sufficiency depicted in state manuals. Many recipients find themselves bouncing between part-time or temporary jobs, suffering income gaps that planners failed to anticipate." Jason DeParle, "Wisconsin Welfare Experiment: Easy to Say, Not so Easy to Do," *New York Times,* 18 October 1998, A1. See also Philip Wilayto, *The Feeding Trough: The Bradley Foundation, "The Bell Curve" and the Real Story Behind W-2, Wisconsin's National Model for Welfare Reform* (Milwaukee: A Job Is a Right Campaign, 1997).

52.   Jeanette Batz, "Poor Excuses," *The Riverfront Times,* 19-25 August 1998, 16. The *Riverfront Times* is published in St. Louis. See also Victor Volland, "Too Few Case Managers and the Lack of Incentives Doom the Plan, They Say," *St. Louis Post-Dispatch,* 17 June 1998, A1.

53.   Rachel L. Swarns, "Welfare as We Know It Goes Incognito," *New York Times,* 5 July 1998, Sec. 4, 1.

54.   At least 39 states and numerous independent agencies as well as the federal government are conducting studies. To assess the postreform status of all low-income families, not just welfare recipients, the U.S. Census Bureau at the direction of Congress is conducting a longitudinal survey of a nationally representative sample of families called the Survey of Program Dynamics, and the Urban Institute is conducting a multiyear project monitoring program changes and fiscal developments along with changes in the well-being of children and families. GAO, *Welfare Reform: States' Implementation Progress and Information on Former Recipients,* 6-16 (see note 22). For a discussion of the difficulties of evaluating welfare reform, see Tom Corbett, *Informing the Welfare Debate: Perspec-*

tives on the Transformation of Social Policy (Madison: Institute for Research on Poverty, April 1997). For a listing of completed and ongoing studies of welfare reform, see the website: http://www.researchforum.org.

55. According to data from New York State analyzed by the Fiscal Policy Institute, New York State had accumulated the nation's second largest TANF surplus, even as it maintained a child poverty rate of 24.6% in 1999. In fiscal year 1999–2000, New York State used federal TANF funds to supplant $403 million in state money previously used for welfare-related programs. New York proposed supplanting even more money in fiscal year 2000–2001. *Poverty Amidst Plenty: Amount of Unspent Federal Anti-Poverty Funds Grows Despite Persistent Need* (Washington, D.C.: National Campaign for Jobs and Income Support, 2000), 6. Available on the Web (4 November 2000) at: http://www.community change.org/nationalcampaign/tanfsurplus.

56. U.S. General Accounting Office, *Welfare Reform: Early Fiscal Effects of the TANF Block Grant*, op. cit., 5 (see note 34).

57. According to the Department of Health and Human Services, states had an unused balance of $3 billion out of $12 billion available in the first 9 months of 1998. See Robert Pear, "States Declining to Draw Billions in Welfare Money," *New York Times*, 8 February 1999, A1. See also General Accounting Office, *Welfare Reform: Status of Awards and Selected States' Use of Welfare-to-Work Grants* GAO/HEHS-99-40 (Washington, D.C.: U.S. Government Printing Office, February 1999).

58. The GAO found that most states have set aside a general "rainy day" fund for economic downturns, but only a minority earmarked funds for future welfare needs, and few have significant balances. In fact, when queried, states reported that given the strength of their economies, they did not see an immediate need to prepare for a recession for their welfare programs. Several felt that by changing the nature of the program toward one focused on moving welfare recipients into the labor market, their caseloads would eventually stabilize at a much lower level. GAO, *Welfare Reform: Early Fiscal Effects*, op. cit., 15-17 (see note 35). Other states complained that since Maintenance of Effort (MOE) requires a designated level

of spending each year, the allocation of state funds to a reserve fund does not count toward MOE, since it is not considered spending. Information supplied by Mark Greenberg, op. cit. (see note 16).

59. National Governors' Association press release, "Governors Warn against Cutting Aid to Nation's Neediest Citizens," 8 March 1999, Washington D.C.

60. David A. Super, Sharon Parrott, Susan Steinmetz, and Cindy Mann, *The New Welfare Law* (Washington D.C.: Center on Budget and Policy Priorities, 1996), Sec. II, "Cash Assistance, Work and Child Care Provisions." Available at: Center on Budget and Policy Priorities (2 August 1999), http://www.cbpp.org.

61. Liz McNichol and Iris J. Lav, *Will States Maintain the Safety Net? Evidence From Bad Times and Good* (Washington, D.C.: Center on Budget and Policy Priorities, 20 February 1996); Robert Greenstein, *The Budgetary Context for Changes in Safety Net Programs* (Washington, D.C.: Center on Budget and Policy Priorities, 27 June 1996).

62. Matsui, quoted in "Some Look at Welfare Plan With Hope, but Others Are Fearful," *New York Times*, 4 August 1996, A26.

63. Price, quoted in ibid.

64. PRWORA, op. cit., sec. 103(a), (see note 3).

65. For a history of the earlier public/private debates, see Michael B. Katz, *In the Shadow of the Poorhouse: A Social History of Welfare in America* (New York: Basic Books, 1986), 42-46. The 1967 amendments to the Social Security Act authorized the states to purchase services from nonprofit or proprietary providers, resulting in "escalated use of these arrangements." See Margaret Gibelman, "Theory, Practice, and Experience in the Purchase of Services," in Margaret Gibelman and Harold W. Demone, Jr., eds., *The Privatization of Human Services: Policy and Practice Issues,* 1 (New York: Springer Publishing Company, 1998), 9. Similarly, two other scholars write: "Although government funding of nonprofit service organizations dates to the colonial period, only in the last 25 years did this government-nonprofit strategy emerge as a widespread and favored tool of public service delivery." Steven Rathgeb

Smith and Michael Lipsky, *Nonprofits for Hire: The Welfare State in the Age of Contracting* (Cambridge, Mass.: Harvard University Press, 1993), 11. Numerous other laws, in addition to the 1967 amendments, including the Community Mental Health Services Act and Titles XVIII and XIX of the Social Security Act (Medicare and Medicaid), facilitated this trend. Smith and Lipsky (p. 209) observe that even during the 1980s, despite widely publicized cuts in federal spending, government funding of nonprofit service agencies in many categories, such as child care and services to the mentally ill and developmentally disabled, continued to rise.

66. Mary R. Mannix, Henry A. Freedman, Marc Cohan, and Christopher Lamb, *Implementation of the Temporary Assistance for Needy Families Block Grant: An Overview* (New York: Center on Social Welfare Policy and Law, November 1996), 5.

67. Cecilia Perry, "Safety-Net for Sale: Private Gatekeepers and Public Dollars," *New Labor Forum* (Spring/Summer 1999), 79. Publication of the Queens College Labor Resource Center, Queens College, City University of New York.

68. PRWORA, op. cit., sec. 104(a), sec. 104(b) (see note 3) has as its purpose "to allow States to contract with religious organizations, or allow religious organizations to accept certificates, vouchers, or other forms of disbursement . . . on the same basis as any other nongovernmental provider. . . ."

69. For documentation on Lockheed Martin's corrupt and unethical efforts to garner government favor, see William D. Hartung and Jennifer Washburn, "Lockheed Martin's New Empire: Targeting Welfare Dollars," *The Nation* 266 (2 March 1998), 11-16.

70. Mark Dunlea, "The Poverty Profiteers Privatize Welfare," *CAQ* 59 (Winter 1996-1997), 6. Available at: Congressional Action Quarterly (1 September 1999), http://caq.com/caq/ caqbackissues.html.

71. After reviewing several studies, Gilbert and Terrell (op. cit., 147 [see note 6]) write that "to date, research findings on the effectiveness of social services delivered under public and private auspices haven't yielded a definitive answer." Kamerman and Kahn conclude that "the evidence var[ies]

with field, time, context, and scale." Sheila B. Kamerman and Alfred J. Kahn, *Privatization and the Welfare State* (Princeton, N.J.: Princeton University Press, 1989), 262. Howard Joseph Karger and David Stoesz (*American Social Welfare Policy: A Pluralist Approach*, 3rd ed. [New York: Longman, 1998], 205-206) cite studies that found that investor-owned hospitals were not more efficient than nonprofit and public hospitals. Karger and Stoesz conclude that "the promise of cost containment through privatization has not been borne out." Margaret Gibelman, who has extensively studied government purchase of social services, writes that "although it is difficult to determine exactly how much money is saved by contracting out, the appearance of substantial costs savings serves an important symbolic agenda" (op. cit., 15 [see note 65]).

72.   American Federation of State, County and Municipal Employees, "Case Study: Child Support Enforcement" in *Government for Sale: An Examination of the Contracting out of State and Local Government Services,* 6th ed., Washington, D.C. Available at: American Federation of State, County and Municipal Employees (1 September 1999), http://www.afscme.org/wrkplace/sale06.htm.

73.   Elliott D. Sclar, "Understanding the Real Costs of Contracting," Remarks to the Executive Council Meeting of the Public Employee Department, AFL-CIO, Bal Harbour, Fla., 17 February 1996; Elliott Sclar, "Privatization and its Discontents, *New Labor Forum* (Spring/Summer 1999), 67. Publication of the Queens College Labor Resource Center, Queens College, City University of New York. For a thorough examination of privatization, see Sclar's *You Don't Always Get What you Pay For: The Economics of Privatization* (Ithaca, N.Y.: Cornell University Press, 2000).

74.   Perry, op. cit., 79 (see note 67).

75.   Cited by Hartung and Washburn, op. cit., 14-15 (see note 69).

76.   AFL-CIO Press release, "Union Membership Climbs According to New Government Data," 25 January 1999, Washington, D.C. Available on the Web at: http://www.aflcio.org/publ/press99/pro0125.htm.

77.   Gilbert and Terrell, op. cit., 147 (see note 6).

78. Perry, op. cit. (see note 67).

79. Felder, quoted in Dunlea, op. cit. (see note 70).

80. Mannix et al., op. cit., 5 (see note 66).

81. In Wisconsin, if a local welfare agency's surplus is less than or equal to 7% of its total expense, it gets to keep it as "profit." Any surplus in excess of 7% is to be distributed as follows: 10% to the local agency for unrestricted use; 45% to the state; and 45% to the local agency for reinvestment in the community for services to low-income people. State contracts with local agencies also have a $5,000 "failure to serve" penalty for failure to provide specified services. American Federation of State, County and Municipal Employees Legislative Council, *Private Profits, Public Needs: The Administration of W-2 in Milwaukee* (Washington, D.C.: American Federation of State, County and Municipal Employees Legislative Council, Wisconsin, October 1998). Report available from: AFSCME, 1625 L St., NW, Washington, D.C. 20036-5687, or on the Web at: (9 September 1999) http://www.afscme.org/pol-leg/pppntc.htm. See also: GAO, *Welfare Reform: States are Restructuring Programs*, op. cit., 93 (see note 11). For information on the Maximus and Goodwill scandals and an overall critique of W-2, see *Credit Where Blame Is Due: Governor Thompson's Record on Low-Income Programs and Policy* (Washington, D.C.: National Campaign for Jobs and Income Support, 16 January 2001).

82. Nina Bernstein, "Deletion of Word in Welfare Bill Opens Foster Care to Big Business," *New York Times*, 4 May 1997, A1.

83. Eric Bates, "The Shame of Our Nursing Homes," *The Nation* 268 (29 March 1999), 11-19.

84. Eric Bates, "Private Prisons," *The Nation* 266, 1 (5 January 1998), 11-17.

85. Perry, op. cit., 81 (see note 65).

86. *Passing the Bucks: The Contracting Out of Public Services* (Washington, D.C.: AFSCME, 1996), 8-9.

87. A Florida TANF privatization pilot program in Flager and Volusia counties raised conflict-of-interest charges when 12

members of a Florida welfare program board awarding the contract chose a vendor for whom they constituted part of the board of directors. Perry, op. cit., 83 (see note 67).

88. Wisconsin provided the first case study of the privatization of all TANF functions. Privatization, along with state TANF policies that seek to deter applicants from getting welfare, have contributed to a drop in Wisconsin's Medicaid and food stamp caseloads among many families that were eligible. In November 1998, U.S. Congressman Thomas Barrett (D-Wisc.) asked the USDA to investigate the W-2 program to determine why the food stamp rolls had declined by almost 10%. He found that applicants waited several hours before they were instructed to return on another day for additional assistance, including food stamps, a violation of the Food Stamp Act. AFSCME, op. cit., 81 (see note 67).

89. Freedman, quoted in Dunlea., op. cit., 8 (see note 70).

90. Dunlea, ibid., 10.

91. Researchers for the Urban Institute who examined the labor markets and caseloads in 20 metropolitan areas across the country concluded that in the majority of these areas, the unemployment rate would continue to be low, even with the entry of welfare recipients into the labor market. However, they cautioned that this scenario varied greatly across areas. Four of the metropolitan areas—significantly those with the highest caseloads—might experience increases. They also did not make any adjustment for the effects on wages or the problem of spatial mismatch. Robert I. Lerman, Pamela Loprest, and Caroline Ratcliffe, *How Well Can Urban Labor Markets Absorb Welfare Recipients*? No. A-33 in Series, "New Federalism: Issues and Options for States" (Washington, D.C.: The Urban Institute, 1999), available at: The Urban Institute (6 September 1999), http://newfederalism.urban.org/html/anf33.html. Gary Burtless points out that BLS projects job growth in low-skill sectors will rise by 13.5%. On the other hand, employer surveys suggest that very few jobs—even low skilled ones—can be filled by applicants who lack general skills such as the ability to read and write or to interact respectfully with customers, suggesting that as states reach down into those left on the rolls, it will become harder to

place them. At any rate, the jobs welfare recipients may get will not be likely to lift them out of poverty any time soon. Gary Burtless, "Can the Labor Market Absorb Three Million Welfare Recipients?" *Focus* 19 (Summer-Fall 1998), 1-6. Focus is a newsletter of the Institute for Research on Poverty, University of Wisconsin, Madison. Examining the history of the labor market and the economic prospects of single mothers with dependent children, Glen Cain concludes that for such women to rise above poverty, macroeconomic growth and increases in wages are key determinants. Glen G. Cain, *The State of the Economy and the Problem of Poverty: Implications for the Success or Failure of Welfare Reform*, Discussion Paper 1183-1198 (Madison, Wisc.: Institute for Research on Poverty, 1998), available from the Institute for Research on Poverty (6 September 1999), http://www.ssc.wisc.edu/irp/dpabs98.htm. Harry Holzer found the demand for welfare recipients in Wisconsin fairly high but cautioned that such jobs might not hold up during a recession. He also found a spatial mismatch between the jobs and welfare clients. Harry J. Holzer, *Will Employers Hire Welfare Recipients? Recent Survey Evidence from Michigan*, Discussion Paper 1177-1198 (Madison, Wisc.: Institute for Research on Poverty, 1998), available at: Institute for Research on Poverty (6 September 1999), http://www.ssc.wisc.edu/irp/dpabs98.htm.

92. Philip Harvey, "How Many Jobs Are There? The Need for a National Job Vacancy Survey," *Uncommon Sense* 15, (New York, National Jobs for All Coalition, March 2000).

93. From the end of 1985 to midyear 1998, the number of inmates in the nation's prisons and jails grew by more than 1,058,000, an annual increase of 7.3%. Darrell K. Gilliard, "Prison and Jail Inmates at Midyear 1998," *Bureau of Justice Statistics Bulletin* (March 1999), 1.

94. Remarks by Humphrey Taylor, president of Louis Harris and Associates, at a conference on "Empowering People with Disabilities," New York City, 21 May 1989. Information given by the International Center for the Disabled.

95. For example, in 1999, the officially unemployed numbered 5.9 million and the unemployment rate averaged 4.2%. However, 3.4 million were involuntary part-timers who wanted

full-time work, and 4.6 million were discouraged workers who had given up looking for a job. If all these categories were added, the "jobless rate" would have been 8.7%, more than twice the official rate. David Dembo and Ward Morehouse, *The Underbelly of the U.S. Economy: Joblessness and the Pauperization of Work in America* (New York: The Apex Press, 2000), 9-15. Statistics are based on data from the U.S. Department of Labor, Bureau of Labor Statistics, *Employment and Earnings*, January 2000.

96.   Lester Thurow, "The Crusade That's Killing Prosperity," *The American Prospect* 25 (March/April 1996), 54-59. See also Vicente Navarro, "'Eurosclerosis' vs. U.S. Dynamism," *Challenge* 41 (July–August 1998), 66-75.

97.   Information on Milwaukee's research can be obtained from the Employment and Training Institute, University of Wisconsin-Milwaukee.

98.   Katharine Abraham, "Structural/Frictional vs. Deficient Demand Unemployment," *American Economic Review* 73 (September 1983), 708-724.

99.   A study of the Milwaukee metropolitan area, which at the time had a booming economy and an unemployment rate lower than the national average, showed there were three to five persons needing work for every available job. Only officially unemployed workers and able-bodied welfare recipients were included in this estimate. If discouraged workers and involuntarily employed part-time workers had been added, the ratio would have been much higher. See Employment and Training Institute, University of Wisconsin/Milwaukee, *Survey of Job Openings in the Milwaukee Metropolitan Area* (biannual), cited in Harvey, op. cit. (see note 92). A study of seven counties in the Hudson Valley of New York projected an almost four-to-one ratio of job seekers to jobs for 1997. Greater Upstate Law Project, *Hudson Valley: 1997, Job Seekers, Job Gap*. Available from the Greater Upstate Law Project, Albany, N.Y. In Minnesota, a state with a below-average unemployment rate, there were 2.7 applicants for every available job. Bruce Steurenagel, *The Job Gap Study, Phase One: First Report of Findings* (St. Paul, Minn.: Jobs Now Coalition, 1995).

100. U.S. Conference of Mayors, *Implementing Welfare Reform,* op. cit. (see note 40).

101. The study was conducted by Paul Kleppner and Nikolas Theodore for the Midwest Job Gap Project, a joint effort of the Chicago Urban League and the Office for Social Policy of Northern Illinois University, 1997. A study of Illinois, published less than a year before passage of the PRWORA, found that there were four workers in need of entry-level jobs for every job opening in the state. Virginia L. Carlson and Nikolas C. Theodore, *Are There Enough Jobs? Welfare Reform and Labor Market Reality* (Chicago: The Job Gap Project of the Center for Urban Economic Development of the University of Illinois at Chicago, the Chicago Urban League and the Office for Social Policy Research at Northern Illinois University, December 1995).

102. Employment and Training Institute, University of Wisconsin/Milwaukee, *Survey of Job Openings in the Milwaukee Metropolitan Area* (biannual), cited in Harvey (see note 92).

103. Katherine Newman and Chauncy Lennon, *Finding Work in the Inner City: How Hard Is It Now? How Hard Will It Be for AFDC Recipients?* (New York: Department of Anthropology, Columbia University, 1996).

104. Congress may be trying to remedy this transportation gap with the $50 billion transportation bill it passed in the Spring 1998, but it will be several years before it is determined if this will be enough. "New Studies Look at Status of Former Welfare Recipients," *CDF Reports* (April/May 1998). *CDF Reports* is published by the Children's Defense Fund, Washington, D.C.

105. U.S. Conference of Mayors, *Implementing Welfare Reform,* op. cit., 15 (see note 39).

106. In Detroit, with an unemployment rate twice that of surrounding suburbs, a poor public transit system and only one in four residents with cars, thousands of credentialed workers went without jobs, while even low-wage jobs in the suburbs went begging. Robyn Meredith, "Jobs out of Reach for Detroiters without Wheels," *New York Times*, 26 May 1998, A12. In Milwaukee, approximately 70% of all full-time vacancies

and 81% of all part-time vacancies were in the suburbs, but 56% of the officially unemployed, plus the vast majority of welfare recipients, lived in the city. Employment and Training Institute, University of Wisconsin/Milwaukee, cited in Harvey, op. cit. (see note 92).

107. Alan Finder, "Welfare Clients Outnumber Jobs They Might Fill," *New York Times*, 25 August 1996, A1. A study by the Federal Reserve Bank of New York yields further data on the likely effects of thrusting more welfare recipients into the labor market. Between the fourth quarter of 1994 and the second quarter of 1997, unemployment in New York City rose 2%, while job growth averaged an annual 1%. The study attributed most of the rise in unemployment—unparalleled in a time of general economic growth—to the increased labor-force participation brought about by more stringent work requirements for welfare recipients imposed by the City even before the new national welfare law went into effect. *Current Issues in Economics and Finance, Second District* Highlights (New York: Federal Reserve Bank of New York, 14 December 1997), 3. A 1997 study by the Community Service Society of New York concluded that under current market conditions (which at the time were relatively good) only about 15–20% of employable welfare recipients would find work each year. Hugh O'Neill, Kathryn Garcia, and Kathryn McCormick, *Where the Jobs Are: How Labor Market Conditions in the New York Area Will Affect the Employment Prospects of Public Assistance Recipients* (New York: Community Service Society of New York, April 1997), 6.

108. U.S. Department of Housing and Urban Development, *Now Is the Time: Places Left Behind in the New Economy.* Washington, D.C.: Author, 1999.

109. For example, average unemployment in Luna County, New Mexico, was 26.9%, or nearly six times the national average in 1998, and in Magoffin County, Kentucky, it was three times the national average. U.S. Department of Housing and Urban Development, ibid. While welfare rolls fell sharply in the Delta, a largely poor, black, rural region, unemployment rates remained above 10% in 1997. Jason DeParle, "Welfare Law Weighs Heavy in Delta, Where Jobs are Few," *New York Times*, 16 October 1997, A1.

110. James Brooke, "Indians' Cruel Winter of Aid Cuts and Cold," *New York Times*, 27 January 1997, A1; Peter T. Kilborn, "For Poorest Indians, Casinos Aren't Enough," *New York Times*, 11 June 1997, A1.

111. Children's Defense Fund Update, Washington, D.C., June 1998.

112. The U.S. Conference of Mayors reported in its 34-city survey that employers appeared willing to hire welfare recipients. United States Conference of Mayors, op. cit., 17 (see note 40).

113. GAO, op. cit., 33-34 (see note 11).

114. Paul Offner, "Jobfare, Familiar and Failed," *New York Times*, 26 September 1996, A27.

115. "Tax Credits for Welfare Hires, *New York Times* editorial, 30 January 1997, A20. See also Ben Wildavsky, "Taking Credit," *National Journal,* 29 March 1997, 610-612.

116. Phil Wilayto, op. cit., 41-42 (see note 51).

117. Press briefing by Shalala et al., op. cit. (see note 1).

118. For business criticism of the public jobs programs of the New Deal, see Nancy E. Rose, *Put to Work: Relief Programs in the Great Depression* (New York: Monthly Review Press, 1994).

119. Clifford M. Johnson, *Toward a New Generation of Community Jobs Programs* (Washington, D.C.: Center on Budget and Policy Priorities, 19 December 1997), 1.

120. As a goad to both the private sector and the states, Clinton offered to hire 10,000 welfare recipients in federal government jobs between 1997 and the year 2001. By the spring of 1998, the White House announced that, with the hiring of 4,800 welfare recipients, it was already exceeding its goal. Press briefing, Shalala, op. cit. (see note 1).

121. Clifford M. Johnson, *Frequently-Asked Questions about Public Job Creation* (Washington, D.C.: Center on Budget and Policy Priorities, December 1998). National League of Cities, *New Directions: Publicly Funded Jobs: A Workforce Development Strategy for Cities* (Washington, D.C.: National League of Cities, undated).

122. Jurisdictions receiving welfare-to-work funds must use 70%
     of them for TANF recipients or noncustodial parents of mi-
     nors whose custodial parent is a TANF recipient. Federal
     guidelines originally specified that this money be targeted
     at individuals with two or three barriers to employment, such
     as the lack of a high school diploma or G.E.D., low reading
     and math skills, the need for substance-abuse treatment, or
     poor work histories. The additional 30% must be spent on
     individuals with long-term welfare dependence. Mark
     Greenberg, *Welfare-to-Work Grants and Other TANF-Related
     Provisions in the Balanced Budget Act of 1997* (Washing-
     ton, D.C.: Center for Law and Social Policy, August 1997),
     8-9; "Education and Job Training under Welfare Reform,"
     Welfare Reform Network News 9/10 (August/September 1997),
     1-2, a newsletter of the Institute for Women's Policy Research,
     Washington, D.C. Amendments enacted in the 2000 appro-
     priations bill remove the requirement that long-term recipi-
     ents must meet additional barriers to employment. Those who
     have received assistance for at least 30 months, or if they
     are within 12 months of becoming ineligible for TANF due
     to time limits, were made eligible, regardless of whether they
     have multiple "barriers to work." See Title VIII, H.R. 3424,
     the Departments of Labor, Health, and Human Services, and
     Education and Related Agencies Appropriations Act, 2000,
     "Welfare to Work and Child Support Amendments of 1999."
     Available on the Web at: http://wtw.doleta.gov/documents/
     99wtw-amend.pdf.

123. National League of Cities, op. cit., 6 (see note 121).

124. Clifford M. Johnson and Ana Carricchi Lopez, *Shattering
     the Myth: Promising Findings from Ten Public Job Cre-
     ation Initiatives* (Washington, D.C.: Center on Budget and
     Policy Priorities, 22 December 1997); Clifford M. Johnson,
     Publicly-Funded Jobs for Hard-to-Employ Welfare Recipients
     (Washington, D.C.: Center on Budget and Policy Priori-
     ties, 14 July 1998); National League of Cities, op. cit. (see
     note 121).

125. Mark Greenberg, op. cit., 2-3 (see note 122).

126. U.S. Conference of Mayors, *Implementing Welfare Reform
     in America's Cities*, op. cit., 10 (see note 40).

127. Among the findings of a 12-state study conducted by the Urban Institute are: (1) Part-time work at the minimum wage increases a family's earnings dramatically—by as much as 51%; (2) as a family moves from part-time work to full-time work at minimum wage, its total income grows by an average of 20%; (3) as a family moves from full-time work at minimum wage to full-time work at $9 an hour, its total income grows by an average of 16%. In calculating income, the researchers considered the family's earnings, its TANF grant, the cash value of food stamps it receives, federal and state EITC credits, any other state credits, and all federal and state tax liabilities. Other public subsidies such as child care, federal housing assistance, and Medicaid were not considered. However, the researchers cautioned that without child-care subsidies, child-care needs might still present a formidable disincentive to staying in the low-wage labor market. Gregory Acs, Norma Coe, Keith Watson, and Robert I. Lerman, *Does Work Pay? An Analysis of the Work Incentives under TANF*, occasional paper no. 9 (Washington, D.C.: The Urban Institute, July 1998).

128. Senators Edward M. Kennedy, Barbara A. Mikulski, Christopher J. Dodd, Paul Wellstone, Tom Harkin, Jack Reed, and Patty Murray, Minimum Wage Sign-On Letter, 15 January 1999. Available from their legislative offices in Washington, D.C.

129. In September 1997, the minimum wage was raised to $5.15 per hour. Poverty thresholds for 1999 are taken from: Joseph Dalaker and Bernadette D. Proctor, U.S. Census Bureau, Current Population Reports Series P60-210, *Poverty in the United States: 1999* (Washington, D.C.: U.S. Government Printing Office, 2000), table 1, 1.

130. Robert Greenstein and Isaac Shapiro, *New Research Findings on the Effects of the Earned Income Tax Credit* (Washington, D.C.: Center on Budget and Policy Priorities, 11 March 1998), 1. See also Jeffrey B. Liebman, "The Impact of the Earned Income Tax Credit on Incentives and Income Distribution, in James M. Poterba, ed., *Tax Policy and the Economy*, (Cambridge, Mass.: MIT Press, 1998), 12. The greatest impact of the EITC is in the South, where earnings

are particularly low. For a comparison of the antipoverty effects of the EITC with other safety net programs see Wendell Primus and Kathryn Porter, *Strengths of the Safety Net: How the EITC, Social Security, and Other Government Programs Affect Poverty* (Washington, D.C.: Center on Budget and Policy Priorities, 9 March 1998). See also Robert Cherry and Gertrude Schaffner Goldberg, "The EITC: What It Does and Doesn't Do," in Ron Baiman, Heather Boushey, and Dawn Saunders, eds., *Political Economy and Contemporary Capitalism: Radical Perspectives on Economic Theory and Policy* (Armonk, N.Y.: M. E. Sharpe, 2000). For discussion of the history and function of the EITC, see Chapter 6, this volume.

131. Although a growing number of states have chosen to exempt poor families from the state income tax, 19 states continue to make those with incomes below the poverty line pay, although some have substantially increased the income level at which income tax is first owed. Of those 19, however, 11 have allowed their thresholds to decline relative to the poverty line during the 1990s. In the states that did levy taxes on some poor families, the average level at which a two-parent family of four began to owe tax was more than $6,200 below the 1998 poverty line of $16,655 for a family of four. For a single-parent family of three, the average tax threshold was almost $4,200 below the poverty line of $13,001. The 19 holdout states were: Illinois, Alabama, Hawaii, Kentucky, Virginia, Montana, New Jersey, Indiana, Michigan, Oklahoma, West Virginia, Ohio, Delaware, Missouri, Louisiana, Georgia, Oregon, Utah, and Arkansas. See Nicholas Johnson, Christina Smith Fitzpatrick, and Elizabeth C. McNichol, *State Income Tax Burdens on Low-Income Families in 1998: Assessing the Burden and Opportunities for Relief* (Washington, D.C.: Center on Budget and Policy Priorities, March 1999). Almost 100,000 poor New York City families pay taxes on incomes that are too low for federal and state taxes. The City's public advocate, Mark Green, concluded that the City's tax system was contributing to the broad gap between rich and poor in the city. Thomas J. Lueck, "New York Taxes Poor Whom U.S. and State Exempt," *New York Times*, 30 April 1998, B2.

132. Diana Pearce and Jennifer Brooks, *The Self-Sufficiency Standard for the Washington, D.C. Metropolitan Area* (Washington, D.C.: Wider Opportunities for Women, Fall 1999).

133. Ibid., 9, 11. Self-Sufficiency Standards have been calculated for several other regions of the country: California, Illinois, Indiana, Iowa, Massachusetts, North Carolina, Pennsylvania, and Texas, and more state studies are underway.

134. Jason DeParle, "Wisconsin Welfare Plan Justifies Hopes and Some Fear," *New York Times*, 15 January 1999, A1.

135. Fact Sheets, "New Welfare Laws Impact on Select Groups, Child Care Resources" (Medford, Mass.: Tufts University Center on Hunger, Poverty and Nutrition Policy, March 1997). Information was supplied by the Institute for Research on Poverty, Madison, Wisc., 1996.

136. Sherman et al., op. cit., 1-2 (see note 39).

137. In 1997, a survey of 15,000 people living in homeless rescue missions found that more than 20% became homeless after being cut off government assistance. See Skip Barry, "The Working Homeless," *Dollars & Sense* 216 (March/April 1998), 10. In a study of 777 homeless families with children living in shelters in 10 cities in late 1997 and early 1998, nearly 1 out of 10 said their homelessness had been caused by TANF reductions or elimination during the past 6 months. See Homes for the Homeless and the Institute for Children and Poverty, *Ten Cities: A Snapshot of Family Homelessness across America, 1997-1998* (New York, 1998), 29, cited in Sherman et al., op. cit. (see note 39). The cities were Atlanta, Salem/Eugene, San Francisco, Dallas/Fort Worth, San Antonio, Norman (Oklahoma), Milwaukee, Chicago, South Bend, and New York City. Among 308 homeless families surveyed in Los Angeles family shelters, 12% said they had experienced benefit reductions or cuts that led directly to their homelessness. Other homeless families reported that benefit cuts had made it harder for them to pay rent or other bills, perhaps contributing to their homelessness. Unpublished tabulations by the Community Welfare Monitoring Project of the Los Angeles Coalition to End Hunger and Homelessness, 13 August 1998, cited in Sherman et al., op. cit. (see note 39).

138. John Tapogna and Ed Whitelaw, "Reforming Welfare Reform, *Oregon Quarterly* (Autumn 1999), 21.

139. During the latter half of the 1990s, low-wage workers began to close the gap with those in the middle, but those at the upper end continued to pull away from the middle and working classes. Lawrence Mishel, Jared Bernstein, and John Schmitt, "Introduction," *The State of Working America 2000-01* (Washington, D.C.: Economic Policy Institute, 2001), 4.

140. Robert Reich describes three types of workers with greatly differing wages and benefits, power over their work, and opportunity for advancement: symbolic analysts; routine production service workers; and in-person service workers. See Robert A. Reich: *The Work of Nations: Preparing Ourselves for the 21st Century* (New York: Vintage Books/ Random House, 1992); James Galbraith describes three industry sectors rather than three types of workers: a high-wage, generally well-protected sector in the monopolistic knowledge industries—especially military-related industries; a middle sector in which wages are dependent largely on the strength of organized labor; and a low-wage sector made up primarily of unskilled service workers where wages are often at poverty level or below and jobs are highly insecure. James K. Galbraith, *Created Unequal: The Crisis in American Pay* (New York: The Free Press, 1998).

141. Wages fell between 1979 and 1995 but began to pick up again in the late 1990s. The wages of those at the lowest end grew fastest, but while productivity rose 20.5% between 1989 and 1999, the median hourly wage among men was slightly less in 1999 than in 1989, while for women it was up just 4%. The divergence between the wage growth of typical workers and productivity growth arises because of rising wage inequality and a shift of income from workers to owners of capital. Mishel et al., op. cit., 9 (see note 139).

142. Mishel et al. put the percentage of workers employed in "nonstandard" work arrangements at nearly one-third of the total labor force in 1997. These "nonstandard" jobs ranged from independent contracting and other forms of self-employment to work in temporary agencies. Nonstandard workers earn less than workers with comparable skills and background who

work in regular, full-time jobs and are less likely to have health or pension benefits. Lawrence Mishel, Jared Bernstein, and John Schmitt, "Executive Summary," *The State of Working America 1998-99* (Ithaca, N.Y.: Cornell University Press, 1999), 21. Paul Osterman, however, defines "contingent" work more narrowly as "an employment situation in which an essential characteristic of the job is that the employee lacks the level of job security that a given employer makes available to 'regular' workers" (p. 55). In 1997, he calculated that temporary employment accounted for 2.7% of total employment and contingent employment 2.4%. Paul Osterman, *Securing Prosperity: The American Labor Market: How It Has Changed and What to Do about It* (Princeton, N.J.: Princeton University Press, 1999), 103.

143. The wage required to lift a family of four headed by a full-time year-round worker out of poverty was $8.19 per hour in 1999. Mishel et al., op. cit., 16 (see note 139).

144. *Paradox of Our Times: Hunger in a Strong Economy* (Medford, Mass.: Tufts University Center on Hunger, Poverty and Nutrition Policy), highlights of the publication available (3 November 2000) at: http://hunger.tufts.edu/pub/paradox_of_our_times. An earlier analysis of food insecurity conducted by the Tuft's Center provided three definitions or levels of food insecurity. The first was defined as "food insecure without hunger." Such households could not afford to insure the nutritional quality of their food. The second and third categories were "food insecure with modest hunger" and "food insecure with severe hunger." Press release, "State-level Study Finds over 15% of Households Food Insecure/Hungry in Seven States, 10% or More in Two-Thirds of States," 22 October 1997.

145. *Statement on the Link Between Nutrition and Cognitive Development in Children* (Medford, Mass.: Tufts University Center on Hunger, Poverty and Nutrition Policy, 1995).

146. Ibid., 5.

147. Mishel et al., op. cit. (see note 142). Unskilled, undereducated workers are not the only ones facing bleak prospects for self-sufficiency from jobs. A college education generally yields about $20,000 more in income than a high school diploma. See U.S. Bureau of the Census, *Current Population*

Reports, P60-193, *Money Income in the United States: 1995* (Washington, D.C.: U.S. Government Printing Office, 1996), table 9, 34. Nevertheless, a growing percentage of college graduates are having difficulty earning enough to support a family. A high school graduate is twice as likely to live in poverty as someone with 1 or more years of college, and a person without a high school diploma is six times as likely to live in poverty as someone with 1 or more years of college. See Jennifer Sturiale, "Relationship between Poverty and Level of Education for Householders 25 Years Old and Over by Race and Hispanic Origin," *Poverty and Income Trends: 1995* (Washington, D.C.: Center on Budget and Policy Priorities, March 1996), 82-83. Based on U.S. Bureau of the Census, Current Populations Reports, unpublished data, March 1996. Unlike past recoveries, this one did not significantly boost the salaries of those in the middle. The MacArthur Foundation found that 9.2% of the working poor in Chicago in 1997 had B.A.s, and one in five college graduates was working in a job for which he or she was overqualified. Thomas Geoghegan, "Overeducated and Underpaid," *New York Times*, 3 June 1997, A23. According to economist Alan B. Krueger, the rosy employment statistics reported by the Labor Department for the economic recovery from the 1991–1992 recession hid a startling phenomenon. While wages for the poorest sector stopped their 20-year fall in 1997 and both employment and wages increased for workers at the top, wages for the vast middle continued to erode, with the median worker's wage falling 5% since 1989. Alan B. Krueger, "The Truth About Wages," *New York Times,* 31 July 1997, A23.

148. A study of census data by the Annie E. Casey Foundation found that the number of poor children with an employed parent or parents increased by 65% over the past two decades, compared with a 25% increase among welfare families in which the parents did not work. It was cited in Steven A. Holmes, "Study Rethinks Relationship between Welfare and Work," *New York Times*, 4 June 1996, D21. Another study by the National Center for Children in Poverty corroborated this trend. Even in families where the single mothers worked full time, 17% of the children under 6 lived in poverty. Without

the EITC, the study found that the rate of children living in poverty would have been 23% higher. Study cited in Tamar Lewin, "Study Finds That Youngest U.S. Children Are Poorest," *New York Times*, 15 March 1998, A15.

149. Kathryn Edin and Laura Lein, *Making Ends Meet: How Single Mothers Survive Welfare and Low-Wage Work* (New York: Russell Sage Foundation, 1997).

150. Lawrence Mishel, Jared Bernstein and John Schmitt, *The State of Working America 1996-97* (Armonk, N.Y.: M.E. Sharpe, 1997), 158.

151. U.S. Bureau of the Census, Current Population Reports, Series P60-211, *Health Insurance Coverage: 1999*, available on the Web (30 September 2000) at: http://www.census.gov/hhes/hlthins/hlthin99.

152. Harry T. Holzer, *What Employers Want: Job Prospects for Less-Educated Workers* (New York: Russell Sage Foundation, 1996).

153. For a discussion of the possible effects of immigrant labor on the wages of native-born, low-income workers, see note 82 in Chapter 5.

154. Solow speculates that wages for unskilled jobs would have to fall by more than 5% to make enough jobs available for all the welfare recipients who will need them. If this drop in wages is checked by minimum wage laws, then more unemployment would be the result. See Robert M. Solow, "Guess Who Pays for Workfare?" *New York Review of Books*, 5 (November 1998), 27-28.

155. An important study on the relation of welfare payments to wages demonstrates that declining welfare packages have already been a major factor in depressing the wages of low-income workers. Michael Hout, *Inequality at the Margins: The Effects of Welfare, the Minimum Wage and Tax Credits on Low-Wage Labor Markets* (New York: The Russell Sage Foundation, March 1997).

156. See Phil Wilayto, op. cit. (see note 51) for a detailed examination of the corporate and philanthropic connections.

157. Kathleen Mullan Harris, *Teen Mothers and the Revolving Door* (Philadelphia: Temple University Press, 1997), cited in Michael Hout, op. cit., 7 (see note 155).

158. Jared Bernstein, *The Challenge of Moving from Welfare to Work: Depressed Labor Market Awaits Those Leaving the Rolls*, 1997 (Washington, D.C.: Economic Policy Institute), 1. Available at: Economic Policy Institute (27 April 1997), http://www.epinet.org.

159. Press briefing by Shalala et al., op. cit., 9 (see note 1). Robert Pear, "Welfare Workers Rate High in Job Retention at Companies," *New York Times*, 27 May 1998, A17.

160. See, e.g., Sharon Parrott, *Welfare Recipients Who Find Jobs*, op. cit. (see note 36); Alan Finder, "Evidence Is Scant That Workfare Leads to Full-time Jobs," *New York Times*, 12 April 1998, A1.

161. Phil Wilayto, op. cit. (see note 51).

162. "Conservatives Say Privatizing Welfare Helps Poor, Nonprofits," *Welfare to Work* 5 (25 March 1996), 236. *Welfare to Work* is published by MII Publications, Washington, D.C. George W. Bush, "Rallying the Armies of Compassion," 29 January 2001, available on the Web (8 February 2001) at: http://www.whitehouse.gov.

163. Bush, ibid.

164. "Conservatives Say Privatizing Welfare Helps Poor, Nonprofits," op. cit. (see note 162).

165. PRWORA, op. cit., Title IX, Sec. 908 (see note 3), "Reduction of Block Grants to States for Social Services; Use of Vouchers."

166. The strong economy and inflated stock market increased charitable giving by 16% between 1995 and 1997, yet philanthropic giving remained at 2% of the GDP—the level of the last three decades. Peter T. Kilborn, "Picking and Choosing among the Truly Needy," *New York Times*, 5 October 1997, Sec. 4, 3.

167. Ruth Coniff, "Girding for Disaster," *The Progressive* 61 (March 1997), 22-24.

168. Peter T. Kilborn, op. cit. (see note 166).

169. John T. Cook and J. Larry Brown, *Analysis of the Capacity of the Second Harvest Network to Cover the Federal Food Stamp Shortfall from 1997 to 2002*, CHPNP, working paper Series FSPSF-070197-1 (Medford, Mass.: Center on Hunger, Poverty and Nutrition Policy, Tufts University School of Nutrition Sciences and Policy, July 1997), 4; U.S. Conference of Mayors, *Hunger and Homelessness in America's Cities 1999*, op. cit. (see note 40).

170. Ibid., see also Andrew C. Revkin, "As Need for Food Grows, Donations Steadily Drop," *New York Times*, 27 February 1999, A1. After studying a number of surveys of social-service provision by churches under Charitable Choice, Eileen Lindner concludes that "while many congregations provided some form of social service ministry, only a small percentage do so in a manner and degree sufficient to obtain public monies and conform to the requirements thereof." The Rev. Eileen Lindner, "Considering Charitable Choice," *2001 Yearbook of American and Canadian Churches* (New York: National Council of Churches of Christ, 2001).

171. Loic J. D. Wacquant and William Julius Wilson, "Poverty, Joblessness and the Social Transformation of the Inner City," in Phoebe H. Cottingham and David T. Ellwood, eds., *Welfare Policy for the 1990s* (Cambridge, Mass.: Harvard University Press, 1989), 70-102. See also Thomas J. Sugrue, "The Structures of Urban Poverty: The Reorganization of Space and Work in Three Periods of American History," in Michael B. Katz, ed., *The "Underclass" Debate: Views from History* (Princeton, N.J.: Princeton University Press, 1993), 114-115.

172. Walter W. Stafford, *Black Civil Society and the Black Family in New York City: A Struggle for Inclusion in Decision-Making* (New York: Black Family Task Force/Manhattan Borough President's Office, 1997), vi.

173. Adam Nagourney, "In Surprise Confrontation during Visit, President Is Criticized on Welfare Law," *New York Times*, 19 February 1997, B6.

174. See, for example: Laurie Goodstein, "Religious Groups See Larger Role in Welfare," *New York Times*, 14 December 1997, A39. For additional views on the implications of and experiences

with Charitable Choice, see Amy L. Sherman, "Churches as Government Partners: Navigating 'Charitable Choice,'" *The Christian Century,* 5 July 2000, 716ff.; Lisa E. Oliphant, "Charitable Choice: The End of Churches as We Know Them?" *Policy and Practice of Public Human Services* 58, June 2000, 8.

175. Steven Greenhouse, "2 Well-Known Churches Say No to Workfare Jobs," *New York Times,* 4 August 1997, B3.

176. GAO, op. cit., 69 (see note 11).

177. "Workfare," *Welfare Reform Network News* 5, 30 April 1997. Newsletter of the Institute for Women's Policy Research, Washington, D.C.

178. "A Workfare Primer," *Welfare News* 2 (September 1997), 7. Newsletter of the Welfare Law Center, New York, N.Y.

179. Steven Greenhouse, "Many Participants in Workfare Take the Place of City Workers," *New York Times,* 13 April 1998, A1. Despite vehement denials by New York's mayor, municipal labor unions filed two suits against the City, charging that it was violating the state's welfare law, which bars public employees from replacing regular workers with workfare participants. Ian Fisher, "Giuliani Drops Workfare Jobs at the Hospitals," *New York Times,* 24 April 1998, A1.

180. "Workfare Workers Win Basic Employment Rights," *NELP Update* (Summer/Fall 1997), 1. Newsletter of the National Employment Law Project, New York, N.Y. In response to a court challenge, a New York State appellate court ruled in September 1998 that New York City's workfare Work Experience Program [WEP] workers did not have to be paid the prevailing wage because "there is a historical recognition that public-assistance recipients performing tasks in exchange for benefits are not public employees." Alan Finder, "Court Backs Giuliani's Way of Assigning Workfare Hours," *New York Times,* 19 September 1998, B3.

181. Liz Schott et al., op. cit., 8 (see note 21).

182. The New York Civil Liberties Union has detailed a host of rights abuses that have been found in New York City's WEP. See *Civil Liberties and Welfare Reform* (New York: New York Civil Liberties Union, March 1997).

183. Although Clinton did not admit that he gave in to union pressure, both critics of the decision and labor leaders concluded that he did. "Making Welfare Work," *New York Times*, 31 May 1997, A18; Jason DeParle, "White House Calls for Minimum Wage in Workfare Plan," *New York Times*, 16 May 1997, A1; Robert Pear, "G.O.P. in House Moves to Bar Minimum Wage for Workfare," *New York Times*, 12 June 1997, B16.

184. "California Rejects DOL Guidance on Minimum Wage Rights of Work Program Participants," *Welfare News* 3, ISSN1091-4064, 30 June 1998, 4-5. Newsletter of the Welfare Law Center, New York, N.Y.

185. Rachel Leon, *Workfare in NYS: Does it Work?* (Albany, N.Y.: Hunger Action Network of New York State, 12 July 1995).

186. Against the wishes of his rank-and-file, Hill had initially made an accommodation with the City over workfare, agreeing to go along with it in exchange for the City's pledge not to displace union members, but he was later forced out of his union leadership post over this and corruption charges. Robert D. McFadden, "Union Chief Calls Workfare 'Slavery,'" *New York Times*, 19 April 1998, A37.

187. "Initial Activities of WLC Workfare Organizing Support Center Include Survey of Workfare Experience," *Welfare News*, 2 (December 1997), 5. Newsletter of the Welfare Law Center, New York, N.Y.

188. Rachel Swarns, "A Wakeup Call for Workfare's Advocates," *New York Times*, 19 April 1998, Sec. 4, 5.

189. Greenhouse, op. cit. (see note 174).

CHAPTER 9
WASHINGTON'S NEW POOR LAW: PART II

1. A study by the Institute for Women's Policy Research of a representative sample of the 2.8 million women receiving AFDC funds showed that over a 2-year period, 70% spent significant time in the labor force. Of that group, 43% worked a substantial amount of time, 30% spent substantial time looking for work or cycling in and out of work, 5% were students

(i.e., preparing themselves for the workforce), and 10% were disabled. Roberta Spalter-Roth, Beverly Burr, Heidi Hartmann, and Lois Shaw, *Welfare That Works: The Working Lives of AFDC Recipients* (Washington, D.C.: Institute for Women's Policy Research, 1995). The New York State Department of Labor concluded that only one-fifth of the welfare recipients required to register with the labor office under New York's welfare reform had virtually no work experience. "Spotlight on Welfare Recipients," *Employment in New York State* (New York: New York State Department of Labor, June 1997), 1. Several other studies have confirmed the extensive work experience of single mothers. Irwin Garfinkel and Sara S. McLanahan, *Single Mothers and Their Children* (Washington, D.C.: The Urban Institute, 1986); Kathleen Mullan Harris, "Work and Welfare among Single Mothers in Poverty," *American Journal of Sociology* 99 (September 1993), 317-352; Christopher Jencks and Kathryn Edin, "The Real Welfare Problem," *American Prospect* 1 (Spring 1990), 31-50; Sar A. Levitan and Isaac Shapiro, *Working but Poor* (Baltimore: Johns Hopkins University Press, 1987); Diana M. Pearce, "The Feminization of Poverty: Women, Work and Welfare," *Urban and Social Change Review* 11 (1978), 28-36; and Marta Tienda, "Welfare and Work in Chicago's Inner-City," *American Economic Review* 80 (1990), 372-376.

2. The in-depth interviews of 379 welfare mothers conducted by Kathryn Edin and Laura Lein generally corroborate these findings on the extensive work experience of welfare mothers, whether or not they report it to the welfare office. Kathryn Edin and Laura Lein, *Making Ends Meet: How Single Mothers Survive Welfare and Low-Wage Work* (New York: Russell Sage Foundation, 1997). A random-sample study of welfare recipients in a county in Michigan added further evidence of the work experience of welfare recipients. The study showed that only 10% had little work experience or failed to recognize workplace norms. Sandra Danziger, Mary Corcoran, Sheldon Danziger, Colleen Haflin, Ariel Kalil, Judith Levine, Daniel Rosen, Kristin Seefeldt, Kristine Siefert, and Richard Tolman, "Barriers to Work among Welfare Recipients," *Focus* 20 (Spring 1999). *Focus* is a publication of the Institute for Research on Poverty, University of Wisconsin, Madison.

3. Judith Combes Taylor, *Learning at Work in a Work-Based Welfare System: Opportunities and Obstacles* (Boston: Jobs for the Future, April 1997), 3. Available at Jobs for the Future (10 September 1999) at: http://www.jff.org/resources/publications/Joyce_ExecSummary.pdf.

4. Spalter-Roth et al. found that completing high school increased the chances of escaping from poverty from 11% to 31%, and some job training more than doubled the chances of escaping from poverty (from 11% to 26%), op. cit. (see note 1).

5. Of first-time recipients 53% had high school diplomas; 34% had from 9–11 years of schooling; and 13% had less than a ninth-grade education. *Aid to Families with Dependent Children: The Baseline* (Washington, D.C.: Office of Human Services, Policy Office of the Assistant Secretary for Planning and Evaluation, U.S. Department of Health and Human Services, June 1998), 116. See also Combes Taylor (see note 3).

6. Judy Mann, "What Welfare Reformers Need to Know," *The Washington Post*, 24 March 1995, E3.

7. Cited by Peter Edelman, "The Worst Thing Bill Clinton Has Done," *Atlantic Monthly,* March 1997, 53.

8. Memo from Mark Greenberg, 30 August 1999.

9. Maurice Emsellem, "Welfare Reforming the Workplace: The Hidden Threat to Workers and Labor Standards," *Uncommon Sense* 18 (New York: National Jobs for All Coalition, April 1997).

10. Comparing 1997 to 1994, the decline in education/training participants ranged from an 84% drop in Maryland to a 30% reduction in California. U.S. General Accounting Office, *Welfare Reform: States Are Restructuring Programs to Reduce Welfare Dependence*, Chapter Report GAO-HEHS-98-109, Washington, D.C.: 17 June 1998, 26-30. Available at: U.S. General Accounting Office (1 September 1999), http://frwebgate.access.gpo.gov/cgi-bin/useftp.cgi.

11. Combes Taylor, op. cit., 3-4 (see note 3); Greg Owen, Ellen Shelton, Amy Bush Stevens, Justine Nelson-Christinedaughter, Corinna Roy, and June Heineman, "Whose Job Is It" Employers' Views of Welfare Reform," *Joint Center for Poverty Research Newsletter* 14 (September 2000).

12. Greenberg, op. cit. (see note 8).

13. The U.S. Department of Education estimates that women with
     some college experience outearn high-school graduates by
     28%. Statistic cited in James M. O'Neill, "New Rules Alter
     Course of Students on Welfare Nationwide: Legislation Re-
     quiring Recipients to Work Is Forcing Some to Drop Out,"
     Philadelphia Inquirer, 25 April 1999, B1. In a study of welfare
     recipients who graduated from eastern Washington Univer-
     sity, Thomas Karier found that "the returns to a college degree
     were sufficiently high to make postsecondary education a
     particularly promising avenue to financial independence."
     Thomas Karier, "Welfare Graduates: College and Financial
     Independence," *Policy Notes* 1998/1 (Annandale, N.Y.: Jerome
     Levy Economics Institute), 1. Available at: Jerome Levy Institute
     (17 January 1999), http://www.levy.org/docs/pn98-1.html. A
     City University of New York Graduate School study of the
     effect of higher education on welfare mothers' earnings and
     employment showed that within a year of graduation, 89%
     had jobs, 87% had earnings high enough to get off welfare,
     75% reported earning more than $10,000 a year, and 42%
     more than $20,000 a year. Similar results were found in Il-
     linois, Pennsylvania, Wyoming, Washington, and Tennessee.
     Diana Spatz, "Welfare Reform Skips School," *The Nation*
     264 (2 June 1997), 18.

14. Interview with Charisse Texeira, 3 April 1997.

15. O'Neill, op. cit. (see note 13).

16. Baime quoted in O'Neill, ibid.

17. "Welfare Reform Is Crunching Higher Ed Enrollment," *On
     Campus* (May/June 1997), 8. Publication of the American
     Federation of Teachers, Washington, D.C.

18. The final regulations are found in: 64 *Federal Register* 17719-
     17931. The Center on Budget and Policy Priorities began a
     series of articles examining the implications of the regula-
     tions. See Liz Schott, Ed Lazere, Heidi Goldberg, and Eileen
     Sweeney, *Highlights of the Final TANF Regulations*, Wash-
     ington, D.C.: Center on Budget and Policy Priorities, 29 April
     1999. Available at: Center on Budget and Policy Priorities
     (17 July 1999), http://www.cbpp.org/4-29-99wel.htm. See also

Mark Greenberg and Stephen Savner, *The Final TANF Regulations: A Preliminary Analysis* (Washington, D.C.: Center for Law and Social Policy, May 1999) available at: CLASP (6 September 1999), http://www.clasp.org/finalregs.PDF.

19.   Activists in Kentucky succeeded in getting a bill passed that secured TANF recipients' "right" to education. It assures that Kentucky TANF recipients will be able to enroll in college, cannot be forced out, and can continue after they reach their 12 months if they are meeting work requirements. TANF recipients will also be informed in writing about their options in education, and the cabinet will make quarterly reports about progress to legislators. Information supplied to authors by Lory Anne Griffy, Women's Center, University of Louisville, Louisville, Ky. She helped write her state's education bill for welfare recipients, House Bill 434.

20.   Mark Greenberg, Julie Strawn, and Lisa Plimpton, *State Opportunities to Provide Access to Postsecondary Education under TANF* (Washington, D.C.: Center for Law and Social Policy, September 1999). Seven states still refuse to allow any higher education to count as work.

21.   "Welfare Reform is Crunching Higher Ed Enrollment,"op. cit. (see note 17).

22.   California allows welfare-to-work participants to attend vocational or academic courses provided that: (1) the participant initiates the program prior to being called in for her or his initial welfare-to-work orientation; (2) the welfare agency determines that the program leads to employment in an occupation for which a demand exists; and (3) the participant does not have a college degree, unless the participant is pursuing a teaching credential. Information supplied by Michael Lichter, senior research analyst, Urban Research Division, Chief Administrative Office, County of Los Angeles, 23 September 1999, and Diana Spatz, executive director, Low-Income Families' Empowerment through Education, Berkeley, Calif., 29 April 1999.

23.   For a description of various options in using the work-study strategy, see Clifford M. Johnson and Esther Kaggwa, *Work-Study Programs for Welfare Recipients: A Job Creation Strategy*

That Combines Work and Education (Washington, D.C.: Center on Budget and Policy Priorities, 18 August 1998). Maine Parents as Scholars Program uses state dollars to set up a work-study program enabling up to 2,000 students to go to college with a cash stipend, medical coverage, child care, and other services they would have received under TANF. Welfare advocates in New York State succeeded in getting the state's Welfare Reform Act of 1997 to require the assessment of all workfare recipients and to honor preferences in assigning TANF recipients to work activities. If a recipient was already enrolled in education or training at the time of call-in, there cannot be a new work assignment unless there is a new assessment. "Organizing and Litigation: Joint Strategies to Secure Protections for Workfare Workers," *Welfare News* 3 (November 5, 1998), 1-2. A newsletter of the Welfare Law Center, New York, N.Y.

24.   O'Neill, op. cit. (see note 13).

25.   Children's Defense Fund, *The State of America's Children Yearbook 1997* (Washington, D.C.: Author, 1997), 2.

26.   Ibid., 38.

27.   Sharon K. Long, Gretchen G. Kirby, Robin Kurka, and Shelley Waters, *Child Care Assistance under Welfare Reform: Early Responses by the States*, occasional paper no. 15 (Washington, D.C.: The Urban Institute, September 1998), 11. See also "TANF Funds Alone Are Not the Child Care Solution," Childrens' Defense Fund Issue Basics. Available from their website (26 September 2000) at: http://www.childrensdefense.org.

28.   U.S. Department of Health and Human Services estimate cited in Arloc Sherman, Cheryl Amey, Barbara Duffield, Nancy Ebb, and Deborah Weinstein, *Welfare to What: Early Findings on Family Hardship and Well-Being* (Washington, D.C.: Children's Defense Fund and National Coalition for the Homeless, December 1998), 28.

29.   United States Conference of Mayors, *Implementing Welfare Reform in America's Cities*, November 1997, Washington, D.C.

30.   "New Studies Look at Status of Former Welfare Recipients," *CDF Reports* (April/May 1998). Publication of Children's

Defense Fund, Washington, D.C. Rachel L. Swarns, "Mothers Poised for Workfare Face Acute Lack of Day Care," *New York Times*, 14 April 1998, B1.

31. Employment and Training Institute, *Removing Barriers to Employment: The ChilD.C.are-Jobs Equation* (Milwaukee: Employment and Training Institute, University of Wisconsin-Milwaukee, May 1998).

32. Jennifer Preston, "Welfare Rules Intensify Need for Day Care," *New York Times*, 11 November 1996, B1.

33. Gina Adams and Nicole Oxendine Poersch, *Who Cares? State Commitment to Child Care and Early Education* (Washington, D.C.: Children's Defense Fund, December 1996).

34. Ann Collins and J. Lawrence Aber, *Children and Welfare Reform*, Issue Brief 1 (New York: National Center for Children in Poverty, 1997), 6-7.

35. Joe Sexton, "Welfare Mothers and Informal Day Care: Is It up to Par?" *New York Times*, 14 October 1996, B1.

36. Peter T. Kilborn, "Child-Care Solutions in a New World of Welfare," *New York Times*, 1 June 1997, A1.

37. The survey by the Center for the Child Care Work Force was based on a sample of child-care centers in Atlanta, Boston, Detroit, Phoenix, and Seattle. The best child care and highest wages for child-care workers were found to be offered by nonprofit centers, but during the decade in which welfare mothers were being pushed into the workforce and public support for child care increased, for-profit chains tripled their revenues from public subsidies. Independent nonprofit centers experienced a 4% decrease in public subsidies. Tamar Lewin, "From Welfare Roll to Child Care Worker," *New York Times*, 29 April 1998, A14.

38. Center on Budget and Policy Priorities, "Developing Innovative Child Support Demonstrations for Non-Custodial Parents," Washington, D.C., 9 January 1998. Available at: Center on Budget and Policy Priorities, http://www.cbpp.org/noncust.htm.

39. U.S. House of Representatives, Committee on Ways and Means, *1998 Green Book: Background Material and Data on*

Programs within the Jurisdiction of the Committee on Ways and Means (Washington, D.C.: U.S. Government Printing Office, 1998), 604-605.

40. Ibid.

41. Clinton's Department of Health and Human Services reported that federal and state child-support enforcement programs broke new records in nationwide collections in fiscal year 2000, reaching $18 billion, a 123% increase over 1992. Press release, "Child Support Collections, Administration for Children and Families, Department of Health and Human Services, 17 January 2001. The program for poor fathers, Parents' Fair Share, failed to increase the earnings or employment of non-custodial fathers. It showed only a small increase (6%) in the average amount of child support paid, and even that finding failed a test of significance. Jason DeParle, "Report on Effort to Aid Poor Fathers Offers Discouraging News," *New York Times*, 29 September 1998, A16.

42. Marguerite Rosenthal, "Sweden: Promise and Paradox," in Gertrude Schaffner Goldberg and Eleanor Kremen, eds., *The Feminization of Poverty: Only in America?* (New York: Praeger, 1990), 142.

43. Edelman, op. cit., 50 (see note 7).

44. One woman in four had health problems, 26.7% suffered from depression, 7.3% suffered from generalized anxiety disorder, 14.6% from post-traumatic stress disorder, probably from severe domestic abuse that had occurred for 14.9% in the last year, and 22.1% of them were caring for children with health, learning, or emotional problems. Significantly, only 2.7% suffered from alcohol dependence, and 3.3% from drug dependence. Danziger et al., op. cit., 32-33 (see note 2).

45. U.S. General Accounting Office, op. cit. (see note 10).

46. David Whitman, "Take This Job and Love It," *U.S. News & World Report*, 14 October 1997, 47.

47. U.S. Department of Health and Human Services, Fact Sheet on "Substance Abuse—A National Challenge," Washington, D.C., 20 December 1997. Available on the Web at: http://www.health.org/mtf/hhsfact.htm.

48. Ruth A. Brandwein and Diana M. Filiano, "Toward Real Welfare Reform: The Voices of Battered Women," *Affilia* 15 (Summer 2000), 225; Jody Raphael and Sheila Haennicke, *Keeping Women Safe through the Welfare-to-Work Journey: How Are We Doing?* (Chicago: The Taylor Institute, 1999), 4. Available on the Web at: http://www.ssw.umich.edu/trapped.

49. The PRWORA addresses domestic violence victims through two measures: the 20% "hardship" exemption, which allows each state to exempt 20% of its caseload from the work requirement for "hardship" reasons; and the Wellstone/Murray Family Violence Amendment, which provides that the governor of a state can opt to establish and enforce standards and procedures to: (a) screen welfare recipients for domestic abuse while maintaining their confidentiality; (b) refer victims to counseling and support services; and (c) exempt individuals with good cause for as long as necessary from certain requirements such as time limits, residency requirements, child-support cooperation, and family cap provisions when compliance with these requirements would make it more difficult for them to escape domestic violence or would unfairly penalize past, present, or potential future victims. "Domestic Violence and Welfare Receipt," *Welfare Reform Network News*, 31 March 1997/revised 11 April 1997, newsletter of the Institute for Women's Policy Research, Washington, D.C. A study released in December 1999 found that most states have adopted the Family Violence Option or are making plans to do so. See Raphael and Haennicke, op. cit. (see note 48). For a summary of the research on domestic violence see: U.S. General Accounting Office, *Domestic Violence: Prevalence and Implications for Employment among Welfare Recipients* GAO/HEHS-99-12 (Washington, D.C., November 1998), 2. Given the lack of trust between welfare recipients and the welfare system, many battered women may be reluctant to divulge the fact that they are battered. As one woman told researchers, "The caseworker would be the last one I'd want to tell." Brandwein and Filiano, ibid., 226, 237.

50. Between 16% and 60% of battered women surveyed in five studies reported that their partner had discouraged them from working, and 33–46% said that their partner prevented them from working. Many experience emotional or physical health

problems that could affect their ability to find and maintain employment. The studies reviewed by the GAO found that women who had been abused often suffered from chronic health problems, low self-esteem, depression and anxiety, and exhibited behaviors associated with post-traumatic stress disorder. U.S. General Accounting Office, ibid., 7-9.

51. Stacy Williams, family violence program manager, Babyland Family Services, New Jersey, in an address to the conference on "The Impact of Welfare Reform on the Delivery of Social Services in New Jersey," Kean University, Union, N.J., 18 March 1999.

52. U.S. General Accounting Office, op. cit., 111 (see note 10).

53. Using a regression model, the researchers concluded that women with 2–3 barriers to work had a 61.7% chance of holding at least a half-time job, women with 4–6 barriers had a 41% chance, while women with 7 or more barriers had only a 5.7% chance of working. Danziger et al., op. cit., 33 (see note 2).

54. Jason DeParle, "As Welfare Rolls Shrink, Load on Relatives Grows," *New York Times*, 21 February 1999, A1.

55. Ann Collins and Barbara Carlson, *Child Care by Kith and Kin—Supporting Family, Friends and Neighbors Caring for Children*. (New York: National Center for Children in Poverty, 1998), 5.

56. *Making Welfare Reform Work: A Report of the NACO Hearings on Welfare Reform Implementation* (Washington, D.C.: National Association of Counties, July 1997), 7.

57. Jason DeParle, "Leftover Money for Welfare Baffles, or Inspires, States," *New York Times*, 29 August 1999, A1.

58. In June 1998, New York City began moving 12,000 mothers, deemed by doctors to be unable to work, into city workfare slots with agencies the City claimed were set up to handle people with disabilities. The policy was challenged by advocates of the poor who said it violated state law and endangered the lives of the City's most vulnerable residents. Several other states, including Florida, Oregon, and Wisconsin, also began the process of putting the disabled to work. Rachel

L. Swarns, "Giuliani to Place Disabled Mothers in Workfare Jobs," *New York Times*, 8 June 1998, A1.

59. Nina Bernstein, "Medicaid Rolls Have Declined in Last Three Years," *New York Times*, 17 August 1998, B1.

60. In the first year of welfare repeal, 675 million people lost Medicaid. Those who lost it were disproportionately families of color. Families USA, *Losing Health Insurance: The Unintended Consequences of Welfare Reform*, Washington, D.C., May 1999, 1. Available at: Families USA (14 June 1999), http://www.familiesusa.org/unintpdt.htm. See also Kathleen A. Maloy, LaDonna A. Pavetti, Julie Darnell, and Peter Shin, *Diversion as a Work-Oriented Welfare Reform Strategy and Its Effect on Access to Medicaid: An Examination of the Experiences of Five Local Communities*, A Report of the Findings of the Second Phase of the Research Funded by the Administration for Children and Families and the Assistant Secretary for Planning and Evaluation, U.S. Department of Health and Human Services, March 1999. Available at: George Washington University School of Public Health and Health Services, Center for Health Policy Research (16 July 1999), http://www.gwumc.edu/chpr/wr/new/welfrfrm.pdf; Pamela Loprest, *Families Who Left Welfare: Who Are They and How Are They Doing?* (Washington, D.C.: The Urban Institute, 1999), available at The Urban Institute (6 September 1999), http://newfederalism.urban.org/html/discussion99-02.html. In one national study of health-care coverage of welfare leavers, the researcher found that most were receiving neither Medicaid nor employer-provided coverage. See Mark Greenberg, *Participation in Welfare Medicaid Enrollment*, Kaiser Foundation Policy Brief, September 1998 available at: Kaiser Foundation (6 September 1999), http://www.kfff.org/kff/library.html.

61. Edin and Lein, op. cit (see note 1).

62. Robert Pear, "Clinton Ordering Effort to Sign up Medicaid Children," *New York Times*, 29 December 1997, A15.

63. "Children's Health Insurance: The Year Ahead," *asap! Update*, April 1999. Newsletter of Families USA Foundation, Washington, D.C.

64.   Robert Greenstein, Richard Kogan, and Marion Nichols, *Bearing Most of the Burden: How Deficit Reduction in the 104th Congress Concentrated on the Poor* (Washington, D.C.: Center on Budget and Policy Priorities, 3 December 1996).

65.   "The Fiscal Year 2000 Military Budget," *The Defense Monitor* XXVIII no. 1 (1999) 1. Newsletter of the Center for Defense Information, Washington, D.C.

66.   Able-bodied adults without children can collect food stamps for 3 months in each 36-month period. After 3 months, they can continue to receive food stamps only if they are working at least half-time or are in a workfare or training slot. There is only one exception to this case: states with high levels of unemployment (10% or more) may request a suspension of the food stamp cut-off. David Super, *Overview of the Food Stamp Time Limits for People Between Ages 18 and 50,* rev. March 1997. Available at: Center on Budget and Policy Priorities (1 September 1999), http//:www.cbpp.org/fs1850ov.htm.

67.   The food-stamp cuts had a more devastating effect than policymakers had anticipated. First, the number of food-stamp workfare slots was only a small fraction of what framers of the bill assumed it would be; second, there is the job gap for undereducated, unskilled workers in the inner cities previously explored; and third, because the tax provisions of the new minimum wage law give employers a tax credit for hiring other types of disadvantaged individuals—welfare recipients, youth living in certain low-income areas, certain ex-felons with low incomes, and certain low-income veterans—but *not* persons in the category affected by this provision. *The Administration's Proposals to Ease Some of the Welfare Law's Harshest Provisions* (Washington, D.C.: Center on Budget and Policy Priorities, 11 April 1997), 10.

68.   Ibid.

69.   Lizette Alvarez, "In Slap at G.O.P. Leadership, House Stops Move to Deny Food Stamps to Immigrants," *New York Times*, 23 May 1998, A11.

70.   *Food Stamp and Nutrition Programs*, available from The Welfare Information Network (9 September 1999) at: http://www.welfareinfo.org/food.htm.

71. Robert Pear, "U.S. to Review Disability Aid for Children," *New York Times*, 28 November 1996, A1.

72. Laura Summer, Sharon Parrott, and Cindy Mann, *Millions of Uninsured and Underinsured Children Are Eligible for Medicaid* (Washington, D.C.: Center on Budget and Policy Priorities, 6 January 1997), 10.

73. "Immigrants and the Medicaid and CHIP Programs," February 1999. Available at: Families USA (1 September 1999), http://www.familiesusa.org/immigrnt.htm.

74. Robert Pear, "A Move to Restore Benefits to Some Immigrants," *New York Times*, 4 May 1997, A30. Nonqualified immigrants would still be able to get certain emergency medical care (including immunizations and testing/treatment for communicable diseases), crisis and disaster relief, community-based services (as defined by the Attorney General), and certain housing assistance if already covered at the time of enactment. Nonqualified immigrants are also ineligible, with certain exceptions, for state and local public benefits unless specifically authorized by state law (including grants, contracts, licensing, retirement, as well as welfare and other benefits). Fredrica D. Kramer, *Welfare Reform and Immigrants: Recent Developments and a Review of Key State Decisions* (Washington, D.C.: The Welfare Information Network, 31 May 1998). Available from the Welfare Information Network (6 June 1999) at: http://www.welfareinfo.org/immigrantissue.htm.

75. Robert Pear, "Administration Welfare Plea Is Scorned," *New York Times*, 14 February 1997, A30.

76. Rachel L. Swarns, "Confused by Law, Nursing Homes Bar Legal Immigrants," *New York Times*, 20 May 1997, A1.

77. Town meeting on Welfare Reform, Yonkers, New York, sponsored by the League of Women Voters of Westchester County, 3 April 1997, attended by one of the authors.

78. John Atlas and Peter Dreier, "America's Housing Crisis: A Grasssroots Strategy and Policy Agenda," *Social Policy* 19 (Winter 1989), 2.

79. Center on Budget and Policy Priorities, *Welfare to Work Vouchers: Making Welfare Work* (Washington, D.C.: Center on Budget

and Policy Priorities, 7 April 1998). Available at: Center on Budget and Policy Priorities (1 September 1999), http://www.cbpp.org/407wel.htm.

80. U.S. Department of Housing and Urban Development, press release, "Housing Study Shows Record 5.3 Million House-holds—Including Growing Numbers of Working Poor—Need Housing Assistance," Washington, D.C., 28 April 1998. The report is entitled, *Rental Housing Assistance—The Crisis Continues* and is available on the Web at: HUD (7 March 1999), http://www.hud.gov.

81. Jennifer Daskal, *In Search of Shelter: The Growing Shortage of Affordable Housing* (Washington, D.C.: Center on Budget and Policy Priorities, 1998). The poverty standard for a family of three was $12,158 in 1995; affordability is defined as 30% of that income.

82. Edward Lazere, *In Short Supply: The Growing Affordable Housing Gap* (Washington, D.C.: Center on Budget and Policy Priorities, July 1995). See also Michael Janofsky, "Shortage of Housing for Poor Grows in U.S.," *New York Times*, 28 April 1998, A14; Jennifer Twombley, Winton Pitcoff, Cushing N. Dolbeare, and Sheila Crowley, *Out of Reach: The Growing Gap Between Housing Costs and Income of Poor People in the United States* (Washington, D.C.: National Low Income Housing Coalition, September 2000).

83. Don Terry, "Chicagoans Split on Housing Plan," *New York Times*, 29 June 1996, A1.

84. *A Tale of Two Nations: The Creation of American "Poverty Nomads"* (New York: Homes for the Homeless, January 1996).

85. Warren Cohen and Mike Tharp, "Fed-up Cities Turn to Evicting the Homeless," *U.S. News and World Report*, 11 January 1999, 28-30. A review of legal actions in 49 cities across the U.S. by the National Law Center on Homelessness and Poverty conducted in 1994 showed that 62% of the cities had passed or enforced measures to restrict the movement and activities of homeless people. Michael Janofsky, "Many Cities in Crackdown on Homeless," *New York Times*, 16 December 1994, A34.

86. James Dao, "Shelter Fee Is Proposed for Homeless," *New York Times*, 21 April 1995, B3.

87. Brosnahan, quoted in ibid.

88. The City University of New York had a policy of "open admissions" for three decades. Under this program, any student with a high-school diploma or equivalent could enter the City University and be given remedial help if needed. The program made it possible for hundreds of thousands from low-income families to obtain a college education. In May 1998, however, the Trustees of the University voted to end the program to the consternation of thousands of students and their professors. Karen W. Arenson, "CUNY to Tighten Admissions Policy at 4-Year Schools," *New York Times*, 28 May 1998, A1.

89. Kramer, op. cit (see note 74).

90. Ibid.

91. Jason DeParle, "Shrinking Welfare Rolls Leave Record High Share of Minorities," *New York Times*, 27 July 1998, A1. The *Times* analyzed data from 14 states and New York City, which accounted for nearly 70% of the nation's caseload. Among the most important findings was the growing Hispanic share of the caseload. See Rachel L. Swarns, "Hispanic Mothers Lagging as Others Leave Welfare," *New York Times*, 15 September 1998, A1.

92. Payne, quoted in DeParle, ibid.

93. For this history, see Mimi Abramovitz, *Regulating the Lives of Women: Social Welfare Policy from Colonial Times to the Present,* rev. ed. (Boston: South End Press, 1996); Linda Gordon, *Pitied but Not Entitled: Single Mothers and the History of Welfare 1890-1935* (Cambridge: Harvard University Press, 1994); and Joel F. Handler and Yeheskel Hasenfeld, *The Moral Construction of Poverty: Welfare Reform in America* (Newbury Park, Calif.: Sage Publications, 1991).

94. Gwendolyn Mink, *Welfare's End* (Ithaca, N.Y.: Cornell University Press, 1998), 118. Mink points out that most married mothers with children under the age of 18 are not full-time, year-round wage workers.

95. According to a Washington policy analyst, only three con-
gresswomen—Patsy Mink, Eleanor Holmes Norton, and Lynn
Woolsey—showed up in the early days of 1995 to support
advocates of poor women who were trying to fight this kind
of welfare reform. Telephone interview with Patricia Reuss,
21 July 1998.

96. The *Time* quote is from 26 July 1996. It was cited in Laura
Flanders, "Compassion Rationed," *Extra!* (November-December, 1996), 9. *Extra!* is a publication of Fairness and Accu-
racy in Reporting, New York, N.Y.

97. The *Washington Post* quote is from 18 July 1996, cited in
Flanders, ibid.

98. Christopher Jencks and Kathryn Edin, "Do Poor Women Have
the Right to Bear Children?" *The American Prospect* 20 (Winter
1995), 43.

99. Mink, op. cit., 121 (see note 95).

100. Edelman, op. cit. (see note 7).

101. Ibid., 46.

102. Robert Scheer, "Trouble Still in Forest City," *The Nation*
256 (22 March 1993), 371-372.

103. Jerry Gray, "House Panel, 31-7, Advances the Balanced-Budget
Deal," *New York Times*, 17 May 1997, A5.

104. Robert Greenstein, *Looking at the Details of the New Budget Legislation: Social Program Initiatives Decline over Time
While Upper-Income Tax Cuts Grow* (Washington, D.C.: Center
on Budget and Policy Priorities, 12 August 1999), 3. Funding for the social program initiatives declines from $10.2
billion in fiscal year 1999 to $8.6 billion in fiscal year 2007,
a decline of 34%, after adjusting for inflation (p. 2).

CHAPTER 10
REAL WELFARE REFORM—THE ROADS NOT TAKEN

1. For the latter point about politicians and business leaders
having to eat their antigovernment words before bringing
Washington to the rescue, see Louis Uchitelle, "Who You

Gonna Call After the Next Bust?" *New York Times*, 22 August 1999, 4:5.

2. Center on Budget and Policy Priorities, *The Poverty Despite Work Handbook,* 2nd ed. (Washington, D.C.: Author, 1999).

3. Poverty-level wages are defined as less than the poverty level for a family of 3 or $13,290 for full-time, year-round work in 1999. For figures on poverty-level wages, see Lawrence Mishel, Jared Bernstein, and John Schmitt, *The State of Working America 2000-01* (Washington, D.C.: Cornell University Press, 2001), tables 2.11-2.13, 133-135.

4. The research of Timothy Bartik led him to conclude that in large East Coast states as well as Illinois and California, slower growing and with more liberal welfare laws and larger caseloads, the labor-supply effects of welfare reform are likely to be particularly large. For example, in New York State, welfare reform could be expected to increase unemployment and reduce wages for less-educated women. See Timothy J. Bartik, "The Labor Supply Effects of Welfare Reform," Kalamazoo, Mich., W. E. Upjohn Institute for Employment Research, 16 July 1998. Available at http://www. upjohninstit.org. It is true that the lowest-wage female workers have shown the largest income gains between 1989 and the first half of 1999 (10.4% increase in real hourly wages for the bottom decile and 6.2% for the bottom quintile, compared to 1.9% for the median gains of all workers). However, the gains for lowest-paid women workers were not even so large as the 16.9% real rise in the minimum wage between 1989 and 1998.

5. Actually, the entitlement for families was largely confined to single-parent families. Among working-age people, most married-couple families as well as childless individuals or couples were excluded.

6. In Chapter 8, we cited *The Underbelly of the U.S. Economy,* the name of an annual publication of the Council on International and Public Affairs that calculates actual joblessness in the United States and finds that it is more than twice the official unemployment rate. Not included in the "underbelly" calculations are jobs that pay less than the poverty level for year-round, full-time work and the large prison and jail

population, nearly two million in 1999. See page 296 for a definition of "disguised unemployment" that focuses on very low-wage jobs.

7. Committee on Economic Security, *The Report of the Committee on Economic Security of 1935, 50th Anniversary Edition* (Washington, D.C.: National Conference on Social Welfare, 1985), 8-9.

8. Compiled by Jim Werner from data of the U.S. Bureau of Labor Statistics, Local Area Unemployment Statistics Program, New York: National Jobs for All Coalition, undated.

9. U.S. Department of Housing and Urban Development, *Now Is the Time: Places Left Behind in the New Economy* (Washington, D.C.: Author, 1999).

10. Frances Perkins, *The Roosevelt I Knew* (New York: Viking, 1946), 190.

11. Franklin Delano Roosevelt, *The Public Papers and Addresses of Franklin D. Roosevelt, 1944-45,* vol. 13, Samuel I. Rosenman, ed. (New York: Russell & Russell, 1950), 40-42.

12. Serge Paugam, "Poverty and Social Disqualification: A Comparative Analysis of Cumulative Disadvantage in Europe," *Journal of European Social Policy* 6 (1996), 287-304.

13. William J. Wilson, *The Truly Disadvantaged: The Inner-City, the Underclass and Public Policy* (Chicago: University of Chicago Press, 1987).

14. Paul Pierson, *Dismantling the Welfare State? Reagan, Thatcher and the Politics of Retrenchment* (Cambridge: Cambridge University Press, 1994), 166.

15. According to Karl Polanyi, the Poor Law reform of 1834 commodified labor by making men entirely dependent on their market incomes or the sale of their labor (*The Great Transformation: The Political and Economic Origins of Our Time* [Boston: Beacon Press, 1944]). Gøsta Esping-Andersen, who draws on Polanyi's work, classifies welfare states by the criterion of decommodification that "refers to the degree to which individuals, or families, can uphold a socially acceptable standard of living independently of market participation." (*The Three*

Worlds of Welfare Capitalism [Princeton, N.J.: Princeton University Press, 1990], 37.)

16. The term *social reproduction* has been used by Marxists to refer to the nonmarket work, not only biological reproduction but the socialization and daily maintenance that creates and sustains the present and future labor force. The "social wage" is another word for government support of social reproduction or social welfare. For example, Bob Russell defines social wages as "the system of state expenditures on public goods and income transfer payments for the ongoing maintenance and renewal of capitalist labour supplies." Bob Russell, "The Crisis of the State and the State of Crisis: The Canadian Welfare Experience," in James Dickinson and Bob Russell, eds. *Family, Economy and State: The Social Reproductive Process under Capitalism* (New York: St. Martin's Press, 1986), 309-310.

17. Bill Clinton, *Between Hope and History: Meeting America's Challenges for the 21st Century* (New York: Random House, 1996), 90.

18. See, for example, Mimi Abramovitz, *Regulating the Lives of Women,* rev. ed. (Boston: South End Press, 1996); and Dorothy C. Miller, *Women and Social Welfare: A Feminist Analysis* (New York: Praeger, 1990).

19. Piven and Cloward argue that "man-in-the-house" rules were intended to prevent nonmarket income from reaching men in the low-wage labor pool. Frances Fox Piven and Richard A. Cloward, "Welfare Doesn't Shore Up Traditional Family Roles: A Reply to Linda Gordon," *Social Research* 55(Winter 1988), 642.

20. Eileen Boris and Peter Bardaglio view the welfare state as a form of patriarchy in which women have shifted their economic dependence from their husbands or family partriarchs to the state. See "The Transformation of Patriarchy: The Historical Role of the State," in Irene Diamond, ed., *Families, Politics and Public Policy* (New York: Longman, Green, 1983).

21. Economist Teresa Amott made this point in a panel on "Poverty and Economics," at a Conference "From Welfare to Mean-

ingful Work through Education," Hamilton College, Utica, N.Y., 16 October 1999.

22. The Speenhamland system, established in the late eighteenth century in England, paid the difference between whatever the laborer earned and an allowance that was intended to prevent him and his family from going hungry; thus, there was no incentive to work harder. The EITC, however, goes up with income until it reaches a maximum range, after which it is gradually phased out. In 1999, the EITC raised earned income by 40% for families with two children who had incomes up to $12,460. For a discussion of how the Earned Income Tax Credit works and some of its rather subtle disincentives for families with incomes beyond the maximum range, see Robert Cherry and Gertrude Schaffner Goldberg, "The Earned Income Tax Credit: What It Does and Doesn't Do," in Ron Baiman, Heather Boushey, and Dawn Saunders, eds. *Political Economy and Contemporary Capitalism: Radical Perspectives on Economic Theory and Policy* (Armonk, N.Y.: M. E. Sharpe, 2000).

23. The charges included out-of-control growth, unacceptable error rates, or cheating and defrauding, and work disincentives resulting from the EITC's phase-out rates. For a discussion of these charges and their refutation, see Dennis J. Ventry, Jr., "The Collision of Tax and Welfare Politics: The Political History of the EITC," unpublished paper, University of California, Santa Barbara, undated. Ventry cites statements of conservatives in Congress who came to regard the EITC as welfare.

24. Martin Luther King, Jr., *Where Do We Go from Here: Chaos or Community?* (Boston: Beacon Press, 1968), 163.

25. A recent publication of the National League of Cities listed as funding sources for local public jobs programs: "grant diversion" funds under TANF whereby monthly TANF checks are used to subsidize recipients' wages; $3 billion in Welfare-to-Work Grants to support work-related services for hardest-to-employ welfare recipients and some noncustodial parents; and the Workforce Investment Act that can be used for paid work experience programs. The latter is the only one that is open to nonwelfare recipients. In the same pub-

lication, public jobs programs in Philadelphia, Minneapolis, Seattle, and Athens, Ohio, were featured. Susan Rosenblum, *New Directions: Publicly Funded Jobs: A Workforce Development Strategy for Cities* (Washington, D.C.: National League of Cities, undated [1999]).

26. Interview with Clifford Johnson, senior fellow, Center on Budget and Policy Priorities, Washington, D.C., 20 September 1999. Johnson, who collected information on job-creation efforts and provided technical assistance to groups attempting to create programs at various levels of government, views present experimentation as the basis for "developing a programmatic infrastructure during good times that would serve as a platform at some point if and when the economy softens."

27. In its policy statement on welfare "reform," the National Jobs for All Coalition called upon Congress to suspend all work requirements and time limits for the receipt of welfare benefits if there are too few suitable job openings to provide work for all unemployed persons, including persons on welfare and involuntary part-time workers. Suitable jobs were defined as being reasonably accessible to the unemployed and roughly matching their qualifications. National Jobs for All Coalition, "Policy Statement on Welfare 'Reform,'" New York, National Jobs for All Coalition, 10 January 1997.

28. This section draws on an article by Gertrude Schaffner Goldberg, "Jobs for All, Economic Justice, and the Challenge of Welfare 'Reform,'" *Journal of Public Health Policy* 18 (1997), 302-323. See also Helen Lachs Ginsburg, June Zaccone, Gertrude Schaffner Goldberg, Sheila D. Collins, and Sumner M. Rosen, eds., "Editorial Introduction" to Special Issue on The Challenge of Full Employment in the Global Economy, *Economic and Industrial Democracy* 18 (February 1997), 5-34.

29. William H. Beveridge, *Full Employment in a Free Society* (London: Allen and Unwin, 1944), 18.

30. Ibid., 19.

31. Martin Luther King, Jr., *The Trumpet of Conscience* (New York: Harper & Row, Publishers, Inc., 1967), 55.

32. *United Nations Charter*, Articles 55 and 56 in *Twenty-five Human Rights Documents* (New York: Center for the Study of Human Rights, Columbia University, 1994), 2.

33. See Gertrude Schaffner Goldberg, "Full Employment and the Future of the Welfare State," in Aaron Warner, Matthew Forstater, and Sumner M. Rosen, eds., *Commitment to Full Employment* (Armonk, N.Y.: M. E. Sharpe, 2000).

34. For two recent examples of this position, see Stanley Aronowitz and William DiFazio, *The Jobless Future: Sci-Tech and the Dogma of Work* (Minneapolis: University of Minnesota Press, 1995); and Jeremy Rifkin, *The End of Work: The Decline of the Global Labor Force and the Dawn of the Post-Market Era* (New York: G. P. Putnam's Sons, 1996). Doug Henwood has written two review essays in which he seriously challenges the factual bases of these works, for example, Aronowitz and DiFazio's inaccuracies in reporting data on total job growth in recent years as well as the increase in part-time employment. See Doug Henwood, "Post What? Economics in the Postmodern Era," *Monthly Review* 48 (September 1996), 1-11; and "Talking about Work," *Monthly Review* 49 (July-August 1997), 18-30.

35. Jörg Huffschmid, "Four More Years? Germany after the Elections," *Debatte* 2 (1994), 44.

36. See, for example, Herbert J. Gans, "Planning for Work Sharing: The Problems and Promise of Egalitarian Work Sharing," in Kai Erikson and Steven Peter Vallas, eds., *The Nature of Work: Sociological Perspectives* (New Haven: American Sociological Series and Yale University Press, 1990).

37. Barry Bluestone and Stephen Rose, "Overworked and Underemployed," *American Prospect* (March-April 1997), 58-69. Juliet Schor estimated substantial increases in annual hours of paid employment between 1969 and 1987—98 additional hours for men and 305 for women. See Juliet B. Schor, *The Overworked American: The Unexpected Decline of Leisure* (New York: Basic Books, 1991), 29.

38. Sheila D. Collins, Helen Lachs Ginsburg, and Gertrude Schaffner Goldberg. *Jobs for All: A Plan for the Revitalization of America* (New York: Apex Press, 1994), 53.

39. Huffschmid, op. cit. (see note 35).

40. Collins et al., op. cit., 46, 56, 61-64, 113-117 (see note 38).

41. William Goodman, "Boom in Day Care Industry the Result of Many Social Changes," *Monthly Labor Review* 118(August 1995), 3-12.

42. See, for example, Jason DeParle, "As Benefits Expire, the Experts Worry," *New York Times,* 10 October 1999, 1, 22. For example, Wisconsin officials are worried about getting Simona Alva into the work force. Alva, a Mexican immigrant with 11 children and a husband who fell ill from epileptic seizures, speaks no English, gets lost on city buses, and is worried that a mentally ill son, 24 years of age, will burn down the house without her supervision. Another one being hustled into the Wisconsin work force is Loretta Tiplett, a high-school graduate who has battled depression all her life and must often care for three young grandchildren, has a son at home who drinks heavily, and a daughter who is susceptible to depression.

43. Women's Committee of 100/ Project 2002, "An Immodest Proposal," undated (2000). Available on the Web at http://www.welfare2002.org.

44. Richard Freeman and William Rodgers, "Area Economic Conditions and the Labor Market Outcomes of Young Men in the 1990s Expansion," in Robert Cherry and William Rodgers, eds., *Prosperity for All? The Economic Boom and African Americans* (New York: Russell Sage, 2000), pp. 50-87.

45. M. Harvey Brenner, "Political Economy and Health," in Benjamin Amick, Alvin R. Tarlow, and Diana Chapman Walsh, eds., *Society and Health* (New York: Oxford University Press, 1995), 213.

46. Robert L. Jin, Chandrakant P. Shah, and Tomislav J. Svoboda, "The Impact of Unemployment on Health: A Review of the Evidence," *Canadian Medical Association Journal* 153 (1995), 538.

47. Ibid., 539.

48. Andrew E. Clark and Andrew J. Oswald, "Unhappiness and Unemployment," *The Economic Journal* 104 (May 1994), 648-659.

49. Kim Moody, *Workers in a Lean World: Unions in the International Economy* (London: Verso, 1997), 106, and passim.

50. Professor June Zaccone suggested this example.

51. Steven Greenhouse, "In Biggest Drive since 1937, Union Gains a Victory," *New York Times*, 26 February 1999, A1, A18.

52. Melissa Fay Greene, *Praying for Sheetrock: A Work of Nonfiction* (New York: Fawcett Columbine, 1991), 31, 43.

53. See, for example, Helen Ginsburg, *Full Employment and Public Policy: The United States and Sweden* (Lexington, Mass.: Lexington Books, 1983); Philip Harvey, *Securing the Right to Employment: Social Welfare Policy and the Unemployed in the United States* (Princeton, N.J.: Princeton University Press, 1989); Bertram Gross, "From Full Employment to Global Human Rights," *International Journal of Sociology and Social Policy* 11 (Summer 1991), 118-158; Jocelyn Pixley, *Citizenship and Employment: Investigating Post-Industrial Options* (Cambridge: Cambridge University Press, 1993); Collins et al., op. cit. (see note 38); John Langmore and John Quiggin, *Work for All: Full employment in the Nineties* (Carlton, Victoria, Australia: Melbourne University Press, 1994); International Labour Organization, *World Employment 1995* (Geneva: ILO, 1995); Ginsburg et al., op. cit. (see note 28); and Warner et al., op. cit. (see note 33).

54. Jörg Huffschmid, "Economic Policy for Full Employment: Proposals for Germany," in Ginsburg et al., ibid., 71-72.

55. Sweden, where full employment was the reigning policy for over 50 years, is a notable exception. See Ginsburg, op. cit. (see note 53). In the 1980s, Göran Therborn pointed to five countries that had consistently maintained very low unemployment rates. See his *Why Some Peoples Are More Employed than Others: The Strange Paradox of Growth and Unemployment* (London: Verso, 1985).

56. Huffschmid (op. cit., 67-86 [see note 54]) argues this position convincingly.

57. Paul Osterman, *Securing Prosperity: The American Labor Market: How It Has Changed and What to Do about It* (Princeton, N.J.: Princeton University Press, 1999), esp. 1-43.

58. The statement is by Jill Claybrook, president of Public Citizen (founded by Ralph Nader). See Angela Bradberry, "From Turtles to Teamsters, Activists Shut Down WTO," *Public Citizen News* 20 (Jan/Feb. 2000), 1, 7, 10. Public Citizen is located in Washington, D.C.

59. U.S. Congress, Pub. Law 104-193, 104th Congress, *Personal Responsibility and Work Opportunity Reconciliation Act of 1996,* Title I, Part A, sec. 407(d).

60. David Howell, "The Skills Myth," *American Prospect* 5 (Summer 1994), 81-90.

61. George T. Silvestri, "Occupational Employment Projections to 2006," *Monthly Labor Review* 120 (November 1997), 78.

62. Linda Weiss, *The Myth of the Powerless State* (Ithaca, N.Y.: Cornell University Press, 1998), 2-3.

63. Lester C. Thurow, *The Future of Capitalism* (New York: William Morrow and Company, 1996), 129-130.

64. Weiss, op. cit., 184-186 (see note 62).

65. Adrian Wood, *North-South Trade, Employment and Inequality* (Oxford: Clarendon Press, 1994).

66. Paul R. Krugman and Robert Z. Lawrence, "Trade, Jobs and Wages," *Scientific American* 270 (April 1994), 44-49.

67. International Labour Organization, op. cit. (see note 53).

68. Robert L. Heilbroner, "The Triumph of Capitalism," *New Yorker*, 23 January 1989, 106.

69. Lawrence Summers, memo on a draft of the World Bank's annual *Global Economic Prospects and the Developing Countries,* December 1991, cited by Henwood, "Post What?" op. cit., 5 (see note 34).

70. Weiss, op. cit., 193 (see note 62).

71. For the figures, see World Bank, *World Development Report 1995* (New York: Oxford University Press, 1995), table 3, 167.

72. Whereas taxes paid by U.S. companies to foreign governments are deducted from total tax liability, taxes paid to state

governments are deducted from income. This is a clear tax incentive for moving businesses offshore. According to a 1993 study published by the National Bureau of Economic Research, a sample of 340 U.S. parent corporations had foreign-source income of $47.3 billion in 1986 (the latest data then available) on which they paid only $1.6 billion in U.S. taxes. Cited in Kevin Phillips, *Arrogant Capital: Washington, Wall Street, and the Frustration of American Politics* (Boston: Little, Brown and Company, 1994), 205. The Reagan and Bush administrations contributed to globalization by channeling tax dollars through the United States Agency for International Development to build "export processing zones" in Central America and the Caribbean and to finance "investment promotion programs" to lure American business to these zones. According to then president of the Amalgamated Clothing and Textile Workers Union, Jack Sheinkman, these U.S. government policies helped to finance manufacturing plants that employed more than 700,000 workers and produced $14 billion in annual exports to the United States. Jack Sheinkman, "How Washington Exports U.S. Jobs, *New York Times*, 18 October 1992, F13.

73. "Clinton's Plea: 'Open the Meetings,'" *New York Times*, 2 December 1999, A17.

74. Richard W. Stevenson, "Still Vigilant, Fed Maintains Steady Rates, *New York Times*, 16 November 2000, C1.

75. Robert L. Heilbroner, *The Worldly Philosophers: The Life, Times, and Ideas of the Great Economic Thinkers*, 6th ed., updated (New York: Simon & Schuster, 1987), 278.

76. Helen Ginsburg, op. cit., 12 (see note 53).

77. Robert Eisner, "Our NAIRU Limit: The Governing Myth of Economic Policy, *American Prospect* 6 (Spring 1995), 58.

78. William Vickrey, "Today's Task for Economists," *American Economic Review* 83 (March), 2.

79. Collins et al., op. cit., 54-55 (see note 38). See also Helen Lachs Ginsburg, "Fall from Grace," *In These Times* 23 (December 1996), 23.

80. Vickrey, op. cit., 7-8 (see note 78).

81. David Alan Aschauer, *Public Investment and Private Sector Growth* (Washington, D.C.: Economic Policy Institute, 1990); Robert L. Heilbroner, "An Economy in Deep Trouble," *Dissent* (1992), 445-450.

82. The housing problem results from a growth of low-income renters (with incomes roughly equal to the three-person poverty line) and a decline in affordable housing (with rent and utility costs totaling less than 30% of the three-person poverty line). Between fiscal years 1977 and 1981, the federal government provided housing subsidies to an average of 260,000 additional low-income households annually, but the number dropped to an average of about 70,000 in the 16 years from 1982 to 1997. See Jennifer Daskal, *In Search of Shelter: The Growing Shortage of Affordable Rental Housing* (Washington, D.C.: Center on Budget and Policy Priorities, 1998). Daskal uses figures from the 1995 American Housing Survey sponsored by the U.S. Department of Housing and Urban Development and from the Congressional Budget Office.

83. John Eatwell, "Disguised Unemployment: The G7 Experience," unpublished paper, Trinity College, Cambridge University, 1992.

84. See Helen Ginsburg and Bill Ayres, "Employment Statistics: Let's Tell the Whole Story," *Uncommon Sense* 4, New York, National Jobs for All Coalition, February 2000.

85. For AFDC benefits, see U.S. House of Representatives, Committee on Ways and Means, *1996 Green Book: Background Material and Data on Programs within the Jurisdiction of the Committee on Ways and Means* (Washington, D.C.: U.S. Government Printing Office, 1996), table 8-12, 437-438. For wages, see *Economic Report of the President* (Washington, D.C.: U.S. Government Printing Office, 1998), table B-47, 336.

86. Mishel et al., op. cit., table 2.4, 120, 2.9, 128 (see note 3).

87. Sydney G. Checkland and Olive Checkland, eds., *The Poor Law Report of 1834* (Harmondsworth, England: Penguin Books, 1974), 21, cited in Gerald Handel, *Social Welfare in Western History* (New York: Random House, 1982), 121.

88. Ethan B. Kapstein, "Workers and the World Economy, *Foreign Affairs* 75 (October 1992), 16.

89. Nancy E. Rose, *Put to Work: Relief Programs in the Great Depression* (New York: Monthly Review Press, 1994).

90. Philip Harvey, "Paying for Full Employment: A Hard-Nosed Look at Finances," *Social Policy* 25 (Spring 1995), 21-30.

91. Raymond Majewski and Edward J. Nell, "Designing an Employer of Last Resort Program for Macroeconomic Effect," paper presented to the Columbia University Seminar on Full Employment, New York, 6 November 2000.

92. Robert Eisner, "Deficits: Which, How Much, and So What," paper delivered to the American Economic Association, New Orleans, July 1992, 5.

93. For a classic statement of this position, see Arthur Okun, *Equality and Efficiency: The Big Trade-Off* (Washington, D.C.: The Brookings Institutions, 1975).

94. See, for example, Andrew Glyn and David Miliband, eds., *Paying for Inequality: The Economic Cost of Social Injustice* (London: Institute for Public Policy Research/Rivers Oral Press, 1994); and Torsten Persson and Guido Tabellini, "Is Inequality Harmful for Growth?" *American Economic Review* 84 (1994), 600-621.

95. Helen Lachs Ginsburg, "Unemployment Means Lost Output and Human Deficits," *Uncommon Sense* 2, New York, National Jobs for All Coalition, August 1995. See also, Eisner, op. cit. (see note 92).

96. For a discussion of such measures, see Collins et al., 53-55 (note 38).

97. The capitalism that conservatives lionize is not the free market of their rhetoric but one that enjoys the stabilizing effect of a wide range of government interventions, not the least of which are social-welfare programs.

98. The Kreisky Commission, named for its chairperson, former Austrian Premier Bruno Kreisky reported to the European Community that "unemployment is a political problem, not an economic one." Commission on Employment Issues in Europe, *A Program for Full Employment in the 1990s: Report of the Kreisky Commission* (Oxford: Pergamon Press, 1989).

99. Joel Blau, *Illusions of Prosperity: America's Working Families in an Age of Economic Insecurity* (New York: Oxford University Press, 1999), 134.

100. Telephone interview with Henry Freedman, executive director of the Welfare Law Center, New York, N.Y., 1 November 1999.

101. Center for Community Change, *Making Welfare Reform Work: How Diverse Organizations Worked to Improve Their States' Welfare Policies* (Washington, D.C.: Center for Community Change, 1999), 8.

102. See the Linc Project website of the Welfare Law Center at: http://www.lincproject.org.

103. "Call to Action" of the "March of the Americas" found on the Kensington Welfare Rights Union's website at: http://www.libertynet.org/kwru.

104. The website of the National Welfare Monitoring and Advocacy Partnership is at: http://www.nwmap.org.

105. "High Tech at the Grassroots," *Responsive Philanthropy* (Summer 1999), 1. *Responsive Philanthropy* is a newsletter of the National Committee for Responsive Philanthropy, Washington, D.C.

106. See "Living Wage Successes: A Compilation of Living Wage Policies on the Books," prepared by ACORN. Available on its website (31 October 1999) at: http://www.livingwage campaign.org/living-wage-wins.html.

107. "Introduction to ACORN's Living Wage Web Site," available from ACORN (31 October 1999) at: http://www.livingwagecampaign.org/introduction.html.

108. Louis Uchitelle, "Minimum Wages, City by City," *New York Times*, 19 November 1999, C1, C19. Uchitelle focuses on the campaign led by the Los Angeles Alliance for a New Economy, an organization encouraged by the Los Angeles County Federation of Labor.

109. See "Summary of Research on Living Wage Ordinances," prepared by ACORN. Available on its website (31 October 1999) at: http://www.livingwagecampaign.org/impact-summary.html.

110. "What is a First Source Agreement?" Available from Center for Community Change on its website (31 October 1999) at: http://www.communitychange.org/1stsource.htm.

111. *New York Times* quoted in "Welfare Recipients Win Residency Case in Supreme Court," *Welfare News* 4, no. 3 (June 1999), 1. *Welfare News* is a newsletter of the Welfare Law Center, New York, N.Y.

112. Alan Finder, "Welfare Clients Outnumber Jobs They Might Fill, *New York Times*, 25 August 1996, A1.

113. Jerome G. Manis, "Assessing the Seriousness of Social Problems," *Social Problems* 22 (1974), 1-15.

114. Joseph Stiglitz, "Democratic Development as the Fruits of Labor," keynote address, Industrial Relations Research Association, Boston, January 2000. Available from Industrial Relations Research Association on its website (9 February 2001) at http://www.irra.uiuc.edu.

Glossary

AALL: American Association for Labor Legislation

ACORN: Association of Communities Organized for Reform Now

ADC: Aid to Dependent Children

ADC-UP/AFDC-UP: Unemployed Parent Program

AFDC: Aid to Families with Dependent Children

AFSCME: American Federation of State, County, and Municipal Employees

AGI: Adjusted Gross Income

CAP: Community Action Program

CCC: Civilian Conservation Corps

CDF: Children's Defense Fund

CEA: Council of Economic Advisors

CES: Committee on Economic Security

CETA: Comprehensive Employment and Training Administration

CHIP: Children's Health Insurance Program

CORE: Congress on Racial Equality

COS: Charity Organization Society

CWA: Civil Works Administration

CWEP: Community Work Experience Program

CWT: Community Work and Training Program

EEA: Emergency Employment Act

EITC: Earned Income Tax Credit

ET: Massachusetts Employment and Training Choices Program

FAP: Family Assistance Plan

FDI: Foreign Direct Investment

FERA: Federal Emergency Relief Administration

FEPC: Fair Employment Practices Commission

FSA: Family Support Act

FVO: Family Violence Option

501

GAO: General Accounting
Office
GDP: Gross Domestic Product

HEW: Department of Health,
Education, and Welfare
HHS: Department of Health
and Human Services

IMF: International Monetary
Fund

JOBS: Jobs, Opportunity, and
Basic Skills
JTPA: Job Training Partnership
Act

LINC: Low Income Networking
and Communications

MDTA: Manpower
Development and Training
Act
MFY: Mobilization for Youth

NAACP: National Association
for the Advancement of
Colored People
NAFTA: North American Free
Trade Agreement
NAIRU: Nonaccelerating
Inflation Rate of
Unemployment
NAM: National Association of
Manufacturers

NIT: Negative Income Tax
NRPB: National Resources
Planning Board
NWMAP: National Welfare
Monitoring and Advocacy
Partnership
NWRO: National Welfare
Rights Organization
NYA: National Youth
Administration

OAI: Old Age Insurance
OEO: Office of Economic
Opportunity

PACs: Political Action
Committees
PBJI: Program for Better Jobs
& Income
PCJD: President's Committee
on Juvenile Delinquency
PRUCOL: Permanently
Residing under Color of
Law Status
PRWORA: Personal
Responsibility and Work
Opportunity Reconciliation
Act
PWA: Public Works
Administration

SEIU: Service Employees
International Union
SSA: Social Security Act
SSI: Supplemental Security
Income

TANF: Temporary Assistance
for Needy Families

TEA-21: Transportation Equity
Act of the 21st Century

TERA: Temporary Emergency
Relief Administration

UI: Unemployment Insurance

WEP: Work Experience Program

WIA: Work Investment Act of
1998

WIC: Special Supplemental
Food Program for Women,
Infants, and Children

WIN: Work Incentive Program

WPA: Works Progress
Administration

WTO: World Trade Organization

Index

Women, single. *See* Mothers,
   single.
Work, 10
   "barriers" to, 251
   "benefit," 16
   ethic, 15, 25
   full-time, 4, 16, 82, 154,
      222-224
   incentives, 44, 77, 151-152,
      154, 179-180
   low-wage, 46, 118, 121
   part-time, 4, 16, 82, 177-178,
      222-224, 252
   program, 60
   reform, 25
   relief, 28, 34, 36, 39, 58-59, 62
   requirements, 1-2, 12, 14-16,
      46, 57, 77, 128, 130-131,
      138-140, 144-145, 150,
      175, 180, 195, 203, 206,

   209, 238, 245-248, 251-
      253, 281
   sharing, 286
   subminimum, 49
"Workers' Unemployment, Old-age
   and Insurance Act," 35
Workfare, 7, 17, 23, 131, 134,
   140, 173-174, 197, 203, 237-
   240, 246, 248, 253
Workforce Investment Act of 1998
   (WIA), 228
Workhouses, 7, 9, 175
Work Incentives (WIN) program,
   130-134, 139, 142, 150, 244
"Work opportunities," 12, 25, 58
Work Opportunity Tax Credit, 226
Workplace, 67
   discrimination in, 13, 118, 139
   transitioning into, 239
Works Progress Administration
   (WPA), 17, 36, 58-62, 158
World Trade Organization (WTO),
   291, 295
World War II, 3, 20, 50, 58-59,
   61-62, 65, 68, 75, 81, 106, 186,
   227, 269, 300